PORTUGAL THE COOKBOOK

PORTUGAL

THE COOKBOOK

LEANDRO CARREIRA

Introduction

When the opportunity to write this book presented itself, I was about to open my first restaurant. I realised what an honour it would be to write such a comprehensive book on the food of my country, but I could also see the amount of work and time involved. On top of opening the restaurant, I felt overwhelmed by the prospect of such a major undertaking. 'I don't think I'm the guy for this,' I told the editor. After a day of reflection, I turned the offer down. A month went by and I received another phone call from the editor, asking to meet again; I knew that meeting was for me to reconsider. Once-in-a-lifetime opportunities rarely present themselves with perfect timing, I realised. I accepted, and my path was set.

For such a small country, Portugal has a huge diversity within its cuisine. For many, many years, however, the food of our nation has stayed under wraps. Now, here was my chance to shine a light on the exciting regional and local distinctiveness that characterises the national cuisine.

As I embarked on this new project, diving into my Portuguese identity, I fell in love with my country and culture so much more than I ever imagined possible. Travel and research were the key ingredients that combined in the recipe for this book, which resulted in the most challenging and exciting period of my life so far. I feel immense gratitude to have had the chance to get to know the food of my country in such a deep and comprehensive way. The experience has contributed to the way I cook, and I still continue to draw constant inspiration from it.

But I am a trained chef, not a writer, and the challenge this book presented gave me cold shivers. What's more, I was living in London, having left Portugal a long time ago. My relationship with my home country was blurry and I felt that I needed to reconnect. But how would I even start? I needed a plan.

During the first few trips to Portugal that I took in the name of research, I thought that in order to collect information I could simply rock up in villages and strike up a conversation with the locals. This turned out to be naïve: often villages were deserted, there was no one on the streets, and those who were around didn't want to chat to a stranger about what they were putting on the family dining table. It was frustrating.

It was my sister Catarina who then helped me to contact all the boroughs of Portugal that are represented within the regions covered in this book. Some were extremely helpful and shared lots of information; others had no records at all relating to local gastronomy and customs. We had to piece everything together slowly. My parents, who travel all over the country for food and have

friends throughout the different regions, played an important role, providing me with openings and contacts who also created a word-of-mouth network of information gathering.

After two-and-a-half years of research that involved reading through an enormous number of documents and scribbled notes from friends and family, poring over recipes from mothers and grandmothers, and even unearthing my own notes from the start of my career as a chef in Portugal, I slowly started to piece together the incredible landscape and uncover the foundations of this remarkable country's food.

The resulting book that you now hold in your hands is not — and cannot be — an exhaustive catalogue and does not include every Portuguese recipe; rather, the most significant cornerstones of each region are represented in detail. Together, the recipes present an overall picture of the diverse and little known nature of the country's extraordinary cuisine. It is the largest collection of traditional Portuguese recipes translated into English to be found between the covers of one book. Portugal, as a travel destination, has become ever more popular over recent years, as has an interest in the national gastronomy. Returning from a special holiday, people want to bring a little of that magic back with them into their kitchens. This book offers just that.

And the best dishes are often so simple to recreate. The recipe for *Amêijoas à Bulhão Pato* (Clams with Coriander and Garlic, page 186), from the Lisbon area and one of my favourites in the book, comprises pristine clams cooked simply with garlic, lemon juice and olive oil. Comforting and easy, it's perfect enjoyed with a cold beer in the sunshine. Or *Perdiz com Amêijoas na Cataplana* (Partridge with Clams, page 204), a special partridge stew from the Algarve that is eaten at the end of summer; so delicious that I can never stop at just one serving. And there's one dish that every single Portuguese person has eaten at least once in their life and is a perennial favourite: *Bacalhau à Brás* (Salt Cod with Eggs, Onions and Potatoes, page 126), a magical combination of shreds of salted cod, caramelised onions and crisp potatoes, finished with creamy egg.

The gastronomy of Portugal is every bit as old, rich and colourful as that of neighbouring France and Spain, and yet it has remained relatively obscure and undiscovered. It's time to put that right. In this book, the sheer diversity of the country's cuisine is mapped through the regions — with their distinct microclimates from north to south that offer rich growing conditions — its history, and its global influence through the centuries, the impact of which is still seen today in cultures across the world. Translating the recipes into English was a real challenge (especially as many were given to me verbally, and sometimes over the phone) but, while being keenly aware of how much can get lost in translation, I hope I have managed to present them in an utterly authentic way, while communicating clearly to a new audience.

You will find that Portuguese cooking is generally simple; the key lies in the different ingredients and how they behave together, and how you treat them. The one thing you will not find covered in these pages is charcuterie. Despite being amazing in Portugal, quite simply it would constitute a complete book in itself and, sadly, it is no longer widely made in the traditional way due to industrialisation and health regulations.

My parents helped me track down the last shop in Portugal to make the special vessel needed to cook the cake *Fatias de Tomar* (Egg 'Cake' Slices Soaked in Vanilla Syrup, page 316), a stainless-steel steamer made now by an 87-year-old artisan with sadly no one to inherit the craft from him. In this particular case, the pot is an incredible vessel that works in the fashion of a 'pressure bain-marie' that makes the cake rise without the aid of flour or yeast, typically used for these cakes. Most of the pot is made in a single sheet of metal, traditionally hand cut either with tinsnips or a machine, which is then welded with precision. For certain, it is a difficult and hard craft that no one now wants to pursue, perhaps for the time-consuming and scant returns. Also, the demand for the *Fatias de tomar* itself is not there anymore. Lucky are the ones who already own one of these pots.

It is precisely these types of lost traditions that lend a book like this such urgency and importance, for us to understand the past as well as how we shape the future of the country's cuisine. I want this book to open up Portuguese food to a wider audience, and go some way in demystifying it. It is my hope that the recipes will transport you straight from your own kitchen to a region of the country; that you will come to appreciate and understand not just the deep gastronomic traditions but also the exciting new and modern developments that have sprung from this oldest of food cultures. As my friend Enrico always says: 'Portugal is the sleeping giant of gastronomy.' Time to wake him up!

Regions and Terroir

Officially the oldest nation state in Europe, Portugal has, over centuries of global exploration and expansion, brought a global larder of ingredients to its shores — potatoes and sugar from the Americas, and spices from India are all still key to our eating habits today. Added to these, Nordic preservation techniques account for the national tradition of salt-curing fish, especially cod. The scaffold of Portuguese cuisine is built from these influences from abroad, as well as the country's influence on the rest of the world.

For the most part of our history, we have been a poor country, with limited access to finer ingredients and a populace fed on the things the monarchy and elites rejected: stale bread, bad wine, vegetable trimmings and animal offal (variety meats). But from such limitations, ingenuity inevitably develops, and some of our most appreciated and classic dishes, like *Açorda* (a sort of bread porridge, page 34) and *Sarrabulho* (Pork Offal Stew, page 232) are testament to this deep tradition. The country was, out of necessity, therefore, an early adopter of 'nose-to-tail' eating. Cured meats, heads, trotters, tails... this is how I grew up, eating fish heads cooked on the grill and boiled, salted pig bones with cornbread.

Despite a history of relative poverty, Portugal has always benefited from a rich and diverse landscape that encompasses fertile, flat farmlands and salt marshes. Just a short drive south from Lisbon, for instance, in the river Sado, rice has been grown since the 1500s.

But the most consumed product in Portugal by far is *bacalhau* (salt cod), with numbers suggesting an average annual consumption of 6 kg/12½ lb per person. It's no wonder that its nickname is *fiel amigo*, or 'faithful friend'. It is said that there are as many as a thousand different recipes for *bacalhau*, and although I think this may well be an exaggeration, it cannot be far off the mark.

For years, the only things known to the world that came out of Portugal were Port wine from the Douro, *Pastéis de Nata* (Custard Tarts, page 390) and *bacalhau* (salt cod). This massive over-simplification has perhaps been standing in the way of a fuller appreciation of the many edible delights the country has to offer. It is my hope that this book will offer an insight into the breadth and richness of the national cuisine, as spread among the various terroirs and regions, that have been a well-kept secret for far too long.

The North

Rivalling Alentejo in the south as the richest and most diverse region of Portugal, Minho covers the area to the north and northwest of Porto. This is a special place where mountains meet the sea, and has some of the greenest areas of the country. Its fertile river banks are home to the most loved (or loathed, by some) freshwater fish species in the country, the lamprey. This fish-like eel even has its own dedicated festival of celebration in March, and a famous dish called *Arroz de Lampreia* (Lamprey Rice, page 276).

A much sought-after product in the Minho region is beef from the *Barrosã* breed of cattle, recognisable from their distinctive, long horns. The cattle occupy the highest lands, grazing on traditional pastures and marshes — a terrain and diet of grass, rye and often potatoes and corn that they are perfectly adapted to. The resulting flesh is dense and red, with a dark yellow marbling of fat and a nutty flavour. Traditionally, the cattle played a crucial part in mountain farming practices, with ideal mobility needed for working in the fields. Following the rural depopulation of recent decades, the government and EU has stepped in to support and protect the cattle, granting protected geographical status (DOC). Today the meat is regarded as a true delicacy.

A sight you will often come across in this area are the *Espigueiros do Lindoso*, granaries on legs made of a combination of granite and wood, dating back to the 18th century and still used to dry out corn and cereals today.

Northeast of the Minho region you will find Trás-os-Montes e Alto Douro, where one of the most famous Portuguese exports — Port — is produced. Crossed by the mighty river Douro, the unique terroir is ideal for wine making generally, not just for fortified wines.

Olive oil is also produced here within 15 boroughs, who supply thirty percent of Portugal's overall output. The special mountainous area provides a particular climate for this almost mythical product, with several varieties of olive flourishing across the region, many with protected status of origin (DOP) and four different grades of oil and varying levels of acidity. Olive oil has a significant impact on the local economy, and some have been awarded the highest distinctions in prestigious competitions, both national and international.

This beautiful area is filled with almond trees that, at the beginning of spring, have magnificent, fragrant displays of blossom, and a big celebration festival at the end of February, the *Festa de Amendoeira em Flor*. The almond also plays a role in the local diet, with the nuts dried and consumed throughout the year. The famous *amendoas de Moncorvo* (caramelised nuts from Moncorvo) can be found all over the region, and you'll find sweet recipes in this book using almonds, such as *Toucinho de Céu* (Bacon from Heaven, page 372), *Broas Castelares* (Cornmeal, Sweet Potato and Cinnamon Cookies, page 394) and *Tosquiados* (Almond Meringues, page 399).

Chestnuts also grow plentifully here, and are a prominent feature of the local agriculture and economy. Known as *Castanha da Terra Fria* (chestnut of the cold land), they too have DOP status and are grown ecologically. The fertile area is also home to many types of game bird and animal, including wild boar and partridge, which feed on the fallen chestnuts and almonds.

The cold, damp climate that dominates for much of the year also creates ideal conditions for wild mushrooms, including girolles and pieds de mouton, which in turn attract foragers and chefs. The famous dishes *Cogumelos Guisados* (Stewed Mushrooms, page 97) and *Perdiz com Cogumelos* (Partridge with Mushrooms, page 202) are fine examples of dishes created from the natural wild bounty. Most are distributed throughout the country's restaurants, with some ending up on the international markets.

As in the Minho, beef is also highly prized, and the *Maronesa* — a primitive, rustic mountain breed of cattle that has a diet that includes potatoes — has succulent meat with delicate aromas. Along with *Posta à Mirandesa* (Mirandesa Steak, page 250) and dishes celebrating the great *Bisaro* breed of pig, beef enriches the culinary landscape and is both celebrated and enjoyed as everyday food.

Central Portugal

Inland towards the northern end of central Portugal is Serra da Estrela, the area with the highest mountain of the country and home to indigenous breeds of sheep, *Bordaleira* and *Churra Mondegueira Serra da Estrela*. The superb milk they produce is turned into the famous creamy, soft cheese of the same name as the mountain range — one of the most famous sheep's cheeses in the world.

Close to these mountains there is another cheese called *Requeijão da Serra da Estrela*, which is often eaten with local honey. This honey is smoother in texture and deeper and stronger in flavour than regular honey, due to the local flora that includes heather.

There is also olive production in this area for the varieties of *galena, verdeal, cobrançosa and cordovil* – all four of them with low acidity.

The mountain slopes are ideal fertile terrain for fruit trees such as apples, pears and cherries. Although most of the fruit that these trees bear end up on the international market, the cherries from Fundão are a true delicacy and find their way into restaurants and markets around the country.

River trout and honey are also prized in this region, with the dish *Truta Abafada* (Stewed River Trout with Spices, page 163) a speciality.

The river Dão, to the west of the mountains and towards the Atlantic, is home to the great wine region of the same name, often referred to as 'the Burgundy of Portugal'. It is an area also renowned for its pastries, including the iconic egg-yolk-based sweets *Ovos Moles de Aveiro* (Soft Sweet Eggs, page 308). First made by Carmelite nuns in the 16th century, the pastry on the *pastéis* was said to be stretched so thin that the Bible could be read through it.

The South

Heading south are other highly fertile areas, including Ribatejo, which translates as 'bank of the river Tejo' (Tagus), and which crosses the province. It is the largest river in the Iberian Peninsula and meets the Atlantic Ocean in Lisbon. The impact of the river on the local agriculture and cuisine is immense, with its huge banks home to important rice production, including the most well-known variety *arroz Carolino*, as well as supplying water for farming, in particular large fields of tomatoes, melons and even grapevines. River fish and eels are abundant and have made their mark on local gastronomy.

Further south, Alentejo is for the most part flat and covers the largest region of Portugal, bordering Spain to the east and the Atlantic on the west. It is home to the most highly prized pig of all, the free-range black foot, or *Pata Negra*, one of the Iberian Peninsula's most sought-after gastronomic treasures. The pig is acorn-fed and roams in the oak forests on the border with Spain, a diet and lifestyle that accounts for its exceptional flavour and high price. It is here that the strongest charcuterie culture of Portugal exists, including the making of *chouriço* (chorizo), *paiolas* (a traditional sausage) and *presunto* (cured ham).

The region also enjoys an outstanding variety of sweet pastries, most of them originating, as in other parts of the country, in convents. Most nuns in medieval Portuguese convents didn't end up there due to spiritual calling. The convent population consisted of the second daughters of the rich, single heiresses, widows and orphaned teenagers with a fortune behind them. Many women even had their maids with them in the convent. These were posh ladies. The maids were crucial to the invention of the convent sweets, as most of them were already used to cooking in sophisticated environments.

The nuns would use the surplus of egg yolks (the whites being used for export and as a purifier in wine production), plentiful native almonds and the easily accessed imported sugar to create rich sweets. Some examples of these that you can find in the region include *Broas Doces de Banha* (Pork Fat Cookies, page 404), *Azevias com Grão* (Sweet Chickpea Pasties, page 338) and *Rebuçados de Ovo de Portalegre* (Egg Yolk Sweets, page 412).

Convent sweets were an elite product and so more egg yolks and less egg whites were used, because the yellow colour was very appealing — the nuns used to sell and make money out of the sweets. There were other convents that cooked sweets that wouldn't be as rich and sophisticated — popular sweets — because they couldn't afford the same ingredients.

With its drier and hotter climate, southern Portugal has always seen the practice of air-drying fish as a means of preservation. Salt production in the Algarve, home to some of the cleanest mineral salt there is, extracted using ancient methods, has played a major part in this curing process, with *muxama* (cured tuna) and *polvo seco* (sun-dried octopus) to name a couple.

With its long coastline, Portugal offers some of the most remarkable diversity of quality fish in the world, and is also home to some of the oldest fishing methods — now no longer applied due to sustainability issues — where two boats would tie nets between them and be pulled ashore by bulls, cows or human strength. Some of the most iconic Portuguese dishes have emerged from this rich coastline, including *Caldeirada de Peixe* (Fish Stew, page 136), *Lagosta Suada à Moda de Peniche* (Stewed Spiny Lobster – Peniche Style, page 178), *Arroz de Marisco* (Seafood Rice, page 280) and, of course, the iconic sun-dried fish of Nazaré, so embedded in local customs.

The Islands

The archipelagos of Madeira and the Azores offer something else altogether. Madeira, with its tropical climate, produces the majestic Madeira wine, as well as outstanding fruits, and has a gastronomy that blends tropical resources with deep tradition. The Azores, a volcanic conglomerate of islands, is home to vast green pastures ideal for grazing, providing high-quality dairy for cheese making. The Azores is also where you will find the famous *Cozido da Logoa das Furnas* ('Furnace' Stew, page 254), a dish of various meats and vegetables that are slow-cooked in a special pot dropped into volcanic hot soil, resulting in its unique flavours.

Naturally, there is a rich supply of seafood and fish on the islands — some of the best in the world — including giant squid, flat-head lobsters and tuna.

A Brief History of Portuguese Food

In the Beginning was Iberia

The premise of *The Stone Raft*, the 1986 novel by the Portuguese Nobel Prize-winning writer José Saramago, is that the Iberian Peninsula has broken off the European continent through a massive geological event and is floating freely in the Atlantic Ocean while its protagonists — five characters from across Portugal and Spain — embark on an imaginary search for a new and common Iberian identity. Saramago's parable rests on the idea that due to geographical location and configuration, and in spite of sovereign borders, 'what brings us together is stronger than what pulls us apart'.

The Iberian Peninsula, between the Mediterranean Sea and the Atlantic Ocean, was the confluence of ancient civilisations, and up until the early 12th century when Portugal gained independence by breaking away from the kingdom of León, the Iberian territories and its populations shared a common history, submitting to the influence of the different civilisations who either conquered or settled in its vast and varied landscape.

Early in the first millennium BCE, waves of Celts from Central Europe invaded and intermarried with the local pre-Celtic tribal populations of the central and northern areas, to form various ethnic groups and tribes and dominated this area. The south, where the heirs to the semi-mythical harbour city of Tartessos lived, retained much of its Tartessian character and ways of life. As they settled and established their territories, most of these tribes evolved from hunter-gathering to farming, herding, pottery making and metallurgy.

These pre-Roman societies anchored their diet in cereals and legumes. Acorns were a plentiful resource; soaked in water to remove their bitterness, they were roasted and pounded into a pulp that could be cooked into porridge or dried and baked into loaves and flatbreads. The more common cereal grains were wheat and buckwheat, barley, spelt, oats and millet, with the Celts having introduced rye. Milled grains would be baked but also eaten as porridge, with water or curded milk.

Legumes such as lentils, broad (fava) beans, peas and grass peas, and vegetables such as chard, coles and onions were staple foods. Endogenous grapes and berries, figs, cherries, plums, quince, pears and apples were common fruits — either eaten fresh or dried. As well as acorns, chestnuts, hazelnuts and pine nuts were also fairly plentiful. Foraging played an important dietary role as a complement to farming: wild leafy greens, herbs, tubers and mushrooms were collected in season.

Iberians were already extracting oil from wild olive trees and using it for frying when the Phoenicians introduced cultivated olive varietals.

Their methods of extraction were inefficient and the wild fruits had little pulp, so the new, plumper fruit and better milling techniques played a pivotal role in the abundant use of olive oil in the diets of the Iberian people from that time onwards.

Milk wasn't served fresh but there's evidence that cheese, curds, whey and butter were commonly consumed. Beer (*caelia*) was the main drink, brewed from barley or millet, and, unlike now, wine was quite rare. At first traded into the peninsula by Phoenicians and Greeks, it was kept for special celebrations and consumed exclusively by the powerful classes.

Meat was sourced mainly from goats, sheep, cows, oxen and horses, and from pigs, which also provided lard (pork fat) for cooking. Celts introduced poultry, and chicken and eggs entered into the Iberian diet, with eggs from wildfowl commonly eaten. Meat from wild animals also played a key dietary role, with hogs, boar, deer, rabbits, hare, pheasant, quail and partridge being regularly enjoyed.

Fishing was an important resource, with freshwater fish being widely eaten and saltwater fish a paramount staple for the people living on the coast, epecially after the Phoenicians promoted preservation methods through salting, in order to supply their trading demand.

Strabo, the Greek geographer and historian, wrote of the Lusitanians — the peoples first associated with a Portuguese identity — that they were 'a warring, agrarian people ... using anointing-rooms twice a day and taking baths in vapours that rise from heated stones, bathing in cold water, and eating only one meal a day; and that in a cleanly and simple way ... They eat goat's-meat mostly, and to Ares they sacrifice a he-goat and also the prisoners and horses ... And the mountaineers, for two-thirds of the year, eat acorns, which they have first dried and crushed, and then ground up and made into a bread that may be stored away for a long time. They also drink beer; but they are scarce of wine, and what wine they have made they speedily drink up in merry feastings with their kinsfolk; and instead of olive-oil they use butter. Again, they dine sitting down, for they have stationary seats builded around the walls of the room, though they seat themselves forward according to age and rank. The dinner is passed round, and amid their cups they dance to flute and trumpet, dancing in chorus, but also leaping up and crouching low.'

This gives us an idea of the backdrop onto which Portuguese foodways were woven.

Phoenicians and Greeks

Phoenician seafarers first reached the southwestern coast of the Iberian Peninsula — in what is now

Portugal — some 3,000 years ago. At first, some small, semi-permanent trading settlements were founded on the southern coast of the Algarve. Their main interest was the mineral wealth of the territory, where they proceeded to acquire metals such as silver, copper and tin that they would trade for textiles, glass, pottery and faience, jewellery and adorning objects, incense, papyrus or carved ivory. As their relationship with local communities evolved, groups of western Phoenicians, probably originating in the areas of Cádiz and Málaga, settled during the eighth century BCE, first in the estuary of the Tagus River and afterwards near important rivers like the Mondego, Sado, Guadiana and Gilão. They named the settlement on the Tagus estuary 'Alis-Ubbo', meaning 'enchanting port', the perfect base for their naval trade.

Fish was so abundant that the Phoenicians introduced fish-processing techniques and, as there were perfect conditions to produce salt, they encouraged local production of salted fish that they could trade elsewhere. As they saw great potential for locally producing more and better commodities, they introduced numerous advanced techniques in ore mining and metallurgy, pottery, jewellery and textile dyeing, but also in viticulture and winemaking, as well as in the cultivation of olive trees and uses for olive oil.

As Phoenicians interacted with local communities, their sophisticated way of life led to marked changes in social habits and even in religious and funerary rituals, but also in dietary practices. This Phoenician influence on Iberian food can be observed in the the products they introduced, such as chickpeas (garbanzos), pomegranates, almonds, figs, grapes and olives and, above all, salted fish products. 'Muxama', a delicacy made from salt-cured tuna loins that can be found in the Algarve and the coast of Andalusia, is believed to have been introduced by the Phoenicians.

As for the Greeks, there really isn't a lot of physical evidence of their presence in the western part of the Iberian Peninsula, apart from fragments of vases and amphorae dug up in archeological excavations that probably arrived there through trade, but legend has it that Lisbon was founded by Ulysses on his journey back home after the war against the city of Troy, albeit 2,500 nautical miles off his course and in another sea. During this long and adventurous journey he battled sea monsters and plenty of strange ocean creatures. One day a bolt of lightning appeared and exploded into flames in an unknown land. According to the legend, Ulysses was instructed by Zeus to build a city named Olisipo on the point of impact. Ulysses or not, ancient Greece's influence on Iberian foodways would be felt only a few centuries later during the Roman occupation.

The Romans

The first Roman invasion of the Iberian Peninsula took place in 219 BCE. Within 200 years, almost the entire Peninsula had been annexed to the Roman Republic and, after the conquest, Rome installed a colonial regime. During this period, Lusitania grew in prosperity and many of modern-day Portugal's cities and towns were founded. The Romanisation of the Peninsula also entailed significant changes in food. Romans were impressed with the fertility and diversity of these territories, considering Hispania 'the land where everything sprouts, even gold'. The new Roman provinces were rich in olive oil, wine and, most of all, *garum*, a highly prized condiment processed from fish that was made in the Peninsula and taken to Rome in large quantities to serve the needs of the more powerful families of the empire. Romans introduced new farming techniques and the use of the Roman plough, new fruit trees and, most importantly, plant grafting. This allowed for a great increase in the production of olive oil and wine that was exported to Rome in dedicated amphoras.

At the mouth of the river Tagus, the Romans renamed the thriving commercial settlement *Felicitas Julia Olisipo*. They improved its docking capacity and created more amphora potteries and fish-processing factories, and Olisipio quickly grew to become a very important trading hub. Luxurious villas were built in the city and in the surrounding countryside, as well as a circus and a theatre, baths and temples, and the inhabitants of the city were given the privileges of Roman citizenship. Lavish banquets were organised to honour the ruling authorities: oysters and seafood from the Tagus, greens and fruit from the fertile orchards of the left bank were served alongside delicacies from remote parts of the Roman world. To the south of the city, on the estuary of the Sado river, the largest garum and fish-processing factories in the whole of the empire were built. Local populations were encouraged to adopt a Roman lifestyle and new foodways. As for many of the old Mediterranean civilizations, the three staples of the Roman diet were wheat, wine and olive oil. The Roman commoner would eat wheat porridge (*puls*) enriched with some legumes if available, seasoned with olive oil and accompanied by some (admittedly very bad-quality) wine. Whereas, according to Strabo, the people of Lusitania ate just a single daily meal consisting of simple ingredients that included the abundance of fish and molluscs along the Tagus.

The Moors

After the decline of the Roman Empire came the havoc of Barbarian invasions, and intermittent phases of peace and war among Germanic Visigoth kings, sub-kings, co-kings and usurpers — a period of plentiful beer, red meat and whole-beast roasts. Then all of a sudden came the Moors — a *razzia* of Arab nomad tribesmen and Berbere soldiers hailing from North Africa, over the straits of Gibraltar — by the thousands. It took less than nine years (711–720 CE) for the Muslim armies to conquer the Iberian Peninsula. Much of the initial conquest was focused on using the established tradition of caravan raiding to claim booty and weaken neighbouring states. One of the major motivating factors of this 'jihad' was less on missionary zeal and more on gaining wealth —

not just on conquest, but from the *jizayh* tax levied on non-Muslims. If Christians and Jews, whom they saw as fellow 'people of the book', paid tribute and accepted the conditions of conquest, they could buy back their right to life, freedom of worship, and security of property. What had been a Roman province became the farthest westernmost province of another empire, the Umayyad Caliphate of Damascus. However, this time it was the invaders who had the more refined culture, including in their culinary habits. To these new rulers, cuisine was an art, and food a gift from God that should be consumed in moderation and shared with those in need. Food was a component of hospitality and socialisation. The invaders introduced new concepts of refinement and indulgence, both in costume and cuisine.

As they settled the *Gharb al-Andaluz*, literally 'West of Andaluz' — the area of the Iberian Peninsula that now corresponds to Portugal — the Moors brought physicians, chemists, architects, mathematicians, astronomers, agronomists and horticulturists, as well as writers, poets, cooks and cookbooks, such as the *Kitāb al Tabīkh*, the recipe bible of Baghdad.

The Moors introduced innovative scientific developments in hydraulics that allowed for the irrigation of farmland, orchards and green gardens. They planted citrus trees along the streets and alleys of cities and villages, both for the fruit and the scent. They introduced rice and sugarcane, two staples that would later tip the scales of Europe's commodity markets. They also introduced the almond and the carob trees that now play an important role in Algarve's economy. Distillation was another of the Moors' major contributions (despite not drinking alcohol), and syrups and infusions such as rose water and orange blossom began to enter recipes. The list of new vegetables, fruits and herbs brought by the Moors to the Peninsula is also extensive: artichokes, cardoons, asparagus and spinach, leeks and celery, lentils and lupin beans, carrots, cauliflower, the all-important aubergine (eggplant), cucumbers and lettuces that would find fame on the sandy vegetable gardens about the Tagus and lend their name to the inhabitants of Lisbon, the 'Alfacinhas' (meaning 'little lettuces'). Sour oranges and lemons, apricots, dates, melons and watermelons became popular. Coriander (cilantro) and garlic topped the list of aromatics, and pennyroyal, mint, thyme, marjoram and oregano were used along with spices such as cumin seeds, pepper, cloves, sesame, fennel seeds, caraway, ginger and the highly prized saffron, which was used in both savoury and sweet dishes. Fish and meats were enriched with spice rubs; marinades of vinegar, verjus or citrus juices with herbs were used as tenderisers. Pickling was a widespread art, and these acidic brines were also used to cure and flavour olives, capers, vegetables and nuts. Another sour marinade introduced by the Moors and widely used to preserve fish was *escabeche*.

The Arabs of Mesopotamia, more familiar with freshwater fish, were delighted with the abundance of sea fish in the Garb al-Andalus.

The Moorish technique of dredging in flour and deep-frying in oil was perfect for preparing red mullet, sardines, mackerel and small eels, a practice that persists to this day. Vegetable soups and broths, lighter than the Celtic porridges, bread soups (*thârida* or *thurda*) led to the famed *açordas* of Alentejo; vinagery chopped salads refreshed with spring water were precursors to *gaspacho* and other cold soups.

Couscous quickly became a staple in the territories' diet and remained so until the late 16th century, when more readily available cereals that required less preparation started to replace it. Extraordinarily, there are villages in the north-western province of Trás-os-Montes, one of the first regions to be re-conquered in the 12th century, where couscous is still made by hand, in exactly the same manner and using the same utensils as the occupying Berbers did more than 900 years ago.

Meat played a major role in the Moorish diet. Christians and Mozarabs (Christians living under Muslim rule) were allowed to consume pig in moderation, though it was forbidden by the Quran. Lamb was the preferred meat, with goat less prized and beef not widely consumed as most oxen were working beasts. Game was also appreciated, and stag was considered a delicacy along with the Iberian red-legged partridge. Birds were very popular and accessible to everyone: fat chickens and roosters were in most demand but pigeons, ducks and geese were also common. Small birds like thrushes, starlings and blackbirds were considered treats. The populace used to feed on tripe (stomach), liver, heart, spleen and lung, and so there were many recipes for offal (variety meats). Lamb heads were nonetheless a choice delicacy, just as they are today in the southern province of Alentejo.

The fact that the Moors introduced sugarcane and its cultivation to the Iberian Peninsula, namely to the Algarve, would change the course of history, as the Portuguese later established plantations in Madeira, making the island at one point the biggest sugar producer in the world and laying the foundations for large-scale plantations that would eventually be established in Brazil, the Americas and the Caribbean Islands. In a few centuries, sugar went from being a scarce spice and a medicine to a widely consumed, daily staple of people of all economic standing, all over the world, but it would, of course, also lead to the abominable trafficking of slaves.

The abundance of sugar, dried fruits and nuts determined the Moorish influence on sweets and confectionery, and the fact that most Portuguese desserts are made using lots of sugar, egg yolks and almonds attests to that. Many of the 'conventual sweets' that brought glory to Catholic convents from the 15th century onwards, bear striking similarities to Arabic sweets found in any souk or teahouse in North Africa today. The oldest known Portuguese cookbook, a 16th-century collection of recipes attributed to Infanta D. Maria, mentions 'moorish' dishes, and in *Arte de Cozinha*

(*Art of Cuisine*, 1680) by Domingos Rodrigues, cook to the Royal Court, two-thirds of all recipes bear strong influences of Arab cuisine. It is an undeniable fact that it was Moorish culture that had the greatest influence over Portuguese foodways. If you browse through a collection of nearly 700 recipes, such as in this book, almost half of them bear a Moorish trait, either within the ingredients or in the cooking technique.

It is worth a mention that Iberia didn't adopt only the recipes from Baghdad, but also the order in which dishes were served: soups and broths first, then fish, birds, meat and sweets at the end. From the Moors, the Portuguese also inherited the table rituals of conviviality, the blessedness of sharing a meal and reverence for old customs passed from generation to generation.

The Iberian Jews

Jews arrived in Sefarad, as they referred to the Iberian Peninsula, before the Roman conquest of Hispania, towards 70 CE, following a harrowing defeat before the legions of Titus Vespasianus that led to the destruction of the Temple of Jerusalem and caused the great Jewish Diaspora. Sephardic Jews remained in Spain until 1492 and in Portugal until 1497, when they were expelled, first by the Spanish Catholic Kings, and then by King Manuel of Portugal.

From the outset, the Sephardi formed thriving communities that became influential due to the combined skills of their members — mostly merchants, artisans, administrators and lenders. During the 10th and 11th centuries, under Muslim rule, the Sephardi culture reached its Golden Age, with a rich and powerful community of important scholars, poets, physicians and courtiers. Arab tolerance allowed for the harmonious coexistence of the three cultures of Arab, Christian and Jewish.

Jewish presence in the Peninsula left a lasting impression on all aspects of life, in customs, the arts, science, language and, of course, gastronomy. Many dishes that are now considered traditional would not exist if not for the influence of Sephardi cuisine. The characteristics of Jewish cuisine are determined by the religious laws of the Kashrut, which sets out which foods are allowed (*kasher*) and which are forbidden (*taref*).

Festivities and the religious calender also determine many food customs: it is, for instance, forbidden to cook during Sabbath, a restriction that led to the development of ways of preserving and cooking food in advance — practising Jews needed to cook their meals the day before Sabbath so that they would be warm and edible on that day. *Adafina*, a savoury stew of meat, chickpeas, collard greens, vegetables and hard-boiled eggs, was the dish that Jews often ate on the day of rest; it is considered the mother of all pot stews, the Spanish *cocido* and the Portuguese *cozido*. The Jewish diet was, in many ways, similar to that of the Moors — using a vast palette of ingredients while following strict religious rules. They ate couscous (savoury as well as sweetened with honey), batter-fried vegetables that the Portuguese ate during Lent and missionaries later took to Japan (which we now know as tempura), salted and pickled fish, unleavened breads, dried fruits and jams (jellies), marzipan and candied nuts such as *amêndoas cobertas de Moncorvo* or *canelões*, similar to Sicilian cannoli. As Sephardic Jews were chased and prosecuted by the infamous Inquisition, many converted to Catholicism, while others concealed their religious practices, pretending to be converts. There's even a story that in order to fool the spying Inquisitiors, the secret Jews invented a sausage that contained no pork meat and instead was stuffed with bread, poultry, olive oil, garlic and paprika — the *alheira*. The historic truth is that this sausage, under that name, only came into existence less than a century ago in the city of Mirandela. It is a delicious sausage.

The Birth of a Nation

After the end of Islamic rule, Spain and Portugal gradually became two separate entities. Afonso I, the first king of Portugal, conquered the country from the Muslim taifa principalities and secured its independence from Spain in the 12th century. Spain became united three centuries later, with the marriage of Isabella of Castille and Ferdinand of Aragon, the two principal Christian kingdoms in the country. The territories were released from Moorish rule and brought together under the flag of the new nation that was inhabited by an amalgam of people from very different roots: the original Lusitanians and Celtiberians had intermarried with late Roman settlers and the invading Suebi Visigoths who stayed behind after being defeated by the Moors, Mozarabs, Jews and Moors. The nobility was made up of knights from Galicia, León and Burgundy, and the elite knights and warriors saw meat as a source of physical and moral strength, while wine, according to the Bible, 'lifted the spirit and gladdened the heart'. Their diet was one of roasted meats placed on thick slices of bread that would soak up the juices. They grabbed their food with their bare hands and sliced it with daggers, eating stews, pottages and soups with wooden spoons.

Ordinary people's diet was necessarily more frugal, but was no doubt healthier for it, based as it was on seasonal farmed or foraged products and cereals for bread or porridge. The population living in the northern territories ate dark, dense breads made from rye, barley or millet, known as *broas*, akin to Germanic *Brot*. Further south, breads were lighter in colour and weight, made from wholegrain wheat, milled on hand-turned stone grinders. The elites ate white bread baked from fine wheat flour. Jews and Moors were given relative religious freedom and allowed to maintain their culture and habits, but were confined to neighbourhoods respectively called *judiarias* and *mourarias* with synagogues, mosques and elected leaders who represented the communities and enforced the law. They were also forced to pay heavy taxes and duties, such as the tithe on production from the land and the *quadragésima* of the value of cattle and all acquired property. In spite of these obstacles, both communities prospered and played a role in the nation's progress. In the High Middle Ages, Lisbon's *Mouraria* had two bathhouses (*hammam*), a prison, a slaughterhouse and corral, a school, a cemetary and two mosques. During the reign of King Pedro I there were fourteen *mourarias* in as many cities of the realm.

Following the Crusades, several monastic orders flourished in Portugal, especially the Benedictines and the Cistercians. Through their religious practice and transmission of knowledge, these religious orders played an important part in the repopulation of the country, in the education of the population and the revitalisation of agriculture. Portugal greatly increased its production of olive oil, and most of all wine, through the influence of monasteries installed throughout the kingdom. Not only did monks teach peasants to make better wines, they encouraged them to produce them at the monasteries, while keeping a tenth of the production in their cellars. Some monasteries were famous for their excellent wines, and monks were renowned for their prodigious appetite for the delights of the table.

Lisbon Past and Present
••

Lisbon has been central in establishing Portugal's culinary identity, playing the leading role for more than three thousand years. The city of seven hills, like Rome, owes its historical prominence to its natural harbour at the mouth of the Tagus river, on the largest estuary in Europe. While there is archaeological proof that the area has been inhabited since 30 thousand years ago, it was really the Phoenicians who put it on the map. Once a peaceful hamlet, *Alis Ubbo* — the 'enchanting port' for the Levantine seafarers — became a thriving trading post. The Phoenicians would create another settlement directly across the river, on the left bank, in similar configuration to their most famous settlement of *Gádir*, today's Cádiz. Ships from all parts of the civilised world arrived to trade and take shelter in the magnificent estuary that was rich in freshwater and ocean fish, a nursery to eels, sole, cuttlefish and octopus, schools of mackerel, sardines and even large creatures such as tuna, dolphins and whales. The surrounding wetlands were rich in oysters and molluscs, the sand banks at the river's mouth full of clams, prawns (shrimp) and other shellfish. There was so much fish to be processed at the salt-fish factories of the left bank that pottery workshops to produce amphora and salt-works had to be installed nearby.

During the Roman period, starting in the second century, Lisbon became one of the most important cities in the Peninsula, with Julius Caesar raising the settlement to the dignity of a *municipium* and naming it Felicitas Julia Olisipo. To suit the lavish lifestyle of the Roman conquerors, many improvements were made in the city. As well as the forum, circus, theatre, temples and baths, fountains and wells were built, and many villas had lead piping and running water. Vast farms were established on both banks of the river to supply the growing population with vegetables, meat and dairy, all sold in open-air markets along with the freshest fish from the nearby river. The Romans also built a large industrial belt, with large *cetárias* for fish salting and preserving — garum from Olisipo was highly prized in Rome.

After the decline of the Roman Empire, Lisbon was successively occupied by the Alans, the Suebi and the Visigoths, who didn't leave much of a legacy other than the thick embankment walls of Lisbon's castle. The Moors stayed in the city for four centuries, restoring it to the glory of Roman times, and more. Al-Usbuna had a great mosque, a magnificent citadel in the heart of the castle, administrative buildings, public baths, terraced orchards with streets and courtyards planted with orange trees. The city enjoyed a relative autonomy from the taifas that fought over its control. The city's mercantile elite, made up of Moors, Christians and Jews, engaged in business partnerships and commercial ventures that were based on bonds of kinship, with trade networks covering most of the civilised world. The elites were allowed to govern the city and trade freely but had to pay the *jizayh* tax based on their earnings. The finest commodities were traded through the port of Lisbon, and the tables of the city's powerful displayed just that.

During the early times of the Christian Reconquest, the city suffered from bloody and destructive battles, but again its strategic location — and the fact that it served as a hub for Crusaders who travelled by sea to the Holy Land — soon made it prosper again. Many British ships were already loading their hulls with wines from the newborn nation of Portugal on their way to the Crusades, so that they could better fight the infidels.

In 1252, Lisbon became the capital of Portugal. The city flourished under the first dynasty of Portuguese kings, only to be besieged under King Ferdinand by his Castilian cousins, who feared that he would claim the Spanish throne. A warrior knight solved the problem by defeating the Castilians and founding the Second Dynasty by becoming King and marrying an English princess, thus sealing Europe's oldest alliance.

Lisbon was the central commercial hub in the Portuguese medieval kingdom, forming large economic areas under its influence that provided it with wine, figs, raisins, olive oil, oranges, animal hides, honey, wax, cork and a surplus of other Iberian products to export to markets in northern Europe.

As the Portuguese set out to conquer territories in North Africa and down the Gulf of Guinea, Lisbon's mercantile class grew stronger and richer. New trading opportunities drew colonies of German, Flemish, Dutch, English and French traders, who established themselves in Lisbon. Greeks, Lombards and Genoese, who had lost their trading

enclaves in Constantinople when the city fell to the Turks in 1453, also came to Lisbon. After the great explorer Vasco da Gama led a Portuguese fleet to India in 1498, the Venetian monopoly on Oriental trade was broken. Lisbon was to become the centre of the world's commerce.

In 1527, the first Portuguese census counted 65,000 inhabitants in Lisbon, occupying 23 parishes. A considerable number of these residents became rich, and the city was endowed with larger and more luxurious buildings. African slaves became a familiar Lisbon sight, with Portugal playing a major role in the trade in slaves.

King Manuel I, known as 'the Fortunate' and who ruled from 1495 to 1521, began the Portuguese colonisation of the Americas and Portuguese India. He also oversaw the establishment of a vast trade empire across Africa and Asia. The income from Portuguese trade monopolies and colonised lands made Manuel the wealthiest monarch in Europe, allowing him to be one of the great patrons of the Portuguese Renaissance, which gave rise to many significant artistic and literary achievements. At this point, the most expensive shopping street in the world was in Lisbon: at *Rua Nova dos Mercadores* you could find jewellery, Ming porcelain, silk, spices and other exotic luxury imports from Africa, Brazil and Asia.

Then a foolish adolescent king led the elite of his armies, most of his able noblemen and a great deal of the country's naval fleet into a disastrous battle against the infidels in Morocco. King Sebastião disappeared in combat, most of the nobility were either killed or taken hostage, and more than 9,000 soldiers were lost. The country went bankrupt through paying ransom to free the survivors, and lost its sovereignty. Felipe II of Spain, one of the contenders to succeed to the throne, became Felipe I of Portugal. Although Spanish for 60 years, Lisbon managed to keep its identity and even came close to becoming the capital of Iberia — King Felipe's mother was Portuguese and he spoke the language, and on being crowned King of Portugal, he moved his court to Lisbon and stayed there for three years, living and dressing like the Portuguese, and eating the food he so loved from his mother's Portuguese table.

Lisbon remained a thriving cosmopolitan city and global commercial hub. Portugal's sovereignty was restored in 1640 and the 'enchanting port' maintained its flurry of vessels of all nations coming and going to all parts of the world.

In the first half of the 18th century, the profits from the plantations and the gold and diamond deposits of Brazil brought a new wave of optimism and excitement to Lisbon. Meanwhile, an aqueduct was being built and manufacturing was flourishing. This period of optimism ended brutally on the morning of 1 November 1755. The churches were all packed with people honouring the dead for All Saints' Day when the city was devastated by one of the most powerful earthquakes ever recorded. Three initial jolts lasted for 10 minutes. Lisbon's quay sank into the Tagus

River. Those who sought safety on boats on the Tagus were drowned by a tsunami. Following the tsunami, massive fires broke out and lasted for days, burning large sections of the city. About 60,000 lives were lost, and more than 12,000 buildings were destroyed; the famous merchant street was razed to the ground, as was the *Paço da Ribeira*, the Royal Palace, nearby.

Lisbon was literally rebuilt from the ashes — and a lot of rubble — with a speed that was astonishing for the time. King José I charged his Prime Minister, Sebastião José de Carvalho, the virtual ruler of the country, with the task of overseeing reconstruction. It is said that the city's reconstruction was funded with 'volunteer donations' collected from gold-producing provinces in Brazil, such was their wealth. The city gained new life through advanced architectural achievements, the Prime Minister was rewarded with the title of Marquis of Pombal, and the new building style became known as *Pombalino* after him.

Western society had been shocked that one of the most beautiful and prosperous cities in Europe could suffer such a fate. The tragedy of Lisbon stirred the conscience of European philosophers and scientists, and arguably contributed towards consolidating the ideals of the Age of Enlightenment. Napoleon's ambitions of greatness also affected Lisbon, as he tried to invade and occupy Portugal three times over a period of six years, forcing the royal family to flee to Brazil. In the first attempt in 1807, the invading force was led by General Junot who, defeated, returned to France in a British Navy ship, carrying his Lisbon loot. His wife, the Duchess of Abrantes, took back a recipe for partridges immortalised by Escoffier in his *Le Guide Culinaire*.

A constitutional war, the independence of Brazil and two feuds about regal succession later, Lisbon entered the 20th century still the capital of a colonial empire... but one in decline. A regicide saw the end of the monarchy and the Republic of Portugal was born. Lisbon still retained its cosmopolitanism, with its harbour ever busy, raw materials still pouring in from the colonies.

In the two World Wars Portugal, under the rule of a dictator, remained neutral. The colonies claimed their freedom and the manna was no longer falling from overseas, leaving Lisbon still beautiful but frugal. The Revolution of the Carnations in 1974 brought freedom to the capital and to the country, and also, finally, independence for the last of the colonies. Lisbon welcomed more than half a million people returning from the former possessions, bringing shattered lives to new beginnings. Lisbon, ex-capital of the empire, was once again cosmopolitan, European and global.

Embraced by the sea and by the river, *Alfacinhas* (Lisboners) make the most of the fresh fish and seafood available, eating it in taverns and restaurants that serve today the memories of flavours from bygone days, with sardines grilled in the open air, freshwater fish stews, oyster soup, fried eels and codfish cakes. Many

A Brief History of Portuguese Food

say that Lisbon is where you can taste the best cuisine from each and every region of Portugal, thanks to migration through the years from the countryside to the capital. I would add that it is where you can taste the best flavours of the former colonies, while dancing to the best music from those countries, because the city is a hub for all Portuguese-speaking cultures. On top of that, Lisbon's citizens come from all four corners of the globe — there is a neighbourhood where people from 92 different nationalities live and work — and there are specialty grocery stores from nearly as many countries. All these people walk today on cobbled slopes that were set by Jewish masons and marched on by Crusaders returning from Jerusalem, sit at miradors where minstrels have sung, drink from the same fountain that has slaked the thirst of the great poet Camões after he had eaten the same salty fried mackerel that we can still enjoy today.

This is why Lisbon embodies Portuguese foodways, old and new.

The Age of Discovery

Portugal's initial motivation to start exploring new sea routes was commercial as well as religious. Henry the Navigator, Prince of Portugal, pursued the objective of finding a sea route to 'Cathay' by sailing south along the African coast and then east, which would also possibly allow him to circle the territories of the Arab 'infidels' and attack them from the rear. While at it, Prince Henry was intent on hijacking the Guinea trade of gold and ivory from the Moors of North Africa by creating a sea route to channel those products directly to Portugal. Half a century before Columbus reached the Americas, the Portuguese were already introducing new products to Europe, like the alligator pepper (*Aframomum melegueta*) that they decided to call 'grains-of-paradise' for marketing purposes. This new and exotic spice garnered instant success among European merchants trading from Lisbon. Columbus himself travelled the African routes in Portuguese trade ships and married the daughter of a captain-donee in Madeira, then the world's biggest producer of sugar. Columbus' discoveries uncovered a whole 'New World' of products — the so-called Columbian Exchange. An interesting exercise is to try to imagine what people ate and how they cooked prior to this interchange. What would Italian cuisine be like without tomatoes, or Thai or even Indian food without chilli peppers? And what would Brazilian cuisine be like without limes or coconuts?

Portugal played a major role in the Columbian Exchange because, unlike Spain who focused their early colonisation efforts on the Americas, Portugal also explored and colonised Africa and Asia. It wasn't just about bringing new products from remote places to Europe, it was the widespread nature of their exploration that made Portugal's role so important. Another factor was that Portugal possessed islands in the Atlantic, such as Madeira, Porto Santo and the Cabo Verde archipelago. These semi-tropical islands allowed Portuguese planters to acclimatise new species to the cooler European climate prior to bringing them to mainland Portugal. These offshore territories in effect became botanical laboratories for the Europeanisation of Asian, African and American foods. Chillies carried by Portuguese seafarers arrived in India around 1510. Twenty years later they had reached Mongolia, and 40 years later Japan. By 1600, chillies were everywhere.

Portugal also played a key role in the Columbian Exchange with the dissemination of corn (maize or *milho* in Portuguese). Although this plant did not originate in Brazil but came from Central America, it was already widespread in the indigenous cultures of Brazil prior to the arrival of Europeans in 1500. The Portuguese carried corn back to Europe with them, and from there carried it to their colonies in Africa. From these colonies it spread throughout the continent, and today corn is the most widely eaten staple food on the African continent.

Exchange wasn't merely about circulating products, it was also about integration and acculturation. As Portugal was a small country both in area and in population, during the early colonisation efforts its rulers promoted a policy of interracial marriage in the new territories, in order to boost the country's number of subjects and citizens. Food and foodways were very much part of the cultural interaction — to this day you will find many examples of dishes, recipes or cooking techniques that bear a Portuguese influence, with Macanese cuisine perhaps the most striking example. From the mid-1500s to 1999, Macau was a Portuguese colony and a platform for the country's interests in the Far East. Portuguese civil servants, soldiers and traders married to Chinese, Malay, Indian, Siamese or Japanese women converged in Macau, and the enclave's cuisine gained an identity of its own; it might well be considered the first 'fusion' cuisine. India is another good example, with the Portuguese first establishing a colony there at the beginning of the 16th century. Portuguese India was ruled first from Cochin, and then Goa. Over the next four centuries, Portuguese control spread to various parts of India, mostly along the west coast of the country, but also in the northeast, in Bengal.

During this time, the Portuguese left their mark on certain Indian cuisines in two ways: by introducing new ingredients to India, and dishes that were then adapted to Indian culinary techniques and tastes. The strongest Portuguese influence was of course in Goa, which Portugal ruled until 1961. Goan Catholic cuisine has a distinct Portuguese flavour and many of its dishes can now be found throughout India and abroad, such as vindaloo and sorpotel. Mumbai's most popular street food, vada pav, a mashed potato fritter (*batata vada*) sandwiched in a bread roll (*pav*) is absolutely Portuguese in influence, just like Bengal's *bandel cheese*.

When the first Portuguese traders arrived in Japan in 1543 they brought with them, among many things, refined sugar, which was valued as a luxury good. Japanese lords enjoyed Portuguese confectionery to a point where some are now part of 'wagashi', the Japanese family of confections served with tea, such as *konpeitō* (candy), *kasutera* (a sponge cake akin to *pão de ló*), and *keiran somen* (the Japanese version of Portuguese *fios de ovos*, also popular in Thailand under the name of *kanom foy tong*). But Portuguese cuisine's most famous gift to Japan is, of course, tempura.

The Persian orange, widely grown in southern Europe from the Moorish invasions onwards, was bitter, and sweet oranges were brought from India to Europe in the 15th century by Portuguese traders. Some Southeast Indo-European languages named the orange, once its main import, after Portugal. Albanians call oranges *portokall*, Bulgarians *portokal*, Greeks *portokali*, Iranians *porteghal*, and Romanians *portocală*. Turks say *Portakal*, and in Arabic it's *al-burtuqal*. In the southern Italian dialect of Naples, the orange is called *portogallo* or *purtualle*, literally 'the Portuguese ones'.

Tea was made fashionable in Britain in the 1660s after the marriage of King Charles II to the Portuguese princess Catherine of Braganza (*Catarina de Bragança*), who brought her fondness for tea, originally from the colony of Macau, to the court. The new queen also introduced marmalade to the British and made the habit of eating with a fork a part of the court's table etiquette.

All over the world, Portuguese immigrants influenced the cuisine of their new 'homelands', such as in Hawaii and parts of New England. *Pão doce* (Portuguese sweet bread), *malassadas*, *sopa de feijão* (bean soup), and Portuguese sausages (such as *linguiça* and *chouriço*) are eaten regularly in the Hawaiian islands by families of all ethnicities. Similarly, the *papo seco*, a crusty bread, has become a staple of cafés in the US cities of Newark or Fall River, where there are substantial Portuguese communities. Nowadays it is not uncommon to find excellent *pastéis de nata* or *bolos de arroz* in pastry shops from London and Paris to Melbourne.

Portuguese gastronomy has of course also been influenced by foreign cuisines, and a fascinating example of that is *canja de galinha*, a comforting and hearty chicken broth traditionally served to people who are convalescing, or to mothers who have just given birth. There are many regional variations and most former Portuguese colonies, including Goa, have their own version. So what is so particular about this chicken broth with rice? It has its origin in India — a plain rice porridge called *kanji* in Kerala and *Pez* in the Konkan region. It was first mentioned in western writings by the great Jewish Portuguese Garcia de Orta in his opus *Colóquios dos Simples e Drogas da India*. The rice broth, or *canje* as he refers to it, would have been a restorative broth made for him by his most faithful servant and cook, Antónia. *Canja* is thus *congee*, the quintessential rice porridge that is a staple food for millions of Asians.

Regional Identity

As significant and vital as rural landscapes, traditional foodways — passed down from generation to generation — help characterise the identity of a region and the soul of a country. In respecting traditions, local cuisines make use of products that thrive in their natural terroir, are available because they are seasonal, and are cooked in their prime. Within one country, regional cuisines differ according to geographic and climatic factors, whether from the mountains or the plains, coast or interior, using rain-fed or irrigated farm products. Biodiversity and the abundance of game, fish or forest-foraged foods can also help determine the food identity of a region. As for recipes in regional cuisines, these are mostly inherited and passed down orally, which is why today it is essential to document and exhaustively register every procedure or gesture with detail. It is also why this book has such importance, because regional cuisines are about proximity — they are local — which is why the same recipe will have subtle differences.

Portuguese cuisine is in essence Atlantic, with similar traits to the Mediterranean diet in the inclusion of fish, seafood and fresh greens. Mediterranean elements also remain in fundamental aspects like climate, geography, economy and culture in the day-to-day life of the Portuguese.

Throughout its history, Portugal has undergone processes of assimilation and acculturation, of integration and exclusion, that have all helped to define the profile of a national identity that is diverse and universal. Likewise, the richess and diversity of Portugal's regional cuisines spring from a symbiosis of livelihood systems, of farmers and fishermen, of monastic and aristocratic traditions, and of influences and ingredients from faraway lands.

As expressed by Reinaldo Ferreira in the popular song *Uma Casa Portuguesa*, made famous by the iconic fado singer Amália Rodrigues, Portuguese foodways, old and new, are expressed 'at the table', with family and friends the elements of summoning and conveyance of communion and conviviality.

Numa casa Portuguesa fica bem /
Pão e vinho sobre a mesa

In a Portuguese house all is fine /
on the table is bread and wine

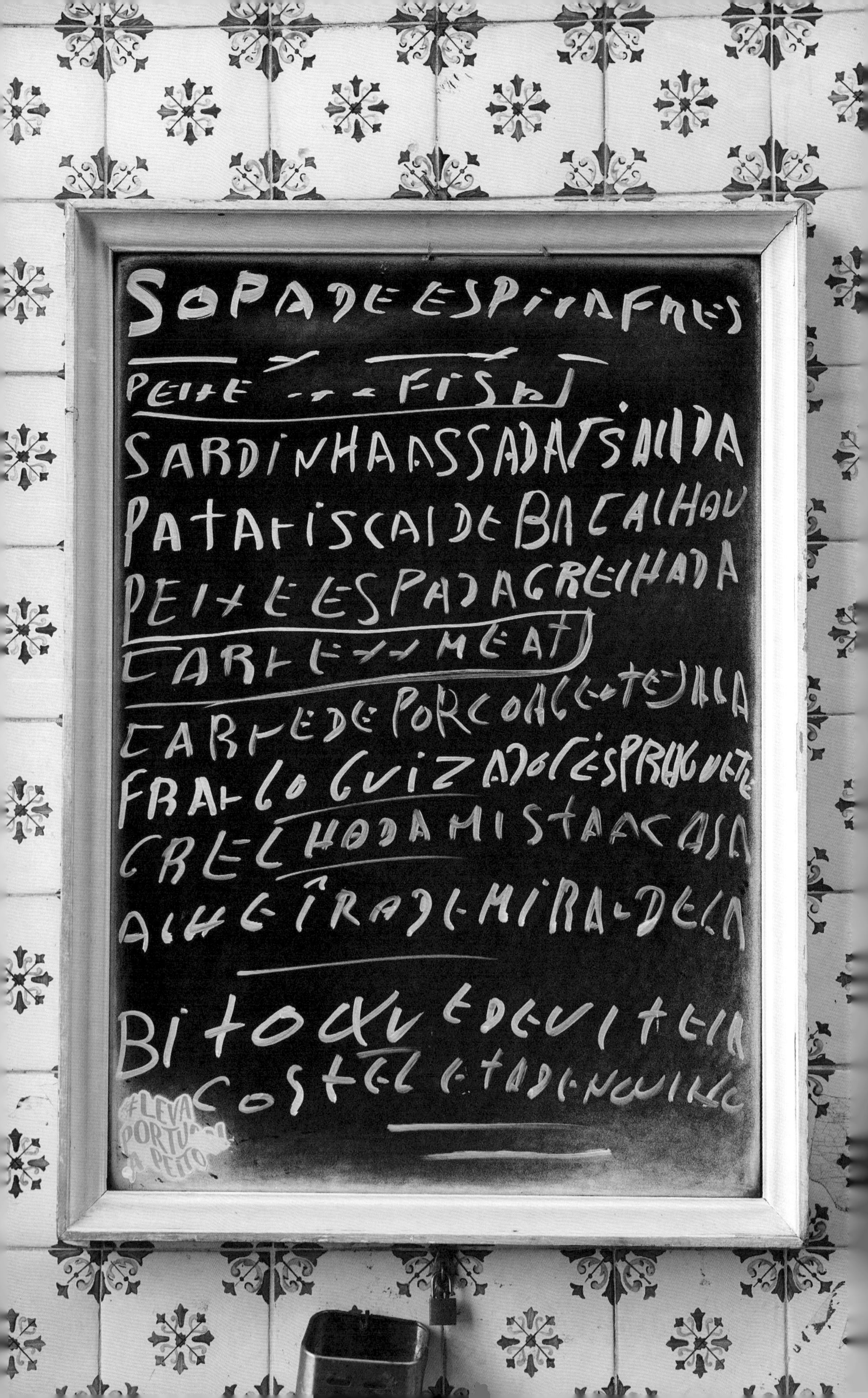

SOPA DE ESPINAFRES

PEIXE --- FISH

SARDINHA ASSADA SALADA
PATANISCA DE BACALHAU
PEIXE ESPADA GRELHADA

CARNE --- MEAT

CARNE DE PORCO A ALENTEJANA
FRANGO GUIZADO C/ESPARGUETE
GRELHADA MISTA CASA
ALHEIRA DE MIRANDELA

BITOQUE DE VITELA
COSTELETA DE NOVILHO

#LEVA PORTUGAL A PEITO

Legend

* Gluten free
* Dairy free
* Vegetarian
* Vegan
* One pot
* 5 ingredients or fewer
* 30 minutes or less

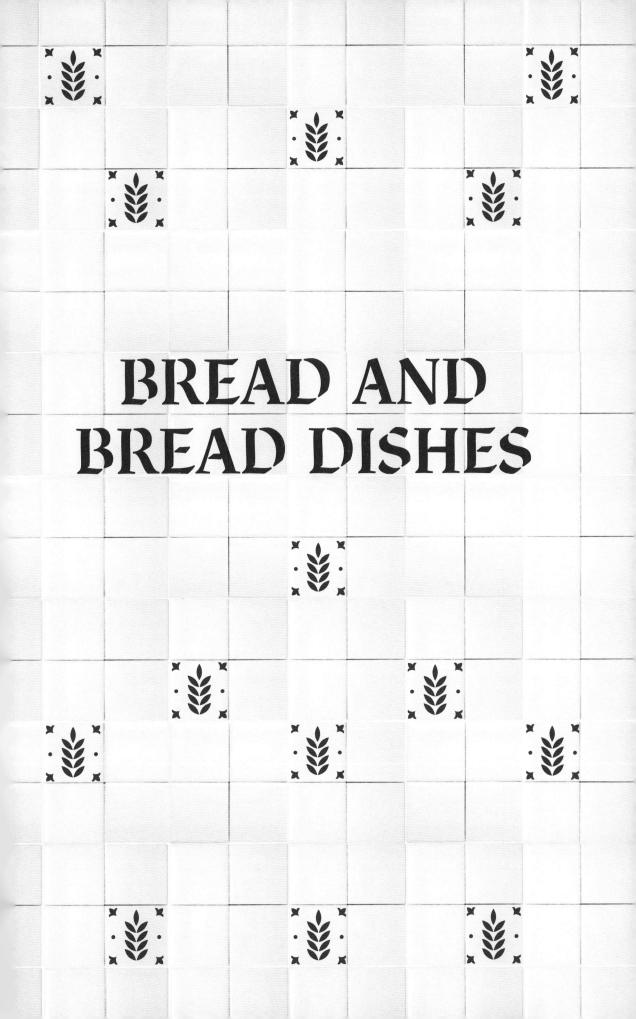

BREAD AND BREAD DISHES

Bread

••

Pão   ⛝ Leiria

Preparation time: 10 minutes, plus 16 hours 20 minutes
fermenting and rising
Cooking time: 45 minutes–1 hour
Makes: 2 medium loaves
⛝ ∅ ∨ ✕

1 kg/2 lb 4 oz (8⅓ cups) flour (T65), plus extra for
    dusting
10 g/¼ oz (2 teaspoons) fresh yeast or
    2.5 g (scant 1 teaspoon) instant dried yeast
10 g/¼ oz (2 teaspoons) salt

For the bread starter:
5 g/¼ oz (1 teaspoon) fresh yeast or
    1.25 g (⅓ teaspoon) instant dried yeast
200 g/7 oz (1⅔ cups) flour (T65)

The day before baking the bread, make the starter.
Put the yeast and 250 ml/8 fl oz (1 cup) water into
a large or medium glass jar or container, add the
flour and mix well. Cover with food wrap and leave
to ferment at room temperature for 12 hours.

The next day, put the 1 kg/2 lb 4 oz (8⅓ cups)
flour into a large bowl. Put the yeast into a small
bowl and a small amount of warm water and stir
to dissolve. Add the salt, then add the leaven and
mix until fully combined. Mix either by hand or
in a stand mixer fitted with a dough hook on low
speed, then add 700 ml/23½ fl oz (2¾ cups plus
2 teaspoons) water, a little at a time, and continue
mixing until a smooth dough forms. Cover the bowl
with a tea (dish) towel and leave to rise at room
temperature for 20 minutes.

Over the next hour, work the dough by folding
each corner into the middle in turn. Do this twice
every 20 minutes — so four sets of eight folds.
Then over the next 3 hours, repeat this folding
process but with intervals of 1 hour.

Once the rising and folding process is completed,
tip the dough out onto a work counter and divide
it into two equal pieces. Shape each piece into a
round. Once the loaves are shaped, leave them to
rest at room temperature for 20 minutes. If using
bread proving baskets (bannetons), dust them
with flour, then place the shaped loaves inside.
Alternatively, use a clean tea (dish) towel dusted with
flour for proving the loaves.

Preheat your wood-fired oven or normal oven
to 240°C/475°F/Gas Mark 9. Put a small roasting
pan on the base of the oven.

Once the oven is hot, fill the roasting tray with
cold water and put the loaves directly on the oven
rack above it. Bake the bread for 45 minutes—
1 hour, or until a golden crust has formed.

Leave the bread to cool on a wire rack before
slicing and serving. This bread can be stored in an
airtight container for up to 5 days or can be frozen.

Bread Dough

••

Massa de Pão   ⛝ Alentejo

Preparation time: 20 minutes, plus 4 hours 20 minutes rising
Cooking time: 50 minutes
Makes: 1 loaf
⛝ ∅ ∨ ✕

1 kg/2 lb 4 oz (8⅓ cups) spelt flour, plus extra for dusting
12 g/½ oz (2 teaspoons) salt
45 g/1½ oz (3 tablespoons) fresh yeast or
    12 g/½ oz (1⅓ tablespoons) instant dried yeast

Put the flour and salt into a bowl. If using fresh yeast,
grate (shred) it into the flour. If using dried then just
add it to the flour. Pour in 620 ml/21 fl oz (2½ cups)
warm water and mix until a smooth dough forms.
Cover with a tea (dish) towel and leave to rise at room
temperature for 4 hours or until doubled in size.

Shape the dough into a round, dust with flour and
leave to rest at room temperature for 20 minutes.

Preheat the oven to 260°C/500°F/Gas Mark 10.
Put the loaf directly on the rack. Bake for 5 minutes
then reduce the temperature to 200°C/400°F/
Gas Mark 6 and bake for a further 45 minutes, or
until golden and sounds hollow when tapped.

Leave the bread to cool on a wire rack before
slicing and serving.

Sweet Potato 'Family Bread'

••

Pão de Família   ⛝ Madeira

Preparation time: 40 minutes, plus 12 hours rising
Cooking time: 40 minutes
Makes: 2 medium loaves
⛝ ∅ ∨ ✕

300 g/11 oz white or regular sweet potatoes, unpeeled
1.2 kg/2 lb 11 oz strong wheat bread flour
1 teaspoon instant dried yeast
½ teaspoon fine sea salt

The day before baking the bread, make the dough.
Put the sweet potatoes into a pan of water, add
a pinch of salt and bring to the boil. Reduce to a
medium heat and cook for 30 minutes, or until soft.
Drain, peel, return to the pan and mash to a purée.

Combine the flour in a bowl with the yeast and
salt. Add the potato purée and mix for 3 minutes
until smooth. Add enough cold water to make a wet
dough. Cover the bowl with a tea (dish) towel and
leave to rise at room temperature for 12 hours.

Preheat your wood-fired oven or normal oven
to 240°C/475°F/Gas Mark 9. Grease two baking
sheets with oil and dust with flour. Divide the dough
into two pieces and shape each into a round.
Put on the baking sheets and bake for 40 minutes,
or until golden and sounds hollow when tapped.

Leave the bread to cool on a wire rack before
slicing and serving.

Stone-baked Wheat Bread (recipe p.32)

Stone-baked Wheat Bread

Bolo do Caco 📷 p.31   ⛿ **Madeira**

Even though it is called *bolo* (cake), this is a flat-bread. Cooked on a *caco* (basalt stone slab) over a wood fire, it has a thin, crunchy crust and a soft, airy crumb. In the Madeira archipelago, *bolo do caco* is sold by street vendors, eaten with melted butter, or served in restaurants paired with regional dishes.

Preparation time: 5 minutes, plus 1 hour rising
Cooking time: 30 minutes
Makes: 4
∅ ✕

20 g/¾ oz (1⅓ tablespoons) fresh yeast or
    5 g/¼ oz (1⅔ teaspoon) instant dried yeast
1 kg/2 lb 4 oz (8⅓ cups) wheat flour, plus extra for dusting
10 g/¼ oz (2 teaspoons) sea salt
garlic butter or salted butter, to serve

Combine the flour and salt in a stand mixer fitted with a dough hook attachment. Alternatively, combine in a large bowl.
    Put the yeast into a bowl, add 160 ml/5½ fl oz (⅔ cup) lukewarm water and stir until dissolved. Add to the flour and mix on medium speed for 15 minutes, or until a smooth dough forms. Cover the bowl with a damp tea (dish) towel and leave to rise at room temperature for 1 hour.
    On a lightly floured work counter, divide the dough into 4 equal balls, then flatten them with your hands to a disc, 2 cm/¾ inch thick.
    Heat a plancha, flat grill or sauté pan. Dust the plancha with flour and cook the *bolos* for 6 minutes on each side, or until golden. Flip them around and cook around the edges, about 2 minutes.
    Serve warm with garlic butter or salted butter.

Sweet Potato Wheat Bread

Bolo do Caco de Batata Doce   ⛿ **Madeira**

Preparation time: 1 hour 10 minutes, plus 1 hour rising
Cooking time: 1 hour 20 minutes
Makes: 9 small or 4 large loaves
∅ ✕

700 g/1 lb 9 oz white sweet potatoes
1 kg/2 lb 4 oz (8⅓ cups) spelt flour, plus extra for dusting
15 g/½ oz (1 tablespoon) salt
20 g/¾ oz (1⅓ tablespoons) fresh yeast or
    5 g/¼ oz (1⅔ teaspoon) instant dried yeast
garlic butter, to serve

Preheat the oven to 190°C/375°F/Gas Mark 5.
    Wrap the sweet potatoes in foil and bake for 45 minutes, or until soft. Leave to rest inside the oven for 10 minutes with the oven off and door open. Remove the skin from the potatoes, then put the flesh into a large bowl and mash to a purée.

Combine the sweet potato purée, flour and salt in a stand mixer fitted with a dough hook attachment. Alternatively, combine in a bowl.
    Put the yeast into a bowl, add 160 ml/5½ fl oz (⅔ cup) lukewarm water and stir until dissolved. Add to the flour and mix on medium speed for 15 minutes, or until a soft dough forms. Cover the bowl with a damp tea (dish) towel and leave to rise at room temperature for 1 hour.
    On a lightly floured work counter, divide the dough into 9 small or 4 medium balls, then flatten them with your hands to a disc.
    This bread was traditionally baked on top of a hot *caco* (piece of stone), but nowadays either heat a steel pan or a wood-fired oven. Cook the *bolos* for 12–15 minutes, or until golden brown all over.
    Preheat the grill (broiler).
    Cut each *bolos* in half, then grill for 5 minutes and brush with garlic butter before serving.

Cornbread

Broa de Milho 📷 p.33   ⛿ **Leiria**

This once-popular recipe has been lost over the years. When I was a kid, my grandmother would give us some of her 'mother dough' so we could make this cornbread, then we would give away some of our 'mother dough' to other households. This was common practice in villages. Ovens were always full of baking cornbread. Freshly baked bread is an aroma to remember forever.

Preparation time: 10 minutes, plus 15 hours fermenting
    and rising
Cooking time: 28 minutes
Makes: 3
⛿ ∅ V ✕

1.5 kg/3 lb 5 oz (12½ cups) corn flour
400 g/14 oz (3⅓ cups) wheat flour,
    plus extra for dusting
20 g/¾ oz (1⅓ tablespoons) fresh yeast or
    5 g/¼ oz (1⅔ teaspoon) instant dried yeast
20 g/¾ oz (3⅓ teaspoons) salt

Combine both flours into a heatproof bowl, then add 1.5 litres/50 fl oz (6¼ cups) boiling water and mix well. Cover with a tea (dish) towel and leave to ferment at room temperature for 12 hours.
    Put the yeast into a bowl, add 80 ml/2¾ fl oz (⅓ cup) water and stir to dissolve. Add to the fermented flour with the salt, then mix until a smooth dough forms. Cover and leave to rise for 3 hours.
    Preheat the oven to 240°C/475°F/Gas Mark 9.
    Divide the dough into 3 equal pieces, then shape each into a round. Dust the loaves with flour and bake for 12 minutes. Reduce the oven to 200°C/400°F/Gas Mark 6 and bake for a further 16 minutes, or until the crust is cracked and golden.
    Leave the bread to cool on a wire rack before slicing and serving. This bread can be stored in an airtight container for up to 5 days or can be frozen.

Bread and Bread Dishes

Cornbread

Corn Flour Flatbread

Bolo da Sertã   ⛉ Açores

This flat, round loaf traditionally made in the islands of São Miguel, São Jorge and Pico, is named after the unglazed clay frying pan — called a *sertã* — in which it is baked. Historically, *bolos da sertã* were improvised, using just three ingredients (corn flour, water and salt), prepared when no wheat flour was available and so 'real' bread was scarce. It is usually eaten warm, from the oven, for dipping or topping other dishes, or simply with butter.

Preparation time: 10 minutes, plus 30 minutes resting
Cooking time: 1 hour
Makes: 9 small breads
⛉ ⌀ V ✕

1 tablespoon sea salt
750 g/1 lb 10 oz (5 cups) corn flour
100 g/3½ oz (¾ cup minus 2 teaspoons) plain
    (all-purpose) flour, plus extra for dusting

Bring 380 ml/13 fl oz (1½ cups) water to the boil in a saucepan, add the salt and stir until dissolved.

Put the corn flour and flour into a bowl and pour over the water. Stir with a spatula to a rough dough, adding more water if necessary. You do not want a smooth dough. Cover the dough with a damp tea (dish) towel and leave to rest for 30 minutes.

Knead the dough on a floured work counter until smooth. Divide it into 9 equal balls, about 130 g/4½ oz each or smaller, if preferred.

Heat a clay or sauté pan over a medium heat. Working one at a time, flatten a ball into a 2-cm/¾-inch cylinder. Rub cold water on one side and cook in the pan for 3 minutes until golden. Flip over and cook on the other side until golden. Remove from the pan and keep warm. Cook the remaining breads in the same way. Serve warm.

Grilled Bread with Olive Oil, Salt and Garlic

Toiras – Vila Chã do Ribatejo   ⛉ Ribatejo

Also known as *Torricado*, this is an important recipe for the Ribatejo region. You can eat this bread on its own or topped with grilled cod or sardines.

Preparation time: 5 minutes
Cooking time: 10 minutes
Serves: 4
⛉ ⌀ V ✕ ⊠

1 x 400-g/14-oz loaf of wheat bread
2 garlic cloves, peeled
extra virgin olive oil, for drizzling
a handful of black olives, to garnish
sea salt

Prepare a barbecue with wood and hot coals. Alternatively, preheat an indoor grill (broiler).

Cut the bread into 2-cm/¾-inch slices. Using a sharp knife, score each slice from top to bottom and then horizontally to make a cross-hatch pattern on both sides. Don't cut all the way through the bread.

Once the coals are glowing, put the bread on the rack or under the grill and cook for 2–3 minutes, or until golden. Rub the garlic over each slice, sprinkle with a pinch of salt and drizzle with olive oil. Return the bread to the grill and cook for a further 2 minutes on both sides, or until the oil starts to 'boil'. Serve while hot garnished with the black olives.

Bread with Pennyroyal Soup — Alentejo Style

Açorda Alentejana   ⌾ p.35   ⛉ Alentejo

The Portuguese word *açorda* derives from the Andalusian Arabic word *thurda/çurda*, from the time in the 8th–13th centuries when the Iberian Peninsula was under Muslim rule. Açorda is Alentejo's most iconic dish. It is a soup with a transparent broth that is merely blanched and served hot, and flavoured with pennyroyal spearmint or coriander (or both), crushed garlic and coarse salt, and drizzled with olive oil. The recipe can vary depending on the area of Alentejo, and can be served with poached or boiled eggs, various types of fish (boiled cod or hake; fried or grilled sardines) and boiled green (bell) peppers.

Preparation time: 20 minutes
Cooking time: 10 minutes
Serves: 4
⛉ ⊠

3 garlic cloves, peeled but left whole
⅓ bunch pennyroyal
⅓ bunch coriander (cilantro)
90 ml/3 fl oz (6 tablespoons) olive oil
1.5 litres/50 fl oz (6¼ cups) fish stock or water
4 eggs
300 g/11 oz stale homemade or sourdough bread
sea salt

Put the garlic into a mortar with the pennyroyal, coriander (cilantro), olive oil and 2 teaspoons of sea salt. Using a pestle, mash to a paste. Transfer to a large heatproof bowl and set aside.

Bring the fish stock or water to the boil in a large saucepan. Reduce the heat to medium and carefully break the eggs into the hot stock, then poach the eggs for 4 minutes.

Add the poached eggs and poaching liquid to the bowl containing the herb paste, then cover with a tea (dish) towel and leave to stand for 5 minutes.

Cut the bread into slices. Place one slice of bread with some paste into individual bowls and top each slice with one egg. Ladle some of the poaching liquid into each bowl before serving.

Bread with Pennyroyal Soup — Alentejo Style

Bread Porridge with Pork

Migas à Alentejana 📷 p.37   ⏲ Alentejo

Traditionally served alongside fried pork, *migas* is made of crusty bread softened in hot water, shaped into large quenelles and cooked in fat from frying the ribs to achieve a golden outer crust. It was made to use up stale bread and is classified as a type of *açorda* (page 429). There are variations of this recipe: the *migas* is not always shaped into a quenelle but cooked loose, served with slices of fried bread and orange (*Migas de Alter do Chão*); it can include potatoes and chorizo (*Migas de Batata*, page 92), boiled salt cod (*Migas de Bacalhau*, page 40), asparagus (*Migas de Espargos*) or can even be a side dish to fried fish or grilled cod (*Migas Gatas*, page 42).

Preparation time: 20 minutes, plus 12 hours marinating
Cooking time: 1 hour 5 minutes
Serves 4
⏲

1 kg/2 lb 4 oz trimmed pork ribs
250 g/9 oz pork loin
30 g/1 oz *Massa de Pimentão* (red bell pepper paste)
2 garlic cloves, crushed with the back of a knife
150 g/5 oz lardo, sliced into thin strips
450 g/1 lb crusty wheat bread, torn into small pieces
sea salt

Cut the pork ribs into single pieces and put into a large bowl with the pork loin. Season with the *Massa de Pimentão*, salt and garlic, rubbing it into the meat, then cover with food wrap and leave to marinate in the fridge for 12 hours.

When ready to cook, put the lardo into a large saucepan and cook over a low heat for 1 minute until melted. Add the pork ribs and cook over a medium heat for 5 minutes, or until golden. Transfer to a baking sheet and keep warm. Add the pork loin to the pan and cook for 10 minutes or until browned. Transfer the pork loin to the baking sheet with the ribs and keep warm.

Pick out the crushed garlic pieces from the marinade, add to the pan and cook for a further 5 minutes, or until golden. Add the bread and stir, then add 1.5 litres/50 fl oz (6¼ cups) water, cover with a lid and cook over a low heat, stirring, for 45 minutes, or until the mixture forms a porridge.

Serve the porridge while warm with the pork ribs and loin.

Bread Porridge with Prawns

Açorda de Camarão da Praia da Vieira   ⏲ Lisbon

A simple dish made of bread, and one of the main food pillars of Portugal, *açorda* has evolved over the centuries, with developments, variations and different names depending on region. It can be more like a soup (*Açorda Alentejana*), served as a side dish (sometimes served with fish roe), or eaten as a complete dish (with shredded cod, lobster, or shrimp). It is to this latter category that *Açorda de Camarão* belongs, with large, rosy, boiled prawns (shrimp) included in the bread stew. This type of *açorda* is generally served in most Lisbon restaurants as a tableside service dish, with waiters bringing the pot to the table and briskly stirring a few egg yolks into the bread mixture in front of guests.

Preparation time: 15 minutes
Cooking time: 45 minutes
Serves: 4
⏲

1 carrot, peeled but left whole
1 onion, peeled but left whole
4 garlic cloves, peeled, one whole and three thinly sliced
1 bay leaf
750 g/1 lb 10 oz tiger or king prawns (shrimp), shell on
600 g/1 lb 5 oz crusty bread
70 ml/2½ fl oz (¼ cup plus 2 teaspoons) olive oil
1 red chilli, finely chopped
4 egg yolks
⅓ bunch coriander (cilantro), finely chopped (optional)
sea salt and freshly ground black pepper

Have a large bowl of iced water nearby. Fill a large saucepan with water, add the carrot, onion, the whole garlic clove and the bay leaf and bring to the boil. Reduce the heat to medium and cook for 15 minutes. Strain the stock through a sieve (fine mesh strainer) into a clean saucepan and bring back to the boil. Add the prawns (shrimp) and blanch for 30 seconds, then transfer them with a slotted spoon to the iced water and leave to cool.

Once cool, remove the shells and heads from the prawns and set these aside. Next, make a small cut in the back of each prawn, then remove and discard the black intestinal thread. Set the prepared prawns aside.

Put the reserved prawn shells and heads into the stock in the pan and cook over a medium heat for a further 10 minutes to extract all the flavour. Line a sieve with muslin (cheesecloth), strain the stock into a heatproof bowl and set aside.

Tear or cut the bread into very small pieces and put them into a large bowl. Add 1.2 litres/40 fl oz (5 cups) of the stock and leave to stand until the bread absorbs the liquid.

Heat the olive oil in a medium saucepan over a low heat, add the sliced garlic and cook for 5 minutes or until soft. Add the bread, stir and increase the heat to medium. Cook for 10 minutes, stirring continuously until the liquid has evaporated and the mixture forms a porridge. Season with the chilli, pepper and salt. Add the prawns and cook, stirring, for 30 seconds, or until warmed through. Remove from the heat, then add the egg yolks and mix very well to combine. Add the coriander (cilantro), if using, and serve.

Bread and Bread Dishes

Bread Porridge with Pork

Bread Porridge with Shellfish

••

Açorda de Marisco ◎ p.39   ◷ **Lisbon**

Preparation time: 20 minutes, plus 10 minutes soaking and
4 hours standing
Cooking time: 45 minutes
Serves: 4
◻

380 g/13½ oz cockles
380 g/13½ oz palourde clams
600 g/1 lb 5 oz tiger prawns (shrimp), shell on
140 ml/4¾ fl oz (½ cup plus 4 teaspoons) olive oil
650 g/1 lb 7 oz sourdough bread, thinly sliced
5 garlic cloves, peeled and chopped
1 bunch coriander (cilantro), chopped,
    plus extra to garnish (optional)
1 bay leaf
2 bird's eye chillies, chopped
2–3 egg yolks
sea salt

The day before, scrub the shells of the cockles
and clams to remove any dirt. Discard any that
don't close when their shells are tapped. Rinse
the cockles and clams several times under cold
running water to remove any sand and grit, then
put them into a large bowl and add enough water
to cover them. Add enough fine sea salt to make
a brine with 1% salt and stir well. Do not add too
much salt this may kill the clams. Leave to stand
in the fridge for 12 hours. This will help to expel
any sand inside the cockles and clams.

    Have a large bowl of iced water nearby. Bring
a large saucepan of water to the boil. Add the
prawns (shrimp) and a pinch of salt and blanch for
1 minute, then transfer them with a slotted spoon
to the iced water and leave to cool. Set 500 ml/
17 fl oz (2 cups plus 1 tablespoon) of the cooking
liquid aside.

    Heat 3 tablespoons of olive oil in two separate
medium saucepans over a medium heat. Add the
clams to one pan and the cockles to the other,
cover both pans with a lid and steam for about
2 minutes, or until they have opened. Transfer the
shellfish to a bowl, reserving any liquid in another
saucepan. Add the prawn cooking liquid to the pan
and boil over a medium heat for 3 minutes, or until
reduced a little. Remove from the heat and add
the bread. Leave to soak for 8–10 minutes.

    Heat the remaining olive oil in a large saucepan
over a low heat, add the garlic and cook for 30
seconds. Add the coriander (cilantro), then the
soaked bread and cook, stirring continuously, for
a further 25 minutes, or until the mixture is smooth.
Add the bay leaf and chillies, then stir through
the shellfish. Taste and adjust the seasoning, if
necessary. Remove from the heat and add the egg
yolks. Garnish with a little chopped coriander, if
liked. Just before serving, mix very well to combine.

Bread Porridge with Eggs

••

Açorda da Madeira   ◷ **Madeira**

Preparation time: 5 minutes, plus 12 hours chilling
Cooking time: 20 minutes
Serves: 4
◻ ⊘ ◻

4 garlic cloves, peeled but left whole
2 thyme sprigs, leaves picked
450 g/1 lb crusty bread, thinly sliced
220 ml/7½ fl oz (1 cup minus 2 teaspoons) olive oil
4 eggs
sea salt

Put the garlic into a mortar with a pinch of salt and
the thyme and, using a pestle, mash to a paste.

    Arrange the bread in a single layer on a baking
sheet. Drizzle with the olive oil and smear with the
garlic paste. Leave to chill in the fridge for 12 hours.

    Fill a saucepan with 2.5 litres/85 fl oz (10 cups)
water and bring to the boil. Once boiling, reduce
the heat to medium, carefully break the eggs into
the simmering water and poach for 4 minutes.
Using a slotted spoon, remove the eggs from the
pan, then pour the water over the bread before
serving with the poached eggs on the side.

Salt Cod Bread Porridge with Tomato

••

Açorda de Bacalhau   ◷ **Beira Alta**
com Tomate

Preparation time: 15 minutes, plus 12–14 hours soaking
Cooking time: 25 minutes
Serves: 4
◻

450 g/1 lb salt cod, desalted (page 40)
60 ml/2 fl oz (4 tablespoons) olive oil
1 large onion, peeled and sliced into rings
100 g/3½ oz (⅔ cup) tomato purée (paste)
850 g/1 lb 14 oz sourdough bread, thinly sliced
3 eggs
sea salt

Check the cod is not too salty before cooking.
If it is, then leave to soak for another 2 hours. Drain.

    Heat the oil in a saucepan over a medium heat.
Add the onion and cod and cook for 15 minutes,
or until the onion is golden. Remove the skin and
any bones from the fish, then flake the flesh.

    Add the tomato purée (paste) to the pan, stir,
then add the cod and 450 ml/15 fl oz (1⅔ cups)
water. Stir the bread into the mixture. Leave to soak
up the liquid for 8–10 minutes. Add a pinch of salt.

    Lightly whisk the eggs in a small bowl with
a fork. Add the eggs to the pan and mix everything
together until well combined before serving.

Bread Porridge with Shellfish

Salt Cod Bread Porridge with Fried Eggs

••

Açorda de Bacalhau   ⎃ **Beira Alta**
com Ovos Estrelados

Preparation time: 20 minutes, plus 12–14 hours soaking
Cooking time: 15 minutes
Serves: 4
⍇

450 g/1 lb salt cod, desalted
500 g/1 lb 2 oz stale bread, thinly sliced
180 ml/6 fl oz (¾ cup) olive oil
6 garlic cloves, peeled and thinly sliced
4 eggs
sea salt

To desalt the salt cod, put it into a bowl of cold water, cover with food wrap and leave to soak in the fridge for 12 hours, changing the water 3 or 4 times during the process. Check the cod is not too salty before cooking. If it is, then leave to soak for another 2 hours. Drain.

Fill a saucepan with enough water to cover the cod and bring to the boil. Reduce the heat to medium and, when simmering, add the cod and cook for 6 minutes, or until the flesh flakes easily. Remove the cod from the pan. Flake the cod into a bowl, removing any bones. Set the cod cooking water aside, checking the salt levels.

Arrange the bread and cod in layers in a deep, rimmed baking sheet, then pour over enough of the cod cooking water to soak the bread. Leave to soak for 2 minutes, then remove the excess water.

Heat 120 ml/4 fl oz (½ cup) of the olive oil in a small pan over a high heat. Once hot, add the garlic and fry for 10 minutes, or until golden. Carefully pour over the cod and bread.

Heat the remaining oil in a frying pan or skillet over a medium heat. Add the eggs and fry for 2 minutes, or to your liking. Season them with salt. Arrange the eggs over the bread before serving.

Salt Cod and Bread Soup

••

Açorda de Bacalhau   ⎃ **Alentejo**

Preparation time: 20 minutes, plus 12–14 hours soaking
Cooking time: 15 minutes
Serves: 4
⍇

600 g/1 lb 5 oz salt cod, desalted (see above)
3 garlic cloves, peeled but left whole
⅓ bunch coriander (cilantro) or pennyroyal
4 eggs
450 g/1 lb bread, preferably sourdough, sliced
sea salt

Check the cod is not too salty before cooking. If it is, then leave to soak for another 2 hours. Drain.

Put the garlic and coriander (cilantro) into a mortar and, using a pestle, mash together until a paste is formed. Add a pinch of salt.

Fill a saucepan with enough water to cover the cod and bring to the boil. Reduce the heat to medium and, when simmering, add the cod and cook for 6 minutes, or until the flesh flakes easily. Remove the cod from the pan. Flake the cod into a bowl, removing any bones, and set aside.

Carefully break the eggs into the cod cooking water, making sure they are kept whole, and poach over a medium heat for 4 minutes. Remove the eggs with a slotted spoon and set aside.

Stir the herb paste into the cooking liquid.

Divide the bread among individual bowls, then pour over the cooking liquid and leave to soak. Top with the cod and poached eggs before serving.

Salt Cod and Bread Sauté

••

Migas de Bacalhau   ▣ p.41   ⎃ **Alentejo**

Preparation time: 20 minutes, plus 12–14 hours soaking
Cooking time: 25 minutes
Serves: 4
⍇

450 g/1 lb salt cod, desalted (see left)
100 ml/3½ fl oz (⅓ cup) extra virgin olive oil
4 garlic cloves, peeled and very thinly sliced
4 eggs
600 g/1 lb 5 oz crusty bread
1 bunch coriander (cilantro), chopped

Check the cod is not too salty before cooking. If it is, then leave to soak for another 2 hours. Drain.

Heat the olive oil in a medium saucepan over a low heat. Add the garlic and fry for 1 minute, or until golden and glossy. Set aside.

Put the cod into a large saucepan, cover with 2.2 litres/76 fl oz (9 cups) water and cook over a low heat for 20 minutes, or until soft. Remove the cod from the pan, setting the cooking liquid aside, and flake the flesh, removing any bones.

Bring a saucepan of water to the boil. Once boiling, reduce the heat, add the eggs and cook for 8 minutes. Remove the eggs from the pan and leave to cool, then peel them and set aside.

Bring the reserved fish cooking liquid to the boil in the pan. Add the sliced bread to the pan, then take it off the heat and leave to stand until the bread becomes soft.

Transfer the soaked bread to the pan with the garlic. Stir in the fish, then cook over a medium heat for 5 minutes, adding more liquid to keep it moist, if necessary. Mix in the coriander (cilantro) and garnish with the reserved eggs, halved or quartered if preferred, before serving.

Salt Cod and Bread Sauté

Bread Porridge

Migas Gatas   ☐ Alentejo

This recipe is a good way of using up any leftover stale bread. It is a typical dish from Alentejo where bread plays a most important role. This dish can be served as an accompaniment to any fried fish.

Preparation time: 20 minutes, plus 12–14 hours soaking
Cooking time: 25 minutes
Serves: 4
☐

3 garlic cloves, peeled but left whole
600 g/1 lb 5 oz stale bread, thinly sliced
120 ml/4 fl oz (½ cup) olive oil
sea salt

To garnish (optional):
450 g/1 lb salt cod, desalted (page 40)
90 ml/3 fl oz (6 tablespoons) olive oil
15 ml/½ fl oz (1 tablespoon) white wine vinegar

If using salt cod in the garnish, check it is not too salty before cooking. If it is, then leave to soak for another 2 hours. Drain.

Put the garlic and 2 teaspoons of salt into a mortar and, using a pestle, mash to a paste.

Put the bread into a bowl with the garlic paste and mix together, then pour 1.5 litres/50 fl oz (6¼ cups) boiling water over the top. Cover with a tea (dish) towel and leave to soak for 10 minutes. Strain, then put the mixture into a large saucepan and add the olive oil. Cook over a medium heat, stirring continuously with a spatula or wooden spoon, for 10 minutes, or until a 'ball' of paste is formed.

If making the garnish, prepare a barbecue or preheat the indoor grill (broiler). When the coals are glowing, put the salt cod on the grill rack and grill for 10 minutes, or until golden. Season with the olive oil and vinegar before serving with the *migas* on the side.

Bread Porridge with Salt Cod and Olive Oil

Migas de Azeite   ☐ Alentejo

Migas, which are dishes made with olive oil, garlic and stale bread, were brought to Portugal by the Arabs in the 8th century. There's another variation of *migas* from Alentejo called *Migas gatas* (above), in which vinegar is added to the final dish. This dish can be served as an accompaniment to any fried fish.

Preparation time: 20 minutes, plus 12–14 hours soaking
Cooking time: 40 minutes
Serves: 4
☐ ✕

600 g/1 lb 5 oz salt cod, desalted (page 40)
600 g/1 lb 5 oz stale bread, cut into thin slices
4 garlic cloves, peeled, 1 thinly sliced, 3 very thinly sliced
220 ml/7½ fl oz (1 cup) extra virgin olive oil

Check the cod is not too salty before cooking. If it is, then leave to soak for another 2 hours. Drain.

When ready to cook, lay the bread slices on a tray that can hold liquid and scatter the very thinly sliced garlic over the bread.

Fill a saucepan with enough water to cover the cod and bring to the boil. Reduce the heat to medium and, when simmering, add the cod and cook for 6 minutes, or until the flesh flakes easily. Remove the cod from the pan. Flake the cod into a bowl, removing any bones, and set aside.

Spread the cod on top of the bread, then pour the cod cooking water over, making sure the bread is soaked. Cover with a tea (dish) towel and leave to soak for 30 minutes. Once the liquid has been absorbed, stir together the cod and bread to form a porridge.

Heat the olive oil in a large saucepan over a medium heat. Add the thinly sliced garlic and cook for 1 minute, or until golden. Add the bread paste and fry, stirring continuously, for 15 minutes, or until it no longer sticks to the sides of the pan. Make the mixture into a roll and cook until it is golden all over.

Rye Bread with Garlic and Paprika — Guarda Style

Migas à Moda da Guarda   ☐ Beira Alta

Preparation time: 15 minutes, plus 5 minutes soaking
Cooking time: 10 minutes
Serves: 4
☐ ⌀ ✕

330 g/11½ oz rye bread, sliced
160 ml/5½ fl oz (⅔ cup) olive oil
1 bay leaf
4 garlic cloves, peeled and finely chopped
1 tablespoon paprika
2 eggs
sea salt

Put the bread into a deep bowl. Set aside.

Bring 750 ml/25 fl oz (3 cups) water to the boil in a saucepan with 60 ml/2 fl oz (4 tablespoons) of the olive oil, the bay leaf, garlic, paprika and season with salt.

Put the eggs into a large heatproof bowl and lightly whisk with a fork.

In another saucepan, heat the remaining olive oil to smoking point over a high heat.

Once the flavoured water is boiling, remove from the heat and mix with the eggs. Pour this mixture over the bread and leave to soak for 5 minutes. Very carefully pour the hot olive oil over the top before serving.

Bread Porridge with Serrano Ham and Fried Eggs

Migas Esturricadas   ♡ **Beira Baixa**

Preparation time: 10 minutes, plus 20 minutes soaking
Cooking time: 20 minutes
Serves: 4
◻

2 parsley sprigs
4 garlic cloves, peeled but left whole
1 teaspoon paprika
700 g/1 lb 9 oz crusty bread, thinly sliced
120 g/4 oz Serrano ham, sliced into thin strips
120 g/4 oz chorizo, thinly sliced
180 ml/6 fl oz (¾ cup) olive oil
4 eggs
sea salt

Bring 500 ml/17 fl oz (2 cups) water, half the parsley, the garlic, paprika and a pinch of salt to the boil in a saucepan. Remove from the heat and strain into a bowl. Discard the parsley and garlic.

Arrange the bread, ham and chorizo in layers in a large shallow dish. Pour in enough flavoured water, about 800 ml/27 fl oz (3¼ cups) to cover the bread and leave to soak for 20 minutes.

Heat a large frying pan or skillet over a medium heat. Add 100 ml/3½ fl oz (⅓ cup) of the olive oil. Strain the water from the bread, ham and chorizo layers, if there is any, and discard. Tip the bread mixture into the frying pan, flatten into an oval shape and cook for 5 minutes, or until it has a light golden crust. Using a spatula, turn it over and cook for a further 3 minutes, or until it has a light golden crust. Transfer to a serving plate and keep warm.

Drizzle the remaining olive oil into a medium frying pan and heat over a medium heat. Once hot, add the eggs and fry for 2 minutes, or to your liking. Sprinkle with salt and put on top of the *migas* with the remaining parsley before serving.

Bread Porridge with Salt Cod and Poached Eggs

Migas Tostadas de Bacalhau   ♡ **Beira Baixa**

Preparation time: 10 minutes, plus 12–14 hours soaking
Cooking time: 40 minutes
Serves: 4
◻

550 g/1 lb 4 oz salted cod, desalted (page 40)
4 garlic cloves, peeled
250 ml/8½ fl oz (1 cup) olive oil, plus extra for drizzling
400 g/14 oz stale bread, thinly sliced
½ teaspoon paprika
5 eggs
sea salt

Check the cod is not too salty before cooking. If it is, then leave to soak for another 2 hours. Drain.

Fill a saucepan with enough water to cover the cod and bring to the boil. Reduce the heat to medium and, when simmering, add the cod, 2 of the garlic cloves and a splash of the olive oil and cook for 6 minutes, or until the flesh flakes easily. Remove the cod from the pan. Flake the cod into a bowl, removing any bones. Strain the cod cooking water into a bowl and set aside.

Arrange a layer of bread in a heatproof dish, then add a thin layer of the cod. Repeat until all the bread and cod are used up. Pour 1.2 litres/40 fl oz (5 cups) of the reserved cod cooking liquid over the layers.

Preheat the oven to 200°C/400°F/Gas Mark 6.

Heat the remaining oil in a saucepan over a medium heat. Add the remaining garlic and fry for 1–2 minutes, or until golden. Remove the garlic from the oil and discard. Stir the paprika into the oil, then pour it over the bread and cod and bake in the hot oven for 20 minutes, or until golden.

Pour the remaining cod cooking water into a saucepan and bring to a simmer over a medium-low heat. Carefully break the eggs into the simmering water, making sure to keep them whole, and poach for 4 minutes. Arrange the eggs on top of the *migas* and drizzle with oil before serving.

Cornbread with Turnip Tops and White Beans

Migas da Lousã   ♡ **Beira Litoral**

Preparation time: 5 minutes, plus 12 hours soaking
Cooking time: 30 minutes
Serves: 4
🥬◻🥚∨

300 g/11 oz (1⅔ cups) dried butter (lima) beans
    or any white beans
1.5 kg/3 lb 5 oz turnip tops, bottom stalks removed
    and roughly chopped
500 g/1 lb 2 oz Cornbread (page 32)
300 ml/10 fl oz (1¼ cups) olive oil
3 garlic cloves, peeled and finely sliced
sea salt

Put the beans into a bowl of cold water and soak for 12 hours. The next day, drain the beans and place in a saucepan. Pour in cold water to cover, add a pinch of salt and cook over a medium heat for 30 minutes, or until soft. Drain and set aside.

Meanwhile, bring a saucepan of water to the boil. Once boiling, add some salt and the turnip tops and cook for 4 minutes. Drain and set aside.

Tear the cornbread into pieces in a large bowl.

Put the cooked beans into a serving bowl, then add the turnip tops and the torn cornbread.

Heat the olive oil and garlic in a small pan over a medium heat. Once the garlic starts to fry, remove from the heat and pour over the beans, turnip tops and cornbread. Sprinkle with salt before serving.

Cornbread Mash with Turnip Tops and Sardines

Migas de Nabo   ◡ Beira Litoral

Preparation time: 15 minutes, plus 12–14 hours soaking
Cooking time: 15 minutes
Serves: 4

◩ ✿

1 kg/2 lb 4 oz sardines
450 g/1 lb Cornbread, crust removed (page 32)
3 garlic cloves, peeled and finely chopped
1 kg/2 lb 4 oz small turnip tops, shredded into fine strips
200 ml/7 fl oz (¾ cup) olive oil
sea salt

Clean the sardines, removing the scales. Make an incision in the belly with a sharp knife and remove the guts, then rinse under cold running water. Season with salt and set aside.

Prepare a barbecue. If you have some wood then add it to the coals. Alternatively, preheat the indoor grill (broiler).

Tear the cornbread into small pieces. Combine with the garlic on a baking sheet, then set aside.

Bring a saucepan of water to the boil and add a pinch of salt. Once boiling, add the turnip tops and cook for 2 minutes. Using a slotted spoon, remove the turnip tops from the pan and put on top of the cornbread. Wait for a few minutes and then drain away any excess water on the baking sheet.

Once the coals are glowing, put the fish onto the grill rack and grill for 5 minutes on each side, or until golden. Alternatively, cook under the grill.

Heat the olive oil in a saucepan to 85°C/185°F. When hot, carefully pour it over the turnip tops and cornbread, before serving with the fish.

Cornbread Mash with Shredded Cabbage

Migas à Moda de Leiria   ◡ Leiria

Preparation time: 10 minutes
Cooking time: 10 minutes
Serves: 4

✿◩◔V◻

1 Portuguese cabbage (couve tronchuda) or Savoy
    cabbage or January King cabbge also work well,
    thick stem removed and very thinly sliced
1 small Cornbread (page 32), crust removed
150 ml/5 fl oz (⅔ cup) extra virgin olive oil,
    plus extra for drizzling
1 large onion, peeled and finely diced
2 bay leaves
4 garlic cloves, peeled and finely chopped
sea salt and freshly ground black pepper

Have a large bowl of iced water nearby. Bring a large saucepan of salted water to the boil. Add the cabbage strips and cook for 1 minute, then transfer them with a slotted spoon or tongs to the iced water and leave to cool. Set aside 250 ml/8 fl oz (1 cup) of the cooking water.

Using your hands, roughly tear or crumble the cornbread and set aside in a medium bowl.

Heat the olive oil in a large, frying pan or skillet over a medium heat. Add the onion, bay leaves and garlic and cook for 2 minutes, or until the onion is soft. Add the cabbage and stir well with a wooden spoon. You can always add a small amount of the reserved cooking water to steam them a little more, then add the cornbread and stir well to finish. Season with salt, pepper and olive oil. Serve hot.

Pan-fried Bread and Potato Mash with Lardo and Garlic

Migas Carvoeiras de Abrantes   ◻ p.45   ◡ Ribatejo

This pan-fried bread and potato mash can be served as an accompaniment to trimmed pork ribs.

Preparation time: 15 minutes
Cooking time: 25 minutes
Serves: 4

◩

400 g/14 oz spelt bread
450 g/1 lb waxy potatoes, peeled and cut into thin slices
150 ml/5 fl oz (⅔ cup) olive oil
3 garlic cloves, peeled and thinly sliced
220 g/7½ oz lardo, cut into long thin slices
sea salt

Tear the bread into small pieces and set aside.

Put the potatoes into a large saucepan, cover with cold water and add a pinch of salt. Bring to the boil, then reduce the heat to low and cook for 10 minutes, or until soft. Drain and set aside.

Heat the olive oil in a large saucepan over a low heat, add the garlic and cook for 1 minute, or until golden brown. Add the lardo, stir and cook for 2 minutes. Add the torn bread pieces and season with salt. Add the cooked potatoes then take the pan off the heat.

Bring 500 ml/17 fl oz (2 cups) water to the boil in a separate saucepan. Once boiling, pour the water into the bread mixture and leave to soak for 2 minutes, then stir the mixture well in the pan to form a 'ball'. Cook over a low heat, drizzled with a little more olive oil, for 6 minutes, or until golden brown. Shape the mixture into a round and transfer to a large serving plate before serving.

Pan-fried Bread and Potato Mash with Lardo and Garlic

Pan-fried Cornbread and Salt Cod Mash

Migas de Broa com Bacalhau de Santarém　　　⛨ Ribatejo

Preparation time: 10 minutes, plus 12–14 hours soaking
Cooking time: 25 minutes
Serves: 4

⛨ ✿

600 g/1 lb 5 oz salt cod, desalted (page 40)
550 g/1 lb 4 oz Cornbread (page 32)
200 ml/7 fl oz (¾ cup) olive oil
3 garlic cloves, crushed with the back of a knife
1 teaspoon sweet paprika
sea salt

Check the cod is not too salty before cooking. If it is, then leave to soak for another 2 hours. Drain.

Tear the bread into small pieces and set aside.

Fill a saucepan with enough water to cover the cod and bring to the boil. Reduce the heat to medium and, when simmering, add the cod and cook for 6 minutes, or until the flesh flakes easily. Remove the cod from the pan, then remove any bones. Flake the cod into a bowl and set aside.

Bring the water in the pan back to the boil, add the torn bread pieces and cook for 5 minutes. Strain into a large bowl. Set aside.

Heat the olive oil in another large saucepan over a medium heat, add the garlic and cook for 30 seconds, or until golden brown, then remove with a slotted spoon. Add the cornbread and flaked cod to the pan and mix well to combine. Season with paprika and keep stirring until a 'ball' has formed. Transfer to a large serving plate.

Cornbread and Spelt Bread Mash with Onions, Potatoes and Cabbage

Magusto à Ribatejana　📷 p.47　　⛨ Ribatejo

Preparation time: 10 minutes, plus 12–14 hours soaking
Cooking time: 35 minutes
Serves: 5

⛨

700 g/1 lb 9 oz salt cod, desalted (page 40), optional
1 medium Portuguese cabbage or any other, leaves separated
6 waxy potatoes, peeled and cut into medium slices
1½ onions, peeled and finely diced
400 g/14 oz Cornbread (page 32)
650 g/1 lb 7 oz spelt bread
250 ml/8 fl oz (1 cup) olive oil
4 garlic cloves, crushed with the flat of a knife
sea salt

If serving with salt cod, check it is not too salty before cooking. If it is, leave to soak for another 2 hours. Drain.

Layer the cabbage leaves in two piles. Using your hands, rip them up into chunks.

Put 3 litres/102 fl oz (12¾ cups) water into a large saucepan, season with salt, then add the potatoes, onions and cabbage and cook over a medium heat for 10–12 minutes.

Meanwhile, tear both breads into small pieces in a large bowl and mix together until combined.

Once cooked, remove the vegetables from the heat. Add the torn bread pieces to the pan and leave to soak for 5 minutes, then mash everything together with the end of a rolling pin until a paste forms. Pour over the olive oil and garlic, then season with salt. Cook over a low heat for 15 minutes, or until some of the liquid evaporates. It should be moist but not totally dry.

If grilling the salt cod, prepare a barbecue or preheat the indoor grill (broiler).

As soon as the coals are glowing, put the salt cod onto the grill rack and grill for 8 minutes, or until golden brown. Alternatively, cook under the indoor grill. Remove from the grill and flake the flesh into a bowl and drizzle with olive oil.

Place the bread and vegetable mash in a large serving dish and then garnish with the salt cod.

Bread Soup with Fried Egg

Migas Ripadas　　　⛨ Trás-os-Montes e Alto Douro

Preparation time: 10 minutes
Cooking time: 10 minutes
Serves: 4

⛨ ✿ ✕ ⊟

450 g/1 lb sourdough bread, thinly sliced
150 ml/5 fl oz (⅔ cup) olive oil
4 garlic cloves, peeled, 2 halved and germ removed, 2 thinly sliced
4 eggs
sea salt

Line individual bowls with the bread slices.

Fill a saucepan with 1.5 litres/50 fl oz (6¼ cups) water, drizzle in about half the olive oil, add a pinch of salt to season and add the halved garlic cloves. Bring to the boil, then reduce the heat to medium and simmer for 5 minutes. Pour the flavoured water into the bowls, cover with a tea (dish) towel and leave to stand for a few minutes.

Meanwhile, heat a drizzle of the remaining olive oil in a frying pan or skillet over a medium heat. Add the eggs and fry for 2 minutes, or to your liking. Season the eggs with salt, then place one egg in each bowl.

Add the remaining olive to the pan and the sliced garlic and fry over a medium heat for 30 seconds, or until golden. Pour the hot olive oil and garlic over the bread and egg before serving.

Cornbread and Spelt Bread Mash with Onions, Potatoes and Cabbage

SOUPS

Sour Soup

It might have *azeda* (sour) in its name, but this soup is not in fact sour — the vinegar added is well balanced by the dish's sweet ingredients (sugar, pumpkin and sweet potatoes) and the cinnamon. Also called *caldo* (broth), *sopa azeda* is usually eaten during popular festivities in the Azores, such as Whitsun. The exact recipe may vary from island to island, and in some parts of the archipelago can be served over a base of bread slices.

Preparation time: 15 minutes, plus 12 hours soaking
Cooking time: 1 hour, plus 10 minutes resting
Serves: 4
▯ ∅ V

250 g/9 oz (1⅓ cups) dried butter (lima) beans or
    any other white bean
60 ml/2 fl oz (4 tablespoons) extra virgin olive oil
1 large silver onion, peeled and chopped
2 garlic cloves, peeled and chopped
1 cinnamon stick
2 bay leaves
3 large sweet potatoes, peeled and chopped into
    small pieces
45 ml/1½ fl oz (3 tablespoons) white wine vinegar
4 thick slices stale crusty bread, preferably sourdough
sea salt

Put the dried beans into a large bowl, pour in enough cold water to cover and leave to soak for 12 hours. The next day, drain the beans and set aside.

Heat the olive oil in a large saucepan over a low heat. Add the onion and garlic and cook gently for 10 minutes, or until soft. Add 2.8 litres/100 fl oz (11¼ cups) water and the soaked beans and cook over a low heat for 30 minutes, or until the beans are soft.

Add the cinnamon stick, bay leaves and salt to the pan, then increase the heat to medium and simmer for 5 minutes.

Add the sweet potatoes to the pan and cook gently over a medium heat for 15 minutes, or until tender. Add the vinegar and stir to combine.

Dip two slices of the bread into the soup and put them into a serving bowl. Leave the dipped bread in the bowl to rest for 10 minutes to soak up the soup. Pour the remaining soup over the bread before serving.

Safflower Soup

Preparation time: 15 minutes
Cooking time: 35 minutes
Serves: 4
▯ ∅ ▯

40 ml/1⅓ fl oz (2⅔ tablespoons) sunflower oil
2 onions, peeled and sliced into thin rings
2 garlic cloves, peeled and finely chopped
½ teaspoon saffron threads
4 slices crusty bread
1 egg yolk
30 ml/1 fl oz (2 tablespoons) white wine vinegar
sea salt

Heat the oil in a saucepan with the onions and garlic over a medium heat and cook for 5 minutes, or until the onions are translucent.

Add 2.5 litres/85 fl oz (10 cups) water to the pan with the saffron, bring to the boil and cook for a further 30 minutes, or until the onion is soft. Remove from the heat, season with salt and cover with a lid.

Toast the bread, then cut into small cubes and divide evenly between four individual bowls. Put the egg yolk and vinegar into a small bowl and lightly whisk until combined, then add it to the pan and stir in.

Pour the soup into the bowls over the bread before serving.

Cheese Soup

Preparation time: 15 minutes
Cooking time: 30 minutes
Serves: 4
∅ ▯

60 g/2¼ oz butter
1 large onion, peeled and chopped
2 celery stalks, chopped into small pieces
35 g/1¼ oz (4¼ tablespoons) plain (all-purpose) flour
320 ml/11 fl oz (1¼ cups) whole (full-fat) milk
50 g/2 oz (½ cup) grated (shredded) cheese (any type
    of hard cheese)
sea salt

Melt the butter in a large saucepan, then add the onion and celery and cook over a medium heat for 15 minutes, or until the vegetables are golden.

Add 1.8 litres/61 fl oz (7¼ cups) water to the pan and bring to the boil for 5 minutes.

Put the flour into a medium bowl and stir in the milk until the flour is fully incorporated. Add it to the pan and gently boil for 10 minutes. Remove the pan from the heat and season with salt.

Pour the soup into four individual bowls and scatter over the grated cheese before serving.

Safflower Soup

Purslane Soup with Poached Eggs

••

Sopa de Beldroegas 🖾 p.53   ⏷ **Alentejo**

A popular soup throughout Portugal, there is a version of this soup from the Algarve that uses potatoes, sweet potatoes, pumpkin, onions and garlic, which are cooked until tender and then blitzed before being warmed through with plenty of purslane leaves.

Preparation time: 10 minutes
Cooking time: 45 minutes
Serves: 4
⌀ ⏢

160 ml/5½ fl oz (⅔ cup) olive oil
2 onions, peeled and sliced into thin rings
3 bunches common purslane, stems removed
2 heads of garlic
3 waxy potatoes, peeled and cut into medium slices
4 eggs
3 slices fresh cheese
350 g/12 oz crusty bread, sliced
sea salt

Heat the olive oil in a saucepan over a medium heat. Add the onion rings and cook for 15 minutes, or until golden. Add the purslane and cook for 2 minutes, or until soft. Add 2 litres/68 fl oz (8½ cups) water to the pan and bring to the boil. Season with salt.

   Peel the outer papery skins from the heads of garlic, leaving the cloves uncovered but whole and in a cluster. Add the heads of garlic to the pan with the potatoes and cook for 25 minutes, or until soft.

   Carefully break the eggs into the pan, making sure they remain whole, and poach for 4 minutes, then add the cheese slices. Taste and adjust the seasoning, if necessary.

   Put the bread slices into a deep serving dish and pour over the soup, including the poached eggs, before serving.

Butter Bean Soup

••

Sopa de Feijão Manteiga   ⏷ **Algarve**

Preparation time: 15 minutes, plus 12 hours soaking
Cooking time: 40 minutes
Serves: 4
🖉 ⏢ ⌀ ∨

300 g/11 oz (1⅔ cups) dried butter (lima) beans
100 ml/3½ fl oz (⅓ cup) olive oil
200 g/7 oz sweet potato, peeled and cut into chunks
250 g/9 oz pumpkin, peeled, de-seeded and cut into chunks
2 small onions, finely chopped
1 bunch flat-leaf parsley, finely chopped
sea salt

Put the dried beans into a bowl, pour in enough cold water to cover and leave to soak for 12 hours.

   The next day, drain the beans and put into a large saucepan. Pour in enough cold water to cover then cook over a medium heat for 20 minutes.

   Meanwhile, heat the olive oil in a saucepan over a medium heat. Add the sweet potato, pumpkin, onions and cook for 15 minutes, or until golden.

   Add the sautéed vegetables and the parsley to the pan with the beans and cook for a further 20 minutes.

   Taste and adjust the seasoning, if necessary, before serving.

Garlic Soup with Bread

••

Sopa de Alho com Ovo   ⏷ **Algarve**

Preparation time: 10 minutes
Cooking time: 10 minutes
Serves: 4
⏢ ⌀ ⏢ ⌧

4 garlic cloves, peeled and very finely chopped
250 g/9 oz crusty bread, thinly sliced
120 ml/4 fl oz (½ cup) olive oil
4 eggs
sea salt

Put the garlic and a pinch of salt into a mortar and, using a pestle, mash to a paste.

   Put the bread slices into a large saucepan, then add the garlic paste and season with a pinch of salt. Add the olive oil and 2.5 litres/85 fl oz (10 cups) water to the pan and bring to the boil.

   Reduce the heat to low. Make a small well in the bread, break the eggs into the well and cook gently over a low heat for 5 minutes, or until the eggs are cooked to your liking.

   Serve the soup in the pan.

Purslane Soup with Poached Eggs

Red Pepper, Tomato and Garlic Cold Soup

Arjamolho ◎ p.55   Ⴘ **Algarve**

Preparation time: 20 minutes
Serves: 4
◻ ⌀ V ✂

400 g/14 oz ripe bull's heart tomatoes
    (or beefsteak tomatoes)
3 garlic cloves, peeled but left whole
1 green (bell) pepper, cored, de-seeded and diced
5 g/¼ oz (1 teaspoon) dried oregano
100 ml/3½ fl oz (⅓ cup) extra virgin olive oil
30 ml/1 fl oz (2 tablespoons) white wine vinegar
200 g/7 oz sourdough bread, sliced
sea salt

Have a large bowl of iced water nearby. Bring
a large saucepan of water to the boil. Using a sharp
knife, score the top of the tomatoes with a small
cross shape. Once the water is boiling, carefully
add the tomatoes and blanch for 30 seconds,
then transfer them with a slotted spoon to the
iced water and leave to cool. Once cool enough to
handle, peel off the skins, cut in half and de-seed,
then cut the flesh into small cubes. Set aside.

Put the garlic and a pinch of salt into a mortar
and, using a pestle, mash to a paste.

Put the diced tomatoes, (bell) peppers,
oregano, olive oil, vinegar and garlic paste into a
large bowl. Add 1.5 litres/50 fl oz (6¼ cups) cold
water and mix until fully combined.

Add the bread slices to the soup before serving.

Red Bean and Bread Soup

Sopa de Alcains   Ⴘ **Beira Baixa**

**Many of these dishes are prepared in traditional
clay pots. If you have access to one, do use it for
this soup as it gives the dish a different flavour.**

Preparation time: 20 minutes, plus 12 hours soaking
Cooking time: 1 hour 20 minutes
Serves: 6
◻ ⌀

500 g/1 lb 2 oz (2¾ cups) dried red beans
120 ml/4 fl oz (½ cup) olive oil, plus an extra
    45 ml/1½ fl oz (3 tablespoons)
2 onions, peeled and finely chopped
1 teaspoon ground cumin
5 eggs
450 g/1 lb stale bread, very thinly sliced
sea salt and freshly ground black pepper

Put the dried beans into a large bowl, pour in
enough cold water to cover and leave to soak for
12 hours.

The next day, drain the beans and put them
into a large saucepan. Add 4.3 litres/145 fl oz (17¼
cups) cold water and a pinch of salt and cook over
a medium heat for 30 minutes, or until soft. Drain
and set aside, reserving the bean cooking water.

Preheat the oven to 200°C/400°F/Gas Mark 6.

To make the stock, heat the 120 ml/4 fl oz
(½ cup) olive oil in a large saucepan over a medium
heat, add the onions and cook for 5 minutes, or
until golden brown. Add the reserved bean cooking
water, season with salt, pepper and cumin and
bring to the boil. Remove the pan from the heat.

Put the eggs into a small bowl and lightly whisk
with a fork. Set aside.

Heat the 45 ml/1½ fl oz (3 tablespoons)
olive oil in a small saucepan over a high heat for
10 minutes or until very hot.

Arrange the bread slices in a large clay tray or
an ovenproof baking dish and pour over a little of
the stock to soak into the bread. Add the cooked
beans, then carefully drizzle the very hot olive oil
over the top and finish with the remaining stock.
Pour the whisked eggs over the top and bake
in the oven for 30–35 minutes, or until the eggs
are set. Serve while hot.

Wild Radish Soup with Beans

Sopa de Saramagos da Moita   Ⴘ **Lisbon**

Preparation time: 20 minutes
Cooking time: 1 hour
Serves: 4
🐟 ◻ ⌀ V ◻ ✕

350 g/12 oz wild radishes, including stems, washed
70 ml/2½ fl oz (¼ cup) olive oil, plus extra to serve
½ onion, peeled and finely chopped
250 g/9 oz (1⅔ cups) fresh butter (lima) beans, shelled
sea salt

Bring a small saucepan of water to the boil, then
add the wild radishes and blanch for 1 minute.
Drain and set aside.

Heat the olive oil in a large saucepan over a
medium heat. Once hot, add the onion and cook
for 10 minutes, or until translucent.

Add the beans to the pan, then pour in
2.5 litres/85 fl oz (10 cups) water and cook over
a medium heat for 45 minutes, or until the beans
are cooked.

Add the blanched radishes to the pan with a
pinch of salt, stir to combine and then bring to the
boil. Drizzle the soup with olive oil before serving.

Red Pepper, Tomato and Garlic Cold Soup

Bean Pod Soup

Caldo de Cascas ⋃ Minho

This strong-flavoured soup, from the north of Portugal, is made with sun-dried green bean pods and local cured meat. In the old days, the locals would eat this when they were working in the fields. It was traditionally consumed during the winter months and used leftover bean shells or pods, so it meant that nothing went to waste.

Preparation time: 15 minutes
Cooking time: 1 hour 45 minutes
Serves: 4
🍲 ▢ ▢

100 g/3½ oz chorizo
90 g/3¼ oz ham
30 g/1 oz lard (pork fat)
300 g/11 oz dried green bean pods
100 ml/3½ fl oz (⅓ cup) olive oil
600 g/1 lb 5 oz waxy potatoes, peeled and
    cut into small pieces
sea salt

Put the chorizo, ham, lard (pork fat) and bean pods into a large saucepan, pour in enough cold water to cover and bring to the boil over a medium heat.
    Once the water is boiling, remove the pan from the heat and drain the meats and bean pods, discarding the water.
    Return the meats and bean pods to the pan and add 2.5 litres/85 fl oz (10 cups) fresh cold water. Add the olive oil and cook over a low heat for 1½ hours, or until the meats are soft.
    Using tongs or a slotted spoon, remove the meats from the pan but leave the cooking water in the pan for the potatoes. Cut or shred the meats into very small pieces and set aside.
    Put the potatoes into the pan and cook over a low heat for 10 minutes, or until soft. Using a potato masher or ladle, mash the potatoes into the cooking liquid to make the soup. Taste and adjust the seasoning, if necessary, then add the shredded meats. Stir the soup before serving.

Broad Bean Pod Soup

Sopa de Vagens de Favas ⋃ Beira Baixa

This is an excellent recipe for using up broad (fava) bean pods, which would otherwise be thrown away as kitchen waste.

Preparation time: 20 minutes
Cooking time: 45 minutes
Serves: 4
▢

900 g/2 lb fresh broad (fava) bean pods
    (chose the softest ones)
2 small onions, peeled and finely chopped
5 waxy potatoes, peeled but left whole
80 ml/2¾ fl oz (⅓ cup) olive oil
1 bunch mint, leaves picked
150 g/5 oz cured lardo, cut into small pieces
4 slices crusty bread
sea salt

Rinse the broad (fava) bean pods under cold running water, then pat dry with paper towels or a tea (dish) towel. Put the pods into a pile and, using a sharp knife, slice them as thinly as possible. Set aside.
    Pour 4 litres/136 fl oz (16 cups) water into a large saucepan. Add the onions, potatoes, olive oil and a pinch of salt to the pan and bring to the boil over a medium heat. Once the water is boiling, add the sliced bean pods, reduce the heat to low and cook for 30 minutes, or until very soft. Once the potatoes are cooked, remove them with a slotted spoon, put them into a medium bowl and crush them with a fork. Return the crushed potatoes to the pan, add the mint leaves and lardo, then taste and adjust the seasoning with salt, if necessary.
    Arrange the bread slices in a large serving dish and pour over the soup before serving.

Black-eyed Pea Soup with Turnip Tops

••

Sopa de Feijão Frade   ᑌ Ribatejo
com Grelos

There are many soups made using black-eyed peas that hail from Ribatejo, including this one with turnip tops. Amongst my favourite alternatives is one soup in which black-eyed peas are cooked with short-grain rice, garlic and bay leaves until soft, then seasoned with salt and white wine vinegar.

Preparation time: 15 minutes, plus 12 hours soaking
Cooking time: 50 minutes
Serves: 6
🐟ᑌ∅∨

400 g/14 oz (2¼ cups) dried black-eyed peas
100 ml/3½ fl oz (⅓ cup) olive oil
2 small onions, peeled and finely chopped
1 bunch turnip tops, about 450 g/1 lb in weight,
    bottom stalks removed
⅓ bunch flat-leaf parsley, leaves picked
sea salt and freshly ground black pepper

Put the dried black-eyed peas into a large bowl, pour in enough cold water to cover and leave to soak for 12 hours.

The next day, drain the black-eyed peas and put them into a large saucepan. Pour in enough cold water to cover, add a pinch of salt and cook over a medium heat for 30 minutes, or until soft. Remove the pan from the heat and set aside, leaving the black-eyed peas in their cooking water.

Heat the olive oil in a large saucepan over a low heat, add the onions and cook for 10 minutes, or until lightly coloured.

Add the black-eyed peas with their cooking water to the pan, then add the turnip tops and simmer for a further 10 minutes. Bring to the boil, then season with salt and pepper. Scatter over the parsley leaves before serving.

Turnip Broth

••

Caldo de Nabos   ᑌ Açores

Turnips are grown on the island of St Maria where they have a more accentuated fragrance than ordinary turnips, as well as a slightly bitter taste, which gives this broth a different aroma and taste. Ordinary turnips are also good in this soup.

Preparation time: 20 minutes, plus 2 days standing and overnight soaking
Cooking time: 45 minutes
Serves: 6
ᑲ

1.5 kg/3 lb 5 oz pig's trotters (feet) halved and cleaned
400 g/14 oz pork belly
200 g/7 oz (1 cup plus 2 tablespoons) lard (pork fat),
    unseasoned
1.5 kg/3 lb 5 oz white turnips, peeled and cut into strips
1 chorizo
4 white sweet potatoes, peeled, but left whole and
    scored on both ends
450 g/1 lb sourdough bread, thickly sliced
1 teaspoon ground cinnamon
sea salt

Three days before cooking, put the pig's trotters, pork belly and lard into a large dish and season with salt. Cover with food wrap and leave to stand in the fridge for two days before making the soup.

The day before cooking, wash the meats and lard a few times in cold water, then put into a large container, cover with water, then cover and leave to stand in the fridge overnight.

When ready to cook, bring a large saucepan of water to the boil, add a pinch of salt and the turnips and blanch for 30 seconds. (This helps to remove the 'punchiness'.) Drain, then repeat the process with fresh water. Drain again and set aside.

Drain the meats and lard, then put them into a large saucepan with the chorizo, cover with a lid and cook over a low heat for 30 minutes, or until very tender.

Put the cooked turnips, meats and chorizo into another large saucepan. Add the sweet potatoes to the pan, pour in enough fresh water to cover, cover with a lid and cook over a medium heat for 15 minutes, or until the sweet potatoes are tender. Remove the pan from the heat.

Arrange the bread slices in the bottom of a large clay pot or serving dish. Dust the bread with the cinnamon. Pour a few ladles of the cooking stock over the bread and leave to soak for 5 minutes. Arrange the meats on a separate plate before serving with the soup.

Wild Asparagus Soup

••

Sopa de Espargos Silvestres   ♡ Alentejo

Preparation time: 20 minutes
Cooking time: 50 minutes
Serves: 4
♤

200 g/7 oz lardo, thinly sliced
130 g/4½ oz *linguiça* (traditional sausage), thinly sliced
1 onion, peeled and finely chopped
3 garlic cloves, peeled and finely chopped
1 teaspoon paprika
450 g/1 lb wild asparagus, bottom stems removed
    and tips cut into chunks
olive oil, for frying
4 slices bread, cut into small cubes
1 egg, lightly beaten
sea salt and freshly ground black pepper

Heat a large saucepan over a medium heat, add the lardo and *linguiça* and cook for 10 minutes, or until lightly coloured. Using tongs or a slotted spoon, remove the meats from the pan, leaving any fat in the pan. Add the onion and garlic to the pan with the paprika and some pepper, then cook for 15 minutes, or until very soft.

Bring a large saucepan of water to the boil and add a pinch of salt. Blanch the asparagus in the boiling water for 30 seconds then drain.

Add 2.5 litres/85 fl oz (10 cups) water to the onion mixture together with the blanched asparagus and the cooked meats. Bring to the boil, then reduce the heat to medium and simmer for 10 minutes.

Meanwhile, heat the olive oil for frying in a large frying pan or skillet over a medium heat. Add the bread cubes and fry for 10 minutes, or until golden. Using a slotted spoon, transfer the bread onto paper towels and leave to drain.

Add the beaten egg to the soup together with the fried bread cubes and stir well. Taste and adjust the seasoning, if necessary, before serving.

Fennel Soup

••

Sopa de Funcho   📷 p.59   ♡ Açores

Preparation time: 20 minutes, plus 12 hours soaking
Cooking time: 2 hours
Serves: 6
🐖 ♤ ♡

450 g/1 lb (2½ cups) dried red beans
500 g/1 lb 2 oz salted pork meat, shoulder,
    ears or any other piece you like
350 g/12 oz pork belly
100 g/3½ oz *linguiça* (traditional sausage)
40 g/1½ oz lard (pork fat)
1 bunch wild fennel tops, finely chopped
3 waxy potatoes, peeled and quartered
2 sweet potatoes, peeled and quartered
sea salt (optional)

Put the dried beans into a large bowl, pour in enough cold water to cover and leave to soak for 12 hours.

Put the meats into a large container, pour in enough cold water to cover and leave to soak for a few hours.

The next day, drain the beans and put them into a large saucepan. Pour in 4 litres/135 fl oz (16 cups) water and cook over a medium heat for 30 minutes, or until soft. Drain, then mash the beans to a purée.

Return the pan to the stove. Add the meats, *linguiça* and lard (pork fat) to the pan along with the fennel tops and cook over a low heat, stirring occasionally, for 45 minutes, or until the meats are nearly cooked.

Add the potatoes and sweet potatoes to the pan, increase the heat to medium and gently cook for a further 15 minutes, or until all the potatoes are tender. Taste and adjust the seasoning, if necessary, adding a pinch of salt.

Using a slotted spoon, remove the meats and potatoes from the pan. Transfer the meats to a chopping board and cut into bite-size pieces.

Divide the meats between six individual bowls and ladle over the soup. Serve the soup with the potatoes alongside.

Fennel Soup

Gaspacho — Alentejo Style

Gaspacho Alentejano ⊡ p.61   ⛉ Alentejo

This ice-cold soup is the ideal refreshment
for the boiling hot summer days in Alentejo,
requiring no stove heat in its preparation since
all the ingredients are used raw. *Gaspacho* varies
depending on the region of Alentejo — finely
sliced ham is one of the toppings in Mértola, but
olives are added in Sobral da Adiça. It is served
in some Alentejo restaurants alongside a tray
of fish (tiny fried sardines, normal-sized grilled
sardines, or fried horse mackerel). This same recipe
is called *arjamolho* in the Algarve region (page 54),
where it is usually eaten with grilled sardines.

Preparation time: 25 minutes
Serves: 6
⛉ ⊞

2 garlic cloves, peeled
3 ripe bull's heart tomatoes (or beefsteak tomatoes),
   de-seeded and cut into strips
1½ large white onions, very thinly sliced
1 green (bell) pepper, cored, de-seeded
   and cut into strips
1 red (bell) pepper, cored, de-seeded and cut into strips
½ tablespoon fresh or dried oregano
150 ml/5 fl oz (⅔ cup) extra virgin olive oil
60 ml/2 fl oz (4 tablespoons) white wine vinegar
250 g/9 oz bread, preferably sourdough,
   cut into small cubes
sea salt

To garnish (optional):
85 g/3¼ oz ham, very thinly sliced
60 g/2¼ oz chorizo, very thinly sliced

Put the garlic and a pinch of salt into a mortar and,
using a pestle, mash to a smooth paste.

Transfer the garlic paste to a large bowl and
add the tomatoes, onions, both (bell) peppers,
oregano, olive oil and vinegar. Pour in 1.6 litres/
54 fl oz (6⅓ cups) cold water and mix together.
Season with salt, then add the bread cubes.

Place the bowl in the fridge and leave to chill
until ready to serve.

Serve the chilled soup when very cold. Garnish
with the sliced meats before serving, if using.

Tomato Soup

Sopa de Tomate   ⛉ Alentejo

Preparation time: 20 minutes
Cooking time: 45 minutes
Serves: 6
⛉

1.5 kg/3 lb 5 oz ripe tomatoes
200 g/7 oz lardo, cut into small pieces
250 g/9 oz *linguiça* (traditional sausage) or chorizo,
   cut into discs
1½ onions, peeled and thinly sliced into half-moons
3 garlic cloves, peeled and thinly sliced into half-moons
1 green (bell) pepper, cored, de-seeded and sliced
2 bay leaves
½ bunch flat-leaf parsley, leaves picked
sea salt
6 slices bread, to serve

Have a large bowl of iced water nearby. Bring a
large saucepan of water to the boil. Using a sharp
knife, score the top of the tomatoes with a small
cross shape. Once the water is boiling, carefully
add the tomatoes and blanch for 30 seconds,
then transfer them with a slotted spoon to the
iced water and leave to cool. Once cool enough
to handle, peel off the skins and cut into quarters.

Put the lardo into a large saucepan and cook
over a medium heat for 5 minutes, or until lightly
coloured and the fat is rendered. Add the *linguiça*
or chorizo slices and cook for a further 10 minutes,
or until slightly crispy. Using tongs or a slotted
spoon, remove all the meats from the pan, leaving
any fat in the pan.

Add the tomatoes, onions and garlic to the pan
and cook for 25 minutes, or until the tomatoes are
soft and starting to break down. Add the green
(bell) pepper, bay leaves and parsley. Season with
a pinch of salt and cook for a further 5 minutes,
stirring until all the ingredients are fully combined.

Add 2.2 litres/75 fl oz (8¾ cups) water to the
pan and bring to the boil over a medium heat.
Taste and adjust the seasoning, if necessary.

Ladle the soup into six individual bowls and
serve with the cooked meats and bread slices.

Gaspacho — Alentejo Style

Kale Soup

••

Caldo Verde ⓞ p.63   ⑬ **Minho**

Found across Portugal, from city restaurants to
remote farmhouses, this green soup is homey,
eaten throughout the year, but especially during
the winter months. Originally from Minho, there
are variations of *caldo verde* across the country
(page 429). Its main ingredients are potato and
onion purée, collard greens and *chouriço*, but the
way the broth is made varies — sometimes meat
bones and hocks are added for flavour — as does
the cooking of the collards (from crunchy to soft).
Different types of *chouriço* and bread can be used
(corn, rye, or wheat and rye mixture).

Preparation time: 20 minutes
Cooking time: 50 minutes
Serves: 6
🐟 ▢ ▢

800 g/1 lb 12 oz waxy potatoes, peeled and quartered
1 onion, peeled and quartered
3 garlic cloves, peeled and halved
400 g/14 oz flat-leaf kale or January King cabbage
130 ml/4½ fl oz (½ cup) olive oil
1 large chorizo, cut into medium slices
sea salt
6 slices Cornbread, to serve (page 32)

Put the potatoes, onion and garlic into a large
saucepan. Pour 4.5 litres/152 fl oz (18 cups) water
into the pan and add a pinch of salt. Cook over
a medium heat for 20 minutes, or until the potatoes
are soft. Transfer the soup to a blender or food
processor and, working in batches, blitz until smooth.
Return the soup to the pan and bring to the boil.
    Separate the kale or cabbage leaves, arrange
them into small piles, roll them up and slice them
as thinly as possible. Add the shredded leaves to
the soup and cook for 30 minutes, or until soft.
Stir in the olive oil, taste and adjust the seasoning.
    Arrange the chorizo slices in the bottom of six
individual soup bowls, then ladle the soup on top.
Serve the soup with slices of cornbread.

Butter Bean Soup with Kale

••

Sopa de Feijão com Couve   ⑬ **Alentejo**

Preparation time: 20 minutes, plus 12 hours soaking
Cooking time: 50 minutes
Serves: 4
▢ 🥦 V

450 g/1 lb (2½ cups) dried butter (lima) beans
1 bay leaf
120 ml/4 fl oz (½ cup) olive oil, plus extra for drizzling
350 g/12 oz potatoes, peeled and cut into chunks
400 g/14 oz flat-leaf kale or January King cabbage
350 g/12 oz bread, sliced

Put the dried beans into a large bowl, pour in
enough cold water to cover and leave to soak for
12 hours.
    The next day, drain the beans and put them
into a large saucepan. Pour in enough cold water
to cover, add a pinch of salt, the bay leaf and olive
oil and cook over a medium heat for 30 minutes,
or until soft. Drain the beans, reserving the cooking
water, and set aside.
    Put the potatoes into a saucepan, add the
reserved cooking water and cook over a medium
heat for 20 minutes, or until soft. Drain, return the
potatoes to the pan and mash with a fork. Set aside.
    Separate the kale or cabbage leaves, arrange
them into small piles, roll them up and shred them
into thick strips. Bring a large saucepan of water to
the boil, add the shredded leaves and blanch for
2 minutes. Transfer to a tray or plate, reserving the
cooking water.
    Add the mashed potatoes, cooked beans and
kale or cabbage to the reserved cooking water in
the pan and mix together until combined. Taste
and adjust the seasoning, if necessary, with salt.
    Arrange the bread slices in a large serving dish
and pour over the soup. Leave the bread to soak
up the soup for a few minutes before serving,
drizzled with a little more olive oil over the top.

Crushed Wheat Soup

••

Sopa de Trigo Pisado   ⑬ **Madeira**

Preparation time: 20 minutes, plus 15 hours soaking
Cooking time: 1 hour 20 minutes
Serves: 6
▢ ▢

450 g/1 lb (2½ cups) dried butter (lima) beans
500 g/1 lb 2 oz whole wheat
600 g/1 lb 5 oz pork belly
800 g/1 lb 12 oz waxy potatoes, peeled
1 Savoy cabbage
3 carrots, peeled and cut into medium-thick discs
1 onion, peeled and finely chopped
sea salt

Put the dried beans into a large bowl, pour in
enough cold water to cover and leave to soak
for 12 hours.
    The next day, put the wheat into a mortar and,
using a pestle, crush it. Transfer to a large bowl,
cover with water and leave to soak for 3 hours.
    Lightly season the pork belly with salt and
drain the soaked beans. Put all the ingredients
into a saucepan, season with salt, add 5 litres/
170 fl oz (20 cups) water and cook over a low heat,
skimming off any foam that rises to the top, for
1 hour 20 minutes, or until the beans are soft and
the vegetables are cooked. Season with salt.
    Remove the potatoes from the pan and transfer
to a serving dish. Remove the meat from the pan,
slice it into small pieces, then return it to the pan.
Serve the soup with the potatoes on the side.

Kale Soup

Cabbage Soup with Ham

Sopa da Beira 📷 p.65   ⛭ **Beira Alta**

Preparation time: 15 minutes
Cooking time: 45 minutes
Serves: 4

🥘 ⬜ ⬜

250 g/9 oz Serrano ham, thickly sliced
300 g/11 oz Savoy cabbage leaves
650 g/1 lb 7 oz baby turnip leaves
130 g/4½ oz (1 cup) cornflour (cornstarch)
30 ml/1 fl oz (2 tablespoons) olive oil
sea salt and freshly ground black pepper

Put the ham into a large saucepan and pour over 2.4 litres/81 fl oz (9⅔ cups) water. Cook over a medium heat for 30 minutes, or until the meat is soft and shreds easily. Remove the meat from the pan, reserving the cooking water, and shred it into strings. Set aside.

Add the cabbage and turnip leaves to the same pan and cook over a medium heat for 10 minutes, or until tender.

Meanwhile, put the cornflour (cornstarch) into a medium bowl, add a little water and stir until it has dissolved and formed a thick paste.

Add the paste to the pan and stir, then return the shredded meat to the pan and cook over a low heat for a further 5 minutes, or until the soup is thick and the flour is cooked.

Season the soup with salt and pepper and then drizzle the olive oil over the top. Stir the soup to mix everything together before serving.

Smoked Pork Fat Broth

Caldo de Unto   ⛭ **Trás-os-Montes e Alto Douro**

Unto is the part of the fat located on the pork belly. It is removed from the animal, then rolled and kept over the fireplace. When some of the fat is needed for cooking, a piece is cut off and used as a fat component in various dishes.

Preparation time: 10 minutes
Cooking time: 15 minutes
Serves: 4

⬜ ✕ ▱

160 g/5¾ oz lard (pork fat) or belly fat, cut into
    small pieces
4 eggs
300 g/11 oz rye bread, sliced
sea salt

Melt the fat in a small saucepan over a low heat.

Pour 1.5 litres/50 fl oz (6¼ cups) water into a saucepan. Add the melted fat and a pinch of salt to the pan and bring to the boil over a high heat.

Reduce the heat to medium, carefully break in the eggs, making sure they are kept whole, and poach for 4 minutes.

Put a slice of bread into the bottom of each individual serving bowl and add a poached egg on top. Ladle the hot soup into each bowl over the bread and eggs before serving.

Pork Offal Stew

Caldo de Entrudo   ⛭ **Beira Baixa**

February is the month of the *entrudo*, a slang word for carnival. It is also the time before Easter when people used to fast and not eat meat, which still happens today in this region. The locals used to gather in groups and make this stew and eat fatty meats like boiled salted pork belly with slabs of cornbread.

Preparation time: 20 minutes
Cooking time: 1 hour 30 minutes
Serves: 6

⬜ ⬜

2 pig's tails
350 g/12 oz pig's snouts
3 pig's ears
2 pig's trotters (feet)
1 large chorizo
1 *farinheira* or smoked sausage
sea salt
6 slices bread, to serve

Clean the pig's tails, snouts, ears and trotters. Remove any remaining hairs, if necessary, by blowtorching and scraping with a sharp knife. Rinse under cold running water. Poke the chorizo and *farinheira* all over with a needle or skewer to prevent them bursting during cooking.

Put all the meats into a large saucepan, pour in enough water to cover and add a pinch of salt. Cook over a low heat for 1 hour 30 minutes, or until the meats are soft. Some of the meats will cook sooner than others, such as the chorizo and *farinheira*, so remove them from the pan, set aside on a plate and keep warm.

Once all the offal (variety meats) is cooked, cut it into small pieces and arrange it in a serving dish. Serve with the chorizo, *farinheira* and bread slices.

Cabbage Soup with Ham

'Stone' Soup

••

Sopa da Pedra de Almeirim 📷 p.67   🛡 Ribatejo

Literally 'stone' soup, *sopa da pedra* is originally from the village of Almeirim, near Santarém. It is made of ingredients that are readily available at home, including dried red beans, potatoes, onions and different types of cured meat (*chouriço*, pig's ears and ham). The tale behind its origin is passed on from generation to generation: a hungry friar arrived in Almeirim carrying only a small stone in his hand. He knocked on the door of a farmer's house and asked if he could cook a soup with the stone. The farmer was intrigued, and accepted. So the friar washed the stone until it was shiny, and asked for a few drops of olive oil. Then he asked for some potatoes, then some beans, and then *chouriço*. The friar cooked the soup, and shared a bowl with the farmer. Finally, the farmer decided to ask what he did with the stone. To which the friar replied: 'The stone? I wash it carefully and take it with me for my next meal!'

Preparation time: 20 minutes, plus 12 hours soaking
Cooking time: 1 hour 30 minutes
Serves: 8
🥘 🗆 🗆

800 g/1 lb 12 oz (4½ cups) dried red beans
2 large pig's ears
1 *morcela*
1 chorizo
250 g/9 oz bacon
2 onions, peeled and quartered
2 garlic cloves, peeled and quartered
1 bay leaf
750 g/1 lb 10 oz waxy potatoes, peeled and cut
    into medium-sized cubes
1 bunch coriander (cilantro), finely chopped
sea salt and freshly ground black pepper

Put the dried beans into a bowl, pour in enough cold water to cover and leave to soak for 12 hours.

The next day, drain the beans and set aside.

Clean the pig's ears. Remove any remaining hairs, if necessary, by blowtorching and scraping with a sharp knife.

Bring a saucepan of water to the boil, add the pig's ears and blanch for 1 minute. Remove from the pan and scrape with the tip of a knife to remove any superficial skin. Set aside.

Pour 3.5 litres/118 fl oz (14 cups) water into a large saucepan, add the beans, pigs' ears, *morcela*, chorizo, bacon, onions, garlic and bay leaf. Season with salt and pepper and cook over a medium heat for 1 hour, or until the meats are soft. Check the meats during cooking and remove them from the pan as soon as they are cooked.

When all the meats are cooked, remove them from the pan and cut them into thin slices. Add the potatoes and coriander (cilantro) to the pan and cook over a medium heat for 10 minutes, or until the potatoes are soft. Return all the meat to the pan, stir to combine. Taste and adjust the seasoning, if necessary, with more salt and pepper.

Wash a stone thoroughly and drop it into the soup pan before serving.

Farmer's Soup

••

Sopa à Lavrador 📷 p.69   🛡 Trás-os-Montes e Alto Douro

This is a rich and heavy soup made for cold winter days. You can add more meat (preferably meat that's been cured in salt over a few weeks or months), but make sure you taste the soup before seasoning — the salt on the meat may be enough to season the soup and you won't need to add any more.

Preparation time: 20 minutes
Cooking time: 50 minutes
Serves: 4
🥘 🗆 🗆

180 g/6 oz (1 cup) dried red beans
4 small potatoes, peeled and halved
400 g/14 oz pointed cabbage or spring greens,
    cut into chunks
2 small onions, peeled and cut into chunks
1 large carrot, peeled and cut into thin disks
2 garlic cloves, peeled and cut into chunks
1 chorizo
300 g/11 oz salted pork belly
30 g/1 oz (1 tablespoon) long-grain rice
80 ml/2¾ fl oz (⅓ cup) olive oil
20 g/¾ oz yellow corn flour (fine polenta-style)
sea salt

Put the dried beans into a bowl, pour in enough cold water to cover and leave to soak for 12 hours.

The next day, drain the beans and set aside.

Pour 2.5 litres/85 fl oz (10 cups) water into a saucepan. Add all the vegetables, chorizo and pork belly to the pan and cook over a low heat for 30 minutes, or until soft. Take the pan off the heat. Using tongs or a slotted spoon, remove the meat from the pan and slice it into small pieces. Set aside.

Remove the cabbage from the pan along with one ladleful of all the other ingredients and set aside.

Mash all the remaining ingredients in the pan, then put the pan over a medium heat and once hot, add the rice. Stir everything in the pan to combine, then add the olive oil and stir again. Cook for 20 minutes, or until the rice is soft. Once cooked, sift the corn flour over the soup, stir to combine and bring to the boil.

Remove the pan from the heat and add the reserved meat, cabbage and ladleful of all the other ingredients.

Taste and adjust the seasoning, if necessary, with salt and stir to combine before serving.

'Dry' Soup

Sopa Seca

♡ Beira Litoral

Preparation time: 15 minutes
Cooking time: 40 minutes
Serves: 4

550 g/1 lb 4 oz beef rump (round steak)
80 g/3 oz chorizo
100 g/3½ oz Serrano ham
3 carrots, peeled and cut into thin irregular shapes
3 turnip tops, cut into thin irregular shapes
1 Savoy cabbage, shredded
1 bunch flat-leaf parsley, leaves picked
330 g/11½ oz bread, thinly sliced
2 mint sprigs, leaves picked
60 g/2¼ oz (½ stick) butter, cut into small cubes
sea salt

Preheat the oven to 200°C/400°F/Gas Mark 6.

Cut the beef into two equal pieces and put it into a large saucepan with the chorizo and ham. Pour in enough water to cover, season with salt and cook over a medium heat, skimming off any foam that rises to the top, for 20 minutes, or until the beef is almost soft. Once the meat is nearly cooked, add the carrots, turnips, cabbage and parsley, then cook over a medium heat for a further 10 minutes. Remove the beef and chorizo from the pan and cut it into small chunks. Set the pan with the cooking liquid aside.

Arrange half the sliced bread in the bottom of a large ovenproof dish. Layer the meats over the bread, then add the vegetables and a few mint leaves. Cover the top with the remaining bread.

Taste and adjust the seasoning of the cooking liquid, or broth, if necessary, then pour a few ladlefuls over the top layer of bread. Dot the butter over the bread and bake for 10 minutes, or until golden brown. Serve immediately.

Meat Soup with Rice

Caldo de Carne

♡ Madeira

Preparation time: 20 minutes, plus 1 hour standing
Cooking time: 1 hour 15 minutes
Serves: 4

🌶 ▢

60 g/2¼ oz (½ stick) butter
80 ml/2¾ fl oz (⅓ cup) olive oil
800 g/1 lb 12 oz beef shin, cut into chunks
2 medium onions, peeled and cut into chunks
2 garlic cloves, peeled and cut into chunks
3 waxy potatoes, peeled and cut into chunks
2 carrots, peeled and cut into chunks
120 g/4 oz (⅔ cup) long-grain rice

Put the butter and olive oil into a saucepan and heat over a medium heat. Add the beef, onions and garlic and cook for 10 minutes, or until the onions are translucent and the meat has coloured.

Pour 2.5 litres/85 fl oz (10 cups) water into the pan, then add the potatoes and carrots. Reduce the heat to low and cook for 45 minutes, or until the meat and vegetables are cooked. Remove the meat from the pan and shred it.

Strain and discard the bones with the vegetables, then pour the stock back into the pan. Add the rice and cook over a medium heat for 20 minutes, or until soft, then add the meat and season with salt. Remove from the heat, cover with a lid and leave to rest for 1 hour.

Gently reheat the soup before serving.

Beef Shin Stew

Caldo da Romaria

♡ Madeira

The name of this red, rich soup made of meat stock, potatoes, carrots and onions literally means 'pilgrimage stock', and the origins of the dish link to the pilgrimage to São Vicente, where there is a chapel built inside a basalt rock at the mouth of the stream that runs through the town. Pilgrims would carry ingredients and stock to make *caldo* when they reached their destination, to replenish their bodies after walking for days.

Preparation time: 20 minutes
Cooking time: 1 hour 35 minutes
Serves: 6

🌶 ▢ ▢

40 g/1½ oz lard (pork fat)
2 onions, peeled and quartered
220 g/7½ oz carrots, peeled and cut into small pieces
2 *pimentas da terra* (sweet peppers) or 1 long red pepper, halved, de-seeded and cut into small pieces
350 g/12 oz ripe tomatoes, cut into small pieces
800 g/1 lb 12 oz beef shin, cut into small pieces
500 g/1 lb 2 oz waxy potatoes, peeled and cut into small pieces
sea salt

Put the lard (pork fat) into a large saucepan and heat over a medium heat until melted. Add the onions, carrots, *pimentas da terra* or pepper, tomatoes and meat and cook for 15 minutes, or until the onions are golden and the meat is tender. Season with salt.

Pour 220 ml/7½ fl oz (1 cup) water into the pan, reduce the heat to low and cook for 1 hour until the meat is completely cooked through. Add the potatoes and cook for a further 20 minutes, or until soft.

Taste and adjust the seasoning, if necessary, before serving.

Farmer's Soup (recipe p.66)

Pumpkin Soup with Vermicelli Noodles

•••

Sopa de Moganga   ♡ Madeira

Preparation time: 15 minutes
Cooking time: 45 minutes
Serves: 6
🥄 ▢

60 g/2¼ oz (½ stick) unsalted butter
2 onions, peeled and finely chopped
4 tomatoes, cut into small cubes
850 g/1 lb 14 oz Malabar gourd pumpkin, peeled,
    de-seeded and thinly sliced
6 waxy potatoes, peeled and cut into small pieces
220 g/7½ oz (1½ cups) fresh peas, shelled (optional)
3 vermicelli noodle nests
sea salt

Melt the butter in a large saucepan over a medium heat. Add the onions and tomatoes and cook for 10 minutes, or until the onions are translucent. Add the pumpkin and cook for 20 minutes, or until tender. Season with salt.

Pour 3 litres/102 fl oz (12¾ cups) water into the pan and bring to the boil. Add the potatoes and peas, if using, reduce the heat to low and cook for 15 minutes, or until the potatoes are soft.

Add the noodle nests, increase the heat to medium and cook for a further 5 minutes, or until the noodles are cooked.

Taste and adjust the seasoning with salt, if necessary, before serving.

Clear Lamb Broth

•••

Canja de Borrego   ♡ Beira Baixa

Preparation time: 15 minutes
Cooking time: 1 hour 40 minutes
Serves: 4
▢

½ lamb's head
500 g/1 lb 2 oz lamb shoulder
40 ml/1⅓ fl oz (2⅔ tablespoons) olive oil
2 small carrots, peeled but left whole
1 onion, peeled and quartered
150 g/5 oz (1¼ cups) orzo pasta
2 bunches mint, leaves picked
sea salt

Put the lamb's head and lamb shoulder into a large saucepan. Pour 3.5 litres/118 fl oz (14 cups) water into the pan, season with a pinch of salt, then add the olive oil, carrots and onion. Cook over a low heat for 1 hour 20 minutes, or until the meat is soft and can be easily pulled from the bones.

Using tongs or a slotted spoon, remove the meat from the pan and strain the cooking liquid, or broth, through a sieve (fine-mesh strainer) into a clean saucepan. Discard the vegetables. Shred the meat and set aside.

Bring the broth to the boil over a high heat. Once boiling, reduce the heat to medium, add the orzo pasta and cook for 10–15 minutes, or until soft. Add the meat and mint leaves.

Taste and adjust the seasoning with salt, if necessary, before serving.

Hare Soup

•••

Sopa de Lebre   ♡ Algarve

For this recipe, you need to buy fresh hare's blood. If you can't find hare's blood, then use chicken blood instead.

Preparation time: 20 minutes
Cooking time: 45 minutes
Serves: 6
▢ ▢

1 medium hare
220 ml/7½ fl oz (1 cup) fresh hare's or chicken blood
1 tablespoon white wine vinegar
250 g/9 oz smoked bacon, diced
3 onions, peeled and finely chopped
100 ml/3½ fl oz (⅓ cup) olive oil
300 ml/10 fl oz (1¼ cups) white wine
8 slices bread, toasted
sea salt and freshly ground white pepper

Clean the hare and chop it into small pieces. Pour the blood into a small bowl, add the white wine vinegar, stir and set aside. (The vinegar stops the blood coagulating.)

Put the bacon into a large saucepan and cook over a low heat for 5 minutes, or until the bacon starts to melt down. Add the chopped onions and olive oil and cook for 12 minutes, or until golden. Add the hare, then mix well and sprinkle over the white wine and cook for 3 minutes.

Add 1.8 litres/61 fl oz (7¼ cups) water to the pan and season with salt and pepper. Cook for 20 minutes, or until the liquid has reduced by half. Add the blood and cook gently for a further 2 minutes, or until thickened.

Arrange the toasted bread in a large serving bowl. Pour the soup over the bread before serving.

Holy Grail Soup

Sopa do Espírito Santo   ⋃ Açores

Made with beef and chicken cooked in a broth of garlic, onion, mint, cinnamon and *malagueta* chilli, this soup is prepared and distributed to the crowds during the *Festas do Espírito Santo* (Festival of the Holy Spirit) parades. Founded by Franciscan monks in Tomar, these Easter-time celebrations later expanded to the Islands during the Crusades. This soup represents the offerings to the Holy Spirit. It is usually the first dish on the festival menu, served alongside a cow's liver cooked in blood, followed by *Alcatra com Molho* (Beef Stew, page 252) with *Massa Sovada* (Sweet Bread Dough, page 352). Traditionally, *Sopa do Espírito Santo* was cooked in a pot that was covered by a linen cloth and some blankets, resting like this for two or three hours until ready to be served.

Preparation time: 15 minutes, plus 2 hours standing
Cooking time: 2–3 hours
Serves 6
⋂

2 onions, peeled and quartered
2 garlic cloves, peeled and quartered
30 g/1 oz (1 tablespoon plus 1 teaspoon) *Massa de Malagueta* (page 102)
2 mint sprigs, plus extra mint leaves
1 cinnamon stick
1 medium whole chicken, cut into 8 pieces
800 g/1 lb 12 oz beef shin (shank) or flank steak, cut into 2-cm/¾-inch chunks
800 g/1 lb 12 oz Savoy cabbage, cut into large chunks
40 g/1½ oz (3 tablespoons) lard (pork fat)
220 g/7½ oz fresh cow's liver, sliced
400 ml/14 fl oz (1⅔ cups) fresh cow's blood (optional)
450 g/1 lb sourdough bread, sliced into long thin strips
100 ml/3½ fl oz (⅓ cup) *Alcatra com Molho* (page 252)
sea salt

Put the onions and garlic into a piece of muslin (cheesecloth) with the *Massa de Malagueta*, mint sprigs and cinnamon stick and wrap them up, tying the top with some butcher's string or kitchen twine, like a 'bouquet garni'.

Pour enough water into a large saucepan to cover the chicken and beef when added. Season the water with a large pinch of salt, then add the 'bouquet garni'. Add the chicken and beef chunks to the pan and cook over a medium heat, skimming off any foam that rises to the top. Check the chicken after 1 hour as it will cook before the beef. As soon as the chicken is cooked, remove from the pan with a slotted spoon and set aside.

Check the beef after 2 hours (it will take between 2 and 3 hours to cook). Once the beef is nearly cooked, add the cabbage and lard (pork fat) to the pan and cook for 10–15 minutes or until tender. Remove the beef from the pan. Shred both the chicken and beef, then set aside.

Meanwhile, fill a separate large saucepan with water, add a pinch of salt, then add the liver and cook over a low heat for 5 minutes, or until cooked through. Remove the liver from the pan, thinly slice and then set aside.

Bring another large saucepan of water with a pinch of salt to the boil. Once the water is boiling, add the blood (if using) and cook over a medium heat for 15 minutes. Strain the blood — by now, the blood will have crumbled. Set aside.

Spread the strips of bread over a deep baking sheet, scatter over a few mint leaves, then pour over the *Alcatra* sauce. Add the cabbage, liver and blood, half of the meat stock and leave to soak for 10 minutes. Pour the remaining stock over the top, then cover with a large, thick tea (dish) towel and leave to soak for 2 hours.

Gently reheat the meats before serving with the 'soup'.

'Dry' Soup — Minho Style

Sopa Seca do Minho   ⋃ Minho

Preparation time: 20 minutes
Cooking time: 3 hours
Serves: 4
⋂

500 g/1 lb 2 oz chicken or ½ chicken, cut into 3 pieces
500 g/1 lb 2 oz beef to boil
140 g/5 oz ham
120 g/4 oz *salpicão* or use *lomo* or chorizo
450 g/1 lb bread, thickly sliced
2 bunches mint, leaves picked
1 Portuguese cabbage, such as tronchuda or use pointed cabbage, leaves separated and halved
sea salt

Pour 3.2 litres/108 fl oz (12¾ cups) water into a large saucepan and bring to a simmer over a medium–low heat. Add the chicken pieces, beef, ham and *salpicao* and cook, skimming off any foam that rises to the top, for 2½ hours, or until all the meats are soft.

Meanwhile, put the bread slices into a large heatproof bowl and scatter over the mint leaves. Set aside.

Preheat the oven to 190°C/375°F/Gas Mark 5.

Once the meats are cooked, remove them from the pan and set aside, then cook the cabbage in the same water for 10 minutes, or until soft.

Meanwhile, cut the meat into small pieces and add them to the pan with the cooked cabbage. Pour the soup over the bread in the heatproof bowl. Add a pinch of salt, if necessary, then pour into a large, deep ovenproof pan and bake in the oven for 20 minutes, or until the top is toasted. Serve immediately.

Chicken Soup

Sopa de Azedo com Galinha   ♡ Açores

Preparation time: 30 minutes, plus 10 minutes standing
Cooking time: 2 hours
Serves 4
♡

1 medium whole chicken, cleaned and trimmed
2 onions, peeled and quartered
3 garlic cloves, peeled and quartered
70 g/2¾ oz tomato pulp
1 teaspoon ground black pepper
1 teaspoon paprika
1 cinnamon stick
4 waxy potatoes, peeled and quartered
sea salt

For the filling:
120 g/4 oz chicken livers, cleaned and trimmed
150 g/5 oz gizzards, cleaned and membrane removed
100 g/3½ oz chicken hearts, excess fat removed
2 slices sourdough bread
1 onion, peeled
2 garlic cloves, peeled
⅓ bunch flat-leaf parsley, leaves picked
1 tablespoon ground *pimenta da terra* or
    long red pepper
1 teaspoon paprika
1 tablespoon lard (pork fat)
2 eggs
sea salt

To make the filling, put the offal (variety meats) in a saucepan and pour in enough water to cover. Add a pinch of salt and cook for 20 minutes. Remove the offal from the pan and finely chop. Set aside.

Soak the bread in a shallow bowl of cold water for 5 minutes, or until the bread has absorbed the water. Gently squeeze the bread to remove the excess water. Set aside.

Finely chop the onion, garlic and parsley together. Transfer to a bowl with the offal and soaked bread. Add the *pimenta da terra*, paprika, lard (pork fat) and eggs, then mix together until well combined. Transfer to a saucepan and cook over a low heat for 20 minutes, or until dried out.

Stuff the filling into the cavity of the chicken, then with a trussing needle and butcher's string or kitchen twine, close up the cavity. Put the chicken into a large saucepan, cover with water, then add the onions and garlic and cook over a medium heat for 1 hour, or until nearly cooked through.

Once the chicken is nearly cooked, add the tomato pulp, then season with salt, pepper, paprika and cinnamon. Add the potatoes and continue to cook for a further 20 minutes, or until the potatoes are soft and the stock has reduced a little more.

Remove the pan from the heat, cover with a lid and leave to rest for 10 minutes before serving.

'Pot' Soup

Sopa da Panela   ♡ Alentejo

Preparation time: 20 minutes
Cooking time: 1 hour
Serves 6
♡ ♡

1 chorizo
550 g/1 lb 3 oz chicken, thighs and legs,
    cut into quarters
600 g/1 lb 5 oz lamb belly, cut into chunks
250 g/9 oz lardo
1½ onions, peeled and halved
800 g/1 lb 12 oz waxy potatoes, peeled and cut into
    chunks
sea salt
1 bunch mint, leaves picked, to garnish
6 slices bread, to serve

Using a skewer or the tip of a sharp knife, prick the chorizo all over to prevent it from bursting during cooking.

Put all the meat into a large saucepan, pour in enough water to cover, season with salt and add the onions. Cook over a medium heat, skimming off the foam that rises to the top with a slotted spoon, for 40 minutes, or until the meat is soft.

Once the meats are cooked, add the potatoes and cook for a further 20 minutes, or until soft. Taste and adjust the seasoning, if necessary.

Garnish the soup with mint leaves before serving with the bread.

Fish Soup from Pico

••

Caldo de Peixe do Pico   ◌ Açores

Caldo de Peixe is neither a stew nor a soup; the fish is removed from the broth and served with boiled potatoes, and the broth served on the side in a bowl, to be sipped slowly. A traditional dish among fishing communities in the Azores, especially on the islands of Pico and Graciosa, different types of fish are cooked very gently in the broth of tomato, onions, bay leaf, white wine and chilli paste, with cumin included in some local variations of the recipe.

Preparation time: 30 minutes
Cooking time: 30 minutes
Serves: 10
◌ ✦

600 g/1 lb 5 oz sea bream
700 g/1 lb 9 oz yellowmouth barracuda
1 medium grey mullet
1 kg/2 lb 4 oz scorpionfish
600 g/1 lb 5 oz grouper
800 g/1 lb 12 oz gulley fish
⅓ bunch flat-leaf parsley, leaves picked
4 bay leaves
60 g/2¼ oz *Massa de Malagueta* (page 102)
½ teaspoon saffron threads
8 large onions, peeled and quartered
12 Jamaican peppercorns
420 ml/14¼ fl oz (1⅔ cups) white wine
800 g/1 lb 12 oz fresh tomatoes, quartered
1.2 kg/2 lb 10 oz small waxy potatoes, cut into thick slices
70 ml/2¼ fl oz (¼ cup) white wine vinegar
10 small waxy potatoes, peeled but left whole
300 ml/10 fl oz (1¼ cups) olive oil
sea salt

For the raw green sauce:
1 large bunch flat-leaf parsley
8 garlic cloves with pink skin
60 g/2¼ oz (⅓ cup) sea salt
80 ml/2¾ fl oz (⅓ cup) white wine vinegar

Clean all the fish, removing the scales. Cut off the fish heads and discard. Make an incision in the bellies with a sharp knife and remove the guts, then rinse under cold running water. Cut all the fish into large chunks.

Put all the fish into a large saucepan with the parsley, bay leaves, *Massa de Malagueta*, saffron, onions, Jamaican peppercorns, white wine, tomatoes, potato slices and the vinegar, then season with salt. Cover with water and cook over a low heat for 30 minutes, or until all the fish is cooked through.

Meanwhile, put the whole potatoes into another saucepan, cover with cold water, add a pinch of salt and cook for 20 minutes, or until soft.

To make the raw green sauce, put the parsley, garlic, saffron, salt and vinegar into a large mortar and, using a pestle, mash it to a paste. Add a splash of water and stir to combine. Set aside.

Using a slotted spoon, transfer the cooked fish to a serving plate. Ladle the soup into individual serving bowls and add a spoonful of the raw green sauce to each bowl. Serve the fish and one whole potato per person alongside the soup.

Dogfish Soup

••

Sopa de Cação   ◌ Alentejo

The star ingredient in this soup is *cação* (dogfish shark). It has a firm, white flesh and is very widely consumed in many guises throughout Alentejo. Historically, this was one of a few fish available in great abundance in the region, thanks to its low cost and longer shelf life (*cação* was one of the sea fish that best endured transport, and therefore arrived in the freshest state). These days, *Sopa de Cação* is made from slices of the fish cooked in a flavourful broth infused with garlic and coriander (or sometimes pennyroyal/spearmint).

Preparation time: 20 minutes
Cooking time: 45 minutes
Serves: 4
◌

800 g/1 lb 12 oz dogfish, cut into large pieces
5 garlic cloves, peeled and halved
⅓ bunch pennyroyal
½ bunch coriander (cilantro)
220 ml/7½ fl oz (1 cup) olive oil
75 g/2¾ oz (½ cup) plain (all-purpose) flour
60 ml/2 fl oz (4 tablespoons) white wine vinegar
1 tablespoon *Massa de Pimentão*
sea salt
300 g/11 oz bread, sliced and toasted, to serve

Put the fish into a large saucepan, pour over enough water to cover and add a pinch of salt. Cook over a medium heat for 20 minutes, then transfer the fish to a plate with a fish slice (spatula) and set aside. Leave the cooking water in the pan to cool.

Put the garlic, pennyroyal and coriander (cilantro) into a mortar and, using a pestle, mash to a paste. Transfer the paste to another large saucepan, add the olive oil and cook gently over a low heat for 10 minutes, or until translucent. Add the dogfish and mix well.

Once the cooking water has cooled, add the flour and stir until smooth. Season with the vinegar and stir in the *Massa de Pimentão*. Stir this mixture into the fish and cook over a low heat for 15 minutes until the flour is cooked.

Serve the soup over the toasted bread slices.

Largehead Hairtail Fish Soup

Sopa de Peixe Espada da Madeira 📷 p.75   ♥ Madeira

Preparation time: 20 minutes
Cooking time: 1 hour
Serves: 6
🗋 🌿

800 g/1 lb 12 oz largehead hairtail fish, gutted, cleaned and patted dry
450 g/1 lb bull's heart tomatoes (or beefsteak tomatoes)
160 ml/5½ fl oz (⅔ cup) olive oil
3 onions, peeled and chopped
4 garlic cloves, peeled and chopped
1 teaspoon dried oregano
1 teaspoon dried thyme leaves
800 g/1 lb 12 oz waxy potatoes, peeled but left whole
sea salt and freshly ground black pepper

Remove the fins and bones from the fish. Remove the head, if there is one, and set aside. Cut the fish into small pieces and set aside.

Have a large bowl of iced water nearby. Bring a large saucepan of water to the boil. Using a sharp knife, score the top of the tomatoes with a small cross shape. Once the water is boiling, carefully add the tomatoes and blanch for 30 seconds, then transfer them with a slotted spoon to the iced water and leave to cool. Once cool enough to handle, peel off the skins, cut in half and de-seed. Cut the flesh into quarters, then into small pieces and set aside.

Put the fish bones and head (if using) into a large saucepan, cover with water and bring to the boil. Reduce the heat to medium and cook for 30 minutes to make a fish stock. Strain the stock through muslin (cheesecloth) into a bowl and discard the bones and head.

Fill another large saucepan with 750 ml/25 fl oz (3 cups) water, then add the olive oil, onions, garlic, oregano, thyme and season with salt and pepper. Add the reserved tomatoes and fish stock. Cook over a medium heat for 10 minutes, or until all the ingredients are cooked.

Transfer the soup to a blender or food processor and blitz until smooth. You may need to do this in batches or use a handheld stick (immersion) blender. Pour the soup back into the pan, add 750 ml/25 fl oz (3 cups) water, stir and bring to the boil. Add the fish pieces, reduce the heat to medium and cook for 20 minutes, or until the fish is cooked through.

Meanwhile, put the whole potatoes into another saucepan, cover with cold water, add a pinch of salt and cook for 20 minutes, or until soft.

Ladle the soup into individual serving bowls. Serve the potatoes alongside the soup.

Freshwater Fish Soup with Pennyroyal

Sopa de Peixe do Rio   ♥ Alentejo

Preparation time: 20 minutes, plus 10 minutes standing
Cooking time: 45 minutes
Serves: 4
🗋

4 large ripe tomatoes
2 barbus fish, gutted, cleaned and patted dry
120 ml/4 fl oz (½ cup) extra virgin olive oil
2 onions, peeled and finely sliced
4 garlic cloves, peeled and finely sliced
⅓ bunch pennyroyal, leaves picked
⅓ bunch water mint, leaves picked
2 red (bell) peppers, cored, de-seeded and sliced into strips
200 ml/7 fl oz (¾ cup) white wine
80 ml/2¾ fl oz (⅓ cup) white wine vinegar
sea salt
4 slices bread, to serve

Have a large bowl of iced water nearby. Bring a medium saucepan of water to the boil. Using a sharp knife, score the top of the tomatoes with a small cross shape. Once the water is boiling, carefully add the tomatoes and blanch for 30 seconds, then transfer them with a slotted spoon to the iced water and leave to cool. Once cool enough to handle, peel off the skins, cut in half and de-seed. Cut the flesh into chunks and set aside.

Put the fish onto a board, grip the head firmly and remove it by cutting across the open edge of the belly and around the head. Remove the tail. Cut down along the length of the backbone following the lateral line with a large, heavy knife. Split the spine in half so each piece of fish has some backbone, then cut the fish into tranches (or slices) by making cuts at 45 degrees to the first cut. Adjust the width of each tranche according to the thickness of the fish. The tranche at the tail will be triangular in shape while the others will be more rectangular. Season the tranches with salt.

Heat the olive oil in a large saucepan over a medium heat. Add the onions and garlic and cook for 10 minutes, or until the onions are translucent. Add the tomatoes, pennyroyal, water mint and the red (bell) peppers and mix together to combine. Add the white wine and 1 litre/34 fl oz (4¼ cups) water. Season with salt and cook for 10 minutes until all the ingredients are cooked through.

Add 2 litres/70 fl oz (8½ cups) water to the pan and bring to the boil. Reduce the heat to medium, add the fish and cook for 25 minutes, or until the flesh separates from the bones. Add the vinegar and leave to stand for 10 minutes.

Taste and adjust the seasoning, if necessary, before serving with sliced bread.

Largehead Hairtail Fish Soup

Salt Cod Broth

•••

Canja de Bacalhau   ♡ Leiria

Preparation time: 15 minutes, plus 12–14 hours soaking
Cooking time: 30 minutes
Serves: 4
◻ ✿

300 g/11 oz salt cod loin, desalted (page 40)
olive oil, for drizzling
4 waxy potatoes, peeled and quartered
50 g/2 oz (¼ cup) long-grain rice
½ teaspoon vinegar
4 eggs
sea salt

Check the cod is not too salty before cooking. If
it is, then leave to soak for another 2 hours. Drain.

Fill a saucepan with enough water to cover
the cod and bring to the boil. Reduce the heat to
medium and, when simmering, add the cod with
a drizzle of oil and cook for 6 minutes, or until the
flesh flakes easily. Remove the cod from the pan
and tear it into fine shreds, removing any bones.

Add the potatoes and rice to the pan with the
cod cooking water. Cook over a medium heat for
15–20 minutes, or until soft. Return the cod to the
pan. Taste and adjust the seasoning, if necessary.

Bring a medium saucepan of water to the boil,
add the vinegar and a pinch of salt. Once boiling,
reduce the heat to medium, carefully break the
eggs into the simmering water so they remain
whole and poach for 4 minutes, or to your liking.
Remove the eggs with a slotted spoon and drain.

Ladle the broth into four individual bowls and
add a poached egg to each bowl before serving.

Glass Blower's Soup

•••

Sopa do Vidreiro   ♡ Leiria

**This soup acquired its name from the huge culture
and industry of glass factories and glass blowers
in the city that it originates from. This soup was
enjoyed by the workers in those factories.**

Preparation time: 10 minutes, plus 12–14 hours soaking
Cooking time: 30 minutes
Serves: 4
◻ ◻

450 g/1 lb salt cod, desalted (page 40)
350 g/12 oz new potatoes, peeled and cut into thick slices
3 eggs
3 slices sourdough bread
2 slices Cornbread (page 32)
3 flat-leaf parsley sprigs, chopped
80 ml/2¾ fl oz (⅓ cup) olive oil

Check the cod is not too salty before cooking. If
it is, then leave to soak for another 2 hours. Drain.

Fill a saucepan with enough water to cover
the cod and bring to the boil. Reduce the heat
to medium and, when simmering, add the cod and
cook for 6 minutes, or until the flesh flakes easily.
Remove the cod from the pan and set aside.

Cook the potatoes in the cod cooking water
for 15–20 minutes, or until soft. Carefully break
the eggs into the simmering water so they remain
whole and poach for 4 minutes, or to your liking.

Put the bread slices into a large terrine, scatter
over the parsley and drizzle with olive oil. Shred
the cod, removing any bones, over the bread in
a single layer. Add the poached eggs to the terrine
and pour a few ladlefuls of the broth over the top.
Leave to soak for 2 minutes before serving.

Fish Soup with Macaroni

•••

Sopa de Peixe com Massa   ♡ Algarve

Preparation time: 15 minutes
Cooking time: 55 minutes
Serves: 6
◻

400 g/14 oz sea bream, de-scaled, gutted,
    cleaned and patted dry
450 g/1 lb skate wing, cleaned and patted dry
120 ml/4 fl oz (½ cup) olive oil
3 onions, peeled and finely chopped
4 garlic cloves, peeled and finely chopped
2 tablespoons chopped coriander (cilantro)
2 bay leaves
1 tablespoon dried oregano
350 g/12 oz canned chopped tomatoes
350 g/12 oz (3½ cups) macaroni
20 ml/¾ fl oz (4 teaspoons) white wine vinegar
6 eggs
4 slices bread
sea salt and freshly ground black pepper

Remove the head from the sea bream, if there is
one, and set aside. Cut both the sea bream and
skate wing into chunks and set aside.

Heat the olive oil in a saucepan over a low heat,
add the onions and garlic and cook for 15 minutes,
or until the onions are golden. Add the coriander
(cilantro), bay leaves, oregano and chopped
tomatoes to the pan and cook for 30 minutes, or
until the tomatoes have broken down into a purée.
Season with salt and pepper.

Add 2.5 litres/85 fl oz (10 cups) water to the
pan and bring to the boil. Reduce the heat to
medium, add the macaroni and cook for 8 minutes,
or until it is nearly cooked. Add the fish and cook for
a further 4 minutes, or until the flesh flakes easily.

Bring a medium saucepan of water to the boil,
add the vinegar. Once boiling, reduce the heat to
medium, carefully break in the eggs so they remain
whole and poach for 4 minutes, or to your liking.
Remove the eggs with a slotted spoon and drain.

Arrange the bread in a serving dish, pour over
the soup and top with poached eggs before serving.

Meagre Fish Soup

Sopa de Estufado
de Corvina de Odeceixe   ⏍ Alentejo

Preparation time: 30 minutes
Cooking time: 1 hour 15 minutes
Serves: 4
⏍ ⏍

1.6 kg/3 lb 8 oz meagre fish, from head to loin piece,
    de-scaled, gutted, cleaned and patted dry
1 kg/2 lb 4 oz ripe tomatoes
150 ml/5 fl oz (⅔ cup) olive oil
120 g/4 oz lardo, thinly sliced
½ linguiça or chorizo, thinly sliced
4 onions, peeled and cut into medium rings
2 garlic cloves, peeled and cut into chunks
2 green (bell) peppers, cored, de-seeded and sliced
    into thin strips
⅓ bunch water mint
⅓ bunch pennyroyal
650 g/1 lb 7 oz new potatoes, peeled and
    cut into quarters
sea salt and freshly ground black pepper
4 slices bread, toasted, to serve

Remove the head from the fish, cut it in half
and season with salt. Cut the remaining fish into
4 tranches or slices and set aside.

Have a large bowl of iced water nearby. Bring
a large saucepan of water to the boil. Using a sharp
knife, score the top of the tomatoes with a small
cross shape. Once the water is boiling, carefully
add the tomatoes and blanch for 30 seconds,
then transfer them with a slotted spoon to the
iced water and leave to cool. Once cool enough to
handle, peel off the skins, cut in half and de-seed,
then cut the flesh into small cubes.

Heat the olive oil in a large, tall saucepan over
a medium heat. Add the lardo and linguiça or
chorizo and cook for 5 minutes, or until the
meat has released its fat and gained some colour.
Remove the meat from the pan and set aside.

Add the onions, garlic, (bell) peppers, water
mint and pennyroyal to the pan and cook for 15
minutes, or until the onions are golden. Add the
tomatoes, season with salt and cook for a further
10 minutes, or until soft. Add 1.8 litres/65 fl oz
(7¼ cups) water and bring to the boil, then reduce
the heat and simmer for 10 minutes.

Add the fish head to the pan together with
the potatoes and cook for 15 minutes, or until the
potatoes are partially cooked. Add the remaining
fish, season with salt and pepper and return the
meat to the pan. Cook gently for 20 minutes, or
until the fish is cooked through. Taste and adjust
the seasoning, if necessary, and leave to stand
for 10 minutes.

Arrange the toasted bread in a serving dish and
pour over the soup before serving.

River Fish Soup

Sopa de Peixe do Rio   ⏍ Ribatejo
de Santarém

Preparation time: 30 minutes
Cooking time: 1 hour
Serves: 4
⏍ ✿

700 g/1 lb 9 oz twait shad fish or allis shad, or other
    freshwater fish, de-scaled, gutted, cleaned and
    patted dry
220 ml/7½ fl oz (1 cup) olive oil, plus extra for drizzling
4 garlic cloves, 2 peeled and crushed and 2 peeled and
    very finely chopped
2 onions, 1 peeled and quartered and 1 peeled and very
    finely chopped
1 bay leaf
⅓ bunch flat-leaf parsley, leaves picked
1 large carrot, peeled and cut into chunks
100 ml/3½ fl oz (⅓ cup) white wine
2 waxy potatoes, peeled and cut into cubes
1 red chilli, finely chopped
300 g/11 oz (3 cups) short macaroni
2 ripe bull's heart tomatoes (or beefsteak tomatoes),
    cut into small pieces
½ teaspoon dried thyme
½ teaspoon dried oregano
sea salt

Remove the head from the fish, if there is one,
and set aside.

Put half the olive oil into a large saucepan with
the crushed garlic, quartered onion, bay leaf, parsley
and carrot and cook over a medium heat for 10
minutes, or until the vegetables are soft. Add the
white wine and 3.5 litres/118 fl oz (14 cups) water,
then add the fish, reduce the heat to low and cook
for 20 minutes, or until the fish is cooked and the
flesh flakes easily. Remove the fish from the pan.
Flake the fish into a bowl, removing any bones,
and set aside. Strain the fish cooking water through
a sieve (fine-mesh strainer) into a large bowl or jug
(pitcher) and set aside.

Heat the remaining olive oil in another large
saucepan over a low heat, add the rest of the
onion and garlic and cook for 10 minutes, or until
the onion is translucent. Add the potatoes and
reserved stock, then add the chilli and season with
salt. Bring to the boil and cook for 10 minutes,
or until the potatoes are al dente.

Add the macaroni and tomatoes to the pan
and cook for a further 8–10 minutes, or until the
macaroni is soft. Add the cooked fish, then taste
and adjust the seasoning, if necessary, with salt.
Add the thyme and oregano and drizzle with olive
oil. Stir everything together before serving.

Wedge Shell Clam Soup

Sopa de Conquilhas ⼑ Algarve

Preparation time: 20 minutes, plus 12 hours standing
Cooking time: 50 minutes
Serves: 4

🐚⼑

3 ripe tomatoes
1.5 kg/3 lb 5 oz fresh *conquilhas* or wedge shell clams
120 ml/4 fl oz (½ cup) olive oil
2 small onions, peeled and cut into chunks
2 bay leaves
90 g/3¼ oz (½ cup) rice
sea salt and freshly ground black pepper

The day before, scrub the shells of the clams to remove any dirt. Discard any that don't close when their shells are tapped. Rinse the clams several times under cold running water to remove any sand and grit, then put them into a large bowl and pour in enough water to cover. Add enough fine sea salt to make a brine with 1% salt and stir well. Do not add too much salt this may kill the clams. Leave to stand in the fridge for 12 hours. This will help to expel any sand inside the clams.

Have a medium bowl of iced water nearby. Bring a saucepan of water to the boil. Using a sharp knife, score the top of the tomatoes with a small cross shape. Once the water is boiling, carefully add the tomatoes and blanch for 30 seconds, then transfer them with a slotted spoon to the iced water and leave to cool. Once cool enough to handle, peel off the skins, cut in half and de-seed, then cut the flesh into small pieces. Set aside.

Heat the olive oil a large saucepan over a medium heat, add the onions and cook for 10 minutes, or until the onions are translucent. Add the tomatoes and bay leaves and cook, stirring frequently, for further 30 minutes, or until a paste has formed. Season with salt and pepper.

Drain the clams and put them into another large saucepan. Cover them with 2 litres/68 fl oz (8½ cups) cold water and cook over a medium heat for 10 minutes, or until they have all opened. Strain the clams through a sieve (fine-mesh strainer) into a large bowl, reserving the clam cooking liquid. Remove the clams from the shells and set aside.

Add the clam cooking liquid to the tomato mixture. Bring to the boil, then add the rice, reduce the heat to medium and cook for 10 minutes, or until the rice is soft. Add the reserved clams to the soup, then taste and adjust the seasoning, if necessary, before serving.

Creamy Prawn Soup

Creme de Camarão 📷 p.79 ⼑ Lisbon

Preparation time: 20 minutes
Cooking time: 40 minutes
Serves: 4

⼑

4 ripe tomatoes
60 g/2¼ oz (½ cup) plain (all-purpose) wheat flour
800 g/1 lb 12 oz prawns (shrimp), head and shells on
60 ml/2 fl oz (4 tablespoons) olive oil
2 onions, peeled and very finely chopped
2 garlic cloves, peeled and very finely chopped
1 red chilli, finely chopped
70 ml/2½ fl oz (¼ cup) white wine
sea salt and freshly ground black pepper
4 slices sourdough bread, toasted, to serve

Preheat the oven to 200°C/400°F/Gas Mark 6.

Have a large bowl of iced water nearby. Bring a large saucepan of water to the boil. Using a sharp knife, score the top of the tomatoes with a small cross shape. Once the water is boiling, carefully add the tomatoes and blanch for 30 seconds, then transfer them with a slotted spoon to the iced water and leave to cool. Once cool enough to handle, peel off the skins, cut in half and de-seed. Cut the flesh into small cubes and set aside.

When the oven is hot, sprinkle a large baking sheet with the flour and bake for 5 minutes, or until golden. Remove from the oven, sift into a bowl and set aside.

Have some ice in a large bowl nearby. Bring a large saucepan of water to the boil and add a pinch of salt. Once boiling, add the prawns (shrimp) and blanch for 30 seconds, then transfer them with a slotted spoon to the bowl of ice and leave to cool. Set the cooking water aside.

Remove the shells from the prawns and set the shells aside. Make a small cut in the back of the prawns, then remove the intestines and discard. Put the shells and heads into a mortar and, using a pestle, mash them. Add them to the cooking water and put the pan over a low heat. Cook for 15 minutes, then strain the stock through a sieve (fine-mesh strainer) into a bowl. Set aside.

Heat the olive oil in a large saucepan over a medium heat, add the onions and garlic and cook for 10 minutes, or until the onions are translucent. Add the chilli and tomatoes and cook for a further 10 minutes, or until the tomatoes are soft. Pour in the wine, then add the sifted flour and mix well to combine. Slowly incorporate the stock, stir well and bring to the boil to cook out the flour. Once the soup has boiled, add the prawns and remove from the heat. Season with pepper, then taste and adjust the seasoning, if necessary.

Ladle the soup into four individual bowls. Cut the toasted bread into small cubes and scatter over the soup before serving.

Creamy Prawn Soup

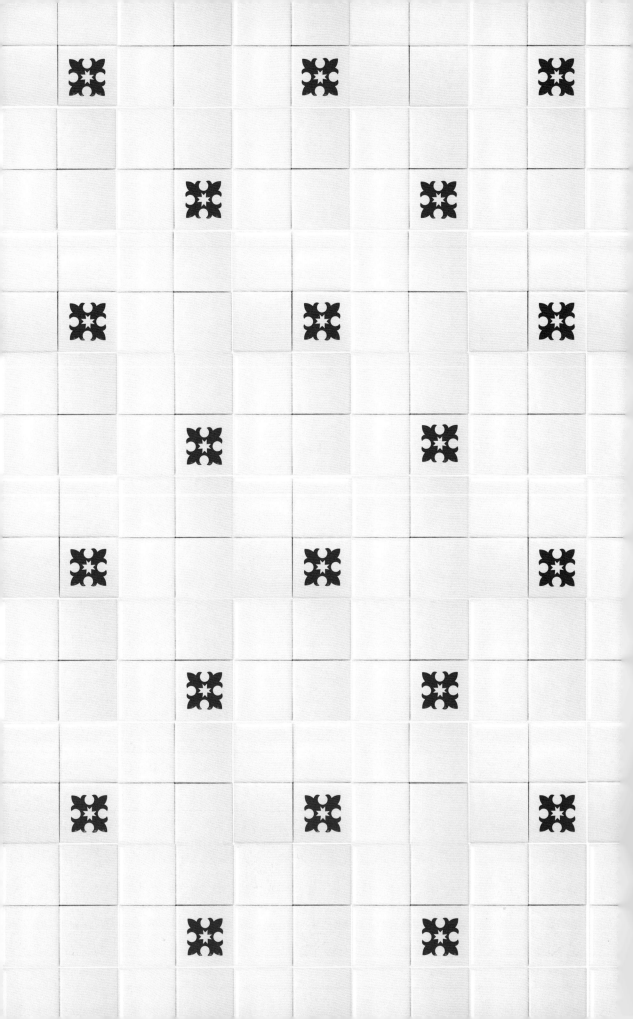

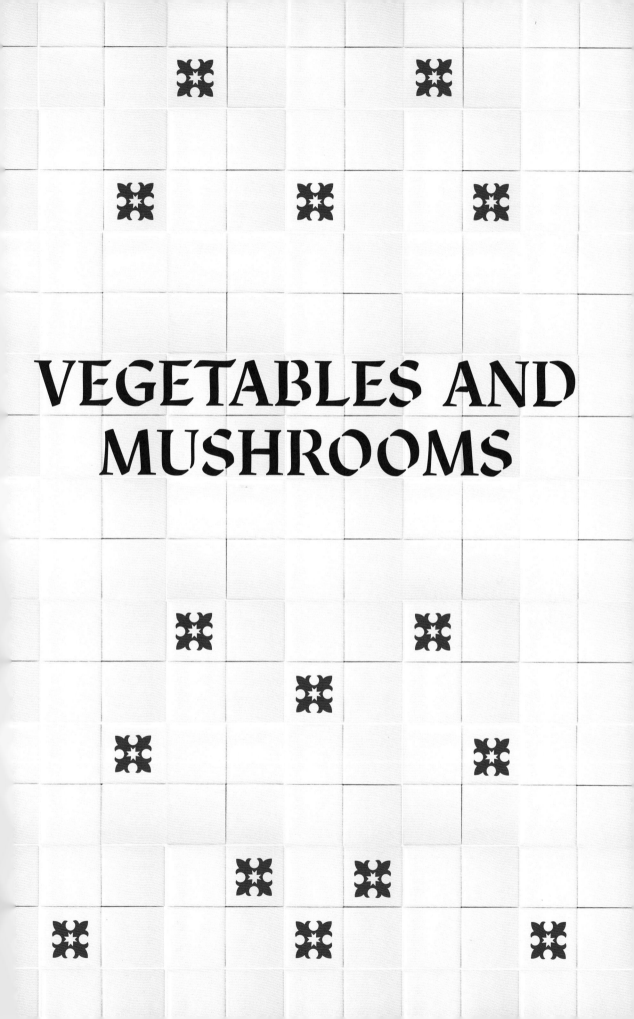

VEGETABLES AND MUSHROOMS

Stewed Peas with Poached Eggs

•••

Ervilhas com   ⬗ **Lisbon**
Ovos Escalfados   📷 p.83

This quick and easy pea stew is usually cooked on cold days, when people want a comforting dish. It may also be called *Ervilhas Guisadas* (braised peas). Poached eggs flavoured with *chouriço* and *toucinho* (pork belly), would have once been cooked to use fresh, seasonal peas in spring.

Preparation time: 5 minutes
Cooking time: 35 minutes
Serves: 4
🐖 ⬭ ⬚

80 ml/2¾ fl oz (⅓ cup) olive oil
50 g/2 oz (3½ tablespoons) butter
1 small onion, peeled and very finely chopped
500 g/1 lb 2 oz (3¼ cups) podded fresh peas
1 teaspoon caster (superfine) sugar
4 eggs
sea salt and freshly ground black pepper

Put the olive oil, butter and onion into a large saucepan and cook over a low heat for 10 minutes, or until the onion is translucent.

Add the peas to the pan, season with salt and add the sugar. Pour in enough water to cover the peas and cook gently for a further 10 minutes.

Make four wells in the peas and break the eggs into them. Cook for 5 minutes, or until the egg whites are set. Season with pepper before serving.

Stewed Peas with Poached Eggs and Linguiça

•••

Ervilhas com Ovos e Linguiça   ⬗ **Algarve**

Preparation time: 20 minutes
Cooking time: 40 minutes
Serves: 4
🐖 ⬚

½ onion, peeled and quartered
½ leek, roughly chopped
1 carrot, peeled and halved
2 garlic cloves, peeled and halved
500 g/1 lb 2 oz (3¼ cups) podded fresh peas
1 large onion, peeled and very finely chopped
nutmeg, for grating
280 g/10 oz *linguiça*, sliced in half and then thinly sliced
40 g/1½ oz (¼ cup) tomato purée (paste)
4 eggs
freshly ground black pepper

First, make a vegetable stock. Put the onion, leek, carrot and garlic into a large saucepan with 1.5 litres/50 fl oz (6¼ cups) water. Bring to the boil, then reduce the heat to medium and cook for 20 minutes. Line a sieve (fine-mesh strainer) with a clean J-cloth or muslin (cheesecloth) and strain the stock through it into a bowl or jug (pitcher). Set aside.

Have a medium bowl of iced water nearby. Bring a medium saucepan of water with a pinch of salt to the boil. Add the peas and blanch for 30 seconds, then drain and plunge them into the iced water to cool. Drain.

Put the chopped onion and peas into a saucepan. Season with grated nutmeg, pepper and a pinch of salt. Add the *linguiça*, tomato purée (paste) and 800 ml/27 fl oz (3¼ cups) of the reserved stock to the pan and cook over a medium heat for 8 minutes.

Break the eggs, one at a time, into the pan, making sure they are kept whole, and poach for 4 minutes, or until done to your liking. Taste and adjust the seasoning, if necessary, before serving.

Stewed Peas with Lardo

•••

Ervilhas à Algarvia   ⬗ **Algarve**

Preparation time: 10 minutes
Cooking time: 15 minutes
Serves: 4
🐖 ⬚ ⬚ ⬚ ✕

200 g/7 oz (1 cup) lard (pork fat), sliced into small pieces
1½ onions, peeled and cut into small pieces
650 g/1 lb 7 oz (4 cups) podded fresh peas
sea salt

Put the lard (pork fat) into a large saucepan and heat over a medium heat for 5 minutes, or until golden. Add the onions and cook for 5 minutes, or until soft, but not coloured.

Add the fresh peas and season with a pinch of salt. Cook for 5 minutes, then add just enough water to cover the peas and bring to the boil. Cover the pan with a lid and leave for 5 minutes before serving.

Stewed Peas with Poached Eggs

Braised Mangetout

Ervilhas Tortas Guisadas　　　○ Beira Baixa

Preparation time: 5 minutes
Cooking time: 20 minutes
Serves: 2
🥩 ◻ ◻ ⊠ ✕

70 g/2½ oz lard (pork fat)
1 onion, peeled and finely chopped
450 g/1 lb mangetout (snow peas)
2 garlic cloves, peeled and finely chopped
sea salt

Heat the lard (pork fat) in a medium saucepan over a low heat, add the onion and cook for 5 minutes until the onion is soft but not coloured.

Add the mangetout (snow peas) to the pan, stir and cook gently for 2–3 minutes. Add the garlic and then pour in 1.2 litres/40 fl oz (5 cups) water or enough to cover the mangetout. Cover with a lid and cook for 15 minutes, or until soft.

Season the mangetout with a pinch of salt before serving.

Battered Green Beans

Peixinhos da Horta　　📷 p.85　　　○ Lisbon

Literally meaning 'little fish from the garden', these battered and fried green beans are served as appetisers in both family restaurants and the home. This technique, which we now call tempura, was actually introduced to the Japanese in the 16th century, when three Portuguese merchants were the first Europeans to arrive in Japan. It has been a staple of Japan's cuisine ever since. The word 'tempura' comes from the Latin word 'tempora', referring to times of fasting, and *Peixinhos da Horta* (and sometimes fried fish) were often eaten when the Catholic church dictated that meat should be avoided.

Preparation time: 10 minutes
Cooking time: 15 minutes
Serves: 4
⌀ ⊠

500 g/1 lb 2 oz green beans, trimmed and strings removed
180 g/6 oz (1½ cups) plain (all-purpose) flour
120 ml/4 fl oz (½ cup) whole (full-fat) milk
1 litre/34 fl oz (4¼ cups) sunflower oil, for deep-frying
juice of 2 lemons, for drizzling
sea salt

Have a large bowl of iced water nearby. Bring a medium saucepan of water to the boil, add the beans and blanch for 30 seconds, or until soft. Transfer with a slotted spoon to the iced water and leave to cool. Once cool, put them in a colander and leave to drip to remove any excess moisture.

Put the flour into a large bowl, add the milk and stir together until a smooth batter forms.

Line a large baking sheet with paper towels. Heat the sunflower oil for deep-frying in a large, deep saucepan or fryer until it reaches 180°C/350°F on a thermometer. Taking three or four beans at a time, dip them into the batter, then carefully drop them into the hot oil and deep-fry for 1 minute, or until golden. Remove with a slotted spoon and leave to drain on the lined baking sheet. Repeat with the remaining beans.

Season the beans with salt and drizzle with lemon juice before serving.

Portuguese-style Broad Beans

Favas à Portuguesa　　　○ Lisbon

Preparation time: 20 minutes
Cooking time: 35 minutes
Serves: 4
🥩 ◻

50 g/2 oz (3½ tablespoons) unsalted butter
2 small onions, peeled and finely chopped
3 garlic cloves, peeled and finely chopped
130 g/4½ oz Serrano ham, cut into thin strips
110 g/3¾ oz pork belly, cut into thin strips
100 g/3½ oz chorizo, cut into medium slices
100 g/3½ oz chorizo with red wine, cut into medium slices
1 bay leaf
2 kg/4 lb 8 oz broad (fava) beans, double podded
⅓ bunch flat-leaf parsley, leaves picked
⅓ bunch coriander (cilantro), leaves picked
1 teaspoon caster (superfine) sugar
sea salt and freshly ground black pepper

For the salad:
60 ml/2 fl oz (4 tablespoons) olive oil
30 ml/1 fl oz (2 tablespoons) white wine vinegar
2 butterhead lettuces, leaves separated
¼ bunch coriander (cilantro), roughly chopped

Melt the butter in a saucepan over a low heat. Add the onions, garlic, ham, pork belly, both chorizos and bay leaf to the pan, then cook for 10 minutes, or until the meat is cooked through and the onions are translucent. Using a slotted spoon, remove all the meat from the pan and set aside.

Add the broad (fava) beans to the pan with the parsley, coriander (cilantro), sugar, a pinch each of salt and pepper and 350 ml/12 fl oz (1½ cups) warm water and stir. Place the reserved meats on top and cover with a lid. Cook over a low heat for a further 10 minutes.

To make the salad, put the oil, vinegar and a pinch of salt into a bowl or jam jar and whisk or seal with a lid and shake to combine. Put the lettuce leaves into a salad bowl and toss in the vinaigrette. Add the coriander and toss again before serving.

Serve the broad beans with the dressed salad.

Battered Green Beans

Broad Beans — Algarve Style

••

Favas à Moda do Algarve ⵔ **Algarve**

Preparation time: 30 minutes
Cooking time: 20 minutes
Serves: 4
🝢 🝢

550 g/1 lb 4 oz (2½ cups) shelled and podded
    (skinned) broad (fava) beans
60 ml/2 fl oz (4 tablespoons) olive oil
3 garlic cloves, peeled and very finely chopped
120 g/4 oz chorizo
100 g/3½ oz *morcela*
120 g/4 oz (⅔ cup) lard (pork fat) combined with some
    meat or bacon (not smoked)
sea salt and freshly ground black pepper

To garnish:
½ bunch coriander (cilantro), roughly chopped
25 g/1 oz fresh garlic tops, chopped
30 g/1 oz fresh onion tops, chopped

Have a medium bowl of iced water nearby. Bring
a medium saucepan of water to the boil, add
the broad (fava) beans and cook for 3 minutes.
Drain and put into the bowl of iced water to cool.
Drain and leave in a colander to drip dry.

Heat the olive oil in a saucepan over a low
heat, add the garlic and cook for 1–2 minutes,
or until golden. Add the beans and sprinkle with
2 tablespoons water. Once it starts to steam, cover
with a lid and cook for 1–2 minutes, or until hot.

Put the chorizo and *morcela* into a large
frying pan or skillet and cook over a low heat for
6–8 minutes, or until the skins are crispy. Slice
the meats and add to the beans, then transfer
to a serving dish and garnish with the coriander
(cilantro), garlic and onions tops.

Broad Beans with Chorizo

••

Favas com Chorizo ⵔ **Ribatejo**

Preparation time: 20 minutes
Cooking time: 25 minutes
Serves: 6
🝢 🝢 🝢

1 chorizo
1 *morcela*
150 g/5 oz pork belly, thinly sliced into small pieces
80 ml/2¾ fl oz (⅓ cup) extra virgin olive oil
4 spring onions (scallions), sliced
green tops of 3 fresh garlic bulbs, chopped
1 large bunch coriander (cilantro), chopped
220 ml/7½ fl oz (1 cup) white wine
2.5 kg/5 lb 10 oz broad (fava) beans, double podded
sea salt

Prick the chorizo and *morcela* all over with the
tip of a sharp knife or skewer to prevent them
bursting during cooking, then put them into a
large saucepan with the pork belly and cook over
a medium heat for 5 minutes, or until the skins
are crispy. Remove all the meat from the pan and
set aside. Leave any fat that has been released by
the meats in the pan for cooking the vegetables.

Pour the olive oil into the pan with the fat from
the meats. Add the spring onions (scallions), garlic
tops and coriander (cilantro), then mix together
over a medium heat. Add the white wine, then add
the broad (fava) beans, season with salt and cover
with lid. Reduce the heat to low and cook gently
for 10 minutes, or until the beans are cooked.

Meanwhile, slice the chorizo and morcela,
then add them to the beans. Taste and adjust the
seasoning with salt, if necessary, before serving.

Stewed Broad Beans with Charcuterie

••

Favas Guisadas com Enchidos 📷 p.87 ⵔ **Trás-os-Montes e Alto Douro**

Preparation time: 30 minutes
Cooking time: 1 hour 20 minutes
Serves: 4
🝢 🝢

2 onions, 1 quartered and sliced and 1 chopped
3 garlic cloves, 2 peeled and chopped and 1 peeled and
    halved
500 g/1 lb 2 oz chicken bones
120 ml/4 fl oz (½ cup) olive oil
80 g/3 oz chorizo, cut into medium slices
80 g/3 oz blood chorizo, cut into medium slices
1 *farinheira*, cut into medium slices
1 *alheira*, cut into medium slices
600 g/1 lb 5 oz (5¼ cups) broad (fava) beans,
    double podded
2 large flat-leaf parsley sprigs
sea salt

First, make a chicken stock. Put the sliced onion,
halved garlic and the chicken bones into a medium
saucepan. Pour in enough water to cover and cook
gently over a low heat for 45 minutes, skimming
off any foam that rises to the top. Strain the stock
through a sieve (fine-mesh strainer) into a bowl
or jug (pitcher) and set aside. Discard the onion,
garlic and chicken bones.

Heat the olive oil in another large saucepan
over a low heat. Add the chopped onion and
garlic to the pan and cook for 10 minutes, or until
translucent. Add the charcuterie and broad (fava)
beans, then pour in 600 ml/20 fl oz (2½ cups) of
the reserved chicken stock and the parsley stems
and cook over a low heat for a further 20 minutes.

Taste and adjust the seasoning, if necessary,
before serving.

Stewed Broad Beans with Charcuterie

'Tasty' Broad Beans

Fava Rica   ⊓ Lisbon

Until the beginning of this century, this was a dish sold on the streets of Lisbon by women who would carry the food in a pot on their head screaming *fava rica*. *Fava rica* means 'good fava bean' or 'tasty fava beans'.

Preparation time: 10 minutes, plus 12 hours soaking
Cooking time: 30 minutes
Serves: 4
🔥 ☐ ⊘ V ☐ ✕

450 g/1 lb (2½ cups) dried broad (fava) beans
3 garlic cloves, peeled and finely chopped
130 ml/4½ fl oz (½ cup) olive oil
20 ml/¾ fl oz (4 teaspoons) white wine vinegar
sea salt and freshly ground black pepper

Put the dried beans into a bowl of water and leave to soak for 12 hours. The next day, drain the beans and remove the black dot with the tip of a knife.

Put the soaked beans into a large saucepan, pour in enough cold water to cover, add a pinch of salt and cook over a medium heat for 30 minutes, or until soft. Drain the beans and put into a large bowl. Add the garlic, olive oil, vinegar and season with salt and a pinch of pepper before serving.

Fried Cornmeal (with Kale or Broad Beans)

Milho Frito   ⊓ Madeira

Milho Frito, or fried corn, has nothing to do with fried cobs of corn but instead small fried cubes made of white cornmeal. It is one of Madeira's most recognised garnishes, usually made with only three ingredients (cornmeal, salt and water). It can also include kale, collard greens or even broad (fava) beans, and is most often served as a side for meat and fish dishes. Historically, *Milho Frito* tells the story of an exchange of recipes and cultures between Madeira and Venezuela, a country with a high number of immigrants from Madeira.

Preparation time: 10 minutes, plus 12 hours chilling
Cooking time: 1 hour
Serves: 8
🔥 ⊘ ✕

500 g/1 lb 2 oz (4¼ cups) white or yellow cornmeal or maize flour
60 g/2¼ oz (½ stick) butter
250 g/9 oz kale, collard greens or spring greens, very thinly sliced, or 250 g/9 oz (2 cups) double podded broad (fava) beans, broken in half
sunflower oil, for shallow-frying
sea salt

The day before, put half the cornmeal or maize flour into a medium bowl and add a small amount of water. Stir until it forms a a paste. Set aside.

Fill a large saucepan with 2.5 litres/85 fl oz (10 cups) water, add the butter and a pinch of salt and bring to the boil. Once boiling, add the cornmeal paste and stir. Return to the boil, then add the kale, greens or broad (fava) beans and cook over a medium heat, stirring continuously, for 5 minutes, or until the vegetables are cooked.

Add the remaining flour to the pan and cook for a further 5 minutes. Season with salt. Spread the cornmeal mixture evenly over a large baking sheet. Leave to cool in the fridge for 12 hours.

The next day, remove the baking sheet from the fridge and turn out the cornmeal mixture from the sheet. Cut the cornmeal mixture evenly into 3-cm/1¼-inch cubes.

Heat the oil for shallow-frying in a large frying pan or skillet over a medium heat. Add the cornmeal cubes and fry for 5 minutes, or until golden and crispy. Remove the cubes from the pan and serve immediately.

Borlotti Beans Stewed with Cabbage

Feijão Catarino com Couves   ⊓ Ribatejo

Preparation time: 20 minutes, plus 12 hours soaking
Cooking time: 55 minutes
Serves: 4
🔥 ☐ ⊘ V

300 g/11 oz (1⅔ cups) dried borlotti beans
60 ml/2 fl oz (4 tablespoons) olive oil
1 large onion, peeled and very finely chopped
2 garlic cloves, peeled and very finely chopped
1 bay leaf
600 g/1 lb 5 oz January king or Savoy cabbage, cored and cut into small pieces
30 ml/1 fl oz (2 tablespoons) white wine vinegar
sea salt and freshly ground black pepper

Put the dried beans into a large bowl of cold water and leave to soak for 12 hours.

The next day, drain the beans and put them into a large saucepan. Pour in enough cold water to cover, add a pinch of salt and cook over a medium heat for 30 minutes, or until soft. Drain and set aside, reserving the cooking water.

Heat the olive oil in a large saucepan over a low heat, add the onion, garlic and bay leaf and cook for 10 minutes, or until the onion is golden.

Add the cabbage to the pan and cook, stirring continuously, for 5 minutes. Add 1.2 litres/40 fl oz (5 cups) of the bean cooking water and cook over a medium heat for a further 5 minutes, or until the cabbage is cooked. Add the soaked beans, bring to the boil, then remove from the heat.

Sprinkle the vinegar over the beans, then season with salt and pepper before serving.

White Beans
with Pig's Head

Feijão Branco ⛉ **Alentejo**
com Cabeça de Porco

Preparation time: 20 minutes, plus 12 hours soaking
Cooking time: 2 hours
Serves: 6
🖋 ⛉

500 g/1 lb 2 oz (2¾ cups) dried butter (lima) beans
1 pig's head, de-boned
1 chorizo
120 ml/4 fl oz (½ cup) olive oil
2 onions, peeled and very finely chopped
3 garlic cloves, peeled and very finely chopped
1 bay leaf
sea salt and freshly ground black pepper

Put the dried beans into a large bowl of cold water and leave to soak for 12 hours.

The next day, drain the beans and put them into a large saucepan. Pour in enough cold water to cover, add a pinch of salt and cook over a medium heat for 30 minutes, or until soft.

Put the pig's head and chorizo into a large saucepan with a pinch of salt. Pour in enough water to cover and cook over a medium heat for 1 hour, or until the meats are soft. Remove the meat from the pan, reserving the cooking stock. Slice all the meats into small pieces and set aside.

Heat the olive oil in another saucepan over a medium heat. Add the onions, garlic and bay leaf and cook for 10 minutes, or until the onions have some colour. Add all the reserved meats, stir well, then add the cooked beans. Pour in enough of the reserved stock to cover the meats and beans and cook for a further 10 minutes.

Taste and adjust the seasoning, if necessary, with salt and pepper before serving.

Wild Sorrel Leaves
with Garlic and Bread

Labaças com Pão e Alho ⛉ **Beira Baixa**

Preparation time: 10 minutes
Cooking time: 10 minutes
Serves: 4
⛉ ⌀ V ⛉ ✕

800 g/1 lb 12 oz wild sorrel leaves (*Rumex acetosa*)
50 ml/1²⁄₃ fl oz (3½ tablespoons) olive oil
5 garlic cloves, peeled and very finely chopped
2 slices bread, crumbled into small pieces
sea salt

Put the sorrel leaves into a pile and slice them very thinly. Rinse the leaves under cold running water and then pat dry.

Heat the olive oil in a large saucepan over a low heat, add the garlic and cook for 30 seconds, or until golden. Add the leaves to the pan and stir. Cook for a further 5 minutes, or until very soft and moist. Stir, then add the bread and mix until well combined. Season with salt before serving.

Curly Dock
with Red Beans

Catacuzes com ⛉ **Alentejo**
Feijão Vermelho

Curly dock belongs to the family of leaves called *Rumex*. There are several varieties and they all have more or less a citrus flavour and meaty leaves, which are best picked when young. Curly dock is one of the first wild leaves that can be harvested in spring.

Preparation time: 20 minutes, plus 12 hours soaking
Cooking time: 1 hour
Serves: 4
🖋 ⌀ V ⛉

350 g/12 oz (2 cups) dried red beans
450 g/1 lb curly dock leaves (*Rumex crispus*), washed, drained and stem removed
80 ml/2¾ fl oz (⅓ cup) olive oil
1 onion, peeled and finely chopped
4 garlic cloves, peeled and finely chopped
1 teaspoon sweet paprika
1 bay leaf
1 teaspoon dried pennyroyal
⅓ bunch coriander (cilantro), roughly chopped
sea salt

Put the dried red beans into a large bowl of cold water and leave to soak for 12 hours.

The next day, drain the beans and put them into a large saucepan. Pour in enough cold water to cover, add a pinch of salt and cook over a medium heat for 30 minutes, or until soft. Drain and set aside, reserving the cooking water.

Have a large bowl of iced water nearby. Bring a medium saucepan of water to the boil. Add the curly dock leaves to the water and blanch for 30 seconds, then transfer to the iced water and leave to cool. Drain and chop the leaves coarsely. Set aside.

Heat the olive oil in a saucepan over a medium heat, add the onion and garlic and cook for 5 minutes, or until softened but not coloured. Add the sweet paprika, bay leaf, pennyroyal and coriander (cilantro) and stir well until combined. Stir in the curly dock leaves, then season with salt.

Finally, add the beans and cook for a further 5 minutes, adding a little of the bean cooking water so they are not too dry. Serve immediately.

Turnip Tops with Corn Porridge

Papas Laberças ♡ **Beira Alta**

This dish was originally created due to the lack of food resources. As it was very nourishing, it was typically eaten on cold winter days. It's similar to porridge (oatmeal) as it is thick. You can make it as thick or as runny as you like, just add in less flour if you prefer it runny. You can also add a garnish of any meat of grilled fish, if you like.

Preparation time: 10 minutes
Cooking time: 25 minutes
Serves: 4
🌱 ⏱ ⊘ ✓ ⏱ ✕

150 g/5 oz (1¼ cups) cornflour (cornstarch)
100 ml/3½ fl oz (⅓ cup) olive oil
800 g/1 lb 12 oz baby turnip tops, bottom stalk removed
    and cut into medium thick strips
20 ml/¾ fl oz (4 teaspoons) cider vinegar
sea salt

Put the cornflour (cornstarch) into a medium bowl, add some warm water and stir to form a paste.

Pour 2.5 litres/85 fl oz (10 cups) water into a large saucepan, add half the olive oil and a pinch of salt and bring to the boil. Add the turnip tops, reduce the heat to medium and cook for 10 minutes, or until tender. When the leaves are cooked, add the cornflour paste, stir and cook for a further 15 minutes, or until thick. Taste and adjust the seasoning with salt, then add the vinegar and remaining olive oil to finish. Serve immediately.

Preserved Carrots with Paprika and Fennel Tops

Cenouras à Algarvia 📷 p.91 ♡ **Algarve**

This is an old pickling method and is best prepared a few days in advance to give all the flavours a chance to develop. Store in an airtight container. This dish is good as a snack before a meal or to garnish fish dishes.

Preparation time: 10 minutes
Cooking time: 15 minutes
Makes: 1 jar
🌱 ⏱ ⊘ ✓ ✉

700 g/1 lb 9 oz carrots, peeled but left whole
4 garlic cloves, crushed with the back of a knife
1 tablespoon sweet paprika
1 tablespoon chopped wild fennel tops
½ bunch flat-leaf parsley, roughly chopped
180 ml/6 fl oz (¾ cup) white wine vinegar
sea salt and freshly ground white pepper

Put the carrots into a large saucepan, pour in enough water to cover and season with a pinch of salt. Cook over a medium heat for 10–15 minutes, or until al dente. Drain and leave to cool to room temperature, then slice the carrots into perfectly round discs. Put the carrot slices into a sterilised, large glass jar or container.

Put the garlic into a medium bowl with the paprika, wild fennel tops, parsley, a pinch of salt and pepper and the vinegar and mix together until combined. Pour this mixture into the jar or container, seal with the lid so it is airtight and shake. Leave to stand for a few days before eating.

Wild Asparagus with Breadcrumbs and Eggs

Espargos Silvestres com Ovos ♡ **Alentejo**

Preparation time: 10 minutes
Cooking time: 20 minutes
Serves: 4
⏱ ⏱

350 g/12 oz wild asparagus spears
75 g/2¾ oz lard (pork fat)
2 garlic cloves, peeled and thinly sliced
80 g/3 oz (1⅔ cups) breadcrumbs
4 eggs, beaten
sea salt and freshly ground black pepper

Prepare the asparagus spears by removing the base, then washing in cold water and leaving them to drain on a perforated tray or in a colander. Cut the asparagus spears into small pieces.

Heat the lard (pork fat) in a frying pan or skillet over a medium heat. Add the garlic and cook gently for 5 minutes, or until it starts to colour. Add the asparagus pieces and toss to coat them in the fat. Add 150 ml/5 fl oz (⅔ cup) water to the pan and cook for 5 minutes before adding another 150 ml/5 fl oz (⅔ cup) water. Cook for a further 5 minutes, or until the asparagus is tender.

Add the breadcrumbs to the pan and mix well with the asparagus, then add the beaten eggs and cook for 5 minutes, or until the eggs are soft and creamy. Season with salt and pepper, if necessary. before serving.

Vegetables and Mushrooms

Preserved Carrots with Paprika and Fennel Tops

Wild Asparagus

Espargos Silvestres ⍾ **Beira Baixa**

Preparation time: 10 minutes
Cooking time: 10 minutes
Serves: 4
◻ ☒

350 g/12 oz wild asparagus spears, cut into small pieces
8 eggs
120 ml/4 fl oz (½ cup) extra virgin olive oil
3 garlic cloves, peeled and sliced
200 g/7 oz stale bread, shredded
sea salt and freshly ground white pepper
½ chorizo, sliced, to garnish

Bring a medium saucepan of water to the boil. Once boiling, carefully add the asparagus pieces and blanch for 2 seconds, then drain. Fill the pan with fresh water, bring it to the boil, then as soon as it is boiling again, add the asparagus and blanch for a further 2 seconds. Drain and set aside.
　Put the eggs into a bowl and whisk them lightly.
　Heat the olive oil in a frying pan or skillet over a medium heat. Add the garlic and cook for 30 seconds, or until golden. Add the bread and fry for 2 minutes. Add the reserved asparagus to the pan, pour in the whisked eggs and mix well with a silicon spatula then cook for 5–7 minutes, or to your liking. Pour into a serving dish, season with salt and pepper and garnish with the chorizo before serving.

Fried Yam

Inhame Frito ⍾ **Madeira**

Preparation time: 10 minutes, plus 3 hours soaking
Cooking time: 1 hour 20 minutes
Serves: 6
◻ ◻ ⌀ ∨ ✕

1.4 kg/3 lb 1 oz yam
220 ml/7½ fl oz (1 cup) sunflower oil, for shallow-frying
sea salt
sugar cane, to serve

Put the yam into a large bowl, pour in enough cold water to cover and leave to soak for 3 hours.
　Using a sharp knife, scrape off the yam's skin, or peel it with a vegetable peeler, then place the yam into a large saucepan. Add 7 litres/238 fl oz (30 cups) water, sprinkle with some sea salt, cover with a lid and cook over a low heat for 25 minutes, or until soft. Drain and peel off the remaining skin, then cut the yam into medium-thick rings.
　Heat the sunflower oil for shallow-frying in a large frying pan or skillet over a medium heat until it reaches 160°C/325°F on a thermometer. Carefully lower the yam into the hot oil and fry for 10 minutes, or until golden on both sides.
　Season before serving with the sugar cane.

Boiled Yam

Inhame Cozido ⍾ **Madeira**

Preparation time: 10 minutes, plus 3 hours soaking
Cooking time: 25 minutes
Serves: 5
◻ ◻ ⌀ ∨ ◻ ✕

1.4 kg/3 lb 1 oz yam, unpeeled and left whole
sea salt
sugar cane, to serve

Put the yam into a large bowl, pour in enough cold water to cover and leave to soak for 3 hours.
　Using a sharp knife, scrape off the yam's skin, or peel it with a vegetable peeler, then place the yam into a large saucepan. Add 7 litres/238 fl oz (30 cups) water, sprinkle with some sea salt, cover with a lid and cook over a low heat for 25 minutes, or until soft. Drain and peel off the remaining skin.
　Season before serving with the sugar cane.

Potato and Lardo Roll with Charcuterie

Migas de Batata ▣ p.93 ⍾ **Alentejo**

Preparation time: 20 minutes
Cooking time: 45 minutes
Serves: 4
◻ ◻

1 kg/2 lb 4 oz new potatoes, peeled and coarsely chopped
4 garlic cloves, 2 peeled and quarted and 2 peeled and roughly chopped
250 ml/8 fl oz (1 cup) olive oil
1 *linguiça*, cut into pieces
1 *farinheira* or smoked sausage, cut into pieces
200 g/7 oz lardo, cut into pieces
2 tablespoons white wine vinegar
1 bay leaf
sea salt and freshly ground black pepper

Put the potatoes and 2 quartered garlic cloves in a large saucepan. Pour in enough water to cover, add a pinch of salt and cook over a medium heat for 15–20 minutes, or until soft. Drain and push through a potato ricer into the pan and set aside.
　Heat the olive oil in another large saucepan over a medium heat. Once hot, add all the meats and cook for 10 minutes. Remove the meats from the pan, leaving the fat behind.
　Add the remaining chopped garlic to the same pan and cook over a medium heat for 5 minutes, or until the garlic just starts to release its aroma but doesn't colour. Add the vinegar, bay leaf and mashed potato, season with salt and pepper, then stir well and roll the mixture into the shape of an omelette.
　Serve with the cooked meats on the side.

Potato and Lardo Roll with Charcuterie

Drunken Potatoes with Pork Ribs

Batatas Bêbadas   Ｕ Beira Baixa

Preparation time: 10 minutes, plus 20 minutes standing
Cooking time: 45 minutes
Serves: 4
Ｏ ＊

750 g/1 lb 7 oz waxy potatoes, unpeeled and left whole
650 g/1 lb 7 oz trimmed pork ribs
80 g/3 oz lard (pork fat)
2 garlic cloves, unpeeled and crushed
250 ml/8 fl oz (1 cup) red wine
sea salt

Put the potatoes into a large saucepan, pour in enough water to cover and cook over a low heat for 20 minutes, or until soft. Drain and set aside.

Cut the pork ribs into separate sections, then put them onto a rimmed baking sheet and season with salt. Leave to stand for 20 minutes.

Heat the lard (pork fat) in a saucepan over a medium heat, add the pork ribs and cook for 5 minutes, or until browned. Remove from the heat.

Put the garlic into a large saucepan, add the pork ribs and red wine and bring to the boil. Reduce the heat to low. Peel the potatoes and cut them into irregular chunks, then stir them into the meat.

Taste and adjust the seasoning, if necessary, with salt before serving.

Poached and Sautéed Potatoes with Paprika

Batatas de Rebolão   Ｕ Ribatejo

Preparation time: 10 minutes
Cooking time: 45 minutes
Serves: 6
＊ Ｏ Ｏ V

1.3 kg/2 lb 14 oz new potatoes
130 ml/4½ fl oz (½ cup) olive oil
5 garlic cloves, peeled and finely chopped
½ teaspoon sweet paprika
2 bay leaves
sea salt and freshly ground black pepper

Put the potatoes into a saucepan, pour in enough water to cover, add a pinch of salt and cook over a low heat for 20 minutes, or until soft. Drain, then peel off the skins with a sharp knife. Set aside.

Heat the olive oil, garlic, paprika and bay leaves in a large saucepan over a medium heat. Once the garlic starts to fry, add the potatoes and stir. Season with pepper and cook the potatoes, stirring, for 30 minutes or until golden all over. Serve immediately.

Chickpea 'Soup'

Cozido de Grão   📷 p.95   Ｕ Alentejo

This soup is a must-have when visiting Alentejo, especially during winter days. There is another variation of this dish which includes green beans that are commonly known in Alentejo as *vajens*. There is also a version from the Algarve that uses rice instead of bread.

Preparation time: 30 minutes, plus 12 hours soaking and salting
Cooking time: 4 hours
Serves: 6
Ｏ

450 g/1 lb trimmed pork ribs
250 g/9 oz beef flank steak
350 g/12 oz lamb shoulder
200 g/7 oz chicken thighs
450 g/1 lb (2½ cups) dried chickpeas (garbanzos)
80 g/3 oz *linguiça*
1 *farinheira* or smoked sausage
200 g/7 oz sweet potatoes, peeled and cut into chunks
200 g/7 oz pumpkin, peeled, de-seeded
    and cut into chunks
250 g/9 oz potatoes, peeled and cut into chunks
3 carrots, peeled and cut into chunks
⅓ bunch mint, leaves picked
sea salt
6 slices bread, to serve

Put all the meats, except the *linguiça* and *farinheira*, onto a large plate and season with salt. Transfer the meats to a large bowl and pour in enough water to cover and leave to soak for 12 hours. Put the chickpeas (garbanzos) into another large bowl, cover with water and leave to soak for 12 hours.

The next day, drain the chickpeas, put them into a saucepan, pour over enough water to cover and cook over a medium heat for 30 minutes, or until soft.

Drain the meat, put it into another large saucepan with the charcuterie, pour over enough water to cover and cook for 20 minutes, or until very soft. The charcuterie will be ready before the rest of the meat is cooked, so keep checking them. Once cooked, remove the charcuterie from the pan and cut into chunky slices. Once all the meat is cooked, return the charcuterie to the pan, remove the pan from the heat and set aside.

Transfer some of the meat cooking liquid to a separate saucepan and add all the vegetables. Add some of the chickpea water, if needed, and cook for 10 minutes. Add the chickpeas, mint leaves and season with salt.

Transfer the meat from the pan to a serving dish, reserving the stock, then put all the vegetables into another serving dish. Put the bread into a third serving dish and pour over the meat stock. Add some mint leaves. Serve the bread, meat and vegetables in their separate dishes.

Corn and Pork Stew

•••

Cozido de Milhos   ⏷ Algarve

Milhos are coarse milled corn that resembles
grains of rice. The corn is 'nixtamalised' exactly
as it is done in Mexico, but how the process
reached the Algarve remains a mystery to this day.
Nixtamalization is a traditional process where the
corn or maize is treated with lime, then cooked
and ground into flour. In Mexico, this corn is made
into hominy or *pozole*. Traditionally, the ashes
used in this recipe are from the fig tree.

Preparation time: 10 minutes, plus 12 hours soaking
Cooking time: 1 hour 30 minutes
Serves: 5
🗱 ▢

1.2 kg/2 lb 10 oz sweetcorn kernels
2 handfuls of wood ashes
1 pig's trotter (foot)
2 pig's ears
1 pig's snout
5 cloves
8 white peppercorns
1 teaspoon fine sea salt

Put the sweetcorn kernels in a large bowl and
cover with water. Leave to soak for 12 hours.

The next day, drain the sweetcorn kernels and
put into a large saucepan. Cover with fresh water
and the ashes and cook over a medium heat for
45 minutes, or until soft.

Drain and rinse the sweetcorn kernels
thoroughly to remove all the ashes, then put into a
clean large saucepan. Add all the meats to the pan
with the cloves, peppercorns and salt then pour in
enough water to cover. Cook over a medium heat
for 45 minutes, or until the meats are soft.

Pour into a serving dish before serving.

Coarse Corn Porridge with Chicken and Chorizo

•••

Milhos com Chouriço   ⏷ Trás-os-Montes
                                e Alto Douro

Preparation time: 15 minutes
Cooking time: 1½ hours
Serves: 4
🗱 ▢

400 g/14 oz (3⅓ cups) coarse corn flour
300 g/11 oz pork belly
100 ml/3½ fl oz (⅓ cup) olive oil
1 onion, peeled and finely chopped
½ chicken
1 *linguiça*
1 *chouriço* (chorizo)
sea salt

Rinse the corn flour a few times in cold water to
remove any loose husks and set aside. Season the
pork belly with salt and set aside.

Heat the olive oil in a large saucepan over a
low heat, add the onion and cook for 10 minutes,
or until translucent. Add 1.8 litres/61 fl oz (7¼
cups) water, the chicken and seasoned pork belly
and cook for 45–50 minutes, or until the meat is
soft. Remove the meat from the pan and cut into
small pieces, then put into a large bowl, add a few
spoonfuls of the stock so the pieces won't dry out
and set aside.

Put the *linguiça* and *chouriço* (chorizo) into
another large saucepan, pour in enough cold water
to cover and cook over a medium heat for 20
minutes, or until cooked. Remove the charcuterie
from the pan and slice into medium discs.

Pour the corn flour into the meat cooking
water, season with a pinch of salt and cook, stirring
continuously, over a low heat for 10 minutes,
or until soft.

Transfer the porridge to a serving dish and
serve with the meat.

Soft Corn Porridge with Thyme and Garlic

•••

Milho Cozido   ⏷ Madeira

Preparation time: 5 minutes
Cooking time: 55 minutes
Serves: 8
🗱 ▢ ▢

450 g/1 lb (3¾ cups) soft corn flour
60 ml/2 fl oz (4 tablespoons) olive oil
2 garlic cloves, peeled and chopped
100 g/3½ oz lardo, cut in half
2 thyme sprigs
sea salt

Put the corn flour into a large bowl, add a small
amount of cold water and stir until all the flour
has dissolved.

Heat the olive oil in a large saucepan over a
low heat. Add the garlic and cook for 5 minutes,
or until golden. Add the lardo and thyme, then stir
and cook for 5 minutes. Add 2.5 litres/85 fl oz
(10 cups) and bring to the boil. Once boiling, slowly
add the corn flour and cook, stirring continuously,
for 45 minutes, or until the corn is cooked and has
thickened into a porridge.

Remove the lardo from the pan and then
pour the corn porridge into a serving dish or onto
individual serving plates and sprinkle with cold
water before serving.

Stewed Mushrooms

••

Cogumelos Guisados   ⛉ Trás-os-Montes
e Alto Douro

Preparation time: 10 minutes
Cooking time: 18 minutes
Serves: 2
◻ ◻ ⊠

250 g/9 oz saffron milk caps
250 g/9 oz chanterelle (girolle) mushrooms
60 ml/2 fl oz (4 tablespoons) olive oil
1 small onion, peeled and thinly sliced
1 garlic clove, peeled and thinly sliced
90 g/3¼ oz Serrano ham, cut into small pieces
sea salt and freshly ground black pepper
4 slices bread, toasted, to serve

Clean all the mushrooms with a brush to remove any dirt or sand, then slice or tear them into large pieces and set aside.

Heat the olive oil in a medium saucepan over a medium heat, add the onion and garlic and cook for 10 minutes, or until golden. Add the ham, stir and cook for a further 2 minutes. Add the mushrooms, stir well with a wooden spoon, then cover with a lid and cook for 5–6 minutes, or until the mushrooms are soft.

Season with salt and pepper before serving with the toasted bread.

Stewed Man on Horseback Mushrooms

••

Míscaros   ⛉ Beira Alta

This mighty wild mushroom is very popular when in season. There are even festivals dedicated to the fungus. There are numerous versions of this recipe, some cooked with rice, charcuterie, eggs or just stewed in their own juices. The yellow night mushroom is also called man on horseback.

Preparation time: 10 minutes
Cooking time: 25 minutes
Serves: 4
🐖 ◻ ⬡ V ◻ ✕

600 g/1 lb 5 oz *míscaros* (man on horseback) mushrooms (page 429) or use any other meaty wild mushrooms
120 ml/4 fl oz (½ cup) olive oil
1 garlic clove, peeled and thinly sliced
sea salt and freshly ground black pepper

Clean all the mushrooms with a brush to remove any dirt or sand, then rinse them under cold running water. Drain then let them drip in a perforated tray or colander for 2 minutes before cooking. Slice the mushrooms in half.

Heat a large frying pan or skillet over a medium heat. Once hot, add the olive oil and garlic and cook for 2–3 minutes, or until the garlic is golden. Add the mushrooms and fry for 2–3 minutes. Reduce the heat to low and cook for a further 5 minutes, or until the mushrooms are soft.

Season with salt and pepper before serving.

Stewed Man on Horseback Mushrooms with Pork and Eggs

••

Míscaros com Ovos e Porco   ⛉ Beira Alta

Míscaros is a variety of mushroom that has been enjoyed all over the world, including Spain, France and Sweden for a few centuries. These mushrooms grow wild in sandy soil and have a distinctive aroma.

Preparation time: 10 minutes
Cooking time: 15 minutes
Serves: 2
🐖 ◻ ◻ ⊠

200 g/7 oz *míscaros* (man on horseback) mushrooms (page 429) or use any other meaty wild mushrooms
3 eggs
40 ml/1⅓ fl oz (2⅔ tablespoons) olive oil
½ onion, peeled and finely chopped
60 g/2¼ oz pork neck, cut into medium pieces
¼ teaspoon paprika
sea salt

Clean all the mushrooms with a brush to remove any dirt or sand, then rinse them under cold running water. Drain then let them drip in a perforated tray or colander for 2 minutes before cooking. Slice the mushrooms into small pieces.

Put the eggs into a medium bowl and whisk with a fork. Set aside.

Put the olive oil, onion and pork neck pieces into a large saucepan. Season with the paprika and heat over a medium heat for 10–15 minutes, or until the meat is fully cooked.

Add the mushrooms to the pan, reduce the heat to low and cook for 5 minutes, or until soft. Add the eggs and cook gently, stirring continuously for a further 5 minutes, or until soft but still moist.

Season with salt before serving.

Cilarca Mushrooms with Eggs

Silarcas com Ovos
◌ **Alentejo**

Cilarca (*Amanita ponderosa*) **is a type of wild mushroom found in Alentejo and Andalusia in Spain from February to April. This particular mushroom fully develops under the soil (almost like a truffle) and is usually heavy and very meaty.**

Preparation time: 15 minutes
Cooking time: 10–12 minutes
Serves 4
🐷◻️🖾

4 cilarcas mushrooms
70 g/2½ oz lard (pork fat)
60 g/2¼ oz chorizo, quartered
1 teaspoon vinegar
7 eggs
sea salt

Clean the mushrooms with a brush to remove any dirt or sand, then wipe them with a wet cloth. Slice them into quarters and set aside.

Melt the lard (pork fat) in a frying pan or skillet, add the chorizo and cook over a medium heat for 2 minutes. Add the mushrooms, cover with a lid and steam for 2 minutes. Sprinkle over the vinegar and season with salt.

Break the eggs into a bowl and lightly whisk with a fork. Pour the whisked eggs into the pan and mix well with a silicone spatula then cook over a medium heat, stirring continuously, for 5–7 minutes, or to your liking.

Taste and adjust the seasoning, if necessary, before serving.

Nori Seaweed and Egg Fritters

Tortas de Erva do Calhau
📷 p.99   ◌ **Açores**

Preparation time: 10 minutes
Cooking time: 20 minutes
Serves 4
◻️∅🖾

250 g/9 oz sea lettuce, washed, drained and cut into
    small pieces
1 tablespoon chopped chives
3 eggs
50 g/2 oz (½ cup) plain (all-purpose) flour
1 garlic clove, peeled and chopped
5 g/¼ oz *Massa de Malagueta* (page 102)
500 ml/17 fl oz (2 cups) sunflower oil
sea salt (optional)

Put the sea lettuce into a large bowl, add the chives and eggs and mix well, then add the flour and garlic and mix well again. Add the *Massa de Malagueta* and stir until everything is combined.

Heat the oil in a large, deep saucepan over a high heat until it reaches 140°C/284°F on a thermometer. Line a large baking sheet with paper towels.

Working in batches, using two spoons, take a scoop of the mixture in one spoon, then pass the mixture repeatedly between the spoons until it forms a smooth oval shape or *torta*. Carefully drop the *torta* into the hot oil and deep-fry for 5 minutes, or until darkly coloured all over. Using a slotted spoon, transfer the *tortas* to the lined baking sheet and leave to drain on paper towels to absorb any excess oil while you continue making and frying the rest.

Season the *tortas* with salt, if you like, before serving immediately.

Fried Truffles with Scrambled Eggs

Túberas Fritas com Ovos
◌ **Alentejo**

Túberas **are a fungus similar to truffles, and some people say they are related to the white truffles now found in Alentejo and Ribatejo due to the climatic conditions during different parts of year. The knowledge of foraging mushrooms and the best locations to find them has been passed from generation to generation within families.**

Preparation time: 10 minutes
Cooking time: 20 minutes
Serves: 4
◻️∅◻️✕🖾

400 g/14 oz *túberas* (truffles)
80 ml/2¾ fl oz (⅓ cup) olive oil
8 eggs
sea salt
4 slices bread, toasted, to serve

Clean the *túberas* with a brush to remove any dirt or sand. Using a vegetable peeler, peel away the outer layers. Rinse them under cold running water. Using a mandolin or a very sharp knife, cut them into thin slices.

Heat a large frying pan or skillet over a medium heat, add a couple of glugs of olive oil, add the sliced *túberas* and cook for 15 minutes, or until golden. Remove from the pan and leave to drain on paper towels to absorb any excess oil.

Break the eggs into a bowl and lightly whisk with a fork. Add a pinch of salt. Pour the whisked eggs into the pan and mix well with a silicone spatula then cook over a medium heat, stirring continuously, for 5–7 minutes, or to your liking.

Stir the mushrooms into the scrambled eggs before serving with the toasted bread.

Nori Seaweed and Egg Fritters

Eggs with Truffles and Chorizo

Criadilhas com Ovos   ꕔ Beira Baixa

Criadilhas or desert truffle (*Terfezia arenaria*) are a close relative of the truffle. They have a mild flavour, similar to truffles and have long been part of the local gastronomy. In the old days, people used to call them 'special potatoes'.

Preparation time: 10 minutes
Cooking time: 20 minutes
Serves: 5
🥜⬜️✕

600 g/1 lb 5 oz *criadilhas* (desert truffle)
30 ml/1 fl oz (2 tablespoons) olive oil
50 g/2 oz (3½ tablespoons) unsalted butter
1 onion, peeled and finely chopped
90 g/3¼ oz chorizo, cut into thin strips
5 eggs, lightly beaten
sea salt and freshly ground black pepper

Remove any soil from the *criadilhas*, rinse under cold running water and then rub with a damp cloth. Cut them into thin strips or quarters. Set aside.

Heat the olive oil and butter in a saucepan over a medium heat, add the onion and cook for 12 minutes, or until translucent. Add the *criadilhas*, chorizo and 150 ml/5 fl oz (⅔ cup) water. Season with salt and pepper and cook gently for 15 minutes, or until the *criadilhas* and chorizo are soft and water has reduced by half. Add the beaten eggs and cook gently, stirring continuously, for 5 minutes, or until the eggs are soft but moist.

Taste and adjust the seasoning, if necessary, before serving.

Tomato Salad with Oregano

Salada de Tomate   ꕔ Algarve
com Orégãos   📷 p.101

This salad can also be made with a red (bell) pepper that has been grilled on the barbecue until blackened and blistered all over, then peeled, de-seeded and cut into strips. Toss the pepper strips through the salad until combined.

Preparation time: 8 minutes
Serves: 4
🥜⬜️⌀V✕

3 ripe bull's heart tomatoes or other good-quality tomatoes
1 small onion, peeled and thinly sliced
1 teaspoon dried oregano
15 ml/½ fl oz (1 tablespoon) white wine vinegar
70 ml/2½ fl oz (¼ cup) olive oil
sea salt

Remove the tip from the top of the tomatoes, then cut each tomato into irregular chunks and put them into a large bowl.

Add the onion and oregano to the bowl and toss together with the tomatoes to combine.

Season with salt and vinegar, then add the oil before serving.

Tomato Stew

Tomatada   ꕔ Alentejo

In the peak of summer, the succulent, vibrant red tomatoes abundant in Alentejo, the Douro and Trás-os-Montes become the star of this dish. *Tomatada* can be both a stand-alone dish, served perhaps with poached eggs, a starter, or a side dish to accompany a plate of grilled sardines. It can even be used as a tomato sauce served over meat or roasted potatoes.

Preparation time: 15 minutes
Cooking time: 1 hour
Serves: 4
⬜️⌀

1.2 kg/2 lb 10 oz ripe bull's heart tomatoes
4 eggs
120 ml/4 fl oz (½ cup) olive oil
1 onion, peeled and thinly sliced
4 garlic cloves, peeled and thinly sliced
2 bay leaves
300 g/11 oz stale bread, crusts removed
sea salt and freshly ground black pepper

Have a large bowl of iced water nearby. Bring a large saucepan of water to the boil. Using a sharp knife, score the top of the tomatoes with a small cross shape. Once the water is boiling, carefully add the tomatoes and blanch for 30 seconds, then transfer them with a slotted spoon to the iced water and leave to cool. Once cool enough to handle, peel off the skins, cut in half and de-seed, then cut the flesh into small cubes. Season with salt and pepper.

Put the eggs into a small bowl and lightly whisk with a fork. Set aside.

Heat the olive oil in a large saucepan over a medium heat. Add the onion, garlic and bay leaves and cook for 5 minutes, or until the onion is translucent. Add the tomatoes and cook for a further 45 minutes until the tomatoes have broken down into a purée.

Using your fingers or a sharp knife, shred or cut the bread into small pieces. Add the bread to the pan and stir well until combined. Add the eggs and cook for a few minutes to dry out the mixture a little.

Taste and adjust the seasoning if necessary, with salt and pepper before serving.

Tomato Salad with Oregano

Spicy Fermented Chilli Paste

Massa de Malagueta   ♡ Açores

This red, intense, spicy pepper paste made of *malagueta* (also known as *pimenta da terra*) — a tiny, tapered chilli pepper — is an indispensable condiment for the Azorean people, and has been made in homes across the archipelago since the 16th century. It is kept in jars throughout the year and used in stews, fritters and soups, as well as in *chouriço* or *linguiça* (spiced sausage). These days, it is served in restaurants, who all have their own version.

Preparation time: 30 minutes
Cooking time: 10 minutes
Makes: 2 medium jars (about 900 g/2 lb/3¾ cups)
🐷 ▢ ⌀ ∨ ✕ ⊠

1.5 kg/3 lb 5 oz *pimenta da terra* or bird's eye chillies, halved and de-seeded
35 g/1¼ oz (1 tablespoon plus 2 teaspoons) fine sea salt
olive oil, for drizzling

Wearing protective gloves, halve and de-seed the peppers or chillies, then put them into a food processor and blitz until puréed. Transfer to a medium saucepan, add the salt and cook over a low heat, stirring occasionally, for 10 minutes, or until the liquid has evaporated.

Transfer the paste to two sterilised, medium-sized, glass jars. Pack the paste in tightly to avoid trapping any air in the jars – once filled, tap the jars sharply against the work counter to expel any air pockets. Drizzle olive oil over the top of the paste to completely cover to a depth of 1 cm/¼ inch, then seal with the lid. Store the jars for 7–10 days in a cool, dark place while the paste ferments. Once opened, store in the fridge.

Pickled Onions

Cebolas em Curtume   📷 p.103   ♡ Açores

This onion pickle is used as a garnish in the Açores for dishes such as fried fish and açordas.

Preparation time: 25 minutes, plus 7 days standing
Makes: 1 medium jar
🐷 ▢ ⌀ ∨ ✕ ⊠

1.8 kg/4 lb small onions
4 *pimenta da terra* or bird's eye chillies
1.6 litres/54 fl oz (6½ cups) vinegar from *vinho de cheiro*
sea salt

Using a sharp knife, cut the onions slightly on the top. Wash and drain them, then put the onions into a large bowl and season with salt.

Tightly pack the onions into a sterilised, medium-sized, glass jar or clay pot with the peppers in the middle. Pour the vinegar over the onions to cover, making sure there is 1 cm/½ inch headspace, then seal with the lid and leave to stand for a week before eating.

Pickled Baby Onions

Cebolinhas de Escabeche   ♡ Madeira

In Madeira, these onions are traditionally eaten at Christmas with *vinha d'alhos* meat (page 429).

Preparation time: 10 minutes, plus 4 days standing
Makes: 1 medium jar
🐷 ▢ ⌀ ∨

1.5 kg/3¼ lb baby onions, unpeeled
1 red chilli, halved
4 cloves
3 bay leaves
10 Jamaican peppercorns
2.5 litres/85 fl oz (10 cups) red wine vinegar
sea salt

Put the onions into a large bowl. Bring a medium saucepan of water to the boil, then pour the boiling water over the onions and leave them to stand for 4 minutes.

Drain and peel off the onion skins, then place the onions in a clay jar or an airtight container large enough to accommodate all of the onions. Season with salt, then add the chilli, cloves, bay leaves and Jamaican peppercorns and cover them with the vinegar. Cover the pot with a tea (dish) towel and leave to stand for 4 days before eating.

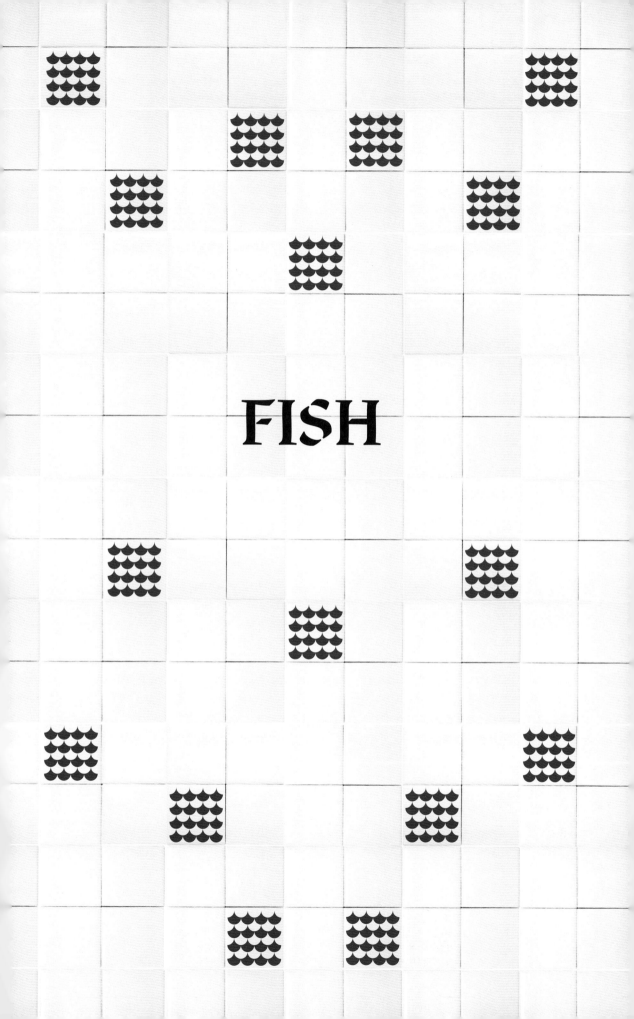

FISH

Boiled Salt Cod with Vegetables

••

Bacalhau com Todos   ⏥ Lisbon

One of the most important and widely consumed cod dishes in Portugal, *Bacalhau com Todos* is a boiled cod loin dish traditionally eaten on Christmas Eve, gathering all (*todos*) around the same table: all is each and every family member, but also every best seasonal vegetable the land has to offer, such as cabbage, turnips, potatoes and carrots. The cod loins always come with a hard-boiled egg on the side, and are drizzled with olive oil.

Preparation time: 20 minutes, plus 12–14 hours soaking
Cooking time: 25–30 minutes
Serves: 4
🔖 🗋

600 g/1 lb 5 oz salt cod, desalted (page 40)
550 g/1 lb 4 oz potatoes, peeled
3 carrots, peeled but left whole
3 onions, peeled but left whole
1 pointed cabbage or small Savoy cabbage,
    leaves separated
3 garlic cloves, peeled but left whole (optional)
4 eggs
120 ml/4 fl oz (½ cup) olive oil
30 ml/1 fl oz (2 tablespoons) white wine vinegar
sea salt and freshly ground black pepper

Check the cod is not too salty before cooking. If it is, then leave to soak for another 2 hours. Drain.

Once the cod is ready, put it into a large saucepan with all the vegetables and pour in enough water to cover the ingredients. Check to see if the water is salty enough, if it isn't then add a pinch and cook over a medium heat for 6 minutes, or until the flesh flakes easily. The cod will be ready first, so remove it from the pan and continue to cook the vegetables for a further 15–20 minutes, or until tender. Drain and set aside.

Meanwhile, bring a medium saucepan of water to the boil. Have a bowl of cold water nearby. Once boiling, carefully lower in the eggs and cook for 8 minutes. Lift the eggs out of the pan and transfer to the iced water to cool. Once cold, peel the shells from the eggs and set aside.

Arrange the cod on a serving plate, add the cooked vegetables, drizzle with the olive oil and vinegar, then season with pepper. Cut the hard-boiled eggs into halves or quarters and serve with the cod and vegetables.

Salt Cod with Indian Peas

••

Bacalhau com Chícharos   📷 p.107   ⏥ Leiria

Preparation time: 30 minutes, plus 12–14 hours soaking
Cooking time: 40–45 minutes
Serves: 6
🔖 🗋

450 g/1 lb (2½ cups) dried Indian peas (chickling peas)
800 g/1 lb 12 oz salt cod, desalted (page 40)
4 eggs
500 g/1 lb 2 oz Cornbread (page 32)
250 ml/8 fl oz (1 cup) extra virgin olive oil
2 garlic cloves, very finely chopped
½ bunch flat-leaf parsley, leaves picked
    and finely chopped
60 ml/2 fl oz (4 tablespoons) cider vinegar
½ teaspoon sea salt

Put the dried Indian peas into a large bowl of cold water and leave to soak for 12 hours.

The next day, check the cod is not too salty before cooking. If it is, then leave to soak for another 2 hours. Drain and set aside.

Prepare a barbecue. If you have some wood, then add it to the coals as this will give a nice aroma to the cod. Alternatively, preheat the indoor grill (broiler).

Drain the Indian peas and put them into a large saucepan. Pour in enough cold water to cover the peas, add a pinch of salt and cook over a medium heat, stirring every 10 minutes, for 30 minutes, or until soft.

Meanwhile, bring a medium saucepan of water to the boil. Have a bowl of cold water nearby. Once bolling, carefully lower in the eggs and cook for 8 minutes, then drain and leave to cool in the cold water. Once cool, peel the shells from the eggs and set aside.

Using your hands, tear the cornbread into large chunks and set aside.

As soon as the barbecue coals are glowing, brush the cod with some of the olive oil, put it on the grill rack and grill for 10–12 minutes depending on the thickness of the fish, or until golden all over with some nice charred areas, but not burnt. Alternatively, cook under the indoor grill.

Once the Indian peas are cooked, drain and put them into a large bowl. Add the garlic and parsley to the bowl and mix everything together.

Flake the cod into a serving bowl then toss in the Indian peas. Cut the hard-boiled eggs into quarters and add to the bowl with the cornbread chunks. Drizzle with olive oil and vinegar, then toss everything together again. Serve with the salt to taste (you may not need the full ½ teaspoon) before serving.

Salt Cod with Indian Peas

Stewed Salt Cod — Lisbon Style

Bacalhau Guisado à Lisboeta   ⛉ **Lisbon**

Preparation time: 30 minutes, plus 12–14 hours soaking
Cooking time: 20–25 minutes
Serves: 4
✿

600 g/1 lb 5 oz salt cod, desalted (page 40)
400 g/14 oz ripe tomatoes
2 large onions, peeled and thinly sliced
3 garlic cloves, peeled and thinly sliced
750 g/1 lb 10 oz waxy potatoes, peeled and thinly sliced
¼ bunch flat-leaf parsley, roughly chopped
1 bay leaf
2 teaspoons paprika
140 ml/4¾ fl oz (½ cup) olive oil
20 g/¾ oz (1½ tablespoons) unsalted butter
sea salt and freshly ground white pepper

Check the cod is not too salty before cooking. If it is, then leave to soak for another 2 hours. Drain.

Have a large bowl of iced water nearby. Bring a saucepan of water to the boil. Using a sharp knife, score the top of the tomatoes with a small cross shape. Once boiling, carefully add the tomatoes and blanch for 30 seconds, then transfer them with a slotted spoon to the iced water and leave to cool. Once cool, peel off the skins, cut in half and de-seed, then cut the tomatoes into slices. Set aside.

Pat dry the cod with paper towels, then slice it into small fillets, removing any skins and bones.

Arrange the tomatoes in a layer in a large, heavy-based saucepan. Seasoning each layer with salt and white pepper, arrange the onions and garlic in a single layer on top, then add the cod in a layer on top of the onions and finish with the potatoes in a layer. Add the parsley, bay leaf and paprika, then drizzle with olive oil and dot with the butter. Cover with a lid and cook over a low heat for 20–25 minutes, or until the potatoes are soft. Do not stir so that everything stays whole. Serve immediately.

Salt Cod with Rye Bread

Bacalhau com Pão de Centeio   ⛉ **Trás-os-Montes e Alto Douro**

Preparation time: 15 minutes, plus 12–14 hours soaking
Cooking time: 25 minutes
Serves: 4
⛉

500 g/1 lb 2 oz salted cod, desalted (page 40)
4 slices rye bread, blitzed into breadcrumbs
3 garlic cloves, peeled and very finely chopped
150 ml/5 fl oz (⅔ cup) olive oil
650 g/1 lb 7 oz small round potatoes
sea salt

Check the cod is not too salty before cooking. If it is, then leave to soak for another 2 hours. Drain.

Preheat the oven to 160°C/325°F/Gas Mark 3.

Remove the skin and any bones from the salt cod, then cut into 150 g/5 oz slices. Put the cod on a clay tray or rimmed metal baking sheet and cover the top of each slice with breadcrumbs.

Sprinkle the garlic over the cod then drizzle with half of the oil. Bake for 25 minutes, or until the flesh flakes easily. Halfway through cooking, drizzle over the remaining oil.

Meanwhile, put the potatoes into a large saucepan and pour in enough cold water to cover. Add a pinch of salt and cook over a medium heat for 15–20 minutes, or until soft. Drain.

Serve the cod with the boiled potatoes.

Salt Cod with Cornbread

Bacalhau à Moda de Viana do Castelo   ⛉ **Minho**

There are a few different versions of this recipe, which originated from the port of Viana do Castelo, in the Duoro region.

Preparation time: 25 minutes, plus 12–14 hours soaking
Cooking time: 35–40 minutes
Serves: 2
✿ ⛉

250 g/9 oz salt cod loin, desalted (page 40)
300 g/11 oz waxy potatoes, peeled and
    cut into 3-cm/1¼-inch chunks
6 Savoy cabbage leaves
150 ml/5 fl oz (⅔ cup) olive oil
2½ onions, peeled, halved and very thinly sliced
3 garlic cloves, peeled and finely sliced
½ teaspoon paprika
sea salt and freshly ground white pepper
200 g/7 oz Cornbread, sliced (page 32), to serve
1 bunch flat-leaf parsley, roughly chopped, to serve

Check the cod is not too salty before cooking. If it is, then leave to soak for another 2 hours. Drain.

Preheat the oven to 160°C/325°F/Gas Mark 3.

Meanwhile, put the potatoes into a saucepan and pour in enough cold water to cover. Add a pinch of salt and cook over a medium heat for 15 minutes, or until soft. Drain and keep warm.

Cut the cod into two loins. Wrap the cod in the cabbage leaves and tie into parcels with butcher's string or kitchen twine. Put the parcels on a baking sheet and roast in the hot oven for 15–20 minutes, or until the cabbage is dry. Unwrap the cod and place in a serving dish. Discard the cabbage leaves.

Heat the olive oil in a saucepan over a medium heat, add the onions and garlic and cook, stirring occasionally, for 5 minutes, or until golden. Add the paprika and season with pepper and a pinch of salt.

Arrange the potatoes around the cod in the serving dish. Pour over the sauce and scatter with parsley before serving with the cornbread.

Salt Cod with Turnip Tops

∷∷∷

Bacalhau com Grelos ⌂ Leiria

Preparation time: 25 minutes, plus 12–14 hours soaking
Cooking time: 35 minutes
Serves: 4
🐟 🗋 ✕

720 g/1 lb 9 oz salted cod, desalted (page 40)
1.2 kg/2 lb 11 oz turnip tops, bottom stalk removed
1 kg/2 lb 4 oz waxy potatoes, peeled
4 garlic cloves, peeled and very finely sliced
350 ml/12 fl oz (1½ cups) extra virgin olive oil

Check the cod is not too salty before cooking. If it is, then leave to soak for another 2 hours. Drain.
Preheat the oven to 180°C/350°F/Gas Mark 4.
Bring a saucepan of water to the boil, but just before it boils add the cod, reduce the heat to medium and cook for 6 minutes, or until the flesh flakes easily. Remove from the pan and set aside.
Bring the water back to the boil, add the turnip tops and cook for 3 minutes, or until tender. Remove from the pan with a slotted spoon and leave to cool. Leave the water in the pan to cool slightly, then add the potatoes. Cook over a medium heat for 10 minutes, or until soft.
Meanwhile, flake the cod, including the skins, into a roasting pan. Sprinkle the garlic over the cod, then cover with the turnip tops. Drizzle half the olive oil over the top.
When the potatoes are cooked, drain them and push them through a sieve (fine-mesh strainer), but don't make a purée. Spread the potatoes evenly over the turnip tops.
Bake for 8 minutes, or until the potato topping is golden. Drizzle with the remaining olive oil before serving.

Salt Cod with Greens

∷∷∷

Migas à Transmontana ⌂ Trás-os-Montes e Alto Douro

Preparation time: 20 minutes, plus 12–14 hours soaking
Cooking time: 10 minutes
Serves: 4
🗋

450 g/1 lb salt cod, desalted (page 40)
140 ml/4¾ fl oz (½ cup) olive oil
4 garlic cloves, peeled and finely chopped
1 collard green or pointed cabbage, leaves separated
350 g/12 oz stale country bread, torn into chunks
½ teaspoon sweet paprika
sea salt and freshly ground black pepper

Check the cod is not too salty before cooking. If it is, then leave to soak for another 2 hours. Drain.
Put the olive oil into a small saucepan with the garlic and set aside.

Bring two saucepans of water to the boil. Add a pinch of salt to one pan. Once boiling, reduce the heat to a simmer, add the cod to the pan without the salt and cook for 6 minutes, or until the flesh flakes easily. Add the cabbage to the other pan and cook for 2–3 minutes, or until tender.
Remove the cabbage from the pan and set aside. Remove the cod from the pan and flake the flesh into a bowl, removing any bones. Reserve 500 ml/17 fl oz (2 cups) of the cod cooking water and keep hot for pouring over the bread.
Arrange the torn bread in a deep serving dish, add the cod and cabbage leaves and pour over the reserved cooking water. Season with salt and pepper and sprinkle with paprika.
Heat the olive oil and garlic over a medium heat and fry for 1–2 minutes, or until golden, then pour over the dish and serve.

Fried Salt Cod Fish Cakes

∷∷∷

Pataniscas de Bacalhau de Lisboa ⌂ Lisbon

It's hard to pinpoint where in Portugal these fish cakes — a popular bar snack — come from as there are variations across the country. For decades, cod was an abundant source of protein, before it became a 'gourmet' ingredient commanding high prices.

Preparation time: 20 minutes, plus 12–14 hours soaking
Cooking time: 30 minutes
Serves: 4

360 g/12 oz salt cod, desalted (page 40)
250 ml/8 fl oz (1 cup) whole (full-fat) milk
80 g/3 oz (⅔ cup) plain (all-purpose) flour
¼ bunch flat-leaf parsley, finely chopped
1 litre/34 fl oz (4¼ cups) sunflower oil, for deep-frying
sea salt and freshly ground black pepper

Check the cod is not too salty before cooking. If it is, then leave to soak for another 2 hours. Drain.
Put the cod into a saucepan, cover with the milk and cook over a low heat for 8 minutes, or until the flesh flakes easily. Remove the cod from the pan and set the milk aside. Flake the cod into a bowl, removing any bones, and set aside.
Put the flour into a bowl, then add the reserved milk and mix together until combined into a batter. Stir in the parsley and cod and season with black pepper. Taste and adjust with salt, if necessary. You may not need to add any as the cod was salted.
Line a large baking sheet with paper towels. Heat enough sunflower oil for deep-frying in a large, deep saucepan or fryer over a high heat until it reaches 180°C/350°F on a thermometer. Working in batches and using a tablespoon, take a scoop of the cod mixture, carefully drop it into the hot oil and deep-fry for 2–3 minutes, or until golden. Remove with a slotted spoon and leave to drain on the lined baking sheet. Continue until all the cod mixture is used up. Serve immediately.

Salt Cod Fritters

Pastéis de Bacalhau

p.111

Lisbon

Made of a shredded cod and potato mixture that is fried until crisp golden brown on the outside and soft on the inside, these quenelle-shaped cod cakes are sold everywhere in Portugal, from pastry shops to roadside cafés and restaurants. They are originally from Minho, where they are still called *Bolinhos de Bacalhau*. They can be eaten warm or cold, as a snack, or a main dish with a side of boiled black-eyed peas, lettuce salad or rice.

Preparation time: 20 minutes, plus 12–14 hours soaking
Cooking time: 30–35 minutes
Serves: 4

280 g/10 oz salt cod, desalted (page 40)
450 g/1 lb waxy potatoes, peeled and quartered
1 onion, peeled and very finely chopped
2 garlic cloves, peeled and very finely chopped
2 tablespoons chopped flat-leaf parsley
4 eggs
1 litre/34 fl oz (4¼ cups) sunflower oil, for deep-frying
sea salt and freshly ground black pepper
lemon wedges, for squeezing

Check the cod is not too salty before cooking. If it is, then leave to soak for another 2 hours. Drain.

Put the potatoes into a large saucepan with the cod, cover with cold water and cook over a medium heat for 10–15 minutes, or until the cod flakes easily and the potatoes are soft. Drain and remove any bones from the fish, then put the cod and potatoes into a large bowl and mash well with a potato masher until smooth. Add the onion, garlic and parsley. Season with pepper and check if any salt is needed. As the cod was salted you may not need any. Add the eggs and mix until everything is well combined.

Line a large baking sheet with paper towels. Heat enough sunflower oil for deep-frying in a large, deep saucepan or fryer over a high heat until it reaches 180°C/350°F on a thermometer. Working in batches and using two tablespoons, take a scoop of the cod mixture in one spoon and then pass it repeatedly between the two spoons to make a smooth, oval-shape quenelle. Carefully drop it into the hot oil and deep-fry for 1–2 minutes, or until golden and crispy. Remove with a slotted spoon and leave to drain on the lined baking sheet. Continue until all the mixture is used up.

Serve the fritters while hot with lemon wedges for squeezing over.

Browned Salt Cod

Bacalhau Albardado

Alentejo

Although Alentejo cuisine might not be best known for its fish recipes — mostly associated with the region's coastal regions and river villages — as in other parts of Portugal, cod takes centre stage in several traditional dishes. In this all-year-round recipe, pieces of soaked salt cod are fried inside a leavened dough that has been made with yeast hydrated with the cod soaking water. They are often served alongside a lettuce or watercress salad, or rice and beans. They also go well with a glass of crisp white wine.

Preparation time: 30 minutes, plus 12–14 hours soaking and 3 hours standing
Cooking time: 25 minutes
Serves: 4

350 g/12 oz salt cod, desalted (page 40)
10 g/¼ oz (2 teaspoons) fresh yeast or
2.5 g/¾ oz (scant 1 teaspoon) instant dried yeast
500 g/1 lb 2 oz (4 cups) plain (all-purpose) flour
olive oil, for deep-frying
20 ml/¾ fl oz (4 teaspoons) extra virgin olive oil
10 ml/2 teaspoons white wine vinegar
1 butterhead lettuce, shredded
sea salt

After soaking and desalting the cod, make sure you reserve 700 ml/23½ fl oz (2¾ cups) of the soaking water. Remove the skin and bones from the cod, then shred the flesh into a bowl and set aside.

Dissolve the yeast in the reserved cod soaking water, then gradually stir in the flour to make a smooth dough. Taste to check the salt levels — it should a slightly salty kick, if not then add a pinch of salt. Cover the bowl with a tea (dish) towel and leave to stand for 3 hours, or until the mixture has a few bubbles on the surface.

Fold the shredded cod into the dough with a wooden spoon.

Line a large baking sheet with paper towels. Heat enough olive oil for deep-frying in a large, deep saucepan or fryer over a high heat until it reaches 180°C/350°F on a thermometer. Working in batches and using two tablespoons, take a scoop of the dough mixture in one spoon and then pass the mixture repeatedly between the two spoons to make a smooth oval-shape quenelle. Carefully lower each quenelle into the hot oil and deep-fry for 1–2 minutes, or until golden and crispy. Remove with a slotted spoon and leave to drain on the lined baking sheet. Continue until all the cod mixture is used up.

Put the extra virgin olive oil and vinegar into a small bowl and whisk with a fork to emulsify. Season with a pinch of salt. This is the dressing for the lettuce.

Before serving, toss the lettuce in the dressing and serve alongside the salt cod fritters.

Salt Cod Fritters

Salt Cod with Black Olives and Fried Potatoes

•••

Bacalhau à Narcisa   ⏷ **Minho**

There are many cod recipes in the Minho and Douro regions due to the proximity of Viana do Castelo, a port town that has been unloading cod from the Atlantic since the 15th century. One of those recipes, *Bacalhau à Narcisa* (also called *Bacalhau à Braga*), was originally invented by a restaurant in Braga (in Minho) called Narcisa in the 19th century. It is made using cod steak fried in olive oil, and lightly sautéed sliced potatoes and onions. *Bacalhau à Narcisa* is served in restaurants particularly in the north of Portugal, in large, oval platters with the cod in the centre, the onions topping it, and the fried potatoes around the edges.

Preparation time: 25 minutes, plus 12–14 hours soaking
Cooking time: 45 minutes
Serves: 4
⚲ ⏷

550 g/1 lb 4 oz salt cod loin, desalted (page 40)
320 ml/11 fl oz (1¼ cups) olive oil
600 g/1 lb 5 oz waxy potatoes, peeled and cut into
    1-cm/½-inch slices
3 onions, peeled and cut into medium-thick rings
1 teaspoon paprika
6 cloves
2 bay leaves, torn into pieces
sea salt
60 g/2¼ oz (⅓ cup) unpitted black olives, to garnish

Check the cod is not too salty before cooking. If it is, then leave to soak for another 2 hours. Drain.

Fill a saucepan with enough water to cover the cod and bring to the boil. Reduce the heat to medium and, when simmering, add the cod and cook for 6 minutes, or until the flesh flakes easily. Remove the cod from the pan and pat dry with paper towels.

Line 2 large baking sheets with paper towels. Heat enough olive oil for shallow-frying in a deep frying pan or skillet until it reaches 180°C/350°F on a thermometer. Carefully add the cod and fry for 10 minutes, or until golden on both sides. Remove the cod from the pan with a fish slice (spatula) and leave to drain on the lined baking sheets.

Add the potato slices to the frying pan with the same oil used to cook the cod and fry for 8–10 minutes, or until golden on both sides. Remove the potatoes from the pan and leave to drain on the lined baking sheets.

Add the onions to the frying pan, a handful at a time, and fry for 5–6 minutes, or until golden. Remove the onions from the pan and leave to drain on the lined baking sheet while you fry the rest. Remove the pan from the heat, leaving the frying oil in there.

Arrange the cod in a large serving dish, scatter the fried onions over the top, then put the fried potatoes around the sides.

Put the frying pan over a medium heat, add the paprika, cloves and bay leaves and add a pinch of salt, then stir to combine. Heat the oil to 130°C/265°F, then remove the pan from the heat.

Pour the hot, fragrant oil over the cod, onions and potatoes in the serving dish, then garnish with the olives before serving.

Fried Salt Cod with Crispy Potatoes

•••

Bacalhau à Algarvia   ⏷ **Algarve**

Preparation time: 20 minutes, plus 12–14 hours soaking
Cooking time: 40 minutes
Serves: 4
⏷

700 g/1 lb 9 oz salt cod, desalted (page 40)
100 g/3½ oz (¾ cup) plain (all-purpose) flour
250 ml/8 fl oz (1 cup) olive oil, plus extra for frying
2 onions, peeled and thinly sliced
3 garlic cloves, peeled and thinly sliced
1 bunch flat-leaf parsley, finely chopped
700 g/1 lb 9 oz small waxy potatoes, unpeeled and
    left whole

Check the cod is not too salty before cooking. If it is, then leave to soak for another 2 hours. Drain.

Remove any skin and bones from the fish, then cut the cod into 1.5-cm/⅔-inch squares.

Spread the flour out on a large plate, then toss the cod in the flour, shaking off any excess.

Line a large baking sheet with paper towels. Heat the olive oil in a large saucepan over a medium heat, add the cod and fry for 2–3 minutes, turning with a slotted spoon until golden all over. Remove the cod from the pan and leave to drain on the lined baking sheet.

Add the onions and garlic to the pan with the same oil used to cook the cod and fry over a low heat for 5–7 minutes until coloured, then remove from the pan and put into a small bowl. Stir through the parsley and set aside.

Put the potatoes into a large saucepan, pour in enough cold water to cover and cook over a medium heat for 10 minutes, or until soft. Drain, leave for a few minutes until cool enough to handle, then rub off the skins.

Heat some more olive oil in a large frying pan or skillet over a medium-low heat. Add the potatoes and fry for 8–10 minutes, or until golden all over.

Serve the cod with the onion mixture and fried potatoes scattered over the top.

Baked Salt Cod with Parsley and Potatoes

••

Bacalhau à Margarida da Praça   ▼ Minho

Preparation time: 30 minutes, plus 12–14 hours soaking
Cooking time: 45 minutes
Serves: 4
🌾 ▯

600 g/1 lb 5 oz salt cod loin, desalted (page 40)
450 ml/15 fl oz (1¾ cups) olive oil
3 onions, peeled and thinly sliced
800 g/1 lb 12 oz waxy potatoes, peeled
salt and freshly ground black pepper
2 bunches flat-leaf parsley, leaves picked, to garnish

Check the cod is not too salty before cooking. If it is, then leave to soak for another 2 hours. Drain.

Once the cod is ready, heat a plancha or flat grill until hot. Once hot, add the cod and cook for 10–12 minutes, or until golden on both sides. Alternatively, cook in a large frying pan or skillet over a high heat with a drizzle of olive oil.

Heat the olive oil in a medium saucepan over a medium heat, add the onions and cook for 7 minutes, or until the onions are translucent. Remove the pan from the heat and set aside.

Put the potatoes into a large saucepan, pour in enough cold water to cover, add a pinch of salt and cook over a low heat for 15–20 minutes, or until tender. Drain and cut them into 1-cm/½-inch slices, then arrange in a large serving dish.

Bring a large saucepan of water to the boil, add the cod and bring it to the boil again, then remove the cod from the pan and place it over the potatoes.

Using a slotted spoon, remove the onions from the pan, leaving any oil in the pan. Spread the onions over the cod and potatoes, then season with pepper.

Reheat the remaining oil from cooking the onions over a medium heat until hot. Pour the hot oil over the cod. Garnish with parsley leaves before serving.

Baked Salt Cod with Cornbread

••

Bacalhau Assado   ▼ Beira Litoral
com Broa de Milho

Preparation time: 20 minutes, plus 12–14 hours soaking
Cooking time: 30 minutes
Serves: 4
🌾

750 g/1 lb 10 oz salt cod loin, desalted (page 40)
1 bay leaf, torn into pieces
430 ml/14½ fl oz (1¾ cups) white wine
180 ml/6 fl oz (¾ cup) olive oil
700 g/1 lb 9 oz Cornbread, crusts removed (page 32)
45 g/1½ oz lard (pork fat)
½ teaspoon paprika
1½ onions, peeled and finely chopped
3 garlic cloves, peeled and finely chopped
600 g/1 lb 5 oz baby new potatoes, peeled
150 g/5 oz (1¼ sticks) unsalted butter
freshly ground black pepper

Check the cod is not too salty before cooking. If it is, then leave to soak for another 2 hours. Drain.

Preheat the oven to 190°C/375°F/Gas Mark 5.

Put the salt cod loins onto a large baking sheet with the bay leaf, 170 ml/5½ fl oz (⅔ cup) white wine and a splash of the olive oil and bake for 8 minutes. Remove from the oven and set aside.

Tear the cornbread into small pieces into a large bowl and combine with the remaining white wine, olive oil, lard (pork fat), paprika, pepper, onions and garlic and mix together until a paste forms. Season with some salt and more pepper, then spread the paste evenly over the fish.

Bake the salt cod for a further 12 minutes, or until golden.

Meanwhile, put the potatoes into a medium saucepan, pour in enough cold water to cover, add a pinch of salt and cook over a medium heat for 15–20 minutes, or until tender. Drain.

Heat the butter in another medium saucepan until melted, then add the potatoes and toss until they are coated in the butter.

Sprinkle the potatoes with salt before serving alongside the cod.

Chargrilled Salt Cod with 'Punched' Potatoes

Bacalhau Assado com Batatas a Murro 📷 p.115   ⛁ Beira Alta

This is one of those dishes that is very hard to pinpoint its actual origin, although some claim it hails from the Beira Alta region. I remember eating this when growing up both in Beira Alta but also when my family moved further south. The potatoes are described as 'punched' because they are flattened with the fist after cooking.

Preparation time: 15 minutes, plus 12–14 hours soaking
Cooking time: 40 minutes
Serves: 4
🌶 ▢ ✕

700 g/1 lb 9 oz salt cod, desalted (page 40)
600 g/1 lb 5 oz small waxy potatoes, unpeeled and
    left whole
300 ml/10 fl oz (1¼ cups) olive oil
5 garlic cloves, peeled and thinly sliced
sea salt and freshly ground black pepper

Check the cod is not too salty before cooking. If it is, then leave to soak for another 2 hours. Drain.

Preheat the oven to 180°C/350°F/Gas Mark 4. Prepare a barbecue or preheat the indoor grill (broiler).

Put the potatoes into a large roasting pan and sprinkle them with salt. Roast in the hot oven for 35 minutes. Remove the pan from the oven and gently 'punch' each potato with your fist.

Meanwhile, as soon as the barbecue coals are glowing, put the cod on the grill rack and grill for 10–12 minutes, or until the fish is golden on both sides. Alternatively, cook under the indoor grill.

Heat the olive oil in a saucepan over a medium heat. As soon as it is hot, remove from the heat and add the garlic and pepper and stir.

Flake the cod into a serving dish, removing any bones, and carefully pour over the hot garlic oil. Add the 'punched' potatoes and stir well to combine everything before serving.

Chargrilled Salt Cod with Onions and Potatoes

Bacalhau Assado com Cebolas e Batatas   ⛁ Beira Litoral

Preparation time: 20 minutes, plus 12–14 hours soaking
Cooking time: 20 minutes
Serves: 4
🌶 ▢ ✕

800 g/1 lb 12 oz salt cod, desalted (page 40)
650 g/1 lb 7 oz small waxy potatoes, unpeeled and
    left whole
200 ml/7 fl oz (¾ cup) extra virgin olive oil
40 ml/1⅓ fl oz (2⅔ tablespoons) white wine vinegar
3 sweet white onions, peeled and very thinly sliced
    (preferably on a mandolin)

Check the cod is not too salty before cooking. If it is, then leave to soak for another 2 hours. Drain.

Prepare a barbecue or preheat the indoor grill (broiler). Have a container of tepid water to the side of the barbecue or grill.

As soon as the barbecue coals are glowing, put the cod onto the grill rack and grill for 10–12 minutes, or until golden on both sides. Alternatively, cook under the indoor grill. Immediately plunge the cod into the container of tepid water for 1 minute. Remove the cod from the container and squeeze, flaking the flesh into a serving bowl.

Meanwhile, put the potatoes into a large saucepan of cold water and cook over a medium heat for 15–20 minutes, or until tender. Drain and set aside in a serving dish.

Put the olive oil and vinegar into a small bowl and whisk with a fork to emulsify.

Scatter the onions over the flaked cod in the serving dish, then pour the olive oil and vinegar mixture over and toss until everything is coated. Serve with the boiled potatoes on the side.

Chargrilled Salt Cod with 'Punched' Potatoes

Baked Salt Cod with Tomato, Mash and Onions

•••

Bacalhau à Santa Luzia   ▢ Minho

Preparation time: 30 minutes, plus 12–14 hours soaking
Cooking time: 1 hour 20 minutes
Serves: 6

1 kg/2 lb 4 oz salt cod loin, desalted (page 40)
380 ml/13 fl oz (1½ cups) olive oil
450 ml/15 fl oz (1¾ cups) whole (full-fat) milk
2 tablespoons plain (all-purpose) flour, for dusting
3 garlic cloves, 2 unpeeled and crushed with the back
    of a knife, 1 peeled and very finely chopped
450 g/1 lb beef tomatoes
4 onions, peeled and very finely chopped
1 teaspoon sweet paprika
50 g/2 oz (⅓ cup) tomato purée (paste)
4 eggs
1.5 kg/3 lb 5 oz waxy potatoes, peeled
sea salt and freshly ground black pepper

For the mayonnaise:
4 egg yolks
15 g/½ oz (1 tablespoon) Dijon mustard
500 ml/17 fl oz (2 cups) sunflower or vegetable oil
10 ml/2 teaspoons white wine vinegar

To garnish:
130 g/4½ oz (¾ cup) black olives, pitted and chopped
20 g/¾ oz flat-leaf parsley leaves, roughly chopped

Check the cod is not too salty before cooking. If it is, then leave to soak for another 2 hours. Drain.
Preheat the oven to 160°C/325°F/Gas Mark 3.
Heat 300 ml/10 fl oz (1¼ cups) of the oil in a large, deep frying pan or skillet over a medium heat.
Meanwhile, put the milk into a large shallow bowl and spread the flour out on a large plate. Put the cod into the milk, then toss it in the flour until coated, shaking off any excess. Add a piece of the cod to the pan with the crushed garlic and fry for 5–6 minutes on both sides, or until golden all over. Remove the cod from the pan and place on a large baking sheet. Repeat with the remaining cod. Once all the fish has been fried, bake in the oven for 12 minutes.
Meanwhile, have a bowl of iced water nearby. Bring a saucepan of water to the boil. Using a sharp knife, score the top of the tomatoes with a small cross shape. Once boiling, add the tomatoes to the pan and blanch for 30 seconds. Transfer with a slotted spoon to the iced water and leave to cool. Once cool enough to handle, peel off the skins, cut into quarters and de-seed, then set aside.
Heat the remaining oil in a saucepan over a low heat, add the onions and remaining garlic and cook for 12 minutes, or until the onions are translucent. Season with paprika and pepper, then add the tomato purée (paste). Cook, stirring, over a low heat for a further 5 minutes.

To make the mayonnaise, put the egg yolks and mustard into a large bowl and slowly whisk in the sunflower oil in a steady stream until thick. Add the vinegar and season with salt. Set aside.
Remove the cod from the oven, increase the temperature to 200°C/400°F/Gas Mark 6 and put the grill (broiler) on. Pour the onion sauce over the top of the cod, then cover it with the mayonnaise.
Bring a saucepan of water to the boil, carefully lower in the eggs and cook for 8 minutes, then remove from the pan and leave to cool. Once cold, peel the eggs and chop them finely. Set aside.
Put the potatoes into a saucepan, cover with cold water, add a pinch of salt and cook over a medium heat for 15–20 minutes, or until soft. Drain. Transfer to a food processor or blender and blitz to a purée. Season with salt and pepper. Set aside.
Meanwhile, grill (broil) the cod for 8 minutes, or until lightly golden. Serve with the mash on the side, garnished with the tomatoes, hard-boiled eggs, chopped olives and parsley.

Quick Salt Cod in the Oven

•••

Bacalhau Rápido da Madeira   ▢ Madeira

Preparation time: 30 minutes, plus 12–14 hours soaking
Cooking time: 45 minutes
Serves: 4

600 g/1 lb 5 oz salt cod, desalted (page 40)
500 g/1 lb 2 oz waxy potatoes, peeled
3 eggs
2 flat-leaf parsley sprigs, chopped
3 onions, peeled and finely chopped
60 ml/2 fl oz (4 tablespoons) olive oil
juice of 1 lemon
sea salt

To garnish
130 g/4½ oz (¾ cup) black olives, pitted and chopped
1 butterhead lettuce, leaves separated (optional)

Check the cod is not too salty before cooking. If it is, then leave to soak for another 2 hours. Drain.
Put the potatoes into a saucepan, cover with cold water, add a pinch of salt and cook over a medium heat for 15–20 minutes, or until soft. Drain. Cut into 1-cm/½-inch slices and set aside.
Remove the skin and bones from the cod, then flake the flesh onto a clean tea (dish) towel. Gather up the towel and rub it into the fish to make strings.
Bring a saucepan of water to the boil, carefully lower in the eggs and cook for 8 minutes, then remove from the pan and leave to cool. Once cold, peel the eggs and chop them finely. Set aside.
Arrange the cod on a serving plate, layer the potatoes on top, then sprinkle with the egg. Put the parsley, onions, olive oil and lemon juice into a bowl and stir with a whisk, then pour over the cod and potatoes. Garnish with olives and lettuce.

Baked Salt Cod with Onions, Potatoes, Turnips, Carrots and Cabbage

••

**Bacalhau Enfornado
de Trás-os-Montes** 　　　□ Trás-os-Montes e
　　　　　　　　　　　　　　Alto Douro

Preparation time: 40 minutes, plus 12–14 hours soaking
Cooking time: 1 hour
Serves: 4
🐟 □

550 g/1 lb 4 oz salt cod, desalted (page 40)
350 ml/12 fl oz (1½ cups) olive oil
2 large onions, peeled and sliced into thin rings
½ teaspoon sweet paprika
9 eggs
2 large bunches flat-leaf parsley, finely chopped
750 g/1 lb 10 oz waxy potatoes, peeled and cut into
　　medium-thick slices
2 turnips, peeled and thinly sliced
2 carrots, peeled and thinly sliced
½ Savoy cabbage, leaves separated
25 ml/1 fl oz (2 tablespoons) white wine vinegar
sea salt and freshly ground black pepper

Check the cod is not too salty before cooking. If
it is, then leave to soak for another 2 hours. Drain.
Remove the skin and any bones from the cod.
　　Heat some of the olive oil in a saucepan over
a medium heat, add the onions and cook for
5 minutes, or until lightly golden. Add the paprika
to the pan and stir, then season with a pinch of salt
and pepper.
　　Line a rimmed baking sheet with paper towels.
Heat the remaining olive oil in a large, deep
saucepan or fryer over a medium–high heat until it
reaches 160°C/325°F on a thermometer.
　　Crack 3 of the eggs into a bowl, add the
chopped parsley and whisk. Flake the cod into the
beaten eggs, then add spoonfuls of the mixture
to the hot oil and deep-fry for 6 minutes, or until
golden all over. Remove with a slotted spoon and
leave to drain on the lined baking sheet. Continue
until all the cod mixture is used up.
　　Using a sieve (fine-mesh strainer), carefully
remove any stray bits of the cod mixture from the
oil. Bring the oil back up to temperature. Working
in batches, carefully drop the potato slices into the
hot oil and deep-fry for 8 minutes, or until golden
and crispy. Leave to drain on the lined baking sheet
and season with salt.
　　Preheat the oven to 200°C/400°F/Gas Mark 6.
　　Arrange a layer of the fried cod and a layer of
the fried potatoes in a large roasting pan, then
layer in the turnips, carrots and cabbage. Repeat
until the all ingredients are used up.
　　Put the remaining eggs into a bowl, add the
vinegar and stir together to combine. Pour the
beaten eggs over the cod, potato and vegetable
layers and stir to combine. Bake for 25–30 minutes,
or until coloured all over. Serve immediately.

Salt Cod 'Brandade' Count of Guarda

••

Bacalhau à Conde da Guarda 　　　□ Beira Alta

This is a comfort dish cooked throughout
Portugal, and is inspired by the similar French
brandade. In this Portuguese version, a creamy
mixture of shredded cod, mashed potatoes
and cream contrasts with a salty, crunchy layer
of melted cheese on top.

Preparation time: 35 minutes, plus 12–14 hours soaking
Cooking time: 1 hour 15 minutes
Serves: 4
🐟

600 g/1 lb 5 oz salt cod, desalted (page 40)
650 g/1 lb 7 oz waxy potatoes, peeled
90 g/3¼ oz (6 tablespoons) unsalted butter
3 small onions, peeled and finely chopped
5 garlic cloves, peeled and finely chopped
270 ml/9 fl oz (1 cup plus 4 teaspoons) double
　　(heavy) cream
75 g/2½ oz (½ cup plus 1 tablespoon) cheddar
　　or other hard cheese, grated (shredded)
sea salt and freshly ground black pepper

Check the cod is not too salty before cooking. If it
is, then leave to soak for another 2 hours. Drain.
　　Preheat the oven to 200°C/400°F/Gas Mark 6.
　　Fill a large saucepan with cold water, add
the potatoes and a pinch of salt and cook over
a medium heat for 15–20 minutes, or until soft.
Drain and return to the pan, then mash with a
potato masher. Set aside.
　　Fill a large saucepan with enough water to cook
the cod, add the fish and cook over a medium heat
for 6 minutes, or until the fish flakes easily. Remove
the cod from the pan. Flake the flesh into a bowl,
removing the skin and any bones, and set aside.
　　Heat the butter in another large saucepan
over a low heat until melted. Add the onions and
garlic and cook for 12 minutes, or until golden.
Add the cod and mix well, then cook for a further
5 minutes. Transfer the mixture to a mortar or food
processor and mash it with a pestle or blitz it until
smooth. Put the mixture into a large bowl, add
the mashed potato and mix well, then add the
cream and season with salt and pepper, mix until
everything is combined.
　　Pour the mixture into an ovenproof dish,
spreading it over the dish and making sure the top
is level. Scatter over the grated (shredded) cheese
and bake for 15–20 minutes, or until the cheese is
golden and bubbling. Serve immediately.

Salt Cod with Eggs, Onions and Potatoes

••

Bacalhau à Gomes de Sá   📷 p.119   ∪ Minho

In creating *Bacalhau à Gomes de Sá*, José Luís Gomes de Sá, a cod merchant and amateur cook in the 18th century, could not have imagined how successful it would become as a dish, still cooked and celebrated all over the country to this day. The key characteristics of this *bacalhau* recipe are flakes of cod infused in milk, then layered with thinly sliced potatoes, onion and eggs, and cooked in a very hot oven until golden and toasted.

Preparation time: 30 minutes, plus 12–14 hours soaking and 2 hours 30 minutes standing
Cooking time: 1 hour
Serves: 4
🐟

600 g/1 lb 5 oz salt cod, desalted (page 40)
700 g/1 lb 9 oz small waxy potatoes, unpeeled and left whole
600 ml/20 fl oz (2½ cups) whole (full-fat) milk
3 eggs
130 ml/4½ fl oz (½ cup) olive oil
2 large onions, peeled and thinly sliced
2 garlic cloves, peeled and thinly sliced
sea salt and freshly ground black pepper
50 g/2 oz (¼ cup) black unpitted olives, to garnish
2 bunches flat-leaf parsley, chopped, to garnish

Check the cod is not too salty before cooking. If it is, then leave to soak for another 2 hours. Drain.

Preheat the oven to 200°C/400°F/Gas Mark 6.

Put the potatoes into a large saucepan, cover with cold water, add a pinch of salt and cook over a medium heat for 15–20 minutes, or until soft. Remove the pan from the heat and set aside.

Bring 1.5 litres/50 fl oz (6¼ cups) water to the boil in a saucepan. Put the cod into a heatproof bowl and pour the boiling water over. Cover with a thick tea (dish) towel and leave to stand for 30 minutes. Drain, then remove the skin and bones, then flake the flesh into a large heatproof bowl.

Pour the milk into a saucepan and heat over a medium heat for 3 minutes until hot but not boiling. Pour over the cod and leave to stand for 2 hours.

Bring a small saucepan of water to the boil, carefully lower in the eggs and cook for 8 minutes, then remove from the pan and leave to cool. Once cold, peel the eggs and slice. Set aside.

Heat the olive oil in a saucepan over a low heat, add the onions and garlic and cook for 12 minutes, or until golden.

Drain the potatoes, rub off the skins and cut into 1-cm/½-inch slices. Add them to the onions together with the flaked cod. Stir gently to avoid breaking the potatoes. Transfer this mixture to an ovenproof dish, add the hard-boiled egg slices and bake in the oven for 12 minutes, or until golden. Garnish with the olives and parsley before serving.

Salt Cod Confit in Olive Oil with Potatoes and Onions

••

Bacalhau à Lagareiro   ∪ Beira Alta

The difference between this dish and *Bacalhau Assado* (page 114) is that this version contains onions and paprika.

Preparation time: 20 minutes, plus 12–14 hours soaking
Cooking time: 45 minutes
Serves: 4
🐟 ▢

750 g/1 lb 10 oz salt cod, desalted (page 40)
600 g/1 lb 5 oz new potatoes
350 ml/12 fl oz (1½ cups) extra virgin olive oil
2 onions, peeled, halved and very finely sliced into half-moons
4 garlic cloves, peeled and very finely sliced
1 teaspoon paprika
sea salt

Check the cod is not too salty before cooking. If it is, then leave to soak for another 2 hours. Drain.

Preheat the oven to 180°C/350°F/Gas Mark 4. Prepare a barbecue. If you have some wood, then add to the coals to give the cod a smoky flavour.

Put the potatoes into a large roasting pan and sprinkle them with 50 g/2 oz (¼ cup) salt. Roast for 45 minutes, stirring them every 15 minutes or so until golden and with a light crisp skin.

Meanwhile, as soon as the barbecue coals are glowing, put the cod on the grill rack and grill for 10–12 minutes, or until the cod has good caramelisation and the flesh turns opaque. If you don't have a barbecue, roast the cod in the oven preheated to 200°C/400°F/Gas Mark 6 with the grill (broiler) on. Transfer to a serving dish.

Heat 100 ml/3½ fl oz (⅓ cup) of the olive oil in a small saucepan over a medium heat, add the onions and garlic and cook for 10 minutes, or until they become glossy. Sprinkle in the paprika and season with a little salt.

Once the potatoes are cooked, add them to the cod, then mix in the onions and garlic and pour over the remaining olive oil. Serve immediately.

Salt Cod with Eggs, Onions and Potatoes

Gratinated Salt Cod with Mashed Potatoes and Mayonnaise

Bacalhau à Zé do Pipo   ⛶ Minho

Although this recipe calls for mayonnaise, an ingredient not commonly used in Portuguese cuisine, it is one of the most acclaimed in the country. *Bacalhau à Zé do Pipo* is named after its creator, José Valentim (nicknamed Zé do Pipo), who was the owner of a popular restaurant in Porto during the 1960s, and who won a national competition called 'A melhor refeição ao melhor preço' ('The best affordable meal'). Many say this is the favourite Portuguese cod recipe and is cooked all over the country.

Preparation time: 25 minutes, plus 12–14 hours soaking
Cooking time: 1 hour 25 minutes
Serves: 4

800 g/1 lb 12 oz salt cod loin, desalted (page 40)
100 ml/3½ fl oz (⅓ cup) olive oil
2 onions, peeled and finely chopped
2 garlic cloves, peeled and finely chopped
1 bay leaf
1.2 litres/40 fl oz (5 cups) whole (full-fat) milk
1 kg/2 lb 4 oz new potatoes, peeled
80 g/3 oz (¾ stick) unsalted butter
sea salt and freshly ground black pepper
30 g/1 oz (¼ cup) pitted black olives, to garnish

For the mayonnaise:
3 egg yolks
450 ml/15 fl oz (1¾ cups) vegetable oil or rapeseed oil
20 ml/¾ fl oz (4 teaspoons) lemon juice

Check the cod is not too salty before cooking. If it is, then leave to soak for another 2 hours. Drain.

Preheat the oven to 200°C/400°F/Gas Mark 6.

To make the mayonnaise, put the egg yolks into a medium bowl and slowly whisk in the vegetable oil in a steady stream until thick. Add the lemon juice and season with salt. Set aside.

Heat the olive oil in a saucepan over a low heat, add the onions, garlic and bay leaf and cook for 12 minutes, or until the onions are lightly coloured. Remove from the heat and set aside.

Put the milk into a large saucepan, add the cod and cook over a low heat for 25 minutes, or until the cod is soft. Don't flake it, keep it whole. Remove from the heat and take the cod out of the milk, discarding the skins and any bones. Flake the cod and set the milk aside.

Put the potatoes into a large saucepan, cover with cold water, add a pinch of salt and cook over a low heat for 20 minutes, or until soft. Drain, then put back into the pan, add the butter and season with salt and pepper. Mash with a potato masher until smooth. Set aside.

Put the cod into a large ovenproof dish, add the onions, then arrange the mashed potato all around the sides of the dish. Cover the cod with the mayonnaise. Bake in the oven for 25 minutes, or until golden on top. Remove from the oven and garnish with olives, before serving.

Salt Cod Roasted in Milk

Bacalhau com Leite   ⛶ Beira Alta

Preparation time: 20 minutes, plus 12–14 hours soaking
Cooking time: 45 minutes
Serves: 4

480 g/1 lb 1 oz salt cod loin, desalted (page 40)
70 ml/2¼ fl oz (¼ cup) olive oil
1½ onions, peeled and finely chopped
1.2 litres/40 fl oz (5 cups) whole (full-fat) milk
50 ml/1¾ fl oz (3½ tablespoons) white wine
350 g/12 oz country or sourdough bread, sliced
4 eggs
sea salt and freshly ground white pepper

Check the cod is not too salty before cooking. If it is, then leave to soak for another 2 hours. Drain.

Heat the olive oil in a saucepan over a medium heat, add the onions and cook for 10 minutes, or until translucent. Shred the cod into the pan, removing the skin and any bones. Add the milk, reduce the heat to low and cook for 6 minutes, or until the flesh flakes easily. Add the wine and season with salt and pepper. Add the bread to the pan, pressing it down into the liquid with a spoon. Remove the pan from the heat and leave the bread to soak for 10 minutes.

Preheat the oven to 200°C/400°F/Gas Mark 6.

Stir the eggs into the bread mixture and then pour it into a roasting pan and bake for 10–15 minutes, or until golden on top. Serve immediately.

Shredded Salt Cod with Chickpeas and Parsley

Meia Desfeita de Bacalhau   ⛶ Lisbon

Preparation time: 25 minutes, plus 12–14 hours soaking
Cooking time: 20 minutes
Serves: 4

350 g/12 oz (2 cups) dried chickpeas (garbanzos)
500 g/1 lb 2 oz salt cod, desalted (page 40)
3 eggs
120 ml/4 fl oz (½ cup) olive oil
1 onion, peeled and thinly sliced
25 ml/1 fl oz (2 tablespoons) white wine vinegar
2 garlic cloves, peeled and thinly sliced
1 teaspoon paprika
sea salt and freshly ground white pepper

Put the chickpeas into a large bowl of cold water and leave to soak for 12 hours.

The next day, check the cod is not too salty before cooking. If it is, then leave to soak for another 2 hours. Drain.

Drain the chickpeas and put them into a large saucepan. Pour in enough cold water to cover, add a pinch of salt and cook over a medium heat, skimming any foam that forms on the surface, for 20 minutes, or until soft. Drain and set aside.

Bring another large saucepan of water to the boil, add the cod and poach over a medium heat for 6 minutes, or until the flesh flakes easily. Drain and remove any bones and skin from the cod.

Meanwhile, have a small bowl of iced water nearby. Bring a saucepan of water to the boil, carefully lower in the eggs and cook for 8 minutes, then remove and put them into the bowl of iced water to cool. Once cool, peel and cut into quarters. Set aside.

Heat the olive oil in a large saucepan over a low heat, add the onion and cook for 12 minutes, or until translucent. Add the cod, chickpeas and vinegar, then stir and bring briefly to the boil. Taste and adjust the seasoning with salt and pepper, if necessary, then sprinkle the garlic and paprika over the top before serving with the egg.

Baked Layered Loaf of Salt Cod, Hard-boiled Eggs and Potatoes

••

Bacalhau à Senhor Prior   ⛓ Beira Litoral

Preparation time: 30 minutes, plus 12–14 hours soaking
Cooking time: 25 minutes
Serves: 4
🐟 ⛓

850 g/1 lb 14 oz salt cod, desalted (page 40)
750 g/1 lb 10 oz waxy potatoes, unpeeled and left whole
6 eggs
3 garlic cloves, peeled and thinly sliced
130 ml/4½ fl oz (½ cup) olive oil
40 g/1½ oz (⅓ cup) black olives,
    pitted and finely chopped
3 bunches flat-leaf parsley, finely chopped
sea salt (optional)

Check the cod is not too salty before cooking. If it is, then leave to soak for another 2 hours. Drain.

Preheat the oven to 200°C/400°F/Gas Mark 6.

Put the cod into a large saucepan with the potatoes and 4 of the eggs and cook over a medium heat for 8 minutes, then remove the cod and eggs and leave the potatoes to cook for another 5 minutes.

Peel the eggs and set aside. Remove the skin and any bones from the fish and flake the flesh onto a plate and set aside.

Drain the potatoes, then peel and slice them into 1-cm/½-inch rings.

Arrange the ingredients in layers, starting with the potatoes, then the garlic, cod and egg in a large ovenproof dish until the ingredients are used up. Drizzle the olive oil over the top.

Put the remaining eggs into a small bowl and whisk with a fork, then pour over the top and bake for 10 minutes.

Scatter over the chopped olives and parsley before serving.

Macaroni with Salt Cod and Potatoes

••

Massa à Barrão de Almeirim   ⛓ Ribatejo

Preparation time: 25 minutes, plus 12–14 hours soaking
Cooking time: 45 minutes
Serves: 4
⛓

450 g/1 lb salt cod, desalted (page 40)
500 g/1 lb 2 oz tomatoes
150 ml/5 fl oz (⅔ cup) olive oil
3 onions, peeled and finely chopped
3 garlic cloves, peeled and finely chopped
2 bay leaves
⅓ bunch flat-leaf parsley, finely chopped
1 bird's eye chilli, chopped
280 ml/9½ fl oz (1 cup plus 2 tablespoons) white wine
850 g/1 lb 14 oz new potatoes, peeled and cut into
    irregular shapes
550 g/1 lb 4 oz (5½ cups) macaroni
sea salt and freshly ground black pepper

Check the cod is not too salty before cooking. If it is, then leave to soak for another 2 hours. Drain.

Cut the cod into small cubes and set aside.

Have a large bowl of iced water ready nearby. Bring a saucepan of water to the boil. Using a sharp knife, score the top of the tomatoes with a small cross shape. Once the water is boiling, carefully add the tomatoes and blanch for 30 seconds, then transfer them with a slotted spoon to the iced water and leave to cool. Once cool enough to handle, peel off the skins, cut in half and de-seed, then cut the flesh into small cubes. Set aside.

Heat the olive oil in a large saucepan over a low heat, add the onions, garlic, bay leaves and parsley and cook for 10 minutes, or until the onions are lightly coloured. Add the tomatoes and chilli, then season with salt and cook for 10 minutes, or until the tomatoes are soft. Add the white wine, increase the heat to medium and cook for 5 minutes. Add the potatoes and macaroni and top up with enough water just to cover. Cook for 10 minutes, or until the potatoes and pasta are soft. Add the cod, reduce the heat to low and cook for a further 10 minutes, or until the fish is cooked.

Taste and adjust the seasoning, if necessary, before serving.

Salt Cod Gratin

••

Bacalhau à Moda   ⛉ Beira Litoral
de Coimbra 🖻 p.123

Preparation time: 20 minutes, plus 12–14 hours soaking
Cooking time: 45–50 minutes
Serves: 4

600 g/1 lb 5 oz salt cod, desalted (page 40)
400 ml/14 fl oz (1⅔ cups) olive oil
3 onions, peeled and very thinly sliced
2 garlic cloves, peeled and very thinly sliced
450 ml/15 fl oz (1¾ cups) whole (full-fat) milk
450 g/1 lb bread, crusts removed
30 ml/1 fl oz (2 tablespoons) white wine vinegar
2 egg yolks
sea salt and freshly ground black pepper

For the salad:
1 large butterhead lettuce, leaves separated
30 ml/1 fl oz (2 tablespoons) olive oil
10 ml/2 teaspoons vinegar

Check the cod is not too salty before cooking. If it is, then leave to soak for another 2 hours. Drain. Flake the flesh into a bowl, removing the skin and any bones, and set aside.

Preheat the oven to 190°C/375°F/Gas Mark 5.

Heat the olive oil in a saucepan over a medium heat, add the onions and garlic and cook for 8 minutes, or until the onions are softened. Add the shredded cod and cook gently for 2 minutes.

Bring the milk to the boil in another saucepan. Add the bread and vinegar to the pan and mix well. Remove the pan from the heat and leave the bread to soak for 10 minutes.

Pour the bread mixture into the pan with the cod and cook over a medium heat for about 10 minutes, then transfer to an ovenproof dish.

Put the egg yolks into a small bowl and whisk with a fork, then brush over the top of the cod mixture in the ovenproof dish. Bake in the hot oven for 15–20 minutes, or until golden on top.

Put the lettuce into a salad bowl and dress with the olive oil and vinegar. Season the lettuce with salt before serving with the gratin.

Salt Cod Salad with Black-eyed Peas and Boiled Egg

••

Salada de Feijão Frade   ⛉ Lisbon
com Bacalhau Cozido

Preparation time: 20 minutes, plus 12–14 hours soaking
Cooking time: 35 minutes
Serves: 4
🐟 ⛉

330 g/11½ oz (1¾ cups) dried black-eyed peas
400 g/14 oz salt cod, desalted (page 40)
1 onion, peeled and finely chopped
2 garlic cloves, peeled and finely chopped
2 flat-leaf parsley sprigs with large leaves, finely chopped
4 eggs
100 ml/3½ fl oz (⅓ cup) olive oil
30 ml/1 fl oz (2 tablespoons) white wine vinegar
sea salt and freshly ground black pepper

Put the black-eyed peas into a large bowl of cold water and leave to soak for 12 hours.

The next day, check the cod is not too salty before cooking. If it is, then leave to soak for another 2 hours. Drain.

Drain the peas and put them into a large saucepan. Pour in enough cold water to cover, add a pinch of salt and cook over a medium heat, skimming any foam that forms on the surface, for 20 minutes, or until soft. Drain and set aside.

Put the onion, garlic and parsley into a small bowl and mix to combine. Set aside.

Bring a saucepan of water to the boil, carefully lower in the eggs and cook for 8 minutes, then remove from the pan and leave to cool. Once cold, peel the eggs and cut into quarters. Set aside.

When the cod is ready, put it into a saucepan and cook over a medium heat for 6 minutes, or until the fish flakes easily with a fork. Drain and leave to cool a little. When cool enough to handle, flake the flesh into a bowl, removing the skin and any bones.

Put the cooked black-eyes peas into a large bowl, add the onion mix and cod, then drizzle with the olive oil and vinegar and toss everything together until combined.

Taste and adjust the seasoning with salt and pepper, if necessary, then transfer the peas and cod mixture to a serving dish. Arrange the eggs on top before serving.

Salt Cod Bladder Stew with White Beans

∙∙

Samos de Bacalhau   ⛉ Beira Litoral
com Feijão Branco   ▣ p.125

Preparation time: 30 minutes, plus 12–14 hours soaking
Cooking time: 1 hour 30 minutes
Serves: 6
⚲ ◻

450 g/1 lb (2½ cups) dried butter (lima) beans
700 g/1 lb 9 oz salt cod air bladder, desalted (page 40)
2 onions, peeled and finely chopped
3 garlic cloves, peeled and finely chopped
60 ml/2 fl oz (4 tablespoons) olive oil
½ teaspoon paprika
½ teaspoon saffron threads
1 bay leaf
1 bird's eye chilli, halved
90 g/3¼ oz chorizo, thinly sliced into discs
2 carrots, thinly sliced into discs
sea salt and freshly ground black pepper

Put the beans into a large bowl of cold water and leave to soak for 12 hours.

The next day, check the salt cod bladder is not too salty before cooking. If it is, then leave to soak for another 2 hours.

Drain the salt cod bladder remove the very fine membrane on the back (the white part).

Drain the beans and put them into a large saucepan. Pour in enough cold water to cover, add a pinch of salt and cook over a medium heat for 30 minutes, or until soft. Leave them to cool in the cooking water, then drain and set both aside.

Put the onions, garlic, olive oil, paprika, saffron, bay leaf and chilli into a large saucepan and cook over a medium heat for 5 minutes, or until the onions are translucent.

Add the chorizo and carrots to the pan, stir, then reduce the heat to low and cook for 2 minutes. Add the cod and mix until everything is combined.

Pour in enough of the bean cooking water to cover all the ingredients and cook over a medium heat for 50 minutes. Add the beans, stir, then add some more cooking water to cover all the ingredients and gently bring to the boil over a low heat. Taste and adjust the seasoning with salt and pepper, if necessary, before serving.

Salt Cod Tongues

∙∙

Línguas de Bacalhau   ⛉ Beira Litoral

In every Portuguese kitchen, in homes and in restaurants, dried, salted cod is more than an essential ingredient; it is a national symbol. The fish has been caught in the North Atlantic waters since the 15th century and brought to Portugal to be salted and stacked outdoors for two to three weeks before being dried indoors. It needs a long soaking in water before being used in any preparation, and can be adapted to a variety of different recipes, from oven-roasted loins to these fried tongues.

Preparation time: 15 minutes, plus 12–14 hours soaking
Cooking time: 45 minutes
Serves: 6
◻

550 g/1 lb 4 oz salt cod tongues, desalted (page 40)
100 g/3½ oz (¾ cup) flour, for dusting
4 eggs
700 ml/23½ fl oz (2¾ cups) sunflower oil, for deep-frying
1½ onions, peeled and very thinly chopped
3 bunches flat-leaf parsley, finely chopped
60 ml/2 fl oz (4 tablespoons) white wine vinegar
170 ml/5½ fl oz (⅔ cup) olive oil
sea salt and freshly ground black pepper

Check the cod is not too salty before cooking. If it is, then leave to soak for another 2 hours. Drain.

Bring a saucepan of water to the boil, then reduce the heat to medium, add the cod and cook for 5 minutes. Remove from the pan, transfer to a perforated tray or colander and let them drip for 2–3 minutes.

Spread the flour out on a plate. Crack 2 of the eggs into a shallow bowl and lightly whisk with a fork. Toss each cod tongue in the flour, shaking off the excess flour then dip into the beaten eggs until coated. Place on a plate.

Line a large baking sheet with paper towels. Heat enough sunflower oil for deep-frying in a large, deep saucepan or fryer over a high heat until it reaches 180°C/350°F on a thermometer. Working in batches, carefully lower the cod tongues into the hot oil and deep-fry for 5 minutes, or until golden. Remove with a slotted spoon and leave to drain on the lined baking sheet. Put the cod tongues on a serving plate.

Meanwhile, have a small bowl of iced water nearby. Bring a saucepan of water to the boil, carefully lower in the remaining eggs and cook for 8 minutes, then remove and put them into the bowl of iced water to cool. Once cool, peel and finely chop.

Put the chopped hard-boiled eggs into a bowl, add the onions, parsley, vinegar and olive oil. Season with salt and pepper, then toss until everything is combined. Pour over the cod tongues before serving.

Salt Cod Bladder Stew with White Beans

Salt Cod with Eggs, Onions and Potatoes

••

Bacalhau à Brás   🖻 p.127   ⛴ Lisbon

There are a thousand-and-one ways to cook *bacalhau* (salted dried cod) across Portugal, but *Bacalhau à Brás* is perhaps the most emblematic of all Lisbon cod recipes. In the 18th century it was known as *Bacalhau Mexido com Ovos*, and it was only in the 19th century, when the city's Bairro Alto neighbourhood became a bohemian area full of bars and *casas de pasto* (taverns) that this dish from a tavern named Brás began to find national acclaim. The old and the more recent recipes are similar, although in the *à Brás* version the fries are very finely cut, almost resembling hay, which remains the most common technique today. My family all love this dish. For the salt cod, I prefer to use loins rather than shredded cod as the shredded fish contains more water and therefore loses more flavour. Desalting cod loins does takes longer, but the flavour is much better.

Preparation time: 30 minutes, plus 24 hours soaking
Cooking time: 35 minutes
Serves: 4–6
🐟 ⛴

400 g/14 oz salt cod loins
600g/1 lb 5 oz large waxy potatoes, peeled
80 ml/2¾ fl oz (⅓ cup) extra virgin olive oil
2 white onions, peeled, halved and cut into half-moons
1 fresh bay leaf
2 garlic cloves, peeled, germ removed and thinly sliced
1 litre/34 fl oz (4¼ cups) sunflower oil, for frying
10 g/¼ oz (¼ cup) flat-leaf parsley, leaves picked
4 eggs
20 g/¾ oz (⅛ cup) pitted black olives, roughly chopped
fine table salt and freshly ground black pepper
extra virgin olive oil, to garnish
green salad, to serve

Rinse the cod in cold running water, then put it into a large bowl of cold water, cover with food wrap and leave to stand in the fridge for 1 day. Keep changing the water every few hours and keep checking the salt level depending on your taste. The cod should not lose its saltiness completely.

When ready to cook, cut the potatoes with the julienne blade on a mandolin. Alternatively, using a sharp knife, slice the potato into very thin matchsticks. Rinse the potato matchsticks under cold running water to remove the starch, pat dry with paper towels and set aside.

Remove the cod from the water and pat dry with paper towels. Remove any bones, then shred.

Heat the olive oil in a large frying pan or skillet over a low heat, add the onions and cook gently, stirring occasionally, for 10–12 minutes, or until golden. Add the bay leaf and garlic and cook for a further 5 minutes. Add the cod and cook gently for 5–6 minutes so it absorbs the flavours.

Remove the pan from the heat and set aside.

Line a baking sheet with paper towels. Heat enough sunflower oil for deep-frying in a large, deep saucepan or fryer over a high heat until it reaches 180°C/350°F on a thermometer. Working in batches, carefully lower the potato matchsticks into the hot oil and deep-fry for 2–3 minutes, or until golden. Remove with a slotted spoon and leave to drain on the lined baking sheet. Season with salt.

Put the parsley leaves into a pile and thinly slice them, then set aside in a bowl.

Put the eggs into another small bowl and whisk lightly with a fork.

Put the cod back over a low heat and warm through for 1–2 minutes. Remove from the heat and add the beaten eggs and parsley at the same time. Mix together until everything is combined. Put it back over the heat for 1 minute to lightly cook the eggs, but not too much as you don't want scrambled eggs, then pour the mixture into a serving bowl and sprinkle with the olives. Add a dash of extra virgin olive oil and serve immediately with the potato matchsticks and a green salad.

Grilled Salt Cod and Bell Peppers

••

Bacalhau com Pimentos Assados   ⛴ Lisbon

Preparation time: 10 minutes, plus 12–14 hours soaking
Cooking time: 20 minutes
Serves: 4
🐟 ⛴

600 g/1 lb 5 oz salt cod, desalted (page 40)
4 red (bell) peppers (or any other colour)
3 large garlic cloves, peeled and very finely chopped
3 tablespoons white wine vinegar
120 ml/4 fl oz (½ cup) olive oil
sea salt and freshly ground black pepper

Check the cod is not too salty before cooking. If it is, then leave to soak for another 2 hours. Drain.

Prepare a barbecue or preheat an indoor grill (broiler).

As soon as the barbecue coals are glowing, put the red (bell) peppers directly on the grill rack and grill for 8 minutes, or until the skins are blackened all over. Alternatively, cook them over a direct flame on the stove. Put them into a large bowl, cover with food wrap or place in a plastic bag and let cool for 15 minutes. Once they are cool enough to handle, peel off the skins, cut them in half, remove the core and seeds and slice them into strips. Set aside.

Put the cod onto the grill rack and grill for 10 minutes, or until golden on both sides. Alternatively, cook the cod under the indoor grill. Shred the cod into a serving bowl, removing any skin and bones.

Add the garlic and pepper to the bowl, season with salt and pepper, then drizzle with vinegar and olive oil. Mix until well combined before serving.

Salt Cod with Eggs, Onions and Potatoes

Raw Salt Cod Salad

Salada de Bacalhau Cru 🖾 p.129   ⛉ **Leiria**

Preparation time: 25 minutes, plus 12–14 hours soaking
Cooking time: 20 minutes
Serves: 4
🖉 ⛉

450 g/1 lb salted cod, desalted (page 40)
2 red (bell) peppers
2 eggs
100 ml/3½ fl oz (⅓ cup) olive oil
30 ml/1 fl oz (2 tablespoons) white wine vinegar
1 small onion, peeled and diced
2 garlic cloves, peeled and diced
⅓ bunch flat-leaf parsley, very finely chopped
sea salt and freshly ground black pepper

Check the cod is not too salty before cooking. If it is, then leave to soak for another 2 hours. Drain.

Prepare a barbecue or preheat the indoor grill (broiler).

As soon as the barbecue coals are glowing, put the red (bell) peppers onto the grill rack and roast for 8 minutes, or until blackened all over. Put inside a plastic bag or cover with food wrap and leave to rest. Alternatively, cook under the grill. Once the peppers are cool enough to handle, remove the skin and seeds, slice the flesh into thin strips and set aside.

Once the cod has the desired saltiness, remove the skin and bones, then shred the flesh. Set aside.

Have a bowl of iced water nearby. Bring a saucepan of water to the boil. Once boiling, add the eggs and cook for 6 minutes, then transfer them to the bowl of iced water and leave to cool. Remove the shells and cut the eggs into slices.

Combine all the ingredients, except the parsley, in a serving bowl and toss everything together. Taste and adjust the seasoning with salt and pepper, if necessary, then add the parsley before serving.

Algarve-style Hake

Pescada à Algarvia   ⛉ **Algarve**

Preparation time: 10 minutes
Cooking time: 20 minutes
Serves: 4
🖉 ⛉ ⛉ ⊠

720 g/1 lb 9 oz hake fillets, skinned and bones removed
2 large onions, peeled and very thinly sliced
4 garlic cloves, peeled and very thinly sliced
1 teaspoon paprika
juice of ½ lemon
2 tablespoons olive oil
½ bunch flat-leaf parsley, finely chopped
sea salt and freshly ground black pepper
boiled potatoes or steamed cauliflower, to serve

Preheat the oven to 180°C/350°F/Gas Mark 4.

Put the hake fillets onto a large baking sheet. Season with salt, then arrange the onions and garlic over the top, making sure the fish is covered. Sprinkle with the paprika, black pepper and lemon juice. Pour over the olive oil and scatter over the parsley. Bake in the oven for 20 minutes, or until the fish flakes easily with a fork.

Serve the hake with either boiled potatoes or steamed cauliflower.

Hake Fillets – Monchique Style

Filletes de Pescada à Monchique   ⛉ **Algarve**

Preparation time: 25 minutes, plus 2 minutes soaking
Cooking time: 20 minutes
Serves: 4

720 g/1 lb 9 oz hake fillets, skinned and bones removed
juice of ½ lemon
60 ml/2 fl oz (4 tablespoons) olive oil
2 onions, peeled and thinly sliced
2 eggs
120 ml/4 fl oz (½ cup) whole (full-fat) milk
110 g/3¾ oz (7¾ tablespoons) butter
70 g/2½ oz (½ cup) plain (all-purpose) flour
800 g/1 lb 12 oz new potatoes, peeled and cut into
    3-cm/1¼-inch chunks
1 red (bell) pepper, halved, cored, de-seeded
    and finely chopped
½ bunch flat-leaf parsley, finely chopped
sea salt

Slice the hake fillets into 5-cm/2-inch steaks, then season with salt and the lemon juice.

Heat the olive oil in a saucepan over a medium heat. Add the onions and cook for 5 minutes, or until translucent. Remove from the heat and set aside.

Have a bowl of iced water nearby. Bring a saucepan of water to the boil. Once boiling, add the eggs and cook for 6 minutes, then transfer them to the bowl of iced water and leave to cool. Remove the shells and cut the eggs in half.

Put the hake fillets into a shallow dish, add the milk and leave to soak for 2 minutes. Heat the butter in a large frying pan or skillet over a medium heat. Spread the flour out on a large plate. Coat the fish with the flour, then fry for 5 minutes, or until golden. If the pieces are thick, finish the fish off in a 180°C/350°F oven for 2 minutes.

Meanwhile, put the potatoes into a saucepan of salted water and cook over a low heat for 15–20 minutes, or until soft. Drain and set aside.

Put the eggs, red (bell) pepper and parsley into a medium bowl and mix until combined. Add them to the onions and mix together.

Put the fish onto a large serving plate and garnish with the egg and onion mixture. Serve with the potatoes on the side.

Raw Salt Cod Salad

Poached Hake with Boiled Eggs and Turnip Tops

••

Pescada à Poveira   ♡ Minho

When making this dish, I actually prefer to steam the hake rather than poach it as I find the fish loses more flavour when cooked in boiling water. However, the traditional method is to poach the hake, as given in this recipe. If you also prefer to steam the fish then cook it for 5 minutes.

Preparation time: 30 minutes, plus 30 minutes standing
Cooking time: 30 minutes
Serves: 4
♢

800 g/1 lb 12 oz hake
600 g/1 lb 5 oz waxy potatoes, peeled and
    cut into 5-cm/2-inch slices
1 kg/2 lb 4 oz turnip tops, bottom stalk removed
4 eggs
250 ml/8 fl oz (1 cup) olive oil
1 onion, peeled and finely chopped
1 teaspoon paprika
35 ml/1¼ fl oz (2 tablespoons) white wine vinegar
5 slices country or sourdough bread
sea salt

Clean and gut the hake, removing all the scales. Cut into tranches of 200 g/7 oz each. Season with salt and leave to stand for 30 minutes.

Put the potatoes into a large saucepan, cover with cold water, add a pinch of salt and cook over a low heat for 10 minutes, or until soft. Remove the potatoes with a slotted spoon and set aside.

Bring the water to the boil in the pan again, then add the turnip tops and cook for 2 minutes. Remove with a slotted spoon and set aside.

Bring the water back to the boil again. Have a bowl of iced water nearby. Once boiling, carefully lower in the eggs and cook for 8 minutes. Lift the eggs out of the pan and transfer to the iced water to cool. Once cold, peel the shells from the eggs and cut into slices. Set aside.

Bring a large, shallow saucepan of water to the boil. Once it is boiling, add the fish, reduce the heat to low and cook gently for 8–9 minutes, or until soft. Remove the fish with a fish slice (spatula) and put onto a plate or tray.

Meanwhile, heat the olive oil in a small saucepan over a low heat, add the onion and paprika and cook for 12 minutes, or until the onion is soft. Add the vinegar and a pinch of salt. This helps to release the sweetness of the onions.

Arrange the bread slices on the bottom of a large serving dish, arrange the fish on top with the turnip tops, potatoes and eggs around the fish, then pour over the hot sauce before serving.

Tuna Steak with White Wine Sauce

••

Bife de Atum   ♡ Madeira

Tuna is an abundant fish in Portugal's Atlantic waters, and tuna fishing is of extreme importance to the country's economy, with most of it exported to countries like the United Kingdom, France and even Japan. In the archipelago of Madeira, tuna is king. There are a number of different regional recipes that include it, although the most common way to honour its freshness is the simplest: steaks resting for a few hours in a white wine and vinegar marinade, pan-fried until golden brown on the outside, then finally basted with the marinade. Tuna steaks are usually served with a side dish of fried cornmeal, or boiled potatoes and onions.

Preparation time: 10 minutes, plus 3 hours 30 minutes marinating
Cooking time: 10 minutes
Serves: 4
🖋♢♢

800 g/1 lb 12 oz lean tuna loin
8 Jamaican peppercorns, crushed
4 garlic cloves, unpeeled and crushed
2 bay leaves
300 ml/10 fl oz (1¼ cups) white wine
250 ml/8 fl oz (1 cup) white wine vinegar
10 g/¼ oz (2 teaspoons) dried oregano
120 ml/4 fl oz (½ cup) olive oil
20 g/¾ oz (4 teaspoons) Dijon mustard
sea salt
Fried Cornmeal (page 88), to serve

Slice the tuna loin into 4 steaks, each 200 g/7 oz, making sure they are not too thick. Put 2 teaspoons salt, the crushed peppercorns, garlic, bay leaves, white wine, vinegar and oregano into a large dish, then add the tuna steaks to the marinade and rub it in until coated. Cover with food wrap and leave and to marinate in the fridge for 3 hours 30 minutes.

Remove the tuna steaks from the marinade, setting the remaining marinade aside. Heat a large frying pan or skillet over a medium heat. Pour in the olive oil and, when hot, add the tuna steaks and cook for 3 minutes on each side, or until golden. Remove the tuna steaks from the pan and add the mustard and remaining marinade to the pan and bring to the boil. Remove from the heat and whisk to emulsify. Put the tuna steaks back into the pan and stir to coat them in the sauce.

Serve the tuna steaks in the sauce alongside the fried cornmeal.

Tuna Steaks with Caramelised Onions

Bifes de Atum de Cebolada ▽ Algarve

There is a variation of this recipe that includes a cinnamon stick and the rind of three lemons, which are added once the onions are starting to colour.

Preparation time: 25 minutes
Cooking time: 40 minutes
Serves: 4

80 g/3 oz (5⅓ tablespoons) unsalted butter
5 onions, peeled, halved and thinly sliced
2 garlic cloves, peeled and thinly sliced
2 bay leaves
1 cinnamon stick (optional)
rind of 3 lemons (optional)
200 ml/7 fl oz (¾ cup) white wine
3 ripe tomatoes, quartered
720 g/1 lb 9 oz tuna steaks
juice of 1½ lemons
plain (all-purpose) flour, for dusting
120 ml/4 fl oz (½ cup) olive oil
sea salt and freshly ground black pepper
Fries (page 180) or green salad, to serve

Heat the butter in a saucepan over a medium heat until melted. Add the onions, garlic, bay leaves and a pinch of salt and cook for 7 minutes, or until the onions are starting to colour. Add the cinnamon stick and lemon rinds (if using), then add the wine. Reduce the heat to low and cook for 10 minutes, or until the onions are golden. Add the tomatoes and cook for a further 10 minutes, or until the tomatoes have broken down. Remove from the heat and set aside.

Season the tuna steaks with salt and pepper, I prefer to use the lemon at the end, but you can also drizzle a little lemon juice over now, if liked.

Sprinkle flour over a large plate, then use to coat the tuna steaks.

Line a large baking sheet with paper towels. Heat a large frying pan or skillet over a medium heat. Once hot, add the olive oil and heat until it reaches 150°C/300°F on a thermometer. Add a tuna steak one at a time and cook for 45 seconds on each side until golden all over, then remove from the pan and leave to rest on the lined baking sheet.

Drizzle lemon juice over the tuna steaks, then arrange on a serving plate and pour over the hot caramelised onions. Serve the tuna steaks alongside some fries or a green salad.

Tuna Steaks with Tomato Sauce

Bifes de Atum de Tomatada ▽ Algarve

Preparation time: 20 minutes
Cooking time: 45 minutes
Serves: 4

600 g/1 lb 5 oz tomatoes
800 g/1 lb 12 oz lean tuna loin
120 ml/4 fl oz (½ cup) extra virgin olive oil
2 onions, peeled and very thinly sliced
2 cloves
1 litre/34 fl oz (4¼ cups) sunflower oil, for deep-frying
6 waxy potatoes, peeled and very thinly sliced
½ bunch flat-leaf parsley, chopped
sea salt and freshly ground black pepper

Have a large bowl of iced water nearby. Bring a large saucepan of water to the boil. Using a sharp knife, score the top of the tomatoes with a small cross shape. Once the water is boiling, carefully add the tomatoes and blanch for 30 seconds, then transfer them with a slotted spoon to the iced water and leave to cool. Once cool enough to handle, peel off the skins, cut in half and de-seed, then cut the flesh into long strips. Set aside.

Cut the tuna into 4 steaks, about 200 g/7 oz each, and season with salt and pepper. Leave the tuna steaks to absorb the seasoning for 2 minutes before cooking.

Heat the olive oil in a large saucepan over a medium heat, add the onions and tomatoes and cook for 7 minutes, or until the onions are soft and the tomatoes have broken down. Add the cloves and tuna steaks and sear the steaks for 5 seconds on each side. Flip them, cover with a lid and cook for 4 minutes. Uncover and remove the pan from the heat.

Line a large baking sheet with paper towels. Heat enough sunflower oil for deep-frying in a large, deep saucepan or fryer over a high heat until it reaches 180°C/350°F on a thermometer. Working in batches, carefully drop the potato slices into the hot oil and deep-fry for 3–4 minutes, or until golden. Remove with a slotted spoon and leave to drain on the lined baking sheet. Season with salt.

Serve the tuna steaks in the sauce with the parsley scattered over the top and the fried potatoes alongside.

Stewed Tuna Steaks

Bifes de Atum Estufados   �♡ Algarve

Preparation time: 30 minutes
Cooking time: 30 minutes
Serves: 4
🖈 ◻

600 g/1 lb 5 oz waxy potatoes, peeled and
    very thinly sliced
680 g/1 lb 8 oz tuna steaks
2 onions, peeled and thinly sliced
650 g/1 lb 7 oz large ripe tomatoes, thinly sliced
120 ml/4 fl oz (½ cup) olive oil
4 bunches flat-leaf parsley, finely chopped
2 bunches coriander (cilantro), finely chopped
2 thyme sprigs, leaves picked
sea salt and freshly ground black pepper

Preheat the oven to 180°C/350°F/Gas Mark 4.
    Spread the potatoes out on a large baking
sheet or in a roasting pan and roast in the oven
for 25 minutes, or until soft.
    Meanwhile, season the tuna steaks with salt
and pepper.
    Put the onions, tomatoes and olive oil into
a large saucepan and cook over a medium heat
for 15–20 minutes to make a sauce. Add the tuna
steaks and herbs, cover with a lid and cook for
5–6 minutes, or until the flesh flakes easily.
    Serve the tuna steaks in the sauce with the
cooked potatoes, seasoned with salt if necessary,
alongside.

Tuna Escabeche

Atum de Escabeche   📷 p.133   �♡ Madeira

Preparation time: 30 minutes, plus 3 hours 30 minutes
standing
Cooking time 10 minutes
Serves 6
🖈 ◻

850 g/1 lb 14 oz lean tuna loin, sliced into 4 pieces
5 garlic cloves, 2 unpeeled and left whole,
    3 peeled and finely chopped
3 bay leaves
220 ml/7½ fl oz (1 cup) olive oil, plus extra for drizzling
2 onions, peeled and sliced into thin rings
120 ml/4 fl oz (½ cup) white wine vinegar
4 large flat-leaf parsley sprigs, finely chopped
2 teaspoons dried oregano
sea salt and freshly ground black pepper

Put the tuna pieces into a large bowl, cover with
cold water and leave to stand in the fridge for
2½ hours.
    Drain the tuna pieces, then put them into
a large saucepan with the 2 unpeeled garlic cloves,
the bay leaves and a pinch of salt. Add a drizzle
of olive oil and cook the tuna over a medium heat
for 6–7 minutes, or until the flesh flakes easily.
    Meanwhile, put the onion rings into a large
bowl, then pour over the vinegar and olive oil.
Add the chopped garlic, parsley and oregano to
the bowl and mix together. Leave to marinate
while the tuna is cooking.
    Remove the tuna pieces from the pan and
flake the flesh into the bowl with the onions.
Mix everything together, cover the bowl with
food wrap and leave to stand for 1 hour at room
temperature before serving.

Tuna Escabeche

Salt-cured Tuna Loin

Estupeta de Atum   ◡ Algarve

Over a thousand years ago, the Romans and Arabs developed a process called *muxuma*, based on packing tuna loins with salt, then leaving them to cure for a couple of days, before washing them in fresh water then leaving them to air-dry in the sun. Tuna prepared this way is now a real treat. There is also another way of preserving tuna called *estupeta* (page 429). This process uses the narrow part of the white muscle on the loins located very near to the dorsal fin that is then cured in saltwater. Use this salt-cured tuna loin in the Salt-cured Tuna Salad (see right).

Preparation time: 15 minutes, plus 30–40 days curing and 2–3 days soaking
𝒥 ◻ ✕

1.5 kg/3 lb 5 oz lean tuna loin
fine sea salt, for soaking and salting

Pour 1.5 litres/50 fl oz (6¼ cups) water into a large bowl. Add 4 g/⅛ oz (1 teaspoon) fine sea salt and stir until all the salt has dissolved to make a brine. Add the tuna pieces to the brine and wash to remove any blood. Remove the tuna pieces from the bowl, drain and pat dry with paper towels.

Transfer the tuna pieces into a large clay or ceramic container, then pack the fish with enough salt to cover. Cover the container with a tea (dish) towel and leave to cure for 30–40 days.

Once ready, remove the tuna pieces from the container and brush off any excess salt. Put into a clean container or large bowl of fresh cold water and leave to soak for 2–3 days until they are desalted, changing the water a few times.

When you want to use the cured tuna, shred it or cut into thin pieces.

Salt-cured Tuna Salad

Salada de Estupeta de Atum   ◡ Algarve

Estupeta (page 429) refers to the dark brown tuna left over from the shavings of *muxama* (salt-dried tuna loin, see left), that are then preserved in a strong brine for more than 30 days. It is sold in plastic tubs of different sizes and can mostly be found in shops in the south of Portugal. It is the main ingredient of this traditional cold salad from the Algarve that is prepared with tomatoes, onions and (bell) peppers.

Preparation time: 30 minutes, plus 4–6 hours standing
Serves: 4
𝒥 ◻

600 g/1 lb 5 oz Salt-cured Tuna Loin (see left), shredded into thin strips
400 g/14 oz bull's heart tomatoes, cut into 3-cm/1¼-inch cubes
2 green (bell) peppers, halved, cored, de-seeded and cut into thin strips
1 onion, halved and very thinly sliced
400 ml/14 fl oz (1⅔ cups) olive oil
300 ml/10 fl oz (1¼ cups) white wine vinegar

Put the cured tuna strips into a large bowl and pour in enough cold water to cover. Leave the tuna strips to soak for 2–4 hours or until they no longer taste salty, changing the water a few times during the process. Remove the tuna strips from the bowl, drain and pat dry with paper towels.

Put the tomatoes, green (bell) peppers, onion and tuna strips into a large serving bowl and toss to combine. Dress with the olive oil and vinegar and mix everything together again. Cover with food wrap and leave to chill in the fridge for 2 hours before serving.

Salt-cured Tuna – São João Style

Atum de São João   ⊓ Madeira

This is an iconic dish from Madeira, traditionally eaten during the celebrations of Saint João. Tuna is a species in danger of overfishing in many parts of the world, where Skipjack tuna is the only sustainable variety. However, in the Azores the Bigeye tuna is less under threat and considered a sustainable fish.

Preparation time: 40 minutes, plus 3 days chilling and 20 minutes soaking
Cooking time: 45 minutes
Serves: 6
⌐ ⊓

1 kg/2 lb 4 oz tuna belly
5 garlic cloves, peeled and thinly sliced
⅓ bunch fresh oregano or 2 teaspoons dried oregano
4 onions, peeled and thinly sliced
500 g/1 lb 2 oz fresh red beans in the pod
4 white sweet potatoes, unpeeled
6 waxy potatoes, unpeeled
4 corn-on-the-cob, husks removed
2 small squash (any variety), peeled, de-seeded and chopped
120 ml/4 fl oz (½ cup) olive oil
50 ml/1⅔ fl oz (3½ tablespoons) vinegar
sea salt

Three days before cooking the tuna, score the tuna belly with a sharp knife, then put it into a large dish, season with salt and rub over the garlic and oregano. Cover with food wrap and chill in the fridge for 3 days.

When ready to cook the tuna, put the fish into a large bowl of cold water for 20 minutes. Drain.

Put the tuna into a medium saucepan. Pour in enough water to cover, then add the onions and beans and cook over a medium heat for 10–15 minutes, or until the tuna is cooked. Drain and put the tuna, onions and beans into a large serving dish. Set aside.

Put the sweet potatoes, potatoes, corn and squash into another large saucepan, cover with cold water, season with salt and cook for 25–30 minutes. They will be ready at different times so remove each one as soon as they are cooked and set aside.

Season the tuna with the olive oil and vinegar before serving with the cooked vegetables.

Wine and Garlic-marinated Grouper

Garoupa de Vinha d'Alhos   ⊓ Açores

Preparation time: 20 minutes, plus 3 days marinating
Cooking time: 30 minutes
Serves: 6
⌐ ⊓

1.2 kg/2 lb 11 oz grouper
1½ tablespoons paprika
8 garlic cloves, peeled and finely chopped
2 bay leaves
2 tablespoons *Massa de Malagueta* (page 102)
600 ml/20 fl oz (2¼ cups) dry white wine
3 eggs
olive or sunflower oil, for shallow-frying
½ bunch flat-leaf parsley, finely chopped
sea salt

Gut and clean the grouper, removing all the scales. Cut off the head and discard, then rinse the fish under cold running water. Season the grouper with salt, then cut it into medium-sized pieces, about 50–100 g/2–3½ oz, and put them into a large bowl. Add the paprika, chopped garlic, bay leaves, *Massa de Malagueta* and wine and rub it into the fish pieces until they are all coated. Cover with food wrap and store in the fridge for 3 days, stirring every day.

When ready to cook, bring a medium saucepan of water to the boil. Have a bowl of cold water nearby. Once boiling, carefully lower in the eggs and cook for 8 minutes. Lift the eggs out of the pan and transfer to the iced water to cool. Once cold, peel the shells from the eggs, coarsely chop and set aside.

Remove the fish pieces from the marinade. Strain the leftover liquid, setting this strained marinade aside.

Line a large baking sheet with paper towels. Heat the oil for shallow-frying in a large sauté pan over a medium-high heat. Once hot enough, add half of the fish pieces and shallow-fry for 3 minutes on each side, or until golden. Remove and leave to drain on the lined baking sheet. Repeat until all the remaining fish has been cooked. Transfer the fried fish to a serving plate.

Put the pan back onto the heat and pour in the reserved strained marinade. Cook, stirring with a wooden spoon, scraping up any crispy bits from the bottom of the pan, for 5 minutes, or until the liquid has reduced a little to make a sauce.

Pour the sauce over the fish on the serving plate. Scatter over the parsley and garnish with the hard-boiled eggs before serving.

Fish Cataplana

Cataplana de Peixe 📷 p.137   ◻ **Algarve**

Cataplana (page 429) is both a traditional Portuguese seafood stew and name of the pot it is prepared in. This dish — a rich, reddish mixture of different fish with potatoes, green (bell) peppers and onions — is today one of the Algarve's main attractions. Its origins are still unknown, there being no official historical records of its creation or origins, but given that Arab occupation of the south of the Iberian Peninsula and North of Africa had a big influence on the crafts of the Algarve for more than 500 years, both pot and dish are likely to link to this period. *Cataplana*, the pot, was once made of zinc, but is now made of a tin interior with a copper-hammered finish and composed of two concave dish-shaped halves that close with a hinge, enabling food to be steamed and giving it a unique and unmistakable flavour. There are still a few artisans who make *cataplanas* by hand.

Preparation time: 50 minutes, plus 40 minutes standing
Cooking time: 20 minutes, plus 10 minutes resting
Serves: 6
🐟 ◻ ◻

400 g/14 oz fresh palourde clams
300 g/11 oz monkfish (flounder) tails
300 g/11 oz grouper or wreckfish
300 g/11 oz red snapper
3 ripe tomatoes
3 onions, peeled and sliced
⅕ green (bell) pepper, cored, de-seeded and
    cut into thin strips
4 garlic cloves, peeled and thinly sliced
2 bird's eye chillies, finely chopped
220 ml/7½ fl oz (1 cup) olive oil
3 bay leaves
1 small bunch flat-leaf parsley, roughly chopped
100 ml/3½ fl oz (⅓ cup plus 1 tablespoon) brandy
160 ml/5½ fl oz (⅔ cup) white wine
12 prawns (shrimp) with heads and shells on
100 g/3½ oz Serrano ham, thinly sliced
80 g/3 oz chorizo, thinly sliced
700 g/1 lb 9 oz new potatoes, peeled and thickly sliced
sea salt

Rinse the clams a few times in cold water to remove any sand and grit, then put them into a large bowl of water, add a pinch of salt and leave to stand for 40 minutes. This helps them to release any remaining sand and grit. Drain.

Gut and clean the fish, removing all the scales, then cut into small pieces and season with salt.

Have a large bowl of iced water nearby. Bring a large saucepan of water to the boil. Using a sharp knife, score the top of the tomatoes with a small cross shape. Once the water is boiling, carefully add the tomatoes and blanch for 30 seconds, then transfer them with a slotted spoon to the iced water and leave to cool. Once cool enough

to handle, peel off the skins, cut in half and de-seed, then cut the flesh into small chunks.

Arrange half of the onions, (bell) peppers, garlic, chillies and tomatoes in a *cataplana*. Season with a pinch of salt, then pour over half of the olive oil. Arrange the fish and clams on top, then crush the bay leaves over the top. Cover the fish with the remaining onions, parsley, peppers, garlic and tomatoes, then pour over the brandy and white wine. Arrange the prawns (shrimp) in a layer on top, then add a layer of ham and chorizo. Cover the *cataplana* with the lid and cook over a medium heat for 20 minutes. Remove the pan from the heat and leave to rest for 10 minutes.

Meanwhile, put the potatoes into a large saucepan of cold water, add a pinch of salt and cook over a medium heat for 15–20 minutes, or until soft. Drain.

Serve the boiled potatoes alongside the fish stew.

Fish Stew — Peniche Style

**Caldeirada de Peixe
à Moda de Peniche**   ◻ **Leiria**

Preparation time: 45 minutes
Cooking time: 25 minutes, plus 10 minutes resting
Serves: 8
🐟 ◻ ◻

4 onions, peeled and thinly sliced into rings
2 garlic cloves, peeled and thinly sliced
1 kg/2 lb 4 oz waxy potatoes, peeled and thinly sliced
    into 3-cm/1¼-inch discs
2 red (bell) pepper, cored, de-seeded and cut into strips
6 large bull's heart tomatoes, cut into small pieces
230 ml/7¾ fl oz (1 cup) olive oil
600 g/1 lb 5 oz monkfish, grey membrane removed
400 g/14 oz skate wing, skin removed
500 g/1 lb 2 oz grouper
600 g/1 lb 5 oz wreckfish
800 g/1 lb 12 oz sea bass
200 g/7 oz monkfish liver
2 bird's eye chillies, finely chopped
sea salt and ground white peppercorns

Arrange the onions and garlic in a layer in the bottom of a saucepan, then arrange the potatoes in a layer on top. Spread the (bell) pepper strips over the potatoes, then spread the tomatoes on top. Add the olive oil, cover the pan with a lid and bring to the boil over low heat, stirring occasionally. Reduce the heat slightly and cook for 10–15 minutes, or until the potatoes are tender.

Meanwhile, cut the fish into large chunks, leaving the bones in. Season with salt and pepper. Add the fish pieces, monkfish liver and chillies, cover the pan again and cook over a low heat for a further 10 minutes, shaking the pan occasionally. Taste and adjust the seasoning with salt, if necessary, then remove the pan from the heat, cover with the lid and leave to rest 10 minutes before serving.

Fish Cataplana

Flathead Grey Mullet

Fataça na Telha   ♡ Ribatejo

Preparation time: 30 minutes
Cooking time: 40–45 minutes
Serves: 4
🐟 ▢

1 grey mullet, about 1.6 kg/3 lb 8 oz
180 ml/6 fl oz (¾ cup) olive oil
1 large onion, peeled and finely chopped
4 garlic cloves, peeled and finely chopped
⅓ bunch flat-leaf parsley, finely chopped
1 bay leaf, crushed
1 tablespoon paprika
juice of 1 lemon
3 waxy potatoes, peeled and cut into 3-cm/1¼-inch cubes
sea salt and freshly ground white pepper
lemon slices, to garnish

Preheat the oven to 160°C/325°F/Gas Mark 3.

Clean and gut the fish, removing all the scales, then rinse under cold running water. Cut the fish into large pieces, about 50–100 g/2–3½ oz, and season with salt and pepper. Brush a little of the olive oil over the fish and set aside.

Combine the onion, garlic, parsley, bay leaf, paprika and lemon juice in a large bowl with the remaining olive oil and set aside.

Put the potatoes into a saucepan of salted water and cook over a medium heat for 10–15 minutes, or until soft. Drain and sprinkle with salt.

Arrange the fish on a clay pantile or curved roof tile and pour over the onion mixture. Arrange the potatoes on top and bake in the oven for 25–30 minutes, or until golden. Check the fish during cooking — it is cooked once the flesh separates from the bone.

Garnish the fish and potatoes with lemon slices before serving.

Red Mullets in Liver Sauce

Salmonetes de Setúbal   ♡ Lisbon

Preparation time: 20 minutes
Cooking time: 30 minutes
Serves: 4
🐟

4 x 250-g/9-oz red mullet
600 g/1 lb 5 oz small waxy potatoes, unpeeled and
    left whole
olive oil, for drizzling
150 ml/5 fl oz (⅔ cup) white wine
2 onions, peeled and finely chopped
60 g/2¼ oz (½ stick) butter, cut into cubes
1 large flat-leaf parsley sprig, finely chopped
1 tablespoon lemon juice
sea salt
green salad, to serve

Prepare a barbecue or preheat an indoor grill (broiler).

Clean the fish, removing the scales. Using a sharp knife, make an incision in the belly and remove the livers, place in a bowl and set aside.

Put the potatoes into a saucepan, cover with water and cook over a medium heat for 15–20 minutes, or until soft. Drain, rub off the skins, then put them into a serving dish and drizzle olive oil over the top. Cover and keep warm.

As soon as the barbecue coals are glowing, season the mullets with salt and grill for 4 minutes on each side, or until golden all over. Alternatively, cook the fish under the grill.

Meanwhile, put the white wine and onions into a saucepan and cook over a medium heat for 10 minutes, or until reduced by a third. Smash the reserved livers with a fork, add them to the pan with the butter and cook for 2 minutes. Remove from the heat, add the chopped parsley and lemon juice and stir until combined.

Pour the sauce over the red mullet and serve alongside the boiled new potatoes and green salad.

Allis Shad in Escabeche

Sável de Escabeche   ♡ Minho

Preparation time: 25 minutes, plus 36 hours chilling over 3 days
Cooking time: 1 hour 15 minutes
Serves: 4
🐟 ▢

1 x 1.6-kg/3 lb 5-oz allis shad (*Alosa alosa*)
6 onions, peeled and cut into rings
6 g/¼ oz (1 teaspoon) white peppercorns
2 bay leaves
¼ bunch flat-leaf parsley
6 cloves
300 ml/10 fl oz (1¼ cups) olive oil
350 ml/12 fl oz (1½ cups) white wine vinegar
sea salt
boiled new potatoes or green salad, to serve
2 lemons, cut into wedges, to serve

Clean the fish, removing the scales. Cut off the head and discard. Using a sharp knife, make an incision in the belly and remove the guts. Next, using a skewer, remove the bloodline. Cut the fish into 4-cm/1½-inch chunks.

Arrange a layer of onion in a large saucepan, followed by a layer of fish, white peppercorns, a bay leaf, a few parsley sprigs and half the cloves. Repeat with another layer to use up all the ingredients. Pour over the olive oil, vinegar and 250 ml/8 fl oz (1 cup) water, then cook over a low heat for 20 minutes. Remove from the heat and once cool leave to rest in the fridge for 12 hours.

Repeat the process on the following 2 days but on the third day, cook for 30 minutes.

Serve with boiled new potatoes or green salad alongside and lemon wedges for squeezing over.

Allis Shad with Fish Roe Porridge

Sável Frito com Açorda de Santarém ⛉ **Ribatejo**

Preparation time: 30 minutes, plus 10 minutes soaking
Cooking time: 50 minutes
Serves: 4
⛉

1 x 1.5-kg/3 lb 5-oz allis shad (*Alosa alosa*)
180 g/6¼ oz allis shad fish eggs
1 bay leaf
420 ml/14¼ fl oz (1⅔ cups) olive oil
2 garlic cloves, peeled and thinly sliced
600 g/1 lb 5 oz spelt bread
juice of 1 lemon
⅓ bunch coriander (cilantro), chopped
500 ml/17 fl oz (2 cups) sunflower oil, for shallow-frying
plain (all-purpose) flour, for dusting
sea salt

Clean and gut the fish, removing all the scales. Cut off the head and set aside. Rinse under cold running water, then cut the fish into pieces, about 1 cm/½ inch thick, and sprinkle with sea salt. Rinse the fish egg sac in cold water and leave to drip on a perforated tray or in a colander.

Bring a saucepan of water to the boil with the bay leaf and a pinch of salt. Once the water is boiling, add the fish heads and fish eggs and cook for 20 minutes, or until the fish eggs are cooked or firm on the outside. Using a slotted spoon, remove the fish eggs and set aside, then cook the heads for a further 10 minutes. Strain the liquid through a sieve (fine-mesh strainer) into a large bowl or jug (pitcher) and set aside. Discard the heads.

Heat the olive oil in another saucepan over a low heat, add the garlic and cook for 30 seconds or until golden. Remove from the heat.

Tear the bread into a large bowl, then pour in enough of the fish stock to cover. Leave to soak for 10 minutes, adding a little more water, if necessary.

Squeeze out the excess water from the bread, then shred the fish eggs into the bread. Add the garlic-flavoured olive oil and mix together very well. Season with salt, then put into a clean saucepan and cook over a low heat for 10 minutes, or until it is a smooth porridge consistency. Remove from the heat and add the lemon juice and chopped coriander (cilantro). Leave to rest, then taste and adjust the seasoning.

Meanwhile, line a large baking sheet with paper towels. Heat enough sunflower oil in a shallow frying pan or skillet over a high heat until it reaches 180°C/350°F on a thermometer. Spread the flour out over a large plate, then working in batches, toss the fish in the flour until coated, shaking off any excess and fry for 4–5 minutes, or until golden and crispy. Remove with a fish slice (spatula) and leave to drain on the lined baking sheet.

Serve the fried fish with the porridge.

Allis Shad with Serrano Ham

Sável na Telha ⛉ **Ribatejo**

Preparation time: 20 minutes
Cooking time: 40 minutes
Serves: 4
🐟 ⛉

1 x 1.5-kg/3 lb 5-oz allis shad (*Alosa alosa*)
olive oil, for brushing and drizzling
180 g/6 oz Serrano ham, sliced
450 g/1 lb baby new potatoes, unpeeled and left whole
juice of 1 lemon
sea salt and freshly ground black pepper

Prepare a barbecue or preheat the oven to 240°C/475°F/Gas Mark 9.

Clean the fish, removing the scales. Cut off the head and set aside. Using a sharp knife, make an incision in the belly and remove the guts, then rinse the fish under cold running water. Make some cuts on both sides of the loins on the fish with a sharp knife, then brush the fish with olive oil, season with pepper and rub some salt over the fish.

Arrange a layer of ham on a clay pantile or curved roof tile, then place the fish on top, then cover the fish with another layer of ham slices. Cover with another tile and use a length of wire to secure them.

Put the potatoes into a large saucepan, cover with cold water, add a pinch of salt and cook over a medium heat for 15–20 minutes, or until soft. Drain, then put the potatoes into a clean tea (dish) towel, gather up the corners and rub the potatoes to remove the skins. Drizzle with olive oil and season with a pinch of salt. Keep warm.

As soon as the barbecue coals are glowing, place the clay tiles holding the fish on the grill rack and grill for 20 minutes, or until the flesh separates from the bone. Keep turning the tiles during cooking so that the fish doesn't burn. Alternatively, cook the fish in the hot oven.

Drizzle the lemon juice over the fish before serving with the boiled potatoes.

Fish Stew – Setúbal Style

....

Caldeirada à Moda de Setúbal   ♡ Lisbon

Preparation time: 1 hour
Cooking time: 55 minutes
Serves: 8
◻ ◻

4 medium red mullet
1 medium sea bass
1 kg/2 lb 4 oz monkfish (flounder)
1 small gurnard
500 g/1 lb 2 oz squid
800 g/1 lb 12 oz sardines, cleaned and gutted
6 large tomatoes
4 large onions, peeled and thinly sliced
4 red (bell) peppers, cored, de-seeded and cut into
    small cubes
1.2 kg/2 lb 11 oz potatoes, peeled and quartered
220 ml/7½ fl oz (1 cup) olive oil
4 cloves
300 g/11 oz penne pasta
sea salt and freshly ground black pepper

Clean and gut all the fish, removing all the scales. Cut off the heads and set aside. Rinse under cold running water, then cut the fish into large tranches.

Have a large bowl of iced water nearby. Bring a large saucepan of water to the boil. Using a sharp knife, score the top of three of the tomatoes with a small cross shape. Once the water is boiling, carefully add the tomatoes and blanch for 30 seconds, then transfer them with a slotted spoon to the iced water and leave to cool. Once cool enough to handle, peel off the skins and cut into small cubes. Set aside.

Arrange the sliced onions in the bottom of a large clay pot (if you don't have a clay pot then use a large, tall saucepan). Arrange the red (bell) peppers and tomatoes over the top of the onions, then add the potatoes. Season with the olive oil, pepper and cloves, then cover with a lid and cook over a medium heat for 30 minutes, or until the vegetables are soft, but still hold their shape. During cooking, keep checking the potatoes. Once the potatoes start to get soft, add all the fish in layers, finishing with the sardines on top. As you add the fish, season each with salt and a pinch of pepper. Cover with the lid and cook for a further 15–20 minutes, or until all the fish is cooked. Transfer all the fish to a serving dish and keep warm.

Add the pasta to the pot and cook in the fish and vegetable juices for 8–10 minutes, or until tender but firm to the bite.

Serve the cooked pasta alongside the fish and vegetables.

Largehead Hairtail with Banana

....

Peixe Espada com Banana   ♡ Madeira

Known as just *espada* in Madeira, black scabbard is a fish species living in the great depths of the Atlantic Ocean. It has an elongated, eel-like body, with a pinkish-white meat that is delicate and tender. *Espada* is a regional delicacy in Madeira, and in this recipe is dipped into a batter made of flour and eggs, then fried until crisp and golden on the outside. You would usually find pieces of fried banana being served with this dish — a small, sweet variety that grows in the southern part of the island.

Preparation time: 20 minutes
Cooking time: 25 minutes
Serves: 4

1 kg/2 lb 4 oz largehead hairtail fish
2 garlic cloves, peeled and finely chopped
juice of 1 lemon
plain (all-purpose) flour, for dusting
3 eggs
500 ml/17 fl oz (2 cups) sunflower oil, for frying
120 g/4 oz (8 tablespoons) unsalted butter
4 bananas, peeled but left whole
1 head butterhead lettuce, leaves separated
30 ml/1 fl oz (2 tablespoons) extra virgin olive oil
10 ml/2 teaspoons white wine vinegar
sea salt and freshly ground black pepper

Cut the fins off the largehead hairtail fish, then remove the skin and cut the fish into medium-size fillets. Put the fish fillets into a large dish and season with the garlic, lemon juice, salt and pepper, then mix well until the fish is well coated.

Spread the flour out on a large plate and lightly whisk the eggs in a medium bowl.

Line a large baking sheet with paper towels. Heat enough sunflower oil for shallow-frying in a large frying pan or skillet over a medium–high heat until it reaches 160°C/325°F on a thermometer.

Dip a fish fillet into the flour shaking off any excess and then dip into the beaten eggs. Working in batches, carefully lower the fish into the hot oil and fry for 3–4 minutes on each side, or until golden all over. Remove from the oil and leave to drain on the lined baking sheet. Repeat with the remaining fish.

Heat the butter in a medium frying pan or skillet over a medium heat until melted. Add the bananas to the pan and fry for 2 minutes on all sides, or until golden all over. Remove from the oil and leave to drain on the lined baking sheet.

Put the lettuce leaves into a salad bowl, dress with the olive oil and vinegar, then season with salt. Toss to coat all the leaves.

Serve the fish with the bananas and dressed lettuce leaves alongside.

Mackerel with Oregano and Shallots

••

Cavala com Molho de Vilão   ♡ Madeira

Cavala (mackerel) is an abundant fish in
Portuguese waters but, because it is very cheap
for Portuguese fishermen, it is either used for
canning or for tuna fattening. But while this is the
fish's destiny in some parts of mainland Portugal,
in Madeira it is turned into a delicacy. Across
the archipelago, this oily and flavourful fish finds
its way into several dishes, such as here where it
is fried and marinated in *molho de vilão* (literally
meaning 'villain sauce'). Locals also use this
slightly spicy sauce to complement tuna steaks
or fried fish.

Preparation time: 20 minutes, plus 3 hours chilling
Cooking time: 35 minutes
Serves: 4
🪰 ⬠

4 medium mackerel
3 garlic cloves, peeled and finely chopped
3 teaspoons dried oregano
½ bunch thyme, leaves picked
2 red chillies, finely chopped
300 ml/10 fl oz (1¼ cups) white wine
120 ml/4 fl oz (½ cup) white wine vinegar
750 g/1 lb 10 oz waxy potatoes, peeled
350 ml/12 fl oz (1½ cups) sunflower oil, for shallow-frying
sea salt

Clean the mackerel, removing the scales. Using
a sharp knife, make an incision in the belly and
remove the guts and bloodline, then rinse under
cold running water. Cut the mackerel into 4 pieces
and put into a large dish. Add the garlic, oregano,
thyme, chillies, white wine and vinegar to the
mackerel, then turn the fish until they are coated all
over. Cover with food wrap and chill in the fridge
for 3 hours.

Remove the mackerel from the marinade and
set the marinade aside, then leave the fish on a
perforated tray or in a colander to drip to remove
any excess liquid.

Put the potatoes into a large saucepan, cover
with cold water, add a pinch of salt and cook over
a medium heat for 15–20 minutes, or until soft.
Drain and set aside.

Meanwhile, line a large baking sheet with paper
towels. Heat enough sunflower oil for shallow-frying
in a large saucepan over a high heat until it reaches
180°C/350°F on a thermometer. Add the fish and
shallow-fry for 3–4 minutes on each side, or until
golden all over. Remove with a fish slice (spatula)
and leave to drain on the lined baking sheet.

Pour the reserved marinade into a saucepan
and bring to the boil over a medium heat. Taste
and adjust the seasoning, if necessary.

Pour the sauce over the mackerel before serving
alongside the boiled potatoes.

Boiled Peeled Horse Mackerel

••

Carapaus Alimados   ♡ Algarve

Carapaus (horse mackerel) has long been,
alongside sardines, one of the most consumed
types of seafood in the Algarve. For centuries,
however, the only way that locals could eat it in
the best condition was to get it salt-cured, with
transportation from the coast to the interior done
by donkeys or bicycle. Preserved that way, the
flesh would be firm and tastier. In this recipe,
carapaus are first salt-cured, and then 'alimado',
which means removing the skin and bones
completely. They are then generously seasoned
with olive oil, vinegar or lemon and plenty of
slivered or crushed garlic, with onion and parsley
often added for extra flavour.

Preparation time: 30 minutes, plus 12 hours chilling
Cooking time: 5 minutes
Serves: 4
⬠ ⬠

1 kg/2 lb 4 oz horse mackerel
2 onions, peeled and very finely sliced
2 garlic cloves, peeled and very finely sliced
250 ml/8 fl oz (1 cup) extra virgin olive oil
200 ml/7 fl oz (¾ cup) white wine vinegar
⅓ bunch flat-leaf parsley, chopped
sea salt
sliced bread, toasted, to serve

Clean the mackerel, removing the scales. Cut off
the head and set aside. Using a sharp knife, make
an incision in the belly and remove the guts and
bloodline, then rinse under cold running water.
Sprinkle some salt over the fish, put into a large
dish, cover with food wrap and leave in the fridge
for 12 hours.

The next day, rinse the fish under cold running
water. Line a large plate or rimmed baking sheet
with paper towels and have a large bowl of cold
water nearby. Bring a large saucepan of water
to the boil, add the mackerel and cook for 2–3
minutes over a medium heat. Don't overcook them.
Remove from the heat and put the fish straight into
the bowl of cold water to cool. Remove the skins
and top bone with your fingers under the water,
then place the fish on the lined plate to dry.

Transfer the fish to a large serving plate, scatter
the onions and garlic over the fish, then pour over
the olive oil and vinegar. Garnish the fish with the
chopped parsley and serve with the toast.

Mackerel with Tomatoes

Cavalas com Tomate ⦿ p.143 ♡ Alentejo

Preparation time: 30 minutes
Cooking time: 45 minutes
Serves 4
🐟 ⬚

4 mackerel
700 g/1 lb 9 oz ripe tomatoes
2 onions, peeled and finely chopped
4 garlic cloves, peeled and finely chopped
120 ml/4 fl oz (½ cup) olive oil
1 green (bell) pepper, halved, cored, de-seeded
    and cut into strips
½ bunch flat-leaf parsley, finely chopped
½ bunch oregano, finely chopped
2 bay leaves
350 ml/12 fl oz (1½ cups) white wine
sea salt and freshly cracked black pepper

Clean the mackerel, removing the scales. Cut off
the heads and discard. Using a sharp knife, make
an incision in the bellies, then rinse under cold
running water. Cut the fish into three pieces.
Set aside.

Have a large bowl of iced water nearby. Bring
a saucepan of water to the boil. Using a sharp knife,
score the top of the tomatoes with a small cross
shape. Once boiling, carefully add the tomatoes
and blanch for 30 seconds, then transfer them with
a slotted spoon to the iced water and leave to cool.
Once cool, peel off the skins, cut in half and de-
seed, then cut the tomatoes into medium cubes.
Set aside.

Put the onions, garlic and olive oil into a large
saucepan and cook over a medium heat for
15 minutes, or until the onions are golden. Add the
tomato cubes and (bell) pepper strips, then add
the chopped parsley, oregano and bay leaves and
cook for 20 minutes, until very soft.

Season the mackerels with salt and cracked
black pepper, add them to the tomato stew and
mix to combine. Pour in the white wine, then
reduce the heat to low and cook for 15 minutes,
or until the fish separates easily from the bones.

Taste and adjust the seasoning with salt, if
necessary, before serving.

Air-dried Horse Mackerel from Nazaré

Peixe Seco da Nazaré ♡ Leiria

This is an old tradition of curing fish. It has always
been prepared by women on the sandy beaches
of Nazaré, while the men go out to sea to catch
the fish. The women clean, gut and butterfly all
the small fish, such as sardines, anchovies and
horse mackerel with their hands. For larger fish,
they use a knife, then wash all the fish in seawater.
The smaller fish are then salted, hung on a special
stand and sun-dried on the beach for three days.
They can be eaten raw. The larger fish are usually
salted for 3 or 4 days, then hung and left to
sun-dry. These fish are either grilled or boiled
after desalting, much like salt cod, and should
not be eaten raw. The most common fish are
sardines, mackerel, horse mackerel, skate wings,
dogfish, octopus and sea bream. 'Enjoado'
means sick in English and it is fish that has been
hung and sun-dried for a couple of hours in the
morning. These are common in the Peixeiras.

Preparation time: 10 minutes
Cooking time: 30 minutes
Serves: 4
🐟 ⬚ ✕

600 g/1 lb 5 oz baby new potatoes
4 horse mackerel, sun-dried from Nazaré
120 ml/4 fl oz (½ cup) olive oil
20 ml/¾ fl oz (4 teaspoons) vinegar

Prepare a barbecue or preheat the indoor grill
(broiler).

Put the potatoes into a large saucepan, cover
with cold water and cook over a medium heat for
15–20 minutes, or until soft.

As soon as the barbecue coals are glowing, put
the mackerel on the grill rack, skin side down, and
grill for 8–10 minutes, or until the skin is golden.
As the skin of the fish can burn easily, it is better
to keep it some distance from the hot coals.
Alternatively, cook under the grill. Flip the fish
onto a baking sheet, skin side up, and leave to rest.

Drain the potatoes, then cut them into quarters.
Drizzle the fish with the olive and vinegar and serve
alongside the boiled potatoes.

Mackerel with Tomatoes

Poached Mackerel with Oregano and Potatoes

Cavalas Salgadas   ⛉ Madeira
Cozidas com Oregãos   📷 p.145

Preparation time: 30 minutes, plus 1 day marinating and
2 hours soaking
Cooking time: 45 minutes
Serves: 4
🐟 ⛉

4 medium mackerel
3 garlic cloves, peeled
3 tablespoons dried oregano
700 g/1 lb 9 oz small waxy potatoes, peeled and
    left whole
2 bay leaves
sea salt

For the sauce:
3 garlic cloves, peeled and finely chopped
100 ml/3½ fl oz (⅓ cup) olive oil
40 ml/1⅓ fl oz (2⅔ tablespoons) white wine vinegar
1½ tablespoons chopped flat-leaf parsley
freshly ground black pepper

Clean the mackerel by making an incision in the
belly with a sharp knife and removing the guts, then
rinse under cold running water. Using a sharp knife,
butterfly the fish and score them on the flesh side
without breaking the skin. Put the mackerel into
a large dish.

Put the garlic into a mortar with 160 g/5½ oz
(⅔ cup) salt and the oregano and, using a pestle,
mash to a paste. Rub the paste over the fish, then
cover with food wrap and leave to marinate in the
fridge for 1 day.

The next day, rinse the fish under cold running
water, then put into a large bowl, cover with cold
water and leave to soak for 2 hours.

Put the potatoes into a large saucepan, cover
with cold water, add a pinch of salt and cook over
a medium heat for 15–20 minutes, or until soft.
Drain and set aside.

Bring a medium saucepan of water to the boil,
then add the mackerel and bay leaves, reduce the
heat to low and cook for 25 minutes, or until the
flesh flakes easily. Using a fish slice (spatula) put the
fish onto a serving dish.

For the sauce, put the garlic, olive oil, vinegar
and parsley into a small bowl, season with pepper
and mix together.

Pour the sauce over the fish before serving
with the boiled potatoes.

Fried Horse Mackerel with Onion Sauce

Carapaus Fritos com Molho   ⛉ Ribatejo
de Cebola do Cartaxo

Preparation time: 25 minutes
Cooking time: 30–40 minutes
Serves: 5
⛉

1.6 kg/3 lb 8 oz horse mackerel
olive oil, for deep-frying
60 ml/2 fl oz (4 tablespoons) white wine vinegar
2 bay leaves
120 ml/4 fl oz (½ cup) olive oil
3 onions, peeled and thinly sliced
6 garlic cloves, peeled and thinly sliced
25 g/1 oz (2 tablespoons) plain (all-purpose) flour
1 bunch breakfast radishes, halved lengthwise
sea salt
⅓ bunch flat-leaf parsley, roughly chopped, to garnish

Clean the mackerel, removing the hard long scale
on both sides of the loins, making an incision in
the belly and removing the guts. Rinse under cold
running water, then leave to drip on a perforated
tray or in a colander. Season the fish with salt.

Line a large baking sheet with paper towels.
Heat enough olive oil for deep-frying in a large,
deep saucepan or fryer over a high heat until it
reaches 180°C/350°F on a thermometer. Working
in batches, carefully lower the mackerel into the
hot oil and deep-fry for 8–10 minutes, or until
golden. Remove the mackerel from the oil with
a slotted spoon and leave to drain on the lined
baking sheet. Put the fish into a large serving dish
and set aside.

Put 50 ml/1⅔ fl oz (3½ tablespoons) water,
the vinegar and bay leaves into a medium bowl
and whisk until well combined.

Heat the 120 ml/4 fl oz (½ cup) olive oil in a
saucepan over a medium heat, add the onions and
garlic and cook for 15 minutes, or until the onions
are golden. Add the water and vinegar mixture and
flour and cook for a further 5 minutes, or until the
sauce has thickened. Season with a pinch of salt.

Pour the sauce over the fish. Arrange the
radishes around the fish on the serving dish, then
garnish with the parsley before serving.

Poached Mackerel with Oregano and Potato

Fried Baby Horse Mackerel with Verjus Sauce

Joaquinzinhos de Agraço / Chicharros de Agraço 📷 p.147   ⛶ Açores

Preparation time: 20 minutes, plus 20 minutes standing
Cooking time: 25 minutes
Serves 4
🐟 ⛶

1.2 kg/2 lb 11 oz baby horse mackerel
cornflour (cornstarch), for coating
2 onions, peeled and finely chopped
4 garlic cloves, peeled and finely chopped
1 *pimenta da terra* or a red long pepper, de-seeded and
    finely chopped
150 ml/5 fl oz (⅔ cup) white wine vinegar
⅓ bunch flat-leaf parsley, finely chopped
220 ml/7½ fl oz (1 cup) olive oil
sea salt

Clean the mackerel, removing the scales. Cut off the head and set aside. Using a sharp knife, make an incision in the belly and remove the guts, then rinse the fish under cold running water and leave to drip on a perforated tray or in a colander. Season the fish with salt.

Preheat the oven to 220°C/425°F/Gas Mark 7. Place a clay baking tray (pan) or a baking sheet in the oven to heat up.

Dust the mackerel with cornflour (cornstarch), shaking off any excess. Place the fish on the hot baking tray or sheet and cook for 20–25 minutes, or until lightly golden. Remove the mackerel from the baking tray or sheet and set aside.

Meanwhile, combine the onions, garlic and pepper together in a large bowl, then season with salt and add the vinegar. Set aside for 10 minutes.

Add the chopped parsley and olive oil to the bowl, then stir thoroughly to combine.

Arrange the fish on a serving plate and pour the sauce over the top. Leave to stand for 10 minutes before serving.

Fried Baby Horse Mackerel Topped with Garlic

Carapaus Fritos Ressoados 📷 p.149   ⛶ Leiria

Ressoados is a term for 'leaving', in this case, leaving the fish to sweat in the pan with the lid on.

Preparation time: 20 minutes, plus 2 days standing
Cooking time: 30 minutes
Serves: 6
🐟 ⛶ ⛶

1.8 kg/4 lb baby horse mackerel
1 litre/34 fl oz (4¼ cups) olive oil
10 garlic cloves, peeled and finely chopped
4 bay leaves, torn in half
150 ml/5 fl oz (⅔ cup) vinegar
sea salt
Cornbread (page 32), to serve

Two days before, clean the mackerel, removing the scales. Cut off the head and set aside. Using a sharp knife, make an incision in the belly and remove the guts, then rinse the fish under cold running water and leave to drip on a perforated tray or in a colander. Season the fish with salt.

Heat enough olive oil for deep-frying in a large, deep saucepan or fryer over a high heat until it reaches 180°C/350°F on a thermometer. Working in batches, carefully lower the fish into the hot oil and fry for 8–10 minutes, or until golden. Remove the mackerel from the oil with a fish slice (spatula) and put straight into a clay pot or glass container. Scatter over the garlic and bay leaves and pour in the vinegar. While still hot, cover with a lid and leave to stand for 2 days.

When ready to eat, serve the mackerel alongside the cornbread.

Fried Baby Horse Mackerel with Verjus Sauce

Sardines Baked
on a Clay Roof Tile

••

Sardinhas na Telha   ♡ Beira Litoral

For this recipe, it is essential to have a couple
of unglazed clay pantiles or curved roof tiles,
which are used for baking the sardines.

Preparation time: 20 minutes, plus 30 minutes salting and
1 hour infusing
Cooking time: 1 hour
Serves: 4
🦐 🗋

1.3 kg/3 lb sardines
200 ml/7 fl oz (¾ cup) olive oil
4 garlic cloves, unpeeled and crushed
700 g/1 lb 9 oz small waxy potatoes, unpeeled and
    left whole
600 g/1 lb 5 oz onions, unpeeled
250 g/9 oz (2 cups) fine polenta (cornmeal)
sea salt

Clean the sardines, removing the scales. Using
a sharp knife, make an incision in the belly and
remove the guts, then rinse under cold running
water. Season the sardines with salt at least
30 minutes before cooking them.
    Heat the olive oil in a medium saucepan over
a low heat, add the garlic and cook gently just
enough to warm the oil, then remove from the heat
and leave to infuse at room temperature for 1 hour.
    Preheat the oven to 180°C/350°F/Gas Mark 4.
    Put the potatoes into a large roasting pan and
sprinkle them with salt. Roast in the hot oven for
35 minutes, or until soft. At the same time, put the
onions into another roasting pan and roast them
alongside the potatoes until cooked. Remove
both pans from the oven and gently 'punch' each
potato with your fist. Peel off the onion skins, then
add them to the potatoes, mix to combine, then
keep warm.
    Put the polenta (cornmeal) into a shallow dish.
Brush two clay pantiles or roof tiles with the garlic-
infused olive oil, then rub the tiles with the garlic
cloves. Dip the sardines into the oil, then into the
polenta to coat and place on the roof tiles. Bake
in the hot oven for 15–20 minutes, or until cooked
and lightly golden.
    Serve the sardines alongside the potatoes
and onions.

Cured Sardines Grilled
with Pine Needles

••

Sardinhas na Telha com Caruma   ♡ Leiria

This recipe is one I have always wanted to try
as my grandmother used to cook this for my
father, although I never understood why he liked
it so much. But after making this dish, I finally
understood. The flavour of the pine needles
infusing the fish is simply superb. A few years ago,
I was inspired by this unusual method of cooking,
using sardines and green pine needles instead of
dried and serving them with pine nuts and vinegar.
Rather than using old oval roof tiles, I used a heavy
iron saucepan with a lid, but you could also use
a large frying pan or skillet, or a saucepan.

Preparation time: 15 minutes, plus 2–3 days curing
Cooking time: 15 minutes
Serves: 4
🦐 🗋 ✕

1.2 kg/2 lb 11 oz sardines
dried pine needles
fine sea salt
100 ml/3½ fl oz (⅓ cup) olive oil, for drizzling
500 g/1 lb 2 oz Cornbread (page 32), to serve

Clean the sardines, removing the scales. Using
a sharp knife, make an incision in the belly and
remove the guts, then rinse under cold running
water. Put the sardines into a large shallow dish
and salt them with a generous amount of fine sea
salt. Cover with food wrap and leave to cure in the
fridge for 2–3 days, depending on their size.
    When ready to cook, prepare a barbecue or
preheat the indoor grill (broiler).
    Rinse the sardines under cold running water to
remove the excess salt, then pat dry with a clean
tea (dish) towel or paper towels. Set aside.
    Cover the bottom of two clay pantiles or roof
tiles with dried pine needles and arrange the
sardines on top in a single layer. Make sure they
are laying flat and not overlapping. Cover the
sardines with more dried pine needles.
    As soon as the barbecue coals are glowing, lay
the roof tiles on the grill rack and grill the sardines
for 15 minutes, or until the flesh flakes easily.
The moisture in the sardines combined with the
heat of the coals will produce smoke, which will
help to cook the fish. Remove the sardines once
cooked and discard the pine needles.
    Drizzle the sardines with the olive oil and serve
alongside the cornbread.

Fried Baby Horse Mackerel Topped with Garlic (recipe p.146)

Fried Crumbled Sardines

Sardinhas Fritas Panadas   ♡ Minho

Preparation time: 30 minutes
Cooking time: 25 minutes
Serves: 4
▢

1 kg/2 lb 4 oz fresh sardines
800 ml/27 fl oz (3¼ cups) olive oil, for shallow-frying
350 g/12 oz (3 cups) plain (all-purpose) flour
4 eggs
400 g/14 oz (8 cups) breadcrumbs
3 bunches flat-leaf parsley, leaves picked
sea salt
2 lemons, cut into wedges, to serve

Clean the sardines, removing the scales. Cut off the head and tail and discard. Using a sharp knife, make an incision in the belly and remove the guts. Butterfly the fish by removing the central bone and opening it out like a book. Sprinkle them with salt.

Line a baking sheet with paper towels. Heat the oil in a frying pan or skillet until it reaches 160°C/325°F on a thermometer. Put the flour into a bowl, whisk the eggs in a second bowl and put the breadcrumbs in third bowl. Dip each sardine first in flour, then in beaten egg and lastly in breadcrumbs to coat. Repeat this twice for each sardine. Working in batches, lower the fish into the hot oil and fry for 5–6 minutes, or until golden. Remove from the oil and leave to drain on the lined baking sheet.

Add the parsley leaves to the hot oil and fry for 5 seconds, or until crispy. Remove from the oil and leave to drain on the lined baking sheet.

Serve the sardines with the fried parsley leaves and lemon wedges for squeezing.

Fish Stew

Caldeirada de Peixe   ♡ Algarve

Preparation time: 20 minutes
Cooking time: 50 minutes
Serves: 6
🐟▢▢

600 g/1 lb 5 oz fresh sardines
450 g/1 lb horse mackerel
400 g/14 oz skate wings
500 g/1 lb 2 oz monkfish (flounder) tail
130 ml/4½ fl oz (½ cup) olive oil
400 g/14 oz ripe tomatoes, cut into medium-thick slices
3 onions, peeled and thinly sliced
3 garlic cloves, peeled and thinly sliced
1½ red (bell) peppers, de-seeded and cut into strips
700 g/1 lb 9 oz waxy potatoes, peeled and sliced
2 bay leaves
⅓ bunch flat-leaf parsley, roughly chopped
1 teaspoon dried oregano
sea salt and freshly ground white pepper

Clean all the fish, removing the scales, if necessary. Using a sharp knife, make an incision in the belly and remove the guts. Cut the skate wings and monkfish (flounder) tail into chunks. Season the fish with salt and pepper, then set aside.

Arrange all the ingredients in a saucepan in layers, starting with the olive oil, then the tomatoes, onions, garlic, red (bell) peppers, potatoes, bay leaves, parsley, oregano and fish. Repeat until all the ingredients are used up. Cover with a lid and cook over a low heat for 50 minutes, or until the fish is cooked. Do not stir during cooking. Gently shake the pan occasionally, if necessary. Serve immediately.

Fisherman's Fish Stew

Caldeirada à Pescador   ♡ Ribatejo

If you have time, make a light stock with the skin and bones leftover from the fish and use it instead of water when cooking this stew. Not only will it make a flavourful dish, it also reduces food waste.

Preparation time: 30 minutes, plus 12 hours soaking
Cooking time: 1 hour
Serves: 6
▢▢

500 g/1 lb 2 oz fresh palorde clams
800 g/1 lb 12 oz allis shad (*Alosa alosa*)
800 g/1 lb 12 oz flathead grey mullet
1 kg/2 lb 4 oz river langoustines
4 onions, peeled and cut into rings
3 garlic cloves, peeled and sliced
2 bay leaves
⅓ bunch flat-leaf parsley, chopped
120 ml/4 fl oz (½ cup) olive oil
1 teaspoon paprika
600 g/1 lb 5 oz ripe tomatoes, quartered
200 g/7 oz bread, sliced
sea salt and freshly ground black pepper

Make a brine with cold water and 1% fine sea salt, pour it over the clams in a bowl and leave to soak for 12 hours, so they release any sand and grit.

The next day, prepare the allis shad and mullet, cutting them into medium-sized pieces. Rinse the langoustines under cold running water. Set aside.

Arrange the onions and garlic in a layer in the bottom of a large clay pot with the bay leaves and parsley. Drizzle with olive oil, then add the paprika and season with salt and pepper. Cook over a medium heat for 15 minutes, or until the onions start to soften. Add the tomatoes, fish and langoustines along with 1.5 litres/50 fl oz (6¼ cups) water. Cover with a lid and cook over a low heat for 35–40 minutes, or until the fish is cooked. Add the clams, but do not stir, then increase the heat to medium, cover with the lid, shake the pot and cook for 5 minutes, or until the clams open. Taste and adjust the seasoning.

Arrange the slices of bread on a large serving plate or dish and pour over the stew.

Stewed Baby Sardines with Potatoes and Tomatoes (recipe p.152)

Stewed Baby Sardines with Potatoes and Tomatoes

••

Caldeirada de Petingas 📷 p.151 ⛉ Beira Litoral

You can find different kinds of this iconic Portuguese cooking method used with other types of seafood as well as river fish, saltwater fish, or even combined freshwater and saltwater fish. Sardines usually take a year to become adults, so catching too many baby sardines has a big impact on the fish stock, so much so that this dish is now very hard to find in restaurants. Nevertheless, I decided to include this recipe for when baby sardines are again allowed to be caught by fishermen.

Preparation time: 20 minutes
Cooking time: 1 hour
Serves: 6
🐟 ▢ ▢

1.5 kg/3 lb 5 oz baby sardines (or herring)
130 ml/4½ fl oz (½ cup) olive oil
3 onions, peeled and thinly sliced
2 bay leaves
2 bunches flat-leaf parsley, roughly chopped
1 kg/2 lb 4 oz oxheart tomatoes, thinly sliced
sea salt and freshly ground white pepper
6 slices Cornbread (page 32), to serve

Clean the sardines, removing the scales. Using a sharp knife, make an incision in the belly and remove the guts, then rinse under cold running water. Season the sardines with salt and set aside.

Heat the olive oil in a large saucepan over a medium heat, add the onions, bay leaves and parsley and cook for 12 minutes, or until the onions are translucent.

Add the tomatoes to the pan and cook for a further 15 minutes, or until the tomatoes start to break down. Add 250 ml/8 fl oz (1 cup) water and bring to the boil. Season with a pinch of salt and white pepper.

Add the fish to the pan, reduce the heat to low and cook gently for 15–20 minutes, or until soft.

Serve the sardine stew with cornbread.

Stewed Sardines with Potatoes, Tomatoes and Peppers

••

Caldeirada de Sardinhas 📷 p.153 ⛉ Leiria

Caldeirada (page 429) is a very popular dish on the west coast, Peniche being the most famous. This dish exists all around the world in coastal areas where access to fish is easy, such as bouillabaisse in Spain. It changes depending on who makes it, as some like to add potatoes while others leave out tomatoes or have no liquid at all, or water or wine or just the juices from the fish, but the key to a successful dish is the freshness of the fish. It must be extremely fresh.

Preparation time: 30 minutes
Cooking time: 40 minutes
Serves: 6
▢ ▢

1.8 kg/4 lb sardines
4 onions, peeled and thinly sliced
4 garlic cloves, peeled and thinly sliced
1 tablespoon paprika
6 waxy potatoes, peeled and thinly sliced
3 bull's heart tomatoes, thinly sliced
2 green (bell) peppers, cored, de-seeded and
    cut into thin strips
1 red chilli, halved
⅓ bunch flat-leaf parsley, roughly chopped
2 bay leaves
150 ml/5 fl oz (⅔ cup) olive oil
sea salt
6 slices sourdough bread, toasted, to serve

Clean the sardines, removing the scales. Using a sharp knife, make an incision in the belly and remove the guts, then rinse under cold running water. Leave the heads on. Season the sardines with salt and set aside.

Arrange the onions and garlic in a layer in the bottom of a large saucepan. Season with salt and paprika, then arrange the potatoes in a layer on top and season with salt and paprika. Spread the tomatoes in a layer on top and season with salt and paprika, then spread the (bell) peppers on top of the tomatoes and season again with salt and paprika. Add the chilli, parsley and bay leaves, then arrange the sardines in a layer on top and pour over the olive oil. Cover with a lid and cook over a medium heat for 40 minutes, or until the potatoes are soft. Do not stir during cooking, instead gently shake the pan occasionally, if necessary.

Taste and adjust the seasoning, if necessary, then serve the sardine stew with the toasted sourdough bread.

Stewed Sardines with Potatoes, Tomatoes and Peppers

Grilled Sardines on Cornbread with Tomato Salad

Sardinhas Assadas com Salada de Tomate   ⎵ Lisbon

It is best to eat these grilled fresh sardines over the cornbread, so that the juices from the fish soak into the bread, which can then be eaten on its own.

Preparation time: 15 minutes, plus 10 minutes salting
Cooking time: 15 minutes
Serves: 4
🌿 ⎵

1.2 kg/2 lb 11 oz fresh sardines
4 large bull's heart tomatoes, cut into chunks
250 ml/8 fl oz (1 cup) extra virgin olive oil
60 ml/2 fl oz (4 tablespoons) white wine vinegar or cider vinegar
1 quantity Cornbread, cut into thick slices (page 32)
sea salt

Prepare a barbecue with wood and charcoal or preheat an indoor grill (broiler).

Clean the sardines, removing the scales. Using a sharp knife, make an incision in the belly and remove the guts. Keep the heads on. Rinse the fish under cold running water and leave to drip on a perforated tray or in a colander.

Season the sardines with a generous amount of salt at least 10 minutes before cooking.

Put the tomatoes onto a large plate and season them with olive oil, vinegar and salt. Set aside.

As soon as the barbecue coals are glowing, put the cornbread directly onto the grill rack and grill for 2–3 minutes on each side, or until golden. Alternatively, cook under the grill. Set aside.

Put the sardines onto the grill rack and grill for 3–4 minutes on each side, or until crispy and golden all over. Alternatively, cook under the grill. Transfer the sardines to a plate and season with olive oil and vinegar.

Arrange the grilled cornbread on individual serving plates and pile the sardines on top. Serve the tomato salad alongside. The juices from the sardines will leech into the bread, so eat that last.

Grilled Sardines on Cornbread with Green Peppers

Sardinhas Assadas com Salada de Pimentos Assados   📷 p.155   ⎵ Leiria

When you gather a group of people together to eat grilled sardines with potatoes and salads, in Portuguese this is called *sardinhada*.

Preparation time: 15 minutes, plus 10 minutes salting and 15 minutes steaming
Cooking time: 35 minutes
Serves: 4
🌿 ⎵

1.2 kg/2 lb 11 oz fresh sardines
3 green (bell) peppers
80 ml/2¾ fl oz (⅓ cup) extra virigin olive oil
600 g/1 lb 5 oz small waxy potatoes, unpeeled and left whole
1 quantity Cornbread, cut into thick slices (page 32)
sea salt

Prepare a barbecue with wood and charcoal or preheat an indoor grill (broiler).

Clean the sardines, removing the scales. Using a sharp knife, make an incision in the belly and remove the guts. Keep the heads on. Rinse the fish under cold running water and leave to drip on a perforated tray or in a colander.

Season the sardines with a generous amount of salt at least 10 minutes before cooking.

As soon as the barbecue coals are glowing, put the (bell) peppers directly onto the grill rack and grill for 8–10 minutes, or until the skins are blackened and blistered. Alternatively, cook under the grill. Put them inside a plastic bag and leave to steam for 15 minutes. To remove the skins, rinse the peppers under cold running water, then cut in half and de-seed. Slice them into thin strips, put into a bowl and drizzle with some of the olive oil. Season with salt and set aside.

Put the potatoes into a large saucepan, cover with cold water, add a pinch of salt and cook over a low heat for 15–20 minutes, or until soft. Drain, put into a bowl and drizzle with some of the olive oil. Set aside.

Meanwhile, put the cornbread directly onto the grill rack and grill for 2–3 minutes on each side, or until golden. Alternatively, cook under the grill. Set aside.

Put the sardines onto the grill rack and grill for 3–4 minutes on each side, or until crispy and golden all over. Alternatively, cook under the grill.

Arrange the grilled cornbread on individual serving plates and pile the sardines on top. Serve the boiled potatoes and charred peppers alongside. The juices from the sardines will leech into the bread, so eat that last.

Grilled Sardines on Cornbread with Green Peppers

Grilled Sardines with Potato, Pepper and Cucumber Salad

••

Sardinhas Assadas com Salada de Pimentos, Pepino e Batata
◡ Lisbon

Preparation time: 20 minutes, plus 15 minutes standing
Cooking time: 35 minutes
Serves: 6
🔥 ◡

3 kg/6 lb 10 oz fresh sardines
1 kg/2 lb 4 oz red (bell) peppers
850 g/1 lb 14 oz baby round potatoes
6 cucumbers, cut in half lengthwise, then cut into chunks
1 onion, peeled and very thinly sliced
160 ml/5½ fl oz (⅔ cup) olive oil
50 ml/1⅔ fl oz (3½ tablespoons) white wine vinegar
fine sea salt

Clean the sardines, removing the scales. Season the fish with a generous amount of salt and leave on a wire rack, perforated tray or in a colander.

Prepare a barbecue or preheat an indoor grill (broiler). As soon as the barbecue coals are glowing, put the (bell) peppers directly onto the grill rack and grill for 8 minutes, or until the skins are blackened and blistered. Alternatively, cook under the grill. Put them inside a plastic bag and leave to steam for 15 minutes. To remove the skins, rinse the peppers under cold running water, then cut in half and de-seed. Slice them into thin strips, put into a large serving dish and set aside.

Put the potatoes into a saucepan of salted water and cook over a medium heat for 15–20 minutes, or until soft. Drain, cut in half and add to the serving dish with the peppers. Add the cucumbers and onion, then toss everything together. Season with salt, drizzle with olive oil and vinegar and toss again.

Put the sardines directly on the grill rack and grill for 3 minutes on each side. Alternatively cook under the grill. Serve alongside the salad.

Shrivelled Skate Wings

••

Raia Enxanbrada – Figueira da Foz
◡ Beira Litoral 📷 p.157

Preparation time: 15 minutes, plus 1 hour 30 minutes drying
Cooking time: 35 minutes
Serves: 4
🔥 ◡

1.2 kg/2 lb 11 oz skate wings, cleaned and rinsed with skin on
600 g/1 lb 5 oz waxy potatoes, unpeeled and left whole
90 ml/3 fl oz (6 tablespoons) olive oil
2 small garlic cloves, peeled and very finely chopped
35 ml/1¼ fl oz (2⅓ tablespoons) white wine vinegar
sea salt and freshly ground black pepper

Salt the skate and hang them in a dry place for at least 1 hour 30 minutes, or until they start to dry out.

Preheat the oven to 180°C/350°F/Gas Mark 4 and prepare a barbecue.

Put the potatoes into a roasting pan and sprinkle with salt. Roast in the hot oven for 35 minutes. Remove from the oven and gently 'punch' each potato with your fist. Drizzle over some olive oil.

Meanwhile, as soon as the barbecue coals are glowing, put the skate wings on the grill rack and grill for 4–5 minutes on each side, or until golden. Flake the skate into a serving dish, removing any bones. Season with the chopped garlic, then drizzle with the olive oil and vinegar and toss.

Season the fish with pepper before serving with the 'punched' potatoes.

Skate Wings in Liver Sauce

••

Raia de Pitau
◡ Beira Litoral

Created by fishermen on the coastal strip between Figueira da Foz and Espinho, *Raia de Pitau* is a dish of skate in a sauce made of its own liver. Because the skate's flesh is firm, lean and with a mild flavour, the liver sauce — which includes paprika, vinegar and garlic — brings a savoury, pungent addition to this dish. In restaurants in the coastal area of the Coimbra district, it is commonly paired with a platter of boiled potatoes.

Preparation time: 15 minutes, plus 45 minutes standing
Cooking time: 20 minutes
Serves: 4
🔥 ◡

800 g/1 lb 12 oz skate wings, cleaned and rinsed with skin on
650 g/1 lb 7 oz waxy potatoes, unpeeled and left whole
50 g/2 oz skate wing liver
100 ml/3½ fl oz (⅓ cup) olive oil
25 ml/1 fl oz (2 tablespoons) white vinegar
5 garlic cloves, peeled and finely chopped
1 bay leaf
1 teaspoon paprika
sea salt and freshly ground black pepper

Salt the skate and leave to stand for 45 minutes. Put the skate into a saucepan of salted water and cook over a medium heat for 10 minutes, or until the skin lifts easily. Remove the skin. Cut the wings vertically into pieces, about 2 cm/¾ inch thick. Set aside with a little of the fish cooking liquid.

Put the potatoes into a saucepan of salted water and cook over a low heat for 15–20 minutes, or until soft. Drain and peel off the skins. Set aside.

Mash the liver in a bowl with a fork. Put the remaining ingredients into a saucepan and cook over a low heat for 5 minutes. Add the liver with a little of the reserved cooking liquid and cook for a further 5 minutes, or until thick. Season to taste.

Place the skate on a serving platter and arrange the potatoes around the fish. Pour the liver sauce over the top before serving.

Shrivelled Skate Wings

Eel Stew

•••

Caldeirada de Eirós   ⋃ Algarve

Preparation time: 35 minutes
Cooking time 50 minutes
Serves: 4
⋂

1.2 kg/2 lb 11 oz eel
1.2 kg/2 lb 11 oz wild sea bream
600 g/1 lb 5 oz ripe tomatoes
160 ml/5½ fl oz (⅔ cup) olive oil
600 g/1 lb 5 oz onions, peeled and sliced into thin rings
4 garlic cloves, peeled and thinly sliced
2 bird's eye chillies, halved
1 bay leaf
1.5 kg/3 lb 5 oz waxy potatoes, peeled and quartered
200 g/7 oz (1¼ cups) peas
1 red (bell) pepper, de-seeded and cut into strips
1 green (bell) pepper, de-seeded and cut into strips
300 g/11 oz palourde clams, cleaned (page 184)
450 ml/15 fl oz (1¾ cups) beer
slices bread, to serve

Clean the eel, removing the head and guts, then cut into medium-sized pieces. Clean the fish, removing the scales. Cut off the head and set aside. Using a sharp knife, make an incision in the belly and remove the guts and bloodline, then cut the fish into large chunks. Set aside.

Have a large bowl of iced water nearby. Bring a large saucepan of water to the boil. Using a sharp knife, score the top of the tomatoes with a small cross shape. Once the water is boiling, carefully add the tomatoes and blanch for 30 seconds, then transfer them with a slotted spoon to the iced water and leave to cool. Once cool enough to handle, peel off the skins, cut in half and de-seed, then cut the flesh into chunks. Set aside.

Heat the olive oil in a saucepan over a low heat, add the onions and garlic and cook for 10 minutes, or until golden. Add the tomatoes and cook for a further 5 minutes. Season with salt, then add the chillies, bay leaf, potatoes and peas. Add enough water to cover and cook for 8 minutes.

Add the fish, eel, (bell) peppers, clams and beer to the pan and cook gently for 25 minutes, or until the fish is cooked and the clams have opened.

Taste and adjust the seasoning, if necessary, then serve with bread.

Eel Stew — Aveiro Style

•••

Caldeirada de Enguias   ⋃ Beira Litoral
à Moda de Aveiro

Preparation time: 20 minutes
Cooking time: 1 hour
Serves: 6
⋂ ⋂

1.5 kg/3 lb 5 oz medium eels, not too thick
5 onions, peeled and sliced into medium-thick rings
600 g/1 lb 5 oz potatoes, peeled and cut into
    3-cm/1¼-inch slices
6 garlic cloves, peeled and sliced
1 tablespoon paprika
1 teaspoon saffron threads
2 bunches flat-leaf parsley, roughly chopped
200 g/7 oz lardo, cured in salt, thinly sliced
120 ml/4 fl oz (½ cup) olive oil
40 ml/1⅓ fl oz (2⅔ tablespoons) white wine vinegar
sea salt and freshly ground black pepper
bread, to serve

Gut and clean the eels. Remove and discard the heads. Rinse thoroughly in cold running water. Cut the eels into medium-sized pieces and set aside.

Arrange a layer of the onions in a saucepan, add a layer of potatoes, then garlic, then eels and season with salt, paprika, saffron and parsley. Repeat until all the ingredients are used up. Arrange the lardo over the top. Drizzle the olive oil over and pour in 400 ml/14 fl oz (1⅔ cups) water. Cover the pan with a lid and cook over a low heat for 1 hour.

Once cooked, remove the lardo from the top and put into a mortar. Add ½ teaspoon of salt and the vinegar and, using a pestle, mash to a paste. Dilute with 2 ladlefuls of the stock from the pan.

Strain the remaining stock from the pan and serve with slices of bread. Pour the sauce made with the lardo over the eels before serving.

Stewed Eels with Bread

•••

Ensopado de Enguias à Ribatejana   ⋃ Ribatejo

Preparation time: 30 minutes
Cooking time: 1 hour 15 minutes
Serves: 4
⋂

1 kg/2 lb 4 oz large eel
120 ml/4 fl oz (½ cup) extra virgin olive oil, plus extra for
    shallow-frying
60 g/2¼ oz lard (pork fat)
2 onions, peeled and cut into rings
½ bunch flat-leaf parsley, roughly chopped
⅓ bunch marjoram, leaves picked
2 bay leaves
2 garlic cloves, peeled and thinly sliced
2 teaspoons white wine vinegar
1 teaspoon sweet paprika
300 g/11 oz sourdough bread, thicky sliced
sea salt and freshly ground black pepper

Gut and clean the eel. Remove and discard the head. Rinse thoroughly in cold running water. Cut the eel into small pieces and season with salt.

Heat the olive oil and lard (pork fat) in a large saucepan over a low heat, add the onions and cook for 12 minutes, or until golden. Add the parsley, marjoram, bay leaves, garlic and eels and mix together to combine all the ingredients.

Put the vinegar into a small bowl, add the paprika and stir to combine, then add to the pan and mix well. Pour in enough water to cover the ingredients and cook over a medium heat for 1 hour, or until the eels are soft.

Meanwhile, heat some olive oil in a frying pan or skillet over a medium heat. Add the bread and fry for 10–15 minutes, or until golden on both sides.

Taste the stewed eels and adjust the seasoning, if necessary. Arrange the fried bread in a large serving dish and pour over the eels before serving.

Poached and Steamed Eels — Mira Style

••

Enguias Suadas de Mira ♡ **Beira Litoral**

Preparation time: 20 minutes
Cooking time: 45 minutes
Serves: 4
◻

1.3 kg/3 lb small eels
½ teaspoon paprika
20 ml/¾ fl oz (4 teaspoons) white wine vinegar
25 g/1 oz lard (pork fat)
1 large white onion, peeled and finely chopped
350 ml/12 fl oz (1½ cups) white wine
2 bunches flat-leaf parsley, roughly chopped
600 g/1 lb 5 oz new potatoes, unpeeled
sea salt and freshly ground black pepper
4 slices sourdough bread, toasted, to serve

Clean the eels, removing the guts. Remove and discard the head. Rinse the eels a few times under cold running water.

Mix together the paprika add vinegar in a small bowl.

Put the eels into a large saucepan with the lard (pork fat), onion, white wine, parsley and the paprika and vinegar mixture. Cover with a lid and bring to the boil over a medium heat. As soon as it is boiling, reduce the heat to low and cook for 40 minutes, stirring occasionally.

Meanwhile, put the potatoes into a large saucepan of salted water and cook over a medium heat for 15–20 minutes, or until soft. Drain the potatoes just before serving.

Serve the cooked eels with the toasted sourdough bread and boiled potatoes alongside.

Fried Eels

••

Enguias Fritas ♡ **Leiria**

Often called Portugal's sea snake, eels are a delicacy in the country, especially in the town of Aveiro. These small, elongated fish are included in many recipes, such as stews (*Caldeirada de Enguias*), in escabeche sauce (*Enguias de Escabeche*), or fried, as in this dish served in restaurants with tomato and pepper rice. At the beginning of the 19th century, eels — which have always been abundant in the Aveiro estuary — were fried and sold by street vendors during popular festivities.

Preparation time: 20 minutes, plus 4 hours infusing, 1 hour 30 minutes soaking and 2 hours marinating
Cooking time: 20 minutes
Serves: 4
🐟 ◻

3 garlic cloves, peeled and thinly sliced
250 ml/8 fl oz (1 cup) white wine
250 ml/8 fl oz (1 cup) white wine vinegar
3 bay leaves
15 g/½ oz (2½ teaspoons) fine table salt
1.2 kg/2 lb 11 oz small eels
2 litres/68 fl oz (8½ cups) sunflower oil, for deep-frying
sea salt

For the sauce, put the garlic into a medium saucepan, add the white wine, vinegar and bay leaves and heat over a medium heat for 5 minutes, or until hot. Remove from the heat and leave to infuse for 2 hours.

Meanwhile, make a brine by putting the fine table salt into a large container and adding 3 litres/102 fl oz (12¾ cups) water. Clean the eels, removing the heads and guts. Rinse the eels under cold running water and leave them in the brine for 1 hour 30 minutes.

Meanwhile, soak wooden skewers in a bowl of water for 30 minutes to prevent them burning during cooking.

Remove the eels from the brine and leave them to drain on a perforated tray or in a colander until dry.

Thread the eels onto the soaked skewers, starting at the tail then crossing the middle loin and passing close to the head.

Line a large baking sheet with paper towels. Heat enough sunflower oil for deep-frying in a large, deep saucepan or fryer over a high heat until it reaches 180°C/350°F on a thermometer. Working in batches, carefully lower the eels into the hot oil and deep-fry for 10 minutes, or until golden. Remove the eels from the hot oil with tongs and leave to drain on the lined baking sheet.

Put the eels into a serving dish and pour over the sauce. Leave to marinate at room temperature for 2 hours before serving.

Fried Eels

Enguias Fritas   ◡ Ribatejo

Preparation time: 15 minutes, plus 3 hours marinating
Cooking time: 30 minutes
Serves: 4
◫

1 kg/2 lb 4 oz medium eels
1.4 litres/47 fl oz (5⅔ cups) sunflower oil, for deep-frying
170 g/6 oz (1½ cups) plain (all-purpose) flour
2 lemons, halved
sea salt and freshly ground black pepper
½ bunch coriander (cilantro), finely chopped, to garnish

Clean the eels, removing the guts. Remove and discard the head. Rinse the insides thoroughly under cold running water. Put the eels into a bowl and season with salt and pepper. Cover with food wrap and leave to marinate in the fridge for 3 hours.

When ready to cook, line a large baking sheet with paper towels. Heat the sunflower oil for deep-frying in a large, deep saucepan or fryer until it reaches 180°C/350°F on a thermometer.

Spread the flour out over a plate. Add the eels to the flour to coat. Working in batches, deep-fry the eels for 10 minutes, or until golden. Remove from the oil with a slotted spoon and leave to drain on the lined baking sheet.

Put the eels into a large serving dish, drizzle them with lemon juice and garnish with coriander (cilantro) before serving.

Conger Eel with Tomato Sauce

Safio com Molho de Tomate   ◡ Leiria

Many have been put off eating conger eels as they are perceived to have too many bones. However, their meat is so tender, juicy and delicious, especially when cooked in a tomato sauce.

Preparation time: 20 minutes, plus 10 minutes resting
Cooking time: 1 hour 10 minutes
Serves: 4
◫ ⬮

4 tomatoes
1 kg/2 lb 4 oz conger eel, cleaned and cut into
    1-cm/½-inch slices
120 ml/4 fl oz (½ cup) olive oil
3 onions, peeled and thinly sliced
2 garlic cloves, peeled and thinly sliced
1 bay leaf
1 teaspoon tomato purée (paste)
120 ml/4 fl oz (½ cup) white wine
¼ bunch flat-leaf parsley, roughly chopped
sea salt and freshly ground black pepper
plain boiled rice or mashed potato, to serve

Have a large bowl of iced water nearby. Using a sharp knife, score the top of the tomatoes with a small cross shape. Bring a saucepan of water to the boil, add the tomatoes and blanch for 30 seconds, then transfer to the iced water to cool. Once cool enough to handle, peel off the skins, cut in half and de-seed, then chop the flesh into chunks.

Season the fish with salt and pepper and leave to rest on a plate for 10 minutes.

Heat the olive oil in a saucepan over a medium heat. Add the onions, garlic and bay leaf and cook for 10 minutes, or until translucent. Add the tomato purée (paste) with the chopped tomatoes, stir, then reduce the heat to low and cook for 30 minutes, or until almost like a purée. Pour in the white wine and bring to the boil, then reduce the heat to medium. Add the fish and stir again. Cover with water, add a lid and cook for 20 minutes. Cook uncovered for a further 10 minutes or until the sauce has reduced.

Taste and adjust the seasoning, if necessary, before serving with either plain boiled rice or mashed potato.

Grilled Eel Skewered On a Bay Tree Branch

Espetada de Eirós   ◡ Ribatejo
em Pau de Loureiro

Preparation time: 20 minutes, plus 15 minutes standing
Cooking time: 45 minutes
Serves: 4
⬮ ◫

1.2 kg/2 lb 11 oz eel
1 red chilli, very finely chopped
juice of 1 lemon
550 g/1 lb 4 oz ripe bull's heart tomatoes, cut into chunks
250 ml/8 fl oz (1 cup) extra virgin olive oil
90 g/3¼ oz (6 tablespoons) unsalted butter, melted
sea salt and freshly ground black pepper

Prepare a barbecue or preheat an indoor grill (broiler). Using a sharp knife, make a skewer from a bay branch.

Clean the eel, removing the guts. Remove and discard the head. Rinse the insides thoroughly with cold running water. Using a sharp knife, make some small cuts over both sides of the eel.

Put the chilli, lemon juice and some salt into a small bowl and mix together, then rub the mixture over the eel and leave to stand for 15 minutes.

Thread the eel onto the bay skewer, creating an 'S' shape along the skewer. Set aside.

Put the tomatoes into a serving dish and season with salt and olive oil. Set aside.

As soon as the barbecue coals are glowing, put the eel on the grill rack and cook, brushing with the melted butter on both sides, for 25–30 minutes. Alternatively, cook the eel under the indoor grill.

Once cooked, remove the eel from the skewer and cut into pieces. Serve with the tomatoes.

Elvers with Lardo

••

Angulas com Toucinho de Valença do Minho ♡ Minho

The Portuguese consume freshwater eels in many ways across the country. I prefer not to blanch elvers (baby eels) before cooking as it drains them of flavour, but in some regions they do, so it is up to you. If you choose to do so, bring a saucepan of salted water to the boil, reduce the heat to medium and blanch the elvers for 30 seconds.

Preparation time: 10 minutes
Cooking time: 15 minutes
Serves: 4
🐟◻◻⊠

400 g/14 oz elvers (baby eels)
40 ml/1⅓ fl oz (2⅔ tablespoons) olive oil
50 g/2 oz lardo, sliced into thin strips
pinch of fine sea salt
pinch of paprika
juice of ½ lemon

Rinse the elvers (baby eels) twice under cold running water to remove any slime.

Heat a large frying pan or skillet over a medium heat and add the olive oil. Once hot, add the lardo and cook for 5 minutes, or until it is very lightly coloured. Add the elvers and fry over a high heat for less than 1 minute. Do not overcook them.

Add a pinch of salt and paprika to the elvers, then drizzle over the lemon juice before serving.

Deep-fried Cured Moray

••

Moreia Frita ♡ Algarve

Portugal has a long history of preserving fish. The technique of sea-salt preserving was introduced to the Iberian Peninsula in the Iron Age, with resident populations (Phoenicians, Greeks and Carthaginians, Romans) all applying the technique. Moray eel, a delicacy from south of the Sado river, is a long, snake-like, yellow-spotted fish. It is gutted and scaled, brined, butterflied and dried in the sun for a few days. Once dried, it is sliced and fried so the skin is crackling. *Moreia Frita* is served in tabernas in the Algarve – you can order it in a sandwich or as a small *petisco* of fried moray strips.

Preparation time: 20 minutes, plus 2 days drying
Cooking time: 10 minutes
Serves: 4
◻◻✕

1 moray eel
olive oil, for brushing
1 litre/34 fl oz (4¼ cups) sunflower oil, for deep-frying
200 g/7 oz (¾ cup) fine table salt
bread slices, to serve

Clean the moray, removing the skin. It is important that the skin is completely removed from the fish, from head to tail, and there are no holes. (You can set the flesh aside to use in other recipes.)

Using large wooden skewers, thread one skewer through one end of the skin, then thread the other skewer through the other end. Repeat with two more skewers, but now on the longitudinal. Brush the moray skin with olive oil and leave to sun-dry for 2 days. Keep checking the skin, when the colour changes it is ready. Slice the skin into square pieces.

Line a large baking sheet with paper towels. Heat the sunflower oil for deep-frying in a large, deep saucepan or fryer until it reaches 180°C/350°F on a thermometer. Working in batches, carefully lower the skins into the hot oil and deep-fry for 2–3 minutes, or until golden. Remove with a slotted spoon and leave to drain on the lined baking sheet.

Season with salt before serving with the bread.

Dogfish Stew

••

Cação Alimado ♡ Alentejo

Preparation time: 30 minutes, plus 15 minutes resting
Cooking time: 55 minutes
Serves: 4
◻◻

8 garlic cloves, peeled but left whole
1 large bunch coriander (cilantro), roughly chopped
130 ml/4½ fl oz (½ cup) olive oil, plus extra for frying the bread
40 g/1½ oz (⅓ cup) plain (all-purpose) flour
1 teaspoon paprika
2 bay leaves
800 g/1 lb 12 oz dogfish, rinsed and cut into large 200-g/7-oz pieces
80 ml/2¾ fl oz (⅓ cup) white wine vinegar
sourdough bread, thickly sliced
sea salt

Put the garlic and coriander (cilantro) in a mortar and, using a pestle, mash into a paste. (This is called *piso*.) Set aside.

Heat the 130 ml/4½ fl oz (½ cup) olive oil in a large saucepan over a low heat, add the paste and cook for 5 minutes. Add the flour, mix well either with a wooden spoon or a silicone spatula and cook for 5 minutes, stirring continuously. Pour in 2.2 litres/76 fl oz (9 cups) water, stir, season with salt, then add the paprika and bay leaves. Add the fish and vinegar and cook for 40 minutes, or until the flesh flakes easily from the bone. Remove the pan from the heat and leave to rest for 15 minutes with the lid on.

Heat enough olive oil for frying the bread in a frying pan or skillet over a medium heat. Add the bread slices and fry for 5 minutes on each side, or until golden all over.

Serve the dogfish stew with the fried bread.

Fish Stew — Fragateiro Style

Caldeirada à Fragateiro   ⬚ Ribatejo

Caldeirada (page 429) is the name of a variety of fish stew cooked in many coastal regions of Portugal, using different types of fish, potatoes and other ingredients, such as onions and tomatoes. This recipe is called *Caldeirada à Fragateiro* because it was cooked by *fragateiros* (boatmen) inside their *fragatas* (traditional Tagus river boats), so it includes fish found in the Tagus, such as eels and monkfish. *Fragateiros* would place old bread in a large, deep bowl, then cover it with the reddish, rich stew.

Preparation time: 45 minutes, plus 12 hours soaking
Cooking time: 1 hour 30 minutes
Serves: 10
✿ ⬚

800 g/1 lb 12 oz fresh clams (cleaned, page 78)
4 sea bream
3 grey mullets
1.2 kg/2 lb 11 oz skate wing
1.5 kg/3 lb 5 oz cuttlefish
1.5 kg/3 lb 5 oz conger eels
4 eels
4 onions, peeled and cut into medium-thick rings
5 waxy potatoes, peeled and cut into medium-thick rings
800 g/1 lb 12 oz ripe tomatoes, cut into thick rings
6 garlic cloves, peeled and thinly sliced
3 red (bell) peppers, halved, cored, de-seeded
    and cut into strips
3 green (bell) peppers, halved, cored, de-seeded
    and cut into strips
2 bay leaves
250 ml/8 fl oz (1 cup) olive oil
200 ml/7 fl oz (¾ cup) white wine
⅓ bunch flat-leaf parsley, roughly chopped
⅓ bunch coriander (cilantro), roughly chopped
5 mint leaves, roughly chopped
sea salt and freshly ground black pepper

For the fish stock:
fish heads, from the sea bream and mullet
1 onion, quartered
1 carrot, sliced
1 bay leaf

The day before, prepare the clams following the instructions on page 78.

Clean the sea bream and mullet, removing all the scales. Cut off the heads and reserve to use in the fish stock. Make an incision in the belly with a sharp knife and remove the guts. Season the fish with salt.

To make the stock, put the fish heads into a large saucepan with the onion, carrot and bay leaf and cover with water. Simmer over a medium heat for 40 minutes, skimming off the foam that rises to the top with a slotted spoon. Strain the stock through a muslin (cheesecloth) or sieve (fine-mesh strainer) into a bowl or jug (pitcher) and set aside.

Clean all the other fish. Remove the skin from the skate wing and cut into 4 pieces. Remove the guts from the cuttlefish and rub the tentacles against each other under cold running water to release any dirt, then cut into strips. Cut the conger eel into medium-sized pieces, still with the bone in. Remove the guts from the eels and rinse under cold running water. Drain the clams.

Arrange the onions in a layer in the bottom of a large saucepan, add a layer of potatoes, then tomatoes, garlic, a mix of (bell) peppers, a bay leaf, clams, cuttlefish, conger eel, skate wings, eel, sea bream and mullet. Drizzle with olive oil and season with salt. Repeat the layers until all the ingredients are used up. Pour over the wine, cover with a lid and cook over a low heat for 20 minutes. At this stage you can add 1 litre/34 fl oz (4¼ cups) of the fish stock, but the water released by all the ingredients should be enough to cook the stew. Scatter over the chopped herbs, before serving.

Oven-baked River Fish with Garlic and Pennyroyal

Assado de Peixe   ⬚ Alentejo

Preparation time: 20 minutes
Cooking time: 45 minutes
Serves: 4
⬚ ✿

1.5-kg/3 lb 5-oz largemouth bass, cleaned and de-scaled
800 g/1 lb 12 oz potatoes, peeled
½ bunch pennyroyal, leaves picked
3 garlic cloves, peeled and thinly sliced
2 bird's eye chillies, finely sliced
350 ml/12 fl oz (1½ cups) olive oil
40 ml/1⅓ fl oz (2⅔ tablespoons) white wine vinegar
sea salt

Prepare a barbecue or preheat the indoor grill (broiler).

Rinse the fish in cold running water, then pat dry with paper towels. Using a sharp knife, make small diagonal cuts over the flesh to help it cook better, then season with salt.

Put the potatoes into a saucepan of cold water, add a pinch of salt and cook over a medium heat for 15–20 minutes, or until soft. Drain and set aside.

As soon as the barbecue coals are glowing, place the fish on the grill rack and cook for 10 minutes on each side. Alternatively, cook under the indoor gril. Transfer to a serving plate and leave to rest.

Meanwhile, put the pennyroyal leaves in a mortar, add the garlic, salt and chillies and, using a pestle, mash to a paste. Transfer the paste to a bowl, add the olive oil, vinegar and any juices that have come out of the fish while resting, and mix together, then season with salt. Pour this mixture over the fish and serve with the boiled potatoes.

Stewed River Trout with Spices

Truta Abafada   ⛉ Beira Alta

Preparation time: 15 minutes, plus 2 days resting
Cooking time: 1 hour
Serves: 2
⛉ 🌢

3 small river trout
250 ml/8 fl oz (1 cup) olive oil
400 ml/14 fl oz (1⅔ cups) white wine vinegar
3 bay leaves
2 sprigs flat-leaf parsley, leaves torn
3 garlic cloves, unpeeled and crushed
nutmeg, for grating
4 black peppercorns
400 g/14 oz small waxy potatoes, peeled
sea salt and freshly ground black pepper

Two days before, clean and scale the trout, keeping the head on. Using a sharp knife, make a cut along the belly and remove the guts. Rinse under cold running water. Season the trout with salt and pepper.

Put the olive oil, vinegar, bay leaves, parsley and garlic into a medium saucepan. Season with grated nutmeg, then add the black peppercorns and bring to the boil over a low heat. Once boiling, add the trout and cook over a low heat for 30–40 minutes, or until soft and tender.

Using a fish slice (spatula), put the trout into a serving dish and leave to cool. Leave the cooking liquid in the pan to cool as well. Once the fish and cooking liquid are cold, combine them, then cover and leave in the fridge for 2 days.

When ready to serve, put the potatoes into a large saucepan of cold water with a pinch of salt and cook over a medium heat for 15–20 minutes, or until soft. Drain and serve with the trout.

Sautéed Bread Mash with River Fish

Migas de Peixe do Rio   ⛉ Beira Baixa

Preparation time: 20 minutes, plus 10 minutes standing
Cooking time: 1 hour
Serves: 6
⛉

1.6 kg/3 lb 8 oz pikeperch
1 kg/2 lb 4 oz common barbus fish
550 g/1 lb 4 oz ripe bull's heart tomatoes
120 ml/4 fl oz (½ cup) olive oil
3 onions, peeled and thinly sliced
4 garlic cloves, peeled and thinly sliced
1 teaspoon paprika
1 bunch dried pennyroyal
500 g/1 lb 2 oz bread, preferably stale, very thinly sliced
1 litre/34 fl oz (4¼ cups) sunflower oil, for deep-frying
140 g/5 oz (1¼ cups) plain (all-purpose) flour
50 ml/1¾ fl oz (3½ tablespoons) white wine vinegar
sea salt and freshly ground black or white pepper

Clean and scale the fish. Using a sharp knife, make a cut along the belly and remove the guts. Rinse the fish under cold running water and season with salt. Cut the pikeperch into 3–4 tranches, depending on the size of the fish.

Have a large bowl of iced water nearby. Bring a saucepan of water to the boil. Using a sharp knife, score the top of the tomatoes with a small cross. Once boiling, carefully add the tomatoes and blanch for 30 seconds, then transfer with a slotted spoon to the iced water and leave to cool. Once cool enough to handle, peel off the skins, cut in half and de-seed, then finely chop and set aside.

Heat the olive oil in another saucepan over a medium heat, add the onions and garlic and cook for 10 minutes, or until translucent. Add the tomatoes and paprika, then reduce the heat to low and cook for 20 minutes, or until a paste has formed. Season with salt and pepper. Add 2.8 litres/95 fl oz (11¼ cups) water and the pennyroyal, then stir and bring to the boil. Once boiling, add the pikeperch, reduce the heat to medium and cook for 30 minutes, or until the flesh flakes easily with a fork. Using a fish slice (spatula), remove the fish from the pan. Remove and discard the skin and bones.

Arrange the bread on a serving plate. Place the fish on top and pour over the stock. Taste and adjust the seasoning, if necessary. Leave to stand for 10 minutes so the bread soaks up the stock.

Line a baking sheet with paper towels. Heat the sunflower oil for deep-frying in a large, deep saucepan or fryer until it reaches 180°C/350°F on a thermometer. Spread the flour out on a large plate. Toss the barbus in the flour, shaking off the excess. Carefully lower the fish into the hot oil and deep-fry for 4–5 minutes on each side, or until golden. Remove with a slotted spoon and leave to drain on the lined baking sheet. Sprinkle with the vinegar.

Serve the bread mash alongside the fried fish.

River Fish Escabeche

Peixe do Rio em Escabeche

⊍ Beira Litoral

Preparation time: 15 minutes
Cooking time: 30 minutes, plus 2 hours standing
Serves: 4

🐟 ⬚ ⬚

1.5 kg/3 lb 5 oz small allis shard (*Alosa alosa*)
350 ml/12 fl oz (1½ cups) olive oil
3 garlic cloves, peeled and thinly sliced
2 bay leaves
1 red chilli
45 ml/1½ fl oz (3 tablespoons) white wine vinegar
3 flat-leaf parsley sprigs, roughly chopped
sea salt and freshly ground black pepper

Clean the fish, removing the scales. Using a sharp knife, make an incision in the belly and remove the guts. Rinse under cold running water. Season the fish with salt.

Line a large baking sheet with paper towels. Heat the olive oil in a large deep-sided frying pan or skillet over a medium heat until it reaches 180°C/350°F on a thermometer. Working in batches, carefully lower the fish into the hot oil and fry for 4–5 minutes on each side, or until golden all over. Remove with a fish slice (spatula) and leave to drain on the lined baking sheet.

Add the garlic, bay leaves, chilli and vinegar to the same pan, reduce the heat to low and cook for 10 minutes, or until the garlic is golden.

Arrange the fish on a serving plate and pour the escabeche mixture over. Scatter the chopped parsley over the top and leave to stand for 2 hours before serving.

Black Scabbardfish in Escabeche

Peixe Espada Preto de Escabeche 📷 p.165

⊍ Madeira

Preparation time: 30 minutes, plus 1 hour 30 minutes marinating
Cooking time: 30 minutes
Serves: 6

⬚

1.2 kg/2 lb 11 oz black scabbardfish
4 garlic cloves, peeled but left whole
2 bay leaves
2 bunches flat-leaf parsley, roughly chopped
3 ripe tomatoes, cut into small pieces
150 ml/5 fl oz (⅔ cup) white wine vinegar
700 g/1 lb 9 oz new potatoes, peeled and quartered
plain (all-purpose) flour, for dusting
olive oil, for shallow-frying
sea salt and freshly ground black pepper

Clean the fish, then cut into slices, about 4 cm/ 1½ inches thick. Put the slices into a large dish.

Put the garlic into a mortar with the bay leaves and parsley and, using a pestle, mash to a paste. Rub the fish with the paste, then season with salt and pepper. Cover with food wrap and leave in the fridge for 45 minutes. Add the tomatoes and vinegar to the fish and leave in the fridge for a further 45 minutes.

Put the potatoes into a large saucepan, cover with cold water and cook over a medium heat for 15–20 minutes, or until soft. Drain and set aside.

Spread the flour out on a large plate. Remove the fish from the marinade and set the marinade aside. Toss the fish in the flour.

Line a large baking sheet with paper towels. Heat the olive oil in a large frying pan or skillet over a medium heat. Carefully lower the fish into the hot oil and fry for 4–5 minutes on each side, or until golden all over. Using a fish slice (spatula), remove the fish from the hot oil and leave to drain on the lined baking sheet.

Add the marinade to the pan and bring to the boil, then pour over the fish. Serve the fish with the boiled potatoes.

Stewed Black Scabbardfish

Peixe Espada Preto Estufado

⊍ Madeira

Preparation time: 15 minutes
Cooking time: 45 minutes
Serves: 6

🐟

1.2 kg/2 lb 11 oz black scabbardfish
4 large ripe tomatoes
100 g/3½ oz (7 tablespoons) butter
½ onion, peeled and thinly sliced
4 garlic cloves, peeled and thinly sliced
1 bay leaf
80 ml/2¾ fl oz (⅓ cup) white wine
sea salt and freshly ground black pepper

Slice the fish into medium-sized pieces and season with salt and pepper.

Have a large bowl of iced water nearby. Bring a saucepan of water to the boil. Using a sharp knife, score the top of the tomatoes with a small cross shape. Once the water is boiling, carefully add the tomatoes and blanch for 30 seconds, then transfer them with a slotted spoon to the iced water and leave to cool. Once cool enough to handle, peel off the skins, de-seed, then slice the flesh into petals.

Heat the butter in another saucepan over a low heat until melted. Add the onion and garlic and cook for 15 minutes, or until translucent. Add the tomato petals and season with a pinch of salt. Stir and add the fish, bay leaf and white wine. Cover with a lid and cook for 30 minutes, or until the fish flakes easily from the bone. Serve immediately.

Black Scabbardfish in Escabeche

Lamprey with Rice – Mértola Style

Arroz de Lampreia – Mértola   ⛉ Alentejo

Preparing lamprey can be a real challenge, as some skill is needed to cut the digestive tract. It is one of the greatest classics of Portuguese cuisine.

Preparation time: 30 minutes, plus 12 hours marinating
Cooking time: 1 hour 20 minutes
Serves: 4
⛉

1 kg/2 lb 4 oz lamprey
1 tablespoon sweet paprika
120 ml/4 fl oz (½ cup) red wine
80 ml/2¾ fl oz (⅓ cup) white wine vinegar
4 garlic cloves, 3 crushed with skin on, 1 peeled and
     finely chopped
2 bay leaves
4 cloves
nutmeg, for grating
2 onions, peeled and finely chopped
250 ml/8 fl oz (1 cup) olive oil, plus extra for frying bread
1 bunch flat-leaf parsley, roughly chopped
350 g/12 oz (1¾ cups) long-grain rice
5 slices bread
sea salt and cracked black pepper

The day before, bring a large saucepan of water to the boil, add the lamprey and poach for 2 minutes. Remove from the pan, leave to cool a little, then rub the fish with some salt to help remove all the viscosity. Clean the lamprey, removing the guts and bones, then rub the fish with the sweet paprika and place in a large bowl. Add the red wine, 1 teaspoon of the vinegar, salt, cracked black pepper, the crushed garlic, the bay leaves, cloves and grated nutmeg. Cover the bowl with food wrap and leave to marinate in the fridge for 12 hours.

The next day, put the onions and chopped garlic into a large saucepan with the olive oil and parsley and cook over a medium heat for 10 minutes, or until the onions have some colour. Add the fish to the onions and cook for a further 30 minutes until soft. Using a slotted spoon, remove the fish from the pan and set aside, then cook the stew for 30 minutes, or until the liquid has reduced by half.

Add the remaining vinegar to the pan and stir, then add the fish, stir into the sauce and warm through for 10 minutes. Taste and adjust the seasoning, if necessary.

Meanwhile, put the rice into a large saucepan of water, add a pinch of salt and cook over a medium heat for 20 minutes, or until cooked.

Heat the olive oil for frying the bread in a frying pan or skillet over a medium heat. Add the bread slices and fry for 5 minutes on each side, or until golden all over.

Serve the fish with the fried bread and rice.

Lamprey Stewed in a Red 'Vinho Verde' Marinade

Lampreia à Bordalesa   ⛉ Minho

Lamprey, a long snake-like fish with a sucker mouth adorned with sharp teeth, is the star ingredient of this dish. Usually in season between January and April, it is a delicacy all over the country, mainly because of its similarity to the texture of slow-cooked meat and its lack of fishy aftertaste. It is commonly prepared as a stew, as here, served with slices of bread on the side, or cooked with rice (*Arroz de Lampreia*). Lamprey has been eaten since the times of the Roman Empire, and it is documented that Roman servants prepared it at Julius Caesar's banquets.

Preparation time: 20 minutes, plus 2 hours marinating
Cooking time: 45 minutes
Serves: 4
⛉

1 kg/2 lb 4 oz lamprey
350 ml/12 fl oz (1½ cups) *Vinho Verde Tinto* (red wine)
350 ml/12 fl oz (1½ cups) good-quality red wine
1 bay leaf
100 ml/3½ fl oz (⅓ cup) olive oil
1 large onion, peeled and cut into chunks
1 red chilli, finely sliced
1 large flat-leaf parsley sprig, coarsely chopped
1 teaspoon dried oregano
2 cloves
3 garlic cloves, peeled and cut into chunks
320 g/11¼ oz long-grain rice
sea salt and freshly ground black pepper
6 slices bread, toasted, to serve

The day before, prepare the lamprey according to the instructions left. Combine both wines, bay leaf, pepper and salt in a bowl. Add the fish and turn until well coated in the marinade. Cover with food wrap and leave to marinate in the fridge for 2 hours.

Heat the oil in a saucepan over a low heat. Add the onion and cook for 10 minutes, or until translucent.

Remove the fish from the marinade, setting the marinade aside and add the fish to the pan with the onion. Add the chilli, parsley, oregano, cloves and garlic. Stir, add the marinade, reduce the heat to low and cook for 15 minutes. Remove the fish to a plate or tray and set aside.

Strain the cooking liquid through a sieve (fine-mesh strainer) into a clean saucepan, pressing down on the mixture. Cook over a low heat for 10 minutes, or until it has reduced. Toss the fish in the sauce to coat. Taste and adjust the seasoning with salt and pepper.

Bring another saucepan of water to the boil. Once boiling, add a pinch of salt and the rice, reduce the heat to low and cook for 10 minutes, or until soft. Strain and put into a serving dish.

Serve the fish with the toasted bread and rice.

Largemouth Bass
with Fish Roe Porridge

Achigã com Açorda
de Ovas de Abrantes   ∪ Ribatejo

The *achigã* (largemouth bass) is a freshwater fish
only introduced in Portugal in the 19th century.
It first appeared in the Tagus river, and later in
the Douro, Tua and Azibo, although it is originally
from southern Canada and northern US. Its
versatility and succulence soon turned this fish
into a tradition in Portuguese cuisine (among
other freshwater fishes, such as *sável*, *boga* or
lúcio). *Achigã* can be roasted in the oven, stewed
or, as in this recipe, grilled over charcoal. It is
usually served with *açorda de ovas*, a bread stew
cooked with *achigã* eggs.

Preparation time: 30 minutes, plus 5 minutes soaking
Cooking time: 30 minutes
Serves: 4
⊡ ⊡

1.6 kg/3 lb 8 oz largemouth bass female including the eggs
1 onion, peeled and very finely chopped
400 ml/14 fl oz (1⅔ cups) olive oil
1 bay leaf
1 garlic clove, peeled and very finely chopped
380 g/13½ oz stale bread
¼ bunch flat-leaf parsley, roughly chopped
sea salt and freshly ground black pepper

Clean the fish, removing the scales. Cut off the
head and discard. Rinse under cold running water,
then cut the fish into pieces, 1 cm/½ inch thick
and season with salt. Rinse the fish egg sac in cold
water and leave to drip on a perforated tray or in
a colander.

Put the onion, fish eggs, black pepper, 80 ml/
2¾ fl oz (⅓ cup) of the olive oil, bay leaf and
garlic into a large saucepan, add 800 ml/27 fl oz
(3¼ cups) water and cook over a medium heat
for 10 minutes, or until the fish eggs are cooked.

Using your fingers, shred the bread into small
pieces into a large bowl.

Pour the onion and egg mixture over the bread
and leave to soak for 5 minutes, stirring with a
wooden spoon until it is a purée. Set aside.

Heat a drizzle of olive oil in a large frying pan
or skillet over a medium heat. Pour in the purée
and bring to the boil, stirring with a spoon. As soon
as it boils, remove from heat and season with salt.
Set aside.

Line a large baking sheet with paper towels.
Heat the remaining olive oil in the frying pan until
it reaches 160°C/325°F on a thermometer. Add
the fish and fry for 4–5 minutes on each side, or
until golden all over. It is important to keep the
temperature consistent. Remove with a slotted
spoon and leave to drain on the lined baking sheet.

Serve the fish with the porridge.

Common Barbel
with Spinach Purée

Barbos de Molhata   ∪ Ribatejo
com Esparregado – Vila Franca

Preparation time: 20 minutes, plus 3 hours 10 minutes
standing
Cooking time: 20 minutes
Serves: 4
⊡

2 common barbel, about 1.2 kg/2 lb 11 oz each
2 onions, peeled and cut into medium-thick slices
4 garlic cloves, peeled and cut into medium-thick slices
1 tablespoon sweet paprika
250 ml/8 fl oz (1 cup) white wine
130 ml/4½ fl oz (½ cup) olive oil
80 ml/2¾ fl oz (⅓ cup) white wine vinegar
⅓ bunch coriander (cilantro), chopped
sea salt and freshly ground white pepper

For the spinach purée:
80 ml/2¾ fl oz (⅓ cup) olive oil
2 garlic cloves, peeled and very thinly sliced
400 g/14 oz (8 cups) baby spinach leaves
30 g/1 oz (2 tablespoons) plain (all-purpose) flour
juice of 1 lemon
15 ml/½ fl oz (1 tablespoon) white wine vinegar

Clean the fish, removing the scales. Cut off the
heads and set aside. Using a sharp knife, make
an incision in the bellies and remove the guts and
inside bloodline. Rinse thoroughly under cold
running water. Cut the fish into chunky pieces and
season with salt, then leave to stand for 3 hours
before cooking.

Arrange the fish, onions and garlic in alternate
layers in the bottom of a large saucepan.

Put the paprika, white wine, olive oil, vinegar,
coriander (cilantro) and white pepper into a large
bowl and mix together until combined. Pour over
the fish. Cover with a lid and cook gently over
a low heat for 20 minutes, or until the fish flakes
easily. Try to avoid lifting the lid during cooking.
Remove from the heat and leave to rest for
10 minutes.

Meanwhile, for the spinach purée, heat a large
frying pan or skillet over a low heat, add the olive
oil and when hot, add the garlic and cook for
30 seconds, or until golden. Add the spinach
and cook gently for 5 minutes, or until wilted.
Transfer to a food processor or blender and blitz
to a smooth purée. Put the purée into a medium
saucepan.

Put the flour into a small bowl, add enough
water to make a smooth paste. Add it to the purée,
then cook over a low heat for 5 minutes, or until it
is very creamy. Season with salt, lemon juice and just
before serving, add the vinegar.

Serve the fish with the spinach purée.

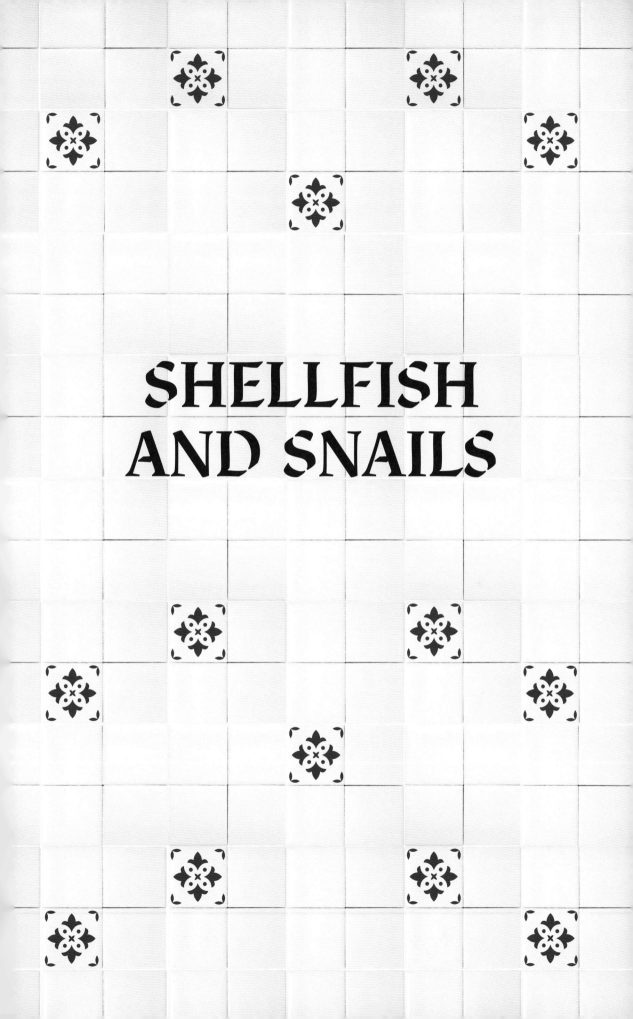

SHELLFISH AND SNAILS

Stewed Octopus with Tomato

•••

Polvo Guisado ⛉ Açores

This octopus stew recipe varies from island to island, but the final result often turns out identical. Its unique characteristics are conferred by the seasonings of ground pepper and *malagueta* chilli, adjusted to one's spicy preferences, and *vinho de cheiro* (literally 'wine of scent') — a light red wine with a perfume-like fragrance found on several of the islands in the Azores, made from American grape variety Isabelle that was introduced when the phylloxera pest struck local vineyards in the 19th century.

Preparation time: 30 minutes
Cooking time: 55 minutes
Serves: 6
🐙 ⛉

2 kg/4 lb 8 oz frozen octopus, thawed and cleaned
70 ml/2⅓ fl oz (4 tablespoons) olive oil
2 onions, peeled and finely chopped
3 garlic cloves, peeled and finely chopped
2 bunches flat-leaf parsley, finely chopped
1 red chilli
400 g/14 oz ripe tomatoes, cut into small squares
sea salt

Rinse the octopus a few times under cold running water to remove the slime. Set aside.

Bring a large saucean of water to the boil with a pinch of salt. Once boiling, lower the octopus into the boiling water and cook for 3 minutes, then remove. Repeat this process three times. On the third time, leave the octopus in the pan and cook for 20 minutes over a medium heat. Remove the pan from the heat and remove the octopus. Set the cooking liquid aside.

Separate the octopus tentacles from the body and cut them into small pieces, then cut the sac into quarters.

Heat the olive oil in a large saucepan over a medium heat, add the onions, garlic and parsley and cook for 5 minutes, or until the onions are golden brown. Add the chilli and tomatoes and stir. Reduce the heat to low and cook for 10 minutes, or until the tomatoes break down to a paste.

Add the octopus to the pan with 300 ml/ 10 fl oz (1¼ cups) of the reserved cooking liquid and cook for a further 10 minutes, or until the liquid has reduced.

Taste and adjust the seasoning with salt, if necessary, before serving.

Octopus Stew — Ribeira do Chão Style

•••

Polvo Guisado – Ribeira do Chão 📷 p.171 ⛉ Açores

Personally, I love the most unusual flavour pairing of octopus with cinnamon. For me, it works really well. This stew is wonderful served with rice.

Preparation time: 15 minutes, plus 20 minutes standing
Cooking time: 45 minutes
Serves 4
🐙 ⛉

1 kg/2 lb 4 oz octopus, cleaned
60 g/2¼ oz (⅓ cup) lard (pork fat)
1 large onion, peeled and finely chopped
3 garlic cloves, peeled and finely chopped
1 tablespoon *Massa de Pimentão*
1 tablespoon tomato purée (paste)
½ teaspoon ground cinnamon
400 ml/14 fl oz (1⅔ cups) *vinho de cheiro*
400 ml/14 fl oz (1⅔ cups) white wine
500 g/1 lb 2 oz waxy potatoes, quartered
sea salt

Cut the octopus into small pieces and wash it in cold running water to remove the slime, then put the octopus into a large bowl. Bring a small saucepan of water to the boil, then pour the water over the octopus and leave to stand for 20 minutes, or until the water cools down, then strain. (I prefer octopus to retain some texture, but if you prefer it to be smooth and creamy, then cook it for longer in a saucepan of boiling water until the desired texture is achieved.) Set aside.

Put the lard (pork fat), onion and garlic into another saucepan and cook over a low heat for 10 minutes, or until the onion is translucent. Add the octopus, then stir in the *Massa de Pimentão*, tomato purée (paste), cinnamon, both wines and a pinch of salt, cover and cook over a low heat for 20 minutes. Check the tenderness of the octopus and when it is nearly cooked, add the potatoes and cook for a further 15 minutes, or until the potatoes and octopus are soft.

Taste and adjust the seasoning with salt, if necessary, before serving.

Octopus Stew — Ribeira do Chão Style

Octopus Stew with Boiled Potatoes

Polvo Guisado   ☉ Açores
com Batatas Cozidas

I disagree with the ancient tradition of beating octopus meat with a stick to supposedly 'tenderise' it. This was practised in Portugal for many years as they didn't know any other way. I prefer to freeze the octopus meat first and then defrost it before preparing and cooking it. During the defrosting process, the fibres break down, making the octopus very tender when cooked.

Preparation time: 20 minutes
Cooking time: 50 minutes
Serves: 4
🐚 ☐

1 medium frozen octopus, thawed and cleaned
100 ml/3½ fl oz (⅓ cup) olive oil
1 large silver onion, peeled and thinly sliced
2 garlic cloves, peeled and thinly sliced
⅓ bunch flat-leaf parsley, roughly chopped
600 ml/20 fl oz (2½ cups) *vinho de cheiro* (red wine)
550 g/1 lb 4 oz small waxy potatoes, unpeeled and
    left whole
sea salt and freshly ground black pepper

Wash the octopus in cold running water a few times to remove the slime, rubbing it with salt.

Bring a large saucepan of water to the boil with a pinch of salt. Once boiling, lower the octopus into the boiling water and cook for 3 minutes, then remove. Repeat this process three times, each time using fresh water. Transfer the octopus to a baking sheet and leave to cool slightly before slicing into small pieces.

Heat the olive oil in a large saucepan over a medium heat, add the onion, garlic and parsley and cook for 10 minutes, or until the onion is translucent. Add the octopus, then pour in the wine and season with salt. Cook for 30 minutes, or until the wine has reduced.

Meanwhile, put the potatoes into a large saucepan, pour in enough water to cover, then add a pinch of salt and cook over a medium heat for 15–20 minutes, or until soft.

Add the boiled potatoes to the octopus, which should be tender, then taste and adjust the seasoning, if necessary, before serving.

Octopus Stew — Faial Style

Polvo Guisado à Moda do Faial   ☉ Açores

Preparation time: 20 minutes
Cooking time: 30 minutes
Serves: 4
🐚 ☐

1 medium octopus, cleaned
60 ml/2 fl oz (4 tablespoons) olive oil
20 g/¾ oz (1½ tablespoons) lard (pork fat)
1 large onion, peeled and finely chopped
2 garlic cloves, peeled and finely chopped
10 g/¼ oz *Massa de Malagueta* (page 102)
1 bay leaf
⅛ bunch flat-leaf parsley, coarsely chopped
10 black peppercorns
3 Jamaican peppercorns
120 ml/4 fl oz (½ cup) white wine
50 ml/1⅔ fl oz (3½ tablespoons) port
220 ml/7½ fl oz (1 cup) *vinho de cheiro* (red wine)
600 g/1 lb 5 oz small waxy potatoes, unpeeled and
    left whole
sea salt

Wash the octopus under cold running water a few times to remove the slime, then cut it into small pieces.

Heat the olive oil and lard (pork fat) in a large saucepan over a medium heat until the pork fat has melted. Add the octopus and cook for 10 minutes, or until the octopus has released its water. Using a slotted spoon, transfer the octopus to a bowl. Add the onions, garlic, *Massa de Malagueta*, bay leaf, parsley and all the peppercorns and stir, then pour in all the wine and cook for 20 minutes, or until reduced by a third.

Meanwhile, put the potatoes into another large saucepan, pour in enough water to cover, then add a pinch of salt and cook over a medium heat for 15–20 minutes, or until soft.

Taste and adjust the seasoning of the octopus, if necessary, and serve with the boiled potatoes.

Stuffed Squid (recipe p.174)

Stuffed Squid

●●●

Lulas Cheias   ◻ **Algarve**
de Monchique 🖼 p.173

Squid, like much of the seafood in the Algarve, is
prepared in a thousand different ways, including
grilled, stewed or stuffed. *Lulas Cheias* are squid
stuffed with a mixture of the squid's tentacles,
presunto (ham), and *linguiça* (spicy sausage),
the ends sealed with toothpicks and then gently
braised in a tomato-based *refogado* (a Portuguese
sofrito). In some recipes, the stuffing also includes
white rice. This is a comfort dish, typically eaten
during the autumn and winter months.

Preparation time: 35 minutes, plus 20 minutes resting
Cooking time: 1 hour 15 minutes
Serves: 4
🐚 ◻

600 g/1 lb 5 oz vine tomatoes
1.5 kg/3 lb 5 oz small squid
180 ml/6 fl oz (¾ cup) olive oil
2 small onions, peeled and chopped
160 g/5¾ oz Serrano ham, chopped into small pieces
    the same size as the onions
220 g/7½ oz (1 cup) long-grain rice
2 bay leaves
200 ml/7 fl oz (¾ cup) white wine
800 g/1 lb 12 oz small waxy potatoes, unpeeled and left
    whole
½ bunch flat-leaf parsley, roughly chopped
sea salt and freshly ground black pepper

Have a large bowl of iced water nearby. Bring a
large saucepan of water to the boil. Using a sharp
knife, score the top of the tomatoes with a small
cross shape. Once the water is boiling, carefully
add the tomatoes and blanch for 30 seconds,
then transfer them with a slotted spoon to the
iced water and leave to cool. Once cool enough to
handle, peel off the skins, cut in half and de-seed,
then cut the flesh into small cubes. Set aside.
    Clean the squid, separating the tentacles and
removing the guts from the body. Rinse them
in salted water, if necessary. Remove the mouth
and very finely chop the heads and tentacles.
    Heat half of the olive oil in a saucepan over a
medium heat, add half of the onions and cook for
5 minutes, or until soft. Add the ham and cook for
2 minutes, then add the squid tentacles and mix
everything together. Season with salt and pepper.
Remove from the heat and set aside.
    Put the rice into a separate large saucepan,
cover with water and bring to the boil. Reduce the
heat to low, cover with a lid and cook for 10–12
minutes until soft. Strain and season with salt and
pepper. Add the rice to the squid mixture in the
pan and mix until combined. Fill the body of the
squid with the mixture, then seal the opening with
a toothpick.
    Heat the remaining olive oil in a large saucepan
over a low heat, add the rest of the onions and

the bay leaves and cook for 12 minutes, or until the
onions are translucent. Add the tomatoes and cook
for 10 minutes, or until they start to break down
into a paste. Add the white wine and stuffed squid,
stir so the squid are submerged in the sauce.
Add enough water to cover the squid, then cover
with a lid and cook for 30 minutes, or until they
are soft. Taste and adjust the seasoning, then
remove from the heat and leave them to rest for
20 minutes.
    Meanwhile, preheat the oven to 180°C/350°F/
Gas Mark 4.
    Put the potatoes into a roasting pan and sprinkle
with salt. Roast in the hot oven for 35 minutes, or
until soft.
    Reheat the squid and scatter with the parsley
before serving alongside the roasted potatoes.

Squid with Roe

●●●

Lulas com Ferrado 🖼 p.175   ◻ **Algarve**

Preparation time: 15 minutes
Cooking time: 25 minutes
Serves: 4
🐚 ◻

1 kg/2 lb 4 oz small squid
200 ml/7 fl oz (¾ cup) olive oil
2 garlic cloves, unpeeled and crushed with the back
    of a knife
10 black peppercorns
2 bay leaves
100 ml/3½ fl oz (⅓ cup) white wine
600 g/1 lb 5 oz baby new potatoes
⅛ bunch flat-leaf parsley, finely chopped
juice of 1 lemon
sea salt and freshly ground white pepper

Clean the squid, separating the tentacles and
removing the guts from the body. Rinse them in
salted water, if necessary. Season the squid with
salt and pepper.
    Heat a large saucepan over a low heat. Once
hot, add the olive oil and garlic and cook for
1 minute. Increase the heat to maximum, add the
squid, whole peppercorns and bay leaves and
fry for 2 minutes. Turn the squid over, add the
white wine, cover with a lid and cook for a further
2 minutes, or until the squid is soft.
    Put the potatoes into a large saucepan, cover
with cold water, add a pinch of salt and cook over
a medium heat for 15–20 minutes, or until soft.
Drain and set aside in a serving dish.
    Put the squid into a large serving dish, scatter
with the parsley and drizzle with the lemon juice
before serving alongside the potatoes.

Squid with Roe

Lobster Rice

Arroz de Lagosta   ▽ Alentejo

Preparation time: 30 minutes, plus 5 minutes resting
Cooking time: 50 minutes
Serves: 4
✿ ▢ ▢

550 g/1 lb 4 oz tomatoes
50 g/2 oz lardo, thinly sliced
2 onions, peeled and finely chopped
3 garlic cloves, peeled and finely chopped
120 ml/4 fl oz (½ cup) olive oil
½ bunch coriander (cilantro), roughly chopped
1 red (bell) pepper, cored, de-seeded and thinly sliced
⅓ bunch parsley, roughly chopped
1 spiny lobster or rock lobster
1.3 litres/44 fl oz (5¼ cups) fish stock
360 g/12¾ oz (1¾ cups) long-grain rice
sea salt and freshly ground black pepper

Have a large bowl of iced water nearby. Using the
tip of a knife, make a small cross on the top of each
tomato, then put into a large heatproof bowl and
carefully pour in enough boiling water to cover.
Leave for 30 seconds, then transfer them to the
iced water. When they are cool enough to handle,
peel off the skins, halve and de-seed. Cut the
tomatoes into small cubes.

Put the lardo into a large saucepan and cook
over a medium heat for 5 minutes, or until lightly
coloured. Remove the lardo from the pan and set
aside. Add the onions and garlic to the pan with
the olive oil, half the coriander (cilantro), red (bell)
pepper, parsley and the cubed tomatoes and cook
over a medium heat for 30 minutes, or until the
onions and tomatoes are cooked down. Transfer
the mixture to a blender or food processor and
blitz until puréed. Pour the tomato purée into a
saucepan and set aside.

Cut the lobster meat into chunks and crack the
head in half.

Add the fish stock to the tomato purée, then
add the rice and a pinch of salt and cook over
a medium heat for 5 minutes before adding the
lobster. Cook for a further 10 minutes, or until
the rice is cooked.

Taste and adjust the seasoning with salt
and pepper, if necessary, then garnish with the
remaining chopped coriander. Leave the rice to
rest for 5 minutes before serving.

Stuffed Spider Crab

Santola Fria Recheada   ▽ Lisbon
de Lisboa   ▣ p.177

Preparation time: 1 hour
Cooking time: 30 minutes
Serves: 4
▢ ▢

1 x 1.3-kg/3-lb spider crab
3 cloves
4 black peppercorns
1 onion, peeled and halved
2 eggs
10 g/¼ oz (2 teaspoons) English mustard
5 ml/¼ fl oz (1 teaspoon) Worcestershire sauce
15 ml/½ fl oz (1 tablespoon) brandy
50 g/2 oz pickles (carrots, onions, gherkins),
     very finely chopped
¼ bunch flat-leaf parsley, very finely chopped
1 red chilli, finely chopped
olive oil, for drizzling
sea salt and freshly ground back pepper
bread slices, toasted, to serve

Fill a large saucepan with enough water to cook
the spider crab, add a pinch of sea salt, the cloves,
peppercorns and onion and bring to the boil.
Reduce the heat to medium, add the spider crab
and cook for 20 minutes exactly. Remove from the
heat and leave the spider crab to cool in the water.

Meanwhile, bring a medium saucepan of water
to the boil. Have a bowl of cold water nearby.
Once boiling, carefully lower in the eggs and cook
for 8 minutes. Lift the eggs out of the pan and
transfer to the iced water to cool. Once cold,
peel the shells from the eggs, chop them finely
and set aside.

Once the crab is cold, remove it from the pan
and start separating the crab into different parts.
Remove the legs, take the middle carapace out,
remove the core from the carapace, scrape out all
the coral and put into a bowl, then scrape out the
meat from inside the carapace and put into a bowl.
Cut the core into 4 pieces, pick out the meat and
put into the bowl. Wash the main crab shell and
set aside.

Using a fork, press the crab meat down to
incorporate the coral and all the liquid from
the inside of the main shell to make a paste.
Add the mustard, Worcestershire sauce, brandy,
pickles, three-quarters of the chopped parsley,
the finely chopped egg and chilli and stir until well
combined. Season with salt and pepper, drizzle
with some olive oil and fill the main shell with
the mixture.

Garnish the crab with the remaining chopped
parsley before serving with the toasted bread.

Stuffed Spider Crab

Steamed Spiny Lobster — Peniche Style

Lagosta Suada à Moda de Peniche   ♡ Lisbon

Preparation time: 35 minutes
Cooking time: 55 minutes
Serves: 4

1 x 1.5-kg/3 lb 5-oz spiny lobster
2 onions, peeled and thinly sliced into rings
750 g/1 lb 10 oz tomatoes, tips removed
    and quartered
3 garlic cloves, peeled and thinly sliced
¼ bunch flat-leaf parsley, finely chopped
1 teaspoon paprika
180 ml/6 fl oz (¾ cup) white wine
50 ml/1⅔ fl oz (3½ tablespoons) firewater or grappa
1 bird's eye chilli, finely chopped
nutmeg, for grating
2 bay leaves
70 g/2½ oz (⅔ stick) unsalted butter
80 ml/2¾ fl oz (⅓ cup) dry port
350 g/12 oz (1¾ cups) long-grain rice
sea salt and freshly ground black pepper

First, prepare the lobster. Twist the lobster tail so the top twists towards you. This should loosen the tail from one side of the body. Next, twist the tail in the opposite direction to loosen it on the other side. Pull the tail straight out to separate it from the base. Break off one of the antenna and push the tip into the anus of the lobster tail and twist it to loosen the digestive tract. The tract should protrude from the middle of the tail meat at the base of the tail. Slowly pull it out and discard.

Put 100 ml/3½ fl oz (⅓ cup) water into a large saucepan, rest the lobster in a colander over the pan and leave it to drip any juices into the water.

Saving any juices that come out and adding them to the water in the pan, cut the lobster by the 'rings', remove the little claws and cut them in half. Do the same for the antennae. Cut the head in half.

Put the lobster claws and antennae into a large saucepan, arrange a few rings of the lobster in a single layer on top, then add a layer of onion, tomatoes, garlic and parsley, season with salt and pepper and sprinkle with a little of the paprika. Repeat the layers with the remaining ingredients.

Add the water with the lobster juices then the white wine, firewater, chilli, some grated nutmeg, the bay leaves and butter to the pan. Cover with a lid and cook over a high heat to gain temperature, then reduce the heat to medium and cook for 45 minutes, stirring every few minutes. Keep checking the lobster as you do not want to overcook it. It is better to leave it 'medium rare'. Uncover, add the port and cook for a further 10 minutes over a medium heat.

Meanwhile, bring 1 litre/34 fl oz (4¼ cups) salted water to the boil in another large saucepan. Add the rice and cook for 10–12 minutes, or until soft. Drain and transfer to a serving bowl.

Serve the boiled rice immediately alongside the lobster.

Cuttlefish Cooked in its Ink

Chocos com Tinta – Vila Real de Santo António   ♡ Algarve   📷 p.179

Preparation time: 10 minutes
Cooking time: 10 minutes
Serves: 5

1.5 kg/3 lb 5 oz small cuttlefish
140 ml/4½ fl oz (½ cup) olive oil
4 garlic cloves, chopped
1½ slices sourdough bread
1 teaspoon paprika
sea salt

Using a sharp knife, make a small incision on the cuttlefish at the end opposite the tentacles and rinse under cold running water. Leave the ink sac inside the body and rub the tentacles. Leave to dry a little.

Heat the olive oil in a large saucepan over a low heat, add the garlic and bread and cook for 3 minutes, or until golden brown. Remove the garlic and bread from the pan, and put them into a mortar. Using a pestle, mash to a coarse mixture, not a paste. Alternatively, blitz in a blender.

Add the paprika and cuttlefish to the pan, cover with a lid and cook over a medium heat for 6–7 minutes depending on the size of the cuttlefish. Add the bread mixture, season with a pinch of salt and stir to combine. Serve immediately.

Cuttlefish Cooked in its Ink

Fried Cuttlefish with Fries

••

Choco Frito   ♡ Lisbon
à Setubalense   🖾 p.181

These crunchy, succulent pieces of cuttlefish (*choco*), coated in seasoned cornflour and deep-fried, are originally from the city of Setúbal, south of Lisbon, but they are now cherished and consumed all over the country. The dish harks back to the days when cuttlefish had no commercial value and the fishermen would keep them for themselves, taking them into Setúbal's tascas where they were fried and served as an accompaniment to drinks and conversation. Today, cuttlefish is the iconic emblem of Setúbal, where there is even a cuttlefish statue, and where restaurants serve platters of *choco frito* with fries, salad and lemon wedges all year round.

Preparation time: 30 minutes, plus 2 hours marinating
Cooking time: 45 minutes
Serves: 4
🗆 🗆

1.2 kg/2 lb 11 oz baby cuttlefish
2 garlic cloves, peeled and thinly sliced
2 bay leaves, torn into pieces
20 g/¾ oz (8 tablespoons) fine sea salt
juice of 2 lemons
1 litre/34 fl oz (4¼ cups) sunflower oil, for deep-frying
800 g/1 lb 12 oz waxy potatoes, peeled and cut into
    thin matchsticks
200 g/7 oz (1⅔ cups) corn flour (cornstarch)
3 eggs
freshly ground black pepper
⅓ bunch curly leaf parsley, finely chopped, to serve
lemon wedges, to serve

Clean the cuttlefish, removing the mouth, ink, innards and skin. Rinse under cold running water, then cut into thin strips. Put the cuttlefish into a bowl, add the garlic, bay leaves, salt and lemon juice and turn until all the strips are well coated. Cover with food wrap and leave to marinate in the fridge for 2 hours.
    Line a baking sheet with paper towels. Heat the oil for deep-frying in a large, deep saucepan or fryer over a high heat until it reaches 190°C/375°F on a thermometer. Working in batches, carefully lower the fries into the hot oil and deep-fry for 4–5 minutes, or until crisp. Remove with a slotted spoon and leave to drain on the lined baking sheet.
    Spread the cornflour (cornstarch) over a large plate. Lightly whisk the eggs in a shallow bowl. Remove the cuttlefish from the marinade, toss in the flour, then dip in the beaten egg until coated.
    Making sure the sunflower oil is at the correct temperature, carefully lower the cuttlefish into the hot oil and deep-fry for 4–5 minutes, or until golden. Remove from the oil with a slotted spoon and leave to drain on the lined baking sheet.
    Scatter the parsley over the cuttlefish before serving with the lemon wedges and fries.

Sautéed Baby Cuttlefish

••

Chocos da Lagoa de Óbidos   ♡ Leiria

Preparation time: 15 minutes, plus 5 minutes resting
Cooking time: 10 minutes
Serves: 4
🍳 🗆 🗆 🖾

800 g/1 lb 12 oz baby cuttlefish
150 ml/5 fl oz (⅔ cup) olive oil
4 garlic cloves, peeled and thinly sliced
2 bird's eye chillies, thinly sliced
100 ml/3½ fl oz (⅓ cup) white wine
50 ml/1⅔ fl oz (3½ tablespoons) Cognac
sea salt and freshly ground black pepper

Clean the cuttlefish, removing the mouth and ink. Rinse under cold running water, then leave to drip on a perforated tray or in a colander.
    Heat a large frying pan or skillet over a medium heat, add the olive oil, then add the garlic and cook for 3 minutes, or until golden.
    Add the cuttlefish to the frying pan and fry for 1–2 minutes. Season with salt, pepper and add the chillies, then cook over a medium heat for a further 1–2 minutes, or until the cuttlefish is soft. Add the white wine and Cognac. Stir, then bring to the boil. Remove from the heat and leave to rest for 5 minutes before serving.

Grey Prawns from the Coast

••

Camarão da Costa   ♡ Leiria

These tiny prawns (shrimp) are similar to what are known as Mylor prawns in the UK. They are packed with an incredible flavour of the sea. Personally, I like to eat them whole with the shell on, or even raw. They are the perfect seafood snack.

Preparation time: 10 minutes
Cooking time: 5 minutes
Serves: 6
🍳 🗆 🗆 🖾 ✕

12 g/¼ oz (2 teaspoons) sea salt
1.2 kg/2 lb 11 oz grey prawns (shrimp)
1 lemon

Fill a saucepan large enough to hold all the prawns (shrimp) with 4 litres/136 fl oz (17 cups) water and bring to the boil. Once boiling, add the salt, then add the prawns (shrimp) and cook for just 40 seconds. Drain and transfer the prawns to a large serving dish.
    Squeeze over the lemon and toss until all the prawns are coated in the juice. Serve immediately.

Fried Cuttlefish with Fries

Mussels — Aveiro Style

Mexilhões
à Moda de Aveiro   ⏍ Beira Litoral

Preparation time: 30 minutes, plus 12 hours chilling and
4 days marinating
Cooking time: 20 minutes
Serves: 4
🐚 ⏍

2 bay leaves, crushed
300 ml/10 fl oz (1¼ cups) vinegar
250 ml/8 fl oz (1 cup) white wine
80 ml/2¾ fl oz (⅓ cup) olive oil
4 cloves
80 live mussels
1 litre/34 fl oz (4¼ cups) sunflower oil, for deep-frying
sea salt and freshly ground black pepper

Prepare the marinade a day in advance. Put the
bay leaves, vinegar, white wine, olive oil, cloves and
pepper into a saucepan and heat over a medium
heat until it just starts to boil. Remove from the heat,
cover and leave to chill in the fridge for 12 hours.

Clean the mussels and remove the beards.
Discard any mussels that do not close when tapped.
Put the mussels into a large saucepan, cover with
a lid and cook over a high heat for 3–4 minutes, or
until they open. Stir the pot. Transfer the mussels
to a rimmed baking sheet and shell them. Discard
any mussels that remain closed.

Stretch a dry tea (dish) towel over a work counter
and spread the mussels out on top. Leave to dry out,
then thread them onto skewers.

Line a large baking sheet with paper towels.
Heat the sunflower oil for deep-frying in a large,
deep saucepan until it reaches 190°C/375°F on a
thermometer. Working in batches, carefully put the
mussels into the hot oil and deep-fry for 2 minutes.
Remove with tongs and leave to drain on the lined
baking sheet.

Put the mussels into a container (typically,
a clay pot is used) and cover them with the
marinade. Cover with a lid and leave in the fridge
for 4 days, stirring them every day, before eating.

Corn Porridge with Wedge Shell Clams

Xerém de Conquilhas   📷 p.183   ⏍ Algarve

Xerém is the Arab name for this *papas de milho*
(corn porridge) that is still cooked in many villages
of the Algarve, especially during winter. Similar
to the Middle Eastern *hares*, a dish of boiled,
cracked or coarsely-ground wheat, *xerém* calls
for fine-ground corn instead of wheat. This is
another recipe that perfectly represents the
Islamic influence on the Algarve, a region once
known as Garb Al-Andalus. *Xerém* is usually served
with clams, but some recipes include cockles,
prawns (shrimp), or even *chouriço*.

Preparation time: 20 minutes, plus 12 hours soaking
Cooking time: 45 minutes
Serves: 4
🐚 ⏍

1.8 kg/4 lb *conquilhas* or wedge shell clams (page 184)
    or palourde clams, surf clams or even cockles
120 g/4 oz smoked bacon, thinly sliced
150 g/5 oz chorizo, thinly sliced
100 g/3½ oz Serrano ham, thinly sliced
280 ml/9½ fl oz (1 cup) white wine
180 g/6 oz (1½ cups) corn flour or 180 g/6 oz (1 cup)
    fine semolina, sifted
sea salt and freshly ground black pepper

The day before, scrub the shells of the clams to
remove any dirt. Discard any that don't close when
their shells are tapped. Rinse the clams several
times under cold running water to remove any
sand and grit, then put them into a large bowl and
pour in enough water to cover. Add enough fine
sea salt to make a brine with 1% salt and stir well.
Do not add too much salt this may kill the clams.
Leave to stand in the fridge for 12 hours. This will
help to expel any sand inside the clams.

The next day, drain the clams and put them
into a large saucepan. Add 150 ml/5 fl oz (⅔ cup)
water, cover with a lid and cook gently over a
low heat for 5 minutes, or until they open. Strain
the clams through a sieve (fine-mesh strainer)
into a large bowl and set the cooking liquid aside.
Remove the clams from their shells and set aside.

Fill a small saucepan with hot water (or other
shellfish stock if you have any) and put over
a low heat. Put the meat into a large saucepan
and cook over a medium heat for 5 minutes.
Add the clams cooking liquid and the wine and
bring to the boil. Remove from the heat, add the
corn flour or semolina and mix well.

Put the pan over a low heat and cook, stirring
continuously, for 10 minutes, or until thick. If it is
becoming too dry during cooking, add some of the
hot water or stock. It should be creamy and moist.
Add half the clams, mix well and taste and adjust
the seasoning with pepper, if necessary. Finish the
dish with the remaining clams and meat on top.

Corn Porridge with Wedge Shell Clams

Wedge Shell Clams — Algarve Style

Conquilhas à Algarvia   ▽ Algarve

Also called *cadelinhas* (literally 'tiny female dogs'), these are small, wedge-shaped clams in a variety of colours ranging from yellow to brown to purple. During the summer months, a trip to the beach almost always means catching *conquilhas*, and it is common to see people with children's buckets or water bottles along the water's edge at low tide, pulling the compact wet sand and plucking a couple of shells from the watery bed they have uncovered. *Conquilhas* are ubiquitous in Algarve cuisine — in soups, *migas*, *xerém*, *açordas* (page 429), and rice — although this recipe, where they are simply opened in olive oil and cooked with browned garlic and chopped coriander, is widely appreciated.

Preparation time: 15 minutes, plus 12 hours soaking
Cooking time: 20 minutes
Serves: 4
🐟 ◻ ◻

1.8 kg/4 lb fresh clams, preferably *conquilhas* or wedge
    shell clams (above) or use palourde or surf
50 ml/1²⁄₃ fl oz (3½ tablespoons) olive oil
3 garlic cloves, peeled and very thinly sliced
juice of 1 lemon
⅓ bunch coriander (cilantro), roughly chopped
fine table salt and freshly ground white pepper

The day before, scrub the shells of the clams to remove any dirt. Discard any that don't close when their shells are tapped. Rinse the clams several times under cold running water to remove any sand and grit, then put them into a large bowl and pour in enough water to cover. Add enough fine sea salt to make a brine with 1% salt and stir well. Do not add too much salt this may kill the clams. Leave to stand in the fridge for 12 hours. This will help to expel any sand inside the clams.

The next day, add the olive oil and garlic to a large saucepan and cook gently over a low heat for 1 minute, or until the garlic is fragrant. Drain the clams and add them to the pan, increase the heat to medium, cover with a lid and cook, stirring occasionally, for 15–20 minutes, or until all the clams have opened. Season the clams with pepper, drizzle with the lemon juice and scatter over the coriander (cilantro) before serving.

Clams in the 'Cataplana'

Amêijoas na Cataplana 📷 p.185   ▽ Algarve

The *cataplana* (page 429) is a staple dish in Portuguese cuisine. The pan, itself, has had a long history and was thought to be brought to Portugal by the Arabs. Since then, it has been created in different fashions including the material from which the pan is made. It was originally zinc and has now changed to copper.

Preparation time: 30 minutes, plus 12 hours soaking
Cooking time: 30 minutes
Serves: 6
🐟 ◻

2.2 kg/5 lb fresh palourde or surf clams
2 teaspoons fine table salt
400 g/14 oz ripe tomatoes
600 ml/20 fl oz (2½ cups) olive oil
2 onions, peeled and cut into chunky pieces
3 garlic cloves, peeled and sliced
1 bay leaf
1 bunch flat-leaf parsley, roughly chopped
200 ml/7 fl oz (¾ cup) white wine
100 g/3½ oz chorizo, quartered
80 g/3 oz Serrano ham cut into small cubes
sea salt and freshly ground black pepper

The day before, scrub the shells of the clams to remove any dirt. Discard any that don't close when their shells are tapped. Rinse the clams several times under cold running water to remove any sand and grit, then put them into a large bowl and pour in enough water to cover. Add enough fine sea salt to make a brine with 1% salt and stir well. Do not add too much salt this may kill the clams. Leave to stand in the fridge for 12 hours. This will help to expel any sand inside the clams.

Have a large bowl of iced water nearby. Bring a large saucepan of water to the boil. Using a sharp knife, score the top of the tomatoes with a small cross shape. Once the water is boiling, carefully add the tomatoes and blanch for 30 seconds, then transfer them with a slotted spoon to the iced water and leave to cool. Once cool enough to handle, peel off the skins, cut in half and de-seed, then cut the flesh into small cubes.

Heat the olive oil in a large saucepan over a low heat, add the onions, garlic, bay leaf and parsley and cook for 7 minutes, or until the onion is starting to gain some colour. Add the white wine and cook for 2 minutes, or until it has reduced. Add the chorizo, ham and tomatoes and cook over a medium heat for 10 minutes. Transfer the mixture to the *cataplana*, remove the parsley and then add the clams on top. Close the lid and seal, then cook over a medium heat, stirring halfway through cooking, for 10 minutes, or until all the clams have opened. Serve immediately.

Clams in the 'Cataplana'

Clams with Coriander and Garlic

Amêijoas à Bulhão Pato   ▽ **Lisbon**

Along the Portuguese coast, and especially in the Lisbon region, clams (*amêijoas*) are picked up by fishermen, but before the advent of this recipe no one had ever thought of the simplest way to cook them: in a frying pan or skillet with coriander, garlic and olive oil, always remembering that the most important ingredient is the delicate water of the clams themselves. They should then be served immediately, because exposure to air turns them dry and stiff. The recipe was created by a Lisbon cook in the 1930s as a tribute to Raimundo António de Bulhão Pato, a poet who was known chiefly for being a *bon vivant* and gourmand.

Preparation time: 20 minutes, plus 12 hours standing
Cooking time: 10 minutes
Serves: 4
▢ ▢

1.2 kg/2 lb 11 oz palourde clams or use any other kind
     of clams or cockles
80 ml/2¾ fl oz (⅓ cup) extra virgin olive oil
4 garlic cloves, peeled and very finely sliced
80 ml/2¾ fl oz (⅓ cup) white wine (optional)
⅛ bunch coriander (cilantro), roughly chopped
juice of 1 lemo
sea salt
4 slices sourdough bread, toasted, to serve

The day before, scrub the shells of the clams to remove any dirt. Discard any that don't close when their shells are tapped. Rinse the clams several times under cold running water to remove any sand and grit, then put them into a large bowl and pour in enough water to cover. Add enough fine sea salt to make a brine with 1% salt and stir well. Do not add too much salt this may kill the clams. Leave to stand in the fridge for 12 hours. This will help to expel any sand inside the clams.

The next day, heat the olive oil in a large saucepan over a medium heat until it reaches 120°C/250°F on a thermometer. Add the garlic and cook for 1 minute to give it a bit of colour, then add the wine, if using, and bring to the boil.

Drain the clams and add them to the pan, then cover with a lid and stir well. Cook for 3 minutes, or until the clams have opened. Add the coriander (cilantro), put the lid back on and stir. Cook for another 1 minute. The clams should just have released all their juices. Season with lemon juice, but not too much as you don't want to mask the flavour of the clams.

Serve the clams with the toasted bread.

Whelk Salad

Salada de Búzios   ▣ p.187   ▽ **Alentejo**

Preparation time: 30 minutes, plus 45 minutes resting
Cooking time: 40 minutes
Serves: 4
🦐 ▢

3 kg/6 lb 10 oz whelks in the shell
2 onions, peeled and cut into very small cubes
2 garlic cloves, peeled and cut into very small cubes
180 ml/6 fl oz (¾ cup) olive oil
80 ml/2¾ fl oz (⅓ cup) white wine vinegar
⅓ bunch coriander (cilantro), roughly chopped
sea salt and freshly ground black pepper
fine table salt

The day before, scrub the shells of the whelks to remove any dirt. Rinse the whelks several times in cold water, using fresh water each time. Drain the whelks and discard the water. Put the whelks into a large bowl and pour in 1.5 litres/50 fl oz (6¼ cups) water to cover. Add 4 g/⅛ oz (1 teaspoon) fine sea salt to make a brine and stir well. Leave to stand in the fridge for 12 hours. This will help to expel any sand inside the whelks.

The next day, fill a saucepan large enough to hold all the whelks with water, add a pinch of salt and bring to the boil. Once boiling, reduce the heat to medium and add the whelks. Cook them for 10–15 minutes. Drain the whelks and leave them to cool. Using a metal skewer pull the meat away from the shells. Remove the 'foot' and remove the guts.

Cut the whelks in half with a sharp knife and place in a bowl, then add the onions and garlic and mix together until combined.

Mix the olive oil, vinegar, pepper, and coriander (cilantro) together in another bowl, and season with salt. Pour the mixture over the whelks and stir well. Leave the whelks to rest for 45 minutes before serving so the meat can absorb all the flavours.

Whelk Salad

Whelk and Bean Stew

••

Feijoada de Búzios   ▽ Algarve

Preparation time: 30 minutes, plus 12 hours soaking
Cooking time: 3 hours 50 minutes
Serves: 4
🦪 ▢

350 g/12 oz (2 cups) dried butter (lima) beans
700 g/1 lb 9 oz whelks muscles or 4 kg/8 lb 13 oz whelks
    in their shells
400 g/14 oz tomatoes
160 ml/5½ fl oz (⅔ cup) olive oil
2 onions, peeled and finely chopped
4 garlic cloves, peeled and finely chopped
120 g/4 oz bacon, cut into small pieces
½ chorizo, cut into small pieces
1 bunch flat-leaf parsley, roughly chopped
2 bird's eye chillies, halved
sea salt and freshly ground black pepper

Put the beans into a large bowl of cold water and leave to soak for 12 hours. If using fresh whelks, rinse them thoroughly under cold running water several times, brushing them to remove the dirt on the shell, then put them into a large bowl, cover with cold water and leave to stand for 12 hours.

The next day, drain the beans and set aside. Drain the whelks, then put them into a large saucepan, cover with water and cook over a medium heat for 3 hours. Strain through a sieve (fine-mesh strainer) into a large bowl. Set both the whelks and the cooking liquid aside.

Using the tip of a knife, remove the whelk meat from the shell. They have a hard bit on the muscle that you need to remove with the knife. Fill a medium bowl with cold water, add a pinch of salt, then wash the whelks in the water. Leave to drain.

Have a large bowl of iced water ready nearby. Bring a large saucepan of water to the boil. Using a sharp knife, score the top of the tomatoes with a small cross shape. Once the water is boiling, carefully add the tomatoes and blanch for 30 seconds, then transfer them with a slotted spoon to the iced water and leave to cool. Once cool enough to handle, peel off the skins, cut in half and de-seed, then cut the flesh into large chunks.

Heat the olive oil in a large saucepan over a low heat, add the onions and garlic and cook for 12 minutes, or until golden brown. Add the bacon, chorizo, tomatoes, parsley and chillies and cook for 2 minutes, or until the tomatoes start to break down. Add the reserved cooking liquid, then add the drained butter (lima) beans, season with salt and pepper and cook gently for 30 minutes, or until soft. Add the sliced whelks and mix until combined. Cook for a further 2 minutes, then remove from the heat and leave to rest before serving. This dish should be served in a clay pot.

Limpets with Pink Peppercorns

••

Lapas com Molho Afonso   📷 p.189   ▽ Açores

The longer you cook limpets, the worse they become. They are one of those shellfish that lose their natural juices and turn rubbery when overcooked, so make sure that you keep it brief.

Preparation time: 20 minutes
Cooking time: 20 minutes
Serves 6
🦪 ▢ ▢

2.5 kg/5 lb 10 oz limpets
150 ml/5 fl oz (⅔ cup) extra virgin olive oil
2 onions, peeled and chopped into small pieces
6 garlic cloves, peeled and thinly sliced
12 pink peppercorns
½ bunch flat-leaf parsley, roughly chopped
sea salt and freshly ground black pepper

Wash the limpets twice in cold water, scrubbing the shells with a small brush to remove any remaining dirt.

Heat the olive oil in a saucepan over a low heat. Add the onions and garlic and cook for 10 minutes without colouring them. Add the peppercorns and cook gently for a further 5 minutes, then add the parsley and season with black pepper.

Add the limpets to the pan and mix well. Increase the heat to medium and cook for 5 minutes, stirring the pan at least twice. Be careful not to overcook the limpets otherwise they will become rubbery. Taste and adjust the seasoning, if necessary, before serving.

Limpets with Pink Peppercorns

Grilled Limpets

....

Lapas Grelhadas ◡ Madeira

Limpets are considered a delicacy in the islands, and are traditionally appreciated as a snack in the Madeira and Azores, either barbecued with butter sauce or just boiled and drizzled with lemon juice. Grilled limpets are also served with cumin on São Jorge island.

Preparation time: 10 minutes
Cooking time: 5 minutes
Serves: 4
⊠

1.2 kg/2 lb 11 oz limpets
120 g/4 oz (1 stick) unsalted butter
2 garlic cloves, peeled and finely chopped
60 g/2¼ oz *Massa de Pimentão*
juice of 2 lemons
4 thick slices sourdough bread, toasted or griddled, to serve

Prepare a barbecue or preheat the indoor grill (broiler).

Scrub the shells of the limpets to remove any dirt. Rinse the limpets several times under cold running water to remove any sand and grit.

As soon as the barbecue coals are glowing, arrange the limpets shell-side down on the grill rack so their juices do not spill out during cooking. Add a knob of butter, garlic, *Massa de Pimentão* and lemon juice to each limpet and grill for 4–5 minutes, or until they come loose from their shells. Alternatively, cook under the indoor grill.

Serve hot with the toasted or griddled bread.

Grilled Limpets with Butter and Chilli Sauce

....

Lapas Grelhadas à Moda dos Açores ◡ Açores

Preparation time: 10 minutes
Cooking time: 15 minutes
Serves: 4
⊠

1.2 kg/2 lb 11 oz limpets
120 g/4 oz (1 stick) unsalted butter, softened
3 garlic cloves, peeled and crushed to a paste
5 g/¼ oz chilli paste or 3 bird's eye chillies, finely chopped
sea salt
4 thick slices sourdough bread, to serve

Prepare a barbecue or preheat the indoor grill (broiler).

Scrub the shells of the limpets to remove any dirt. Rinse the limpets several times under cold

running water to remove any sand and grit.

Meanwhile, put the softened butter into a bowl, add the garlic paste, then add the chilli paste or chopped chillies. Season with salt and mix together until well combined.

As soon as the barbecue coals are glowing, arrange the limpets shell-side down on the grill rack so their juices do not spill out during cooking. Place a small spoonful of the chilli butter to each limpet and grill for 4–5 minutes, or until they come loose from their shells. Alternatively, cook under the indoor grill.

Serve hot with the bread.

Ground Stew Limpets

....

Sarrabulho de Lapas de São Jorge ◡ Açores

Preparation time: 15 minutes
Cooking time: 20 minutes
Serves 4
◻

1.8 kg/4 lb limpets
4 thick slices bread, crusts removed
70 ml/2¼ fl oz (⅓ cup) olive oil
2 onions, peeled and finely chopped
4 garlic cloves, peeled and finely chopped
1 tablespoon *Massa de Malagueta* (page 102)
1 teaspoon ground black pepper
4 flat-leaf parsley sprigs, finely chopped
1 tablespoon lemon juice
sea salt and freshly ground black pepper

Scrub the shells of the limpets to remove any dirt. Rinse the limpets several times under cold running water to remove any sand and grit.

Bring a large saucepan of salted water to the boil, then reduce the heat to medium, add the limpets and blanch them for 4 minutes, or until the meat can be released from the shells. Drain, reserving the limpet cooking liquid, then remove the limpets from their shells. Put the limpet meat into a blender or food processor and blitz until finely chopped. Alternatively, chop the meat finely with a knife and set aside.

Put the bread into a food processor and blitz to breadcrumbs. Set aside.

Heat the olive oil in a large saucepan over a low heat. Add the onions and garlic and cook for 10 minutes, or until the onions are translucent. Add the breadcrumbs, increase the heat to medium and cook for 5 minutes. If it is too dry add a little of the reserved cooking liquid, then add the *Massa de Malagueta* and season with the ground pepper. Add the limpets, parsley and lemon juice and mix until everything is well combined.

Taste and adjust the seasoning, if necessary, before serving.

Limpets Escabeche

••

Lapas de Escabeche da Madeira   ⛊ Madeira

Preparation time: 15 minutes, plus 3 days standing
Cooking time: 45 minutes
Serves: 4
🌿 ▢

2 kg/4 lb 8 oz limpets
220 ml/7½ fl oz (1 cup) olive oil
2 onions, peeled and thinly sliced
3 garlic cloves, peeled and thinly sliced
130 ml/4½ fl oz (½ cup) white wine
60 ml/2 fl oz (4 tablespoons) white wine vinegar
1 red chilli, finely chopped
2 flat-leaf parsley sprigs, roughly chopped
2 bay leaves
sea salt and freshly ground black pepper

Scrub the shells of the limpets to remove any dirt. Rinse the limpets several times under cold running water to remove any sand and grit.

Bring a large saucepan of salted water to the boil, then reduce the heat to medium, add the limpets and blanch them for 4 minutes, or until the meat can be released from the shells. Drain, then remove the limpets from their shells and set aside.

Heat the olive oil in a large frying pan or skillet over a medium heat. Add the onions and garlic and cook for 15 minutes, or until the onions are golden brown. Remove from the heat and add the white wine, vinegar, pepper, chilli, parsley and bay leaves. Put the pan back on the heat and bring to the boil.

Put the limpets into a sterilised, large glass jar or other container and pour over the escabeche, leaving a 1-cm/½-inch head space. Leave to cool, then cover with a lid and leave in the fridge for 3 days before eating.

Limpets Rice

••

Arroz de Lapas   ⛊ Madeira

Preparation time: 20 minutes
Cooking time: 45 minutes
Serves: 4
🌿 ▢

1.8 kg/4 lb limpets
150 ml/5 fl oz (⅔ cup) olive oil
2 onions, peeled and finely chopped
3 garlic cloves, peeled and finely chopped
1 bay leaf
2 tomatoes, cut into small cubes
3 cloves
60 ml/2 fl oz (4 tablespoons) Madeira wine
350 g/12 oz (1¾ cups) rice
⅓ bunch flat-leaf parsley, roughly chopped
sea salt and freshly ground black pepper

Scrub the shells of the limpets to remove any dirt. Rinse the limpets several times under cold running water to remove any sand and grit.

Bring a large saucepan of salted water to the boil, then reduce the heat to medium, add the limpets and blanch them for 4 minutes, or until the meat can be released from the shells. Drain, reserving the limpet cooking liquid, then remove the limpets from their shells and cut in half.

Strain the limpet cooking water into a bowl or jug (pitcher). You will need about 1 litre/34 fl oz (4¼ cups). Set aside.

Heat the olive oil in a medium saucepan over a low heat. Add the onions, garlic, bay leaf, tomatoes, cloves and pepper and cook for 15 minutes, or until the onions are golden brown.

Add the Madeira and 900 ml/30 fl oz (3¾ cups) of the reserved cooking liquid, bring to the boil, then add the rice and parsley. Reduce the heat to medium and gently cook the rice for 20 minutes. Depending on the type of rice you are using, it may take more or less time to cook, so keep an eye on it and check when it is nearly ready.

Just before the rice is fully cooked, add the limpets to warm through, stir, then season with salt, if necessary. Serve immediately.

Azorean Barnacles with Garlic

Cracas com Alho   ⛉ Açores

Until the middle of the 18th century *cracas* were wrongly considered a mollusc, but scientists confirmed at the end of the 19th century that they are in fact small marine crustaceans. They live all their life attached to rocks, generally about 10 to 15 metres deep, and they are caught on the coast in an apnea dive. Similar to barnacles, *cracas* are boiled in water and eaten with the help of a small hook after they have cooled down. The water that comes from inside of the shell is usually sipped afterwards.

Preparation time: 20 minutes
Cooking time: 15 minutes
Serves 4
⬗ ⬜ ⬜

1.5 kg/3 lb 5 oz goose barnacles
1 small onion, peeled and quartered
2 *pimentas*, quartered
5 garlic cloves, peeled and crushed with the back
    of a knife
1 small bunch flat-leaf parsley, roughly chopped
sea salt and freshly ground white pepper

If you have access to seawater that is ideal, otherwise, make a brine with 3% sea salt to cook the barnacles.

Put the barnacles, cavities facing upwards, into a saucepan large enough to accommodate all of them, and cover them with water. Add the onion, *pimentas*, garlic, parsley and white pepper and cook over a medium heat for 15 minutes.

Remove the barnacles carefully from the pan, making sure the cavities remain facing upwards so that some of the cooking liquid remains inside and serve. You can drink the liquid that remains in the cavity.

Poached Goose Barnacles

Percebes ao Natural   ⛉ Algarve

Percebes, or goose barnacles, are a *petisco* in many *marisqueiras* or *cervejarias* all over Portugal, but it's in the Algarve (and sometimes in Peniche), especially along the rugged southwest coast, that they are prised by experienced fishermen from rocks that are repeatedly pummelled by the pounding waves. *Percebes*, named after the Latin word *pollicipes* in reference to the crustacean's resemblance to a thumb, have a somewhat unappetising appearance, but diners pay a high price and fishermen take great risks to capture this pure taste of the sea that no other seafood offers. The best way to enjoy their full sweet, succulent, seawater flavour is to boil them for no more than 15 to 20 seconds, and eat them while still warm, or blanched in an ice bath.

Preparation time: 5 minutes
Cooking time: 2 minutes
Serves: 4
⬗ ⬜ ⬜ ⊠ ✕

1 kg/2 lb 4 oz goose barnacles
sea salt

Bring 3 litres/102 fl oz (12¾ cups) water and 10 g/¼ oz (2 teaspoons) salt to the boil in a large saucepan. You can also use 3 litres/102 fl oz (12¾ cups) seawater. If you do use seawater, then do not add any extra salt. Once it starts boiling, add the barnacles and cook for 2 minutes over a high heat. Drain and eat hot or cold. The Portuguese prefer to eat these cold.

Boiled Periwinkles

Caramujos Cozidos   ⛉ Madeira

Preparation time: 10 minutes
Cooking time: 15 minutes
Serves: 4
⬗ ⬜ ⬜ ⊠ ✕

1.5 kg/3 lb 5 oz periwinkles
4 garlic cloves, unpeeled and crushed
juice of 2 lemons
sea salt

Wash the periwinkles under cold running water a few times to remove any dirt. Check them carefully as sometimes they harbour other creatures inside.

Fill a saucepan with 4 litres/136 fl oz (17 cups) water, add the crushed garlic and season with salt. Bring to the boil, then add the periwinkles and cook for 10 minutes. Drain and put into a serving dish. Drizzle with lemon juice, then use suitable metal forks to remove the meat from the shells.

Snails — Portuguese Style

Caracóis à Portuguesa

Lisbon

Many people in Lisbon wait anxiously for the warmer months when restaurants put up signs announcing 'Há caracóis!' ('snails available here'). Portuguese snails are different from their French *escargot* counterpart, being smaller and greyer, and are here drowned in a savoury broth that includes piri-piri (chilli pepper sauce). *Caracóis à Portuguesa* is a *petisco*, served either as a snack alongside a few beers, as an appetiser before a meal, or as a bite while watching a soccer game.

Preparation time: 20 minutes, plus 12 hours standing
Cooking time: 3 hours
Serves: 4

1.6 kg/3 lb 8 oz medium snails
100 ml/3½ fl oz (⅓ cup) olive oil
½ white onion, peeled and cut into large chunks
3 garlic cloves, peeled and quartered
2 bird's eye chillies, finely chopped
1 bay leaf
1 bunch dried oregano
sea salt and freshly ground black pepper

Wash the snails several times under cold running water to remove as much slime as possible.

Heat the olive oil in a large saucepan over a medium heat, add the onion and garlic and cook for 2 minutes, or until the onion is soft, then add the chillies, bay leaf, snails and oregano and season with salt. Pour in enough water to cover and cook over a low heat for 3 hours. Using a slotted spoon, keep skimming the foam off the top during cooking.

Remove the pan from the heat and leave the snails to cool in the stock. Taste and adjust the seasoning with salt and pepper. Once cool, transfer the snails and stock to a large bowl or container, cover and leave to chill in the fridge for 12 hours.

Serve the next day.

Snails — Algarve Style

Caracóis à Algarvia

Algarve

I have fond memories of this dish when I used to live in the south, going out for a *petisco* with my parents and eating snails; the smell of the stewed oregano is quite incredible. Ideally, you need to buy the snails a few days before cooking this dish as they need to be washed extremely well to get rid of their slime.

Preparation time: 20 minutes
Cooking time: 1 hour
Serves: 6

2.5 kg/5 lb 10 oz small snails
2 heads garlic, 1 smashed and 1 separated into cloves
rind of 1 orange
rind of 1 lemon
2 thyme sprigs
2 teaspoons dried oregano
2 red chillies, finely chopped (optional)
sea salt

Wash the snails several times under cold running water to remove as much slime as possible.

Put the snails into a saucepan, large enough to accommodate them all, then cover with water and place over a low heat. Slowly increase the heat so the snails start to come out of their shells and bring to a boil. Once the water starts to boil, remove the snails from the pan and put them into another large pan. Cover with fresh water, then add the garlic, some salt, the citrus rind, thyme, oregano and chilli, if using. Cook over a low heat for 45 minutes. Taste and adjust the seasoning, if necessary, before serving.

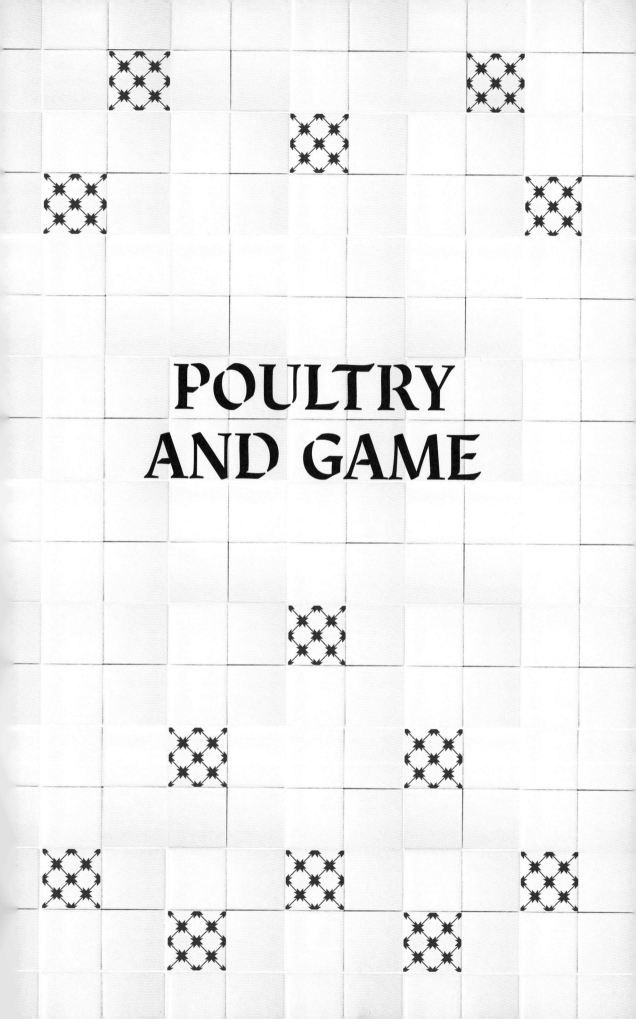

POULTRY
AND GAME

Chicken Pies

••

Empadas de Galinha   🖼 p.197   🖰 Alentejo

These golden puff-pastry pies are seasoned with a spice mix of nutmeg, black pepper and cloves. Originally from Alentejo, *Empadas de Galinha* are made in other parts of the country with a variety of pastry (shortcrust, for example) and fillings (such as veal or partridge). Most commonly they are eaten as a main dish or a snack.

Preparation time: 50 minutes
Cooking time: 1 hour 20 minutes
Makes: 12
🖰

1 whole chicken
1 chorizo
150 g/5 oz lardo
2 onions, peeled and sliced
½ bunch flat-leaf parsley, roughly chopped
5 white peppercorns
5 cloves
70 g/2¾ oz (½ cup) plain (all-purpose) flour, plus extra
    for dusting
4 egg yolks, plus an extra 2 yolks for the egg wash
50 ml/1⅔ fl oz (3½ tablespoons) white wine vinegar
50 ml/1⅔ fl oz (3½ tablespoons) lemon juice
1 kg/2 lb 4 oz readymade puff pastry
sea salt and freshly ground black pepper

Clean the chicken, trim away any excess fat and chop it into small pieces. Put the chicken, chorizo, lardo, onions, parsley, peppercorns and cloves into a large saucepan and cover with cold water. Season with salt and cook over a medium-low heat for 30 minutes, or until the chicken is cooked through. Using a slotted spoon, skim off any foam that forms on the surface during cooking. Remove the meat from the pan and set aside. Strain the chicken cooking liquid into a bowl through a sieve (fine-mesh strainer) lined with muslin (cheesecloth). Set aside the stock to cool.

    Shred the chicken, discarding the skin and bones, then cut the chorizo and lardo into small pieces. Set aside.

    Put the flour into a small bowl, add 100 ml/ 3½ fl oz (7 tablespoons) of the cold stock and stir together until smooth. Add the 4 egg yolks.

    Put 700 ml/23 fl oz (scant 3 cups) of the stock into a large saucepan, then stir in the flour and egg yolk mixture. Cook over a low heat, stirring continuously for 20 minutes, or until it thickens and the flour is fully cooked. Remove from the heat, stir in the meats, season with salt and pepper, then add the vinegar and lemon juice to taste. Chill in the fridge.

    Preheat the oven to 190°C/375°F/Gas Mark 5.

    Roll out the pastry on a lightly floured work surface to a thickness of 2 mm/1/16 inch. Using a 12-cm/4¾-inch pastry cutter, cut out 12 rounds, from the puff pastry. Line 12 pans, about 9 cm/ 3½ inch wide, with the pastry rounds. Fill the lined pans with the meat filling. Cut out another 12 rounds of pastry, this time measuring 9 cm/ 3½ inches and place on top. Seal, crimp the edges and brush the tops of the pastries with the beaten egg yolk. Make a small slit in the top of each pie to let the steam escape. Bake in the hot oven for 25–30 minutes, or until the pastry is golden. Remove from the pans and leave to rest on a wire rack for 20 minutes before serving.

Chicken Broth — Alentejo Style

••

Canja de Galinha Alentejana   🖰 Alentejo

Prepared by all Portuguese grandmothers and mothers as a salve for bouts of flu or stomach ache, *Canja de Galinha* can be a comforting, simple chicken broth all year round and on all occasions. It is made from chicken poaching liquid, garnished with pasta (alphabet pasta for kids) or rice, eggs in shells, and flavoured with parsley or, most commonly, mint. *Canja* is also very popular in Asia, from Japan and Korea to Vietnam and Malaysia, where it is originally from. Known there as congee, it is a thick rice porridge.

Preparation time: 20 minutes
Cooking time: 55 minutes
Serves: 6
🖋 🖰 🖰

1 whole chicken
90 g/3¼ oz *linguiça*
1 large onion, peeled and halved
1 bunch flat-leaf parsley, roughly chopped
1 bay leaf
200 g/7 oz (1 cup) long-grain rice
sea salt and freshly ground black pepper

Clean the chicken, trim away any excess fat and cut it in half and then into quarters. Keep the offal (variety meats). Season the chicken with salt, then put it into a large saucepan with the *linguiça*, onion, parsley and bay leaf, together with the offal. Cover the chicken with water and cook over a medium heat for 45 minutes. The offal should be cooked before the chicken, so when it is cooked, remove and set aside. Once the meat comes easily off the bones, remove the chicken from the pan, and strain the cooking liquid through a sieve (fine-mesh strainer). Chop the offal into small pieces.

    Pour the strained stock back into the pan, add the rice and cook over a medium heat for 10–12 minutes, or until soft.

    Stir the offal into the rice, season with salt and pepper, if necessary, and serve with the rest of the chicken meat.

Chicken Pies

Poached and Roasted Hen

••

Galinha Cerejada

◊ Algarve

This traditional dish from Loulé owes its name to the fact that the skin of the chicken acquires a colour similar to that of a cherry (*cereja*) when slowly poached in water with *linguiça* (spicy sausage) added. In other recipe variations, the chicken acquires a dark red colour from being roasted in olive oil with garlic and chilli, or rubbed with a paste of lard, paprika, garlic, onion and white wine. *Galinha cerejada* is usually prepared to use the chicken left over from the *canja* (chicken broth soup) cooked the day before.

Preparation time: 30 minutes
Cooking time: 40 minutes
Serves: 4
🐟 ◊

1 whole chicken
120 g/4 oz lardo, halved
80 g/3 oz *linguiça* (Portuguese sausage) or use chorizo, halved
1 carrot, peeled but left whole
1 bunch flat-leaf parsley, finely chopped
2 small onions, 1 peeled and halved and 1 peeled and very finely chopped
50 g/2 oz lard (pork fat)
80 ml/2¾ fl oz (⅓ cup) olive oil
3 garlic cloves, peeled and finely chopped
500 ml/17 fl oz (2 cups) white wine
320 g/11¼ oz (1⅔ cups) long-grain rice
sea salt and freshly ground black pepper
green salad, to serve

Clean the chicken, trim away any excess fat and chop it into small pieces. Season the chicken with salt, then put it into a large saucepan with the lardo, *linguiça*, carrot, half of the parsley and the halved onion. Cover with water and cook over a medium heat for 15 minutes, or until the chicken is cooked through. Remove the meat from the pan and set aside. Set aside the chicken cooking liquid.

Heat the lard (pork fat) and olive oil in a medium saucepan over a low heat, add the chopped onion and garlic and cook for 5 minutes. Don't let the onions colour. Add the chicken to the pan and stir, then cook for 5 minutes. Add the white wine, cover with a lid and cook over a medium heat for 2 minutes, or until the wine has reduced. Taste and adjust the seasoning, if necessary.

Meanwhile, put the rice into a medium saucepan and pour in 700 ml/23½ fl oz (2¾ cups) of the reserved chicken cooking liquid. Bring to the boil, then reduce the heat to low, cover with a lid and cook for 10–12 minutes until soft. Season with salt, then arrange the rice in a large serving dish, add the chicken on top, with the *linguiça*, and lardo sliced over and garnish with the remaining parsley. Serve with a green salad.

Chicken Stewed in a Clay Pot

••

Frango na Púcara 📷 p.199

◊ Leiria

Preparation time: 30 minutes, plus 10 minutes resting
Cooking time: 1 hour
Serves: 4
🐟

1 whole chicken
100 g/3½ oz Serrano ham
50 g/2 oz smoked bacon, rind removed
4 tomatoes
10 small onions, peeled and quartered
2 garlic cloves, peeled and crushed
2 tablespoons mustard
200 ml/7 fl oz (¾ cup) white wine
120 ml/4 fl oz (½ cup) port
120 ml/4 fl oz (½ cup) firewater or grappa
30 g/1 oz (2 tablespoons) butter
2 butterhead lettuces, leaves separated
60 ml/2 fl oz (4 tablespoons) olive oil
30 ml/1 fl oz (2 tablespoons) white wine vinegar
1 litre/34 fl oz (4¼ cups) sunflower oil, for deep-frying
1 kg/2 lb 4 oz new potatoes, peeled and cut into thin fries
sea salt and freshly ground black pepper

Clean the chicken, trim away any excess fat and chop it into small pieces. Slice the ham and bacon into pieces the same size as the chicken. Set aside.

Have a large bowl of iced water ready nearby. Bring a saucepan of water to the boil. Using a sharp knife, score the top of the tomatoes with a small cross shape. Once the water is boiling, carefully add the tomatoes and blanch for 30 seconds, then transfer with a slotted spoon to the iced water and leave to cool. Once cool enough to handle, peel off the skins and cut into quarters. Set aside.

Preheat the oven to 200°C/400°F/Gas Mark 6.

Season the chicken with 2 teaspoons salt and 1 teaspoon pepper, then place it inside a *púcura* (clay cooking pot). Add the ham, bacon, tomatoes, onions, garlic, mustard, white wine, port, firewater or grappa and butter. Cover with a lid and cook for 45 minutes, then check the chicken. If it almost ready, uncover and cook for a further 10 minutes, or until golden brown. Leave to rest for 10 minutes.

Put the lettuce leaves into a salad bowl. Combine the olive oil and vinegar in a small bowl, add a pinch of salt, then drizzle over the lettuce.

Line a large baking sheet with paper towels. Heat the sunflower oil for deep-frying in a large, deep saucepan until it reaches 180°C/350°F on a thermometer. Working in batches, carefully lower the potato fries into the hot oil and deep-fry for 2–3 minutes, or until golden brown. Remove with a slotted spoon and leave to drain on the lined baking sheet. Season with salt.

Serve the stewed chicken with the green salad and fries alongside.

Chicken Stewed in a Clay Pot

'White' Chicken with Garlic and Chilli

Galinha Branca ⏏ Leiria

This is another recipe that I grew up watching my grandmother make for us. It is slow cooking at its best and is often made in a three-legged iron pot hung over the fire. It was incredibly special.

Preparation time: 20 minutes
Cooking time: 1 hour
Serves: 4
🌿 ⏏

1 whole chicken
150 ml/5 fl oz (⅔ cup) olive oil
8 garlic cloves, unpeeled and crushed
1 red chilli, finely chopped
fine sea salt
boiled plain white rice, to serve

Clean the chicken, trim away any excess fat and cut it in half, removing the backbone. Chop the chicken into medium-sized pieces and season with salt. Set aside.

Wash the backbone to remove any remaining blood, then put it into a large saucepan and cover with 1.5 litres/50 fl oz (6¼ cups) cold water to make a stock. Cook over a medium heat for 20 minutes, skiming off the foam that rise to the top with a slotted spoon. Remove the stock from the heat and set aside.

Heat the olive oil in another large saucepan over a low heat. Add the chicken, garlic and chilli and cook for 5 minutes, or until one side is golden. Flip over and cook for a further 5 minutes. Once the chicken is coloured on both sides, add a few ladlefuls of the reserved stock, stir and cover with the lid. Cook gently for 20–30 minutes, or until the stock has reduced and the meat is cooked. If not, add more stock and reduce again. The meat should be very soft and golden with a thick flavourful sauce.

Serve the chicken with the sauce and boiled plain white rice alongside.

Partridge with Shredded Fried Potatoes — Coimbra Style

Perdiz à Moda de Coimbra 📷 p.201   ⏏ Beira Litoral

Preparation time: 30 minutes
Cooking time: 2 hours 5 minutes
Serves: 4
🌿 ⏏

4 small partridges
3 onions, peeled and thinly sliced
6 white peppercorns
18 cloves
1 teaspoon ground cumin
250 ml/8 fl oz (1 cup) white wine
180 ml/6 fl oz (¾ cup) olive oil
100 ml/3½ fl oz (⅓ cup) white wine vinegar
sea salt and ground white pepper
green salad, to serve

For the potatoes:
600 g/1 lb 5 oz new potatoes, peeled
1.5 litres/50 fl oz (6¼ cups) sunflower oil,
    for deep-frying

Clean the partridges, trim away any excess fat and tie them up tightly with butcher's string or kitchen twine. Season the partridges with salt and ground white pepper.

Arrange the onions in a layer on the bottom of a saucepan large enough to accommodate the partridges. Add all the ingredients to the pan on top of the onions, including the partridges, and cover with a lid. Cook over a low heat for 2 hours, or until the onions are very soft and the partridges are cooked.

Meanwhile, grate (shred) the potatoes very thinly on a mandolin, then rinse them under cold running water a few times to help remove the excess starch.

Line a large baking sheet with paper towels. Heat the sunflower oil for deep-frying in a large, deep saucepan until it reaches 180°C/350°F on a thermometer. Working in batches, carefully lower the potatoes into the hot oil and deep-fry for 2 minutes, or until golden brown. Remove with a slotted spoon and leave to drain on the lined baking sheet, then season with salt.

When the partridges are cooked, transfer them to a large serving dish. Remove the cloves and most of the peppercorns from the saucepan, then transfer the onions and cooking liquid to a blender and process until smooth.

Pour the sauce over the partridges and serve either hot or cold with the fried potatoes and a green salad alongside.

Partridge with Shredded Fried Potatoes – Coimbra Style

Chicken Offal with Tomato and Cumin Sauce

Pipis com Molho de Tomate   ♡ Leiria

Pipi has a several meanings in Portuguese, including the name that children give to birds, or the onomatopoeic word derived from 'pio', which in Portugal is the sound emitted by birds. However, it is this traditional *petisco* made of chicken giblets and served in tabernas or bars that is the best known meaning of the word all over Portugal.

Preparation time: 25 minutes, plus 5 minutes resting
Cooking time: 1 hour 30 minutes
Serves: 4
🐟 □ ▢

250 g/9 oz chicken gizzards
150 g/5 oz chicken livers
150 g/5 oz chicken hearts
8 chicken feet
150 ml/5 fl oz (⅔ cup) olive oil
2 onions, peeled and finely chopped
3 garlic cloves, peeled and finely chopped
500 ml/17 fl oz (2 cups) white wine
400-g/14-oz can chopped tomatoes
30 g/1 oz (2 tablespoons) tomato purée (paste)
1 red chilli, cut into small pieces
2 bay leaves
60 ml/2 fl oz (4 tablespoons) white wine vinegar
1 teaspoon ground cumin
sea salt and freshly ground black pepper

Clean all the offal (variety meats), the membrane around the gizzards, the fat on the liver and hearts, and cut the chicken feet in half. Rinse thoroughly under cold running water and let them drip on a perforated tray or in a colander.

Heat half the olive oil in a large saucepan over a medium heat. Add the hearts and fry for 5 minutes, then remove to one side of a plate. Add the gizzards and fry for 5 minutes, then transfer to the other side of the plate. Add the livers to the pan and fry for 5 minutes. Transfer to the plate with the rest of the offal, but keep them all separated.

Add the remaining olive oil to the same pan used to fry the offal, put the onions and garlic into the pan and cook over a medium heat for 15 minutes, or until golden brown. Add the white wine and bring to the boil. Add the canned tomatoes, tomato purée (paste), schilli and bay leaves. Reduce the heat to low and cook for 20 minutes, or until the tomatoes have broken down. Return the offal to the pan, then add the chicken feet, vinegar, cumin and a pinch of salt and cook for a further 40 minutes. Taste and adjust the seasoning with salt and pepper and add a little water, if it is too thick.

Remove the pan from the heat and leave to rest for 5 minutes before serving.

Partridge with Mushrooms

Perdiz com
Cogumelos 📷 p.203   ♡ Trás-os-Montes
e Alto Douro

Preparation time: 20 minutes
Cooking time: 50 minutes
Serves: 4
🐟 □

1 large or 2 medium partridges
150 ml/5 fl oz (⅔ cup) olive oil
90 g/3¼ oz Serrano ham, sliced into small pieces
2 small onions, peeled and very finely chopped
1 garlic clove, peeled and very finely chopped
500 g/1 lb 2 oz miscaros (man on horseback) mushrooms (page 429) or wild girolles, cleaned and torn or cut into chunks
sea salt and freshly ground black pepper

Clean the partridges, trim away any excess fat and cut down the backbone, then remove and discard the central bone. Cut the partridge into small pieces, season with salt and pepper and set aside.

Heat the olive oil in a saucepan over a medium heat. Add the partridge, ham, onions and garlic and cook for 5 minutes, or until the onions are translucent. Add the mushrooms, cover with a lid, reduce the heat to low and cook gently for 45 minutes. Do not overcook the mushrooms. Taste and adjust the seasoning, if necessary, before serving.

Stewed Partridge

Perdiz Estufada à Portuguesa   ♡ Lisbon

Preparation time: 20 minutes
Cooking time: 1 hour
Serves: 4
🐟 □

4 medium partridges
250 g/9 oz Serrano ham, thinly sliced
100 g/3½ oz lard (pork fat) or unsalted butter
2 onions, peeled and thinly sliced
500 ml/17 fl oz (2 cups) white wine
sea salt and freshly ground black pepper

Clean the partridges, trim away any excess fat and remove any offal (variety meats). Rinse any blood from the insides under cold running water. Leave to drip on a perforated tray or in a colander.

Season the partridges with salt and pepper, then wrap in the ham and secure with butcher's string or kitchen twine.

Heat the lard (pork fat) or butter in a saucepan over a medium heat. Add the onions and cook for 15 minutes, or until golden. Add the wine, bring to the boil, add the partridges, cover with a lid, reduce the heat to low and cook for 45 minutes, or until cooked through. Serve immediately.

Partridge with Mushrooms

Partridges Cooked in a Clay Pot

Perdizes na Púcara de Tomar ♡ Ribatejo

Preparation time: 20 minutes, plus 10 minutes resting
Cooking time: 45 minutes
Serves: 4
🌶 🍲

2 grey partridges
80 g/3 oz Serrano ham, thinly sliced
60 ml/2 fl oz (4 tablespoons) olive oil
2 small onions, peeled and quartered
70 g/2½ oz (⅔ stick) unsalted butter
80 ml/2¾ fl oz (⅓ cup) white wine
60 ml/2 fl oz (4 tablespoons) white wine vinegar
2 garlic cloves, peeled and finely chopped
1 bird's eye chilli, finely chopped
sea salt

Leaving them whole, clean the partridges from any offal (variety meats). Rinse any blood from the insides under cold running water. Leave to drip on a perforated tray or in a colander.

Season the partridges with salt, then wrap the birds in the ham so they are completely covered.

Put the partridges into a *púcara* (clay cooking pot) or large saucepan with all the other ingredients. Cover with a lid and cook over a low heat for 45 minutes, or until the meat is soft, turning the birds during cooking. If too dry, add a little water – there should be juices left at the end of cooking. Leave to rest for 10 minutes before serving.

Stewed Partridge

Perdiz Estufada ♡ Algarve

In this recipe it is very important to keep an eye on the cooking time, as an overcooked partridge is dry with little to no flavour. When the meat is cooked, remove it from the saucepan and set it aside, then leave the remaining ingredients to stew a bit more if they need to.

Preparation time: 1 hour
Cooking time: 1 hour
Serves: 4

4 small partridges
250 ml/8 fl oz (1 cup) olive oil, plus extra for frying the bread
200 ml/7 fl oz (¾ cup) white wine
8 garlic cloves, peeled but left whole
4 cloves
½ bunch flat-leaf parsley, roughly chopped
800 g/1 lb 12 oz waxy potatoes, peeled
100 g/3½ oz (1 stick) butter
sea salt and freshly ground black pepper
4 slices sourdough bread, to serve

Clean the partridges, trim away any excess fat and remove any offal (variety meats). Rinse any blood from the insides under cold running water. Leave to drip on a perforated tray or in a colander.

Season the partridges with salt, then put into a large casserole dish (Dutch oven) with the olive oil, white wine, garlic, cloves and parsley, and cook over a low heat for 1 hour, or until the birds are tender.

Meanwhile, put the potatoes into a large saucepan, cover with cold water, add a pinch of salt and cook over a low heat for 15–20 minutes, or until soft. Drain and put them into a food processor or blender. Add the butter and salt and pepper to taste and process until a smooth purée has formed. Set aside.

Heat enough olive oil for frying the bread in a frying pan or skillet over a medium heat, add the bread and fry for 5 minutes on each side, or until golden all over.

Serve the partridges with the potato purée and fried bread alongside.

Partridge with Clams

Perdiz com Amêijoas na Cataplana ♡ Algarve

This dish requires a special copper pan called a *cataplana* (page 429), which has a lid with an airtight rubber seal.

Preparation time: 15 minutes, plus 2 hours standing and 10 miunutes rest
Cooking time: 1 hour 15 minutes
Serves: 4
🌶 🍲

1 kg/2 lb 4 oz fresh palourde or surf clams
2 teaspoons fine table salt
2 partridges
2 bird's eye chillies, finely chopped
2 large onions, peeled and finely chopped
4 garlic cloves, peeled and crushed
2 bay leaves
80 g/3 oz (¾ stick) butter
250 ml/8 fl oz (1 cup) red port
200 ml/7 fl oz (¾ cup) white wine
1 teaspoon smoked paprika
½ bunch flat-leaf parsley, roughly chopped

Rinse the clams a few times in cold water to remove any sand and grit, then put them into a large bowl of water, add the fine table salt, stir and leave to stand for 2 hours. This helps them to release any remaining sand and grit.

Clean the partridges, removing any traces of offal (variety meats). Rinse any blood from the insides under cold running water. Leave to drip on a perforated tray or in a colander. Cut the partridges into quarters, season with salt and sprinkle with the chopped chillies.

Put the onions, garlic, bay leaves and butter into a *cataplana* and cook over a low heat for 15 minutes, or until the onions are golden. Add the partridges and cook for 45 minutes, or until coloured all over.

Add the port, a little at a time, then add the white wine, a little at a time. Drain the clams and add them to the pan, stir, then put the lid on and cook for 15 minutes. Add the paprika and stir. Remove from the heat and leave to rest with the lid on for 10 minutes. Uncover, scatter the parsley over the top and stir. Taste and adjust the seasoning, if necessary, before serving.

Partridge 'Escabeche'

Perdiz de Escabeche   ♡ Beira Baixa

A traditional dish from Alentejo and Beira Interior, this *escabeche* preparation (page 429) was historically applied to game birds. During the hunting season (September through spring), men would hunt and women would preserve the meat so that it could be eaten all winter. *Perdiz de Escabeche* can be served cold, warm or at room temperature.

Preparation time: 30 minutes, plus 2 days marinating
Cooking time: 1 hour
Serves: 4
🦴 ♡

2 grey partridges, about 450g/1 lb each
200 ml/7 fl oz (¾ cup) white wine
6 garlic cloves, peeled and finely chopped
1 bunch rosemary
1 bunch carqueja
3 bay leaves
150 ml/5 fl oz (⅔ cup) olive oil
sea salt
green salad or boiled potatoes, to serve

For the escabeche:
120 ml/4 fl oz (½ cup) olive oil
3 small onions, peeled and finely chopped
2 carrots, peeled and cut into medium-thick slices
1 green (bell) pepper, cored, de-seeded and thinly sliced
3 garlic cloves, peeled and finely chopped
8 black peppercorns
1 teaspoon paprika
100 ml/3½ fl oz (⅓ cup) white wine vinegar

Clean the partridges, trim away any excess fat and remove any offal (variety meats). Rinse any blood from the insides under cold running water. Leave to drip on a perforated tray or in a colander.

Cut the partridges in half lengthwise, season with salt and put them into a large bowl with the white wine, garlic, rosemary, carqueja and bay leaves. Season with salt and toss everything together until the birds are well coated in the marinade. Cover with food wrap and leave in the fridge for 2 days, turning the birds in the marinade once a day.

When ready to cook, remove the partridges from the marinade, reserving the marinade. Heat a large saucepan over a high heat. Once hot, reduce the heat to medium, add the olive oil and the birds and cook for 45 minutes, or until browned all over. Add the marinade, reduce the heat to low, then remove the birds from the pan and set aside. Cook the marinade for 5 minutes, or until it has reduced a little. Put the birds back into the pan, taste and adjust the seasoning, if necessary. Remove the pan from the heat and set aside.

For the escabeche, heat the olive oil in a saucepan over a medium heat. Add the onions, carrots, green (bell) pepper, garlic and peppercorns and cook for 10 minutes, or until the vegetables are al dente, then add the paprika, stir and add the vinegar and a pinch of salt. Stir again. Add the escabeche to the pan with the partridges and stir until well combined.

Serve the partridges and escabeche with a green salad or boiled potatoes alongside.

Wild Pigeon Rice

Arroz de Pombo Bravo   ♡ Beira Baixa

Preparation time: 20 minutes
Cooking time: 1 hour
Serves: 4
🦴 ♡ ♡

3 wild (wood) pigeons
70 ml/2¼ fl oz (4⅔ tablespoons) olive oil
40 g/1½ oz lardo, cut into pieces
1½ onions, peeled and finely chopped
4 garlic cloves, peeled and finely chopped
2 bunches flat-leaf parsley
2 bay leaves
260 g/9 oz (1¼ cup) short-grain rice, such as Carolino
sea salt

Prepare the pigeons, removing any remaining feathers and all the offal (variety meats). Rinse any blood from the insides under cold running water. Cut the pigeons into small pieces, watching for any shot that might be still in the meat, then cut the heart and liver into small pieces and season them with salt.

Heat the olive oil in a large saucepan over a low heat. Add the lardo, onions, garlic, parsley and bay leaves to the pan. Add the pigeons with any offal, cover with a lid and cook for 45 minutes, or until the onions and meat are soft. Add a splash of water, if necessary, to prevent it drying out during cooking. Add 800 ml/27 fl oz (3¼ cups) water and bring to the boil, then add the rice, reduce the heat to low and cook, stirring occasionally, for 15 minutes, or until the rice is soft. Taste and adjust the seasoning, if necessary, before serving.

Hunter's Rabbit Stew

••

Coelho à Caçadora
◻ Lisbon

Preparation time: 20 minutes
Cooking time: 1 hour 10 minutes
Serves: 4
🔪 ◻ ◻

1 x 1.3-kg/2 lb 14-oz rabbit, halved lengthwise, jointed
    and cut into chunks
100 g/3½ oz lard (pork fat)
130 g/4½ oz lardo, sliced into small pieces
2 onions, peeled and thinly sliced
2 garlic cloves, crushed
5 sprigs flat-leaf parsley, roughly chopped
2 bay leaves
8 black peppercorns
200 ml/7 fl oz (¾ cup) red wine
sea salt and freshly ground black pepper

Season the rabbit pieces with salt and pepper.

Heat the lard (pork fat) and lardo in a saucepan over a medium heat. Add the rabbit and cook for 8–10 minutes, or until golden all over. Add the remaining ingredients except the wine and cook for 15 minutes, or until the onions are golden. Add the wine and 250 ml/8 fl oz (1 cup) water, cover with a lid, reduce the heat to low and cook for 1 hour, or until the meat is tender. The loins will be ready before the legs, so remove them after 45 minutes.

Rabbit with Vinha d'Alhos

••

Coelho de Vinha d'Alhos
de Vale de Santarém
◻ Ribatejo
📷 p.207

Vinha d'Alhos marinade (page 429) is an important part of the pillars of traditional cooking, based on a mixture of wine, garlic and vinegar together with different aromatics, such as cumin, paprika and cinnamon. This dish gave origin to the famous Indian curry, Vindalho, or vindaloo.

Preparation time: 45 minutes, plus 5 hours marinating
Cooking time: 1 hour
Serves: 4
🔪 ◻

1 x 1-kg/2 lb 4-oz rabbit, halved lengthwise, jointed and
    cut into small pieces
3 garlic cloves, peeled and bashed
180 ml/6 fl oz (¾ cup) white wine
60 ml/2 fl oz (4 tablespoons) white wine vinegar
2 bay leaves
600 g/1 lb 5 oz waxy potatoes, peeled and cut into fries
1.5 litres/50 fl oz (6¼ cups) sunflower oil, for deep-frying
120 ml/4 fl oz (½ cup) olive oil
80 g/3 oz lard (pork fat)
2 onions, peeled and cut into thin rings
sea salt and freshly ground black pepper
slices of crusty bread, to serve (optional)

Put the rabbit pieces into a bowl with the garlic, white wine, vinegar, bay leaves and enough salt to season the meat. Rub the marinade into the meat, then cover with food wrap and leave to marinate in the fridge for 5 hours.

When ready to cook, rinse the potatoes a few times under cold running water, then set aside.

Line a large baking sheet with paper towels. Heat the sunflower oil for deep-frying in a large, deep saucepan or fryer until it reaches 180°C/350°F on a thermometer. Working in batches, carefully drop the fries into the hot oil and deep-fry for 2–3 minutes, or until golden and crispy. Remove with a slotted spoon and leave to drain on the lined baking sheet. Season with salt.

Remove the meat from the marinade, setting the marinade aside and pat the meat dry with a tea (dish) towel or paper towels.

Heat the olive oil and lard (pork fat) in a large saucepan over a medium heat, add the rabbit, a few pieces at a time, and cook for 10 minutes, or until browned all over. Remove the meat to a plate and continue cooking the rest.

Add the onions to the fat left in the pan and cook over a low heat for 10 minutes, or until soft and with a bit of colour. Add the marinade and bring to the boil, then remove from the heat.

Arrange the rabbit on a serving plate, pour the marinade with the onions over the top and serve with the fries and bread, if preferred.

Stewed Rabbit with Savory

••

Coelho
à Transmontana
◻ Trás-os-Montes
e Alto Douro

Preparation time: 30 minutes, plus 30 minutes standing
Cooking time: 1 hour 20 minutes
Serves 4
🔪 ◻

1 x 1.3-kg/2 lb 14-oz rabbit, halved lengthwise, jointed
    and cut into chunks
3 bunches summer savory, torn into small pieces
100 ml/3½ fl oz (⅓ cup) olive oil
200 g/7 oz bacon, chopped
1 large onion, peeled and chopped
2 sprigs flat-leaf parsley, roughly chopped
2 bay leaves
80 ml/2¾ fl oz (⅓ cup) white wine
650 g/1 lb 7 oz waxy potatoes, peeled
sea salt and freshly ground black pepper

Put the rabbit pieces into a bowl. Add the summer savory, salt and pepper, then leave for 30 minutes.

Heat the olive oil in a saucepan over a low heat. Add the rabbit, bacon, onion, parsley, bay leaves and wine. Cover with a lid and cook, stirring occasionally, for 1 hour, or until the meat is tender.

Meanwhile, put the potatoes into a saucepan of cold water, add a pinch of salt, and cook over a medium heat for 15–20 minutes, or until soft.

Serve the stewed rabbit with the potatoes.

Rabbit with Vinha d'Alhos

Rabbit Stew

••

Coelho   ⛉ Algarve

Preparation time: 30 minutes, plus 5 minutes resting
Cooking time: 1 hour 10 minutes
Serves: 4

1 medium rabbit, halved lengthwise and cut into chunks
60 g/2¼ oz (½ stick) butter
60 ml/2 fl oz (4 tablespoons) olive oil, plus extra
    for frying the potatoes
2 onions, peeled and quartered
3 garlic cloves, peeled and thinly sliced
400-g/14-oz can chopped tomatoes
½ red (bell) pepper, halved, cored, de-seeded
    and cut into thin strips
1 bird's eye chilli, finely chopped
600 ml/20 fl oz (2½ cups) white wine
80 ml/2¾ fl oz (⅓ cup) firewater or brandy
6 bay leaves
800 g/1 lb 12 oz new potatoes, peeled and left whole
sea salt and freshly ground black pepper
8 slices crusty bread, toasted, to serve

Season the rabbit pieces with salt. Heat the
butter and olive oil in a saucepan large enough to
accommodate all the meat over a medium heat.
Add the rabbit, onions and garlic and cook for
15 minutes, or until the onions are golden. Add
the tomatoes, (bell) pepper, chilli and some
black pepper and cook over a medium heat for
5 minutes. Add the white wine, firewater or brandy
and bay leaves. Cover the pan with a lid and cook
for 40 minutes, or until the meat is soft.
    Meanwhile, put the potatoes into a large
saucepan, cover with cold water, add a pinch of salt
and cook over a medium heat for 15–20 minutes,
or until soft. Drain and set aside.
    Heat a frying pan or skillet over a medium
heat. Once the pan is hot, drizzle in some olive oil,
add the potatoes and fry for 10 minutes, or until
golden brown all over. Season with a pinch of salt.
    Taste and adjust the seasoning of the stew,
if necessary, with salt and pepper. Remove from
the heat and leave to rest for 5 minutes before
serving with the fried potatoes and toasted bread.

Wild Rabbit Stew

••

Coelho Bravo   ⛉ Ribatejo

Preparation time: 30 minutes, plus 28 hours marinating
Cooking time: 1 hour 30 minutes
Serves: 4
🖉 ▢ ▢

1 wild rabbit, halved lengthwise and cut into chunks
3 garlic cloves, peeled and finely chopped
2 onions, peeled and cut into thin rings
⅓ bunch flat-leaf parsley
1 bay leaf
8 white peppercorns
50 ml/1⅔ fl oz (3½ tablespoons) olive oil
1.2 litres/40 fl oz (5 cups) white wine
20 g/¾ oz gum rockrose (wild plant)
sea salt and freshly ground black pepper

Put the rabbit pieces into a bowl, add the garlic and
salt and rub it into the meat until well coated. Cover
with food wrap and leave in the fridge to marinate
for 4 hours.
    Add the onions and the remaining ingredients
to the bowl with the meat and season with pepper.
Mix until well combined, cover again and leave in
the fridge for 24 hours.
    When ready to cook, put all the ingredients into
a large saucepan and cook over a low heat for 1 hour
30 minutes, or until the meat is soft. Check the meat
during cooking – if it is getting too dry, add a little
water. Once the rabbit is cooked, remove the meat
from the pan with a slotted spoon and set aside,
then pour the remaining contents of the pan into a
blender and process to a smooth sauce.
    Serve the rabbit with the sauce over the top.

Wild Rabbit Stew with White Beans

••

Coelho Bravo com Feijão Branco   ⛉ Ribatejo

Preparation time: 30 minutes, plus 12 hours soaking,
4 hours marinating and 5 minutes resting
Cooking time: 2 hours 40 minutes
Serves: 4
🖉 ▢

600 g/1 lb 5 oz (3⅓ cups) dried white beans
1 wild rabbit
3 garlic cloves, peeled and crushed
2 bay leaves, crushed
3 bull's heart tomatoes
50 ml/1⅔ fl oz (3½ tablespoons) olive oil
2 onions, peeled and finely chopped
1 red (bell) pepper, halved, cored, de-seeded and
    cut into thin strips
220 ml/7½ fl oz (1 cup) red wine
sea salt and freshly ground black pepper

The day before, put the beans into a large bowl of cold water and leave to soak for 12 hours. The next day, drain the beans and set aside.

Prepare the rabbit, cutting it into small pieces. Rub the meat with the garlic, bay leaves and salt, then put into a large bowl, cover with food wrap and leave to marinate in the fridge for 4 hours.

Meanwhile, place the beans in a saucepan, pour in enough cold water to cover and cook over a low heat for 1 hour, or until soft. Remove from the heat, leave in the pan and set aside

Have a large bowl of iced water nearby. Bring a large saucepan of water to the boil. Using a sharp knife, score the top of the tomatoes with a small cross shape. Once the water is boiling, carefully add the tomatoes and blanch for 30 seconds, then transfer them with a slotted spoon to the iced water and leave to cool. Once cool enough to handle, peel off the skins, cut in half and de-seed, then cut the flesh into small pieces. Set aside.

Heat the olive oil in another large saucepan over a medium heat, add the onions and cook for 5 minutes, or until the onions are translucent. Add the tomatoes, (bell) pepper, wine, rabbit pieces and the marinade to the pan, then simmer over a low heat for 1 hour 30 minutes, or until the meat is soft.

Reserving the cooking liquid, strain the beans. Add the beans to the pan with the rabbit along with 3 ladlefuls of the bean cooking liquid. Bring to the boil and cook for a further 10 minutes, or until the liquid has reduced. Remove from the heat and leave to rest for 5 minutes before serving.

Hare Scallops

•••

Bifes de Lebre   ⍔ **Beira Baixa**

Preparation time: 20 minutes, plus 2 hours 30 minutes marinating
Cooking time: 20 minutes
Serves: 4
⍔

loins and back legs of 2 medium hares, cut into thick steaks
2 bay leaves, crushed
50 ml/1²⁄₃ fl oz (3½ tablespoons) white wine vinegar, plus an extra 2 tablespoons for the salad dressing
6 garlic cloves, peeled and finely chopped
1 bunch flat-leaf parsley, roughly chopped
250 ml/8 fl oz (1 cup) olive oil, plus an extra 4 tablespoons for the salad dressing
1 butterhead lettuce, leaves separated
4 slices crusty bread, to serve
sea salt

Put the hare steaks into a large bowl, season with salt, then add the crushed bay leaves, vinegar, garlic and parsley. Cover with food wrap and leave to marinate in the fridge for 2 hours 30 minutes.

When ready to cook, remove the hare steaks from the marinade, setting the marinade aside. Heat a large frying pan or skillet over a medium heat. Add the olive oil and, when hot, add the

meat and cook for 10 minutes, or until browned all over. Pour in the reserved marinade and cook for a further 10 minutes, or until the meat is fully cooked.

Put the lettuce into a serving bowl and dress the leaves with the olive oil and vinegar. Serve the hare steaks in the sauce with the lettuce and bread.

Hare Stew with White Beans

•••

Lebre com Feijão Branco   ⍔ **Alentejo**

Despite its similarity to rabbit, hare meat is very dark and lean, and provides a stronger and sweeter flavour, leading to more creative and interesting dishes. *Lebre com Feijão Branco*, **or just** *Feijoada de Lebre*, **is a white bean and hare casserole made in Alentejo, where hunting is allowed on the extensive green plains. This dish is usually cooked after** *montarias* **(hunting days).**

Preparation time: 30 minutes, plus 12 hours soaking
Cooking time: 2 hours 30 minutes
Serves 6
⍔

450 g/1 lb (2½ cups) butter (lima) beans
1 medium hare, halved lengthwise and cut into chunks
60 g/2¼ oz lard (pork fat)
40 ml/1⅓ fl oz (2⅔ tablespoons) olive oil, plus extra for frying the bread
1½ onions, peeled and very finely chopped
3 garlic cloves, peeled and very finely chopped
¼ bunch flat-leaf parsley, roughly chopped
120 ml/4 fl oz (½ cup) white wine
6 slices bread, cubed
sea salt and freshly ground black pepper

The day before, put the beans into a large bowl of cold water and leave to soak for 12 hours. The next day, drain the beans, put them into a large saucepan, cover with cold water, add a pinch of salt and cook over a medium heat for 30 minutes, or until soft. Remove from the heat, leave in the pan and set aside.

Heat the lard (pork fat) and olive oil in a large saucepan over a medium heat, add the onions garlic, parsley, white wine, a pinch of salt and pepper and cook for 15 minutes, or until the onions are golden. Season the hare pieces with salt, add to the pan and mix everything together. Pour in enough water to cover the meat, then simmer over a low heat for 1 hour 30 minutes, or until the meat is soft.

Reserving the cooking liquid, strain the beans. Add the beans to the pan with the hare along with a little of the bean cooking liquid, if needed. Bring to the boil and cook for a further 10 minutes, or until the liquid has reduced.

Heat the olive oil for frying the bread in a frying pan or skillet over a medium heat. Add the bread cubes and fry for 5 minutes, or until golden and crispy all over. Serve with the stewed hare.

Hare Meatballs

••

Almondegas de Lebre   ◊ Beira Baixa

Preparation time: 40 minutes
Cooking time: 1 hour
Serves: 4
◻

1 medium hare
3 bunches flat-leaf parsley, roughly chopped
80 g/3 oz lardo
3 eggs
25 ml/1 fl oz (2 tablespoons) white wine vinegar
2 small onions, peeled and finely chopped
120 ml/4 fl oz (½ cup) olive oil
60 g/2¼ oz (½ cup) plain (all-purpose) flour
500 ml/17 fl oz (2 cups) meat or vegetable stock
sea salt
4 large slices crusty bread, toasted, to serve

Debone the hare. (Use the bones to make stock for another recipe.) Finely chop the hare meat and put it into a food processor. Add 1 bunch of the parsley and the lardo and process until combined. Add the eggs, vinegar and half of the onions and process until combined.

Meanwhile, heat the olive oil in a large saucepan over a low heat. Add the remaining onions and cook for 15 minutes, or until golden. Add the remaining parsley and mix well.

Spread the flour out on a large plate. Using damp hands, take a small portion of the meat mixture, shape it into a small ball and roll the meatball in the flour until lightly coated. Repeat to use up all the meat mixture.

Add the meatballs to the onions in the pan and cook over a high heat for 20 minutes, or until browned all over. Reduce the heat to medium, add the stock, partially cover the pan with a lid and cook for 20 minutes. Remove the lid and cook uncovered for a further 5 minutes.

Serve the meatballs with toasted bread.

Green Eggs

••

Ovos Verdes   ◙ p.211   ◊ Lisbon

Preparation time: 20 minutes
Cooking time: 25 minutes
Serves: 4
◻

6 eggs
55 g/2 oz (½ stick) unsalted butter
50 g/2 oz onion, peeled and very finely chopped
⅓ bunch flat-leaf parsley, finely chopped
plain (all-purpose) flour, for dusting
olive oil, for shallow-frying
sea salt and freshly ground black pepper

Bring a medium saucepan of water to the boil. Have a bowl of iced water nearby. Once boiling, carefully lower in four of the eggs and cook for 8 minutes. Lift the eggs out of the pan and transfer to the iced water to cool. Once cold, peel the shells from the eggs and cut them in half lengthwise. Using a teaspoon, scoop out the yolks into a small bowl, taking care to keep the whites intact. Crush the egg yolks with a fork and set them and the egg whites aside.

Melt the butter in a medium saucepan, add the onion and cook over a low heat for 10 minutes, or until soft. Remove the pan from the heat, add the crushed egg yolks, parsley and season with salt and pepper. Mix well to combine.

Using a teaspoon, fill the cavities in the egg whites with the onion and egg yolk mixture.

Sprinkle some flour over a plate. Break the remaining two eggs into a shallow bowl and whisk with a fork. Add the filled egg whites to the plate and carefully coat them in the flour, then transfer them to the bowl and carefully coat them in the beaten egg.

Line a large baking sheet with paper towels. Heat the oil, for shallow-frying in a large, deep frying pan or skillet until it reaches 160°C/325°F on a thermometer. Working in batches, carefully lower the eggs into the hot oil and fry for 2 minutes, or until golden all over. Remove with a slotted spoon or fish slice (spatula) and leave to drain on the lined baking sheet.

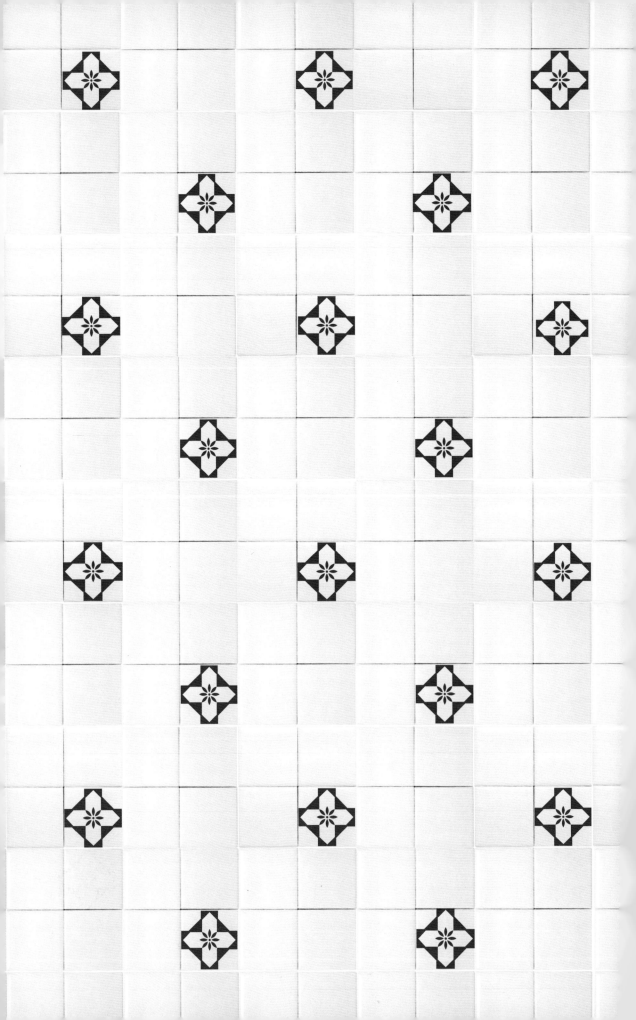

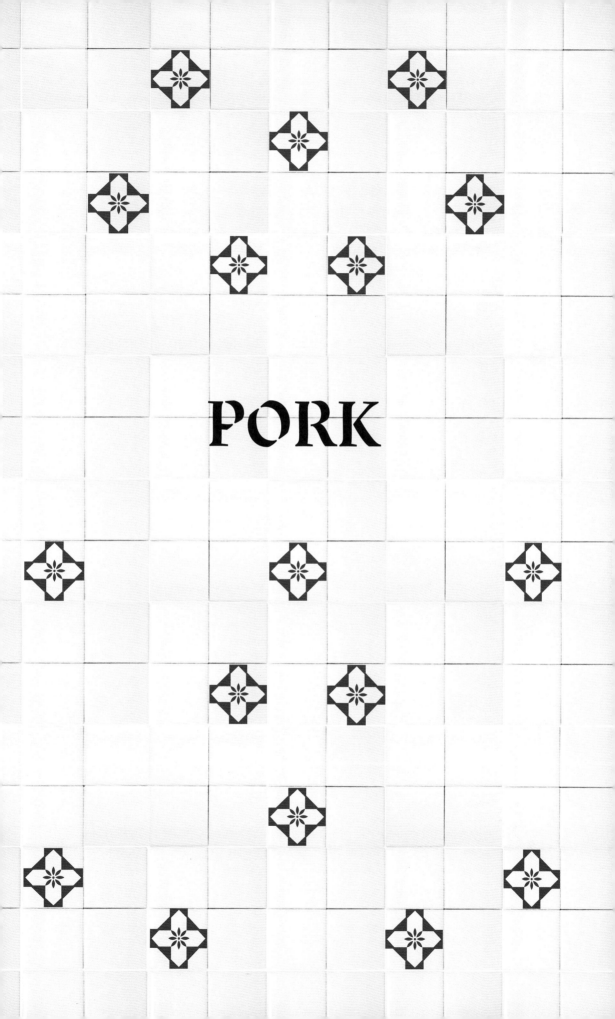

PORK

Pork Loin Preserved in Pork Fat and Paprika

Lombo de Porco na Banha 📷 p.215   ♡ Algarve

This recipe represents an old way of preserving food in lard (pork fat). This was common practice in my grandparents' house.

Preparation time: 15 minutes, plus 5 days chilling
Cooking time: 35 minutes
Serves: 4
▢ ▢

800 g/1 lb 12 oz pork loin
80 g/3 oz *Massa de Pimentão*
300 ml/10 fl oz (1¼ cups) white wine
10 garlic cloves, peeled and finely chopped
60 ml/2 fl oz (4 tablespoons) vinegar
4 bay leaves, crushed
700 g/1 lb 9 oz lard (pork fat)
sea salt
12 slices sourdough bread, to serve

Remove any excess fat from the pork loin, then cut it into medium-sized chunks.

Put all the ingredients, except the lard (pork fat), into a large bowl and season with salt. Cover with food wrap and leave in the fridge for 4 days, turning the meat every day.

When ready to cook, heat a large saucepan over a medium heat, add some of the pork fat and the meat and cook for 10 minutes, or until the meat is browned all over. Transfer the meat to a large, deep tray or bowl. Add the remaining pork fat to the pan and cook until melted. Pour over the meat and leave to cool. Leave the meat resting in the fat for at least one day before serving cold with bread. It can be kept for a long time covered with the fat.

Pork Crackling

Torresmos da Guarda   ♡ Beira Alta

This is eaten as a snack in some villages or as a garnish for other dishes. It can be kept for some time in an airtight container.

Preparation time: 15 minutes, plus 20 minutes standing
Cooking time: 30 minutes
Serves: 4
🏷 ▢ ▢ ✕

700 g/1 lb 9 oz pork belly
180 g/6 oz (1 cup) lard (pork fat)
sea salt

Cut the pork belly into 2-cm/¾-inch cubes. Put them into a large dish, season with salt and leave for 20 minutes.

Line a large baking sheet with paper towels. Heat a large saucepan over a medium heat. Add some of the lard (pork fat), then, when melted, add one-third of the meat and fry for 10 minutes, or until golden brown. Remove and set aside on the lined baking sheet and repeat with the remaining meat and pork fat.

Pork Bits Sautéed in Pork Fat

Picos Salteados   ♡ Algarve

Picos in the title refers to chunky 'bits' of pork. Before fridges in everyone's homes, this recipe was a way to preserve meat for a long time. There is also a variation of this recipe that doesn't use vinegar and oregano.

Preparation time: 20 minutes, plus 4 days standing
Cooking time: 30 minutes
Serves: 4
🏷 ▢ ▢

1 kg/2 lb 4 oz pork loin
4 garlic cloves, peeled but left whole
1 teaspoon dried oregano
70 g/2½ oz *Massa de Pimentão*
30 ml/1 fl oz (2 tablespoons) white wine vinegar
180 ml/6 fl oz (¾ cup) olive oil
1.8 kg/4 lb lard (pork fat)
7 bay leaves
sea salt

To serve:
vegetable pickles
black olives

Remove any excess fat from the pork loin and cut it into large chunks.

Put the garlic, oregano, *Massa de Pimentão* and vinegar into a large mortar and, using a pestle, mash to a paste.

Put the pork loin into a large shallow bowl and spread the paste over the meat. Cover with food wrap and keep in a cold place for 4 days, stirring the meat once a day.

When ready to cook, heat a large frying pan or skillet over a medium heat, add some of the lard (pork fat) and cook until melted. Add the pork loin and cook for 10 minutes, or until the meat is browned all over.

Transfer the pork to a large container or bowl and arrange the bay leaves over the top of the meat. Put the remaining pork fat into the pan and cook until melted. Pour the melted fat over the meat in the container to cover it completely, then cover with baking (parchment) paper. Whenever you need it, take the meat out and cook with the same pork fat that it has been preserving in, seasoning with salt. Serve with vegetable pickles and black olives.

Pork Loin Preserved in Pork Fat and Paprika

Pork Loin Marinated in Wine and Garlic

•••

Carne de Vinha d'Alhos　　　🗇 **Madeira**
da Madeira 📷 p.217

This dish spread to India and Pakistan in the 15th century, where it took the name vindaloo (a garbled pronunciation of *Vinha d'Alhos* – page 429). The recipe was modified to cater for local conditions and tastes, including palm oil instead of wine and vinegar, plus spices such as cinnamon, cardamom and chilli peppers.

Preparation time: 30 minutes, plus 4 days chilling
Cooking time: 40 minutes
Serves: 4
🗇

1 kg/2 lb 4 oz pork loin (or pork neck)
5 garlic cloves, peeled and very finely chopped
150 ml/5 fl oz (⅔ cup) white wine vinegar
220 ml/7½ fl oz (1 cup) white wine
2 bay leaves, crushed
1 red chilli, finely chopped
850 g/1 lb 14 oz baby new potatoes, peeled
2 sweet potatoes, peeled
6 large slices crusty bread
50 g/2 oz lard (pork fat)
1 lemon, cut into slices
2 oranges, cut into slices
sea salt

Rinse the meat in warm water, then pat dry with paper towels. Cut the meat into small chunks, then put it into a medium bowl.

Put the garlic into another medium bowl, add the vinegar, white wine, bay leaves and chilli and mix well to combine. Pour over the meat and mix well. Cover the bowl with food wrap and leave to chill in the fridge for 4 days.

When ready to cook, put the potatoes and sweet potatoes into a large saucepan of cold water and cook over a medium heat for 10–12 minutes, or until soft. Drain and set aside.

Meanwhile, put the meat into a large saucepan and cook over a medium heat for 20 minutes until it is medium-rare. Take the pan off the heat, remove the meat and set aside. Dip the bread slices into the juices and arrange on a large serving plate. Strain the juices and leave to cool in the fridge.

Remove the fat that has formed on the top of the juices and add it to a frying pan or skillet. Add the lard (pork fat) and melt over a medium heat. Add the meat and cook for a further 10 minutes, or until the meat is cooked. Remove and set aside.

Cut the potatoes and sweet potatoes into thick slices, then add to the pan and cook for 10 minutes, or until golden all over. Serve the pork over the bread with slices of lemon and orange, and with the potatoes alongside.

Pork Loin with Clams

••

Lombo de Porco com Amêijoas　　🗇 **Alentejo**

Preparation time: 30 minutes, plus 24 hours marinating and 3 hours standing
Cooking time: 30 minutes
Serves: 4
🐟 🗇 🗇

1.2 kg/2 lb 11 oz clams
2 teaspoons fine table salt
8 garlic cloves, peeled but left whole
2 tablespoons *Massa de Pimentão*
800 g/1 lb 12 oz pork loin, excess fat removed
130 g/4½ oz lard (pork fat)
250 ml/8 fl oz (1 cup) white wine
⅓ bunch flat-leaf parsley, finely chopped
sea salt

To serve:
1 lemon, cut into wedges
fried potatoes (optional)

Rinse the clams a few times in cold water to remove any sand and grit, then put them into a large bowl of water, add the fine table salt, stir and leave to stand for 2 hours. This helps them to release any remaining sand and grit.

Put the garlic and a pinch of salt into a mortar and, using a pestle, crush to form a paste. Alternatively, use a blender. Add the *Massa de Pimentão* and mix well to combine. Put the meat into a container and rub the meat with the pimentão mixture to coat. Cover with food wrap and leave to marinate in the fridge for 24 hours.

When ready to cook, slice the meat into 3-cm/1¼-inch cubes. Make sure the cubes are not too thick. Heat a frying pan or skillet over a medium heat. Once hot, add the lard (pork fat), then add the meat and cook for 10 minutes, or until seared. Once all the meat is seared, add the clams and mix together, then pour over the wine and cover with the lid. Cook for a further 20 minutes, or until all the clams open. Discard any clams that remain closed.

Scatter the parsley over the top of the pork and clams before serving with the lemon wedges and fried potatoes, if liked.

Pork Loin Marinated in Wine and Garlic

Sautéed Pork with Mustard Sauce

Pica-pau do Ribatejo p.219 Ⓤ Ribatejo

Preparation time: 20 minutes, plus 45 minutes marinating
Cooking time: 40 minutes
Serves: 4

500 g/1 lb 2 oz pork neck, boned
½ bird's eye chilli, finely chopped
1 bay leaf
2 garlic cloves, peeled and thinly sliced
220 ml/7½ fl oz (1 cup) white wine
50 g/2 oz (½ stick) unsalted butter
50 g/2 oz (3½ tablespoons) mustard
⅕ bunch flat-leaf parsley, finely chopped

To serve:
vegetable pickles
black olives

Cut the pork neck into 1-cm/½-inch slices, then into thin strips. Put it into a large bowl and season with salt, then add the chilli, bay leaf and garlic. Add the white wine, cover with food wrap and leave to marinate for 45 minutes.

Remove the meat from the marinade and set the marinade aside. Heat a medium saucepan over a medium heat, then add the butter and, once melted, add the meat and fry for 10 minutes, or until the meat is cooked. Add the reserved marinade, stir, then reduce the heat to low-medium and cook for a further 30 minutes until the marinade has reduced. Add the mustard and stir again.

Scatter the parsley over the pork in the sauce before serving alongside the vegetable pickles and black olives.

Braised Pork with Cloves and Peppercorns

Torresmos de Molho de Fígado Ⓤ Açores

These succulent pork ribs emerged from the time when, around January, pig slaughtering was a common annual practice across the archipelago. The meat, preserved using various methods such as in fat or salt, ensured there was food for the following months (*torresmos* would keep well in lard for an entire year). The chunks of pork are immersed for 24 hours in *Vinha d'Alhos* (a spicy, vinegary wine; page 429), olive oil and garlic marinade, then cooked until tender in a liver sauce. They are always served hot out of the pot.

Preparation time: 30 minutes, plus 12 hours marinating
Cooking time: 1 hour
Serves: 10

8 garlic cloves, peeled but left whole
12 pink peppercorns
120 ml/4 fl oz (½ cup) vinegar
150 ml/5 fl oz (⅔ cup) white wine
1.2 kg/2 lb 11 oz pork ribs, de-boned, or shoulder, cut into small pieces
200 g/7 oz lardo, cut into small pieces
10 black peppercorns
400 g/14 oz pork liver, cut into medium-sized slices
1 bay leaf
8 cloves
250 g/9 oz pork belly
sea salt

Put the garlic and pink peppercorns into a mortar and, using a pestle, mash them to a paste. Add the vinegar and most of the white wine, reserving a little for the liver. This paste is the *vinha d'alhos*.

Put the pork rib pieces and lardo into a large container, add the paste and rub it into the meat until the paste is well incorporated. Cover and leave to marinate in the fridge for 12 hours.

When ready to cook, toast half of the black peppercorns in a dry frying pan or skillet over a medium heat for 5 minutes, or until they start smoking. This will help to release the oils and aromatic components. Put them into a mortar and smash them with the pestle.

Season the liver with salt, the remaining white wine and the smashed peppercorns. Set aside.

Put the bay leaf, the remaining peppercorns and the cloves into a large frying pan or skillet, then add the fatty meat and cook gently over a medium heat for 10 minutes until they start to render the fat and become golden and lightly crispy. Add the remaining meat and cook for a further 20 minutes, stirring continuously so the colouring and cooking is even. Add the liver with all the marinade to the pan and cook for a further 20 minutes. Serve immediately.

Sautéed Pork with Mustard Sauce

Crispy Pork Belly with Potatoes

Torresmos da Beira   ♡ Beira Alta

Preparation time: 20 minutes, plus 24 hours marinating
Cooking time: 50 minutes
Serves: 4
🐖 ♡

800 g/1 lb 12 oz pork belly
650 g/1 lb 7 oz trimmed pork ribs
1 teaspoon paprika
1 bay leaf
250 ml/8 fl oz (1 cup) white wine
650 g/1 lb 7 oz waxy potatoes, unpeeled and left whole
100 g/3½ oz (½ cup) lard (pork fat)
sea salt and freshly ground black pepper

Cut the pork belly into 3-cm/1¼-inches squares, then cut the pork ribs into individual ribs and put them into a large dish. Season with salt, pepper and paprika, then add the bay leaf and half the wine and toss until the meat is well coated in the marinade. Cover with food wrap and leave to marinate in the fridge for 24 hours, tossing the meat twice.

When ready to cook, fill a large saucepan with cold water, add the potatoes and a pinch of salt and cook over a medium heat for 15–20 minutes, or until soft. Remove the pan from the heat and set aside the potatoes in their cooking water until ready to serve.

Heat a large frying pan or skillet over a medium heat. When hot, add a good amount of the lard (pork fat) then, when melted, add small batches of the meat and cook for 10 minutes, or until golden all over. Repeat with the remaining meat, adding more lard for every new batch.

Return all the meat to the pan, then add the remaining wine together with the rest of the marinade and bring to the boil. reduce the heat to low and cook for 5 minutes. Taste and adjust the seasoning, if necessary.

Peel the cooked potatoes and cut them into thick slices. Arrange the potatoe slices on a serving platter and put the meat over them before serving.

Grilled Pork Belly Strips with Bean Rice

Lentrisca com Arroz de Feijão   ♡ Leiria

Lentrisca **is the name given only in the Leiria region for thin slices of pork belly.**

Preparation time: 15 minutes, plus 12 hours soaking and 5 minutes resting
Cooking time: 1 hour 5 minutes
Serves: 4
🐖

300 g/11 oz (1⅔ cups) dried red butter (lima) beans
12 slices lean pork belly with just a string of fat
80 g/3 oz (¾ stick) butter
1 onion, peeed and very finely chopped
1 garlic clove, peeled and very finely chopped
1 bay leaf
250 g/9 oz (1¼ cups) long-grain rice
1 lemon, halved
sea salt

Put the beans into a large bowl of cold water and leave to soak for 12 hours. The next day, drain the beans and put them into a large saucepan. Pour in enough cold water to cover, add a pinch of salt and cook over a medium heat for 30 minutes, or until soft. Drain and set aside, reserving the bean cooking liquid.

Meanwhile, season the pork belly slices with a pinch of salt.

Melt the butter in a medium saucepan over a low heat. Add the onion and garlic and cook for 10 minutes, or until the onion is translucent. Add the beans and stir, then add 750 ml/25 fl oz (3 cups) of the bean cooking liquid and the bay leaf and bring to the boil. Add the rice, reduce the heat to low and cook for 20 minutes, or until soft. Remove the pan from the heat and leave to rest for 5 minutes.

Preheat the grill (broiler).

Grill (broil) the pork belly slices for 15 minutes, turning frequently, or until golden and cooked through. Squeeze the lemon juice over the meat and serve with the beans and rice.

Pork Stew with White Beans

Caldo Branco ♡ Leiria

This is an old recipe that has been eaten by my family for over three generations. I remember as a kid, checking the big copper pot on side of the fire and put off eating it due to the intense aroma of the cooked turnip tops and dense aspect of the dish. However, I now enjoy eating this dish a lot.

Preparation time: minutes, plus 3 days resting, 1 hour soaking (optional) and 1 hour resting
Cooking time: 1 hour 15 minutes
Serves: 10
⊘ ▯ ▯

350 g/12 oz pork belly
300 g/11 oz pork loin
800 g/1 lb 12 oz trimmed pork ribs
1 pig's snout
3 pig's ears
1 chorizo
1 *negrito*
2 bunches turnip tops, bottom stalk removed or 1 large
    January King cabbage
4 waxy potatoes, peeled and cut into chunks
200 g/7 oz (1 cup) long-grain rice
extra virgin olive oil, for drizzling
sea salt

Season the pork belly, pork loin and pork ribs with a little more salt than you would usually use. Put it into a large dish, cover with food wrap and leave to rest in the fridge for 3 days.

When ready to cook, rinse the pork meat a few times under cold running water to remove the excess salt. If necessary, leave it soaking in a large bowl of cold water for 1 hour to remove the excess salt. The meat should have a degree of saltiness.

Put the pork meat, pig's snout, pig's ears, chorizo and *negrito* into a large saucepan and cover with cold water. Cook over a medium heat for 45 minutes, or until the meat is soft. Using a slotted spoon or tongs, remove the meat from the pan and put into a large dish and set aside. Keep the cooking liquid.

Cut the turnip tops into small pieces, or if using the cabbage, cut this into long thin strips. Add the turnip tops or cabbage to the meat cooking liquid with the potatoes and cook over a medium heat for 15–20 minutes, or until soft. Add the rice and cook for a further 10 minutes, then turn off the heat and leave to rest.

Chop the pork meat into chunks, cut the chorizo and *negrito* into slices and return them to the pan. Cover with a lid and leave to rest for 1 hour. Drizzle some extra virgin olive oil over the top of the stew before serving.

Portuguese Pork and Bean Stew

Feijoada à Portuguesa ♡ Lisbon

This dish is much better prepared in advance so the flavours can develop overnight.

Preparation time: 30 minutes, plus 12 hours soaking
Cooking time: 3 hours
Serves: 8
⊘ ▯

650 g/1 lb 7 oz (3⅔ cups) dried butter (lima) beans
2 large pig's ears
2 pig's feet
500 g/1 lb 2 oz trimmed pork ribs
3 onions
3 cloves
100 ml/3½ fl oz (⅓ cup) olive oil
1 large *farinheira* (smoked sausage)
180 g/6 oz *morcela* or black pudding
130 g/4½ oz chorizo
4 garlic cloves
4 tomatoes, cut into small pieces
250 g/9 oz lardo, cut into small pieces
2 bay leaves
2 sprigs flat-leaf parsley
sea salt and freshly ground black pepper

Put the beans into a large bowl of cold water and leave to soak for 12 hours. The next day, drain the beans and set aside.

Singe the pig's ears with a blowtorch to remove any hairs, then rinse under cold running water and put into a large saucepan with the pig's feet. Cover with water, add a pinch of salt and cook over a medium heat for 30 minutes, or until soft. Remove from the pan and leave to cool. Cut the ears into thin slices, then remove the bones from the trotter and set aside.

Cut one of the onions in half and stud with the cloves. Put the soaked beans into another large saucepan. Pour in enough cold water to cover, add a pinch of salt, the onion studded with cloves and a drizzle of olive oil and cook over a medium heat for 30 minutes, or until soft. Strain and set aside, reserving the cooking water in the pan.

Prick the *farinheira* and *morcela* all over with a skewer so they don't burst during cooking, then put them into the pan with the bean cooking water and cook over a medium heat for 45 minutes, or until soft. Drain and set the cooking water aside.

Poke the chorizo all over with a skewer. Put the onions, garlic and tomatoes into a saucepan and cook over a medium heat for 30 minutes, or until very soft. Add the lardo, bay leaves, chorizo and parsley. Add enough of the charcuterie cooking liquid to cover the ingredients and cook over a low heat for 30 minutes, or until the chorizo is cooked. Add the beans and pig's ears, season with salt and pepper and bring to the boil. Reduce the heat to low and simmer for a further 10 minutes.

Portuguese Meat Stew

••

Cozido à Portuguesa 📷 p.223   ⊍ **Lisbon**

Preparation time: 45 minutes, plus 12 hours soaking
and 1 hour standing
Cooking time: 3 hours
Serves: 10
◻

450 g/1 lb (2½ cups) dried butter (lima) beans
2 pig's feet
3 pig's ears
450 g/1 lb pork belly
400 g/14 oz beef rump (round)
550 g/1 lb 4 oz beef flank
700 g/1 lb 9 oz beef short ribs
600 g/1 lb 5 oz chicken
2 *morcela* or Portuguese black pudding
2 chorizo
1 *farinheira* (smoked sausage)
3 turnips, quartered
½ January king cabbage, or Savoy cabbage
   or collard greens
⅓ squash, peeled, de-seeded and cut into chunks
6 potatoes, peeled and cut into chunks
4 carrots, peeled and halved
800 g/1 lb 12 oz (4 cups) long-grain rice
600 g/1 lb 5 oz sourdough bread, thickly sliced
½ bunch mint (optional)
sea salt

Put the beans into a large bowl of cold water and
leave to soak for 12 hours. The next day, drain the
beans and set aside.

Singe the pig's feet and pig's ears with a blowtorch to remove any hairs. Make a small cut on the
bottom of the ears and clean them with the tip of
the knife. Rinse thoroughly under cold running
water then leave to drain on a perforated tray or in
a colander.

Salt the meats for 1 hour before cooking.

When ready to cook, prick the charcuterie with
a skewer all over so they don't burst, then put them
into a large saucepan with the rest of the meats,
cover with water and cook over a medium heat for
45 minutes, or until cooked through. Some of the
meats will cook faster than others, so keep checking
during cooking and remove them from the pan as
soon as they are cooked. The chicken will be the
first one to be ready.

Once all the meats and charcuterie are cooked,
remove them from the pan and put them onto
a large rimmed baking sheet. Spoon a few ladles
of the cooking liquid over them to prevent them
drying out while the vegetables are cooking. Set
the remaining cooking liquid aside.

Put the beans into another large saucepan.
Pour in enough cold water to cover, add a pinch of
salt and cook over a medium heat for 30 minutes,
or until soft. Drain and set aside in a bowl, covered
in some of the reserved meat cooking liquid.

Put the turnips, cabbage and squash into a
large saucepan, cover with water and cook over

a medium heat for 14 minutes, or until tender.
Put the potatoes and carrots into another saucepan,
cover them with some of the meat cooking water
and cook over a medium heat for 20 minutes, or
until soft.

Put the rice into another saucepan and add
some more of the meat cooking liquid; you may
also need to add some water. Cook over a low
heat for 10–12 minutes until soft.

Put the bread into a large serving dish, then
pour the meat stock over the bread and add the
mint, if using. Cut all the charcuterie into slices,
then cut all the meat into small pieces and arrange
them together on a large serving platter. Serve
with the rice, beans and all the vegetables.

Stewed Cabbage – Odeceixe Style

••

Couvada de Odeceixe   ⊍ **Algarve**

Preparation time: 20 minutes, plus 1 hours standing
Cooking time: 1 hour 30 minutes, plus 20 minutes resting
Serves: 6 ·
🐟◻◻

350 g/12 oz pork belly
70 g/2½ oz lard (pork fat)
1 ham bone, cut into pieces
400 g/14 oz pork shoulder
200 g/7 oz pork loin
400 g/14 oz trimmed pork ribs
1 pig's foot, halved
2 Savoy cabbages or January king cabbages
4 carrots, halved
5 turnips, peeled and quartered
1½ chorizo
1 large *morcela* or Portuguese black pudding
1 tablespoon ground cumin
sea salt

Put the pork belly into a large dish, season with
salt, cover with food wrap and leave to stand for
1 hour. Cut the pork belly into pieces.

Put the lard (pork fat) into a large saucepan
over a medium heat and cook until melted. Add
the bones and pork belly and cook for 15 minutes,
or until browned all over. Fill the pan with water,
add the pork shoulder, loin, ribs and trotter (foot)
and cook for 1 hour, or until all the meat is soft.
Do not season.

When the meat is cooked, add the cabbage,
carrots, turnips, chorizo, *morcela* and cumin and
bring to the boil over a medium heat, giving time
for the charcuterie to cook.

Remove from the heat and leave to rest for
20 minutes before eating.

Portuguese Meat Stew

Chunky Pork – Minho Style

Rojões à Moda do Minho   ▽ Minho

This was usually prepared the day after pig slaughter, with parts of the pig that could not be used elsewhere, or needed fast preparation. The recipe features *beloura*, which are sausage-shaped cakes made of wheat, rye, corn flour and pig's blood. *Rojões* can also be served with *Papas de Sarrabulho* (see page 232).

Preparation time: 30 minutes, plus 3 hours marinating
Cooking time: 1 hour
Serves: 6
🐷 ◻

160 g/5¾ oz (1¼ cups) chestnuts
1 kg/2 lb 4 oz pork leg, cut into 8-cm/3¼-inch pieces
3 garlic cloves, peeled and very finely chopped
1 teaspoon sweet paprika
2 bay leaves, broken in half
150 ml/5 fl oz (⅔ cup) *vinho verde branco* or any white wine with good acidity
150 g/5 oz lard (pork fat), plus extra if needed
250 g/9 oz *belouras* (blood sausage)
250 g/9 oz *Tripas Enfarinhadas* (page 236)
180 ml/6 fl oz (¾ cup) fres pig's blood, cooked (page 225)
1 litre/34 fl oz (4¼ cups) sunflower oil, for deep-frying
800 g/1 lb 12 oz small round potatoes, peeled and quartered
sea salt and freshly ground black pepper
fine table salt
2 bunches flat-leaf parsley, to garnish
2 lemons, cut into wedges, to serve

Preheat the oven to 180°C/350°F/Gas Mark 4.
Spread the chestnuts out on a large baking sheet and roast in the oven for 30 minutes, then remove and leave until cool enough to handle. Peel off the skins and set aside.
Put the meat into a large bowl with the garlic, paprika, bay leaves and wine. Season with salt and pepper, then cover with food wrap and leave to marinate for 3 hours.
When ready to cook, put a large saucepan over a medium heat, add the lard (pork fat) and, when hot, cook the meat in batches for 10 minutes, or until browned all over. Transfer to a plate, reserving the remaining marinade.
Put some of the meat cooking fat into a medium saucepan, add the *Belouras* and *Tripas Enfarinhadas* and cook for 5 minutes, or until crispy on both sides. Add a little more pork fat if needed.
When all the meat is cooked, combine it in the pan with the marinade and cook over a low heat for 5 minutes, or until the marinade has reduced.
Cut the cooked blood into small squares, add them to the meat, stir and cook for a further 5 minutes. Taste and adjust the seasoning with salt and pepper.
Line a large baking sheet with paper towels. Heat the sunflower oil in a large, deep saucepan or fryer until it reaches 180°C/350°F on a thermometer. Working in batches, carefully drop the potatoes into the hot oil and deep-fry for 5–6 minutes, or until golden brown. Remove with a slotted spoon and leave to drain on the lined baking sheet. Season with fine table salt.
Arrange the meat, *Belouras, Tripas Enfarinhadas*, chestnuts and potatoes in a large serving dish and mix everything together. Pour liquid over the top, garnish with parsley and lemon wedges to serve.

Poached Blood and Flour 'Cakes'

Belouras – Farinhatos   ▽ Minho

Preparation time: 30 minutes, plus 2 hours standing
Cooking time: 45 minutes
Serves: 5
◻

100 ml/3½ fl oz (⅓ cup) fresh pig's blood
350 g/12 oz (3 cups minus 2 teaspoons) fine corn flour (cornmeal)
170 g/6 oz (1½ cups minus 2 teaspoons) plain (all-purpose) flour
170 g/6 oz (1½ cups minus 2 teaspoons) rye flour
2 teaspoons ground cumin
4 orange leaves
2 bay leaves
2 garlic cloves
1 bunch flat-leaf parsley stems
15 g/½ oz (1 tablespoon) fresh yeast or 4 g/¼ oz (1⅓ teaspoons) instant dried yeast
pingue (fat from cooking pork) or lard (pork fat)
sea salt and freshly ground black pepper

Combine the pig's blood with 280 ml/9½ fl oz (1 cup plus 2 tablespoons) water in a large bowl or jug (pitcher) and stir.
Put all the flours into a large bowl with the cumin and season with salt and pepper. Add the blood mixture and mix to a stiff dough. Cover the bowl with a tea (dish) towel or food wrap and leave to stand at room temperature for 2 hours.
Have a large bowl of cold water ready. Wet your hands, then take pieces of the dough and shape into logs. Repeat with the remaining dough.
Put the orange leaves, bay leaves, garlic, parsley stems and a pinch of salt into a large saucepan with 3.5 litres/118 fl oz (14 cups) water and bring to the boil. Reduce the heat to low, add the logs and cook gently for 30 minutes, or until they float to the surface. Using a slotted spoon, remove them onto a plate or tray, then cover with food wrap or a (dish) towel and leave them to cool.
When they cylinders are cool, thinly slice them. Heat a frying pan or skillet over a medium heat. Once it is hot, add the *pingue* or lard (pork fat) and the logs and fry them for 6–7 minutes on each side, or until they are crispy. Serve immediately.

Roast Suckling Pig – Bairrada Style

Leitão Assado à Moda da Bairrada   ♡ **Beira Litoral**

Suckling pig plays a big role in Portuguese cuisine as it's served at large festivals, ceremonies or just in communal eating. The old-fashioned way of roasting suckling pigs was in a specially made clay brick oven heated by wood. Nowadays, modern industrial ovens are used, but they roast the pigs much in the same way, usually with a long metal 'skewer' rather than a wooden one, traditionally made from bay leaf wood. At the end of roasting, the pig should have a brown and very crispy skin. It is served with oranges slices, sour salads and crispy potatoes with a glass or two of regional white wine from Bairrada. When the pig is removed from the oven a small cut is made on the belly and the juices are drained out, which are used in another typical dish called *Cabidela de Leitão*.

Preparation time: 45 minutes
Cooking time: 2 hours 20 minutes
Serves: 10
🐖 ♡

1 x 5-kg/11-lb whole suckling pig
18 garlic cloves, peeled and crushed
60 g/2¼ oz (⅓ cup) lard (pork fat)
65 g/2¼ oz (¼ cup) fine sea salt
30 ml/1 oz (2 tablespoons) white wine from Bairrada
2 bay leaves, crushed
4 oranges, thinly sliced

For the salad:
2 butterhead lettuces, leaves separated
45 ml/1½ fl oz (3 tablespoons) olive oil
20 ml/¾ fl oz (4 teaspoons) white wine vinegar
sea salt

Preheat the oven to its hottest temperature.

Clean the inside of the pig, removing any remaining blood and offal (variety meats).

Put all the remaining ingredients, except the orange slices, into a large mortar and, using a pestle, mash to a paste.

Rub the pig inside and outside with the paste then, using a trussing needle and butcher's string or kitchen twine, stitch the belly of the pig closed. Cover the ears with foil so they don't burn while cooking. Push the 'skewer' through the pig starting at the mouth and going out through the tail and roast in the very hot oven. If you have an oven with a rotisserie this will be perfect. Spray some saltwater (3% salt) onto the skin during cooking to prevent the skin bursting. Roast for 2 hours, or until the skin is dark brown and crispy, then remove from the oven and leave to rest for 10 minutes.

Using a sharp knife, make a small cut in the belly and drain the juices. (Set the juices aside for use in another recipe.) Put the pig back into the oven for a further 8–10 minutes to dry out.

To serve, remove the string, cut the pig in half, then cut into small pieces, making sure each piece has some skin. Place on a large serving platter.

Put the lettuce leaves into a large salad bowl, add the olive oil, vinegar and sprinkle with some salt, then toss together.

Arrange the orange slices around the slices of pork on the platter and serve with the dressed salad leaves.

Suckling Pig Offal Stewed in Blood Sauce

Cabidela de Leitão   ♡ **Beira Litoral**

Whenever you roast a suckling pig in the oven, place a tray underneath to catch all the delicious roasting juices, so they can be added to this stew.

Preparation time: 20 minutes
Cooking time: 55 minutes
Serves: 6
🐖 ♡

1 suckling pig's blood or fresh pig's blood
50 g/2 oz lard (pork fat)
1 small white onion, peeled and finely chopped
1 garlic clove, peeled and finely chopped
1 bay leaf
2 bunches flat-leaf parsley, roughly chopped
1 suckling pig offal (variety meats), heart, lung and liver, cut into small pieces
150 ml/5 fl oz (⅔ cup) white wine
sea salt and freshly ground black pepper

Bring a medium saucepan of salted water to the boil, then pour in the pig's blood and cook for 30 minutes. Strain the cooked blood and leave to cool. Once cold, shred it with your hands into small pieces and set aside.

Heat the lard (pork fat) in a large saucepan over a medium heat, add the onion, garlic, bay leaf and parsley and cook for 15 minutes, or until the onion is golden. Add the offal (variety meats), then season with a pinch of salt. Stir and cook over a low heat, gradually adding the wine with 120 ml/4 fl oz (½ cup) water, a little at a time.

Once the offal is cooked, add the shredded pig's blood together with some of the juices that have collected in the tray placed underneath a suckling pig that has been roasted in the oven. Cook over a low heat for a further 8 minutes, then taste and adjust the seasoning with salt and pepper, if necessary. Serve immediately.

Suckling Pig and Bean Casserole

Feijoada de Leitão   ⛉ Beira Litoral

If there are any leftovers from the suckling pig (*Leitão Assado*, page 225) then this recipe from Anadia in the Bairrada region is the perfect way to use them up.

Preparation time: 20 minutes, plus 12 hours soaking
Cooking time: 1 hour 5 minutes
Serves: 6
⛉

350 g/12 oz (2 cups) dried white butter (lima) beans
or other bean of your choice
35 g/1¼ oz lard (pork fat)
40 ml/1⅓ fl oz (2⅔ tablespoons) olive oil, plus extra
for drizzling
2 onions, peeled and very finely chopped
3 garlic cloves, peeled and very finely chopped
100 g/3½ oz chorizo, cut into small cubes
⅕ bunch flat-leaf parsley, roughly chopped
1 bay leaf
1 kg/2 lb 4 oz leftover roasted suckling pig (from *Leitão assado*, page 225)
3 suckling pig's feet, halved lengthwise and then the
meat cut into small pieces
2 suckling pig's ears
2 small carrots, peeled and sliced
½ cabbage, cut into small pieces (optional)
400 g/14 oz (2 cups) white long-grain rice
sea salt

Put the dried beans into a large bowl of cold water and leave to soak for 12 hours. The next day, drain the beans and put them into a large saucepan. Pour in enough cold water to cover, add a pinch of salt and cook over a medium heat for 30 minutes, or until soft. Drain and set aside, reserving the bean cooking liquid.

Heat the lard (pork fat) and olive oil in a saucepan over a low heat, add the onions, garlic, chorizo, parsley and bay leaf and cook for 12 minutes, or until the onions are translucent. Add the meat and stir, then increase the heat to medium and cook for 5 minutes. Add the beans, carrots and cabbage (if using) and mix well. Pour in enough of the reserved bean cooking liquid to cover all the ingredients and cook for a further 15 minutes, or until the liquid has reduced. Taste and adjust the seasoning, if necessary, with salt and pepper. Bear in mind that the suckling pig was seasoned before roasting so you may not need to add any more.

Meanwhile, cook the rice in a medium saucepan of water over a medium heat for 10–12 minutes, or until soft. Drain and put into a serving dish, then drizzle with olive oil.

Serve the pork and bean casserole with the boiled rice on the side.

Fried Suckling Pig

Leitão Frito   ⛉ Alentejo

Preparation time: 20 minutes, plus 12 hours marinating
Cooking time: 1 hour
Serves: 10
🐖 ⛉

1 x 5-kg/11-lb whole suckling pig (or ½ suckling pig to
serve 5 people)
8 garlic cloves, peeled and crushed
80 g/3 oz *Massa de Pimentão*
120 ml/4 fl oz (½ cup) white wine vinegar
400 g/14 oz lard (pork fat)
sea salt

Clean the suckling pig of any remaining hairs, blow torching them if necessary, then scrape the pig with a knife and rinse under cold running water. Remove any offal (variety meats). Cut the pig in half, then into small pieces.

Put the garlic, *Massa de Pimentão* and vinegar into a mortar. Season with salt and, using a pestle, mash to a paste. Rub the pieces of suckling pig meat with this mixture and leave in the fridge for 12 hours to marinate.

Heat a large frying pan or skillet over a medium heat. Once hot, add some of the lard (pork fat) and a small batch of the meat and cook for 10 minutes, or until golden and crispy. Remove from the pan and continue cooking the meat until all the pieces are used up. Serve immediately.

Roast Suckling Pig with Offal Stuffing

Leitão Recheado à Beira Alta   ⛉ Beira Alta

Preparation time: 45 minutes, plus 40 minutes resting
Cooking time: 3 hours 30 minutes
Serves: 10
🐖 ⛉

1 x 5-kg/11-lb whole suckling pig
400 g/14 oz Serrano ham, sliced into small pieces
130 g/4½ oz chorizo, sliced into small pieces
1 litre/34 fl oz (4¼ cups) white wine
750 g/1 lb 10 oz lardo, halved
80 g/3 oz (5⅓ tablespoons) butter
180 g/6 oz (1 cup) lard (pork fat)
2 onions, peeled and finely chopped
4 garlic cloves, peeled and finely chopped
3 bunches flat-leaf parsley, roughly chopped
5 egg yolks
1 tablespoon sweet paprika
sea salt and freshly ground black pepper

To serve:
½ bunch flat-leaf parsley, leaves picked
2 large bunches radishes

Clean the suckling pig of any remaining hairs, blow torching them if necessary, then scrape the pig with a knife and rinse under cold running water. Remove any offal (variety meats). Rinse the kidneys and heart under cold running water, then cut them into pieces the same size as the charcuterie. Discard the lungs and tripe (stomach lining). Cut half the lardo into pieces the same size as the charcuterie. Set aside.

Wash the inside of the pig with most of the white wine and leave to drip over a perforated tray or in a colander.

Heat a saucepan over a medium heat. When hot, add 30 g/1 oz (2 tablespoons) of the butter and 70 g/2½ oz (½ cup) of the lard (pork fat), the lardo, offal, ham, chorizo, onions, half the garlic, and parsley. Cook over a low heat for 20 minutes, stirring occasionally. When all the meat is cooked, remove the pan from the heat, add the egg yolks and stir. Put the pan over a medium heat and cook for 5 minutes, or until the egg yolks are cooked. Remove the pan from the heat and leave to cool.

Preheat the oven to 200°C/400°F/Gas Mark 6.

Once cold, stuff the pig with the filling. Close the opening with a trussing needle and butcher's string or kitchen twine. Put the pig on a large rimmed baking sheet with a wire rack underneath.

Put the remaining lardo, butter, lard, garlic, paprika and pepper onto a cutting board and chop together into very fine pieces. Rub the pig with some of this mixture, then roast for 1 hour. Remove from the oven and leave to rest somewhere with good airflow for 30 minutes.

Increase the oven temperature to its highest setting, rub the pig with the lardo mixture again and roast for a further 1 hour 20 minutes, brushing halfway through cooking with the leftover white wine and rubbing in the remaining lardo mixture. Remove from the oven and leave to rest for 10 minutes before serving with the parsley and radishes.

Pig's Head Terrine

Cabeça de Xara   Ʊ **Alentejo**

Commonly known as *Queijo de Cabeça de Porco* (pork's head cheese), *Cabeça de Xara* is a *petisco* (shared plate) made of pork cartilage, skin and pieces of meat, eaten in slices alongside bread and regional wine. It is usually found in cafés and tabernas all over Alentejo throughout the year, but many people still prepare it at home — a hefty stone slab used as a weight in its preparation is still a presence in many Alentejo kitchens. The origin of this *petisco* is the subject of disagreement. Some claim it was inspired by the French *tête d'achard*, others that it might have had an Arab influence, linked to the Arabic word *xa'ara*, meaning 'tangled' and made using the flesh from a calf's head. One of the oldest recipes in Portugal for *Cabeça de Xara* dates back to 1788, as documented in the book *Cozinheiro Moderno ou Nova Arte de Cozinha*, written by Lucas Rigaud.

Preparation time: 30 minutes, plus 3 days standing
Cooking time: 1 hour 40 minutes
Serves: 4
☐

1 pig's head
2 onions, peeled and cut into chunks
5 garlic cloves, peeled and cut into chunks
½ bunch marjoram, roughly chopped
½ bunch sage, roughly chopped
½ bunch flat-leaf parsley, roughly chopped
1 g (¼ teaspoon) ground white peppercorns
70 ml/2¼ fl oz (¼ cup) olive oil
300 ml/10 fl oz (1¼ cups) white wine
sea salt
crusty bread, to serve (optional)

Clean the pig's head of any remaining hairs with a blow torch, then scrape the skin with a knife and wash thoroughly. Open the pig's head with a cleaver and remove the brains and discard. Sprinkle the pig's head with salt and leave for 24 hours, then sprinkle again with more salt and leave again for another 24 hours. Rinse the head in cold running water, then leave to soak in a large container of cold water for 2 hours to remove any remaining salt.

Put the head into a large saucepan and cover with water. Add the onions, garlic and herbs and cook over a medium heat for 1 hour 30 minutes, or until the meat is soft and can easily be pulled away from the bones with a fork. Using a slotted spoon, skim off any foam that forms on the surface during cooking.

Remove the head from the pan and cut it into chunks. Line a sieve (fine-mesh strainer) or colander with muslin (cheesecloth), place over a bowl and pour the stock through it. Pour back into a saucepan, add the oil and wine and bring to the boil. Reduce the heat and simmer for 10 minutes. Strain the meat from the pot and place it on a tea (dish) towel.

Either place the towel with the meat on inside a 16 x 25-cm/6 x 10-inch cake pan and add a weight on top or just tie up the towel with some butcher's string or kitchen twine and place a weight on top, then leave in the fridge overnight.

Once cold, cut into thin slices and serve with slices of crusty bread.

Black Iberian Pig's Brain

Miolos de Porco
Alentejano 📷 p.229

Ơ Alentejo

Preparation time: 30 minutes, plus 24 hours standing
Cooking time: 45 minutes
Serves: 6
▢

400 g/14 oz pork loin, cut into chunks
750 g/1 lb 10 oz pork ribs, trimmed and ribs separated,
     then cut in half
300 g/11 oz pork jowl, cut into chunks
40 g/1½ oz *Massa de Pimentão*
300 ml/10 fl oz (1¼ cups) white wine
6 garlic cloves, peeled and finely chopped
150 g/5 oz lard (pork fat)
550 g/1 lb 4 oz crusty bread, preferably sourdough
1 pig's brain
5 eggs
juice of 1 orange
juice of 1 lemon
sea salt

Put all the meats, except the brains, the *Massa de Pimentão*, white wine and garlic into a large bowl and season with salt. Cover with food wrap and leave to marinate in the fridge for 24 hours.

When ready to cook, heat the lard (pork fat) in a large saucepan over a medium heat. Add the meats and cook for 30 minutes, or until they are golden and cooked through. Taste and adjust the seasoning, if necessary. Remove the meats from the pan and set aside, then set the pan with the fat aside, too.

Put the bread into a food processor and process until breadcrumbs form. Set aside.

Put the pork brains into a large bowl and, using a fork, crumble it into pieces. Add the eggs, breadcrumbs, orange and lemon juice and mix together until combined. Set aside.

Put the breadcrumb and brains mix into the same pan used to cook the meats and fry in the leftover fat over a medium heat for 15 minutes. Season with salt.

Serve the bread and brain mixture with the meats piled on top.

Pig's Brain Scrambled with Kidney, Eggs and Bread

Miolos de Porco,
Rim, Ovos e Pão

Ơ Beira Baixa

Preparation time: 20 minutes
Cooking time: 45 minutes
Serves: 4
▢

1 pig's brain
1 pig's kidney
350 g/12 oz lean pork fillet (tenderloin)
140 g/5 oz bread, blitzed into large breadcrumbs
50 g/2 oz lard (pork fat)
150 ml/5 fl oz (⅔ cup) white wine
3 eggs
10 ml/¼ fl oz (2 teaspoons) white wine vinegar
sea salt and freshly ground black pepper

Remove any sinew from the pig's brain and kidney, then rinse them under cold running water and pat dry with paper towels or a clean tea (dish) towel. Cut the pork fillet (tenderloin) and kidney into small pieces. Set aside.

Bring a medium saucepan of water to the boil, with a pinch of salt. Once boiling, add the brain, reduce the heat to medium and cook for 10 minutes. Drain and put it into a large bowl. Add the bread and mash slightly with a fork.

Heat a large saucepan over a medium heat. Once hot, add the lad (pork fat), then add the kidney and pork fillet and cook for 15 minutes, or until browned all over. Add the wine and cook for a further 5 minutes, or until the wine has reduced by half. Add 120 ml/4 fl oz (½ cup) water and bring to the boil.

Mix the eggs into the brain and bread mixture together until combined. Add to the meat, then reduce the heat to low and cook for 15 minutes until the eggs are soft but still moist. Drizzle with vinegar and serve.

Black Iberian Pig's Brain

Stewed Pig's Brain
with Eggs

••

Miolos de Porco
com Ovos do Cartaxo   ♡ Ribatejo

Preparation time: 15 minutes
Cooking time: 35 minutes
Serves: 4

1 pig's brain
25 ml/1 fl oz (2 tablespoons) white wine vinegar
50 g/2 oz (3½ tablespoons) unsalted butter
50 g/2 oz lard (pork fat)
1 large onion, peeled and cut into small pieces
2 garlic cloves, peeled and thinly sliced
⅓ bunch flat-leaf parsley, finely chopped
300 g/11 oz lean pork meat, cut into small pieces
6 eggs
sea salt and freshly ground black pepper

Remove the thin membrane from the brain.

Bring a medium saucepan of water to the boil with a pinch of salt and the vinegar. Add the brain and poach for 12 minutes, then remove from the pan and chop it into pieces.

Heat the butter and lard (pork fat) in a medium saucepan over a medium heat, add the onion and garlic with half the parsley and cook for 8 minutes, or until the onion is soft. Add the lean meat and cook for 5 minutes, then add the pig's brain and stir until everything is combined. Season with salt.

Put the eggs into a small bowl and whisk them a little with a fork. Add the eggs to the meat and cook over a low heat for 10 minutes, or until creamy. Don't overcook the eggs. Sprinkle with the remaining parsley and serve.

Pork Kidneys –
Anadia Style

••

Rins de Porco   ♡ Beira Litoral
à Moda da Anadia

Preparation time: 20 minutes, plus 30 minutes marinating
Cooking time: 55 minutes
Serves: 4

4 pig's kidneys
juice of 2 lemons
70 ml/2¼ fl oz (¼ cup) olive oil, plus extra for drizzling
60 g/2¼ oz lard (pork fat)
1 large onion, peeled and finely chopped
1 large sprig flat-leaf parsley, roughly chopped
10 g/¼ oz (3½ teaspoons) plain (all-purpose) flour
200 ml/7 fl oz (¾ cup) sparkling wine from Bairrada
750 g/1 lb 10 oz potatoes, peeled and cut into chunks
sea salt and freshly ground black pepper

Clean the kidneys of any remaining fat, then thinly slice and put them into a large glass dish. Season with the lemon juice and pepper, then cover with food wrap and leave to marinate for 30 minutes.

Heat the olive oil and lard (pork fat) in a saucepan over a low heat, add the onion and cook for 15 minutes, or until golden. Add the kidneys and parsley and toss, then add the flour and wine. Reduce the heat to low and cook for 20 minutes, or until the alcohol has evaporated and the sauce has reduced. Taste and adjust the seasoning, if necessary, then remove from the heat and leave to rest while making the mashed potatoes.

Put the potatoes into a large saucepan, cover with water and a pinch of salt, then cook over a medium heat for 15–20 minutes, or until soft. Drain, put them back into the pan and mash. Season with salt and drizzle with olive oil.

Serve the kidneys with the mashed potatoes.

Pork Liver
with Onion Stew

••

Fígado de Porco   ♡ Ribatejo
de Cebolada   📷 p.231

Preparation time: 25 minutes, plus 4 hours marinating
Cooking time: 35 minutes
Serves: 4

400 g/14 oz very fresh pork liver
5 garlic cloves, peeled and thinly sliced
200 ml/7 fl oz (¾ cup) white wine
750 g/1 lb 10 oz new potatoes, peeled
60 ml/2 fl oz (4 tablespoons) olive oil
40 g/1½ oz lard (pork fat)
3 large onions, peeled and thinly sliced
1 teaspoon paprika
½ teaspoon ground cumin
50 ml/1⅔ fl oz (3½ tablespoons) white wine vinegar
sea salt and freshly ground black pepper

Cut the liver into thin slices and put into a large bowl. Season with salt and pepper, then add half the garlic and the white wine and toss everything together. Cover with food wrap and leave to marinate for 4 hours.

When ready to cook, put the potatoes into a large saucepan, cover with cold water, add a pinch of salt and cook over a medium heat for 15–20 minutes, or until soft. Drain and set aside.

Meanwhile, heat the olive oil and lard (pork fat) in a large saucepan over a low heat, add the onions and remaining garlic and cook for 12 minutes, or until the onions are translucent. Add the liver, paprika, cumin and vinegar and mix until well combined. Cover with a lid and stew gently for 20 minutes, or until the liver is cooked. Taste and adjust the seasoning, if necessary, with salt.

Serve the stew with the boiled potatoes on the side.

Pork Liver with Onion Stew

Pork Offal Stew

••

Sarrabulho   ▢ Beira Litoral

The killing of pigs has been embedded in the
local culture for years, as people bred the pigs
throughout the year or just for a few months
and then killed them in their back yard or farm
for for their own consumption. This was until
the 1990s when the government passed a bill
that the killing of animals in people's yards and
farms was no longer permitted due to health and
safety reasons. This bill took away the cultural
tradition of people getting together to slaughter
their pigs. Nevertheless, if you show you have the
right hygiene conditions you can still do it. This
stew was usually made on slaughter day when the
whole family and some locals gathered to take
part. I was lucky enough to grow up in a family
that took this tradition very seriously. You can
garnish this dish with small boiled potatoes.

Preparation time: 30 minutes
Cooking time: 50 minutes
Serves: 10
🔥 ▢

400 ml/14 fl oz (1⅔ cups) fresh pig's blood (if available)
25 ml/1 fl oz (2 tablespoons) white wine vinegar
750 g/1 lb 10 oz new potatoes, unpeeled
30 ml/1 fl oz (2 tablespoons) olive oil
3 bunches flat-leaf parsley, chopped
250 g/9 oz pork crepinette, cut into small pieces
1.2 kg/2 lb 11 oz pork meat, shoulder neck pieces with
    some fat, cut into small pieces
700 g/1 lb 9 oz pork liver, cut into small pieces
4 garlic cloves, peeled and coarsely chopped
1 bay leaf
350 ml/12 fl oz (1½ cups) red wine from Bairrada
sea salt and freshly ground black pepper

If you have some fresh blood, pour into a large bowl
and stir in the vinegar to prevent it coagulating.
    Put the potatoes into a medium saucepan with
a pinch of salt, cover with cold water and cook
over a medium heat for 15–20 minutes, or until
soft. Drain, peel and cut them into small pieces.
Set aside.
    Meanwhile, bring another medium saucepan of
water to the boil. Pour in the pig's blood (if using)
and cook over a medium heat for 20 minutes, or
until curds form. Strain and set aside.
    Put a clay pan or saucepan over a medium heat,
add the olive oil, parsley and meat, except the liver,
and cook for 15 minutes. Season with salt, pepper
and add the garlic and bay leaf. Pour in the red
wine and cook for a further 10 minutes, or until the
wine has reduced by half, then add the shredded
blood and mix well. Add the liver, reduce the heat to
low and cook for 5 minutes. Add the potatoes and
mix well. Don't overcook the liver otherwise it will
become rubbery; it should be nice and soft. Taste
and adjust the seasoning, if necessary, with salt and
pepper. Serve immediately.

Creamy Polenta with Various Meats and Pig's Blood

••

Papas de Sarrabulho   ▢ Minho

This hearty, traditional stew from Minho that
almost resembles a porridge, was originally served
on pig slaughter days during the colder winter
months, so includes pork offal (variety meats)
and blood, with different types of pork sausage
(*salpicão* and *chouriço*), and *presunto* (ham)
added. Today, *Sarrabulho* (page 429) is offered
in restaurants in the north of Portugal, usually
enjoyed on its own, or served with a side of *Rojões
à Moda do Minho* (see page 224).

Preparation time: 15 minutes
Cooking time: 1 hour 45 minutes
Serves: 6
🔥 ▢

350 g/12 oz beef shoulder
250 g/9 oz bacon
230 g/8 oz ham
150 g/5 oz pork liver
1 medium pork backbone
350 g/12 oz pork chops
½ chicken
220 ml/7½ fl oz (1 cup) fresh pig's blood
250 g/9 oz (2 cups) fine polenta (cornmeal)
1 teaspoon ground white pepper
1 tablespoon ground cumin
sea salt

Put all the meat into a large saucepan with enough
water to cover and cook over a medium heat for
1 hour, or until all the meat is cooked through. The
ham and bacon will cook first so remove them and
set aside on a large plate, then remove the others
once they are cooked. Remove the meats from
the pan and transfer to a plate or tray and leave
until cool enough to handle. Once cool, remove
any bones and shred the meat. Put the liver to one
side, away from the other meat, and shred it – it
will be incorporated with the pig's blood later on.
Leave the meat cooking liquid to cool in the pan.
    Bring a medium saucepan of water to the boil.
Once boiling, add the pig's blood, season with salt
and cook for 25 minutes. Strain the blood and put
it into a food processor or blender. Add 200 ml/
7 fl oz (¾ cup) cold water and blitz until smooth.
Set aside.
    Once the meat cooking liquid is cold, add the
polenta (cornmeal) and cook over a medium heat
for 20 minutes. Halfway through cooking, add
the pig's blood and reserved shredded liver, keep
cooking until the polenta is completely smooth.
Add all the meat, white pepper and cumin, then
taste and adjust the seasoning, if necessary, with
salt. Serve.

'Pot in the Oven' Meat Stew

Panela no Forno ♡ Beira Baixa

Preparation time: 25 minutes
Cooking time: 2 hours 30 minutes
Serves: 4
🖋 ▢

1 pig's ear
400 g/14 oz cow's bladder
1 pig's foot
120 g/4 oz Serrano ham
90 g/3¼ oz streaky (lean) bacon
90 ml/3¼ fl oz (6 tablespoons) olive oil
1 small onion, peeled and finely chopped
100 g/3½ oz chorizo, half thinly sliced
3 cloves
300 g/11 oz (1½ cups) long-grain rice
1 small *farinheira* (smoked sausage)
sea salt and freshly ground black pepper

Singe the pig's ears with a blowtorch to remove any hairs, then rinse under cold running water. Rinse the cow's bladder under cold running water then, if necessary, scrape it clean with a sharp knife. (You can ask your butcher to do this.) Put the bladder into a large saucepan and cover with water. Cook over a medium heat for 40 minutes, or until soft. Remove from the pan and set 600 ml/20 fl oz (2½ cups) of the bladder cooking liquid aside.

Put the pig's ear, pig's foot, ham and bacon into another large saucepan and add 5 litres/169 fl oz (20 cups) water. Cook over a low heat for 1 hour, or until all the meat is soft. The ham and bacon will cook first so remove them and set aside on a large plate, then remove the others once they are cooked. Strain the cooking liquid and set 1 litre/ 34 fl oz (4¼ cups) aside.

Cut all the meat into small pieces. Combine both reserved cooking liquids in a jug (pitcher).

Heat the olive oil in a ovenproof casserole dish (Dutch oven) over a low heat, add the onion and the thinly sliced chorizo and cook for 10 minutes, or until the onion is translucent. Add all the meat and cloves, season with salt and pepper, then gently cook for 10 minutes.

Preheat the oven to 160°C/325°F/Gas Mark 3.

Add 1 litre/34 fl oz (4¼ cups) of the combined cooking liquids to the pan, bring to the boil, then add the rice and stir. Once boiling, cover with a lid. remove from the heat and place in the hot oven to finish cooking the rice, about 20 minutes. Keep checking the rice as you don't want it to overcook.

Meanwhile, prick the *farinheira* and remaining chorizo all over with a needle, then cut them into medium-thick slices and put them into another large saucepan. Cover with cold water and cook over a medium heat for 10 minutes, or until soft.

Once the rice is cooked, remove the dish from the oven and arrange the chorizo and *farinheira* on top. Serve immediately.

Pork Offal Stew with Paprika

Tachada ♡ Leiria

This original dish has vanished from the villages in Leiria as the slaughter of pigs is now not allowed. As the locals don't have access to fresh pig's offal (variety meats), this dish has been adapted over the years and today most use pork belly and ribs. Nevertheless, if you can find pig's offal then you should try this dish. While the men used to kill and prepare the pigs, including cleaning and butchering them, the women were in the kitchen preparing the offal, including the lungs and kidneys, and mixed it together with some fresh lean meat and left it to marinate for a couple of hours before cooking it. I remember this tradition when I was growing up. It usually occurred in autumn (the fall) and we would eat the *friginada* (fried pork offal) in the wine cellar where the pig would be hung to dry overnight as it was usually the coolest place on the farm.

Preparation time: 15 minutes
Cooking time: 25 minutes
Serves: 8
▢ ▢

400 g/14 oz pork liver
300 g/11 oz pig's heart
250 g/9 oz pig's lungs
120 g/4 oz lard (pork fat)
2 teaspoons sweet paprika
2 bay leaves
400 ml/14 fl oz (1⅔ cups) red wine
sea salt
400 g/14 oz crusty bread, thickly sliced, to serve

Prepare all the offal (variety meats), by removing any excess fat and cutting them into small pieces. Keep them all on separate plates as they have different cooking times.

Heat a large frying pan or skillet over a medium heat, add the lard (pork fat) and liver and cook for 5 minutes, flipping the pieces over so they cook on both sides. Add the heart and cook for 2 minutes, flipping the pieces over and, finally, add the lungs and cook for a further 3 minutes. Season with salt, the paprika and bay leaves and cook over a medium heat for 5 minutes before adding the wine. Cover partially with a lid to allow the steam to evaporate and cook for 10 minutes, or until the wine has reduced by a third.

Serve the offal with slices of crusty bread.

Meat Stew with Beans and Spices — Porto Style

Tripas à Moda do Porto 📷 p.235   ⋃ Minho

During the 15th century, people from Porto donated the best parts of their cows to the Armada of Prince Henry the Navigator, when they were busy discovering remote lands. The locals were left with the tripe (stomach lining), so they came up with this rich and nourishing dish as a way of using it. Do not confuse this dish with *Dobrada* (page 255), another tripe recipe from south of Porto. There are some long cooking times, so I prefer to cook the meat the day before.

Preparation time: 1 hour, plus 12 hours soaking
Cooking time: 6 hours 30 minutes
Serves: 10
🐖 ⍭

1.3 kg/3 lb (7¼ cups) dried white butter (lima) beans
400 g/14 oz carrots, cut into medium-thick slices
2 pig's feet
1 cow's hoof
4 pig's ears
400 g/14 oz pork belly, seasoned with salt and paprika
1.5 kg/2½ lb pork ribs, trimmed
1 medium chicken
1.2 kg/2 lb 11 oz cow's stomach
2 lemons, cut into wedges
250 g/9 oz chorizo
230 g/8 oz ham
60 g/2¼ oz lard (pork fat)
100 ml/3½ fl oz (⅓ cup) olive oil
3 onions, peeled and chopped into small pieces
4 garlic cloves, peeled and chopped into small pieces
3 bay leaves
6 cloves
2 tablespoons sweet paprika
2 teaspoons ground cumin
⅓ bunch flat-leaf parsley, roughly chopped
100 ml/3½ fl oz (⅓ cup) white wine vinegar
800 g/1 lb 12 oz (4 cups) long-grain rice
sea salt

Put the beans into a large bowl of cold water and leave to soak for 12 hours. The next day, drain the beans and put them into a large saucepan with the carrots. Pour in enough cold water to cover and cook over a low heat for 1 hour, or until soft. Drain and set aside, reserving the cooking liquid.

Singe the pig's feet, pig's ears and cow's hoof with a blowtorch to remove any hairs. Set aside.

Rinse the cow's stomach under cold running water, then rub it with lemon and salt until cleaned.

Bring a large saucepan of water to the boil. Add the stomach and as soon as the water returns to the boil, remove it from the pan. Refill the pan with fresh water, add the stomach and cook over a medium heat for 3 hours, or until very soft. Remove from the pan and leave to cool on a plate or tray. Once cool, cut into chunks. Set aside.

Put all the other meat into another large saucepan. Cover with water and cook over a medium heat for 1 hour, or until the meat is soft and can easily be pulled apart. Remove each piece as soon as it is cooked. Once all the meat is cooked, cut it into small pieces. You can also pull the bones out of the ribs and the chicken if you like. Set aside. Reserve the stock.

Put a large saucepan over a medium heat, add the lard (pork fat), olive oil, onions and garlic and cook for 5 minutes, or until the onions are lightly coloured. Add the bay leaves and cloves and stir. Add all the meat to the pan, stir, cover with enough of the reserved cooking liquid and bring to the boil. Season with paprika, salt and cumin, add the drained beans and cook for 10 minutes, or until the liquid has reduced a little to intensify the flavour. Taste and adjust the seasoning with cumin and salt, sprinkle with the parsley, add the vinegar and stir.

Meanwhile, bring another large saucepan of water to the boil. Add the rice, cook for 12 minutes, or until soft. Drain the rice and serve with the stew.

Pork Blood Stew

Laburdo – Castelo Branco   ⋃ Beira Baixa

Preparation time: 20 minutes, plus 5 minutes soaking
Cooking time: 15 minutes
Serves: 4
⍭

3 garlic cloves, peeled and crushed
2 teaspoons ground cumin
½ teaspoon sweet paprika
60 g/2¼ oz lardo, chopped into small pieces
1 small onion, peeled and finely chopped
600 ml/20 fl oz (2½ cups) fresh pig's blood
2 bay leaves
300 g/11 oz stale bread, thinly sliced
sea salt

Put the garlic, cumin and paprika into a mortar with a little salt, and, using a pestle, mash to a paste. Set aside.

Melt the lardo in a saucepan over a low heat. Add the onion and cook for 5 minutes, or until lightly coloured. Remove the pan from the heat.

Bring a saucepan of water to the boil, then add the onion and garlic paste and boil for 5 minutes.

Strain the pig's blood through a sieve (fine-mesh strainer) or chinois into a bowl, then gradually pour the blood into the boiling water, stirring continuously so it doesn't coagulate. Reduce the heat to low and cook for 3 minutes.

Arrange the bread in a large serving dish, then pour over the pig's blood stew. Cover the dish with a tea (dish) towel and leave to soak for 5 minutes before serving.

Meat Stew with Beans and Spices – Porto Style

Pig's Ear Salad

Salada de Orelha de Porco 📷 p.237 | ▽ Leiria

I remember my dad ordering this dish from an old tavern in our city – chewy, vinegary pieces of meat served with thick slices of cornbread.

Preparation time: 20 minutes, plus 12 hours chilling with an additional 12 hours chilling (optional)
Cooking time: 2 hours 30 minutes
Serves: 4
🐖 ▢

4 pig's ears
1 onion, peeled and cut into small cubes
2 garlic cloves, peeled and cut into small cubes
2 tablespoons finely chopped flat-leaf parsley or
    coriander (cilantro)
100 ml/3½ fl oz (⅓ cup) olive oil
60 ml/2 fl oz (4 tablespoons) white wine vinegar
½ teaspoon paprika (optional)
sea salt and freshly ground black pepper

Wash the pig's ears and put them into a large dish and season with salt. Cover with food wrap and leave in the fridge for 12 hours.

The next day, rinse the pig's ears to remove the salt, then put them into a saucepan and cover with cold water. Cook over a medium heat for 2 hours 30 minutes, or until soft. Drain and leave to cool. Once the ears are cold, cut them into small pieces, put into a medium bowl and set aside.

Put the onion and garlic into a small bowl, add the parsley or coriander (cilantro) and mix well to combine. Add the mixture to the ears, then season with the olive oil, vinegar and salt and pepper and mix until well combined. It is best to leave to chill in the fridge for 12 hours but it can be eaten now.

Sprinkle the ears with paprika before serving.

Pig's Ears and Tails with Garlic and Coriander

Orelha e Rabo de Porco de Coentrada | ▽ Alentejo

Preparation time: 20 minutes, plus 45 minutes resting
Cooking time: 2 hours 45 minutes
Serves: 4
🐖 ▢

3 pig's ears
4 pig's tails
5 garlic cloves, peeled and very finely chopped
½ bunch coriander (cilantro), finely chopped
150 ml/5 fl oz (⅔ cup) olive oil
70 ml/2¼ fl oz (¼ cup) vinegar
sea salt and freshly ground black pepper

Clean the pig's ears removing any leftover hairs, blow torching them if necessary, then scrape them with the tip of a knife and rinse under cold running water. Do the same for the tails. Put the pig's ears and tails into a large saucepan, cover with cold water, add a pinch of salt and cook over a medium heat for 2 hours 30 minutes, or until soft. Remove them from the pan and leave to cool a little.

Heat the grill (broiler), then place the ears and tail on the grill rack and cook for 15 minutes, or until golden brown.

Put the garlic and coriander (cilantro) into a large bowl and mix together to combine. Add the olive oil, vinegar and a little pepper, then combine.

Slice the pig's ears into thin strips and cut the tails into small pieces. Add the meat to the garlic and coriander mixture and toss together until the meat is well coated. Cover with food wrap and leave to rest for 45 minutes before serving.

Fried Pork Tripe

Tripas Enfarinhadas | ▽ Minho

This dish can be eaten as a *petisco* or snack or as part of *Rojões á Moda do Minho* (page 224).

Preparation time: 30 minutes, plus 12 hours soaking
Cooking time: 15 minutes
Serves: 4
🐖 ▢

250 g/9 oz pork tripe (stomach lining)
6 lemons, cut into medium-thick slices
600 g/1 lb 5 oz (5 cups) fine corn flour (cornmeal)
2 teaspoons ground cumin
fat from *Rojões á Moda do Minho* (page 224) or lard
    (pork fat), for frying
freshly ground black pepper

Rinse the pork tripe (stomach lining) under cold running water until clean. Put the tripe into a large bowl with 2 lemon slices and cover with water. Leave to soak for 12 hours. It is important to change the water and lemon slices at least three times during the soaking process.

The next day, drain the tripe and dry it as well as possible with a clean tea (dish) towel. Put the corn flour, cumin and some pepper on a large plate or tray and mix well.

Turn the tripe inside out, then toss in the corn flour mixture until well coated. Using fine butcher's string or kitchen twine tied at one end, fold the tripe back into its normal shape. Add a little more flour to the inside, but without filling it up.

Bring a saucepan of salted water to the boil. Add the tripe and leave for 5 minutes, then remove to a plate or tray and cut into small pieces, each about 6 cm/2½ inches.

Melt the fat or lard (pork fat) in a large frying pan or skillet over a medium heat. Add the tripe and fry for 10 minutes, or until crisp. Serve.

Pig's Ear Salad

Pig's Feet Stew with Coriander

••

Pezinhos de Coentrada ⛭ Alentejo

Pork is the choice of meat in Alentejo, where almost all pigs, especially black pigs, are acorn-fed. The resulting tasty, juicy meat is used in a variety of recipes, and here pig's feet are stewed in garlic, coriander, cloves and an olive oil paste. *Pézinhos de Coentrada* is a *petisco*, cooked in many restaurants throughout the country, and traditionally served with thin slices of bread on the side.

Preparation time: 25 minutes, plus 12 hours standing
Cooking time: 1 hour 30 minutes
Serves: 4
⛭

3 pig's feet
2 onions, peeled and finely chopped
50 g/2 oz lard (pork fat)
2 bay leaves
45 g/1½ oz (⅓ cup) plain (all-purpose) flour
3 teaspoons paprika
¼ bunch coriander (cilantro), roughly chopped
6 garlic cloves, peeled but left whole
2 eggs
60 ml/2 fl oz (4 tablespoons) white wine vinegar
sea salt
450 g/1 lb crusty bread, sliced and toasted, to serve

The day before you want to cook, clean the pig's feet, cut them in half and rinse under cold running water. Put them into a large bowl and season with salt. Cover with food wrap and leave in the fridge for 12 hours.

When ready to cook, put the pig's feet into a large saucepan, cover with water and cook over a medium heat for 2 hours, or until the cartilage starts to separate from the bone. Once cooked, remove the pan from the heat and set aside.

Put the onions into another saucepan with the lard (pork fat) and bay leaves and cook over a medium heat for 10 minutes, or until the onions are translucent. Add the flour and paprika, then mix well.

Meanwhile, put the coriander (cilantro), garlic and a pinch of salt into a mortar and, using a pestle, mash to form a paste. Set aside.

Add the pig's feet to the pan with the onions along with enough of their cooking liquid to cover them and cook over a low heat for 6 minutes, stirring continuously to prevent them sticking. Remove the pan from the heat, add the eggs and mix them into the pig's feet stew, stirring continuously. Finish with the vinegar.

Serve the pig's feet stew with toasted bread.

Pig's Feet with White Beans

••

Chispe com Feijão Branco de Almeirim ⛭ Ribatejo

Preparation time: 20 minutes, plus 12 hours soaking (optional)
Cooking time: 55 minutes
Serves: 6
🐷 ⛭ ⛭

450 g/1 lb (2½ cups) dried beans or fresh if available
1 chorizo
1 *morcela* (black pudding)
2 pig's ears
3 pig's feet
350 g/12 oz pork belly
5 waxy potatoes, peeled and diced
½ Portuguese cabbage, or January King cabbage, sliced into thin strips
sea salt

If using dried beans, put the beans into a large bowl of cold water and leave to soak for 12 hours. The next day, drain the beans and put them into a large saucepan. Set aside.

Using a skewer, prick holes over the chorizo and *morcela* to prevent them bursting during cooking. Singe the pig's feet and pig's ears with a blowtorch to remove any hairs, then rinse under cold running water.

Put the ears, feet, chorizo, *morcela* and pork belly into the pan with the beans and cook over a low heat with a pinch of salt for 30 minutes, or until the beans and meat are soft. Keep checking the meat regulary during cooking as some meat will be ready before the others, so remove them as soon they are cooked.

Once all the meat and beans are cooked, add the potatoes and cabbage to the pan and cook them over a low heat for 20 minutes. Slice the pork belly into chunks, the ears into strips and the feet in half lengthwise. Cut the chorizo and *morcela* into thick slices, then add all the meat back to the pan and cook for a further 5 minutes. Taste and adjust the seasoning, if necessary, with salt, then stir and serve.

Boiled Salted Pork Bones

••

Ossos Salgados de Porco   ♡ Leiria

I remember eating this with my family, especially during the winter. The meat was removed from the *salgadeira*, a salt box that sat outside all year round, and where pieces of pork were covered in salt and cured for months. This recipe needs to be done at least three weeks ahead in order to enjoy the full flavour of the cured meat, but the meat can but the meat can be kept in the salt for months. You also need enough time to eat it, as you have to scrape all the meat off the bones. It makes an excellent mid-afternoon snack for the winter months.

Preparation time: 40 minutes, plus 3 weeks curing and
2 days soaking
Cooking time: 45–60 minutes
Serves: 12
🐟 ▢

5 pig's ears
5 pork neck bones, cut in half
1 kg/2 lb 4 oz pork belly
2 pork ribs
10 kg/22 lb rock salt
2 Cornbreads (page 32), to serve

Singe the pig's ears with a blowtorch to remove any hairs, then rinse under cold running water.

Rub the pig's ears, pork neck bones, pork belly and pork ribs with some of the salt. Put all the meats into a plastic container that is large enough to accommodate all the meat and cover with the remaining salt. Making sure the food wrap is touching the salt, cover the container with food wrap, place some weights on the top and leave to cure for 3 weeks.

When the pork has cured, remove the meats from the salt and wash under cold running water. Cut the ribs into sections of two and the pork belly into 5-cm/2-inch chunks. Leave the pig's ears whole.

Fill up the same container with cold water, then add the meat and leave to soak for 2 days to desalt them, changing the water twice a day.

When ready to cook, put all the meat into a large saucepan, cover with cold water and bring to the boil. Cook over a medium heat for 45–60 minutes, or until the meat is soft. Once the meat is cooked, remove it from the pan and put into a large serving dish.

Serve the meats with hunks of cornbread.

São Miguel Cornbread Porridge

••

Papas de São Miguel   ♡ Beira Litoral
– Oliveira de Azeméis

Vinha d'Alho was made and eaten in almost all the houses of Oliveira de Azeméis on 29 September, the day of the patron saint São Miguel. This porridge can be as thick or thin as you like, if you prefer it thinner then use less cornflour (cornstarch).

Preparation time: 30 minutes, plus 2 days marinating and
12 hours soaking
Cooking time: 50 minutes
Serves: 6
🐟 ▢ ▢

3 pork loin bones
200 g/7 oz pork skin
6 garlic cloves, 4 peeled and coarsely chopped,
     2 peeled and very finely chopped
650 ml/22½ fl oz (2⅔ cups) red wine
450 g/1 lb (2½ cups) dried white butter (lima) beans
2 onions, peeled and very finely chopped
3 bunches flat-leaf parsley, very finely chopped
350 g/12 oz turnip tops, bottom stalks removed and
     cut into very thin strips
300 g/11 oz (2½ cups) cornflour (cornstarch)
1 teaspoon ground cumin
sea salt

Put the pork loin bones and skin into a large bowl with the coarsely chopped garlic and red wine. Season with salt and leave in the fridge for 2 days, turning them around in the marinade every day.

The day before cooking, put the dried beans into a large bowl, pour in enough water to cover and leave to soak for 12 hours.

When ready to cook, remove the bones and skin from the marinade and rinse under cold running water. Drain the beans.

Fill a large saucepan with water, then add the meat and soaked beans and cook over a low heat for 30 minutes, or until the beans and meat are soft. Remove the meat from the pan, then using a knife, remove the meat from the bones and cut the skin into small pieces. Set aside.

Add the very finely chopped garlic, onions, parsley and baby turnip leaves and cook over a medium heat for 10 minutes. Return the meat back to the pan.

Put the cornflour (cornstarch) into a medium bowl, add some cold water and stir until it has dissolved into a thick paste. Add the paste to the pan and cook over a low heat, stirring continuously, for a further 5 minutes, or until thick. Add the cumin, then taste and adjust the seasoning, if necessary. Serve immediately.

Linguiça and Yams

Linguiça com Inhame 📷 p.241   ⊍ Açores

Inhame (yam), also called '*tocas*', is a tuber that in the Azores enjoys the same levels of importance as a potato. It is used in many dishes, including *Cozido da Lagoa das Furnas* (a local meat and vegetable stew that is buried in the ground and cooked using natural heat of the volcanic soil, page 254), or simply eaten as a snack. The yam's bark varies in colour from dark brown to light pink, and its edible portion consists of a pulp ranging from white to yellow, pink or purple. The raw skin is rough and difficult to peel, so they are cooked with the skinl on; it softens as it cooks and does not cause skin irritation or itching (hence the use of gloves when touching yam). Yam is boiled in this recipe and served with fried *linguiça*, a smoke-cured sausage seasoned with garlic and paprika, commonly used as a side dish to many pork recipes in the Azores.

Preparation time: minutes
Cooking time: 55 minutes
Serves: 4
🐖 ▢ ✕

2 yams, peeled
100 g/3½ oz pork fat
2 *linguiças* or chorizo
sea salt

Put the yams into a saucepan and pour in enough water to cover, then add a pinch of salt. Cook over a medium heat for 20–25 minutes, or until soft. Drain and cut into small pieces. Set aside.

Melt the lard (pork fat) in a large frying pan or skillet over a medium heat. Add the *linguiças* and cook for 10 minutes, or until the skins are crispy. Remove from the pan and pat dry with paper towels, then cut them into small pieces, the same size as the yams.

Combine the cooked yam and meat before serving together.

Chorizo with Turnip Tops

Chouriça com Grelos   ⊍ Beira Alta

As a kid I never liked turnip tops, though in my grandparent's house they ate them on a regular basis. The bitterness of them used to put me off. Things change, however, and I love them now. In this recipe, I love the contrast of the turnips and chorizo, the bitterness and fattiness working together is just brilliant, simple and nourishing.

Preparation time: 25 minutes
Cooking time: 40–45 minutes
Serves: 4
🐖 ▢ ▢ ✕

250 g/9 oz chorizo
400 g/14 oz Serrano ham
700 g/1 lb 9 oz new potatoes, peeled and quartered
1 kg/ 2 lb 4 oz turnip tops, bottom stalks removed

Bring a large saucepan of water to the boil. Add the chorizo and ham and cook over a medium heat for 20 minutes. Remove the meats and set aside, then add the potatoes and cook for 15–20 minutes, or until soft. Add the turnip tops and cook for another 5 minutes, or until tender.

Slice the meat, then serve with the boiled potatoes and turnip tops on the side.

Cabbage-wrapped Chorizo Cooked in Hot Ashes

Chouriço Assado com   ⊍ Leiria
Folhas de Couve na Cinza

The people in my village, including my grandmother, once used this cooking method. Before going to bed, she would wrap chorizo in several layers of cabbage leaves, tie them up nicely and then put them into the white-hot ashes of the fire. She covered them with more ashes and left them in there until the morning. The result was pretty spectacular, as the chorizo was cooked with a superb smokiness. I have applied this method to some dishes in the restaurants and it works wonderfully with charcuterie, figs and stone fruits.

Preparation time: 10 minutes, plus 12 hours smoking
Serves: 4
🐖 ▢ ✕

4 chorizo
2 cabbages, such as Savoy or January King

Prepare an open fire with wood and coals in order to produce plenty of hot ashes.

Remove the leaves from the cabbages and cut the thickest part from the heart. Arrange the cabbage leaves into four piles each with two or three layers of leaves. Place a chorizo on each pile of cabbage leaves and wrap to make a parcel. Tie the leaves with butcher's string or kitchen twine to secure.

Once the fire has died down, put all the cabbage parcels into the fireplace, covering them with the hot ashes. It's important that the parcels are covered only in ashes and are not in contact with any live coals, otherwise the leaves may burn and damage the chorizo. Leave for 12 hours.

The next day, remove the parcels from the ashes that should now be cold. Remove the cabbage leaves carefully so that the ashes do not come into contact with the chorizo.

Serve the chorizo on their own or with cheese.

Linguiça and Yams

BEEF AND VEAL

Meat Pies from Castelo Branco

Empadas de Castelo Branco   📷 p.245   ▽ Beira Baixa

Preparation time: 45 minutes, plus 50 minutes resting
Cooking time: 1 hour 20 minutes
Makes: 13

For the dough:
260 g/9 oz (2 cups plus 4 teaspoons) plain (all-purpose)
     flour, plus extra for dusting
30 g/1 oz lard (pork fat) or butter
1 egg, for the egg wash
sea salt
butter, for greasing

For the filling:
1 onion, peeled and finely chopped
2 garlic cloves, peeled and finely chopped
10 g/¼ oz flat-leaf parsley, finely chopped
1 small bunch marjoram, leaves picked
1 bay leaf
50 ml/1⅔ fl oz (3½ tablespoons) olive oil
600 g/1 lb 5 oz flank or any other cut suitable
     for braising, any sinew removed and
     cut into small cubes
nutmeg, grated
100 ml/3½ fl oz (⅓ cup plus 1 tablespoon) white wine
sea salt and freshly ground black pepper

To make the dough, put the flour and lard (pork fat) or butter into a large bowl, with a pinch of salt and mix together until a smooth dough forms. Cover with food wrap and leave to rest for 50 minutes.

For the filling, put the onion, garlic, parsley, marjoram and bay leaves into a large saucepan with the olive oil and cook over a medium heat for 15 minutes, or until the onions are golden. Add the meat, season with salt, pepper and grated nutmeg, then increase the heat to high and cook for 5 minutes, or until the meat is lightly browned. Reduce the heat to low, add the wine, partially cover with a lid and cook for a further 30 minutes, or until the meat is soft. Remove from the heat and leave to cool.

Preheat the oven to 180°C/350°F/Gas Mark 4. Grease 13 baking pans, 8 cm/3¼ inches in diameter and 2.5 cm/1 inch high, with butter.

Divide the dough into two equal portions. Roll out one portion of the dough on a lightly floured work counter into a large rectangle and, using a 9-cm/3½-inch ring cutter, cut out 13 circles. Use them to line the pans. Roll out the other portion of dough into a large thin rectangle, and cut out 13 more circles of dough. These are the lids.

Fill the pie bases with the filling, then place a lid on top and seal tightly with your fingers. Put the egg into a small bowl and whisk lightly with a fork, then brush the egg over the tops of the pastries. Put the pans on a large baking sheet and bake in the oven for 30 minutes, or until golden brown.

Deep-fried Beef Pasties

Pastéis de Massa Tenra   ▽ Lisbon

These individual savoury pockets of pastry (pie dough) crust are often stuffed with a stewed meat mixture, sealed with a fork, then deep-fried until crisp and golden. They are made using a traditional pastry, *massa tenra*, meaning 'tender pastry', are usually eaten as a snack, and can be found all over Portugal, but especially in cafés and restaurants in Lisbon and Porto.

Preparation time: 15 minutes
Cooking time: 45 minutes
Serves: 5

1½ onions, peeled and very finely chopped
30 g/1 oz (2 tablespoons) unsalted butter
350 g/12 oz (1½ cups) minced ground beef or other
     minced meat
20 g/¾ oz (2⅓ teaspoons) plain (all-purpose) flour, plus
     extra for dusting
250 ml/8 fl oz (1 cup) meat or vegetable stock
3 egg yolks
juice of 1 lemon
¼ bunch flat-leaf parsley, chopped
1 quantity *Massa Tenra* dough (page 293)
1.5 litres/50 fl oz (6¼ cups) sunflower oil, for deep-frying
sea salt and freshly ground black pepper
green salad leaves, to serve

Put the onions and butter into a saucepan and cook over a low heat for 10 minutes, or until the onion is translucent. Add the meat and cook for a further 10 minutes, stirring to break up any clumps, until browned all over. Sprinkle the flour over and stir, then add the stock. Increase the heat to medium and cook for 15 minutes, or until the mixture becomes a moist paste, but not dry. Remove the pan from the heat, add the egg yolks and mix until well combined. Season with salt, pepper, lemon juice and add the chopped parsley.

Divide the dough into two portions. Roll out each piece of dough on a floured work counter to give you two thin rectangular sheets of the same size. Using a teaspoon, put filling in mounds down the middle of one of the sheets of dough, spacing the mounds evenly apart. Cover the filling with the other sheet of dough, press down gently between the mounds and cut out the pasties with a round pasta cutter.

Line a large baking sheet with paper towels. Heat the sunflower oil for deep-frying in a large, deep saucepan or fryer until it reaches 180°C/350°F on a thermometer. Working in batches, carefully lower the pasties into the hot oil and deep-fry for 2–3 minutes, or until golden. Remove with a slotted spoon and leave to drain on the lined baking sheet.

Serve the pasties with some green salad leaves.

Meat Pies from Castelo Branco

Savoury Pasty with Saffron Broth and Vinegar

Pastéis de Molho da Covilhã   ∪ Beira Baixa

This iconic dish from the city of Covilhã dates back to 1920, when the many factory workers in this region had to find a nutritious lunch that didn't take long to prepare. These pastries could be made in advance and lasted for weeks. They are similar to the UK's Cornish pasties.

Preparation time: 30 minutes, plus 10 minutes resting
Cooking time: 2 hours
Makes: 5

For the dough:
325 g/11¾ oz (2¾ cups) plain (all-purpose) flour,
    plus extra for dusting
325 g/11¾ oz (3 sticks) butter or lard (pork fat)
20 ml/¾ fl oz (4 teaspoons) firewater

For the meat filling:
30 ml/1 fl oz (2 tablespoons) olive oil, plus extra for greasing
1 onion, peeled and very finely chopped
300 g/11 oz flank steak
sea salt and freshly ground black pepper

For the stock:
75 ml/2½ fl oz (5 tablespoons) white wine vinegar
1 g/⅓ oz saffron threads
5 sprigs flat-leaf parsley

To make the filling, heat the olive oil in a saucepan over a medium heat, add the onion and cook for 10 minutes, or until the onion is translucent.

Meanwhile, put the meat into another saucepan, cover with water and add a pinch of salt. Cook over a low heat for 50 minutes, or until soft. Transfer the meat to a food processor and blitz until ground. Add it to the onion and cook over a low heat for a further 10 minutes. Taste and adjust the seasoning with salt and pepper. Set aside.

Put all the ingredients for the dough into a large bowl, add 140 ml/4¾ fl oz (⅔ cup) cold water and mix together until a smooth dough is formed. Tip the dough onto a lightly floured work counter and roll out to a large rectangle, then fold the bottom third into the middle, then the top third into the middle and roll out again. Repeat this, roll out, then lay the butter in pieces over the dough. Fold the dough over the butter into thirds and roll out into a thick rectangle. Cut the dough into 5 pieces and flatten them with the rolling pin, leaving one side a bit thicker. Put 50 g/2 oz of the filling into the middle of the pastry, then flip the thinner part of the dough over the thicker part and press down gently with your fingers to seal.

For the stock, put 1.6 litres/56 fl oz (6½ cups) water, the vinegar, saffron and parsley into a large saucepan and bring to the boil, then reduce the heat to medium and simmer for 15 minutes. Remove from the heat, discard the parsley and set aside.

Preheat the oven to 240°C/475°F/Gas Mark 9 and grease a large baking sheet with olive oil.

Put the pastries onto the baking sheet and bake for 30 minutes, or until golden. Serve the pastries on a rimmed plate, or shallow bowl with some of the stock poured around. Cover with a large plate and leave for 10 minutes before serving.

Beef Rissoles

Rissóis de Carne   ∪ Lisbon

Half-moon-shaped, hand-sized savoury *rissóis* (singular *rissol*) are popular deep-fried turnovers that can be found everywhere in Portugal, from cafés to house parties to receptions. They are most commonly filled with prawns (*Rissol de Camarão*), but they can also include minced meats, cod (*Rissol de Bacalhau*) or suckling pig (*Rissol de Leitão*). *Rissóis* are usually eaten cold, as a snack or starter, or warm as a main course with salad or rice, such as tomato rice or turnip greens rice.

Preparation time: 30 minutes, plus 1 hour chilling
Cooking time: 1 hour
Serves: 5

For the filling:
60 ml/2 fl oz (4 tablespoons) olive oil
1 onion, peeled and finely chopped
2 garlic cloves, peeled and finely chopped
350 g/12 oz (1½ cups) minced (ground) beef
80 g/3 oz ripe tomatoes, peeled and finely chopped
50 g/2 oz (⅓ cup) tomato purée (paste)
1 bay leaf
40 g/1½ oz chorizo, cut into very small pieces
75 ml/2½ fl oz (5 tablespoons) white wine
5 eggs
350 g/12 oz (7 cups) breadcrumbs
1.5 litres/50 fl oz (6¼ cups) sunflower oil, for deep-frying
1 lemon, halved
sea salt and freshly ground black pepper

For the dough:
25 ml/1 fl oz (2 tablespoons) olive oil
120 ml/4 fl oz (½ cup) milk
65 g/2¼ oz (¾ stick) butter
330 g/11¾ oz (2¾ cups) plain (all-purpose) flour, plus
    extra for dusting

To make the filling, heat the olive oil in a saucepan over a medium heat, add the onion and garlic and cook for 10 minutes, or until the onion is translucent. Add the beef and cook for a further 10 minutes, or until browned. Add the tomatoes, tomato purée (paste), bay leaf, chorizo, wine and a pinch of salt. Reduce the heat to low and cook for 20 minutes, or until all moisture has evaporated and the mixture looks like a paste. Remove and discard the bay leaf. Transfer to a plate to cool. Season with salt and pepper.

For the dough, put 170 ml/6 fl oz (¾ cup)

water into a saucepan with the olive oil, milk, butter and a pinch of salt, then bring to the boil. Reduce the heat to low and add all the flour in one go, stirring until incorporated. Increase the heat to medium and cook for 5 minutes, stirring until the dough starts to come off the sides of the pan.

Tip the dough out onto a floured work counter and knead until cold. Roll the dough out into a long thin sheet. Using a round pasta cutter, cut out as many rounds of dough as possible. Put a teaspoonful of the filling onto one side of each round and fold the dough over to enclose the filling. Press down gently to seal. Repeat until all the dough and filling is used up.

Put the eggs into a shallow bowl and whisk lightly with a fork. Spread the breadcrumbs out over a large plate. Dip each rissole into the egg and then roll in the breadcrumbs until well coated. Repeat this process twice, then place them on a large baking sheet and leave to chill in the fridge for 1 hour. You can freeze these rissoles, too. Just take them out 1 hour before deep-frying them.

When ready to cook, line a large baking sheet with paper towels. Heat the sunflower oil for deep-frying in a large, deep saucepan until it reaches 180°C/350°F on a thermometer. Working in batches, carefully lower the rissoles into the hot oil and deep-fry for 3–4 minutes, or until golden. Remove with a slotted spoon and leave to drain on the lined baking sheet. Squeeze a few drops of lemon juice onto each rissole before serving.

Beef Skewers – Madeira Style

Espetadas à Madeirense   ◡ Madeira

Espetadas are juicy cubes of beef seasoned with crushed garlic and bay leaves, and skewered on bay wood or metal skewers. In the past they were served only at pilgrimages, with bread and wine, which presented a rare opportunity for pilgrims to eat expensive beef. Today, restaurants in the archipelago, especially in the village of Estreito de Câmara de Lobos, have hooks for hanging the skewers at the tables; meat is ordered by weight and grilled on charcoal, then served with *Bolo do Caco* (page 32) and *Milho Frito* (pages 32 and 88).

Preparation time: 15 minutes
Cooking time: 25 minutes
Serves: 4

3 garlic cloves, peeled but left whole
6 bay leaves
800 g/1 lb 12 oz beef tenderloin, trimmed of sinew
100 g/3½ oz (1 stick) unsalted butter, melted
sea salt

To serve:
Fried Cornmeal (*Milho Frito*) (page 88)
Stone-baked Bread (*Bolo de Caco*) (page 32)

Prepare a barbecue or preheat the indoor grill (broiler).

Put the garlic and bay leaves into a mortar and, using a pestle, mash them to a paste.

Cut the beef into medium-sized cubes, season them with salt and rub them with the garlic and bay leaf paste. Thread the meat onto metal skewers.

As soon as the barbecue coals are glowing, put the skewers on the grill rack and grill for 10–15 minutes, brushing the meat with the melted butter and turning until cooked. Alternatvely, cook under the grill.

Serve with Fried Corn and Stone-baked Bread.

Pan-fried Steak with Cream Sauce

Bife à Marrare   ◡ Lisbon

This pan-seared steak with a rich cream sauce is also known as *Bife à Café* but was the precursor of all the various *Bife à Café* versions found on Lisbon menus these days (most restaurants have modified the original to include mustard and garlic). The original recipe was created at the end of the 18th century by António Marrare, an Italian entrepreneur with a restaurant empire in Lisbon who owned a café called Marrare das Sete Portas. This and other steak dishes were served to writers, poets, artists and bohemians.

Preparation time: 10 minutes
Cooking time: 15 minutes
Serves: 4
🥩 ☒

100 g/3½ oz (1 stick) unsalted butter
600 g/1 lb 5 oz rump (round) or sirloin (Porterhouse) steak, any excess fat removed and cut into 4 steaks about 200 g/7 oz each
120 ml/4 fl oz (½ cup) single (light) cream
sea salt and freshly ground black pepper

Put a wire rack over a large rimmed baking sheet or roasting pan. Heat a cast-iron or non-stick frying pan or skillet over a medium-high heat. Once hot, add half the butter and leave to melt. Season the steaks with salt, then put two steaks in the pan at a time and cook for 1½ minutes on each side. Transfer the steaks to the wire rack and leave to rest while you cook the remaining steaks.

Once the meat is resting, add the cream to the pan, season generously with pepper and cook over a medium heat for 1 minute. Add the steaks and all the juices that have dripped into the sheet or pan and cook for a further 2 minutes, or until the sauce has reduced. Serve immediately.

Portuguese Steak with an Egg on Horseback

••

Bife à Portuguesa
com Ovo a Cavalo 📷 p.249   ⛿ **Lisbon**

This and other recipes, like *Bife à Marrare* (page 247), are some of the most unmissable Portuguese beef steak dishes, created in Lisbon's cafés and *cervejarias* in the 18th and 19th centuries. 'A cavalo' means 'on horseback', an allusion to the appearance that the fried eggs placed on top are 'riding' the steak. It is usually served with fries and salad.

Preparation time: 15 minutes
Cooking time: 25 minutes
Serves: 4
🐟

600 g/1 lb 5 oz rump (round) steak, any excess fat
    removed and cut into 4 portions, 150 g/5 oz each
1 litre/34 fl oz (4¼ cups) sunflower oil, for deep-frying
700 g/1 lb 9 oz waxy potatoes, peeled and cut into
    thin fries
10 g/¼ oz (1⅔ teaspoons) fine table salt
85 g/3 oz (¾ stick) brown butter
2 bay leaves
3 garlic cloves, peeled and thinly sliced
10 g/¼ oz (2 teaspoons) Dijon mustard
180 ml/6 fl oz (¾ cup) white wine
4 eggs
1 butterhead lettuce, leaves separated
½ white onion, peeled and thinly sliced
50 ml/1⅔ fl oz (3½ tablespoons) extra virgin olive oil
10 ml/¼ fl oz (2 teaspoons) white wine vinegar
15 g/½ oz (2½ teaspoons) sea salt
freshly ground black pepper

Season the steaks with salt and pepper. Leave to marinate for 15 minutes.

Meanwhile, line a large baking sheet with paper towels. Heat the sunflower oil for deep-frying in a large, deep saucepan or fryer until it reaches 180°C/350°F on a thermometer. Working in batches, carefully lower the fries into the hot oil and deep-fry for 10 minutes, or until golden. Remove with a slotted spoon and leave to drain on the lined baking sheet. Season with the fine table salt and set aside.

Heat a large frying pan or skillet over a medium-high heat. Once hot, add 25 g/1 oz (2 tablespoons) of the butter and leave to melt. Add the steaks, one or two at a time, and sear for 2 minutes on both sides, or until golden brown all over. Transfer the steaks to a plate and leave to rest.

Add the bay leaves, garlic and mustard to the pan and cook, stirring, for 1 minute. Add a splash of the white wine and stir with a wooden spoon to release all the crispy bits from the bottom of the pan, then add the rest of the wine and cook over a medium heat for 2 minutes, or until reduced by half. Add the remaining 60 g/2¼ oz (½ stick) of the butter, then remove the pan from the heat and stir to emulsify the sauce. Return the steaks to the pan

and leave to rest for a few minutes before warming them again.

Meanwhile, break the eggs into a large, non-stick, dry frying pan or skillet and fry over a medium heat for 5 minutes. Bringing it slowly up to heat in this way cooks the eggs evenly without browning on the outside.

Put the lettuce leaves and white onion into a salad bowl and mix together. Dress with the olive oil and vinegar, then season with a pinch of salt.

Serve the steaks in the sauce with a fried egg on top of each steak and with the fries and green salad on the side.

Pan-fried Steak with an Egg on Horseback

••

Bife com Ovo a Cavalo   ⛿ **Lisbon**

This is a dish that every single Portuguese person living in the country has probably eaten at some point in their lives. It is a popular menu item in almost all *cervejarias*. (Yes, we serve meat in seafood restaurants).

Preparation time: 10 minutes, plus 15 minutes marinating
Cooking time: 25 minutes
Serves: 4
🐟 ⛿

600 g/1 lb 5 oz rump (round) steak or sirloin
    (Porterhouse) steak, any excess fat removed, and
    cut into 4 portions about 150 g/5 oz each
5 garlic cloves, peeled and thinly sliced
1 litre/34 fl oz (4¼ cups) sunflower oil, for deep-frying
700 g/1 lb 9 oz waxy potatoes, peeled and cut into
    thin fries
40 g/1½ oz lard (pork fat)
30 ml/1 fl oz (2 tablespoons) olive oil
4 eggs
sea salt and freshly ground black pepper

Season the steaks with salt and pepper and sprinkle over the garlic. Leave to marinate for 15 minutes.

Meanwhile, line a large baking sheet with paper towels. Heat the sunflower oil for deep-frying in a large, deep saucepan or fryer until it reaches 180°C/350°F on a thermometer. Working in batches, carefully lower the fries into the hot oil and deep-fry for 10 minutes, or until golden. Remove with a slotted spoon and leave to drain on the lined baking sheet.

Heat a large frying pan or skillet over a medium heat. Once hot, add the lard (pork fat) and leave to melt. Add the steaks, one or two at a time, and sear for 2 minutes on both sides, or until golden brown all over. Transfer the steaks to a plate and leave to rest.

Heat the olive oil in another large frying pan over a medium heat. Break the eggs into the pan and fry for 5 minutes, or until fried to your liking.

Serve the steaks with a fried egg on top of each steak and with the fries on the side.

Portuguese Steak with an Egg on Horseback

Mirandesa Steak

Posta à Mirandesa 🖾 p.251 ♡ Trás-os-Montes
e Alto Douro

Posta à Mirandesa is a large, juicy, thick tenderloin steak sprinkled with salt and brushed with an olive oil mixture, then grilled over a fire until seared on the outside and medium-rare on the inside. It is usually found in restaurants in northern Portugal, because this cut of meat comes from free-range *Mirandesa* calves, sourced directly from Trás-os-Montes, which is the only region where this breed is found. The steak is usually served with a side of roasted potatoes and sautéed turnip tops. Until the end of the 20th century, it would be grilled over hot charcoals at fairs, and placed on a large slice of rye bread so that the meat juices soaked into it.

Preparation time: 15 minutes
Cooking time: 40 minutes
Serves: 4
🖋 ▢

650 g/1 lb 7 oz new potatoes, unpeeled and left whole
120 ml/4 fl oz (½ cup) olive oil, plus extra for drizzling
30 ml/1 fl oz (2 tablespoons) white wine vinegar
2 garlic cloves, peeled and very finely chopped
1 teaspoon sweet paprika
720 g/1 lb 9 oz Mirandesa steak (sirloin) or any other
    good-quality sirloin steak
1 kg/2 lb 4 oz turnip tops, bottom stalk removed
sea salt

Prepare a barbecue or preheat the oven to 200°C/400°F/Gas Mark 6.
    Wrap the potatoes individually in foil and either roast them directly in the barbecue coals for 20 minutes, or until soft. Alternatively, bake them in the oven.
    Put the olive oil, vinegar, garlic, paprika and a little salt into a small bowl and stir with a fork. This is the sauce for the meat and potatoes.
    Season the meat with salt then put onto the barbecue grill and cook over the coals for 2 minutes on each side, or until golden brown and crispy all over.
    Meanwhile, bring a large saucepan of water to the boil. Add a pinch of salt and the turnip tops and cook for 1 minute, then drain and place on a tray or plate and drizzle with some of the olive oil.
    Arrange the steak in a serving dish with the baked potatoes and cooked turnip tops. Drizzle the sauce over both the steak and potatoes before serving.

Braised Steak and Onions

Bifes de Cebolada ♡ Lisbon

Preparation time: 20 minutes
Cooking time: 1 hour
Serves: 4
🖋

300 g/11 oz tomatoes
20 g/¾ oz lard (pork fat)
80 g/3 oz (¾ stick) butter
3 onions, peeled and thinly sliced
600 g/1 lb 5 oz rump (round) steak, any excess fat
    removed and cut into 4 portions, 150 g/5 oz each
3 garlic cloves, peeled and thinly sliced
¼ bunch flat-leaf parsley, finely chopped
1 bay leaf
100 ml/3½ fl oz (⅓ cup) white wine
600 g/1 lb 5 oz waxy potatoes, peeled but left whole
sea salt and freshly ground black pepper

Have a large bowl of iced water nearby. Bring a large saucepan of water to the boil. Using a sharp knife, score the top of the tomatoes with a small cross shape. Once the water is boiling, carefully add the tomatoes and blanch for 30 seconds, then transfer them with a slotted spoon to the iced water and leave to cool. Once cool enough to handle, peel off the skins, cut in half and de-seed.
    Add the lard (pork fat) and butter to a large saucepan, then arrange the onions in a single layer on the bottom of the pan. Add the meat in a layer over the onions, then add the garlic in another layer, then the tomatoes and finally, add the parsley. Season each layer with a pinch of salt and pepper. Add the bay leaf and white wine and cook over a medium heat for 30–35minutes. Reduce the heat to low, cover with a lid and cook for a further 25 minutes. Check during the cooking time to make sure it is not getting too dry.
    Meanwhile, put the potatoes into a large saucepan, cover with cold water, add a pinch of salt and cook over a medium heat for 15–20 minutes, or until soft. Drain and put into a serving dish.
    Serve the steak and onions with the boiled potatoes on the side.

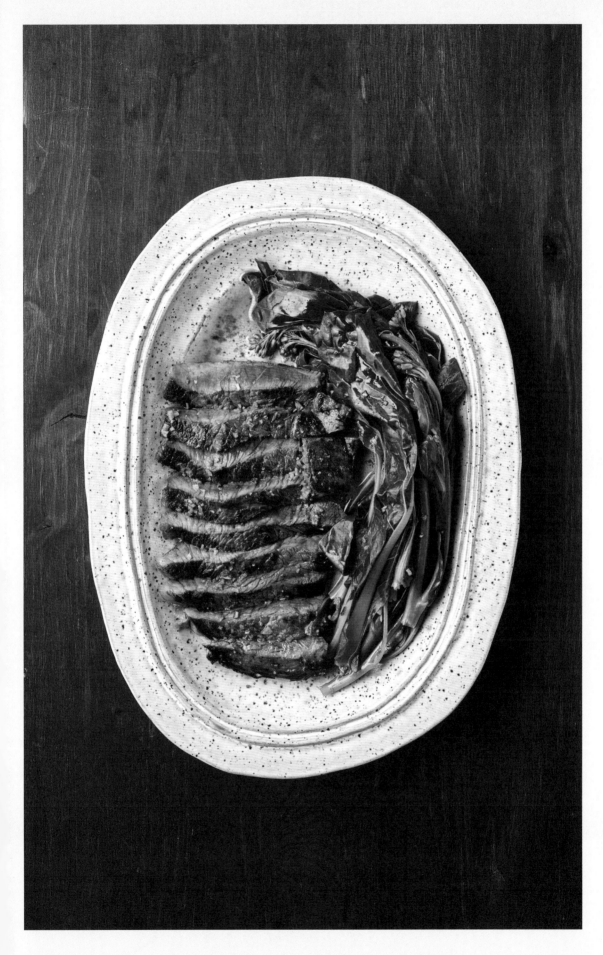

Mirandesa Steak

Beef Stew

••

Alcatra da Terceira   ⛶ Açores

One of the most well-known dishes in the Azores archipelago, the recipe for *alcatra* is different in every parish on Terceira, although without substantial modifications. Its origins link to the arrival of the first settlers on the island, in around 1450, particularly to those who came from the Trás-os-Montes region on the mainland, where there is a very similar dish called *chanfana* made with goat. Historically, however, there were two main recipes for this dish of beef cooked in a large clay pot: one that called for rump steak, considered the best cut of beef and therefore only served in manor houses; and another, with less known and inexpensive cuts of beef, found in farmers' houses at the time. It was the latter that became the main recipe today.

Preparation time: 30 minutes
Cooking time: 4 hours 30 minutes
Serves: 6
⛶

1.2 kg/2 lb 11 oz beef shin (shank), cut into large chunks
800 g/1 lb 12 oz topside beef (top round), cut into
     large chunks
10 black peppercorns, crushed
12 pink peppercorns, crushed
1 bay leaf, crushed
80 g/3 oz lard (pork fat)
140 g/5 oz (1¼ sticks) butter
4 onions, peeled and thinly sliced
4 garlic cloves, peeled and chopped
130 g/4½ oz smoked bacon, diced
1 cinnamon stick
2 cloves
2.2 litres/76 fl oz (9 cups) white wine
50 ml/1⅔ fl oz (3½ tablespoons) white wine vinegar
sea salt
Massa Sovada (page 352), to serve

Preheat the oven to 160°C/325°F/Gas Mark 3. Season the beef shin (shank) and topside beef (top round) with salt and rub it in. Set aside.

Put the black peppercorns, pink peppercorns and bay leaf into a mortar and, using a pestle, crush.

Using a bay leaf branch or a large metal skewer, make small holes all over the beef, then rub the spice mix into the holes.

Melt the lard (pork fat) and butter in a large clay pot or saucepan, then arrange the onions in a single layer on the bottom of the pan. Add the garlic, bacon and beef in more layers. Repeat these layers, finishing with a final layer of onions.

Add the cinnamon stick and cloves to the pot and pour in the white wine, vinegar and 250 ml/ 8 fl oz (1 cup) water. Place in the hot oven to braise, stirring occasionally, for 4 hours 30 minutes. Check during the cooking time to make sure it is not getting too dry – if so, add add a little more wine and water. Serve with *Massa Sovada*.

Pot-roast Beef

••

Carne Assada na Panela   📷 p.253   ⛶ Madeira

Preparation time: 20 minutes, plus 4 hours marinating and 10 minutes resting
Cooking time: 1 hour 10 minutes
Serves: 4
🔥 ⛶

4 black peppercorns
6 pink peppercorns
5 cloves
1 kg/2 lb 4 oz rump (round) steak
3 bay leaves, crushed
80 ml/2¾ fl oz (⅓ cup) Madeira wine
1 onion
1 large tomato
60 ml/2 fl oz (4 tablespoons) olive oil
30 g/1 oz lard (pork fat)
1 litre/34 fl oz (4¼ cups) meat stock
650 g/1 lb 7 oz new potatoes, peeled or scrubbed
80 g/3 oz (⅔ cup) black olives
sea salt and freshly ground black pepper

Season the steak with salt and pepper and rub it in. Set aside.

Put the black peppercorns, pink peppercorns and cloves into a mortar and, using a pestle, crush.

Using a bay leaf branch or a large metal skewer, make small holes all over the meat, then rub the spice mix into the holes. Put the meat into a large dish, scatter over the crushed bay leaves and pour over half the Madeira wine. Cover with food wrap and leave to marinate in the fridge for 4 hours.

Using a sharp knife, score the onion on the opposite side to the root, then make a small cross shape in the top of the tomato.

When ready to cook, heat the olive oil and lard (pork fat) in a large saucepan over a medium heat. Add the meat and sear for 5 minutes, or until it is coloured all over. Reduce the heat to low then, while stirring, add small amounts of meat stock to scraping up any crispy bits from the bottom of the pan. Repeat.

Add the onion and tomato to the pan and cook for 40 minutes, or until the the meat is cooked. Remove the onion and tomato, add the potatoes and a little more of the meat stock, if needed. Increase the heat to medium and cook for a further 20 minutes, or until the potatoes are soft. Reduce the heat to low, add the remaining Madeira wine and the olives and cook for a further 5 minutes. Remove from the heat, cover the pan with a lid and leave the meat to rest for 10 minutes.

Pot-roast Beef

'Furnace' Stew

••

Cozido da Lagoa das Furnas   ▽ Açores

In the Furnas Valley, on the island of São Miguel, this *cozido* (stew; page 429) is cooked with the help of volcanic steam. All the ingredients are layered inside a pot, with no liquid added; the pot is covered with a lid tied on to leave a long length of rope for lifting it out later, and buried in the ground. The *cozido* is cooked very slowly, for about six hours, in the steamy heat of the hot springs, with juices slowly released into the pot by the ingredients. You can adapt this at home by using a regular lidded pot with a cup of water added, and cooking it on the stove.

Preparation time: 40 minutes
Cooking time: 4–5 hours
Serves 8
◻ ◻

1.7 kg/3 lb 12 oz beef shin (shank), chopped into
    medium-sized pieces
1.2 kg/2 lb 11 oz pork leg meat, cut into medium-
    sized pieces
1 whole chicken, cut into medium-sized pieces
2 big *chouriços* or meaty chorizo would also work
    with less fat, cut into medium-sized pieces
350 g/12 oz smoked pork belly, cut into medium-
    sized pieces
1 kg/2 lb 4 oz potatoes, peeled and any large
    ones cut into quarters
800 g/1 lb 12 oz carrots, cut into long sticks
5 turnips, peeled and cut into chunks
2 Savoy cabbages, cut into chunks
1 Portuguese cabbage (*tronchuda*) or January king
    cabbage, cut into chunks
3 g/⅛ oz pink peppercorns
salt

To serve:
mint leaves
bread

Layer all the ingredients into a large saucepan, finishing with a final layer of cabbage leaves. If you don't have any natural volcanic cooking holes on the ground nearby, then either cook in an open fire as mentioned above or cook on the stove over a very low heat for 4–5 hours until the meat is tender. Keep checking the pan every hour as the temperature can be variable, depending on your cooking method.

    Once all the ingredients are cooked through, remove the top cabbage leaves and serve the vegetables on a plate with the meat on another. The juices released from the cooking are used to make a '*cozido* soup' which is topped up with mint leaves to infuse the stock and served with bread.

Beef Stew from Pico

••

Caçoila do Pico   ▽ Açores

Preparation time: 10 minutes
Cooking time: 2 hours 30 minutes
Serves: 4
🍷 ◻ ✕

600 g/1 lb 5 oz beef rump (rump roast)
60 g/2¼ oz lard (pork fat)
60 g/2¼ oz (½ stick) unsalted butter
1 onion, peeled and sliced into rings
3 garlic cloves, peeled and chopped
⅓ bunch flat-leaf parsley, roughly chopped
40 g/1½ oz (¼ cup) tomato purée (paste)
220 ml/7½ fl oz (1 cup) *vinho de cheiro*
10 white peppercorns
500 g/1 lb 2 oz small round potatoes
sea salt

Season the beef with salt and set aside.

    Melt the lard (pork fat) and butter in a saucepan over a low heat. Add the onion, garlic, parsley and tomato purée (paste), then add the meat, pour in the wine and add the peppercorns. Cover with a lid and gently cook for 2 hours 30 minutes, or until the meat is very soft and tender.

    Twenty minutes before the stew has finished cooking, put the potatoes into another saucepan, cover with cold water and season with a pinch of salt. Cook over a medium heat for 15–20 minutes, or until soft. Drain and serve the boiled potatoes with the meat stew.

Mixed Meats Stew

••

Rancho à Moda de Viseu   ⛎ Beira Litoral

Preparation time: 20 minutes, plus 12 hours soaking and
30 minutes resting
Cooking time: 1 hour 25 minutes
Serves: 6
◻ ◻

180 g/6 oz (1 cup) dried chickpeas (garbanzos)
200 g/7 oz beef flank
300 g/11 oz trimmed pork ribs
150 g/5 oz lardo
½ chorizo
450 g/1 lb whole chicken or half chicken
3 carrots, peeled and thinly sliced
600 g/1 lb 5 oz potatoes, peeled and cubed
1 Savoy cabbage or Portuguese cabbage (tronchudo),
    shredded
200 g/7 oz macaroni
60 ml/2 fl oz (4 tablespoons) olive oil
½ teaspoon ground cumin
sea salt

Put the dried chickpeas (garbanzos) into a large
bowl, pour enough cold water over to cover and
leave to soak for 12 hours.

The next day, drain the chickpeas and put them
into a large saucepan. Pour over enough water to
cover and add the beef flank and pork ribs. Add
some salt and cook over a medium heat for 20
minutes. Add the lardo, chorizo and chicken, then
reduce the heat to low and cook for 40 minutes,
or until the meat is cooked.

Remove the meat from the pan and set aside,
then add the carrots, potatoes and cabbage to the
pan and cook over a medium heat for 15 minutes,
or until al dente. You may need to add some more
water to the pan during cooking. Add the macaroni
and a pinch of salt and cook for a further 10
minutes, or until the pasta is cooked.

Meanwhile, cut the meat into small pieces,
then put them back into the pan and stir. Taste
and adjust the seasoning, if necessary. Drizzle
the olive oil over the top and add the cumin.
Stir, remove from the heat and leave to rest for
30 minutes before serving. You can cook this
the day before you want to eat it and leave it in
the fridge overnight, then just reheat it.

Cow's Bladder, Tripe and Beans

••

Dobrada com Feijão   ⛎ Açores

Preparation time: 45 minutes, plus 12 hours soaking
Cooking time: 1 hour 30 minutes
Serves: 4
🐖 ◻

450 g/1 lb (2½ cups) dried red beans
1 cow's bladder
2 lemons, halved
800 g/1 lb 12 oz beef tripe (stomach lining)
2 onions, peeled and finely chopped
2 garlic cloves, peeled and finely chopped
1 bay leaf
3 tomatoes, chopped
60 ml/2 fl oz (4 tablespoons) olive oil
½ pimenta da terra or long red pepper or
    1 bird's eye chilli, chopped
½ Savoy cabbage, cut into chunks
½ linguiça, sliced into 1-cm/½-inch chunks
½ morcela, sliced into 1-cm/½-inch chunks
2 large sprigs flat-leaf parsley, chopped
sea salt

Put the dried red beans into a large bowl of cold
water and leave to soak for 12 hours.

The next day, wash the cow's bladder under
cold running water a few times. Set aside. Rub one
of the lemons all over the tripe (stomach lining),
then rinse a few times in cold water. Set aside.

Drain the beans and put them into a large
saucepan. Pour in enough cold water to cover,
add a pinch of salt and cook over a medium heat
for 30 minutes, or until soft. Drain and set aside,
reserving the cooking water.

Meanwhile, fill a large saucepan with water, add
a pinch of salt, and bring to the boil. Once the water
is boiling, add the tripe and cook over a medium
heat for 30 minutes, or until soft, skimming the
surface with a ladle to remove the foam on the top.
Using a slotted spoon, remove the stomach from
the pan and cut it into small pieces, about 4 cm/1½
inches, and set aside. Set the cooking liquid aside.

Put the onions, garlic, bay leaf and tomatoes
into a medium saucepan, drizzle with the olive oil
and cook over a medium heat for 15 minutes until
all the ingredients are softened. Add the pimenta
da terra or red pepper and cabbage and cook for
10 minutes over a medium heat, adding 200 ml/
7 fl oz (¾ cup plus 1 tablespoon) of the reserved
cooking water and bringing it to the boil.

Add the beans to the pan with the linguiça
and morcela, then cover with more of the reserved
cooking liquid and bring to the boil. Cook for
10 minutes to gain some texture. Add the bladder,
reduce the heat to low and cook for a further
20 minutes, or until the liquid has reduced.

Taste and adjust the seasoning, if necesary,
then scatter over the parsley. Rest the stew for
10 minutes before serving.

Cow's Hoof with Chickpeas

Mão de Vaca com   ☐ **Lisbon**
Grão de Malveira

This is a very old dish that has its origins in the area of Mafra in central Portugal. It is unique as it uses a cow's hoof (foot), chilli sauce and chickpeas (garbanzos), and is very popular in the north and south of the country.

Preparation time: 30 minutes, plus 12 hours soaking
Cooking time: 1 hour 30 minutes
Serves: 6

450 g/1 lb (2½ cups) dried chickpeas (garbanzos)
1 cow's hoof (foot)
2 lemons, halved
4 tomatoes
olive oil, for drizzling
100 g/3½ oz (1 stick) unsalted butter
2 onions, peeled and finely chopped
4 garlic cloves, peeled and finely chopped
150 g/5 oz lardo, cut into thin strips
150 g/5 oz chorizo, thinly sliced
2 carrots, peeled and finely chopped
2 bay leaves
¼ bunch flat-leaf parsley, roughly chopped
200 ml/7 fl oz (¾ cup plus 1 tablespoon) white wine
450 g/1 lb (2¼ cups) white rice
sea salt and freshly ground black pepper
chilli sauce or 1 fresh red chilli, chopped, to garnish

Put the chickpeas (garbanzos) into a large bowl of cold water and leave to soak for 12 hours. The next day, drain the chickpeas and set aside.

Clean the cow's hoof (foot) under cold running water to remove any dirt. Rub them all over with the lemons and then in salt. Put the hoof into a tall saucepan or a pressure cooker, cover with water and cook over a medium heat for 30 minutes, or until soft. Cut the meat into chunks.

Meanwhile, put the chickpeas into a large saucepan, pour in enough cold water to cover, add a pinch of salt and a drizzle of olive oil and cook over a low heat for 30 minutes, or until soft. Remove from the heat and leave to cool in the cooking water.

Have a large bowl of iced water nearby. Bring a large saucepan of water to the boil. Using a sharp knife, score the top of the tomatoes with a small cross shape. Once the water is boiling, add the tomatoes carefully and blanch for 30 seconds, then transfer them with a slotted spoon to the iced water and leave to cool. Once cool enough to handle, peel off the skins, cut in half and de-seed, then cut the flesh into small cubes.

Put the olive oil and butter into another large saucepan over a medium heat. Add the onion, garlic and tomatoes and cook for 20 minutes, or until the mixture looks like a paste. Add the hoof meat, lardo, chorizo, carrots, bay leaves and parsley and mix to combine, then add the white wine and chickpeas. Bring to the boil over a high heat, then reduce the heat to medium and cook for 5 minutes, or until the liquid has reduced.

Put the rice into another large saucepan, cover with water, add a pinch of salt and bring to the boil. Cook the rice for 10–12 minutes, or until soft. Drain and serve with the meat, garnished with a bit of chilli sauce or fresh chilli sprinkled over the top.

Meat and Bread Sausage

Alheiras de Açoreira   ☐ **Trás-os-Montes
e Alto Douro**

This is a classic meat product from Portugal. The local people in the northern villages get together to make *alheiras* (page 429) using traditional methods, which then last for a couple of months.

Preparation time: 45 minutes, plus 24 hours standing
Cooking time: 3 hours 50 minutes
Makes: 16

1.2 kg/2 lb 11 oz pork belly, cut into 3 pieces
500 g/1 lb 2 oz pork bones
500 g/1 lb 2 oz beef, such as shin or shoulder
1 chicken
2 cloves
3 large onions, 1 halved
5 garlic cloves, 3 unpeeled and left whole, 2 peeled and finely chopped
80 g/3 oz sweet paprika
3 bay leaves
750 g/1 lb 10 oz stale crusty bread (not white bread), thinly sliced
400 g/14 oz (2¼ cups) lard (pork fat) or 700 g/1 lb 9 oz fat from cooking the pork, for melting
40 g/1½ oz hot paprika
¼ bunch flat-leaf parsley, finely chopped
300 g/11 oz fine pork tripe (stomach lining), cleaned
sea salt

Put the pork belly pieces and pork bones into a large container and season them with salt. Cover with a lid and put into the fridge overnight.

The next day, put the pork belly, bones, beef and chicken into a large saucepan. Stick a clove in each half of the halved onion, add it to the pan with the 3 whole garlic cloves, half of the sweet paprika and all the bay leaves. Pour in enough water to cover the meat, plus a little more, then cook over a low heat for 3 hours 30 minutes, or until all the meat is tender and cooked through, topping up the water, if necessary. The chicken will cook first, so remove it when cooked and place on a plate. When all the meat is cooked, remove with a slotted spoon or fish slice (spatula) and place on a large plate or tray and leave to cool slightly. Strain the cooking liquid into a separate clean saucepan and set aside. Shred the meat into a large bowl, scraping the pork bones of any meat it might have. Set aside.

Arrange the bread in a large dish. Bring the meat cooking liquid in the pan to the boil, then pour over enough of this stock to soak the bread. It needs to be well soaked. Cover the bread with a clean tea (dish) towel and leave to stand for 10 minutes.

Put the lard (pork fat) into a saucepan and heat over a low heat until melted. It needs to be very hot.

Add the finely chopped garlic to the bread together with the hot paprika, remaining sweet paprika and the parsley, then add to the meat and stir with a wooden spoon in the same direction to combine. Add the melted pork fat and keep stirring until the mixture is smooth. Adjust the seasoning with salt, if necessary, then leave to cool slightly.

Prepare the fine pork tripe (stomach lining). Cut the tripe into 20-cm/8-inch pieces. The pieces can be smaller, but not too small otherwise it becomes difficult to tie them. Tie one end of the tripe and, using a funnel, fill the tripe pieces with the meat mixture, then tie the other end to secure. Repeat with the remaining tripe and filling. The *alheiras* can be dried and smoked for a couple of days and kept in a dry environment. Some people like to keep them in olive oil for a few months.

To eat the *alheiras*, prick holes all over them to prevent them bursting during cooking, then either grill or pan-fry them whole in olive oil.

Meat and Bread Sausage with Turnip Tops and a Fried Egg

Alheiras com Grelos e Ovo Estrelado   ⛶ Trás-os-Montes e Alto Douro

This is a classic way of serving *alheira* (page 429). The crispy skin and smooth filling of the sausage combined with the bitterness from the turnip tops makes it a unique dish. Some people like to eat this with plain boiled rice or a crisp green salad on the side.

Preparation time: 10 minutes
Cooking time: 25 minutes
Serves: 4
🖉 ⛶

1.2 kg/2 lb 11 oz turnip tops, bottom stalk removed
130 ml/4½ fl oz (½ cup) olive oil
4 *Alheiras de Açoreira* (see left)
4 eggs
sea salt

Fill a medium saucepan with water, add a pinch of salt and bring to the boil over a medium heat. Once boiling, add the turnip tops and cook for 3 minutes, or until tender. Drain and set aside.

Heat a medium frying pan or skillet over a medium heat. Once hot, drizzle in some of the olive oil, then two at a time, add the *alheiras* and pan-fry for 10 minutes, or until golden and crispy. Remove from the pan and keep warm, then repeat with the remaining *alheiras*.

Meanwhile, heat enough oil to fry the eggs in another frying pan or skillet over a medium heat. Crack the eggs into the pan and fry for 5 minutes, or to your liking.

Serve the *alheiras* each with a fried egg on top and the turnip tops on the side.

Veal Steak with Wild Gorse

Nacos de Vitela com Carqueja   ⛶ Ribatejo

Preparation time: 25 minutes, plus 12 hours marinating and 10 minutes resting
Cooking time: 35 minutes
Serves: 4
🖉 ⛶

700 g/1 lb 9 oz veal rump (top round), cut into chunks
1 teaspoon paprika
200 ml/7 fl oz (¾ cup) olive oil
6 garlic cloves, peeled and finely chopped
3 bay leaves, crushed
120 g/4 oz lard (pork fat)
3 onions, peeled and finely chopped
17.5 ml/½ fl oz (3½ tablespoons) white wine
17.5 ml/½ fl oz (3½ tablespoons) red wine
1 bunch *carqueja*
500 g/1 lb 2 oz new potatoes, peeled but left whole
sea salt and freshly ground black pepper

Put the veal into a large bowl. Season with salt, pepper and the paprika, then add the garlic, bay leaves and the olive oil and toss until the meat is well coated in the marinade. Cover with food wrap and leave to marinate in the fridge for 12 hours, tossing the meat twice.

The next day, heat the lard (pork fat) in a large saucepan over a medium heat, add the veal and cook for 5 minutes, or until it is browned all over. Add the onions and cook for 15 minutes, or until golden brown. Add the wines and *carqueja*, then cover with a lid, reduce the heat to low and cook for 15 minutes, or until the meat is soft. Taste and adjust the seasoning, then remove from the heat and leave to rest for 10 minutes.

Meanwhile, put the potatoes into a saucepan, cover with cold water, add a pinch of salt and cook over a medium heat for 15–20 minutes, or until soft. Drain and serve with the meat.

Roasted Veal – Lafões Style

Vitela Assada à Moda de Lafões   Ⓤ Beira Alta

Preparation time: 40 minutes, plus 12 hours marinating
Cooking time: 3 hours 30 minutes
Serves: 6
🍖 ▢

3 onions, peeled and thinly sliced
6 garlic cloves, peeled and thinly sliced
2 bay leaf
2 red chillies, finely chopped
1.2 kg/2 lb 11 oz flank steak with any fat left on, cut into
    large chunks
90 g/3¼ oz *Massa de Pimentão*
80 g/3 oz (½ cup) tomato purée (paste)
90 g/3¼ oz (½ cup) lard (pork fat)
90 ml/3 fl oz (6 tablespoons) olive oil
500 ml/17 fl oz (2 cups) white wine
700 g/1 lb 9 oz waxy potatoes, peeled and cut into
    medium-sized cubes
2 large bunches turnip tops, bottom stalk removed
sea salt

Spread the onions, garlic, bay leaf and chillies over a large rimmed baking sheet.

Put the meat into a large bowl and season with salt, then add the *Massa de Pimentão*, 30 g/1 oz (¼ cup) of the tomato purée (paste), the lard (pork fat), half the olive oil and wine. Toss the meat until it is well coated in the marinade. Arrange the meat in a layer on top of the onions and leave in the fridge for 12 hours.

The next day, spread the cubed potatoes out on another large baking sheet, add the onions and garlic from the marinatig ingredients, the remaining tomato purée and drizzle with the rest of the olive oil. Season with salt and toss until well coated.

Preheat the oven to 190°C/375°F/Gas Mark 5. Once hot, reduce the oven temperature to 150°C/300°F/Gas Mark 2.

Pour 140 ml/4¾ fl oz (½ cup) water over the meat and toss, then cook slowly in the low oven for 3 hours 30 minutes, turning it every hour, until the meat is soft, lightly caramelised and there is a sauce of the meat juices.

One hour before the meat is ready, add the potatoes to the oven and cook until golden, stirring the tray two or three times during cooking.

Meanwhile, bring a large saucepan of salted water to the boil. Add the turnip tops and cook for 3 minutes. Drain, put into a serving bowl and drizzle with olive oil.

Serve the meat on a tray with the potatoes on the side and the turnip tops.

Veal Liver with Soft-boiled Potatoes

Iscas com Elas   📷 p.259   Ⓤ Lisbon

Often seen as a traditional Lisbon *petisco*, this dish was very popular at the beginning of the 20th century. Thin slices of calf's liver are marinated for 24 hours in a vinegar-based sauce, then fried in lard. *Iscas* would once have been permanently on offer at tascas and tabernas, usually served with a plate of boiled potatoes, known as '*elas*' (meaning 'them'), or alternatively eaten between two slices of bread.

Preparation time: 20 minutes, plus 24 hours marinating
Cooking time: 25 minutes
Serves: 4
🍖 ▢

500 g/1 lb 2 oz veal or beef liver, sliced into thin steaks
150 ml/5 fl oz (⅔ cup) white wine
30 ml/1 fl oz (2 tablespoons) white wine vinegar
4 garlic cloves, peeled and thinly sliced
2 bay leaves, crushed
600 g/1 lb 5 oz waxy potatoes, peeled
60 g/2¼ oz lard (pork fat)
¼ bunch flat-leaf parsley, finely chopped
sea salt and freshly ground black pepper

Put the liver into a large bowl, add the white wine, vinegar, garlic and bay leaves. Toss the liver until it is well coated in the marinade and leave to marinate in the fridge for 24 hours.

When you are ready to cook, put the potatoes into a large saucepan, cover with cold water, add a pinch of salt and cook over a medium heat for 15–20 minutes, or until soft. Drain and keep warm.

Meanwhile, remove the liver steaks from the marinade, reserving the marinade. Heat a large frying pan or skillet over a medium heat. Add the lard (pork fat), then add the liver in batches and fry for 5 minutes, or until coloured on both sides. Don't cook the liver for too long otherwise it will become dry and tough. Remove to a plate and continue frying the rest.

Remove all the liver from the pan, keep the frying liquid and add the marinade, then cook over a medium heat for 10 minutes, or until it the liquid has reduced a little and is starting to thicken. Remove the pan from the heat and add the liver. Mix well without breaking up the meat, then serve with the potatoes, sprinkled with chopped parsley.

Veal Liver with Soft-boiled Potatoes

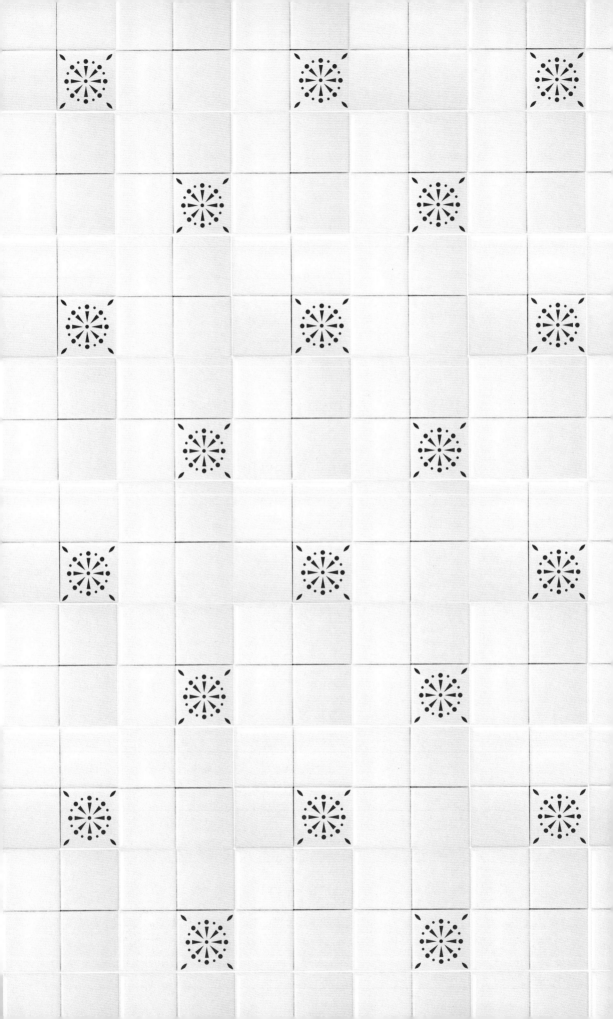

MUTTON, LAMB AND GOAT

Oven-roasted Mutton Leg

Perna de Carneiro   ⍟ Trás-os-Montes
Assado à Transmontana   e Alto Douro

Preparation time: 20 minutes, plus 2 hours marinating
Cooking time: about 2 hours
Serves: 8

1 mutton leg, trimmed of any excess fat
100 g/3½ oz (1 stick) butter
100 g/3½ oz (½ cup) lard (pork fat)
700 ml/23½ fl oz (2¾ cups) white wine
2 onions, peeled and thinly sliced
350 ml/12 fl oz (1½ cups) meat stock
3 eggs
160 g/5¾ oz (3¼ cups) breadcrumbs
sea salt

Rub the mutton leg with salt and then place it in a large roasting pan. Melt half of the butter in a small saucepan over a low heat. Coat the leg in the lard (pork fat) and melted butter. Pour over the wine, then add the onions and leave to marinate in the fridge for 2 hours before roasting.

Preheat the oven to 180°C/350°F/Gas Mark 4, or if you have a wood-fired oven heat it until hot.

Pour the stock over the mutton leg and then roast it in the hot oven for 1 hour 30 minutes for medium-rare meat, or until golden brown all over. You can check the doneness of the meat by inserting a probe thermometer into the middle of the leg. If its internal temperature is between 55–60°C/131–140°F it is ready. During roasting, brush the leg with the remaining butter and baste it with all the meat juices in the pan. Once cooked, remove the leg from the oven.

Increase the oven temperature to 200°C/400°F/Gas Mark 6.

Put the eggs into a bowl and whisk with a fork. Brush the mutton leg with the beaten egg and then sprinkle the breadcrumbs all over. Return the leg to the oven for a further 30 minutes, or until the breadcrumbs are golden brown. Remove from the oven and leave to rest before serving.

Mutton Stewed in Red Wine

Chanfana de Borrego   ⍟ Beira Litoral
(Lampatana)

This recipe is traditionally cooked in a black clay pot in a wood-fired oven or over an open fire. There are a few different stories related to the creation of this recipe, but one was that this was created in a convent during the French invasion. During their occupancy they contaminated the water, so the locals' only option for cooking the meat was in wine, hence the generous use of red wine in this recipe.

Preparation time: 45 minutes, plus 12 hours marinating
Cooking time: 2 hours 30 minutes
Serves: 8

3.3 kg/7 lb 4 oz mutton with bones, cut into small pieces
120 g/4 oz lardo, cut into thin strips
1½ onions, peeled and finely chopped
3 garlic cloves, peeled and crushed
1 red chilli, finely sliced
2 bay leaves, crushed
2 bunches flat-leaf parsley, roughly chopped
3 litres/102 fl oz (12¾ cups) red wine
800 g/1 lb 12 oz waxy potatoes, unpeeled
3 bunches turnip tops, bottom stalk removed
olive oil, for drizzling
sea salt

Put the mutton pieces into a large bowl, add the lardo, onions, garlic, chilli, bay leaves and parsley and season with salt. Mix everything together, then put into a large black clay pot or casserole dish (Dutch oven), cover with a lid and leave to marinate in the fridge for 12 hours.

The next day, preheat a wood-fired oven. Pour the wine over the meat, cover the pan with a lid and cook in the hot oven for 2 hours 30 minutes.

Meanwhile, put the potatoes into another large saucepan, cover with cold water, add a pinch of salt and cook over a medium heat for 15–20 minutes, or until soft. Drain, put them into a serving dish and set aside.

When the meat is nearly cooked, bring a large saucepan of water to the boil, add a pinch of salt, then add the turnip tops and cook for 3 minutes, or until tender. Drain, put them into a serving dish and drizzle with the olive oil. Set aside.

For the last 10 minutes of the cooking time for the mutton, remove the lid so that the meat can crisp up a little.

Serve the mutton stew with the boiled potatoes and turnip tops on the side.

Mutton Stew with Boiled Potatoes

Carneiro Guisado   ⍟ Ribatejo
à Moda de Alpiarça

This recipe was something that used to be offered to guests on the morning of a wedding before the ceremony. However, over the years it became less popular, although recently it has had something of a resurgence and people are now starting to make it again. I remember going to weddings with my family where this was one of the dishes served.

Preparation time: 25 minutes
Cooking time: 3 hours 30 minutes
Serves: 8

350 g/12 oz lard (pork fat)

3 onions, peeled and finely chopped

5 garlic cloves, peeled and finely chopped

¼ bunch flat-leaf parsley, finely chopped

3 kg/6 lb 10 oz mutton with bones, cut into medium-sized pieces

1 teaspoon ground pepper

1 teaspoon paprika

100 ml/3½ fl oz (⅓ cup) white wine

700 g/1 lb 9 oz new potatoes, peeled and quartered

sea salt

Melt the lard (pork fat) in a large saucepan over a low heat. Add the onions, garlic and parsley to the pan and cook for 10 minutes, or until the onions are translucent.

Season the mutton pieces with salt, then add to the pan with the pepper and paprika, then cook for 10 minutes. Pour in enough wine to cover the meat. Cover the pan with a lid and gently simmer for 3 hours, or until the meat is soft. Check the meat regularly during cooking and top up with a little water, if necessary, to prevent it drying out. Don't stir the meat when adding more wine.

Meanwhile, put the potatoes into another large saucepan, cover with cold water, add a pinch of salt and cook over a medium heat for 15–20 minutes, or until soft. Drain, put them into a serving dish.

Serve the mutton stew with the boiled potatoes on the side.

Lamb Stew

Ensopado de Borrego   ☐ Alentejo

Preparation time: 30 minutes

Cooking time: 2 hours

Serves: 6

☐ ☐

800 g/1 lb 12 oz lamb breast (belly), cut into small pieces

500 g/1 lb 2 oz lamb leg, cut into small pieces

400 g/14 oz lamb ribs, cut into individual ribs

250 ml/8 fl oz (1 cup) olive oil

2 garlic cloves, peeled and finely chopped

3 bay leaves

½ bunch mint, leaves picked

6 thick slices crusty bread, preferably sourdough

sea salt

Put all the meat into a stock pot or large saucepan, season with salt and pour in enough water to cover. Cook over a medium heat for 10 minutes. Once the water is boiling, add the olive oil, garlic and bay leaves and cook for 1 hour 30 minutes, or until the meat is tender, skimming off the foam that rises to the top with a slotted spoon.

Arrange the bread on a serving platter. Place the meat on top and pour over some of the lamb cooking liquid. Leave to rest for 2 minutes. Scatter over the mint leaves before serving with the bread.

Lamb Stewed in Red Wine – Coimbra Style

Chanfana de Borrego à Moda de Coimbra   ☐ Beira Litoral

A black clay pot will always give a better end result to this stew, but if you don't have one then use an ordinary saucepan. The cooked dish can be left for three or four weeks in the fridge as the layer of fat on the top of the stew helps to preserve it.

Preparation time: 30 minutes

Cooking time: 4 hours

Serves: 6

🐷 ☐

30 g/1 oz lard (pork fat)

2.5 kg/5½ lb lamb meat, bone-in, such as rack, leg, shoulder, cut into small pieces

2 bay leaves, crushed

8 cloves

3 garlic cloves, peeled and crushed

45 ml/1½ fl oz (3 tablespoons) olive oil

2 onions, peeled and quartered

2 litres/68 fl oz (8½ cups) red wine

800 g/1 lb 12 oz waxy potatoes, unpeeled

sea salt and freshly ground black pepper

Preheat the oven to 190°C/375°F/Gas Mark 5.

Melt the lard (pork fat) in a large saucepan over a low heat.

Put the lamb pieces into a large bowl and season with salt and pepper. Add the bay leaves, cloves, olive oil and the melted lard, then mix well.

Transfer the meat to a large clay pot or casserole dish (Dutch oven), add the onions and pour in enough wine to cover the meat. Cover the pan with a lid and gently simmer for 4 hours, or until the meat is soft. Check the meat regularly during cooking and top up with a little more wine, if necessary, to prevent it drying out. Don't stir the meat when adding more wine.

Meanwhile, put the potatoes into another large saucepan, cover with cold water, add a pinch of salt and cook over a medium heat for 15–20 minutes, or until soft. Drain, put them into a serving dish and set aside.

For the last 10 minutes of the cooking time for the lamb, remove the lid so that the meat can crisp up a little.

Serve the lamb stew with the boiled potatoes on the side.

Lamb Offal Stew Cooked with Blood

●●●

Sarapatel   ⏍ **Beira Baixa**

Preparation time: 20 minutes
Cooking time: 55 minutes
Serves: 6
⏍

offal (variety meats) from 1 lamb, including liver, heart
    and lungs
fresh lamb's blood mixed with a little white wine vinegar
    (optional)
200 g/7 oz lard (pork fat)
1 large onion, peeled and very finely chopped
3 garlic cloves, peeled and very finely chopped
2 bay leaves
½ tablespoon sweet paprika
2 tablespoons ground cumin
3 cloves
350 g/12 oz stale bread, thinly sliced
½ bunch flat-leaf parsley, roughly chopped
sea salt and freshly ground black pepper

Clean the offal (variety meats), then cut them into
small pieces. If you can get fresh lamb's blood,
bring a medium saucepan of water to the boil,
add a pinch of salt, then add the blood and cook
for 30 minutes.

Put the lard (pork fat) into a large saucepan,
add the onion, garlic, bay leaves and a pinch of salt
and cook over a low heat for 5 minutes, or until the
onion is lightly coloured.

Add the offal to the pan and cook for 10 minutes.
Add the paprika, cumin, cloves and 2.2 litres/
75 fl oz (8¾ cups) water. Once all the offal is
cooked, shred the blood into the pan and cook
for a further 10 minutes, or until the blood has
dissolved into the stew. Taste and adjust the
seasoning, if necessary, with salt and pepper.

Arrange the bread in a large serving dish and
pour the offal stew over the top. Scatter over the
parsley before serving.

Stuffed Sheep's Stomach Sausages

●●●

Maranhos   ⏍ **Beira Baixa**

Maranho is a fresh sausage made using sheep or
goat stomach (also known as *bandouga*), which
is stuffed with sheep or goat meat, rice and mint.
It is still hand sewn with a needle and thread before
the filling is added, and always uses natural rather
than synthetic casings. Its C-shaped curve and
minty, muttony or goaty flavour mark it out from
any other traditional Portuguese sausage. Its origins
are linked to Sertã, a village very close to Portugal's
geographical centre, where sheep and goat existed
in abundance, and by necessity every part of the
animal would be used. Today, *Maranho* is a delicacy
served in restaurants throughout the region.

Preparation time: 45 minutes, plus 2 hours resting
Cooking time: 2 hours
Serves: 5
🌿⏍

1 sheep's stomach
1 lemon, halved
1 garlic clove, peeled but left whole
160 g/5¾ oz ham with fat cap, very finely chopped
100 g/3½ oz chorizo, very finely chopped
60 g/2¼ oz streaky (lean) bacon, very finely chopped
800 g/1 lb 12 oz lean mutton, very finely chopped
1 mint sprig, very finely chopped
1 flat-leaf parsley sprig, very finely chopped
350 g/12 oz (1¾ cups) white rice
220 ml/7½ fl oz (1 cup) white wine
olive oil, for drizzling
450 g/1 lb turnip tops, bottom stalks removed
sea salt and freshly ground black pepper

Rinse the sheep's stomach several times under cold
running water until it is clean. Have a large bowl
of cold water nearby. Bring a large saucepan of
water to the boil, dip the stomach into the boiling
water for 20 seconds, then put it into the bowl of
cold water. Using a sharp knife, scrape the inside,
then repeat the boiling, cooling and scraping three
times until the stomach is completely clean. Rub
the lemon all over the stomach.

Cut the stomach open to form a large sheet,
then cut it into 5 pieces to form the sausage
casings. Fold each piece in half and stitch along
one long side with a trussing needle and medium-
thick butcher's string or kitchen twine. Set aside.

Put the garlic into a mortar with some salt and,
using a pestle, mash to form a paste.

Put the ham, chorizo, bacon, lean mutton, mint
and parsley into a large bowl and mix together.
Add the garlic paste, rice and wine, then drizzle
with some olive and stir well to combine. Cover
with a clean tea (dish) towel or food wrap and leave
in a cool place for 2 hours.

Fill the sausage casings with the rice and meat
mixture. The rice will expand during cooking so do

not overfill them but leave a gap. Seal the sausage casings by stitching them closed.

When ready to cook, bring a large saucepan of water to the boil with a pinch of salt. Carefully lower the sausages into the boiling water, then reduce the heat to medium, cover the pan with a lid and cook for 1 hour 30 minutes. Halfway through the cooking time, prick the sausages with a fork to prevent them bursting. Once cooked, remove the sausages from the pan and transfer to a baking sheet. Drizzle with some olive oil.

Preheat the oven to 200°C/400°F/Gas Mark 6.

Bake the sausages in the oven for 20 minutes, or until golden brown, then remove and set aside on the baking sheet.

When the sausages are nearly ready, bring a large saucepan of water to the boil, add a pinch of salt, then add the turnip tops and cook for 3 minutes, or until tender. Drain, put them into a serving dish and drizzle with the olive oil. Set aside.

Cut the sausages into thick slices and serve with the turnip tops on the side.

Stuffed Sheep's Stomach

••

Burilhões da Beira Alta ◔ Beira Alta

Preparation time: 45 minutes, plus 10 minutes resting
Cooking time: 30–45 minutes
Serves: 4–6
🐖 ◻ ◻

1 sheep's bladder
300 g/11 oz sheep tripe (stomach lining)
120 g/4 oz lardo, cut into very small pieces
130 g/4½ oz Serrano ham, cut into very small pieces
150 g/5 oz chorizo, cut into very small pieces
2 flat-leaf parsley sprigs with leaves, finely chopped
130 ml/4½ fl oz (½ cup) olive oil
sea salt and freshly ground black pepper

Preheat the oven to 160°C/325°F/Gas Mark 3.

Rinse the sheep's bladder several times under cold running water until it is clean. Have a large bowl of cold water nearby. Bring a large saucepan of water to the boil, dip the bladder into the boiling water for 20 seconds, then put it into the bowl of cold water. Using a sharp knife, scrape the inside, then repeat the boiling, cooling and scraping three times until the bladder is completely clean.

Repeat the same cleaning process with the tripe (stomach lining), then, using a sharp knife or scissors, cut the intestines into very small pieces.

Combine the lardo, ham, chorizo and parsley in a bowl. Add the intestines, season with salt and pepper and mix well.

Using a sharp knife, cut as many small rounds from the bladder as possible. Fill each round with some of the meat mixture, then close up the opening with a trussing needle and medium-thick butcher's string or kitchen twine. Repeat to use up all of the filling.

Fill an ovenproof casserole dish (Dutch oven) with 3 litres/102 fl oz (12¾ cups) water. Add the olive oil and a pinch of salt and bring to the boil. Carefully lower the filled pouches into the water, cover with a lid and cook in the oven for 45 minutes. Check after 30 minutes and if the pouches are soft, they are ready. Leave to rest in the dish for 10 minutes before serving.

Goat Stewed in Red Wine

••

Chanfana de Chainça ◔ Leiria

Preparation time: 30 minutes, plus 12 hours marinating
Cooking time: 3 hours
Serves: 6
◻

1.5 kg/3 lb 5 oz goat or mutton meat
240 g/8½ oz onions, peeled and halved
3 garlic cloves, peeled and germ removed
½ bunch flat-leaf parsley, roughly chopped
20 g/¾ oz (4 teaspoons) black peppercorns
5 g/¼ oz cloves
5 red chillies, finely sliced
2 bay leaves
1.5 litres/50 fl oz (6¼ cups) red wine
200 ml/7 fl oz (¾ cup) extra virgin olive oil
1.2 kg/2 lb 11 oz new potatoes, peeled
12 slices sourdough or stale crusty bread, toasted
sea salt

The day before, using a sharp knife, clean all the meat of any excess fat, then cut it into medium-sized pieces.

Chop the onions, garlic and two-thirds of the parsley together and put into a large bowl. Set aside the rest of the parsley for the garnish.

Put the peppercorns and cloves into a dry frying pan or skillet and heat over a medium heat for 5 minutes, or until the spices start to release their aromatic oils. Remove the pan from the heat, add the chillies and bay leaves, then stir together with the onion mixture. Add the red wine and the meat pieces, then cover with food wrap and leave to marinate in the fridge for 12 hours.

The next day, remove the meat from the marinade and season with 25 g/1 oz (5 teaspoons) of salt. Remove the onions and garlic from the marinade and transfer to a large saucepan and cook over a low heat for 10 minutes. Add the meat to the pan and cook for a further 10 minutes, or until browned. Add the wine and cook over a low heat for 3 hours, or until tender. The cooking time may vary depending on the meat, so check every 30 minutes. Taste and adjust the seasoning, if necessary.

Put the potatoes into another large saucepan, cover with cold water, add a pinch of salt and cook over a medium heat for 15–20 minutes, or until tender but not losing their shape or texture.

Arrange the toasted bread in a serving dish, then pour over the meat stew and finish with the remaining parsley. Serve with the boiled potatoes.

Roasted Kid

Cabrito Assado 🖼 p.267   ⛾ Alentejo

Roast kid goat is considered a true icon of Portugal's cuisine, found from the north to the south of the country. *Cabrito* meat is tender, with a pale pink colour that is the result of being fed almost exclusively on breast milk, making it a perfect dish for children and grown-ups in family reunions, weddings, popular festivities, Christmas and Easter. Historically, kid goat meat is associated with Catholicism, and is a central dish of an abundant Easter, when people would celebrate the end of 40 days of eating only fish.

Preparation time: 30 minutes, plus 3 hours marinating
Cooking time: 2 hours
Serves: 6
🖉 ⛾

2.5 kg/5 lb 10 oz kid goat meat, leg or rack, cut into
    medium-size chunks
4 heads garlic, halved
100 ml/3½ fl oz (⅓ cup) olive oil
250 ml/8 fl oz (1 cup) white wine
60 ml/2 fl oz (4 tablespoons) white wine vinegar
60 g/2¼ oz lard (pork fat)
2 onions, peeled and thinly sliced
1 tablespoon paprika
1 teaspoon freshly ground black pepper
2 bay leaves
⅓ bunch flat-leaf parsley, roughly chopped
sea salt

Rub the kid goat meat with the halved garlic heads, then season with salt. Transfer the meat to a large rimmed baking sheet along with the used garlic heads.

Mix the olive oil, white wine, vinegar lard (pork fat), onions, paprika, pepper, bay leaves and 250 ml/8 fl oz (1 cup) water together in a large bowl. Pour this mixture over the meat on the baking sheet and leave to marinate in the fridge for 3 hours.

Preheat the oven to 160°C/325°F/Gas Mark 3.

Scatter the parsley over the meat and roast in the hot oven for 2 hours, or until browned all over. The cooking time may vary depending on the meat, so check every 30 minutes. Top up with a little more water or wine, if necessary, to prevent it drying out. Taste and adjust the seasoning, if necessary.

Whole Roasted Kid

Cabrito Estonado   ⛾ Beira Baixa

Kid, goat and sheep all played an important role in Portuguese communities as they supply milk for cheese production as well as meat. This dish is a delicacy that is at risk of disappearing, because of rules implemented by the health authorities on the slaughtering of animals. When the kid is slaughtered, the meat is poached in boiling water. This helps to remove the fur, leaving just the skin. *Estonado* (page 428) means removing on the surface. This recipe is cooked in a wood-fired oven, on a rack made from bay branches. During roasting the fragrance from the bay leaves infuses into the meat.

Preparation time: 45 minutes, plus 4 hours drying
Cooking time: 2 hours 30 minutes
Serves: 10
🖉 ⛾

1 kid goat, about 6 kg/13 lb
18 garlic cloves, peeled but left whole
1½ tablespoons ground white pepper
1 teaspoon paprika
350 g/12 oz lard (pork fat)
2 bay leaves
600 ml/20 fl oz (2½ cups) white wine
sea salt

Take a stock pot large enough to accommodate the kid goat, fill it with water and bring it to the boil over a high heat. Grab the kid goat by the front and back legs and plunge it into the boiling water. Poach it for 30 seconds, then remove and put it onto a work counter. Carefully remove the hair from the skin with your fingers. Repeat this process until all the fur has been removed. Don't leave the kid got in the water for too long — you don't want to boil it. Using a sharp knife, scrape the skin all over the kid goat to remove any remaining hair.

Open the kid goat and remove the offal (variety meats). Drain the blood into a bowl and set aside for use in another recipe, such as *Sarapatel* on page 264. Hang the kid goat for 4 hours in a dry place covered with a clean tea (dish) towel.

When ready to cook, put the garlic, paprika, salt and pepper and into a large mortar and, using a pestle, mash it to a paste. Add the lard (pork fat) and mix well to combine. Crush the bay leaves into the mix, then add enough salt to season the whole kid goat and mix well. Rub the meat with this mixture inside and outside, reserving a little of the mixture. Stir the reserved mixture into the wine in a bowl, then pour this inside the kid.

Create a rack from bay tree branches and put them inside the oven, arraging them so that the meat will not touch the bottom of the oven. Heat a wood-fired oven or preheat the oven to 180°C/350°F/Gas Mark 4. Put the kid goat on the branches and roast in the hot oven for 2 hours 30 minutes, or until golden brown all over.

Roasted Kid

Roasted Kid in Red Wine

Chanfana de Cabrito   ℧ Beira Litoral

This recipe requires a clay pot, but in case you don't have access to one, an ordinary roasting pan or heavy-duty pan can be used instead.

Preparation time: 30 minutes, plus 10 minutes resting
Cooking time: 3 hours 35 minutes
Serves: 4
🥬 ▯

1.5 kg/3 lb 5 oz kid goat
4 bay leaves
90 g/3¼ oz (½ cup) lard (pork fat)
⅓ bunch flat-leaf parsley, roughly chopped
2 onions, peeled and finely chopped
2 garlic cloves, peeled and finely chopped
1 tablespoon paprika
4 cloves
10 white peppercorns
3 litres/102 fl oz (12¾ cups) red wine
sea salt

Preheat the oven to 160°C/325°F/Gas Mark 3.

Clean the kid goat, then chop the meat into small pieces. Bring a large saucepan of water to the boil, add the bay leaves and cook for 1 minute.

Arrange the meat on a large rimmed baking sheet and pour over the bay leaf-infused water. Leave for 1 minute, then drain and wash the kid goat under cold running water. Leave to drip over a perforated tray or in a colander. Season with salt.

Put the lard (pork fat) into a large roasting pan and heat over a medium heat for 5 minutes, or until the fat starts to render, then add all the remaining ingredients except the red wine. Add the meat and stir well to combine. Pour in the red wine and roast the meat in the hot oven for 3 hours 30 minutes, or until cooked through. Leave to rest for 10 minutes before serving.

Roasted Kid with Turnip Tops

Cabrito Assado   ℧ Ribatejo
com Grelos   📷 p.269

Preparation time: 40 minutes, plus 1 hour standing and 10 minutes resting
Cooking time: 1 hour
Serves: 8
🥬 ▯

5 kg/11 lb kid goat
12 garlic cloves, peeled but left whole
1 red chilli, roughly chopped
2 tablespoons paprika
2 bay leaves
150 ml/5 fl oz (⅔ cup) olive oil, plus extra for drizzling
120 g/4 oz lard (pork fat)
200 ml/7 fl oz (¾ cup) white wine
2 large bunches turnip tops, bottom stalk removed
sea salt

Heat a wood-fired oven or preheat the oven to 220°C/425°F/Gas Mark 7.

Clean the kid goat, then chop the meat into small to medium-sized pieces.

Put the garlic into a large mortar with the chilli, paprika, bay leaves, olive oil, lard (pork fat) and enough salt to season the kid goat. Using a pestle, mash everything to a paste. Rub the mixture over the kid goat inside and outside and leave to stand for 1 hour.

Put the kid goat onto a large rimmed baking sheet and drizzle the wine all over the meat. Roast in the hot oven for 35 minutes. If using a regular oven, reduce the temperature to 190°C/375°F/Gas Mark 5 and roast for a further 15 minutes, or until the meat is tender and be easily pulled away from the bones. Check the meat regularly and turn it over so it doesn't burn. Remove from the oven and leave to rest for 10 minutes.

Meanwhile, bring a large saucepan of salted water to the boil. Once boiling, add the turnip tops and cook for 3 minutes. Drain, transfer to a serving dish and drizzle with olive oil. Serve the meat with the turnip tops on the side.

Roasted Kid with Turnip Tops

Roasted Stuffed Kid – Barril de Alva Style

Cabrito Recheado à Moda de Barril de Alva   ♡ Beira Litoral

There are lots of different recipes for kid goat all over Portugal, from grilled (broiled) to roasted, some stuffed while others are just rubbed with pastes or simply seasoned with salt and pepper. Roast kid are usually cooked in wood-fired ovens on traditionally made large clay black or red trays. In this region, black clay is very popular.

Preparation time: 1 hour, plus 1 hour standing
Cooking time: 3 hours 30 minutes
Serves: 8

1 x 3.5-kg/7 lb 12-oz milk-fed kid goat
180 ml/6 fl oz (¾ cup) olive oil
5 onions, 2 peeled and finely chopped, 3 peeled and thinly sliced
12 garlic cloves, 4 peeled and finely chopped, 8 peeled and left whole
offal (variety meats) from 1 lamb, including kidneys, heart, liver, any excess fat removed and cut into small pieces
130 ml/4½ fl oz (½ cup) white wine
½ tablespoon sweet paprika
330 g/11½ oz lard (pork fat)
sea salt and freshly ground black pepper
5 bunches watercress
60 ml/2 fl oz (4 tablespoons) extra virgin olive oil
20 ml/¾ fl oz (4 teaspoons) white wine vinegar

Prepare the kid goat by removing the head and part of the neck, then cut off the tail. If necessary, follow the instructions on page 266 to remove the hair from the skin, remove the offal (variety meats) and drain the blood.

Heat the olive oil in a large saucepan over a medium heat, add the finely chopped onions and finely chopped garlic and cook for 15 minutes, or until golden. Add all the offal and stir. Add one-third of the wine, season with salt and pepper and mix together. Cook for 30 minutes, or until cooked through. Taste and adjust the seasoning, if necessary, then remove the pan from the heat and set aside.

Put the remaining whole garlic cloves into a large mortar, add the paprika and, using a pestle, mash to a paste. Add half the lard (pork fat) and mix well to combine. Add enough salt and pepper to season the whole kid goat and mix well. Rub the meat with this mixture inside and outside, then leave to stand for 1 hour.

Open up the kid's belly and stuff the offal mixture inside. Using a trussing needle and medium-thick butcher's string or kitchen twine, stitch the opening together to close.

Heat a wood-fired oven or preheat the oven to 180°C/350°F/Gas Mark 4.

Spread the remaining lard over the kid goat. Put the sliced onions into a medium bowl and pour over the remaining wine. Arrange the onions on a large baking sheet, put the kid goat on top and roast in the hot oven for 2 hours 45 minutes, or until golden brown all over.

Arrange the watercress in a salad bowl. Combine the extra virgin olive oil and vinegar in a small bowl and mix together to emulsify. Drizzle the dressing over the watercress, season with salt, then toss until the watercress is well coated.

Serve the kid goat meat with the dressed watercress salad on the side.

Roasted Young Kid

Cabrito Novo 🖾 p.271   ♡ Beira Baixa

Preparation time: 40 minutes
Cooking time: 1 hour 30 minutes
Serves: 4

1.5 kg/3 lb 5 oz kid goat meat, cut into medium-thick slices
3 large onions, 1 peeled and cut into large chunks, 2 peeled and thinly sliced
1 bunch flat-leaf parsley, roughly chopped
2 bay leaves, crushed
700 g/1 lb 9 oz squash, peeled, de-seeded and cut into chunks
1 fennel bulb, cut into chunks
5 garlic cloves, peeled and finely chopped
150 ml/5 fl oz (⅔ cup) olive oil
60 g/2¼ oz (½ cup) unpitted olives, roughly chopped
180 g/6 oz (1⅓ cups) walnut halves, roughly chopped
sea salt

Preheat the oven to 200°C/400°F/Gas Mark 6. Put the kid goat meat, onion chunks and parsley into a large saucepan, cover with water and cook over a medium heat for 30 minutes, or until tender but not falling off the bone. Remove the meat from the pan and transfer to a plate, then set aside the cooking liquid.

Season the meat with salt and the crushed bay leaves. Arrange a layer of the meat over the base of a large clay pot or roasting pan, then add a layer of the squash, fennel and garlic. Repeat until all the meat and vegetables are used up. Drizzle over the olive oil, then pour some of the reserved cooking liquid over the top and roast in the hot oven for 1 hour, or until the vegetables are cooked and the meat is soft and easily falls off the bone. Check the meat regularly during cooking and top up with a little more of the reserved cooking liquid, if necessary, to prevent it drying out.

Scatter the olives and walnuts over the kid goat meat before serving.

Roasted Young Kid

Roasted Kid
with Offal Rice

For maximum flavour, the kid goat should be roasted in a wood-fired oven sat on thick bay branches in a large clay tray. Always buy a whole kid goat that is as fresh as possible, and ask your butcher to include the offal (variety meats) too. Traditionally, the front and back legs of the kid goat are tied together with butcher's string or kitchen twine, but you can skip this stage as it doesn't change the flavour of the cooked meat.

Preparation time: 45 minutes, plus 12 hours marinating
Cooking time: 55 minutes
Serves: 8
🦴 ▢

1 x 5-kg/11-lb kid goat, with the offal (variety meats) for the rice
1 large onion, peeled and coarsely chopped
4 garlic cloves, peeled but left whole
250 ml/8 fl oz (1 cup) *Vinho Verde* vinegar or red wine vinegar
1 teaspoon sweet paprika
1½ teaspoons ground white pepper
150 g/5 oz lardo, thinly sliced
120 g/4 oz lard (pork fat)
sea salt

For the rice:
1 teaspoon saffron threads
25 g/1 oz lard (pork fat)
1 onion, peeled and finely chopped
120 g/4 oz Serrano ham
½ chorizo
offal (variety meats) from the kid goat, cut into small pieces
450 g/1 lb (2 cups) short-grain rice, preferably Carolino
¼ bunch flat-leaf parsley, coarsely chopped
1 bay leaf
2 onions, peeled and cut into thin rings

Prepare the kid goat by removing the head and part of the neck, then cut off the tail. If necessary, follow the instructions on page 266 to remove the hair from the skin, remove the offal (variety meats) and drain the blood.

Put the onion, garlic, vinegar, paprika, white pepper and enough salt to season the whole kid goat into a large mortar, and, using a pestle, mash to a paste. Rub the meat with this mixture inside and outside, then leave in the fridge for 12 hours to marinate.

Heat a wood-fired oven or preheat the oven to 160°C/325°F/Gas Mark 3.

Wrap the saffron threads for the rice in foil and toast in the hot oven for 5 minutes. Remove from the oven and set aside. Increase the oven temperature to 180°C/350°F/Gas Mark 4.

Using a sharp knife, make small cuts all over the meat and push the pieces of lardo into them.

Create a bed of bay tree branches in a large ovenproof clay tray or large roasting pan. Put the kid goat on the branches and roast in the hot oven for 50 minutes, or until golden brown all over. Turn the kid goat over halfway through the cooking time to ensure it cooks evenly.

Meanwhile, prepare the rice. Heat the lard (pork fat) in a large casserole dish (Dutch oven) over a low heat, add the onion and cook for 15 minutes or until lightly coloured. Add the ham, chorizo and offal, stir, then add 1.5 litres/50 fl oz (6¼ cups) water and cook gently for 30 minutes, or until everything is cooked through. Remove the offal and meat from the dish and set aside on a large plate or tray. Add the rice, parsley, bay leaf, onion rings and toasted saffron to the dish, then cover with a lid and place in the hot oven with the meat to finish cooking for 20 minutes.

Once cooked, remove the kid goat and rice from the oven. Slice the meat then arrange it on top of the rice before serving.

Chargrilled Kid

Preparation time: 15 minutes, plus 12 hours standing
Cooking time: 1 hour 20 minutes
Serves: 5
🦴 ▢

1 x 2.5-kg/5 lb 10-oz kid goat half
8 garlic cloves, peeled but left whole
150 g/5 oz (¾ cup) lard (pork fat)
1 tablespoon paprika
850 g/1 lb 14 oz baby new potatoes, unpeeled and left whole
sea salt and freshly ground black pepper

Season the kid goat half with salt and leave to stand in the fridge for 12 hours.

Put the garlic and enough salt to season the kid goat into a large mortar and, using a pestle, mash to a paste.

Put the lard (pork fat), paprika and some freshly ground black pepper into a medium bowl, add the garlic paste and mix to combine. Cover with food wrap and leave in the fridge for 12 hours.

The next day, prepare a barbecue. If you have some wood, add that to the coals as well. Preheat the oven to 160°C/325°F/Gas Mark 3.

Put the potatoes into a large roasting pan, sprinkle with salt and roast for 35 minutes, or until soft on the inside and crispy on the outside.

As soon as the barbecue coals are glowing, brush the kid goat with the garlic paste, then put it on the grill rack and grill for 45 minutes, or until the skin is crispy and the meat is cooked through.

Slice the meat then serve with the roasted potatoes on the side.

Roasted Kid
with Carqueja Rice —
Serra d'Arga Style

Cabrito Assado à Serra d'Arga   ♡ **Minho**
com Arroz de Carqueja

Preparation time: 45 minutes, plus 24 hours marinating
Cooking time: 1 hour 45 minutes
Serves: 5
🍖🗋

3 kg/6 lb 10 oz kid goat meat
3 garlic cloves, peeled but left whole
40 g/1½ oz *Massa de Pimentão*
80 ml/2¾ fl oz (⅓ cup) white wine vinegar
300 ml/10 fl oz (1¼ cups) white wine
juice of 1 lemon
2 bay leaves, crushed
2 onions, peeled and thinly sliced
1 carrot, peeled and thinly sliced
2 large bunches flat-leaf parsley, roughly chopped
50 g/2 oz lard (pork fat)
600 ml/20 fl oz (2½ cups) *Vinho Verde Branco* wine or
    other white wine with good acidity
700 g/1 lb 9 oz small round potatoes, peeled
sea salt and freshly ground white pepper

For the rice:
500 g/1 lb 2 oz chicken
120 g/4 oz Serrano ham
100 ml/3½ fl oz (⅓ cup) olive oil
1 large onion, peeled and finely chopped
1 garlic clove, peeled and finely chopped
¼ bunch flat-leaf parsley, finely chopped
50 g/2 oz carqueja, finely chopped
450 g/1 lb (2 cups) short-grain rice, preferably Carolino

Clean the kid goat, then chop the meat into medium-sized pieces.

Put the garlic and *Massa de Pimentão* into a mortar and, using a pestle, mash to a paste.

Put the vinegar, white wine, lemon juice, bay leaves, pepper and enough salt to season the meat into a large bowl and stir. Add the garlic paste and mix well to combine. Pour this marinade over the kid goat and rub the meat with this mixture inside and outside, then leave in the fridge for 24 hours to marinate.

When ready to cook, heat a wood-fired oven or preheat the oven to 180°C/350°F/Gas Mark 4.

Remove the kid goat from the marinade. Arrange the onions, carrots and parsley in the bottom of a large ovenproof clay tray or roasting pan. Spread the lard (pork fat) over the vegetables, then lay the kid goat on top. Pour the wine into the tray and roast in the oven for 1 hour, basting the meat with the wine and juices in the tray during cooking.

Halfway through the cooking time, add the potatoes to the tray and mix well in the juices. Once the kid goat is cooked through, turn off the oven but leave the meat in the oven to rest until ready to serve with the rice.

Meanwhile, prepare the rice, put the chicken into a large saucepan with the ham and cook over a medium heat for 45 minutes, skimming off the foam that rises to the top with a slotted spoon. Remove from the heat and strain the stock through a sieve (fine-mesh strainer) into a large heatproof bowl or jug (pitcher). You will need 1 litre/34 fl oz (4¼ cups).

Heat the olive oil in a large saucepan over a low heat, add the onion, garlic, parsley and *carqueja* and cook for 12 minutes, or until the onion is translucent. Add the rice to the pan, stir, then pour in the stock and gently cook for 25 minutes, or until the rice is soft.

Slice the meat then arrange it on top of the rice before serving.

Scrambled Kids' Brains
with Eggs

Mioleira de Cabrito   ♡ **Beira Baixa**

Preparation time: 10 minutes
Cooking time: 25 minutes
Serves: 4
🗋

2 kids' brains, washed
6 eggs
320 g/11¼ oz bread, blitzed into large breadcrumbs
110 ml/3¾ fl oz (½ cup) olive oil
sea salt

Bring a medium saucepan of water to the boil. Add the kids' brains and cook for 3–5 minutes, or until soft. Remove the brains from the pan and transfer to a large bowl. Using a fork or wooden spoon, mash the brains into small pieces. Add the eggs and mix together until everything is combined. Add the breadcrumbs and mix together.

Heat a large frying pan or skillet over a high heat. Add the olive oil and, once hot, reduce the heat to medium and pour the brain mixture into the pan. Cook for 20 minutes, or until it is a creamy consistency. Season with salt and serve.

RICE DISHES AND SAVOURY CAKES

Creamy Cod Rice

•••

Arroz de Bacalhau 📷 p.277   ⏷ Minho

One of the very few traditional dishes to mix cod and rice, *Arroz de Bacalhau* was originally created to make use of all parts of the fish; there are even documented recipes that use the skin, roasted or fried. These days, *Arroz de Bacalhau* is made with cod steak that is shredded, stewed with onions and tomatoes, mixed with uncooked rice, then gently cooked until the rice is tender.

Preparation time: 10 minutes, plus 12–14 hours soaking
Cooking time: 45 minutes
Serves: 2
🌱 ◻ ✕

220 g/7½ oz salted cod, desalted (page 40)
1 small onion, peeled and finely chopped
1 garlic clove, peeled and finely chopped
170 g/6 oz (¾ cup) short-grain rice,
    preferably Carolino
sea salt and freshly ground black pepper

Check the cod is not too salty before cooking. If it is, then leave to soak for another 2 hours. Drain.
    Put the cod into a medium saucepan, cover with water and cook over a low heat for 6 minutes, or until the cod is soft. Remove from the pan, then remove the skin and any fish bones. Flake the flesh into chunks. Set aside 600 ml/20 fl oz (2½ cups) of the cooking water.
    Put the onion and garlic into a large saucepan and cook over a low heat for 10 minutes, or until the onion is translucent and lighter in colour. Add the rice and cod, stir, then add the reserved cooking water. Increase the heat to medium and cook for 25 minutes, or until the rice is soft and creamy. You may need to add a little more of the cod cooking water, if it's drying out, so keep checking.
    Season with salt and pepper and serve.

Lamprey Rice — Minho Style

•••

Arroz de Lampreia   ⏷ Minho
à Moda do Minho

There are a lot of recipes for lamprey rice even in the Minho area, but they are all slightly different. Lamprey rice can be cooked with chorizo, such as in this recipe, or a different kind of wine like *vinho verde tinto*.

Preparation time: 30 minutes, plus 2 hours marinating
Cooking time: 1 hour
Serves: 4
🌱 ◻ ◻

1 lamprey
300 ml/10 fl oz (1¼ cups) white wine
4 garlic cloves, peeled and halved
1 bay leaf
1 bunch flat-leaf parsley, leaves picked
100 ml/3½ fl oz (⅓ cup) olive oil
1 onion, peeled and thinly sliced
90 g/3¼ oz chorizo, thinly sliced
350 g/12 oz (1½ cups) short-grain rice,
    preferably Carolino
sea salt

Prepare the lamprey according to the instructions on page 166. Cut the fish into pieces, about 3 cm/1¼ inches.
    Put the wine, garlic, salt, bay leaf and parsley into a large bowl. Mix together, then add the fish and turn so the fish is coated in the marinade. Cover with food wrap and leave to marinate in the fridge for 2 hours.
    Heat the olive oil in a large saucepan over a low heat, add onion and chorizo and cook for 12 minutes, or until the onion is soft.
    Add the fish and all the marinade to the pan, increase the heat to medium and cook for 15 minutes. Remove the fish from the pan with a slotted spoon, add 1.2 litres/40 fl oz (5 cups) water, taste and adjust the seasoning with salt and pepper, then bring to the boil. Add the rice and cook for 25 minutes, or until the rice is soft.
    Return the fish to the pan to warm through, then stir before serving.

Creamy Cod Rice

Lamprey Rice — Montemor-o-Novo Style

‹‹‹

Arroz de Lampreia   ◊ Beira Litoral
à Montemor-o-Novo

Preparation time: 25 minutes, plus 12 hours marinating
Cooking time: 45 minutes
Serves: 6

🌿 ◻

1 medium lamprey
60 ml/2 fl oz (4 tablespoons) vinegar
2 bay leaves
1 litre/34 fl oz (4¼ cups) red wine
3 large sprigs flat-leaf parsley, roughly chopped
4 garlic cloves, peeled and crushed
2 onions, peeled and finely diced
150 ml/5 fl oz (⅔ cup) olive oil
1 teaspoon paprika
450 g/1 lb (2 cups) short-grain rice,
    preferably Carolino
sea salt and freshly ground black pepper

Bring a large saucepan of water to the boil. Once boiling, place the lamprey in a colander and blanch for 30 seconds. Remove from the pan and scrape off the slime.

Put the vinegar into a large bowl. Using a sharp knife, make a cut next to the gills on both sides of the lamprey and hold over the bowl to drain the blood into the vinegar. Set aside. Remove the head and gills. Cut the belly lengthwise and remove the guts and cartilage, then cut the fish horizontally with the bone still in, into 8-cm/3¼-inch slices. Set aside.

Add the bay leaves, red wine, parsley and garlic to the blood and vinegar mixture, then season with salt. Put the fish into the marinade and mix until the fish is coated. Cover with food wrap and leave to marinate in the fridge for 12 hours.

The next day, put the onions, olive oil, paprika and a pinch of salt and pepper into a medium saucepan and cook over a low heat for 7 minutes, or until the onions are golden brown.

Remove the lamprey from the marinade, keeping the marinade, and add the fish to the onions. Cook, stirring frequently, over a low heat for another 30 minutes.

Strain the marinade through into a bowl or jug (pitcher), discarding what is left in the sieve (fine-mesh strainer). You will need about 1.8 litres/61 fl oz (7¼ cups) of the marinade to cook the rice, so you may need to top up with water.

Once the fish is cooked, pour in the marinade and bring it to the boil over a low heat. Stir then, using a slotted spoon, remove the fish from the pan and set aside on a plate. Let the marinade reduce for 2 minutes to intensify the flavour. Gradually add the rice to the pan and cook over a low heat, stirring continuously, for 15 minutes, or until the rice is cooked. Serve the fish on top of the rice.

Cockle Rice

‹‹‹

Arroz de Berbigão   📷 p.279   ◊ Algarve

I grew up on the west coast of the Algarve where my father used to collect all sorts of seafood with his friends, from the barnacles on the cliffs to crabs and ultimately cockles inshore of the Praia da Amoreira.

Preparation time: 20 minutes, plus 3 hours standing
Cooking time: 45 minutes
Serves: 4

🌿 ◻

1.6 kg/3 lb 8 oz fresh cockles
2 teaspoons fine table salt
150 ml/5 fl oz (⅔ cup) olive oil
3 garlic cloves, peeled and thinly sliced
½ bunch coriander (cilantro), leaves picked
260 g/9 oz (1¼ cups) short-grain rice,
    preferably Carolino
sea salt and freshly ground black pepper

Rinse the cockles several times under cold running water, then put them in a large bowl covered with water and the fine table salt. Stir the cockles, then leave to stand for 3 hours so they can release all the grit and sand.

Using a slotted spoon, remove the cockles from the brine into another container. Line a chinois or sieve (fine-mesh strainer) with muslin (cheesecloth) then pour the brine through it into a large bowl. Set aside.

Add a drizzle of the olive oil in a large saucepan, add the cockles, cover with a lid and cook over a medium heat for 5 minutes, or until they open. Using a slotted spoon, remove them from the pan into a large bowl and strain the juices through a sieve or a lined chinois. Mix the cockle juices and the brine together. You should have 800 ml/27 fl oz (3¼ cups).

Heat the remaining olive oil in a large saucepan, add the garlic, the mixed cockle juices and brine and half the coriander (cilantro) and bring to the boil. Remove the coriander, add the rice and cook over a low heat for 15 minutes, or until the rice is nearly cooked. Make sure the rice doesn't dry out during cooking, if it does add some more liquid.

Once the rice is nearly cooked, add the cockles and season with pepper. You can remove the cockle meat from the shells before adding them to the rice, if you like.

Taste and adjust the seasoning with salt if necessary, then chop the remaining coriander finely and scatter over the rice before serving.

Cockle Rice

Seafood Rice

Arroz de Marisco 📷 p.281   ✆ Leiria

This is a very popular dish in Praia da Vieira, a coastal town close to Leiria. Always buy shellfish fresh from a good supplier or fishmonger.

Preparation time: 30 minutes, plus 12 hours standing
Cooking time: 1 hour
Serves: 6
🌱 ☐

500 g/1 lb 2 oz fresh clams
4 large tomatoes, bull's heart if available or other
    good-quality ripe tomatoes
200 ml/7 fl oz (¾ cup) extra virgin olive oil, plus extra
    for drizzling
2 white onions, peeled and very finely chopped
2 garlic cloves, peeled and very finely chopped
1 bay leaf
150 g/5 oz (1 cup) tomato pulp
1 spiny lobster or rock lobster
450 g/1 lb (2¼ cups) long-grain rice
1 medium brown crab
200 g/7 oz prawns (shrimp)
60 ml/2 fl oz (2 tablespoons) lemon juice
½ bunch coriander (cilantro), roughly chopped
2 red chillies, finely chopped
sea salt and freshly ground black pepper

The day before, scrub the shells of the clams to remove any dirt. Discard any that don't close when their shells are tapped. Rinse the clams several times in cold water to remove any sand and grit, then put them into a large bowl and add enough water to cover them. Add enough fine sea salt to make a brine with 1% salt and stir well. Leave to stand in the fridge for 12 hours. This will help to expel any sand inside the clams.

Have a large bowl of iced water nearby. Bring a large saucepan of water to the boil. Using a sharp knife, score the top of the tomatoes with a small cross shape. Once the water is boiling, carefully add the tomatoes and blanch for 30 seconds, then transfer them with a slotted spoon to the iced water and leave to cool. Once cool enough to handle, peel off the skins, cut in half and de-seed, then dice the flesh. Set aside.

Heat the olive oil in a large saucepan over a low heat. Add the onions, garlic and bay leaf and cook for 10 minutes, or until the onions have softened but not coloured. Add the tomato pulp and mix well. Cook gently for 5 minutes, then add the fresh tomatoes and cook gently for another 45 minutes.

Have a large bowl of iced water ready nearby. Bring a large saucepan of water to the boil, add 50 g/2 oz (¼ cup) salt then, once the water is boiling, reduce the heat so it is simmering and add the lobster. Cook for 4 minutes. Remove the lobster from the pan and leave to cool in the iced water. Set the cooking water aside. You will need about 1.6 litres/54 fl oz (6½ cups).

Remove the shells from the lobster, keep the head juices together with the coral in a bowl for later, then remove the back vein and discard. Cut the meat into chunks and put into a bowl. Cover with food wrap and set aside.

Add the rice to the tomato base and dry cook for 5 minutes, then cover the rice with the reserved lobster cooking water and cook gently over a medium heat. Cut the crab into 4 pieces and add it to the rice, adding more water if necessary, then add the clams and prawns (shrimp). Keep cooking over a medium heat until the rice is nearly cooked. Season with salt and pepper.

Remove from the heat and leave the rice to rest in the pan before serving. Stir in the lobster coral, then drizzle with extra virgin olive oil and lemon juice. Add the coriander (cilantro) and chilli and taste and adjust the seasoning, if necessary.

Limpet Rice — Faial Style

Arroz de Lapas – Faial   ✆ Açores

Preparation time: 15 minutes
Cooking time: 20 minutes
Serves: 4
🌱 ☐

1 kg/2 lb 4 oz fresh limpets
100 ml/3½ fl oz (⅓ cup) olive oil
1 onion, peeled and very finely chopped
2 garlic cloves, peeled and very finely chopped
½ teaspoon paprika
1 bay leaf
360 g/12¾ oz (1¾ cups plus 2 teaspoons)
    long-grain rice, but short-grain also works well
¼ bunch flat-leaf parsley, finely chopped
sea salt and freshly ground black pepper

Wash the limpets in cold water, scrubbing them with a small brush. Bring a large saucepan of water to the boil, then add the limpets and blanch for 30 seconds. Using a slotted spoon, transfer the limpets to a baking sheet, then strain the cooking water through a sieve (strainer) or a fine muslin (cheesecloth) into a jug (pitcher) and set aside. You will need about 800 ml/27 fl oz (3¼ cups) cooking water.

Heat the olive oil in a large saucepan over a low heat, add the onion and garlic and cook for 10 minutes, or until the onion is translucent. Season with salt, pepper, paprika and add the bay leaf. Pour in the reserved cooking water, then add the rice, season with salt and cook over a medium heat for 15 minutes, or until the rice is tender. Depending on the quality and variety of the rice the amount of liquid may vary so keep an eye on it as it cooks.

Meanwhile, remove the limpets from their shells, discarding the shells. Once the rice is cooked, stir in the limpets, then sprinkle with parsley and serve.

Razor Clam Rice

••

Arroz de Lingueirão   ▯ **Algarve**

Razor clams are common around the Algarve
coastline, and are still collected by hand across
most beaches in the south. Their name derives
from their resemblance to an old-fashioned
barber's razor and, while once a poor relative
of clams and cockles, they are today the star
of several dishes, including this dish found
throughout the Algarve, where they are served
in a tomato and coriander (cilantro) rice stew.

Preparation time: 30 minutes, plus 3 hours standing
Cooking time: 25 minutes
Serves: 4
🐟 ▯

1.5 kg g/3 lb 5 oz razor clams in the shell
80 ml/2¾ fl oz (⅓ cup) olive oil
2 garlic cloves, peeled and finely chopped
1 small onion, peeled and finely chopped
1 red chilli, finely chopped
280 g/10 oz (1¼ cups) short-grain rice
3 bunches flat-leaf parsley, roughly chopped
fine table salt
sea salt and freshly ground black pepper

Scrub the shells of the razor clams to remove any
dirt. Discard any that don't close when their shells
are tapped. Rinse the razor clams several times
under cold running water to remove any sand
and grit, then put them into a large bowl and add
enough water to cover them. Add enough fine
sea salt to make a brine with 3% salt and stir well.
Leave to stand in the fridge for 3 hours. This will
help to expel any sand inside the clams.

Put 1.5 litres/50 fl oz (6¼ cups) water into
a large saucepan with a pinch of salt and bring
to the boil. Add the razor clams and poach for
45 seconds to shock them, then remove them with
tongs and put them onto a large plate or tray and
remove them from their shells. Strain the poaching
water through a sieve (fine-mesh strainer) or a
chinois lined with muslin (cheesecloth) into another
bowl or jug (pitcher) and set aside. You will need
about 800 ml/27 fl oz (3¼ cups).

Remove and discard the digestive sac from
the razor clams and cut them in half. Set side.

Put the olive oil, garlic and onion into a small
saucepan and cook over a low heat for 10 minutes,
or until the onions are translucent. Add the chilli
and season with salt and pepper. Add the reserved
poaching liquid, stir and bring to the boil. Add
the rice, then reduce the heat to low and cook
for 15 minutes, or until the rice is soft. About
2 minutes before the rice is ready, add the razor
clams, stir and finish cooking the rice. Remove
from the heat, sprinkle the parsley over the top
and leave to rest for 5 minutes before serving.

Octopus Rice

••

Arroz de Polvo 📷 p.283   ▯ **Algarve**

Preparation time: 25 minutes, plus 12 hours freezing
Cooking time: 45 minutes
Serves: 4
🐟 ▯

1 medium octopus, fresh or frozen
380 g/13½ oz tomatoes
170 ml/5¾ fl oz (⅔ cup) olive oil
170 g/6 oz onions, peeled and very finely chopped
4 garlic cloves, peeled and very finely chopped
1 large green (bell) pepper
2 bird's eye chillies, finely chopped
270 ml/9 fl oz (1 cup) red wine
380 g/13½ oz (2 cups) long-grain rice
1 bunch flat-leaf parsley, roughly chopped
sea salt

If you are using fresh octopus, rinse it in cold
running water and then freeze it. Thaw the octopus
before cooking. This will help to break down
the texture of the octopus, making it soft when
cooked, rather than beating it with a wooden
spoon or rolling pin.

Cut the octopus into pieces, removing all the
tentacles. Use the head too.

Have a large bowl of iced water nearby. Bring
a large saucepan of water to the boil. Using a sharp
knife, score the top of the tomatoes with a small
cross shape. Once the water is boiling, carefully
add the tomatoes and blanch for 30 seconds,
then transfer them with a slotted spoon to the
iced water and leave to cool. Once cool enough
to handle, peel off the skins, cut in half and
de-seed, then cut the flesh into medium pieces.
Set aside.

Heat the olive oil in a large saucepan over a
medium heat, add the onions and garlic and cook
for 5 minutes, or until they gain a little colour.
Add the tomatoes and green (bell) pepper and
cook for 5 minutes. Add the octopus and cook
for a few minutes. Add the chillies, red wine and
1.2 litres/40 fl oz (5 cups) water and cook for
a further 15–20 minutes, or until the octopus is
cooked. Keep checking the octopus as you do not
want to overcook it.

Once the octopus is cooked, add the rice
and cook for 15 minutes, or until the rice is soft.
Remove from the heat, scatter the parsley over the
top and leave to rest for 5 minutes before serving.

Octopus Rice

Octopus Rice — Pico Style

••

Arroz de Polvo   ⏺ Açores
à Moda do Pico

As I have already mentioned, you can freeze
and then thaw octopus to tenderise the meat
and achieve a better texture when cooking it.
Personally, I prefer to eat octopus with a bit
of a bite, rather than melting in the mouth, but it
is totally up to you.

Preparation time: 20 minutes
Cooking time: 1 hour 20 minutes
Serves: 4
🐙 ▢ ▢

1 x 1.5-kg/3 lb 5-oz octopus
2 onions, peeled and finely chopped
2 garlic cloves, peeled and finely chopped
220 ml/7½ fl oz (1 cup) red wine
80 ml/2¾ fl oz (⅓ cup) olive oil
360 g/12¾ oz (1¾ cups) long-grain rice
sea salt and cracked black pepper
½ bunch flat-leaf parsley, roughly chopped, to serve

If you are using fresh octopus, rinse it in cold
running water and then freeze it. Thaw the octopus
before cooking. This will help to break down
the texture of the octopus, making it soft when
cooked, rather than beating it with a wooden
spoon or rolling pin.

Wash the octopus in cold water a few times,
rubbing it. Slice the octopus into small pieces.

Put the octopus into a large saucepan with the
onions and garlic, pour in enough water to cover
and bring to the boil. When it starts to boil,
add the wine and olive oil, reduce the heat slightly
and simmer gently over a medium heat for 1 hour.

You will need 800 ml/27 fl oz (3¼ cups) water
to cook the rice, so check how much liquid there
is in the pan by straining the liquid through a sieve
(fine-mesh strainer) into a jug (pitcher). If there
is not enough, then add water to make it up to
800 ml/27 fl oz (3¼ cups). Pour the cooking water
back into the pan with the octopus, garlic and
onions and bring to the boil. Add the rice, reduce
the heat to low and cook for 15 minutes, or until
the rice is tender.

Remove the pan from the heat, then season
with salt and pepper. Leave to rest for 5 minutes.
Scatter over the chopped parsley before serving.

Octopus Rice — Minho Style

••

Arroz de Polvo   ⏺ Minho
à Moda do Minho

This stewed, tender octopus, served with boiled
potatoes and cabbage, is part of the Christmas
Eve banquet in the northern regions of Portugal
— Minho and Trás-os-Montes. In villages, octopus
substitutes the ubiquitous cod during Christmas
festivities, which is owing to the proximity of
Spain's Galicia, the octopus fishing region, as
well as the religious fervour of generations that
imposed meatless meals during the Christmas
season, a limitation that only ended with Christmas
day lunch. When stewed octopus is combined
with rice, the result is this *arroz de polvo*.

Preparation time: 25 minutes, plus 12 hours freezing
Cooking time: 1 hour 45 minutes
Serves: 4
🐙 ▢

1 x 1.5-kg/3 lb 5-oz octopus
60 g/2¼ oz lard (pork fat)
50 ml/1⅔ fl oz (3½ tablespoons) olive oil
1 onion, peeled and finely chopped
1 garlic clove, peeled and finely chopped
⅓ bunch flat-leaf parsley, roughly chopped
1 small chilli, finely chopped
80 ml/2¾ fl oz (⅓ cup) red wine vinegar
380 g/13½ oz (1¾ cups) short-grain rice,
    preferably Carolino
40 g/1½ oz (⅓ cup) pitted black olives
sea salt and freshly ground white pepper

If you are using fresh octopus, rinse it in cold running
water and then freeze it. Thaw the octopus before
cooking. This will help to break down the texture
of the octopus, making it soft when cooked, rather
than beating it with a wooden spoon or rolling pin.

Wash the octopus in cold water a few times,
rubbing it. Slice the octopus into small pieces.
Remove the tentacles and sac, then cut the
tentacles in half and the sac in quarters.

Bring 4 litres/136 fl oz (16 cups) water to the
boil in a large saucepan.

Heat both fats in a large ovenproof saucepan
or casserole dish (Dutch oven) over a low heat,
add the onion and garlic and cook for 10 minutes,
or until the onion is translucent and lightly
coloured. Add the parsley, stir, then add the chilli
with a pinch of pepper and cook for a further
5 minutes. Add the octopus, stir, then pour in half
the vinegar. Increase the heat to medium, cover
with a lid and cook for 10 minutes. Add the hot
water, reduce the heat to low and cook with the
lid on for 50 minutes, or until the octopus is soft.

Preheat the oven to 150°C/300°F/Gas Mark 2.

Strain the water through a sieve (fine-mesh
strainer) into a large bowl or jug (pitcher). You will
need about 800 ml/27 fl oz (3¼ cups).

Put the octopus and onions back into the pan, add 800 ml/27 fl oz (3¼ cups) of the cooking water, taste and adjust the seasoning with salt and pepper, then add the remaining vinegar and bring to the boil. Add the rice and when it starts to boil, remove from the heat and cover with the lid. Bake in the oven for 25 minutes, or until the rice is soft.

Serve with the olives scattered over the top.

Rooster Blood Rice

Arroz de Cabidela ♡ Minho

Preparation time: 20 minutes
Cooking time: 1 hour
Serves: 6
🌿 ▢

1 rooster, cut into small pieces
80 ml/2¾ fl oz (⅓ cup) olive oil
½ onion, peeled and finely chopped
2 garlic cloves, peeled and finely chopped
1 bay leaf
1 teaspoon sweet paprika
2 bunches flat-leaf parsley, roughly chopped
350 g/12 oz (1¾ cups) long-grain rice
fresh blood from the rooster mixed with 1 teaspoon white wine vinegar to prevent coagulation
juice of 1 lemon
sea salt

Bring a large saucepan of water with a pinch of salt to the boil. Once the water is boiling, add the rooster, reduce the heat to medium and cook for 10 minutes, or until it is soft and partially cooked. Do not overcook. Remove the rooster from the pan and set the cooking liquid aside. You will need about 1.1 litres/37 fl oz (4¼ cups).

Heat the olive oil in a large saucepan over a low heat, add the onion, garlic and bay leaf and cook for 10 minutes, or until the onion is translucent.

Add the rooster to the pan and mix until well combined. Add the sweet paprika and stir. Add the reserved cooking liquid and cook for 20 minutes, or until the rooster is completely cooked. Remove the meat from the pan and set aside.

Add the parsley and rice to the pan, stir and cook for 15 minutes, or until the rice is soft. Return the meat to the pan together with the blood, stir and cook for 5 minutes over a low heat. Taste and adjust the seasoning, adding a splash of lemon juice to finish before serving.

Carqueja Rice

Arroz de Carqueja ♡ Beira Alta

This is a typical dish from the Viseu area. The original recipe is made with chicken blood, but this can be left out, it just means there is less depth of flavour and it is a lighter colour. Carqueja or gorze is widely used in game and poultry dishes and it gives these dishes a unique flavour. Most recipes use a simple infusion, or it can just be added to the dish.

Preparation time: 20 minutes, plus 6 hours infusing
Cooking time: 1 hour
Serves: 4
🌿 ▢

1 large bunch *carqueja* or gorze
1 medium chicken, cut into small pieces
80 ml/2¾ fl oz (⅓ cup) olive oil
30 g/1 oz (2 tablespoons) lard (pork fat)
1 large onion, peeled and finely chopped
2 garlic cloves, peeled and finely chopped
1 bay leaf
2 large bunches flat-leaf parsley, halved
360 g/12¾ oz (1⅔ cups) short-grain rice
sea salt and freshly ground black pepper

Bring 1.2 litres/40 fl oz (5 cups) water to the boil in a large saucepan over a high heat. Remove from the heat, add the *carqueja*, cover with food wrap or a lid and leave to infuse for 6 hours.

If you can obtain some fresh chicken blood (drained when slaughtering), put it into a bowl and add 1 teaspoon white wine vinegar to prevent coagulation, then stir and set aside. If you don't have access to live poultry, the blood can be omitted.

Season the chicken pieces with salt and pepper and set aside.

Put the olive oil, lard (pork fat), onion, garlic, bay leaf and parsley into a large saucepan. Add the chicken pieces, cover with a lid and cook over a low heat for 10 minutes, or until the meat is soft. Add the rice, stir, then add 1 litre/34 fl oz (4¼ cups) of the infused water and bring to the boil. Reduce the heat to low and cook for 20 minutes, or until the rice is cooked. During cooking check to see how much liquid there is as it should be runny, so add a little more of the infused water, if necessary.

Taste and adjust the seasoning, if necessary, before serving.

Duck Rice from Braga

••

Arroz de Pato de Braga   ⛶ Minho

Mostly known as old duck rice (*Arroz de Pato à Antiga*), there are different versions throughout the country. Some use orange, like in my village, others are runnier without being toasted, while others use different meat, such as chicken. You can replace some of the charcuterie with local cured meat or whatever you can buy. At my house back home, Mum cooks this in a wood-fired oven, which gives the dish another layer of flavour.

Preparation time: 25 minutes
Cooking time: 1 hour 20 minutes
Serves: 6
🐷 ⛶

1 x 1.5-kg/3 lb 5-oz duck
1 pig's ear
80 ml/2¾ fl oz (⅓ cup) olive oil
2 small onions, peeled and finely chopped
2 garlic cloves, peeled and finely chopped
2 bunches flat-leaf parsley, finely chopped
600 ml/20 fl oz (2½ cups) white wine
100 g/3½ oz *salpicão* or *lomo*
90 g/3¼ oz chorizo
60 g/2¼ oz bacon
550 g/1 lb 4 oz (2¾ cups) long-grain rice
juice of 1 lemon
sea salt and freshly ground black pepper

Prepare the duck, removing any offal (variety meats) and blood left inside and removing any feathers. Clean the pig's ear by rinsing under cold running water. Cut the duck in half through the back and season with salt.

    Preheat the oven to 200°C/400°F/Gas Mark 6.

    Heat the olive oil in a saucepan over a medium heat, add the duck and cook for 5 minutes, or until it is browned all over. Remove from the pan and set aside. Add the onions, garlic and chopped parsley to the pan and cook for 15 minutes, or until the onions are soft and golden brown. Add the white wine, charcuterie, pig's ear and duck. Top up the pot with 3.5 litres/118 fl oz (14 cups) water, season with salt and pepper and cook over a medium heat for 30 minutes, or until the meat is soft. Keep checking on the meat during cooking and remove each piece as soon as it is ready.

    Once all the meat is cooked, shred the duck and cut the charcuterie into medium-thick disks. Cut the pig's ear into small pieces too. Set aside. Strain the stock through a sieve (fine-mesh strainer) into a jug (pitcher) and pour 1.3 litres/44 fl oz (5¼ cups) back into the pan. Bring to the boil, then add the rice, stir and reduce the heat to medium. Cook the rice for 25 minutes, or until soft. Add the shredded duck and stir. Taste and adjust the seasoning with salt, pepper and lemon juice.

    Transfer the duck rice to a large ovenproof dish, arrange the charcuterie and the pig's ear on top and crisp up in the oven for 10 minutes. Serve.

Wild Pigeon Rice

••

Arroz de Pombo Bravo   ⛶ Beira Baixa

Preparation time: 20 minutes
Cooking time: 50 minutes
Serves: 4
🐷 ⛶ ⛶

3 wild pigeons
80 ml/2¾ fl oz (⅓ cup) olive oil
1½ onions, peeled and finely chopped
4 garlic cloves, peeled and finely chopped
40 g/1½ oz lardo, cut into pieces
2 bay leaves
260 g/9 oz (1¼ cup) short-grain rice, preferably Carolino
2 bunches parsley, roughly chopped
sea salt

Prepare the pigeons, removing any remaining feathers and all the offal (variety meats), then rinse the insides under cold running water. Cut the pigeons into small pieces, watching out for any shot that might still be in the meat. Cut the heart and liver into small pieces and season them with salt.

    Heat the olive oil in a large saucepan over a low heat. Add the onions, garlic, lardo and pigeons with the offal. Cover with a lid and cook for 15 minutes, or until the onions and meat are soft. Add a splash of water if necessary to prevent it drying out during cooking. Add 800 ml/27 fl oz (3¼ cups) water and bring to the boil, then add the bay leaves and rice, reduce the heat to low and cook, stirring occasionally, for 30–35 minutes, or until the rice is soft. Taste and adjust the seasoning, if necessary. Scatter over the parsley before serving.

Pork Offal Rice

••

Arroz de Cachola   ⛶ Alentejo

Preparation time: 20 minutes
Cooking time: 45 minutes
Serves: 4
🐷 ⛶

180 g/6 oz lardo, sliced
1 onion, peeled and very finely chopped
2 garlic cloves, peeled and very finely chopped
1 bay leaf
2 cloves
5 white peppercorns
250 g/9 oz pork liver, cleaned and sliced into pieces
250 g/9 oz pork lungs
320 g/11¼ oz (1⅔ cups) long-grain rice
1 teaspoon ground cumin
35 ml/1¼ fl oz (2⅓ tablespoons) white wine vinegar
sea salt

Put the lardo into a large saucepan and cook over a medium heat for 10 minutes, or until coloured. Remove from the pan and set aside, then add the onion, garlic, bay leaf, cloves and peppercorns to the pan and cook for 15 minutes, or until the onion becomes golden. Add the pork liver, season with salt and stir to combine with the onions.

Heat 700 ml/23½ fl oz (2¾ cups) water in another large saucepan until warm. Pour over the liver, add the rice and cook over a medium heat for 10 minutes, or until the rice is cooked. Add the cumin and vinegar, then taste and adjust the seasoning, if necessary.

Serve, garnished with the slices of cooked lardo over the top.

The dish can be finished with some pork blood.

Beef, Chicken and Pork Rice with Blood and Cumin – Minho Style

••

Arroz de Sarrabulho   ⛌ Minho
à Moda do Minho
– Ponte de Lima

This dish has its origins in Ponte de Lima, a city in the north of Portugal in the Minho region and is one of the most emblematic dishes from this region. The combination of chicken, pork and beef with the fragrance of cumin and finished with pork blood makes it unique in taste, as most recipes only include pork offal (variety meats).

Preparation time: 15 minutes
Cooking time: 1 hour 40 minutes
Serves: 6
🌾 ⛌

120 g/4 oz chorizo
350 g/12 oz beef topside (top round)
450 g/1 lb trimmed pork ribs
300 g/11 oz chicken, thighs and breast
550 g/1 lb 4 oz pork bones from the loin
nutmeg, for grating
2 bay leaves
450 g/1 lb (2 cups) short-grain rice
1½ teaspoons ground cumin
2 cloves
juice of 1 lemon
150 ml/5 fl oz (⅔ cup) fresh pork blood mixed
    with 1 teaspoon white wine vinegar
sea salt and freshly ground black pepper

Put all the meat and bones into a large saucepan and add 4.5 litres/152 fl oz (18 cups) water. Grate in a little nutmeg, season with salt and pepper then cook over a low heat for 1 hour 15 minutes, or until all the meat is soft. During cooking, skim off the foam that rises to the top with a slotted spoon and keep checking the meat, removing each piece as soon as it is ready. Once all the meat is cooked, shred it from the bones and set aside. Reserve 1.4 litres/47 fl oz (5⅔ cups) of the cooking liquid, topping up with water if there is not enough.

Remove any fat that may be sitting on the top of the stock.

Pour the stock into a clean, large saucepan and bring to the boil over a medium heat. Once it starts boiling, reduce the heat to low and add the bay leaves and rice. Cook for 10 minutes, then add all the shredded meat to the pan, stir and finish cooking the rice for 15 minutes, or until soft. Season with the cumin, cloves and lemon juice and serve.

Oven-baked Rice with Serrano Ham

••

Arroz de Forno   ⛌ Minho

This is the basic recipe but you can add other ingredients to it, such as different charcuterie or other meats, and chicken stock can be replaced with beef stock, if you prefer.

Preparation time: 20 minutes
Cooking time: 1 hour 40 minutes
Serves: 4
🌾 ⛌

1 teaspoon saffron threads
60 ml/2 fl oz (4 tablespoons) olive oil
2 onions, peeled and cut into chunks
150 g/5 oz Serrano ham
½ chorizo
2 bunches flat-leaf parsley, coarsely chopped
360 g/12¾ oz (1¾ cups) long-grain rice

For the stock:
400 g/14 oz chicken bones
1 onion, peeled but left whole
1 garlic clove, peeled but left whole

Start by making a light chicken stock. Put the chicken bones and onion into a saucepan, add the garlic and 1.5 litres/50 fl oz (6¼ cups) water and cook over a medium heat for 40 minutes, skimming off the foam that rises to the top during cooking with a slotted spoon. Strain the stock and discard the bones. Set about 1 litre/34 fl oz (4¼ cups) of the stock aside.

Preheat the oven to 160°C/325°F/Gas Mark 3.

Wrap the saffron in foil and toast in the oven for 5 minutes.

Heat the olive oil in a medium ovenproof saucepan or casserole dish (Dutch oven) over a low heat, add the onions and cook for 15 minutes, or they are golden brown. Add the ham, chorizo and parsley, stir, then add the reserved chicken stock and cook for 10 minutes over a medium heat to release the flavour from the meat. Remove the meat from the pan and set aside. Add the saffron to the pan and bring to the boil. Once it starts boiling, add the rice. Cover with a lid and bake in the oven for 25 minutes, or until the rice is soft. About 5 minutes before the rice is ready, remove the lid to toast the top. Serve the rice with the meat.

Pork Offal Rice Stew with Pig's Blood

••

Arroz de Golada com Sangue ♡ **Lisbon**

Preparation time: 50 minutes
Cooking time: 2 hours
Serves: 5
🌿 ⬜

100 g/3½ oz pig's heart
100 g/3½ oz pig's tongue
250 g/9 oz trimmed pork ribs
100 g/3½ oz pig's lungs
100 g/3½ oz pork sweetbreads
1 pork neck bone
160 g/5¾ oz chicken thighs or legs
150 g/5 oz flat-iron steak
1 chorizo
2 cloves
80 ml/2¾ fl oz (⅓ cup) olive oil
2 onions, peeled and very finely chopped, keep the skins
1 bay leaf
⅓ bunch flat-leaf parsley, roughly chopped
650 g/1 lb 7 oz (3 cups) short-grain rice
160 ml/5½ fl oz (⅔ cup) pig's blood
sea salt and freshly ground black pepper

Prepare all the meats, removing any excess fat from the heart, scraping the tongue with a sharp knife and washing it under cold running water. Poke the chorizo with the tip of the knife so it releases more flavour during cooking.

Put all the meats into a large saucepan, season with salt, add the cloves, the onion skins and pepper. Cover generously with water as the meat will be cooked for a long time, and cook over a medium heat for 1 hour 20 minutes, or until all the meat is cooked. Some of the meats will cook faster than others, such as the lungs, sweetbreads and chicken so remove them as soon as they are cooked and transfer them to a large plate and set aside. Keep skimming off the foam that rises to the top with a slotted spoon.

Once all the meat is cooked, using tongs or a fish slice (spatula), remove them from the pan to a large plate and set aside. Line a sieve (fine-mesh strainer) with muslin (cheesecloth) and strain the cooking water through it into a large bowl. You should have about 2 litres/68 fl oz (8½ cups) cooking water.

Heat the olive oil in a large saucepan over a low heat, add the onions, bay leaves and parsley, stir and cook for 10 minutes, or until the onions are translucent. Add the meat cooking water and bring to the boil.

Meanwhile, shred the steak, chicken, pork ribs and neck bone, removing the bones. Cut the lung, heart, tongue, sweetbread and chorizo into small pieces.

Once the cooking water is boiling, add the rice, reduce the heat to medium and cook for 15 minutes. Add the pig's blood, stir and cook for a further 10 minutes, or until the rice is soft, creamy, loose and not dry. Add the shredded meat, then season with salt and pepper.

Put the rice into a large serving dish and arrange the sliced offal (variety meats) pieces over the rice to serve.

Roasted Kid Rice

••

Arroz de Cabrito ♡ **Ribatejo**
– Santarem 📷 p.289

Preparation time: 30 minutes, plus 4 hours standing
Cooking time: 1 hour 40 minutes
Serves: 10
🌿 ⬜

1.6 kg/3 lb 8 oz kid goat meat
300 ml/10 fl oz (1¼ cups) white wine
1 teaspoon ground white pepper
120 ml/4 fl oz (½ cup) olive oil
1 bunch flat-leaf parsley, roughly chopped
5 small onions, 3 peeled and halved, 1 peeled and sliced
  into small pieces and 1 peeled and chopped
1 kg/2 lb 4 oz chicken
65 g/2¼ oz rendered beef fat
550 g/1 lb 4 oz (2½ cups) short-grain rice
juice of 2 lemons
sea salt

Cut the kid goat into small pieces, then arrange the meat on a large baking sheet, season with the white wine, pepper, olive oil, salt, parsley and the onion sliced into small pieces, and toss everything on the meat. Cover with food wrap and leave in the fridge for 4 hours to absorb the flavours.

Meanwhile, cut the chicken into small pieces and put them into a large saucepan. Cover with cold water, add the halved onions and a pinch of salt and cook over a medium heat, skimming off the foam that rises to the top with a slotted spoon, for 1 hour, or until the chicken is cooked. Remove the chicken from the pan with a slotted spoon and set aside for use in other recipes. Strain the stock through a sieve (fine-mesh strainer) into a large bowl or jug (pitcher) and set aside.

Preheat the oven to 180°C/350°F/Gas Mark 4.

Put the remaining onions and the beef fat into a large ovenproof saucepan or casserole dish (Dutch oven) over a medium heat and cook for 5 minutes, or until the onions are soft but with no colour. Add the rice and stir for 2 minutes, then add enough of the chicken stock to cook the rice. Bring to the boil, then finish cooking in the oven for 15 minutes, or until the rice is soft but still has a bit of a bite. Spoon the rice into a large roasting pan and spread it out until it covers the bottom of the pan. Add 1 ladleful of the remaining chicken stock, stir, then place a wire rack over the roasting pan and arrange the kid on the rack. Bake for 20 minutes, or until the meat is golden brown. All the juices will fall into the rice during cooking. Squeeze over the lemon juice before serving.

Roasted Kid Rice

Rice Black Pudding

Morcelas de Arroz   ♡ Leiria

This recipe has been passed down through three generations of my family. In the Leiria region, blood sausage with rice is very popular and one of the most famous recipes is from a small town called Mira de Aire. Sadly, these old recipes are now being forgotten, so this is my version.

Preparation time: 30 minutes
Cooking time: 2 hours
Serves: 10
🔥 ▢

1 teaspoon ground cumin
1 teaspoon fine table salt
1 teaspoon wild fennel tops, finely chopped
1 teaspoon ground cloves
½ bunch parsley, very finely chopped
2 large onions, peeled and very finely chopped
1.5 kg/3 lb 5 oz lean pork meat, finely diced
400 g/14 oz crepinette, finely diced
2 kg/4 lb 8 oz (9 cups) short-grain rice
1.2 litres/40 fl oz (5 cups) fresh pig's blood
1.5 kg/3 lb 5 oz fresh pork tripe (stomach lining)
120 ml/4 fl oz (½ cup) olive oil (optional)
sea salt

Put all the spices and parsley into a small bowl and stir until combined. Set aside.

In a large saucepan, bring 2 litres/68 fl oz (8½ cups) salted water to the boil. Add the onions and cook for 5 minutes, then, add the meat and crepinette and cook over a medium heat for 25 minutes, or until the meat is cooked. Add the rice, reduce the heat to low and cook for about 10 minutes, or until al dente, but not totally cooked at this point. Remove the rice and meat mixture from the pan and pour into a large bowl. Add the mixed spices and parsley, then add the blood, stirring with a wooden spoon as you pour so the blood doesn't curdle. Adjust the seasoning, if necessary.

Cut the tripe (stomach lining) into 25-cm/10-inch pieces. This depends on personal taste as you can use different sizes of the pork tripe. Use some butcher's string or kitchen twine to tie up one end of the tripe pieces then, using a funnel that fits into the tripe pieces, start to fill the tripe and tie the ends to seal. Don't fill them up too much as they may burst while cooking. Stir the filling after each piece of tripe is filled as you want a mixture of meat and rice.

Bring a large, deep saucepan of water to the boil, add a pinch of salt, then reduce the heat and, once it is simmering, add the filled tripe and cook for 1 hour 20 minutes, or until the skin is easily poked with a toothpick. Make sure the water is simmering and not boiling. Using a slotted spoon, transfer to a serving plate and leave to rest before eating. You can grill (broil) or pan-fry them in olive oil afterwards or eat as they are, hot or cold.

Turnip Tops Rice

Arroz de Grelos   ♡ Lisbon

Grelos is a term that refers to the stems of cruciferous plants in which the flower will open, but only turnip tops are exclusively called *grelos*. These leafy greens have a light, bitter taste (although leaving the leafy parts of the vegetable intact during cooking, and the florets in particular, reduces the bitterness caused when the *grelos* are cut or chewed). When mixed with a creamy rice, they create a perfect side dish to cut through rich, fatty sausages, such as *alheira* (page 429) or *morcela*, or pastries, such as *Pastéis de Massa Tenra* (page 293) or *Rissóis* (page 246).

Preparation time: 15 minutes
Cooking time: 35 minutes
Serves: 4
🔥 ⌀ ▢

1½ onions, peeled and very finely chopped
2 garlic cloves, peeled and very finely chopped
60 ml/2 fl oz (4 tablespoons) olive oil, plus extra
    for drizzling
30 g/1 oz (2 tablespoons) butter
650 g/1 lb 7 oz turnip tops, bottom stalks removed
    and cut into small pieces
300 g/11 oz (1½ cups) long-grain rice
sea salt and freshly ground black pepper

Put the onions and garlic into a saucepan, mix together, then add the olive oil and butter. Cook over a low heat for 10 minutes, or until the onions are translucent. Add the turnip tops and cook for a further 5 minutes, until soft. Season with salt and pepper, then add 850 ml/28¾ fl oz (3½ cups) water and bring to the boil. Add the rice, reduce the heat to medium and cook for about 15 minutes, depending on the rice.

Once the rice is cooked, remove from the heat and leave to rest for 5 minutes before drizzling some olive oil over the top and serving.

Wild Radish Rice

••

Arroz de Saramagos   ⛉ **Beira Baixa**

The wild radishes can be replaced by turnip tops or mustard leaves, if you prefer.

Preparation time: 15 minutes
Cooking time: 30 minutes
Serves: 4
🌱 ◻ ⌀ ∨ ◻

50 ml/1⅔ fl oz (3½ tablespoons) olive oil, plus extra
    for drizzling
1 large onion, peeled and finely chopped
3 garlic cloves, peeled and finely chopped
1 bay leaf
350 g/12 oz wild radishes with stems, cut into chunks
250 g/9 oz (1 cup) short-grain rice, preferably Carolino
sea salt

Heat the olive oil in a large saucepan over a low heat, add the onion, garlic and bay leaf and cook for 10 minutes, or until the onion is translucent and soft.

Add 800 ml/27 fl oz (3¼ cups) water and a pinch of salt to the pan and bring to the boil. Add the radishes and cook for 2 minutes, then add the rice, reduce the heat to low and cook for 15 minutes, or until the rice is soft. Drizzle with olive oil before serving.

Rice with Chickpeas

••

Arroz de Grão   ⛉ **Trás-os-Montes
                                    e Alto Douro**

Preparation time: 15 minutes, plus 12 hours soaking
Cooking time: 1 hour
Serves: 4
🌱

400 g/14 oz (2¼ cups) dried chickpeas (garbanzos)
60 ml/2 fl oz (4 tablespoons) olive oil
50 g/2 oz (½ stick) butter
1 onion, peeled and finely chopped
1 garlic clove, peeled and finely chopped
100 g/3½ oz ham, cut into small squares
300 g/11 oz (1⅓ cups) short-grain rice,
    preferably Carolino
sea salt

Put the chickpeas (garbanzos) into a large bowl of cold water and leave to soak for 12 hours.

The next day, drain the chickpeas, put into a medium saucepan, pour in about 2 litres/68 fl oz (8½ cups) water and cook over a medium heat for 30 minutes, or until soft. Remove the pan from the heat and set aside, keeping the chickpeas in the cooking liquid. You will need about 1.3 litres/ 44 fl oz (5¼ cups).

Melt the olive oil and butter in another saucepan. Add the onion and garlic and cook over a low heat for 15 minutes, or until the onion is golden. Add the ham and then the rice and stir to combine. Pour in 1.3 litres/44 fl oz (5¼ cups) chickpea cooking liquid. Bring to the boil, then reduce the heat to medium and cook for 15 minutes, or until the rice is soft.

Just before the rice is cooked, add the chickpeas and gently stir to combine but not break them up. Leave the chickpeas to warm through and the rice to finish cooking. Taste and adjust the seasoning, if necessary, with salt and before serving.

Red Bean Rice

••

Arroz de Feijão Vermelho   ⛉ **Leiria**

This is one of those dishes that can easily be found in restaurants that offer quick and more affordable meals. It is usually garnished with grilled (broiled) thin strips of pork belly seasoned with salt and a splash of vinegar.

Preparation time: 15 minutes, plus 12 hours soaking
Cooking time: 1 hour
Serves: 4
🌱 ◻ ⌀ ∨

350 g/12 oz (2 cups) dried red beans
80 ml/2¾ fl oz (⅓ cup) olive oil, plus extra for drizzling
1 onion, peeled and chopped
1 garlic clove, peeled and chopped
400 g/14 oz (2 cups) long-grain rice
sea salt and freshly ground black pepper

Put the beans into a large bowl of cold water and leave to soak for 12 hours.

The next day, drain the beans and put them into a large saucepan. Pour in enough cold water to cover, add a pinch of salt and cook over a medium heat for 30 minutes, or until soft. Drain and set aside, reserving the cooking liquid. You will need about 1.2 litres/40 fl oz (5 cups).

Heat the olive oil in a large saucepan over a low heat. Add the onion and garlic, and cook for 10 minutes, or until the onion is translucent. Add the rice, mix well and cook for 5 minutes, then add the reserved bean cooking liquid and increase the heat to medium. Season with a pinch of salt and pepper and cook for about 12 minutes, or until soft.

Just before the rice is cooked, add the beans and gently stir to combine but not break them up. Once the rice is cooked, remove from the heat and drizzle with olive oil before serving.

'Man on Horseback' Mushroom Rice

Arroz de Míscaros ⛉ Beira Alta

'Man on horseback' mushrooms are very popular across Portugal when in season and are added to everything from rice to eggs and stews. Be very careful when foraging mushrooms: never pick any mushrooms that you aren't certain are safe to eat.

Preparation time: 15 minutes
Cooking time: 40 minutes
Serves: 4
🌿 ⊘ ⛉

80 ml/2¾ fl oz (⅓ cup) olive oil
2 small onions, peeled and finely chopped
2 garlic cloves, peeled and finely chopped
2 bunches flat-leaf parsley, finely chopped
1 red chilli, finely chopped
30 g/1 oz (2 tablespoons) unsalted butter
450 g/1 lb *míscaros* (man on horseback) mushrooms, or any other wild meaty mushrooms
250 ml/8 fl oz (1 cup) red wine
330 g/11½ oz (1⅔ cups) long-grain rice
sea salt and freshly ground black pepper

Put the olive oil, onions, garlic, parsley, chilli and butter into a saucepan and cook over a low heat for 15 minutes, or until the onions are golden.

Clean the mushrooms with a damp cloth. Cut them into chunks, add to the pan and cook for 5 minutes, or until soft. Add the red wine and cook gently until the wine has reduced by half.

Add 850 ml/28½ fl oz (3½ cups) water or use vegetable stock and bring to the boil over a medium heat. Add the rice, season with salt, then stir and cook for 15 minutes, or until the rice is cooked. During cooking check to see how much liquid there is as it should be runny, so add a little more water, if necessary. Taste and adjust the seasoning, if needed, with pepper before serving.

Chestnut Porridge

Caldudo — Idanha-a-Nova ⛉ Beira Baixa

Chestnut trees are more common in the north of Portugal than in the region of Idanha-a-Nova, but it is thanks to the Oleiros and Carters — who travelled north in the 1960s, trading pottery and oranges in exchange for chestnuts — that this soupy rice dish is found there. While it's not often made any more, the memory survives among elders.

Preparation time: 15 minutes
Cooking time: 45 minutes
Serves: 4
🌿 ⊘ ⛉

200 g/7 oz chestnuts, peeled
1 litre/34 fl oz (4¼ cups) whole (full-fat) milk
200 g/7 oz (1 cup) unrefined or caster (superfine) sugar
60 g/2¼ oz (⅓ cup) long-grain rice
1 teaspoon ground cinnamon
sea salt

The day before, prepare the chestnuts. The next day, put the chestnuts into a large saucepan, cover with water, add a pinch of salt and bring to the boil. Once the chestnuts start to break down, add the milk and sugar and stir. Reduce the heat to low and cook for 25 minutes, or until fully cooked.

Add the rice to the pan and cook for a further 15 minutes until the rice is soft with a light, creamy consistency. Add the cinnamon, then remove from the heat and mash everything together with a fork before serving.

Chestnut Rice

Arroz de Castanhas ⛉ Minho

Preparation time: 15 minutes
Cooking time: 1 hour 15 minutes
Serves: 4
🌿 ⛉

400 g/14 oz chicken bones or any other meat bones
1 carrot, peeled but left whole
2 onions, 1 peeled and halved, 1 peeled and finely chopped
4 garlic cloves, 2 peeled and left whole, 2 peeled and finely chopped
85 ml/2¾ fl oz (⅓ cup) olive oil
280 g/10 oz (2 cups) peeled chestnuts, quartered
330 g/11¾ oz (1⅔ cups) long-grain rice (or use short-grain rice)
sea salt and freshly ground black pepper

Put the chicken bones, carrot, halved onion, 2 whole garlic cloves and 2.5 litres/85 fl oz (10 cups) water into a large saucepan and cook over a low heat for 45 minutes, skimming off the foam that rises to the top with a slotted spoon. Strain the stock through a sieve (fine-mesh strainer) into a large heatproof bowl or jug (pitcher) and discard the bones and vegetables. You will need about 1 litre/34 fl oz (4¼ cups) stock.

Heat the olive oil in a medium saucepan over a low heat, add the finely chopped onion and garlic and cook for 15 minutes, or until the onion is golden. Add the chestnuts, stir, season with salt and pepper, then add the rice and cook gently for 5 minutes, stirring frequently. Add the hot stock, increase the heat to medium and cook for a further 5–7 minutes until the rice is soft.

Taste and adjust the seasoning, if necessary, with salt and pepper before serving.

Soft Dough

Massa Tenra   ♡ **Lisbon**

This base recipe can be used in both savoury and sweet recipes and can be made into pastries, which are baked or fried with different fillings.

Preparation time: 20 minutes
Makes: 400 g
✕ ⊠

350 g/12 oz (3 cups) plain (all-purpose) flour
15 g/½ oz (1 tablespoon) unsalted butter
20 g/¾ oz lard (pork fat)
sea salt

Put the flour into a large bowl, add the butter and lard (pork fat) and mix them into the flour until well incorporated.
    Pour 210 ml/7 fl oz (¾ cup) water into a jug (pitcher) and season with a pinch of salt. Gradually stir the water into the flour and mix well to form a dough. Tip the dough out onto a work counter and knead until smooth. Use as directed in the recipe.

Easter Cakes from Guarda

Bolo Folar da Guarda   ♡ **Beira Alta**

As in many regions of Portugal, Easter cakes were very important and used to be offered to kids as a present from their godparents.

Preparation time: 15 minutes, plus 15 minutes standing and 3 hours 30 minutes rising
Cooking time: 35–40 minutes
Makes: 3
◻ ∅

25 g/1 oz (2 tablespoons) fresh yeast or 7 g/¼ oz
    (2¼ teaspoons) instant dried yeast
800 g/1 lb 12 oz (6⅔ cups) spelt flour, plus extra for dusting
5 g/⅛ oz (1 teaspoon) sea salt
65 ml/2¼ fl oz (¼ cup) olive oil, plus extra for brushing
8 eggs
30 ml/1 fl oz (2 tablespoons) firewater

Put the yeast into a bowl, add a small amount of lukewarm water and stir until dissolved. Leave to stand at room temperature for 15 minutes.
    Put the flour and salt into a bowl. Heat the olive oil in a saucepan over a medium heat until it reaches 120°C/248°F on a thermometer. Stir the hot oil into the flour. Add the yeast mixture and stir well to combine, then add the eggs and mix until a smooth dough forms. Pour over the firewater and knead to a smooth, elastic dough. Cover the bowl with food wrap and leave to rise at room temperature for 1 hour 30 minutes, or until doubled in size.
    Turn the dough out onto a floured work counter and cut it into 3 equal pieces. Stretch each piece

of dough into a rectangle, about 25 x 15 cm/ 10 x 6 inches. Brush each with some olive oil, then fold one side over onto the other side and brush with oil. Repeat with all the pieces. Cover with a tea (dish) towel and leave to prove at room temperature for 2 hours, or until doubled in size.
    Preheat the oven to 200°C/400°F/Gas Mark 6.
    Arrange the dough on a baking sheet and bake for 35–40 minutes, or until golden all over and a toothpick inserted into the middle comes out clean. Leave to cool on a wire rack before serving.

Savoury Salt Cod Cake

Bola de Bacalhau   ♡ **Trás-os-Montes**
de Lamego   **e Alto Douro**

Preparation time: 25 minutes, plus 45 minutes rising
Cooking time: 1 hour
Makes: 1

70 ml/2¼ fl oz (4⅔ tablespoons) olive oil,
    plus extra for oiling and brushing
2 onions, peeled and chopped into small pieces
250 g/9 oz salt cod, desalted (page 40), bones removed
60 ml/2 fl oz (4 tablespoons) whole (full-fat) milk
12 g/½ oz (2½ teaspoons) fresh yeast or 3 g/⅛ oz
    (1 teaspoon) instant dried yeast
140 g/5 oz (1¼ sticks) unsalted butter
3 whole eggs
400 g/14 oz (3⅓ cups) plain (all-purpose) flour
sea salt

Grease a 25 x 30-cm/10 x 12-inch baking sheet with olive oil.
    Heat the olive oil in a saucepan over a low heat, add the onions and cook for 10 minutes, or until translucent. Flake the cod flesh into the onions and mix together. Cook for a further 6 minutes, then remove the pan from the heat and set aside.
    Heat the milk in a saucepan over a low heat until warm (no hotter than 32°C/90°F or the yeast won't activate). Pour the milk into a bowl, add the yeast and stir until dissolved. Set aside for 5 minutes.
    Put the butter into a saucepan and heat over a low heat until melted.
    Put the eggs into a large bowl and whisk lightly, then add the milk and yeast mixture and the melted butter and mix together well. Add the flour with a pinch of salt and mix until a dough forms.
    Tip the dough onto a lightly floured work counter and knead until smooth. It will be sticky at first but once kneaded it will be fine. Transfer the dough to the prepared baking sheet and leave to rise in a warm place for 45 minutes.
    Preheat the oven to 190°C/375°F/Gas Mark 5.
    Divide the dough in half and stretch one half over the baking sheet, then add the cod mixture in a single layer. Cover with the remaining stretched-out dough. Brush oil over the top, then bake for 35 minutes, or until a toothpick is inserted into the middle of the cake comes out clean. Leave to cool on a wire rack before serving.

Savoury Cake Stuffed with Sardines

Bola de Sardinhas   ♡ Trás-os-Montes e Alto Douro

I also like this cake made with ordinary bread dough instead of the cornbread one, as it is less dense. There are two ways of making this cake. If using the cornbread dough, divide it into two 'flatbreads', about 2 cm/¾ inch thick, then layer the onions on top then the sardines and bake. However, if using the bread dough, stretch out half of the dough over a baking sheet, then put the sardines on top with the onions and cover with the remaining dough, before leaving to rise at room temperature for 2 hours and then baking.

Preparation time: 25 minutes, plus 2 hours rising (optional)
Cooking time: 45 minutes
Makes: 1
◻ ✂

600 g/1 lb 5 oz sardines
1 onion, peeled, halved and thinly sliced into half moons
100 ml/3½ fl oz (⅓ cup) olive oil
1 kg/2 lb 4 oz Cornbread dough (page 32) or bread dough
sea salt and freshly ground black pepper

Clean the fish, removing the scales. Make an incision in the belly with a sharp knife and remove the guts, then rinse under cold running water. Season the sardines with salt and pepper. Set aside.
　　Put the onion into a medium bowl with the olive oil, season with salt and pepper and mix together.
　　If using the Cornbread dough, divide it into two 'flatbreads', about 2 cm/¾ inch thick, then place them on a large baking sheet and add a layer of onions on the top of each. Arrange the sardines over the top of the onions.
　　If using the bread dough, stretch out half of the dough over a large baking sheet, then arrange the sardines and onions in a layer on top and cover with the remaining dough. Leave to rise at room temperature for 2 hours.
　　Preheat the oven to 220°C/425°F/Gas Mark 7.
　　Bake for 45 minutes, or until the bread is cooked. The cornbread will be lightly crusted on the sides. Serve.

Savoury Cake Stuffed with Ham

Bola de Lamego   ♡ Trás-os-Montes e Alto Douro

Personally, I enjoy eating this savoury cake at breakfast. I lightly toast it in the oven then spread over a layer of good-quality butter. It also makes a good starter (appetiser) before any meal or simply as a snack.

Preparation time: 15 minutes, plus 20 minutes rising and 5 minutes resting
Cooking time: 35 minutes
Makes: 1

140 g/5 oz (1¼ sticks) unsalted butter, plus extra for greasing
60 ml/2 fl oz (4 tablespoons) whole (full-fat) milk
12 g/½ oz (2½ teaspoons) fresh yeast or 3 g/⅛ oz (1 teaspoon) instant dried yeast
3 eggs
400 g/14 oz (3⅓ cups) plain (all-purpose) flour
1 teaspoon caster (superfine) sugar
350 g/12 oz Serrano ham or ham of your choice, cut into thin pieces
1 egg yolk, for brushing
sea salt

Grease a 25 x 30-cm/10 x 12-inch baking sheet with butter.
　　Heat the milk in a small saucepan over a low heat until warm (the milk should be no more than 32°C/90°F, otherwise the yeast won't activate), then pour into a small bowl, add the yeast and stir until dissolved. Set aside for 5 minutes.
　　Put the butter into a saucepan and heat over a low heat until melted.
　　Put the eggs into a large bowl and whisk lightly, then add the milk and yeast mixture and the melted butter and mix together well. Add the flour and sugar with a pinch of salt and mix until a smooth dough forms. Add the ham, then knead until it is fully incorporated. Put the dough onto the prepared baking sheet, cover with a clean tea (dish) towel and leave to rise in a warm place for 20 minutes.
　　Preheat the oven to 190°C/375°F/Gas Mark 5.
　　Put the egg yolk into a small bowl, whisk lightly, then brush over the top of the dough. Bake for 35 minutes, or until a toothpick or skewer is inserted into the middle of the cake comes out clean. Leave to cool on a wire rack before serving.

Savoury Cake Stuffed with Charcuterie and Chicken

Folar de Carnes Transmontano

♡ Trás-os-Montes e Alto Douro

Also known as *Folar de Valpaços* or *Folar de Chaves*, this stuffed bread is usually made in the northeast region of Trás-os-Montes. Its shape, content and preparation vary from village to village, and even between families: it can be round or rectangular; filled with chicken or veal; fluffy or compact. But all recipes include *presunto* (ham), as well as different types of sliced pork sausages, such as *chouriço*, *salpicão* (salami) and *linguiça* (spicy sausage). Historically, *folar* was baked by godparents so they could offer it to their godchildren as an Easter gift.

Preparation time: 1 hour, plus 4 hours rising and 5 minutes resting
Cooking time: 1 hour
Makes: 1

For the dough:
420 ml/14¼ fl oz (1⅔ cups) whole (full-fat) milk
30 g/1 oz (2 tablespoons) fresh yeast or 7 g/¼ oz (2¼ teaspoons) instant dried yeast
55 g/2 oz (3⅔ tablespoons) butter
40 g/1½ oz (¼ cup) lard (pork fat)
450 g/1 lb (3¾ cups) plain (all-purpose) flour, plus extra for dusting
5 eggs

For the chicken:
½ medium chicken, jointed into pieces
1 onion, peeled and finely chopped
2 garlic cloves, peeled and finely chopped
60 g/2¼ oz (½ stick) butter
50 g/2 oz (¼ cup) lard (pork fat)
sea salt and freshly ground black pepper

For the filling:
80 g/3 oz ham, cut into small thin pieces
90 g/3¼ oz chorizo, skinned and cut into thin pieces
80 g/3 oz *salpicão* or use lomo or similar, skinned and cut into thin pieces
50 ml/1⅔ fl oz (3½ tablespoons) olive oil, plus extra for oiling
1 egg yolk, for brushing

Put the chicken into a large bowl and season with salt and and pepper. Set aside.

Put the onion and garlic into a saucepan with the butter and lard (pork fat) and cook over a low heat for 15 minutes, or until the onion is golden. Add the chicken pieces, stir, then cover with a lid and cook for 10 minutes over a low heat. Add 120 ml/4 fl oz (½ cup) water and cook for a further 20 minutes, adding a little more water if the pan is getting dry, or until the chicken is cooked through.

Remove the pan from the heat and leave to cool. Remove the chicken from the pan, then take the meat off the bones and shred into pieces, not too small though. Set aside.

Strain the chicken cooking liquid into a bowl and set aside.

For the dough, heat the milk in a medium saucepan over a low heat until warm (the milk should be no more than 32°C/90°F, otherwise the yeast won't activate), then pour into a medium heatproof bowl, add the yeast and stir until dissolved. Set aside for 5 minutes.

Heat the butter and lard in two separate saucepans over a low heat until melted.

Dust a large bowl with flour and set aside. Put the flour and a pinch of salt into another large bowl. Add the eggs, melted butter, pork fat and the milk and yeast mixture and mix well for 10 minutes until a dough forms. Knead to a smooth dough, then put the dough into the floured bowl, cover with a clean tea (dish) towel and leave to rise for 3 hours, or until doubled in size.

Mix all the charcuterie meat together in a bowl.

Once the dough has risen, add the shredded chicken, charcuterie meat and 2 tablespoons of the reserved chicken cooking liquid to the dough and knead it in until the dough has a smooth consistency.

Oil a round cake tin, 28 cm/11 inch diameter and 10 cm/4 inches high with olive oil and place the dough inside. Cover with a clean tea (dish) towel and leave to prove for 1 hour.

Preheat the oven to 180°C/350°F/Gas Mark 4.

Put the egg yolk into a small bowl, whisk lightly, then brush over the top of the dough. Bake for 40 minutes, or until golden brown on top and a toothpick or skewer inserted into the middle of the cake comes out clean. Remove from the pan and leave to cool on a wire rack. Serve.

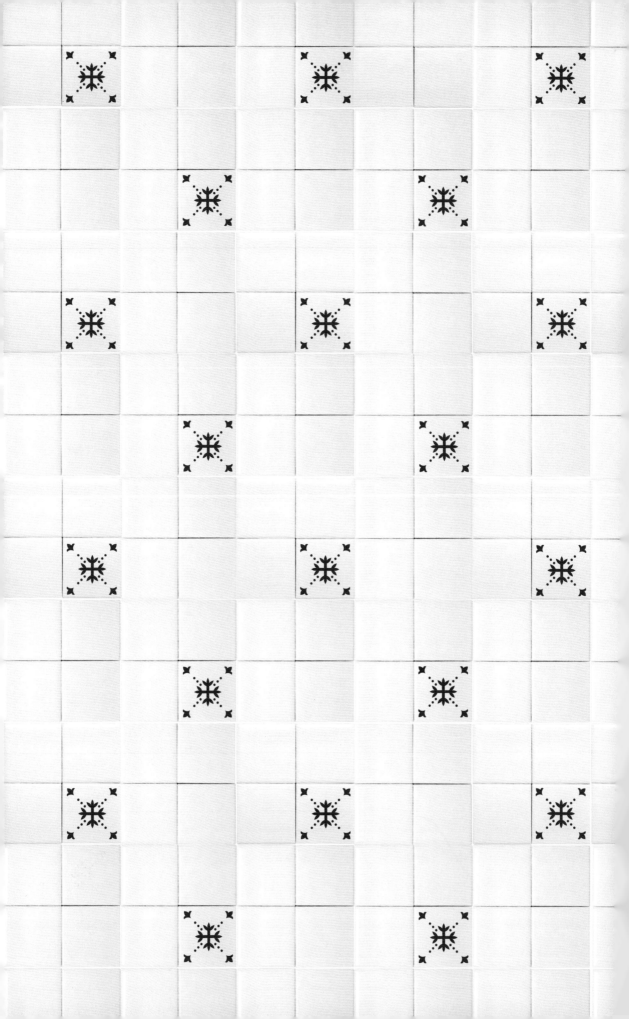

DESSERTS

Egg Flan

•••

Pudim Flan   ⋃ Lisbon

Flan adorns the dessert displays of almost every
family-run restaurant in Portugal, either baked
in large moulds with fluted edges, or in small,
individual pudding basins. Very similar to the
French crème caramel, *Pudim Flan* has a creamy
texture and mild flavour, with the caramel lending
it its sweetness and depth. There are variations
of the recipe that can include orange or lemon
zest, cinnamon or port.

Preparation time: 20 minutes, plus 15 minutes resting
Cooking time: 45 minutes
Serves: 6–8
🥄 🖉 ✕

380 g/13½ oz (2 cups minus 4 teaspoons) caster
    (superfine) sugar
zest of 1 lemon
11 eggs
1 litre/34 fl oz (4¼ cups) whole (full-fat) milk
15 g/½ oz (1 tablespoon) cornflour (cornstarch)

Preheat oven to 180°C/350°F/Gas Mark 4.
    To make the caramel, put 180 g/6 oz (1 cup
minus 4 teaspoons) of the sugar into a small
saucepan and heat over a low heat until the sugar
crystals have dissolved and turned dark brown.
Do not stir the sugar but tilt the pan to swirl the
caramel, if needed. Once the sugar has dissolved,
add 3 tablespoons water and cook over a medium
heat for 5 minutes. Set aside.
    Put the remaining 200 g/7½ oz (1 cup) sugar,
lemon zest, eggs and milk into a large bowl and
mix with a balloon whisk until well combined. Add
the cornflour (cornstarch) and mix until combined.
Leave the mixture to rest for 15 minutes to release
the air bubbles, then add the caramel.
    Pour the mixture into a 28-cm/11-inch ring cake
pan or savarin mould with a hole in the middle.
    Bake in the hot oven for 25 minutes. Remove
from the oven then leave to cool completely in the
cake pan. Once cold, carefully turn out the flan from
the cake pan onto a plate. Keep refrigerated until
ready to serve.

Egg and Bacon Flan

•••

Pudim do Abade   ⋃ Minho
de Priscos   📷 p.299

This large, velvety, caramel-coloured egg-yolk
pudding's main characteristic is that it includes
fresh lard (pork fat) in its preparation. It is baked
in a bain-marie in the oven, in a traditional mould
with the outside ridges coated in caramel. Its
creator, the abbot (*abade*) of Priscos village in
Braga for 40 years, was a notable 19th-century
cook who prepared sumptuous and grand
banquets for the kings of Portugal. These days,
Pudim do Abade de Priscos (Abbot of Priscos
Pudding) is served as a dessert in a handful of
restaurants in Portugal, where its original recipe
is still respected, and is the symbol of the village
of Priscos' flag.

Preparation time: 20 minutes
Cooking time: 45 minutes
Serves: 6–8
🥄 🏳

320 g/11¼ oz (1⅔ cups) caster (superfine) sugar,
    plus an extra 230 g/8 oz (1 cup plus 2 tablespoons)
    for the dry caramel
1 cinnamon stick
pared rind of 1 lemon
50 g/2 oz lard (pork fat), sliced into small pieces
12 egg yolks
50 ml/1⅔ fl oz (3½ tablespoons) red port

Preheat the oven to 200°C/400°F/Gas Mark 6.
    Put the 320 g/11¼ oz (1⅔ cups) sugar,
240 ml/8 fl oz (1 cup minus 2 teaspoons) water,
the cinnamon stick, lemon rind and lard (pork fat)
into a large saucepan and heat over a medium heat
for 10–12 minutes until it reaches 103°C/217°F on
a thermometer. Strain the syrup through a sieve
(fine-mesh strainer) into a large heatproof bowl
and leave to cool.
    Put the egg yolks and port into a large bowl
and whisk, then strain through a sieve and add to
the sugar syrup. Stir gently to combine.
    Put the 230 g/8 oz (1 cup plus 2 tablespoons)
sugar for the dry caramel into a saucepan and heat,
without stirring, over a low heat for 5 minutes or
until a caramel forms. Once the caramel starts to
form, stir with a silicone spatula until smooth.
    Pour the caramel into a 28-cm/11-inch ring cake
pan or savarin mould with a hole in the middle and
tilt to evenly coat the inside of the pan.
    Pour the egg yolk mixture into the caramel-
filled cake pan and cover with a lid. Carefully place
the cake pan into a large roasting pan and pour in
enough hot water to reach halfway up the sides of
the cake pan.
    Bake in the hot oven for 55 minutes. Remove
from the oven and the bain-marie, then leave
to cool completely in the cake pan. Once cold,
carefully turn out the flan from the cake pan onto
a plate. Keep refrigerated until ready to serve.

Egg and Bacon Flan

Egg White Flan with Caramel and Egg Yolk Cream

Molotofe de Leiria

Leiria

This recipe is not easy to make as it has long cooling times and the shape of the flan can be tricky to master, but it is definitely worth the effort as it is a very light and fluffy pudding.

Preparation time: 15 minutes
Cooking time: 20 minutes
Serves: 6–8

unsalted butter, for greasing
160 g/5¾ oz (¾ cup plus 4 teaspoons) caster (superfine) sugar, plus an extra 200 g/7 oz (1 cup) for the dry caramel
8 large egg whites

For the egg yolk cream:
8 egg yolks
80 g/3 oz (½ cup minus 4 teaspoons) caster (superfine) sugar
150 ml/5 fl oz (⅔ cup) whole (full-fat) milk

Preheat the oven to 180°C/350°F/Gas Mark 4. Grease a 28-cm/11-inch fluted cake pan with butter.

Put the 200 g/7 oz (1 cup) sugar for the dry caramel into a large saucepan and heat, without stirring, over a low heat for 5 minutes or until a caramel forms. Once the caramel starts to form, stir with a silicone spatula until smooth.

Put the egg whites into a stand mixer fitted with a whisk attachment and whisk at medium speed until soft peaks form. Alternatively, put them into a large bowl and use electric beaters. While whisking, add the 160 g/5¾ oz (¾ cup plus 4 teaspoons) sugar, a little at a time, until it is all used up. Reduce the speed and, while whisking, add the caramel. Make sure the caramel is well incorporated and the mixture is an even brown.

Pour the caramel mixture into the prepared cake pan. Carefully place the cake pan into a large roasting pan and pour in enough hot water to reach halfway up the sides of the cake pan.

Bake in the hot oven for 8 minutes. Turn the oven off, open the door slightly and leave the flan to rest inside the oven for 10 minutes. Remove from the oven and the bain-marie, then leave to cool completely in the cake pan.

For the egg yolk cream, combine all the ingredients in a large saucepan and cook over a low heat, stirring continuously for 5 minutes, or until thick. Remove from the heat and leave to cool.

Carefully turn out the flan from the cake pan onto a plate and place it in the fridge to chill. Once cold, spread the egg yolk cream over the top. Keep refrigerated until ready to serve.

Cottage Cheese Flan

Pudim de Requeijão

Beira Alta

***Requeijão* is a fresh cheese made from sheep or goat's milk. It has a medium dense texture and a deep flavour, and can be easily found in the Beiras.**

Preparation time: 15 minutes
Cooking time: 1 hour
Serves: 6–8

135 g/4¾ oz (1 cup plus 1 tablespoon) almond flour
13 egg yolks
500 g/1 lb 2 oz (2½ cups) caster (superfine) sugar, plus an extra 300 g/11 oz (1½ cups) for the dry caramel
1 egg white
400 g/14 oz *requeijão* or similar fresh textured cheese
1 teaspoon ground cinnamon

Preheat the oven to 180°C/350°F/Gas Mark 4.

Put all the ingredients except the sugar for the dry caramel into a large bowl and, using a wooden spoon or a silicone spatula, mix until thoroughly combined.

Put the 300 g/11 oz (1½ cups) sugar for the dry caramel into a large saucepan and heat, without stirring, over a low heat for 5 minutes or until a caramel forms. Once the caramel starts to form, stir with a silicone spatula until smooth. Pour the caramel into a 28-cm/11-inch fluted cake pan, and tilt to evenly coat the inside of the pan.

Pour the cheese mixture into the cake pan over the caramel layer. Carefully place the cake pan into a large roasting pan and pour in enough hot water to reach halfway up the sides of the cake pan.

Bake in the hot oven for 55 minutes. Insert a toothpick into the middle of the flan. If it comes out clean, then the flan is ready. If not, bake for a further 2 minutes. Remove from the oven and the bain-marie, then leave to cool completely in the cake pan. Once cold, carefully turn out the flan from the cake pan onto a plate. Keep refrigerated until ready to serve.

Curdled Milk Flan

Pudim de Coalhada   ⵔ Açores

Preparation time: 30 minutes, plus 3 hours setting and
overnight straining
Cooking time: 30 minutes
Serves: 6–8
Ø

2 litres/68 fl oz (8½ cups) whole (full-fat) milk
8 g/¼ oz vegetable rennet
80 g/3 oz (5⅓ tablespoons) unsalted butter, plus extra
    for greasing
2 eggs, plus 1 extra (optional)
230 g/7¾ oz (1 cup plus 2 tablespoons) caster
    (superfine) sugar
75 g/2¾ oz (½ cup) plain (all-purpose) flour, sifted
1 teaspoon ground cinnamon
200 g/7 oz (1 cup) caster (superfine) sugar
100 g/3½ oz breadcrumbs, toasted

Heat the milk in a saucepan over a medium heat,
stirring frequently, until it reaches 75°C/167°F on
a sugar thermometer. Once it is at temperature,
remove the pan from the heat and leave to cool
to between 30–32°C/86–89.6°F. Add the rennet
and mix well with a balloon whisk, then cover with
food wrap and leave to rest for 3 hours, or until set.
Apply some cuts once the milk has set to make it
easier to release the whey.
    Line a sieve (fine-mesh strainer) with a piece
of muslin (cheesecloth), then place the sieve over
a large bowl. Gently ladle the set milk into the
muslin and leave it to drip through overnight.
    The next day, remove the *coalhada* or set milk
from the muslin, making sure it is dry, and set aside.
    Preheat the oven to 160°C/325°F/Gas Mark 3.
Grease a 25-cm/10-inch fluted cake pan with butter.
    Melt the butter in a small saucepan. Add the
eggs to another saucepan and lightly whisk. Add
the melted butter and the 230 g/7¾ oz (1 cup
plus 2 tablespoons) sugar and bring to the boil.
Remove from the heat and leave to cool.
    Once the egg and sugar mixture is cold, mix
with the set milk, flour, cinnamon and remaining
200 g/7 oz (1 cup) sugar. Mix well, leaving the
dough a bit loose. If it is not soft, add another egg.
    Put the 200 g/8½ oz (1¼ cups) sugar for the
dry caramel into a large saucepan and heat, without
stirring, over a low heat for 5 minutes or until a
golden caramel forms. Once the caramel starts to
form, stir with a silicone spatula until smooth. Pour
the caramel into the prepared cake pan and tilt
to evenly coat the inside of the pan. Spread the
toasted breadcrumbs evenly over the caramel in
the cake pan then pour in the filling.
    Bake in the hot oven for 25 minutes. Insert a
toothpick into the middle of the flan. If it comes
out clean, then the flan is ready. If not, bake for a
further 2 minutes. Remove from the oven and leave
to cool completely in the cake pan. Once cold,
carefully turn out the flan from the cake pan onto
a plate. Keep refrigerated until ready to serve.

Chestnut Flan

Pudim de Castanhas   ⵔ Trás-os-Montes
                 e Alto Douro

**Chestnuts play a big role in the local economy
and agriculture of the Trás-os-Montes region so
are an important part of the local people's diet.**

Preparation time: 20 minutes
Cooking time: 1 hour 30 minutes
Serves: 6–8
Ø

80 g/3 oz (5⅓ tablespoons) unsalted butter, plus extra
    for greasing
plain (all-purpose) flour, for dusting
250 g/9 oz (2 cups) chestnuts, peeled or 350 g/12 oz
    (3 cups) whole
10 egg yolks
620 ml/21 fl oz (2½ cups plus 4 teaspoons) whole
    (full-fat) milk
1 teaspoon ground cinnamon
240 g/8½ oz (1¼ cups) caster (superfine) sugar, for the
    dry caramel
sea salt (optional)

Preheat the oven to 190°C/375°F/Gas Mark 5.
Grease a 28-cm/11-inch fluted cake pan with
butter, then sprinkle with flour, tipping off
the excess.
    If the chestnuts are whole, put them into a
large saucepan, pour in enough water to cover, add
a pinch of salt and cook over a medium heat for
45 minutes, or until soft. Omit this stage if you are
using peeled chestnuts. Put the chestnuts into a
large bowl and add the butter, then mash.
    Put the egg yolks and sugar into a stand mixer
fitted with a whisk attachment and whisk on medium
speed until light and fluffy. Alternatively, put them
into a large bowl and beat with a balloon whisk.
Add the mashed chestnuts and milk and mix until
well combined. Add the cinnamon.
    Put the sugar for the dry caramel into a large
saucepan and heat, without stirring, over a low
heat for 5 minutes or until a golden caramel
forms. Once the caramel starts to form, stir with
a silicone spatula until smooth. Pour the caramel
into the prepared cake pan and tilt to evenly coat
the inside of the pan.
    Pour in the chestnut mixture into the cake
pan over the caramel layer. Carefully place the
cake pan into a large roasting pan and pour in
enough hot water to reach halfway up the sides
of the cake pan.
    Bake in the hot oven for 45 minutes. Remove
from the oven and the bain-marie, then leave
to cool completely in the cake pan. Once cold,
carefully turn out the flan from the cake pan onto
a plate. Keep refrigerated until ready to serve.

Almond Flan

•••

Pudim de Amêndoas ▽ **Algarve**

Preparation time: 15 minutes
Cooking time: 55 minutes
Serves: 6–8
⌀

10 egg yolks
1 egg
20 g/¾ oz (2⅓ tablespoons) plain (all-purpose) flour,
    plus extra for dusting
420 g/14¾ oz (2 cups plus 4 teaspoons) caster
    (superfine) sugar
110 g/3¾ oz (1 cup minus 2 teaspoons) almond flour
40 g/1½ oz (3 tablespoons) unsalted butter, cut into
    small cubes, plus extra for greasing

Put the egg yolks, egg and plain (all-purpose) flour
into a large bowl and whisk until smooth.
   Put the sugar and 180 ml/6 fl oz (¾ cup) water
into a saucepan and heat over a medium heat for
10–12 minutes until it reaches 116°C/241°F on a
sugar thermometer. Add the almond flour and stir
to combine, then remove from the heat and add
the egg mixture. Put the pan over a low heat and
gently cook for 10 minutes, or until the yolks are
cooked and thick. Remove from the heat, add
the butter, stir and leave to cool until it is
completely cold.
   Preheat the oven to 180°C/350°F/Gas Mark 4.
Grease a 27-cm/10¾-inch fluted cake pan
with butter, then line the bottom with baking
(parchment) paper. Grease the paper too.
   Pour the cold mixture into the prepared pan
and bake in the hot oven for 45 minutes, or until
golden brown. Remove from the oven, then leave
to cool completely in the cake pan. Once cold,
carefully turn out the flan from the cake pan onto
a plate. Keep refrigerated until ready to serve.

Orange Flan

•••

Pudim de Laranja 📷 p.303 ▽ **Algarve**

Preparation time: 15 minutes
Cooking time: 45 minutes
Serves: 6–8
⌀

35 g/1¼ oz (2 tablespoons) unsalted butter, plus extra
    for greasing
280 g/10 oz (1½ cups minus 4 teaspoons) caster
    (superfine) sugar
⅔ teaspoon instant dried yeast
zest and juice of 2½ oranges
25 g/1 oz (2 tablespoons) plain (all-purpose) flour
10 egg yolks
1 egg white

Preheat the oven to 160°C/325°F/Gas Mark 3.
Grease a 28-cm/11-inch fluted cake pan with butter.
   Put all the ingredients into a large bowl and
mix well until combined. Pour into the prepared
cake pan. Carefully place the cake pan into a large
roasting pan and pour in enough hot water to
reach halfway up the sides of the cake pan.
   Bake in the hot oven for 45 minutes, or until
golden brown all over and a toothpick inserted
into the flan comes out clean. Remove from
the oven and the bain-marie, then leave to cool
completely in the cake pan. Once cold, carefully
turn out the flan from the cake pan onto a plate.
Keep refrigerated until ready to serve.

Orange Flan with Madeira

••

Pudim de Laranja ▽ **Madeira**
com Vinho da Madeira

**This soft, sweet pudding, also known as *Pudim
de Veludo* (velvet pudding), is typically made of
eggs, sugar, milk and orange zest, although it
can also include Madeira wine. It is the Madeira
version of *Pudim Flan* (Egg Flan, page 298),
and can be made in a large ring mould, often
embossed with decorative designs, and baked in
a bain-marie. It is commonly served as a dessert
at family gatherings.**

Preparation time: 20 minutes
Cooking time: 1 hour 15 minutes
Serves: 6–8
🐖 ▯ ⌀ ✕

350 g/12 oz (1¾ cups) caster (superfine) sugar,
    plus 150 g/5 oz (¾ cup) sugar for the caramel
7 egg yolks
5 egg whites
30 ml/1 fl oz (2 tablespoons) Madeira wine
100 ml/3½ fl oz (7 tablespoons) orange juice

Preheat the oven to 180°C/350°F/Gas Mark 4.
   Put the sugar for the caramel into a saucepan
and heat over a low heat to slowly caramelise the
sugar. Add 30 ml/1 fl oz (2 tablespoons) warm
water and stir for 3 minutes. Pour the caramel into
a 23-cm/9-inch fluted cake pan and tilt the pan
until it is coated all over.
   Put the remaining sugar, the egg yolks, whites,
Madeira and orange juice into a large bowl and whisk
with a fork. Pour the mixture over the caramel in
the pan, then cover with a lid or foil and seal tightly.
Carefully place the cake pan into a large roasting
pan and pour in enough hot water to reach halfway
up the sides of the cake pan.
   Bake in the hot oven for 50 minutes. Remove
from the oven and the bain-marie, then leave
to cool completely in the cake pan. Once cold,
carefully turn out the flan from the cake pan onto
a plate. Keep refrigerated until ready to serve.

Orange Flan

Papaya Flan with Caramel

Pudim de Papaia da Madeira   ᘉ **Madeira**

Preparation time: 25 minutes
Cooking time: 1 hour 20 minutes
Serves: 6–8
∅

180 g/6 oz (1 cup minus 4 teaspoons) caster (superfine)
    sugar, plus 150 g/5 oz (¾ cup) for the caramel
1 papaya, peeled
150 ml/5 fl oz (⅔ cup) whole (full-fat) milk
65 g/2¼ oz (½ cup) self-raising (self-rising) flour
zest of 1 lemon
100 g/3½ oz (1 stick) unsalted butter, softened
3 eggs

Preheat the oven to 200°C/400°F/Gas Mark 6.

Put the sugar for the caramel into a saucepan and heat over a low heat to slowly caramelise. Add 30 ml/1 fl oz (2 tablespoons) warm water and stir for 5 minutes. Pour the caramel into a 28-cm/11-inch fluted cake pan and tilt the pan to coat it.

Cook the papaya in a saucepan of water over a medium heat for 15 minutes. Alternatively, cook it in a steamer to reduce the water absorbed. Drain, cut in half and de-seed. Put the flesh into a blender and blitz to a purée. Transfer to a bowl.

Put the milk and flour in another bowl and whisk until smooth, then stir in the papaya purée, lemon zest, butter, eggs and remaining sugar. Pour the mixture over the caramel in the pan. Carefully place the cake pan into a large roasting pan and pour in enough hot water to reach halfway up the sides of the cake pan. Bake in the hot oven for 1 hour. Remove from the oven and the bain-marie, then leave to cool completely in the cake pan. Once cold, carefully turn out the flan from the cake pan onto a plate. Keep refrigerated until ready to serve.

Honey Flan

Pudim de Mel   ᘉ **Algarve**

Preparation time: 10 minutes
Cooking time: 55 minutes
Serves: 6–8
🐷

unsalted butter or lard (pork fat), for greasing
400 g/14 oz (2 cups) caster (superfine) sugar
60 g/2¼ oz (¼ cup) honey
25 ml/1 fl oz (2 tablespoons) olive oil
10 whole eggs
zest of ½ lemon
1 teaspoon ground cinnamon

Preheat the oven to 160°C/325°F/Gas Mark 3 and grease a 28-cm/11-inch fluted cake pan.

Put all the ingredients into a large bowl and mix well until combined. Pour into the prepared pan.

Carefully place the cake pan into a large roasting pan and pour in enough hot water to reach halfway up the sides of the cake pan. Bake in the hot oven for 55 minutes, or until golden brown and sticky. Remove from the oven and the bain-marie, then leave to cool completely in the cake pan. Once cold, carefully turn out the flan from the cake pan onto a plate. Keep refrigerated until ready to serve.

Baked Egg Pudding

Sericá   📷 p.305   ᘉ **Alentejo**

This soft, moist pudding — also known as *Sericaia*, *Siricaia*, or *Cericá* — is one of the most popular desserts in Portugal. It was introduced to the country in 1562 by the Viceroy of India, Constantino de Bragança, and given to the nuns at Chagas de Cristo convent in Vila Viçosa, who then handed it to the Santa Clara convent in Elvas, the city where *Sericá* is most celebrated. At that time, it would have been baked on tin plates in wood-fired ovens, the only type of oven that guaranteed a cracked crust. Today, it is common to see *Sericá* cooked in and sold direct from a large clay dish.

Preparation time: 25 minutes
Cooking time: 1 hour 45 minutes
Serves: 6–8
∅

600 ml/20 fl oz (2½ cups) whole (full-fat) milk
1 cinnamon stick
pared rind of 1 lemon
pinch of sea salt
7 eggs, separated
400 g/14 oz (2 cups) caster (superfine) sugar
100 g/3½ oz (¾ cup plus 2 teaspoons) plain
    (all-purpose) flour
2 teaspoons ground cinnamon

Put the milk, cinnamon stick, lemon rind and salt into a large saucepan and bring to the boil. Once boiling, strain through a sieve (fine-mesh strainer) into a heatproof bowl and set aside.

Put the egg yolks and sugar into a stand mixer fitted with a whisk attachment and whisk on medium speed until creamy and doubled in volume.

Preheat the oven to 200°C/400°F/Gas Mark 6.

Add the flour to the milk and stir until smooth, then stir in the egg mixture and pour into a large saucepan. Cook over a medium heat for 5 minutes, or until thick. Leave the mixture to cool.

Put the egg whites into a clean bowl and whisk into soft peaks, then add to the cooled milk mixture and gently fold in with a silicon spatula. Pour the mixture into a shallow ovenproof dish and sprinkle with the ground cinnamon. Bake in the hot oven for 1 hour, or until the top is cracked and a toothpick inserted into the centre comes out clean. Remove from the oven, then leave to cool completely. Once cold, keep refrigerated until ready to serve.

Baked Egg Pudding

Egg Yolk Sheets Poached in Syrup

Trouxas das Caldas ⬚ p.307   ⏷ Lisbon

These vibrant, shiny egg rolls soaked in sugar syrup are extremely sweet, and their main characteristic is the technique used to cook them: *trouxas* (meaning 'bundles'; page 429) are made of tissue-thin layers of egg yolk and sugar in the thread stage rolled up like bales of hay. *Trouxas de Ovos das Caldas*, which are associated with the city of Caldas da Rainha, just north of Lisbon, are mainly eaten on special occasions, usually served with a piece of fruit on the side.

Preparation time: 20 minutes
Cooking time: 35 minutes
Serves: 5
🌶 ▢ ∅ ✕

16 egg yolks
2 egg whites
1 kg/2 lb 4 oz (5 cups) caster (superfine) sugar

Line a large baking sheet with food wrap. Have a spray bottle filled with cold water nearby.

Put the egg yolks and whites into a stand mixer fitted with a whisk attachment and whisk at medium speed for 2 minutes. Alternatively, put them into a large bowl and whisk with electric beaters. Strain the egg mixture through a sieve (fine-mesh strainer) into a large bowl and set aside.

Put the sugar and 600 ml/20 fl oz (2½ cups) water into a large saucepan and heat over a medium heat for 10–12 minutes until it reaches 108°C/226°F on a sugar thermometer. Reduce the heat to low.

Using a 20 g/¾ oz measuring spoon, scoop a spoonful of the egg mixture and pour it over the syrup. Use a fork to stretch the egg mixture out to form a sheet and cook for 5 minutes, or until the sheet is firm. Remove the sheet and put it onto the lined baking sheet. Repeat this process. As you cook the egg mixture, the sugar syrup will reduce, so in between each cooking, spray some cold water into the syrup.

Once all the egg sheets are cooked, lay the sheets out and trim the sides to neaten. Lay the trimmings over the sheet., then roll up the sheet with the trimmings inside. Brush the rolls with the remaining sugar syrup before serving.

Egg Yolk Noodles Poached in Syrup

Encharcada do Convento de Santa Clara   ⏷ Alentejo

Preparation time: 10 minutes
Cooking time: 25–30 minutes
Serves: 6
🌶 ▢ ∅ ✕

600 g/1 lb 5 oz (3 cups) caster (superfine) sugar
18 egg yolks
3 egg whites
1 tablespoon ground cinnamon, for dusting

Put the sugar and 160 ml/5½ fl oz (⅔ cup) water into a large saucepan and heat over a medium heat for 10–12 minutes until it reaches 108°C/226°F on a sugar thermometer.

Meanwhile, put the egg yolks into a large bowl and whisk with a balloon whisk. Pour the whisked egg yolks through the mesh of a sieve (fine-mesh strainer) into the pan of sugar syrup, moving in a circular motion. Alternatively, you can fill up a squeezy bottle with the egg yolks and squeeze them into the pan in circles. Using a wet silicone spatula, keep stirring the sugar syrup from the side to the centre to avoid any sugar crystallisation and let the egg yolks cook over a medium heat for 5 minutes until the eggs have a bite but remain slightly wet.

Preheat the oven to 200°C/400°F/Gas Mark 6 and heat the grill (broiler).

Transfer the eggs noodles to an ovenproof dish and dust with the cinnamon. Cook for 10 minutes, or until the top is golden brown. Serve.

Egg Yolk Sheets Poached in Syrup

Sweet Egg 'Lamprey'

Lampreia de Ovos   ♡ Beira Litoral

This dessert from Aveiro is extraordinarily special. The amount of time and the skill that goes into making something that looks like a lamprey fish from eggs and sugar is quite staggering.

Preparation time: 45 minutes
Cooking time: 45 minutes
Makes: 1
🦐 ▢ ⬤

For the soft sweet eggs:
500 g/1 lb 2 oz (2½ cups) caster (superfine) sugar
28 egg yolks
½ teaspoon ground cinnamon

For the egg strings:
1 egg white
18 egg yolks
450 g/1 lb (2¼ cups) caster (superfine) sugar

For the egg sheets:
750 g/1 lb 10 oz (3¾ cups) caster (superfine) sugar
36 egg yolks
2 almonds
1 cherry

For the soft sweet eggs, put the sugar and 260 ml/9 fl oz (1 cup plus 2 teaspoons) water into a large saucepan and heat over a medium heat for 10–12 minutes until it reaches 101°C/214°F on a sugar thermometer. Remove the pan from the heat and gradually add the egg yolks, then put the pan over a low heat and cook, stirring continuously, but not in zigzags for 15 minutes, or until the eggs are thick.

To make the egg strings, put the egg white into a large bowl and whisk lightly with a fork. Add the egg yolks and strain through a sieve (fine-mesh strainer). Set aside.

Put the sugar and 280 ml/9½ fl oz (1 cup plus 2 tablespoons) water into a large saucepan and heat over a medium heat for 10–12 minutes until it reaches 106°C/222°F on a sugar thermometer.

Sprinkle a large rimmed baking sheet with cold water and have it nearby. Make sure the syrup is simmering, then pour some of the egg mixture into the special funnel for making *Fios de Ovos* or a squeezy bottle and, holding the funnel or nozzle about 20 cm/8 inches above the surface of the syrup, pour the eggs into the syrup in circles. When all the egg in the funnel has been added, remove the pan from the heat and remove the egg strings from the pan to the baking sheet. Repeat the process with the remaining eggs.

For the egg sheets, put the sugar and 230 ml/ 7¾ fl oz (1 cup) water into a large saucepan and heat over a medium heat for 10–12 minutes until it reaches 103°C/217°F on a sugar thermometer.

Sprinkle a large rimmed baking sheet with cold water and have it nearby. Make sure the syrup is

over a low heat and simmering gently. Put the egg yolks into a large bowl and break up with a fork, then strain through a sieve (fine-mesh strainer) into another bowl. Using a large spoon, pour a spoonful of the eggs over the sugar, making an egg sheet, and cook for about 1 minute, or until cooked. Remove the egg sheet to the baking sheet and then repeat the process with the remaining egg yolks.

To assemble the dessert, arrange some of the egg sheets to make a shape of a lamprey, larger over the head becoming thinner towards the tail, on a large serving plate. Top the sheets with some of the egg strings, then spread some of the soft sweet eggs over the top. Set aside a few of the egg strings to put around the finished egg lamprey, then repeat the layers until all the ingredients are used up, the last layer should be egg sheets. Using a blowtorch or a spoon that has been heated on the stove until it is very hot, carefully spot the top of the egg lamprey to represent the fish skin.

Cut the almonds in half and then into thin sticks (these are for the teeth). Position the cherry to make the mouth on the head and add the almond teeth, then put the remaining egg strings around the finished lamprey before serving.

Soft Sweet Eggs — Aveiro Style

Ovos Moles de Aveiro   ♡ Beira Litoral

Literally translating as 'soft eggs', *Ovos Moles* are one of the most famous sweet delicacies in Portugal. The vibrant yellow or orange egg yolk and sugar combination is key to a multiplicity of recipes, harmonising small cakes or filling other sweets. However, they are most acclaimed in the Aveiro district, where they are either sold in hand-painted wooden barrels, or wrapped in finger-sized, bright white communion wafers, shaped to replicate marine creatures such as fish, whelks and clams.

Preparation time: 5 minutes
Cooking time: 30 minutes
Serves: 8
🦐 ▢ ⬤ ▢ ✕

500 g/1 lb 2 oz (2½ cups) caster (superfine) sugar
28 egg yolks
½ teaspoon ground cinnamon

For the soft sweet eggs, put the sugar and 260 ml/9 fl oz (1 cup plus 2 teaspoons) water into a large saucepan and heat over a medium heat for 10–12 minutes until it reaches 101°C/214°F on a sugar thermometer. Remove the pan from the heat and gradually add the egg yolks, then put the pan over a low heat and cook, stirring continuously, but not in zigzags for 15 minutes, or until the eggs are thick.

Transfer the eggs to a serving dish and sprinkle with cinnamon.

Sweet Vermicelli

••

Aletria   ▽ Minho

Aletria has a special place on the Portuguese
Christmas dinner table and during other
festivities, especially in the north of Portugal.
Much like rice pudding, this angel-hair pasta
pudding is a vibrant yellow, sweet, comforting
treat for kids and adults alike. It is always
decorated with cinnamon, but it can include
more or less pasta and can be made with or
without egg yolks. In Beira Alta and Beira Baixa,
aletria should be compact enough to be able to
cut into slices, but in Minho it is a creamier affair.

Preparation time: 5 minutes
Cooking time: 30 minutes
Serves: 8
⏀

1.6 litres/54 fl oz (6½ cups minus 2 tablespoons) whole
    (full-fat) milk
pared rind of 2 lemons, finely cut
320 g/11¼ oz (1⅔ cups) caster (superfine) sugar
380 g/13½ oz vermicelli
12 egg yolks
ground cinnamon, for dusting

Put the milk, lemon rinds and sugar into a large
saucepan and heat over a low heat for 10 minutes,
or until the sugar has dissolved.
    Bring a large saucepan of water to the boil, add
the vermicelli and cook for 8–10 minutes, or until
soft. Drain and add the vermicelli to the milk, then
bring to the boil. Remove from the heat and leave
to cool.
    Once the mixture is cold, add the egg yolks,
stir and cook over a low heat for 10 minutes, or
until it is creamy and the yolks are cooked. Pour
into a large serving dish and dust with cinnamon
before serving.

Sweet Scrambled Eggs with Almonds, Sultanas and Pine Nuts

••

Mexidos de Guimarães   ▽ Minho

This dish is always on the table at Christmas and
is extremely rich. *Mexidos* means 'stirred'.

Preparation time: 5 minutes
Cooking time: 40 minutes
Serves: 6
⏀

500 g/1 lb 2 oz (2½ cups) caster (superfine) sugar
80 g/3 oz (⅓ cup) honey
100 ml/3½ fl oz (⅓ cup plus 1 tablespoon) white wine
60 g/2¼ oz (4 tablespoons) unsalted butter
50 g/2 oz (⅓ cup) sultanas (golden raisins)
70 g/2¼ oz (½ cup) pine nuts
250 g/9 oz (5 cups) breadcrumbs
8 egg yolks
70 ml/2¼ fl oz (¼ cup plus 2 teaspoons) orange
    blossom water
ground cinnamon, for dusting
sea salt

Put the sugar and 900 ml/30 fl oz (3¾ cups) water
into a large saucepan and bring to the boil. Reduce
the heat to low and add a pinch of salt, the honey,
wine and butter. Stir and cook for 5 minutes.
Add the sultanas (golden raisins), pine nuts and
breadcrumbs and gently stir for 25 minutes until
the mixture starts to come off the sides of the pan.
Remove from the heat and leave to cool.
    Put the egg yolks into a medium bowl and
whisk lightly with a fork, then add them to the
honey and sugar mixture together with the orange
blossom water. Put the pan over a low heat and
cook for 8 minutes, or until the egg yolks are
cooked. Pour into a large serving dish and dust
with cinnamon before serving.

Sweet Egg Cream Rolls

Pampilhos   ⏷ Ribatejo

These cakes were created in honour of the Ribatejo *campinos* (cattle herders) who use a long stick to lead the cattle, which is called *pampilho*.

Preparation time: 20 minutes, plus 30 minutes resting
Cooking time: 1 hour
Makes: 8
∅

180 g/6 oz (scant 1 cup) caster (superfine) sugar
180 g/6 oz (1½ sticks) unsalted butter, softened
1 egg, plus 1 egg yolk
410 g/14 oz (3½ cups minus 2 teaspoons) self-raising (self-rising) flour, plus extra for dusting
2 egg yolks, for egg wash

For the filling:
250 g/9 oz (1¼ cups) caster (superfine) sugar
12 egg yolks
ground cinnamon, for dusting

Put the sugar, softened butter and eggs into a stand mixer fitted with a paddle attachment and whisk at medium speed for 3–4 minutes or until pale and fluffy. Alternatively, whisk with electric beaters in a large bowl. Add the flour and mix until a smooth dough forms. Cover with food wrap and leave to chill in the fridge overnight.

For the filling, put the sugar into a large saucepan with 150 ml/5 fl oz (⅔ cup) water and heat over a medium heat for 10–12 minutes until it reaches 108°C/226°F on a sugar thermometer. Remove from the heat.

Put the egg yolks into another large saucepan and lightly whisk them with a fork. While whisking, pour the syrup over the egg yolks in a steady stream to produce *Ovos Moles*. Cook, stirring continuously, over a very low heat for 20 minutes, or until thick enough to coat the back of a spoon. Remove from the heat and leave to chill in the fridge overnight.

Preheat the oven to 230°C/450°F/Gas Mark 8. Line a baking sheet with baking (parchment) paper.

Roll out the dough on a lightly floured work counter to a thickness of about 4 mm/¼ inch, then cut the dough into 9 small rectangles, each measuring 15 x 12 cm/6 x 4½ inches. Pour the filling into the middle of each rectangle, dust with cinnamon and roll it up like a cannelloni to cover. Arrange the rolls on the prepared baking sheet, seam side down. Chill in the fridge until completely cold.

Brush with the beaten egg yolk. sprinkle a pinch of cinnamon over each roll and bake in the hot oven for 15–20 minutes, or until golden brown. Remove from the oven and turn on the grill (broiler) on your oven. When hot, grill (broil) for 2–3 minutes, or until the top is a caramel colour. Remove from the grill and leave to cool on a wire rack before serving.

Floating Islands

Farófias   📷 p.311   ⏷ Lisbon

These fluffy, sweet egg-white dumplings boiled in sugared milk and bathed in a rich custard, are usually sprinkled with powdered cinnamon, although the topping may vary according to individual taste, and can include caramel, *Ovos Moles* (Soft Sweet Eggs, page 308), and/or sliced almonds. The origin of *Farófias*, once called 'nuvens' (literally meaning 'clouds') is not entirely known, but there is a very similar recipe in documents from the 18th century from the Nossa Senhora da Conceição convent in the Algarve. Today they are eaten warm or cold at weddings and anniversaries, or simply on the family meal table.

Preparation time: 10 minutes
Cooking time: 30–40 minutes
Serves: 4
🐚 ∅

4 eggs, separated
160 g/5¾ oz (¾ cup plus 4 teaspoons) caster (superfine) sugar
pared rind of ⅕ lemon
800 ml/27 fl oz (3¼ cups) whole (full-fat) milk
10 g/½ oz (2 teaspoons) cornflour (cornstarch)
ground cinnamon, for dusting

To make the meringue mixture, put the egg whites into a stand mixer fitted with a whisk attachment and whisk at medium speed until soft peaks form. Alternatively, whisk with electric beaters in a large bowl. While whisking, add the sugar until it is a thick and smooth consistency.

Put the lemon rind and milk into a large saucepan and bring to the boil. Reduce the heat to low and simmer for 2 minutes.

Working in batches, scoop up a spoonful of the meringue and carefully lower it into the simmering milk. Cook for 2 minutes, then carefully flip them over and cook for another 2 minutes. Using a slotted spoon, remove them from the pan and put them onto a wire rack with a tray underneath to catch all the drips. Once they are all cooked, pour all the milk that has dripped from the meringues back into the pan and leave the milk to cool.

Put the cornflour (cornstarch) into a small bowl and add 2 tablespoons of cold milk, then add the egg yolks and mix until well combined. Pour this into the pan with the rest of the milk and cook, stirring continuously with a silicone spatula, over a medium heat for 10 minutes, or until thick.

Place the meringues in a large serving dish and cover them with the custard. Dust with cinnamon before serving.

Floating Islands

Sweet Egg Yolk Strands

••

Fios de Ovos   📷 p.313   ⛉ Beira Litoral

This is a classic egg dessert made all over
Portugal, but it is in Aveiro where it has its roots.
To prepare the fine strands of egg, which are then
boiled in sugar syrup, this recipe requires a special
funnel with a narrow opening, but you can use a
squeezy bottle. It can be eaten by itself or as part
of another dessert as a decoration or filling.

Preparation time: 10 minutes
Cooking time: 30 minutes
Serves: 8
🔥🍶⊘◻✕

1 egg white
18 egg yolks
450 g/1 lb (2¼ cups) caster (superfine) sugar

Put the egg white into a large bowl and whisk
lightly with a fork. Add the egg yolks and strain
through a sieve (fine-mesh strainer). Set aside.

Put the sugar and 280 ml/9½ fl oz (1 cup plus
2 tablespoons) water into a large saucepan and
heat over a medium heat for 10–12 minutes until
it reaches 106°C/222°F on a sugar thermometer.

Sprinkle a large rimmed baking sheet with cold
water and have it nearby. Make sure the syrup is
simmering, then pour some of the egg mixture
into the special funnel for making *Fios de Ovos* or
a squeezy bottle and, holding the funnel or nozzle
about 20 cm/8 inches above the surface of the
syrup, pour the eggs into the syrup in circles. When
all the egg in the funnel has been added, remove
the pan from the heat and remove the egg strings
from the pan to the baking sheet. Repeat the
process with the remaining eggs.

Either serve on their own or use as directed in
another recipe.

Parcels of Sweet Egg Yolk Strands with Almonds

••

Dom Rodrigo   ⛉ Algarve

This conventual sweet made of egg yolks and
sugar has the appearance of a ball of wool, or
yarn, although its serving style has been modified
throughout history. It started by being sold as
it was, but soon changed to being served in
porcelain or glass bowls to be eaten with a spoon,
and most recently wrapped in a coloured metallic
wrap with a twisted top. *Dom Rodrigo* is widely
consumed at any time but especially during festive
times, and it is usually on display in pastry shops
throughout the Algarve.

Preparation time: 10 minutes
Cooking time: 35 minutes
Makes: about 10
🔥🍶⊘✕

90 g/3¼ oz (⅔ cup) blanched almonds
240 g/8½ oz (1¼ cups minus 2 teaspoons) caster
    (superfine) sugar, plus an extra 120 g/4 oz (⅔ cup)
    sugar for the syrup
5 egg yolks
ground cinnamon, for dusting
220 g/7½ oz Sweet Egg Yolk Strands (*Fios de Ovos*,
    see left)

Grate (shred) the almonds on a box grater or blitz
them in a food processor. Set aside.

Put the 240 g/8½ oz (1¼ cups minus
2 teaspoons) sugar and 500 ml/17 fl oz (2 cups
plus 1 tablespoon) water into a large saucepan
and heat over a medium heat for 10–12 minutes
until it reaches 108°C/226°F on a sugar
thermometer. Remove from the heat and add
the almonds, then add the egg yolks and stir to
combine. Put the pan over a low heat and cook
for 10 minutes, or until thick. Sprinkle some
ground cinnamon over the top and mix well.
Remove from the heat and leave to cool.

To make the syrup, put the remaining sugar
and 100 ml/3½ fl oz (⅓ cup plus 1 tablespoon)
water into another large saucepan and heat over
a medium heat for 10–12 minutes until it reaches
108°C/226°F on a sugar thermometer. This will be
used to cook the parcels when they are rolled up.

Splash a spoonful of the *Fios de Ovos* onto
your hand, then add a spoonful of the almond
paste and roll the *Fios de Ovos* in the paste until
covered. It should look like a small round pellet.
Repeat until you have used up all the ingredients.

Pour the sugar syrup into a large frying pan or
skillet and bring to the boil, then add the parcels
and 'sear' for 5 minutes, or until coloured. Remove
from the pan and leave to cool. When cool,
wrap them in baking (parchment) paper and silver
coloured paper.

Sweet Egg Yolk Strands

Crispy Egg Yolk Strands with Almonds

••

Palha de Abrantes   ♡ Ribatejo

There are many different Portuguese recipes that include *Fios de Ovos* (Sweet Egg Yolk Strands, page 312), but there is one that seems to be this sweet's greatest complement: *Palha de Abrantes*. This vivid yellow, small round cake is no more than sweet egg yolk strands placed on top of a communion wafer, covered with a thin layer of *Ovos Moles* (Soft Sweet Eggs, page 308), then toasted in a very hot oven. Part of the conventual confectionery culture that took place in Portugal between the 15th and 18th centuries, this sweet's name is associated with the fact that the town of Abrantes was once a Tagus port that supplied, among other products, bales of straw (*palha*), as well as the fact that the egg yolk strands resemble straw.

Preparation time: 15 minutes
Cooking time: 35 minutes
Makes: 26
🐚 ◻ ⊘ ✕

330 g/11½ oz (1⅔ cups) caster (superfine) sugar
18 egg yolks
80 g/3 oz (⅔ cup) almond flour
edible rice paper sheets

Put the sugar and 350 ml/12 fl oz (1½ cups) water into a large saucepan and heat over a medium heat for 10–12 minutes until it reaches 108°C/226°F on a sugar thermometer.

Meanwhile, put 10 egg yolks into a large bowl and whisk with a balloon whisk. Pour the whisked egg yolks through the mesh of a sieve (fine-mesh strainer) into the pan of sugar syrup, moving in a circular motion. Alternatively, you can fill up a squeezy bottle with the egg yolks and squeeze them into the pan in circles. Using a wet silicone spatula, keep stirring the sugar syrup from the side to the centre to avoid any sugar crystallisation and let the egg yolks cook over a medium heat for 5 minutes until the eggs have a bite but remain slightly wet.

Put the almond flour and remaining egg yolks into a bowl and mix to combine. Heat the remaining syrup from making the egg noodles until it reaches 101°C/214°F on a sugar thermometer, then remove from the heat and add the almond flour. Gently cook, stirring continuously, over a low heat for 20 minutes, or until the egg yolks are cooked and you can see the bottom of the pan when stirring. Remove from the heat and leave to cool.

Preheat the oven to 240°C/475°F/Gas Mark 9.

Cut the rice paper sheets into 26 circles, each measuring 6 cm/2½ inches in diameter, then arrange them on 12 large baking sheets. Put 1 teaspoon of the almond mixture onto each circle and cover it with egg noodles. Bake in the hot oven for 2 minutes, or until golden brown on top. Remove from the oven and leave to cool before serving.

Egg Sheets with Egg Cream

••

Túberas Fritas com Ovos   ♡ Alentejo

Preparation time: 15 minutes, plus 4 hours chilling
Cooking time: 45 minutes
Makes: 1
🐚 ⊘

For the egg sheets:
250 g/9 oz egg yolks
1 whole egg
320 g/11¼ oz (1⅔ cups) caster (superfine) sugar
unsalted butter, for greasing

For the creamy eggs:
540 g/1 lb 3 oz (2¾ cups) caster (superfine) sugar
350 g/12 oz egg yolks

To make the egg sheets, pour 2.5 litres/85 fl oz (10 cups) water into a deep roasting pan. This is to hold your egg sheet once it is cooked. Have a clean spray bottle filled with cold water nearby.

Put the egg yolks and whole egg into a large bowl and, using a fork, mix together. Don't whisk, as you don't want any foam and as little air as possible.

Put the sugar and 270 ml/9 fl oz (1 cup) water into a large 23-cm/9-inch frying pan or skillet and heat over a medium heat for 10 minutes until it reaches 103°C/217°F on a sugar thermometer. Remove the pan from the heat.

Using a ladle, scoop the eggs from the bowl and carefully pour them into the sugar syrup in the pan. Using a silicone spatula, spread the eggs out on top of the syrup to make a large sheet. Gently bring the sugar syrup to the boil and cook the egg sheet for 5 minutes. Transfer the egg sheet to the prepared roasting pan and spray with cold water.

For the creamy eggs, put the sugar and 440 ml/ 15 fl oz (1¾ cups) water into a large saucepan and heat over a medium heat for 10–12 minutes until it reaches 108°C/226°F on a sugar thermometer. Meanwhile, put the egg yolks into a large bowl and whisk with a balloon whisk. Once the sugar syrup has reached the correct temperature, remove from the heat and leave to cool for 10 minutes.

Stirring continuously with a whisk or silicone spatula, gradually add the egg yolks to the syrup. Return the pan to the heat and cook, stirring continuously, over a low heat for 10 minutes until it reaches 110°C/230°F on a sugar thermometer. Transfer the mixture to a bowl, cover with food wrap and leave in the fridge until completely cold.

Grease a 18-cm/7-inch loose-bottomed cake pan well with butter. Line the base and sides of the pan with the egg sheet, making sure some hangs over the rim. Pour the creamy eggs into the centre and fold the overhanging pieces over the top. Using a blowtorch, torch the top until it is lightly coloured with some black spots. Leave to chill in the fridge for 4 hours, then carefully remove from the pan before serving.

Egg Yolk and Almond-stuffed Wafers

Queijinhos de Hóstia   ᴗ Alentejo

I'm always excited to make this recipe, as the creative side of it just amazes me. An egg and almond dough is rolled into rings, filled with creamy sweet eggs and sandwiched between a light, crispy top and base made from *hostia* or edible rice paper. I hope the Portuguese people never stop making them.

Preparation time: 30 minutes
Cooking time: 20 minutes
Makes: 8–10
🌱 ▢ ⌀

14 egg yolks
400 g/14 oz (2 cups) caster (superfine) sugar
250 g/9 oz (2 cups) almond flour
2 egg whites
edible rice paper sheets
1 quantity Soft Sweet Eggs (*Ovos Moles*, page 308),
    to fill the *queijinhos*

Put the egg yolks into a large bowl and whisk with a fork to break them down a little. Set aside.

Put the sugar and 160 ml/5½ fl oz (⅔ cup) water into a medium saucepan and heat over a medium heat for 10–12 minutes until it reaches 106°C/222°F on a sugar thermometer. Add the almond flour and stir until well combined. Remove from the heat, add the egg whites then put the pan back over a medium heat and cook for 10 minutes, or until it thickens. Remove from the heat, then either leave the mixture in the pan or transfer to a bowl, cover with a clean tea (dish) towel and leave to cool until completely cold.

Using a medium ring cutter, cut out rounds from the rice paper. The size of the rounds can vary, depending on the size you prefer, but they should be at least 5 cm/2 inches in diameter, and you will need two rounds of rice paper per portion.

Once the almond dough is cold, stretch it over a work counter into a rectangle, about 3 mm/⅛ inch thick, then cut out strips from the dough, each measuring 3 x 11 cm/1¼ x 4¼ inches.

Bring the two ends of each strip of dough together to make a ring and seal the ends. There should be a hole in the middle like a doughnut. Place this ring on one round of rice paper, then fill the centre of the ring with the *Ovos Moles* and place another round of rice paper on top and press down gently.

'Nun's Necks'

Pescoços de Freiras   ᴗ Beira Baixa

Pescoços de Freira, which literally translates as 'Nuns' Necks', are communion wafers rolled and filled with a sweet egg yolk mixture, and are another sweet that came out of the convent confectionery culture. Historically, the name, and others such as *Suspiros* (Sighs), *Beijos de Freira* (Nuns' Kisses), *Papos de Anjo* (Angel's Double Chin) and *Mexericos de Freira* (Nuns' Gossip,) evoked dating, sex and the body, which caught people's imagination and helped attract business; the sweets being the nuns' main source of income. The nuns perfected these egg yolk and sugar recipes, which were passed down through generations with all the required secrecy of a commercially successful product.

Preparation time: 25 minutes
Cooking time: 30 minutes
Makes: 17
🌱 ⌀

250 g/9 oz (1¼ cups) caster (superfine) sugar, plus an
    extra 250 g/9 oz (1¼ cups) for the syrup
260 g/9 oz (2 cups plus 4 teaspoons) almond flour
25 g/1 oz (2 tablespoons) unsalted butter
6 egg yolks
almond oil, for brushing
edible rice paper sheets
1 egg white

Put the sugar and 125 ml/4¼ fl oz (½ cup) water into a large saucepan and heat over a medium heat for 10–12 minutes until it reaches 108°C/226°F on a sugar thermometer. Remove from the heat, add the almond flour and stir until smooth. Add the butter and stir again. Add the egg yolks, then put the pan over a low heat and cook, stirring continuously for 10 minutes, or until a thick paste forms. Remove from the heat, then pour the mixture into a large heatproof bowl, cover the surface of the mixture with food wrap to stop it drying out and leave to cool.

Meanwhile, to make the syrup, put the extra sugar and 100 ml/3½ fl oz (⅓ cup plus 1 tablespoon) water into a large saucepan and heat over a medium heat for 10–12 minutes until it reaches 101°C/214°F on a sugar thermometer.

Brush 1 or 2 baking sheets with almond oil.

Cut the edible rice paper sheets into pieces, 6 cm/2½ inches wide and 10 cm/4 inches long. Put the egg white into a small bowl and whisk with a fork. Brush the sheets with the egg white, then put a spoonful of the almond and egg filling on one side and roll them up into a cylinder.

Using a fork, dip them into the syrup and then put them on the prepared baking sheets and leave to dry.

'Nun's Bellies'

◆◆

Barrigas de Freiras   ♡ Beira Litoral

You will need a well-polished copper pot for this recipe, as the mixture needs to simmer constantly and caramelise on the bottom.

Preparation time: 10 minutes
Cooking time: 45 minutes
Serves: 4
🥄 🗓 ☐ ✕

18 egg yolks
2 whole eggs
500 g/1 lb 2 oz (2½ cups) caster (superfine) sugar
100 g/3½ oz (1 stick) unsalted butter, cut into small cubes and softened

Put the egg yolks and whole eggs into a large bowl and, using a fork, mix together. Don't whisk, as you don't want any foam and as little air as possible. Set aside.
   Pour 300 ml/10 fl oz (1¼ cups) water into a 25-cm/10-inch copper pot. Add the sugar and cook over a medium heat for 10–12 minutes until it reaches 101°C/214°F on a sugar thermometer.
   Add the eggs and gently cook over a medium-low heat for a few seconds, then using two forks, start moving the eggs around in the pan and poke the middle of the eggs with the fork. Start to add small amounts of the butter around the pan and stir the eggs, poking again. If it foams too much remove a little of the syrup with a spoon. Repeat the process until you have used all the butter. There should be a light caramelisation on the bottom. Transfer to a serving dish and leave to cool before serving.

Egg 'Cake' Slices Soaked in Vanilla Syrup

◆◆

Fatias de Tomar 📷 p.317   ♡ Ribatejo

This recipe requires a special cooking pan which was created in Tomar and can only be bought there. I sent my dad on a mission to find someone that makes one, and he found an artisan who still makes a few a week. It is an extraordinary piece of kit, as it is a special double boiler pan; the result is a light, fluffy cake.

Preparation time: 50 minutes, plus 20 minutes cooling
Cooking time: 1 hour
Makes: 1
🥄 🗓 ✕

unsalted butter, for greasing
16 egg yolks
2 eggs

For the syrup:
380 g/13½ oz (2 cups minus 4 teaspoons) caster (superfine) sugar
2 vanilla pods (beans), split in half and with seeds scraped out

Grease the *Fatias de Tomar* pan with butter.
   Put the egg yolks and eggs into a stand mixer fitted with a whisk attachment and whisk at medium speed for 45 minutes. Alternatively, whisk with electric beaters in a large bowl. Pour the mixture into the prepared pan, then bring to the boil over a high heat. Reduce the heat to medium and cook for 40 minutes. Set a timer then, when it goes off, remove the pan from the heat and leave to cool with the lid on for 20 minutes.
   Remove the egg cake from the pan and put it onto a large plate and set aside.
   To make the syrup, put the sugar and vanilla pods (beans) and seeds into a large saucepan with 550 ml/18½ fl oz (2¼ cups) water. Bring to the boil, then reduce the heat to medium and simmer for 10 minutes. Remove from the heat, cover with a lid and leave to rest for another 10 minutes. Remove the vanilla pods from the syrup.
   Cut the egg cake into slices, then dip each slice into the syrup, and put them in layers on a large serving plate.

Egg 'Cake' Slices Soaked in Vanilla Syrup

Angels' Double Chins

Papos de Anjos   ⋃ Minho

Preparation time: 10 minutes, plus 6 hours soaking
Cooking time: 10–12 minutes
Serves: 4–6
⊘ ⊘

unsalted butter, for greasing
6 egg yolks
1 large whole egg
320 g/11¼ oz (1⅔ cups) caster (superfine) sugar
pared rind of 2 lemons
1 cinnamon stick

Preheat the oven to 160°C/325°F/Gas Mark 3.
Generously grease 8 cake pans, 6 cm/2½ inches
in diameter and 1.5 cm/⅝ inch high with butter.
    Put the egg yolks and whole egg into a stand
mixer fitted with a whisk attachment and whisk at
high speed until they are pale and have doubled
in volume. Alternatively, whisk with electric beaters
in a large bowl. Pour the egg mixture into the
prepared pans and bake in the hot oven for
10–12 minutes, or until puffed up and golden brown.
Remove from the oven, cool slightly, then turn
them out of the pans onto a wire rack. Using the
tip of a knife, make a small incision in the back of
them and leave to cool completely.
    Meanwhile, make the syrup. Put the sugar,
190 ml/6½ fl oz (¾ cup) water, the lemon rinds
and cinnamon into a large saucepan and bring
to the boil, then reduce the heat to medium and
simmer for 10 minutes. Remove from the heat,
cover with a lid and leave to cool completely.
(This takes about 2 hours.)
    Arrange the *Papos de Anjos* in a shallow serving
dish. Remove the cinnamon stick and lemon rinds
from the cooled syrup and pour over. Leave to
soak for 6 hours before serving.

Creamy Egg and Milk Curd

Leite Creme   ◙ p.319   ⋃ Beira Alta

**This highly traditional yellow, creamy, caramelised
pudding is most commonly seen on restaurant
menus in every city in Portugal, but is easy to make
at home using simple and inexpensive ingredients.
Similar to, but not to be confused with, French
crème brûlée, *Leite Creme* is cooked in a pan
on the stove rather than baked, and is flavoured
with vanilla rather than lemon peel. What they
both have in common, however, is the distinctive
caramelised topping made from burnt sugar.**

Preparation time: 5 minutes
Cooking time: 35 minutes
Serves: 5
⊘ ⊘ ⊓ ✕

40 g/1½ oz (⅓ cup) cornflour (cornstarch)
80 ml/2¾ fl oz (⅓ cup) whole (full-fat) milk
8 egg yolks
1 vanilla pod (bean), cut lengthwise
240 g/8½ oz (1¼ cups) caster (superfine) sugar, plus an
    extra 150 g/5 oz (¾ cup), for caramelising

Put the cornflour (cornstarch) and milk into a
saucepan and stir. Add the egg yolks and vanilla
pod (bean). Cook over a low heat, stirring with
a rubber spatula for 30 minutes, or until thick.
    Divide the mixture between individual ramekins
or pour into a large heatproof dish. Sprinkle the
150 g/5 oz (¾ cup) sugar over the top. Blowtorch
to caramelise the sugar. Serve immediately.

Cream of Egg Yolks and Roasted Almonds — Évora Style

Torrão de Ovos – Évora   ⋃ Alentejo

Preparation time: 10 minutes
Cooking time: 35 minutes
Serves: 4–6
⊘ ⊓ ⊘ ✕

600 g/1 lb 5 oz crystallised sugar
350 g/12 oz (2⅔ cups) blanched almonds
12 egg yolks, whisked

Preheat the oven to 190°C/375°F/Gas Mark 5.
    Put the sugar and 300 ml/10 fl oz (1¼ cups)
water into a medium saucepan and heat over a
medium heat for 10–12 minutes until it reaches
117°C/243°F on a sugar thermometer. Remove the
pan from the heat and leave to cool.
    Spread the almonds out on a large baking sheet
and toast them in the hot oven for 10–15 minutes, or
until golden brown. Remove from the oven, leave to
cool a little, then put them into a mortar and break
them up a bit with a pestle. Do not mash them.
    Add the almonds to the sugar syrup, then add
the egg yolks and bring to the boil over a medium
heat, stirring continuously. As soon as it boils, pour
the mixture into a serving bowl and leave to cool
before serving.

Creamy Egg and Milk Curd

Milk Custard Dessert

••

Leite Creme à Moda do Minho   ▽ Minho

In some parts of Minho the locals use dry biscuits (cookies) to decorate this dessert. If you wish to use some plain ones, then break them up coarsely and place them in the bottom of the serving dish.

Preparation time: 15 minutes
Cooking time: 30 minutes
Serves: 6
🌿 🖉

850 ml/28½ fl oz (3½ cups plus 2 tablespoons) whole (full-fat) milk
25 g/1 oz (2 tablespoons) cornflour (cornstarch)
1 large cinnamon stick
pared rind of 2 lemons
5 egg yolks
170 g/6 oz (¾ cup plus 4 teaspoons) caster (superfine) sugar, plus extra for sprinkling

Put 50 ml/1⅔ fl oz (3½ tablespoons) of the milk into a small bowl, add the cornflour (cornstarch) and stir until smooth. Put the remaining milk, the cinnamon and lemon rind into a large bowl, add the egg yolks and sugar mix together.

Combine the egg yolk mixture with the milk and cornflour mixture in a medium saucepan and heat over a low heat for 20 minutes, stirring continuously with a wooden spoon until it starts to thicken, then keep stirring for a further 5 minutes. Pour into a large serving dish. Sprinkle a thin layer of sugar over the top. Heat up a flat large spoon on the stove or use a blowtorch to caramelise the sugar and serve.

Gooey Custard Cakes

••

Tigeladas   📷 p.321   ▽ Beira Litoral

These cakes used to be cooked in red clay pots in a wood-fired oven, but if you don't have one, a normal oven works just fine.

Preparation time: 10 minutes
Cooking time: 35 minutes
Makes: 12
🖉

unsalted butter, for greasing
30 g/1 oz (3⅔ tablespoons) plain (all-purpose) flour
430 ml/14½ fl oz (1¾ cups) whole (full-fat) milk
5 eggs
190 g/7 oz (1 cup) caster (superfine) sugar
6 ml/1 teaspoon lemon juice
ground cinnamon, for dusting

Heat a wood-fired oven, making sure it isn't too hot. Alternatively, preheat the oven to 180°C/350°F/Gas Mark 4. Grease 12 baking pans, about 12 cm/4½ inches in diameter and 1.5 cm/⅝ inch high with butter.

Put the flour into a large bowl, add the milk and mix well. Set aside.

Put the eggs, sugar and lemon juice into a stand mixer fitted with a whisk attachment and whisk for 5 minutes, or until doubled in volume. Alternatively, use a large bowl with electric beaters. Gradually, add the flour and milk mixture to make a smooth batter.

Divide the batter equally between the pans, but do not fill them to the rim. Bake in the hot oven for 35 minutes, or until the tops are brown but still slightly runny. It is better to slightly undercook them. Remove from the oven and dust with cinnamon before serving.

Gooey Custard Cakes

Gooey Cakes from Oliveria do Hospital

••

Tigeladas de
Oliveira do Hospital   ⏰ Beira Alta

These particular gooey custard cakes are made
with no starch, so they are better to eat the
following day when they have rested.

Preparation time: 10 minutes
Cooking time: 40–45 minutes
Makes: 15
🌶 ⊘ ✕

500 g/1 lb 2 oz (2½ cups) caster (superfine) sugar
10 eggs
20 ml/¾ fl oz (4 teaspoons) lemon juice
850 ml/28¾ fl oz (3½ cups plus 2 teaspoons) whole
    (full-fat) milk
½ teaspoon ground cinnamon

Preheat the oven to 180°C/350°F/Gas Mark 4.
    Put all the ingredients into a medium bowl and
mix together until combined. Pour the mixture
into 15 baking pans, about 12 cm/4½ inches in
diameter and 2 cm/¾ inch high or use round
clay containers.
    Bake in the hot oven for 40 minutes, or until
the cakes are slightly puffed up and have spots
of caramelisation on the top and a toothpick
inserted into the middle comes out clean. If they
are not ready, cover with foil and bake for a further
5 minutes. Leave to cool and then refrigerate
overnight before serving. These cakes will keep for
up to 3 days when stored in the fridge.

Gooey Cakes with Honey

••

Tigeladas de Mel   ⏰ Beira Alta

Preparation time: 20 minutes
Cooking time: 50 minutes
Makes: 16
⊘

olive oil, for oiling
5 eggs
zest of ½ lemon
360 g/12¾ oz (1¾ cups plus 2 teaspoons) caster
    (superfine) sugar
1 tablespoon honey
30 g/1 oz (3⅔ tablespoons) plain (all-purpose) flour
730 ml/24½ fl oz (3 cups minus 4 teaspoons) whole
    (full-fat) milk
ground cinnamon, for dusting (optional)

Preheat the oven to 200°C/400°F/Gas Mark 6. Oil
16 cake pans, about 12 cm/4½ inches diameter, or
use round clay containers, with olive oil.
    Put the eggs, lemon zest, sugar and honey into
a large bowl and mix well to combine. Add the flour
and milk and whisk until smooth.
    Once the oven is hot, put the prepared cake
pans in the oven for 6 minutes to heat up, then
carefully remove them from the oven and pour
in the egg mixture. Don't fill them up to the rim.
Bake in the hot oven for 50 minutes, or until
they are caramelised on top and golden brown.
A toothpick inserted into the middle comes out
clean. If they are not ready, cover with foil and
bake for a further 5 minutes.

Gooey Cakes with Honey from Beira Baixa

‧‧

Tigeladas com Mel da Beira Baixa ◌ Beira Baixa

Preparation time: 35 minutes
Cooking time: 25 minutes
Makes: 20
Ø

olive oil, for oiling
11 eggs
zest of 1 lemon
300 g/11 oz (1½ cups) golden caster (superfine) sugar
80 g/3 oz (⅓ cup) honey
30 g/1 oz (¼ cup) plain (all-purpose) flour
½ teaspoon ground cinnamon

Preheat the oven to 200°C/400°F/Gas Mark 6. Oil 20 cake pans, about 11 cm/4¼ inches diameter and 1 cm/½ inch high, with olive oil.

Put the eggs, lemon zest, sugar and honey into a stand mixer fitted with a whisk attachment and whisk at medium speed for 25 minutes. Alternatively, whisk with electric beaters in a large bowl.

Put the flour and cinnamon into a small bowl and mix to combine, then sift it over the egg mixture and fold it in gently until everything is fully combined.

Once the oven is hot, put the prepared cake pans in the oven for a 6 minutes to heat up, then carefully remove them from the oven and pour in the egg mixture. Don't fill them up to the rim. Bake in the hot oven for 25 minutes, or until they are caramelised on top and golden brown. A toothpick inserted into the middle comes out clean. If they are not ready, cover with foil and bake for a further 5 minutes.

Gooey Cakes from Ferreira do Zêzere

‧‧

Tigeladas de Ferreira do Zêzere ◌ Ribatejo

Preparation time: 10 minutes
Cooking time: 35 minutes
Makes: 14
Ø

260 g/9 oz (1⅓ cups) caster (superfine) sugar
110 g/3¾ oz (1 cup minus 2 teaspoons) spelt flour
7 eggs
50 ml/1⅔ fl oz (3½ tablespoons) whole (full-fat) milk
zest of 1 lemon
½ teaspoon ground cinnamon

Preheat the oven to 200°C/400°F/Gas Mark 6. Put 14 x 12-cm/4½-inch cake pans into the oven to warm.

Put the sugar and flour into a stand mixer fitted with a whisk attachment and mix to combine, then add the eggs, milk, lemon zest and cinnamon and whisk at medium speed for 5 minutes, or until smooth. Alternatively, whisk with electric beaters in a large bowl or whisk by hand until smooth.

Carefully pour the batter into the warm cake pans and bake in the hot oven for 30 minutes, or until dark brown on the top. Remove from the oven, then carefully turn them out of the cake pans and leave to cool on a wire rack.

Blancmange (18th century)

Manjar Branco – Portalegre   ⛿ Alentejo

Manjar Branco are quenelle-shaped, gelatinous cakes prepared using only white ingredients (milk, rice flour and sugar) then lightly toasted. These ones are from Portalegre, where they are plated decoratively in overlapping rows on a large tray. They date back to the Middle Ages, and similar recipes appear in many cookbooks of European countries, such as blancmange in France and the UK, and *manjar blanco* in Spain. This recipe is from the Convent of Santa Clara de Portalegre, and bears no relation to the recipe from Coimbra, which is made of chicken and served in a bowl.

Preparation time: 10 minutes
Cooking time: 40 minutes
Serves: 6–8
🍃 ⌀ ✕

450 g/1 lb (2¼ cups) caster (superfine) sugar
140 ml/4¾ fl oz (½ cup plus 4 teaspoons) whole (full-fat) milk
180 g/6 oz (1½ cups plus 2 teaspoons) rice flour
75 g/2¾ oz (½ cup) corn flour

Put the sugar and 400 ml/14 fl oz (1⅔ cups) water into a saucepan and heat for 10 minutes, or until it reaches 106°C/222°F on a sugar thermometer. Remove from the heat and add half the milk.

Put both flours and the remaining milk into a bowl and stir to combine, then add the mixture to the sugar mixture. Cook, stirring continuously, over a low heat for 10 minutes, or until it thickens. The mixture should have the consistency of a paste but not be too wet. During cooking, remove a little of the mixture with a spoon and if it sticks to your fingers continue cooking until it doesn't.

Preheat the oven to 200°C/400°F/Gas Mark 6.

Using two spoons, scoop up some of the 'dough' and pass the mixture repeatedly between the spoons to make a smooth oval shape. Place on a large baking sheet and repeat until all the 'dough' has been used. Cover with a damp tea (dish) towel and bake in the hot oven for 30 minutes, or until coloured. Leave to cool before serving.

Blancmange (medieval)

Manjar Branco   🖼 p.325   ⛿ Beira Litoral

This is the oldest sweet from the city of Coimbra. The recipe was created in the convent of Celas where the current shape was made, the 'nun's breast'. Nevertheless, it is the use of chicken breast in a sweet that really makes this stand out as it is very unusual and shows how creative and original cooking is on the Portuguese culinary landscape.

Preparation time: 10 minutes
Cooking time: 1 hour
Makes: 16
🍃

1 skinless, boneless chicken breast
zest of 1 orange
700 ml/23½ fl oz (2¾ cups) whole (full-fat) milk
420 g/14¾ oz (2 cups plus 4 teaspoons) caster (superfine) sugar
220 g/7½ oz (1¾ cups plus 4 teaspoons) rice flour
sea salt

Put the chicken into a small saucepan, cover with water, add a pinch of salt and cook over a low heat for 20 minutes, or until cooked. Remove from the pan, setting the cooking water aside and shred the meat into thin shreds, then put into a mortar and, using a pestle, mash to a paste.

Transfer the paste to a large saucepan and add the milk, sugar, orange zest, rice flour and 180 ml/ 6 fl oz (¾ cup) of the cooking water and mix well to combine. Bring to the boil over a low heat and cook, stirring continuously with a wooden spoon or silicone spatula for 10 minutes until a thick paste forms. Remove from the heat and leave to cool.

Preheat the oven to 220°C/425°F/Gas Mark 7.

Use 16 clay disks, 13 cm/5 inches in diameter as serving trays. Divide the batter between the clay disks, heaping the mixture in mounds to make the shape of a breast. Bake in the hot oven for 30 minutes, or until dark brown on top. Leave to cool before serving.

Blancmange (medieval)

Rice Pudding

••

Arroz Doce 📷 p.327   ⛶ Beira Litoral

Rice pudding is one of the most comforting desserts in Portugal, appreciated by kids and grown-ups alike. Short-grain rice (usually a Portuguese variety called *Carolino*) is cooked gently in milk on the stove, with or without egg yolks. It can be very sweet or just a little, and served either creamier or more set, warm or cold. It is typically decorated with a dusting of ground cinnamon, sometimes with initials or elaborate drawings, sometimes plain, and in a big platter or in tiny, individual plates. There are ten (or more) different recipes for this sweet dessert across the regions (Minho, Trás-os-Montes, Beira Litoral, Alentejo and Lisbon in particular) but no party or festivity, wedding or celebration, is complete without *Arroz Doce*.

Preparation time: 5 minutes
Cooking time: 40 minutes
Serves: 4
🐚 ∅

170 g/6 oz (¾ cup) short-grain rice, preferably Carolino
320 ml/11 fl oz (1¼ cups plus 4 teaspoons) whole (full-fat) milk
pared rind of 1 lemon
180 g/6 oz (1 cup minus 2 teaspoons) caster (superfine) sugar
½ teaspoon ground cinnamon
sea salt

Bring 260 ml/9 fl oz (1 cup plus 2 teaspoons) water to the boil with a pinch of salt in a medium saucepan. Add the rice, reduce the heat to low and cook for 6 minutes.

Meanwhile, bring the milk and lemon rind to the boil in a separate saucepan, then remove from the heat.

While stirring, gradually add the warm milk to the rice, keeping the temperature low so the rice cooks evenly. Cook over a low heat for 30 minutes, stirring, until the rice is soft. Still stirring, add the sugar. At this point you should have a creamy rice pudding. Remove and discard the lemon rind and pour into a serving dish. Dust cinnamon over the top before serving.

Baked Rice Pudding with Egg Whites

••

Arroz Doce com Claras   ⛶ Lisbon

Preparation time: 30 minutes
Cooking time: 50 minutes
Serves: 5
🐚 ∅

pared rind of 2 lemons
130 g/4½ oz (⅔ cup) short-grain rice, preferably Carolino
40 g/1½ oz (3 tablespoons) unsalted butter
500 ml/17 fl oz (2 cups plus 1 tablespoon) whole (full-fat) milk
4 egg yolks
220 g/7¾ oz (1 cup plus 4 teaspoons) caster (superfine) sugar
1 teaspoon ground cinnamon
3 egg whites
sea salt

Preheat the oven with the grill (broiler) to 200°C/400°F/Gas Mark 6.

Put 650 ml/22 fl oz (2¾ cups) water, the lemon rind and a pinch of salt into a large saucepan and bring to the boil. Add the rice, stir, reduce the heat to medium and cook for 15 minutes, or until soft. Add the butter, mix in, then gradually add the milk. Remove from the heat and leave to cool to room temperature.

Meanwhile, put the egg yolks into a small bowl and whisk lightly with a fork. Once the rice mixture is at room temperature, add the egg yolks, then cook over a low heat for 10 minutes, or until very creamy. Add 160 g/5¾ oz (¾ cup plus 2 teaspoons) of the sugar and stir well. Pour the rice into an ovenproof dish and sprinkle with the cinnamon.

Put the egg whites into a stand mixer fitted with a whisk attachment and whisk until soft peaks form. While whisking, gradually add the remaining 60 g/2 oz (⅓ cup) sugar. Alternatively, whisk the egg whites in a large bowl with electric beaters.

Spoon the meringue over the rice to cover, then grill (broil) for 25 minutes, or until golden brown.

Rice Pudding

Doughnuts with Lemon and Cinnamon

••

Sonhos   ∪ Minho

Sonhos, which literally means 'dreams', are an essential presence at the Portuguese Christmas table. These spherical cakes, fried until the outside turns crisp while its sweet centre remains creamy, are usually drizzled with a syrup made of sugar, cinnamon, lemon zest and port. Similar to *Malassadas* (pages 329) and *Bilharacos* (page 332), they are served piled high on large, round platters.

Preparation time: 15 minutes
Cooking time: 45 minutes
Serves: 4
⊘

75 g/2¾ oz (5 tablespoons) butter
pared rind of 1 lemon
40 g/1½ oz (¼ cup minus 2 teaspoons) caster
    (superfine) sugar
1 teaspoon ground cinnamon
250 g/9 oz (2 cups) plain (all-purpose) flour
7 eggs
1 litre/34 fl oz (4¼ cups) sunflower oil, for deep-frying
sea salt

For the syrup:
450 g/1 lb (2¼ cups) caster (superfine) sugar
pared rind of 2 lemons
1 cinnamon stick

Put 440 ml/15 fl oz (1¾ cups) water, the butter, lemon rind, sugar, cinnamon and a pinch of salt into a large saucepan. Bring to the boil over a medium heat.

Once boiling, gradually sift the flour into the mixture and stir quickly until is everything is combined. When all the flour is incorporated, transfer the dough to a work counter and knead until the dough is cold. Once cold, add the eggs, one at a time, mixing between each addition, until you have a smooth, elastic dough.

When ready to cook, line a large baking sheet with paper towels. Heat the sunflower oil for deep-frying in a large, deep saucepan or fryer over a medium-high heat until it reaches 160°C/325°F on a thermometer. Working in batches, using a tablespoon, scoop a ball of the dough and carefully drop it into the hot oil. Deep-fry for 5 minutes, or until golden brown. Remove with a slotted spoon and leave to drain on the lined baking sheet. Repeat until all the dough has been used.

To make the syrup, put all the ingredients into a large saucepan with 270 ml/9 fl oz (1 cup plus 4 teaspoons) water and heat over a medium heat for 10–12 minutes until it reaches 101°C/214°F on a thermometer. Remove from the heat and set aside.

Dip the doughnuts into the syrup until well coated before serving warm.

Doughnuts with Orange

••

Sonhos com Xarope   ∪ Lisbon
de Açúcar

Preparation time: 15 minutes, plus 30 minutes resting
Cooking time: 1 hour 20 minutes
Serves: 4
⊘

55 g/2 oz (3⅔ tablespoons) unsalted butter
pared rind of 1 orange
45 g/1½ oz (3½ tablespoons) caster (superfine) sugar
140 g/5 oz (1 cup plus 4 teaspoons) spelt flour
4 eggs
1 litre/34 fl oz (4¼ cups) sunflower oil, for deep-frying
sea salt

For the syrup (optional):
330 g/11¾ oz (1⅔ cups) caster (superfine) sugar
pared rind of 1 large lemon
1 cinnamon stick

For the cinnamon sugar (optional):
65 g (1/3 cup) caster (superfine) sugar, for dusting
½ teaspoon ground cinnamon, for dusting

Put 200 ml/7 fl oz (¾ cup) water, the butter, orange rind, sugar and a pinch of salt into a large saucepan. Bring to the boil over a medium heat.

Once boiling, gradually sift the flour into the mixture and stir quickly until everything is combined. When all the flour is incorporated, transfer the dough to a heatproof bowl and leave to cool completely. Once cold, add the eggs, one at a time, mixing well between each addition. Work the dough for 5 minutes until it is very smooth and elastic, then leave to rest for 30 minutes.

When ready to cook, line a large baking sheet with paper towels. Heat the sunflower oil for deep-frying in a large, deep saucepan or fryer over a medium-high heat until it reaches 160°C/325°F on a thermometer. Working in batches, using two oiled tablespoons, scoop up balls of the dough and carefully drop them into the hot oil. Deep-fry for 5 minutes, or until golden brown. Remove with a slotted spoon and leave to drain on the lined baking sheet. Repeat until all the dough has been used.

To make the syrup, if using, put all the ingredients into a large saucepan with 150 ml/5 fl oz (⅔ cup) water and heat over a medium heat for 10–12 minutes until it reaches 108°C/226°F on a thermometer. Remove from the heat and set aside.

To make the cinnamon sugar, if using, put the sugar and cinnamon into a shallow dish and mix together to combine.

Either dip the doughnuts into the syrup or roll the doughnuts in the cinnamon sugar until well coated before serving warm.

Rice Doughnuts with Cinnamon

Sonhos de Arroz – Alpiarça   ♡ Ribatejo

Preparation time: 15 minutes
Cooking time: 40 minutes
Serves: 4
♢ ⌀

270 g/9½ oz (1⅓ cups) long-grain rice
300 g/11 oz (2½ cups) plain (all-purpose) flour
90 g/3¼ oz (½ cup minus 2 teaspoons) caster
    (superfine) sugar, plus extra
½ teaspoon ground cinnamon
5 eggs, separated
1 litre/34 fl oz (4¼ cups) sunflower oil, for deep-frying

To finish:
65 g (⅓ cup) caster (superfine) sugar, for dusting
½ teaspoon ground cinnamon, for dusting

Put the rice into a large saucepan and cover with 1.2 litres/40 fl oz (5 cups) water. Cook over a low heat for 20 minutes, or until all the water has evaporated. Transfer the rice to a large heatproof bowl, add the flour, sugar, cinnamon and egg yolks and whisk very well until combined. Leave to cool.

Put the egg whites into another bowl and, using either electric beaters or a stand mixer fitted with a whisk attachment, whisk until soft peaks form, then gently fold the whites into the rice mixture until they are incorporated.

When ready to cook, line a large baking sheet with paper towels. Heat the sunflower oil for deep-frying in a large, deep saucepan or fryer over a medium-high heat until it reaches 180°C/350°F on a thermometer. Working in batches, scoop some of the mixture out with an oiled spoon and carefully drop into the hot oil and deep-fry for 5 minutes, or until golden brown. Remove with a slotted spoon and leave to drain on the lined baking sheet. Repeat until all the dough has been used.

Put the sugar and cinnamon into a shallow dish and mix together to combine. One at a time and while still hot, add the doughnuts to the cinnamon sugar and toss until well coated before serving warm.

Deep-fried Dough

Malassadas   ♡ Açores

Malassadas are small, light cylinders or rectangles of leavened doughs that are deep-fried and then coated with granulated sugar, and sometimes cinnamon. Usually eaten on Mardi Gras, these sweets are a specialty of São Miguel. Originally created on the island in preparation for Lent, with the intention of using up home ingredients such as lard and sugar, the tradition spread to Hawaii, where Shrove Tuesday is known as Malassadas Day. This celebration dates back to the 19th century, when the Portuguese (mostly from the Azores) went to Hawaii to work in sugarcane plantations. They took not only their Catholic traditions with them, but also their *Malassadas* recipes.

Preparation time: 20 minutes, plus 3 hours rising
Cooking time: 40 minutes
Makes: 16
⌀

20 g/¾ oz (1 tablespoon plus 1 teaspoon) fresh yeast or
    4 g/¾ oz (1 teaspoon) instant dried yeast
250 ml/8½ fl oz (1 cup) whole (full-fat) milk, warmed
550 g/1 lb 4 oz (4½ cups) plain (all-purpose) flour
45 g/1½ oz (¼ cup) caster (superfine) sugar
1 teaspoon salt
3 whole eggs
1 litre/34 fl oz (4¼ cups) sunflower oil, for deep-frying,
    plus extra for oiling

To finish:
65 g (⅓ cup) caster (superfine) sugar, for dusting
½ teaspoon ground cinnamon, for dusting

If using fresh yeast, dissolve it in 125 ml/4¼ fl oz (½ cup) of the milk. Put the flour into a bowl and stir in the sugar and salt. Add the yeast and eggs and mix together, then mix in enough milk to make a soft, slightly sticky dough. Cover the bowl with a clean tea (dish) towel and leave to rise at room temperature for 3 hours.

When ready to cook, line a large baking sheet with paper towels. Heat the oil for deep-frying in a large, deep saucepan or fryer over a medium-high heat until it reaches 160°C/325°F on a thermometer. Working in batches, lightly oil your hands, take small amounts of the dough, about 40 g/1½ oz (2 tablespoons), and stretch the dough to the size of your hand (about 10 x 7.5 cm/4 x 2 inches, and about 1 cm/½ inch thick). Carefully drop into the hot oil and deep-fry for 4–5 minutes, turning halfway through, or until golden brown on both sides. Remove with a slotte spoon and leave to drain on the lined baking sheet. Repeat until all the dough has been used.

Put the sugar and cinnamon into a shallow dish and mix together to combine. One at a time and while still hot, add the doughnuts to the cinnamon sugar and toss until well coated before serving warm.

Doughnuts Dusted with Cinnamon Sugar

Filhoses 📷 p.331   ⛉ Beira Baixa

Preparation time: 30 minutes, plus 3 hours rising
Cooking time: 30 minutes
Serves: 6
⛉ ∅ V

10 g/¼ oz (2 teaspoons) fresh yeast or
      2.5g (scant 1 teaspoon) instant dried yeast
110 ml/3¾ fl oz (½ cup minus 2 teaspoons) olive oil,
      plus extra for oiling
15 ml/½ fl oz (1 tablespoon) firewater
50 ml/1⅔ fl oz (3½ tablespoons) orange juice
5 eggs
750 g/1 lb 10 oz (6 cups) flour (T55)
4 g/¼ oz (scant 1 teaspoon) sea salt
1.5 litres/50 fl oz (6¼ cups) olive oil, for deep-frying

To finish:
65 g (1/3 cup) caster (superfine) sugar, for dusting
½ teaspoon ground cinnamon, for dusting

If using fresh yeast, put it into a small bowl and add a tiny bit of warm water. Stir until dissolved.

Put 110 ml/3¾ fl oz (½ cup minus 2 teaspoons) olive oil, firewater and orange juice into a small saucepan and heat gently over a low heat for 5 minutes. Do not boil.

Put the eggs into a large bowl and whisk, then add the warm liquids and the yeast and mix well until combined. Add the flour and mix with your hands to form a smooth dough. Cover the bowl with a clean tea (dish) towel or food wrap and leave to rise at room temperature for 3 hours.

When ready to cook, line a large baking sheet with paper towels. Heat the olive oil for deep-frying in a large, deep saucepan or fryer over a medium-high heat until it reaches 180°C/350°F on a thermometer. Once it has reached temperature, carefully drop a little dough into the hot oil to test; if it sizzles and turns golden brown within 30 seconds, it is ready.

Working in batches, lightly oil your hands, take small amounts of the dough, about 40 g/1½ oz (2 tablespoons), and flatten and stretch it. Carefully drop into the hot oil and deep-fry for 4–5 minutes, turning halfway through, or until golden brown on both sides. Using with a slotted spoon or fish slice (spatula), remove from the oil and leave to drain on the lined baking sheet. Repeat until all the dough has been used.

Put the sugar and cinnamon into a shallow dish and mix together to combine. One at a time and while still hot, add the doughnuts to the cinnamon sugar and toss until well coated before serving warm or cold.

Deep-fried Dough Dusted with Cinnamon Sugar

Coscorões de Almeirim   ⛉ Ribatejo

Preparation time: 30 minutes, plus 25 minutes resting
Cooking time: 45 minutes
Makes: 32
∅

195 g/7 oz (1 stick plus 5 tablespoons) unsalted butter
650 g/1 lb 7 oz (5¼ cups) plain (all-purpose) flour, plus
      extra for dusting
1½ teaspoons instant dried yeast
2 eggs
2 egg yolks
zest and juice of 1 orange
150 ml/5 fl oz (⅔ cup) white wine at room temperature
1.2 litres/40 fl oz (5 cups) sunflower oil, for deep-frying
sea salt

To finish:
100 g (½ cup) caster (superfine) sugar, for dusting
1 teaspoon ground cinnamon, for dusting

Put the butter into a saucepan and heat over a low heat for 2–3 minutes, or until melted. Remove from the heat and set aside.

Put the flour and yeast into a large bowl and make a well in the middle of the flour. Add the egg, egg yolks, orange juice, melted butter and a pinch of salt, then mix the dough with your hands, slowly incorporating the wine, a little at a time, using just enough to form a smooth dough. Cover with a clean tea (dish) towel or food wrap and leave to rest at room temperature for 25 minutes.

Divide the dough into two portions. Roll out one portion of the dough on a lightly floured surface to 2 mm/1/16 inch thickness. Cut out small rectangles, about 7.5 x 5 cm/3 x 2 inches, then score each rectangle with three slashes. Repeat with the rest of the dough. Cover the dough rectangles with a clean tea (dish) towel and keep covered until ready to cook.

Line a large baking sheet with paper towels. Heat the sunflower oil for deep-frying in a large, deep saucepan or fryer over a medium-high heat until it reaches 180°C/350°F on a thermometer. Working in batches, carefully drop the dough into the hot oil and deep-fry for 3 minutes, turning them halfway through, or until golden brown all over. Remove with a slotted spoon and leave to drain on the lined baking sheet.

Put the sugar and cinnamon into a shallow dish and mix together to combine. One at a time and while still hot, add the fried pastries to the cinnamon sugar and toss until well coated before serving warm or cold.

Doughnuts Dusted with Cinnamon Sugar

'Drunken' Doughnuts

••

Borrachos ⋃ Alentejo

As in the Beiras region, in Alentejo, they also came up with the recipe that includes a strong spirit, in this case white wine, which when fried, you can really taste the alcohol. You can keep these cooked *Borrachos* for a long time in an airtight container.

Preparation time: 25 minutes, plus 45 minutes resting
Cooking time: 20 minutes
Serves: 6
⋂

380 g/13½ oz (3 cups plus 2 teaspoons) plain
    (all-purpose) flour, plus extra for dusting
1½ teaspoons instant dried yeast
1 teaspoon ground cinnamon
160 g/5¾ oz lard (pork fat)
145 ml/5 fl oz (½ cup) white wine
25 ml/1 fl oz (2 tablespoons) firewater
juice of 1 orange
1 whole egg
1 litre/34 fl oz (4¼ cups) sunflower oil, for deep-frying

To finish:
100 g (½ cup) caster (superfine) sugar, for dusting
1 teaspoon ground cinnamon, for dusting

Sift the flour into a large bowl, add the yeast and cinnamon and mix together until combined.

Put the lard (pork fat) into a medium saucepan and heat over a medium heat until melted, then add the white wine. Add the lard and wine mixture to the flour and mix until combined. Add the firewater, orange juice and egg to the pan and mix until a soft dough forms, then knead the dough well for 5 minutes. Cover the bowl with a clean tea (dish) towel or food wrap and leave to rest at room temperature for 45 minutes. The dough should have an elastic consistency and, when poked with your finger, it should come out clean.

Turn the dough out on a floured work counter and spread it into a thin sheet. Using a large ring cutter, cut out rounds from the dough. Next, using a medium ring cutter, punch out smaller rounds from the centre of each of the larger rounds to make rings.

Line a large baking sheet with paper towels. Heat the sunflower oil for deep-frying in a large, deep saucepan or fryer over a medium-high heat until it reaches 180°C/350°F on a thermometer. Working in batches, carefully drop the dough rings into the hot oil and deep-fry for 3 minutes, turning them halfway through, or until golden brown all over. Remove with a slotted spoon and leave to drain on the lined baking sheet.

Put the sugar and cinnamon into a shallow dish and mix together to combine. One at a time and while still hot, add the doughnuts to the cinnamon sugar and toss until well coated before serving warm or cold.

Pumpkin Doughnuts

••

Bilharacos ⋃ Beira Litoral

These small, spherical fritters are indispensable during Christmas season, although they are also sold in pastry shops and cafés throughout the year. They have been given the name *Bilharacos* in the Aveiro district, but are known as *Sonhos* (literally 'dreams') in other regions of Portugal. *Bilharacos* are usually made of pumpkin, which gives them a brown tint on the outside and a vivid orange inside. They sometimes include port, nuts and dried fruits (walnuts, pine nuts or raisins) and, after they are fried, it is common to sprinkle them with cinnamon sugar.

Preparation time: 30 minutes, plus overnight standing and 30 minutes resting
Cooking time: 1 hour
Serves: 6
🥜 ⋂ ⊘

1.25 kg/2 lb 12 oz pumpkin, peeled, de-seeded and cut
    into chunks
1 cinnamon stick
pared rind of 1 lemon
90 g/3¼ oz (¾ cup) fine polenta (cornmeal)
4 eggs, lightly beaten
25 ml/1 fl oz (2 tablespoons) white port
1 teaspoon ground cinnamon
zest and juice of 1 orange
1 teaspoon instant dried yeast
1 litre/34 fl oz (4¼ cups) sunflower oil, for deep-frying,
    plus extra for oiling
90 g/3¼ oz (½ cup plus 2 teaspoons) caster (superfine)
    sugar
sea salt

To finish:
100 g (½ cup) caster (superfine) sugar, for dusting
1 teaspoon ground cinnamon, for dusting

The day before, put the pumpkin into a medium saucepan, pour in enough water to cover, add the cinnamon stick, lemon rind and a pinch of salt and cook over a low heat for 20 minutes, or until soft. Drain the pumpkin, discarding the cinnamon and lemon, and transfer to a perforated tray or colander. Leave to drip overnight.

The next day, put the pumpkin onto a clean tea (dish) towel and squeeze out any remaining moisture to form a dry, thick paste.

Put the pumpkin purée into a large bowl, add the polenta (cornmeal), eggs, port, ground cinnamon, orange zest and juice, and yeast and mix well to form a smooth dough. Cover with a clean tea (dish) towel and leave to rest at room temperature for 30 minutes.

When ready to cook, line a large baking sheet with paper towels. Heat the sunflower oil for deep-frying in a large, deep saucepan or fryer over a medium-high heat until it reaches 180°C/350°F on a thermometer. Working in batches, using two oiled tablespoons, scoop up balls of the dough and carefully drop them into the hot oil. Deep-fry for 5 minutes, or until golden brown. Remove with a slotted spoon and leave to drain on the lined baking sheet.

Put the sugar and cinnamon into a shallow dish and mix together to combine. One at a time and while still hot, add the doughnuts to the cinnamon sugar and toss until well coated before serving warm or cold.

Pumpkin Doughnuts with Cinnamon

••

Filhoses de Abóbora   ▢ **Leiria**

Preparation time: 30 minutes, plus 45 minutes resting
Cooking time: 1 hour
Serves: 4
▢ ⌀

300 g/11 oz pumpkin flesh, cut into chunks
3 g/⅛ oz (½ teaspoon) sea salt
500 g/1 lb 2 oz (4¼ cups minus 2 teaspoons) plain (all-purpose) flour
zest of 2 oranges
150 ml/5 fl oz (⅔ cup) orange juice
2⅔ teaspoons instant dried yeast
2 whole eggs
1 litre/34 fl oz (4¼ cups) sunflower oil, for deep-frying

To finish:
100 g (½ cup) caster (superfine) sugar, for dusting
1 teaspoon ground cinnamon, for dusting

Put the pumpkin into a medium saucepan, pour in enough water to cover, add the salt and cook over a low heat for 20 minutes, or until soft. Drain the pumpkin and transfer to a perforated tray or colander and leave to drip. Transfer to a blender or food processor and blitz to a purée.

Put the pumpkin purée into the bowl of a stand mixer fitted with a paddle attachment or in a large bowl, add the flour, orange zest and juice, yeast and eggs and mix well to form a smooth dough. Cover with a damp tea (dish) towel and leave to rest at room temperature for 45 minutes.

When ready to cook, line a large baking sheet with paper towels. Heat the sunflower oil for deep-frying in a large, deep saucepan or fryer over medium-high heat until it reaches 180°C/350°F on a thermometer. Working in batches, using two oiled tablespoons, scoop up balls of the dough and carefully drop them into the hot oil. Deep-fry for 5 minutes, or until golden brown. Remove with a slotted spoon and leave to drain on the lined baking sheet.

Put the sugar and cinnamon into a shallow dish and mix together to combine. One at a time and while still hot, add the doughnuts to the cinnamon sugar and toss until well coated before serving warm or cold.

Oven-baked Doughnuts

••

Filhoses no Forno   ▢ **Açores**

Preparation time: 20 minutes
Cooking time: 40–50 minutes
Serves: 4
⌀

For the dough:
350 g/12 oz (3 cups) self-raising (self-rising) flour, plus extra for dusting
1 teaspoon instant dried yeast
25 g/1 oz (1 tablespoon plus 2 teaspoons) caster (superfine) sugar
finely grated zest of 1 lemon
700 ml/23½ fl oz (2¾ cups plus 2 tablespoons) whole (full-fat) milk
8 eggs
unsalted butter, for greasing

For the filling:
320 ml/11 fl oz (1¼ cups) whole (full-fat) milk
10 g/¼ oz (2 teaspoons) cornflour (cornstarch)
280 g/10 oz (1½ cups minus 4 teaspoons) caster (superfine) sugar
2 egg yolks
45 g/1½ oz (3 tablespoons) unsalted butter
pared rind of 1 lemon

To make the dough, sift the flour and yeast into a bowl and mix together.

Combine the sugar, lemon zest and milk in a medium saucepan and bring to the boil. As soon as it is boiling, remove from the heat, add the flour and whisk well until combined. Add the eggs, one by one, stirring with a silicone spatula between each addition and making sure each egg is incorporated before adding the next. Return the pan to the heat and cook over a low heat for 10 minutes, or until smooth and the eggs are cooked. Remove from the heat and take the dough out of the pan. Leave to cool slightly.

Preheat the oven to 180°C/350°F/Gas Mark 4. Grease a large baking sheet with butter.

Divide the dough into 8 equal-sized balls, place them on the prepared baking sheet and bake for 20–30 minutes, or until golden brown and when a toothpick is inserted into the middle comes out clean. Place the doughnuts on a wire rack to cool while you make the filling.

To make the filling, put all the filling ingredients into a large saucepan and cook over a medium heat for 10 minutes, or until it thickens up. Remove from the heat and leave to cool.

Once both doughnuts and filling have cooled, make a small hole in each of the baked doughnuts and spoon a little of the filling into the cavity before serving.

Portuguese Churros

Farturas   ♡ Lisbon

Ask any Portuguese person from north to south, and they will immediately tell you that *Farturas* remind them of popular festivities and fairs that take place throughout the year from the interior to the coast. These large, soft sweets, usually sold from flashing, brightly coloured food trucks, are made of a light dough extruded from a piping (pastry) bag into a big fryer to form a large spiral shape. The fried dough is then cut into smaller pieces using a pair of scissors and eaten plain, or sprinkled with either sugar or cinnamon, or both.

Preparation time: 5 minutes
Cooking time: 30 minutes
Serves: 4
▯ ⌀ ∨ ▯ ✕

1.5 litres/50 fl oz (6¼ cups) sunflower oil, for deep-frying
320 g/11¼ oz (2⅔ cups) self-raising (self-rising) flour
1 teaspoon fine table salt

To finish:
100 g (½ cup) caster (superfine) sugar, for dusting
1 teaspoon ground cinnamon, for dusting

Line a large baking sheet with paper towels. Heat the sunflower oil for deep-frying in a large, deep saucepan or fryer until it reaches 200°C/400°F on a thermometer.

Meanwhile, put the flour and salt into a large bowl with 600 ml/20 fl oz (2½ cups) cold water and mix quickly. It shouldn't be too thick so you may need to add a little more water.

Spoon the dough into a piping (pastry) bag fitted with a star-shaped nozzle (tip). Once the oil is at temperature, working in batches, pipe the dough directly into the hot oil, from the rim of the pan to the middle. Deep-fry for about 5 minutes — it should fry fairly fast. As soon as it is golden brown all over, remove with a slotted spoon and leave to drain on the lined baking sheet. Using a pair of scissors, cut into pieces, about 10 cm/4 inches long.

Put the sugar and cinnamon into a shallow dish and mix together to combine. One at a time and while still hot, add the churros to the cinnamon sugar and toss until well coated before serving warm.

'Pumpkin Stem' Churros

Pés de Abóbora   ♡ Ribatejo

Pés de Abóbora translates as 'pumpkin feet' or 'pumpkin stems'. They are fried pastries, similar to churros, but with added port.

Preparation time: 5 minutes, plus 15 minutes resting
Cooking time: 35 minutes
Serves: 4
⌀

25 g/1 oz (2 tablespoons) unsalted butter
zest of 2 lemons
230 g/8 oz (2 cups minus 2 teaspoons) plain (all-purpose) flour
65 ml/2¼ fl oz (¼ cup) white port
2 eggs
1 litre/34 fl oz (4¼ cups) sunflower oil, for deep-frying
sea salt

To finish:
100 g (½ cup) caster (superfine) sugar, for dusting
1 teaspoon ground cinnamon, for dusting

Bring 200 ml/7 fl oz (¾ cup plus 1 tablespoon) water, the butter, lemon zest and a pinch of salt to a simmer in a large saucepan. When simmering, add the flour and stir for 5 minutes until thick. Remove from the heat and, stirring continuously, add the port then the eggs, one at a time, stirring well between each addition, until it is a smooth batter. Leave to rest for 15 minutes.

When ready to cook, line a large baking sheet with paper towels. Heat the sunflower oil for deep-frying in a large, deep saucepan or fryer until it reaches 180°C/350°F on a thermometer.

Spoon the dough into a piping (pastry) bag fitted with a star-shaped nozzle (tip). Once the oil is at temperature, working in batches, pipe the dough directly into the hot oil, cutting it into 15-cm/6-inch pieces as you pipe. Deep-fry for 5 minutes, or until golden brown all over. Remove with a slotted spoon and leave to drain on the lined baking sheet.

Put the sugar and cinnamon into a shallow dish and mix together to combine. One at a time and while still hot, add the doughnuts to the cinnamon sugar and toss until well coated before serving warm.

Deep-fried Polenta Cakes with Orange and Fennel

Broas Fritas de Benavente   ♡ Ribatejo

Preparation time: 20 minutes, plus 15 minutes resting
Cooking time: 40 minutes
Makes: 16
◻ ⌀ V

210 g/7½ oz (1¾ cups) fine polenta (cornmeal)
250 g/9 oz (2 cups) spelt flour, plus extra for dusting
260 g/9 oz (1⅓ cups) caster (superfine) sugar, plus
     extra for sprinkling
5 g/¼ oz chopped wild fennel tops
zest and juice of 1 orange
80 ml/2¾ fl oz (⅓ cup) olive oil
1 litre/34 fl oz (4¼ cups) sunflower oil, for deep-frying

Put the polenta (cornmeal), flour, sugar, wild fennel tops and the orange zest and juice into a large heatproof bowl and mix together with your hands.
　Heat 80 ml/2¾ fl oz (⅓ cup) water in a small saucepan until warm. Remove from the heat.
　Heat the olive oil in a medium saucepan over a medium-high heat until it reaches 160°C/325°F on a thermometer. Pour it into the flour mixture, then add the warm water and knead the dough well for 10 minutes. Cover with a tea (dish) towel or food wrap and leave to rest for 15 minutes.
　When ready to cook, line a large baking sheet with paper towels. Heat the sunflower oil for deep-frying in a large, deep saucepan or fryer over a medium-high heat until it reaches 180°C/350°F on a thermometer.
　Divide the dough into 16 small balls, each of 50 g/2 oz. Dust your hands with flour, then flatten each ball a little with your hands. Working in batches, carefully drop the balls into the hot oil and deep-fry for 5 minutes, or until golden brown all over. Remove with a slotted spoon and leave to drain on the lined baking sheet.
　Sprinkle with some extra sugar before serving.

Deep-fried Dough with Orange and Cinnamon

Filhoses   ♡ Alentejo

These pillowy, golden, deep-fried leavened cakes are usually eaten for Christmas or Carnival in Alentejo. There are two traditional ways to shape *Filhoses* (page 429): by hand, making large, flat rounds and cutting four or five parallel cuts that stop short of the edges, then twisting the dough before frying; or using thin, metallic moulds on a stick to stamp out a lacy round, square or flower shape (called *Filhoses de Forma* or *Floreta*). *Filhoses* are usually sprinkled with sugar and cinnamon, or honey syrup, after being fried.

Preparation time: 15 minutes, plus 10 minutes resting
Cooking time: 30 minutes
Serves: 4–6
◻ ⌀ V

800 g/1 lb 12 oz (6⅔ cups) plain (all-purpose) flour
200 ml/7 fl oz (¾ cup plus 1 tablespoon) olive oil
zest and juice of 2 oranges
100 ml/3½ fl oz (⅓ cup plus 1 tablespoon) firewater
     or brandy
pinch of sea salt
pinch of ground cinnamon
2 litres/68 fl oz (8½ cups) sunflower oil, for deep-frying

To finish:
100 g (½ cup) caster (superfine) sugar, for dusting
1 teaspoon ground cinnamon, for dusting

Sift the flour into a large bowl. Heat the olive oil in a medium saucepan over a medium heat until warm.
　Pour the olive oil over the flour and mix in. Add the orange juice and zest, the firewater, salt and cinnamon and mix together until a smooth dough has formed. Cover with food wrap and leave to rest for 10 minutes.
　Tip out the dough onto a lightly floured work counter and roll into rectangles, about 5 mm/ ¼ inch thick.
　Line a large baking sheet with paper towels. Heat the sunflower oil for deep-frying in a medium, deep saucepan over a medium-high heat until it reaches 180°C/350°F on a sugar thermometer. Working in batches, carefully lower the pastries into the hot oil and deep-fry for 5 minutes, or until golden brown, then remove and leave to drain on the lined baking sheet.
　Put the sugar and cinnamon into a shallow dish and mix together to combine. One at a time and while still hot, add the doughnuts to the cinnamon sugar and toss until well coated before serving warm.

Deep-fried Rolled Dough

Filhoses de Enrolar 📷 p.337 ⛛ Alentejo

Filhoses de Enrolar, or *Filhoses de Vila Viçosa*, are golden, long strips of dough, rolled into a snail's shell shape, fried, then dipped in sugar syrup or honey. These candy fritters were traditionally cooked on the Thursday preceding Carnival, in sufficient quantities to last the entire week. In some parts of Alentejo, such as the region of Montemor-o-Novo, the recipe for the *Filhoses* (page 429) batter calls for orange juice, and these would usually be sprinkled with sugar and cinnamon instead of sugar syrup.

Preparation time: 20 minutes, plus 20 minutes resting
Cooking time: 30 minutes
Serves: 4

70 g/2½ oz lard (pork fat)
80 g/3 oz (5⅓ tablespoons) unsalted butter
650 g/1 lb 7 oz (5½ cups minus 2 teaspoons) plain
   (all-purpose) flour, plus extra for dusting
50 ml/1⅔ fl oz (3½ tablespoons) olive oil
60 ml/2 fl oz (4 tablespoons) firewater or brandy
juice of 1 orange
3 eggs
1.5 litres/50 fl oz (6¼ cups) olive oil, for deep-frying

For the syrup:
450 g/1 lb (2¼ cups) caster (superfine) sugar

Put the lard (pork fat) and butter into a saucepan and heat over a medium-low heat until melted.

Sift the flour into a large bowl and add the melted fats, olive oil, firewater, orange juice and eggs. Using your hands, mix everything together until a smooth dough forms. Cover with a clean tea (dish) towel and leave to rest at room temperature for 20 minutes.

Turn the dough out onto a floured work counter and, using your hands, stretch the dough into a thin sheet, 3 mm/⅛ inch thick, then cut the dough into strips, about 6 x 12 cm/2½ x 4½ inches.

When ready to cook, line a large baking sheet with paper towels. Heat the olive oil for deep-frying in a large, deep saucepan or fryer over a medium-high heat until it reaches 170°C/344°F on a thermometer. Working in batches, take a dough strip and carefully dip one end into the oil then, using two forks, roll the strip up into a coil. Deep-fry for 5 minutes, or until golden brown. Remove with a slotted spoon and leave to drain on the lined baking sheet. Repeat with the remaining dough strips.

To make the syrup, put the sugar into a medium saucepan with 200 ml/7 fl oz (¾ cup) water and heat over a medium heat for 10–12 minutes until it reaches 110°C/230°F on a thermometer. Remove the pan from the heat and dip each *Filhose* into the sugar syrup until well coated. Place them on a plate before serving.

Sweet Potato Pastries

Pastéis de Batata Doce ⛛ Algarve

Preparation time: 30 minutes, plus 1 hour resting
Cooking time: 40 minutes
Makes: about 16
⌀

25 g/1 oz (2 tablespoons) unsalted butter
25 ml/1 fl oz (2 tablespoons) olive oil
300 g/11 oz (2½ cups) plain (all-purpose) flour
1 litre/34 fl oz (4¼ cups) sunflower oil, for deep-frying
100 g (½ cup) caster (superfine) sugar, for dusting
sea salt

For the filling:
350 g/12 oz sweet potatoes
200 g/7 oz (1 cup) caster (superfine) sugar
1 teaspoon ground cinnamon
grated zest of 1 lemon

Put the butter into a small saucepan and heat over a low heat for 2 minutes, or until melted. Remove from the heat, add the olive oil and stir to combine. Sift the flour into a large bowl, add the melted butter and olive oil mixture with a pinch of salt, then add 150 ml/5 fl oz (⅔ cup) warm water. Using your hands, mix everything together until a smooth dough forms. Knead the dough for 10 minutes, then cover with food wrap and leave to rest at room temperature for 1 hour.

Meanwhile, make the filling. Preheat the oven to 180°C/350°F/Gas Mark 4. Wrap the sweet potatoes in foil and bake in the hot oven for 20 minutes, or until very soft. Leave for a few minutes until cool enough to handle, then peel off the skins. Transfer to a blender or food processor and blitz to a purée.

Put the sweet potato purée into a large bowl with the sugar, cinnamon and lemon zest. Mix everything together well and leave to cool.

Turn the dough out onto a floured work counter and roll it into a thin sheet, 3 mm/⅛ inch thick. Using a large ring cutter, cut out rounds from the dough. Using a teaspoon, put a small pile of the filling onto one half of each round, then fold the other half of the round over to cover. Gently press down with your fingertips around the edge to seal in the filling.

When ready to cook, line a large baking sheet with paper towels. Heat the sunflower oil for deep-frying in a large, deep saucepan or fryer over a medium-high heat until it reaches 180°C/350°F on a thermometer. Working in batches, carefully drop the pastries into the hot oil and deep-fry for 5 minutes, or until golden brown. Remove with a slotted spoon and leave to drain on the lined baking sheet.

Put some sugar into a shallow dish and toss the pastries in the sugar until well coated before serving.

Deep-fried Rolled Dough

Sweet Chickpea Pasties

••

Azevias com Grão 🖼 p.339   ⋃ Alentejo

A few years ago, I put these sweet chickpea (garbanzo) filled pasties on the menu for a project that I ran in London's east end. The guest's loved the original idea of chickpeas in a sweet pasty.

Preparation time: 25 minutes, plus 12 hours soaking
Cooking time: 1 hour
Serves: 6

For the dough:
1 quantity *Massa Tenra* (page 293)

For the filling:
1 kg/2 lb 4 oz (5½ cups) dried chickpeas (garbanzos)
700 g/1 lb 9 oz (3½ cups) caster (superfine) sugar
pared rind of 1 lemon
1 cinnamon stick
⅛ teaspoon ground cinnamon
1 litre/34 fl oz (4¼ cups) sunflower oil, for deep-frying

To finish:
100 g (½ cup) caster (superfine) sugar, for dusting
1 teaspoon ground cinnamon, for dusting

The day before, put the chickpeas (garbanzos) into a large bowl of cold water and leave to soak for 12 hours.

The next day, drain the chickpeas then rub them to release their skins. Rinse under cold running water to wash the skins off. Put the chickpeas into a large saucepan, pour in enough cold water to cover and cook for 30 minutes, or until soft. Drain, then put the chickpeas into a food processer and process to a purée. Set aside.

Put the sugar and lemon rind into a large saucepan with 200 ml/7 fl oz (¾ cup) water and heat over a medium heat for 10–12 minutes until it reaches 108°C/226°F on a thermometer. Add the chickpea purée to the pan together with the cinnamon stick and ground cinnamon, then cook, stirring continuously, for a further 5 minutes, or until you can see the bottom of the pan. Remove the lemon rind and cinnamon stick and leave the filling to cool before making the *Azevias*.

Turn the dough out onto a floured work counter and divide it in half. Roll out each piece into a thin sheet roughly the same size. Placing them at regular intervals, pile tablespoons of the filling along the centre of one sheet. Lay the second sheet on top to cover the filling. Using a pasta cutter, cut around the mounds of filling to make round parcels. Press down around the edges of each parcel to seal in the filling.

When ready to cook, line a large baking sheet with paper towels. Heat the oil for deep-frying in a large, deep saucepan or fryer over a medium-high heat until it reaches 180°C/350°F on a thermometer. Working in batches, carefully lower the pasties into the hot oil and deep-fry for 5 minutes, or until golden brown all over. Remove with a slotted spoon and drain on the lined baking sheet.

Put the sugar and cinnamon into a shallow dish and mix together to combine. One at a time and while still hot, add the pasties to the cinnamon sugar and toss until well coated before serving warm.

Sugar-glazed Pastry Puffs from Reguengo do Fetal

••

Cavacas do Reguengo do Fetal   ⋃ Leiria

Cavacas are hollow, dry cakes, similar to a popover or profiterole, which are coated with a bright white sugar glaze. They are usually consumed during Easter and Christmas, as they have a strong connection to some religious practices.

Preparation time: 30 minutes
Cooking time: 25–30 minutes
Makes: 20
⬠ ⌀

For the dough:
7 whole eggs
7 egg yolks
70 ml/2½ fl oz (¼ cup) extra virgin olive oil
3 g (¼ teaspoon) sea salt
600 g/1 lb 5 oz (5 cups) plain (all-purpose) flour,
    plus extra for dusting

For the glaze:
450 g/1 lb (2¼ cups) caster (superfine) sugar
4 egg whites
zest and juice of 1 lemon

Preheat the oven to 160°C/325°F/Gas Mark 3.
Put the whole eggs and egg yolks into a bowl, add the olive oil, salt and half the flour, then mix well until the flour is fully incorporated. Gradually add the remaining flour until a smooth dough forms.

Turn the dough out onto a floured work counter and roll it out until 2 cm/¾ inch thick. Cut the dough into 8-cm/3¼-inch strips, then cut on the horizontal. *Cavacas* are traditionally a wobbly shape, so bake them on top of some rolls made from folded foil, sprinkled with a little flour. Place the dough strips over the top and bake in the hot oven for 10 minutes, or until golden brown. Remove from the oven and leave to cool on a wire rack until completley cold.

Meanwhile, make the glaze. Put the sugar, egg whites, lemon zest and juice into a stand mixer fitted with a whisk attachment and whisk until creamy and resembles meringue.

Preheat the oven to 140°C/275°F/Gas Mark 1.
Once cold, brush one side of each *Cavacas* with the glaze, then put them on a baking sheet and bake in the low oven for 8 minutes, or until the glaze is dry. Remove from the oven and repeat the process on the other side. Leave to cool on a wire rack before serving.

Sweet Chickpea Pasties

Sugar-glazed Pastry Puffs from Caldas da Rainha

Cavacas das Caldas   ⏚ Lisbon

The distinctive concave shape of *cavacas* once served as a receptacle for wine, poured in to soften and moisten them. *Cavacas das Caldas*, a symbol of the city of Caldas da Rainha, were, in the 19th century, cooked in *cavacarias* — places that baked and sold *cavacas* to the many pilgrims who passed through on their way to Fátima (the cake keeps for a long time without going stale), and to people frequenting the region's thermal springs.

Preparation time: 30 minutes
Cooking time: 45 minutes
Makes: 15
Ø ✕

55 g/2 oz (3⅔ tablespoons) unsalted butter,
    plus extra for greasing
220 g/7½ oz (1¾ cups plus 2 teaspoons) spelt flour,
    plus extra for dusting
7 eggs

For the syrup:
380 g/13½ oz (2 cups minus 4 teaspoons) caster
    (superfine) sugar

Preheat the oven to 180°C/350°F/Gas Mark 4. Grease 15 small cake pans, each measuring 10 cm/4 inches in diameter, with butter then sprinkle with flour, tipping out the excess.

Put the butter into a small saucepan and heat over a low heat for 2 minutes, or until melted. Remove from the heat and set aside.

Put the eggs into a stand mixer fitted with a whisk attachment, add the flour and whisk at medium speed for 20 minutes, or until smooth. Alternatively, whisk with electric beaters in a large bowl. While stirring, slowly add the melted butter and keep stirring until it is well incorporated and makes a smooth batter.

Divide the batter evenly between the prepared cake pans, filling them to no more than 5 mm/ ¼ inch from the rim as they will rise during cooking. Bake in the hot oven for 20 minutes, then reduce the oven temperature to 160°C/325°F/ Gas Mark 3 and bake for a further 10 minutes. Remove from the oven, then turn the *Cavacas* out of the pans and leave to cool on a wire rack until completely cold.

To make the syrup, put the sugar into a large saucepan with 220 ml/7½ fl oz (1 cup) water and heat over a medium heat for 10–12 minutes, or until it reaches 101°C/214°F on a thermometer. Remove from the heat.

Once cold, dip each *Cavacas* into the syrup, then leave to dry on a wire rack before serving.

Sugar-glazed Pastry Puffs from Romaria

Cavacas da Romaria   ⏚ Beira Alta

Cavacas da Romaria are a sweet treat made during Easter. There are two varieties, one covered with a sugar syrup and one without. These ones, which are concave, are typical from the Viseu region. After they have cooled, the locals fill them with red wine or port.

Preparation time: 30 minutes
Cooking time: 30–35 minutes
Makes: 26
⏚ Ø

750 g/1 lb 10 oz (6¼ cups) self-raising (self-rising) flour,
    plus extra for dusting
3 g/⅛ oz (½ teaspoon) sea salt
75 ml/2½ fl oz (5 tablespoons) olive oil
3 eggs
700 g/1 lb 9 oz egg whites
red wine, to serve

For the syrup:
380 g/13½ oz (2 cups minus 4 teaspoons) caster
    (superfine) sugar

Preheat the oven to 200°C/400°F/Gas Mark 6. Dust several large baking sheets with flour.

Put the flour, salt and olive oil into a large bowl and mix with your hands. Add the eggs, one at a time, mixing between each addition, until a smooth dough forms. Alternatively, mix in a stand mixer at medium speed. While stirring, gradually add the egg whites until the dough is light and aerated.

Using a large dessertspoon, scoop the dough onto the prepared baking sheets, leaving space in between them as they will spread. Bake in the hot oven for 20 minutes, or until light golden brown. Remove from the oven and leave to cool on wire racks until completely cold.

To make the syrup, put the sugar into a large saucepan with 700 ml/23½ fl oz (2¾ cups) water and heat over a medium heat for 10–12 minutes, or until it reaches 117°C/243°F on a thermometer. Remove from the heat and whisk until it becomes opaque.

Once cold, brush each *Cavacas* with the syrup, then leave to dry on a wire rack before serving with red wine.

Glazed Pastry Puffs from Pinhel

••

Cavacas do Pinhel ⛛ Beira Alta

Preparation time: 1 hour 15 minutes
Cooking time: 20 minutes
Makes: 24
⛉

lard (pork fat), for greasing
320 g/11¼ oz (2⅔ cups) plain (all-purpose) flour
6 g/¼ oz (1 teaspoon) sea salt
15 ml/½ fl oz (1 tablespoon) firewater
12 eggs
350 ml/12 fl oz (1½ cups) olive oil

For the glaze:
2 egg whites
25 ml/1 fl oz (2 tablespoons) white wine vinegar

Preheat the oven to 220°C/425°F/Gas Mark 7.
Grease the cups of two 12-hole muffin pans, 8 cm/
3¼ inches in diameter, with the lard (pork fat).

Put the flour, salt and firewater into a large bowl
and mix together. Put the eggs and olive oil into
a stand mixer fitted with a whisk attachment and
whisk at medium speed for 10 minutes. Add the
flour and whisk for 40 minutes until super fluffy.

Divide the batter evenly between the prepared
muffin pans, filling them to no more than 5 mm/
¼ inch from the rim as they will rise during cooking.
Bake in the hot oven for 20 minutes, or until a deep
caramel colour. Remove from the oven and leave to
cool on a wire rack until completely cold.

To make the glaze, put the egg whites into
a stand mixer fitted with a whisk attachment and
whisk until soft peaks form. Add the vinegar and
whisk again until well incorporated.

Once cold, brush each *Cavacas* with the glaze,
the leave to dry on a wire rack before serving.

Glazed Ear-shaped Pastry Puffs

••

Cavacas da Ilha ⛛ Açores
de Santa Maria

Preparation time: 25 minutes, plus 15 minutes resting
Cooking time: 30 minutes
Makes: 8
⬙

120 ml/4 fl oz (½ cup) extra virgin olive oil
135 g/4¾ oz (1 cup plus 1 tablespoon) self-raising
    (self-rising) flour, sifted, plus extra for dusting
11 whole eggs
40 g/1½ oz (3 tablespoons) unsalted butter

For the syrup:
430 g/15 oz (2¼ cups) caster (superfine) sugar

Heat the olive oil in a large saucepan over a medium
heat until it reaches 160°C/325°F on a thermometer,
then remove from the heat.

Add the flour to the pan with the warm oil. Add
the eggs, one at a time, mixing well between each
addition, until a dough forms. Once the eggs are
incorporated, add 65 ml/2¼ fl oz (4⅓ tablespoons)
water and mix well for a further 5 minutes until the
mixture becomes a smooth dough. Cover the pan
with a clean tea (dish) towel and leave to rest at
room temperature for 15 minutes.

Preheat the oven to 180°C/350°F/Gas Mark 4.
Melt the butter in a small saucepan over a low heat.
Brush 8 small round baking pans, about 10 cm/4
inches in diameter and 5 cm/2 inches high, with the
melted butter. Dust the pans with flour, tipping out
the excess flour.

Using a tablespoon, scoop the dough evenly into
the prepared pans, leaving a few millimetres from the
rim of the pans to allow the cakes to expand. Place
the pans on a baking sheet and bake in the hot oven
for 20 minutes, or until golden brown. Remove from
the oven and leave to cool in the pans on a wire rack
until completely cold.

To make the syrup, put the sugar into a large
saucepan with 220 ml/7½ fl oz (¾ cup) water
and heat over a medium-high heat for 10–12
minutes, or until it reaches 125°C/257°F on a
thermometer. Remove from the heat and whisk
until it becomes opaque.

Remove the *Cavacas* from the pans. If they
are not completely cold, leave to cool. Once cold,
pour the syrup over the top of each *Cavacas* and
leave to dry on a wire rack before serving.

Sweet Pasties Filled with Almond Rice

••

Pastéis de Arroz   ▢ Açores

Preparation time: 30 minutes, plus 1 hour and overnight
resting
Cooking time: 50 minutes
Serves: 6
⌀

For the dough:
300 g/11 oz (2½ cups) self-raising (self-rising) flour
20 g/¾ oz (1½ tablespoons) unsalted butter
25 g/1 oz (2½ tablespoons) caster (superfine) sugar
4 egg yolks
plain (all-purpose) flour, for dusting

For the filling:
320 g/11¼ oz (1½ cups) short-grain rice
150 g/5 oz (1½ cups) ground almonds
600 g/1 lb 5 oz (3 cups) caster (superfine) sugar
12 egg yolks
85 g/3 oz (¾ cup) icing (confectioners') sugar

The day before, make the filling. Wash the rice
twice under cold running water to remove the
excess starch, then put into a large saucepan,
cover with boiling water, add the salt and cook over
a medium heat for 20 minutes, or until soft. Strain
the rice, place in a food processor and process to
a smooth purée. Set aside.

Preheat the oven to 160°C/325°F/Gas Mark 3.
Line a baking sheet with baking (parchment) paper.

Spread the ground almonds out on the
prepared baking sheet and toast in the oven for
8–10 minutes. The almonds should not take on a
lot of colour, you are only looking to enhance their
flavour. Set aside.

Put the sugar into a large saucepan with
450 ml/15 fl oz (1⅔ cups) water and heat over a
medium-high heat until it reaches 116°C/241°F on
a thermometer. Once it is at temperature, remove
from the heat, add the rice purée, then cook over
a low heat for 5 minutes. Remove the pan from
the heat again and add the egg yolks and toasted
almonds. Put the pan back on a medium heat for
5 minutes to cook the egg yolks. At this stage you
should have a smooth, thick purée. Leave to rest
overnight in the fridge.

The next day, make the dough, sift the flour
onto a work counter, then add the butter, caster
sugar, egg yolks and 150 ml/5 fl oz (⅔ cup) water
and mix together until well combined. Using your
hands, knead the dough for 10 minutes until a
smooth dough forms, adding a drop of cold water
if necessary. Cover with food wrap or a damp tea
(dish) towel and leave to rest for 1 hour.

Preheat the oven to 160°C/325°F/Gas Mark 3.
Line a baking sheet with baking (parchment) paper.

Roll the dough out on a floured work counter
until into a thin sheet. Place the sweet filling in
a long line over half of the dough as you would

do when making ravioli, then fold over the other
half of the dough. Gently press around the the
filling to seal each parcel. Sprinkle the parcels with
icing (confectioners') sugar and place them on the
prepared baking sheet. Bake in the hot oven for
about 10 minutes, or until golden brown. Leave
them to cool slightly before serving.

Puff Pastry 'Pillows' Filled with Egg and Almond Cream

••

Travesseiros de Sintra   ▢ Lisbon

Preparation time: 15 minutes
Cooking time: 35–40 minutes
Serves: 6
⌀

500 g/1 lb 2 oz ready-made puff pastry
plain (all-purpose) flour, for dusting
280 g/10 oz (1½ cups minus 4 teaspoons) caster
    (superfine) sugar
6 egg yolks
50 g/2 oz (½ cup minus 2 teaspoons) almond flour
icing (confectioners') sugar, for dusting

Roll out the puff pastry on a floured work counter
to a large sheet, 3 mm/⅛ inch thick. Cut out
rectangles measuring 14 x 6 cm/5½ x 2½ inches.

Put the sugar into a large saucepan with
100 ml/3½ fl oz (⅓ cup) water and bring to the
boil, then reduce the heat to low and cook for
7 minutes. Remove from the heat and leave to
cool a little before gradually adding the egg yolks,
stirring well between each addition. Stir in the
almond flour then put the pan back over a low heat
and cook, stirring continuously, for 5 minutes, or
until thick.

Preheat the oven to 180°C/350°F/Gas Mark 4.
Line a baking sheet with baking (parchment) paper.

Pour some of the egg and almond filling onto
each of the puff pastry rectangles, then fold the
puff pastry over horizontally and fold the end bits
under the rectangle to close. Put onto the lined
baking sheet and bake in the hot oven for 20–25
minutes, or until golden brown. Remove from the
oven, leave to cool slightly and the dust with icing
(confectioners') sugar before serving.

Pastry Cones Filled with Almond Custard

Canudos de Leiria   ◡ **Leiria**

Similar to *Cornucópias de Alcobaça*, these are crispy, fried, cone-shaped sweets filled with bright yellow *Ovos Moles* (Soft Sweet Eggs, page 308). It is their cooking method that marks them out as unusual: the dough is cut into thin strips that are then spiralled around cane straws that grow wild in the Leiria region, then the pastry cones are removed from the straws after being fried.

Preparation time: 30 minutes, plus 15 minutes resting
Cooking time: 45 minutes
Makes: 8
⌀

For the dough:
140 g/5 oz (1¼ cups minus 2 teaspoons) plain
    (all-purpose) flour, plus extra for dusting
36 g/1¼ oz (2⅓ tablespoons) unsalted butter
1 litre/34 fl oz (4¼ cups) sunflower oil, for deep-frying

For the cinnamon sugar:
40 g/1½ oz (3¼ tablespoons) golden unrefined caster
    (superfine) sugar
2 teaspoons ground cinnamon

For the filling:
55 g/2 oz (½ cup) flaked (slivered) almonds
120 g/4 oz (⅔ cup) unrefined golden caster (superfine) sugar
60 g/2¼ oz bread, crusts removed
4 eggs

To make the dough, put the flour and butter into a large bowl, add 20 ml/¾ fl oz (4 teaspoons) water and mix well until a smooth dough forms. Cover with food wrap and leave to rest for 15 minutes.

To make the cylinders, you will need a cone-shaped metal or wooden mould, 10 cm/4 inches long by 1.5 cm/⅝ inch. Roll out the dough on a lightly floured work counter to make a large sheet, 3 mm/⅛ inch thick. Cut the dough into strips that are long enough to wrap all the way round and along the cone-shaped mould, making sure that the tip of the cone is covered.

Line a large baking sheet with paper towels. Heat the sunflower oil for deep-frying in a large, deep saucepan or fryer over medium-high heat until it reaches 180°C/350°F on a thermometer. Working in batches, carefully lower the pastry cones to the hot oil and deep-fry for 5 minutes, or until golden brown. Remove with a slotted spoon and leave to drain on the lined baking sheet.

To make the cinnamon sugar, put the sugar and cinnamon into a shallow dish and mix together to combine. One at a time, add the pastry cones to the cinnamon sugar and roll until lightly coated. Set aside while you make the filling.

Preheat the oven to 160°C/325°F/Gas Mark 3. Line a baking sheet with baking (parchment) paper.

Spread the ground almonds out on the prepared baking sheet and toast in the oven for 10–12 minutes, or until golden. Set aside.

Put the sugar into a large saucepan with 100 ml/3½ fl oz (⅓ cup) water and heat over a medium heat for 10–12 minutes until it reaches 112°C/234°F on a thermometer. Add the toasted almonds, then crumble the bread into the pan using your hands. Remove the pan from the heat and mix well. Add the eggs, then put the pan over a medium heat and cook for 20 minutes, stirring continuously so it doesn't stick to the pan. Remove the pan from the heat and leave to cool.

Once cold, spoon or pipe the filling into the pastry cones before serving.

Waffles

Talassas   ◡ **Beira Baixa**

Preparation time: 10 minutes
Cooking time: 20–30 minutes
Serves: 4
⌀

Traditionally these waffles are cooked over a wood fire in a flat plan and then rolled up into a cigar shape.

90 g/3¼ oz (6 tablespoons) unsalted butter, at room
    temperature
130 g/4½ oz (⅔ cup) caster (superfine) sugar
6 eggs
130 g/4½ oz (1 cup plus 4 teaspoons) self-raising
    (self-rising) flour
pinch of salt (optional)
butter or olive oil, for greasing
icing (confectioners') sugar, for dusting

Put the butter and sugar into the bowl of a stand mixer fitted with a whisk attachment. Whisk on a medium speed until pale and creamy. Alternatively, whisk with electric beaters in a large bowl. Beat in the eggs, one at a time. Gently fold in the flour and salt, if using, until everything is well combined. (The mixture will look slightly curdled, but this is fine.)

Grease and heat an electric waffle machine. Alternatively, if you have an old-school flat iron pan, heat it over hot coals. Depending on the size of the waffle machine or the flat iron pan, pour in 1½–2 spoonfuls of the batter, and cook for 3–4 minutes, or follow the instructions for the waffle maker until golden brown. Remove and set aside. Repeat until the rest of the batter has been used up. Serve immediately, dused with icing (confectioners') sugar.

Puffed Pastry Triangles with Egg Cream and Meringue Topping

Jesuítas 📷 p.345 ♡ Minho

As Portuguese Jesuit priests were persecuted in Japan in 1633, and later in Portugal in the 1800s, little did they know they would end up being adored as a pastry. *Jesuítas* contrast with other pastries with their brown, fragile triangles of puff pastry layered with an egg-yolk filling, and crisp, shiny royal icing (frosting) topping. Their origin divides opinion, but all point in one direction: Confeitaria Moura, a 200-year-old pastry shop in Santo Tirso (Porto) claims they hired a Spanish baker who created the pastry in the 18th century before it spread out to other pastry shops across the country.

Preparation time: 30 minutes
Cooking time: 40 minutes
Serves: 6
∅

500 g/1 lb 2 oz ready-made puff pastry
plain (all-purpose) flour, for dusting

For the filling:
220 g/7½ oz (1 cup plus 4 teaspoons) caster (superfine) sugar
4 eggs

For the topping:
2 egg whites
30 g/1 oz (¼ cup) icing (confectioners') sugar
½ teaspoon ground cinnamon

Preheat the oven to 200°C/400°F/Gas Mark 6. Line a large baking sheet with baking (parchment) paper.
To make the filling, put the sugar and eggs into a stand mixer fitted with a whisk attachment and whisk at medium speed until creamy. Alternatively, whisk with electric beaters in a large bowl.
Roll out the puff pastry on a lightly floured work counter to a large rectangle, about 4 mm/¼ inch thick.
Spread the filling over one half of the puff pastry sheet, then fold the other half over to cover the filling. Gently press down around the edges to seal.
To make the topping, put the egg whites into a small bowl with the icing (confectioners') sugar and cinnamon and whisk to emulsify. Spread the topping over the folded puff pastry.
Using a sharp knife, cut the puff pastry into elongated triangles. Transfer the triangles onto the lined baking sheet and bake in the hot oven for 20 minutes, or until the pastry is risen and flaky with a crispy top. Remove from the oven and leave to cool before serving.

Priest's Ears

Orelhas de Abade ♡ Trás-os-Montes e Alto Douro

Preparation time: 10 minutes
Cooking time: 15 minutes
Serves: 6
∅ ⌀ V

450 g/1 lb Bread Dough (page 30)
800 ml/27 fl oz (3¼ cups) olive oil, for deep-frying
caster (superfine) sugar, for dusting
ground cinnamon, for dusting

On a lightly floured work counter, stretch out the bread dough so that it is as thin as possible. Using a pasta cutter, cut out rough ear shapes from the stretched-out dough.
Line a large rimmed baking sheet with paper towels. Heat the olive oil in a large, deep saucepan or fryer over a medium-high heat until it reaches 150°C/300°F on a thermometer. Working in batches, carefully lower the 'ears' into the hotl oil and deep-fry for 3 minutes. Once they start frying, use a ladle to throw some of the hot oil over the 'ears' so they curl up. Using a slotted spoon, remove the 'ears' and leave to drain on the paper towels. Repeat until you have fried all the dough.
While still warm, dust the 'ears' with sugar and cinnamon before serving.

Golden Fried Eggy Bread

Fatias Paridas ♡ Alentejo

Preparation time: 15 minutes
Cooking time: 35–40 minutes
Serves: 4
∅

550 ml/18½ fl oz (2¼ cups) whole (full-fat) milk
4 eggs
500 ml/17 fl oz (2 cups) sunflower oil, for shallow-frying
8 large slices bread

To finish:
caster (superfine) sugar, for dusting
ground cinnamon, for dusting

Line a large baking sheet with paper towels.
Pour the milk into a shallow bowl. Crack the eggs to another bowl and whisk them with a fork.
Heat the sunflower oil in a large frying pan or skillet over a medium heat.
Dip a slice of bread first into the milk and then into the beaten egg, making sure the bread is fully soaked. Carefully lower the bread into the hot oil and fry for 2–3 minutes on each side, or until golden brown all over. Transfer to the lined baking sheet. Repeat with the remaining slices of bread.
Dust both sides of the fried eggy bread with sugar and cinnamon before serving.

Puff Pastry Triangles with Egg Cream and Meringue Topping

Golden Bread Slices

Rabanadas Douradas   ◊ Beira Litoral

Preparation time: 20 minutes, plus 3 hours drying
Cooking time: 30 minutes
Makes: 8–10
▯ ∅ ✕

1 medium loaf white bread
1 lemon
500 g/1 lb 2 oz (2½ cups) caster (superfine) sugar
14 egg yolks
½ teaspoon ground cinnamon

Cut the bread into thick slices and leave at room temperature for a few hours to dry out slightly.

Remove the rind from the lemon with a vegetable peeler, then slice it into fine strips, as fine as possible. Set aside.

Put 150 g/5 oz (¾ cup) of the sugar into a large saucepan with 330 ml/11 fl oz (1⅓ cups) water and heat over a medium-high heat until it reaches 101°C/214°F on a thermometer. Once it is at temperature, remove from the heat.

Prepare the Soft Sweet Eggs (Ovos Moles) with the remaining 350 g/12 oz (1¾ cups) sugar and the egg yolks following the recipe on page 308. Don't cook the mixture until it is too thick, as you need to be able to dip the bread in it. Leave to cool.

Sit a large wire rack over the top of a large baking sheet. The wire rack must be large enough to accommodate a few slices of bread at the time. Put the sugar syrup next to the Ovos Moles.

One at a time, dip the slices of bread into the syrup, then place the bread on the wire rack and leave to drip for a few seconds. Next, dip the bread into the Ovos Moles and leave to drip for a few seconds. Transfer the slices to a serving platter. Repeat until all the bread is used up.

Finish each slice of bread with a little of the finely shredded lemon rind, then dust some cinnamon over the top before serving.

Fried Eggy Bread Soaked in Red 'Vinho Verde'

Rabandas Doces   ◊ Minho
com Vinho Verde Tinto

Preparation time: 30 minutes, plus 12 hours standing
Cooking time: 55 minutes
Makes: 10
∅

35 g/1¼ oz (2 tablespoons) unsalted butter
360 g/12¾ oz (1¾ cups plus 2 teaspoons) caster (superfine) sugar, plus extra for sprinkling
2 cinnamon sticks
pared rind of 2 lemons
1 litre/34 fl oz (4¼ cups) sunflower oil, for deep-frying
3 egg yolks
2 egg whites
600 g/1 lb 5 oz bread, cut into 1.5-cm/⅝-inch thick slices
ground cinnamon, for sprinkling

For the wine soaker:
800 ml/27 fl oz (3¼ cups) red Vinho Verde wine
150 g/5 oz (⅔ cup) honey
80 g/3 oz (½ cup) caster (superfine) sugar
1 teaspoon ground cinnamon

The day before, put 250 ml/8 fl oz (1 cup) water, the butter, sugar, cinnamon sticks and lemon rind into a large saucepan and heat over a medium heat for 10–12 minutes until it reaches 103°C/217°F on a sugar thermometer. Remove from the heat.

Line a large baking sheet with paper towels. Heat the sunflower oil for deep-frying in a large, deep saucepan or fryer over a medium-high heat until it reaches 150°C/300°F on a thermometer.

Meanwhile, put the egg yolks and whites into a small bowl and whisk with a fork.

Sit a large wire rack over the top of a large baking sheet. The wire rack must be large enough to accommodate a few slices of bread at the time.

One at a time, dip the slices of bread into the syrup and leave for 2 minutes, then place the bread on the wire rack and leave to drip for a few seconds. Next, dip the bread into the eggs. Carefully lower them into the hot oil and deep-fry for 5 minutes, or until golden brown. Remove with a slotted spoon and leave to drain on the lined baking sheet.

Dust each slice of bread with sugar and cinnamon until lightly coated, then place in a large rimmed baking sheet.

Prepare the wine soaker by combining all the ingredients in a medium saucepan and bringing them to the boil. Remove from the heat then pour the wine soaker over the bread and leave to stand for 12 hours or overnight.

Serve the next day.

Bread and Almond Cake

Tiborna

◌ Alentejo

Preparation time: 40 minutes, plus resting overnight
Cooking time: 45 minutes
Serves: 6–8
◌

17 eggs
630 g/1 lb 6 oz (3 cups plus 2 tablespoons) caster (superfine) sugar
220 g/7¾ oz bread, crusts removed and cut into small cubes
220 g/7¾ oz (1¾ cups minus 2 teaspoons) almond flour
pared rind of 1 lemon
1 teaspoon ground cinnamon
edible rice paper
280 g/10 oz *Doce de Chila* (page 414)

The day before, separate the egg yolks from the whites. Set 3 egg yolks aside, then put the remaining egg yolks into a large bowl and whisk with a whisk. Pour the beaten egg yolks into a squeezy bottle.

Dampen a large baking sheet with cold water. Put the sugar into a large saucepan with 630 ml/21½ fl oz (2½ cups) water and bring to the boil, then reduce the heat and simmer while drizzling in the whisked egg yolks to make noodles. Cook the egg noodles for 1 minute. Using a slotted spoon, transfer the noodles to the damp baking sheet and set aside.

Remove the sugar syrup from the heat. Add the bread cubes and leave them to soak for 2 minutes. Using a slotted spoon, transfer the soaked bread to another baking sheet, making sure they are separated out and not clinging to one another.

Shred any remaining bread into very small pieces and set aside.

Add the almond flour to the remaining sugar syrup in the pan and bring to the boil. Remove from the heat and leave to cool slightly before adding the reserved 3 egg yolks, lemon rind and cinnamon. Stir to combine, then return the pan to a medium heat and cook for 5 minutes, or until thick. Transfer the mixture to a bowl, cover with food wrap and leave to rest overnight.

The next day, cut the rice paper into rounds, each measuring 4 cm/1½ inches in diameter. Arrange a layer of the bread cubes onto each paper round, then 2 teaspoons of the almond mixture and 1 teaspoon of *Doce de Chila*. Top each one with some of the sweet shredded breadcrumbs and egg noodles.

Put each cake one onto a square of baking (parchment) paper, about 7 x 7 cm/2¾ x 2¾ inches, and tie with string before serving.

Caramelised Eggy Bread Pudding

Barrigas de Freira – Baixo Alentejo

◌ Alentejo

Preparation time: 10 minutes
Cooking time: 35 minutes
Serves: 6–8
◌

450 g/1 lb crystallised sugar
90 g/3¼ oz slice of bread, crusts removed
30 g/1 oz (2 tablespoons) unsalted butter
6 egg yolks
5 whole eggs
caster (superfine) sugar, for sprinkling

Put 150 ml/5 fl oz (⅔ cup) water into a medium copper saucepan, add the crystallised sugar and bring to the boil over a medium heat. Remove from the heat and leave to cool slightly.

Dampen the slice of bread with a little water, then gently squeeze the bread to remove any excess. Put the bread into a small bowl, add the butter, egg yolks and whole eggs, and mix well.

Combine the mixture with the crystallised sugar in the copper saucepan and cook over a low heat for 10–15 minutes, or until some dark bits appear at the side. Don't stir the mixture, just shake the pan.

Pour the mixture onto a plate. Sprinkle some sugar over the top before serving.

Sweet Bread and Egg Yolk Porridge

Migas Doces

◌ Alentejo

Preparation time: 10 minutes
Cooking time: 30–35 minutes
Serves: 6–8
◌

300 g/11 oz crystallised sugar
120 g/4 oz stale bread, torn into small pieces
7 egg yolks, lightly beaten
ground cinnamon, for dusting

Put the sugar into a large saucepan with 120 ml/4 fl oz (½ cup) water and bring to the boil. Boil for 10–12 minutes over a medium-high heat or until it reaches 101°C/214°F on a thermometer. Add the bread, reduce the heat to low and cook, stirring frequently, for 10 minutes, or until it forms a paste. Remove the pan from the heat and leave to cool.

Add the egg yolks to the bread mixture and mix well. Put the pan back over a low heat and cook, stirring continuously, for 20 minutes. Remove from the heat and leave to cool. Transfer to a serving bowl and dust with cinnamon before serving.

Sweet Porridge with Eggs, Almonds and Bread

Manjar Celeste   ⋃ **Ribatejo**

Preparation time: 30 minutes
Cooking time: 25 minutes
Serves: 4
◻ ⌀

90 g/3¼ oz (⅔ cup) blanched almonds
160 g/5¾ oz (3¼ cups) fresh breadcrumbs
400 g/14 oz (2 cups) caster (superfine) sugar
7 egg yolks
3 egg whites
320 g/11¼ oz *Fios de Ovos* (Sweet Egg Yolk Strands,
    page 312), to decorate

Grate (shred) the almonds on a box grater or blitz in a food processor. Set aside.

Put the breadcrumbs into a shallow bowl and cover with water. Leave to soak for 2 minutes, then squeeze out all the water you can with your hands.

Put 200 g/7 oz (1 cup) of the sugar into a saucepan with 100 ml/3½ fl oz (⅓ cup) water and heat over a medium heat for 10–12 minutes or until it reaches 101°C/214°F on a thermometer. Remove from the heat, add the almonds and breadcrumbs and bring to the boil over a medium heat.

Meanwhile, put the egg yolks, egg whites and remaining sugar into a stand mixer fitted with a whisk attachment and whisk at medium speed for 10 minutes. Alternatively, whisk with electric beaters in a large bowl.

Remove the pan from the heat. Stirring continuously, add the egg mixture to the pan and put over a medium heat and cook, while stirring, for 10 minutes, or until thick and coming away from the pan. Pour the porridge into a serving dish and decorate with the *Fios de Ovos* before serving.

Sweet Porridge with Cracked Wheat

Frangolho da Madeira   ⋃ **Madeira**

Preparation time: 10 minutes
Cooking time: 1 hour 10 minutes
Serves: 6
⌀ ⌂

500 g/1 lb 2 oz (4¼ cups minus 2 teaspoons) plain
    (all-purpose) flour
130 ml/4½ fl oz (½ cup) whole (full-fat) milk
35 g/1¼ oz (2⅓ tablespoons) unsalted butter
zest of 1 lemon
100 g/3½ oz (½ cup) caster (superfine) sugar
ground cinnamon, for dusting
sea salt

Put the flour, milk, butter, lemon zest and a pinch of salt into a large saucepan and cook over a low heat for about 1 hour, stirring continuously. When the flour is cooked, add the sugar, increase the heat to medium and cook for a few more minutes. Pour the porridge into a serving dish and dust with cinnamon before serving.

Sweet Porridge with Curdled Pig's Blood and Walnuts

Sarrabulho Doce   ⋃ **Minho**

The sweet version of *Papas de Sarrabulho* (Pork Offal Stew, page 232) was originally served as a dessert on pig slaughter days, and is still prepared in some villages in northern Portugal. It consists mainly of boiled and crumbled blood and leftover pieces of bread, mixed together with honey or sugar, port and cinnamon, until dark brown, thick and rich.

Preparation time: 15 minutes, plus 10 minutes standing
Cooking time: 25 minutes
Serves: 4
◻ ◻

200 g/7 oz (1 cup) caster (superfine) sugar
1 cinnamon stick
90 ml/3 fl oz (6 tablespoons) port
50 g/2 oz (¼ cup) honey
90 g/3¼ oz bread, cut into small cubes
90 g/3¼ oz pig's blood cooked and shredded
    (page 225)
80 g/3 oz (⅔ cup) walnuts, halved

Put the sugar, cinnamon stick, port and honey into a medium saucepan with 100 ml/3½ fl oz (⅓ cup plus 1 tablespoon) water. Heat over a medium heat for 10–12 minutes until it reaches 106°C/223°F on a thermometer. Remove from the heat, add the bread, without stirring, cover with a tea (dish) towel and leave to stand for 10 minutes.

Stir in the bread cubes with a fork, then add the cooked, shredded blood and stir in. Put the pan over a low heat and cook, stirring continuously, for 10–15 minutes, or until a paste forms. Add the walnuts and stir to mix. Pour the porridge into a serving dish before serving.

Sweet 'Pudding' with Bread and Saffron

Bucho de Porco Doce   ʊ Trás-os-Montes e Alto Douro

Although it resembles a meat sausage, this large pudding is not in fact savoury but a sweet that was typically cooked in a festive environment after the pig slaughter. It would once have been made using the pig's stomach, which was cleaned and smoked, then filled with a mixture of leftover bread, eggs, sugar and cinnamon; these days, a linen cloth rather than a pig's stomach is used. It is served cut into slices, to be savoured with jam (jelly) or honey.

Preparation time: 45 minutes, plus 20 minutes soaking
Cooking time: 3 hours 40 minutes
Serves: 6–8

200 g/7 oz fine pork tripe (stomach lining)
250 ml/8 fl oz (1 cup) whole (full-fat) milk
750 g/1 lb 10 oz stale bread, cut into very small pieces
80 g/3 oz (⅔ cup) plain (all-purpose) flour
13 eggs
320 g/11¼ oz (1⅔ cups) caster (superfine) sugar, plus extra for sprinkling
20 ml/¾ fl oz (4 teaspoons) lemon juice
3 g/¹⁄₁₆ oz (1 tablespoon) saffron threads
1 teaspoon ground cinnamon
sea salt

Clean and dry the pork tripe (stomach lining).

Put the milk into a small saucepan and heat over a medium heat until hot. Put the bread into a heatproof bowl, then pour over the hot milk and leave to soak for 20 minutes. Using your hands, squeeze out the excess milk.

Put the flour, eggs, sugar, lemon juice, saffron threads, a pinch of salt and the soaked bread into a large bowl. Using your hands, mix for 15 minutes until everything is well incorporated.

After the stomach is cleaned and dried, fill it with the bread mixture, making sure to leave a gap at the opening so you can stitch it up. Stitch the gap closed, then put the pudding inside a bag, tie tightly then place inside a linen bag and tie tightly again.

Fill a large saucepan with water, add the pudding and cook over a low heat for 3 hours 30 minutes. Remove the pudding from the linen bags and leave to dry for a few minutes.

Sprinkle more sugar over the top of the pudding before serving.

Sweet 'Sausages' with Almonds

Morcelas Doces de Arouca   ʊ Minho

These are also known as *Morcelas de Amêndoa*. The *morcelas* resemble the blood sausage, but in this case, it only resembles the shape of them.

Preparation time: 20 minutes
Cooking time: 40 minutes
Serves: 6–8

180 g/6 oz (1⅓ cups) blanched almonds
450 g/1 lb (2¼ cups) caster (superfine) sugar
⅓ teaspoon ground cinnamon
pinch of ground cloves
140 g/5 oz (2¾ cups) breadcrumbs
110 g/3¾ oz (1 stick) unsalted butter, softened, plus extra for frying
200 g/7 oz fine pork tripe (stomach lining)
sea salt

Grate (shred) the almonds either on a box grater or blitz in a food processor until ground. Set aside.

Put the sugar into a large saucepan with 200 ml/7 fl oz (¾ cup) water and heat over a medium heat for 10–12 minutes until it reaches 106°C/223°F on a thermometer. Remove from the heat, add the almonds, cinnamon, cloves, breadcrumbs and softened butter, stir, then cook over a low heat for 15 minutes, or until it is a smooth, dry paste. Transfer the mixture to a large bowl and leave to cool.

Rinse the tripe (stomach lining) under cold running water. Usually shop-bought ones are ready to go, nevertheless, rinse them, then cut the tripe into 12 cm/5 inch pieces. Tie one end with butcher's string or kitchen twine and fill them with the almond mixture. Don't fill them up to the top. Seal the opening with string and repeat until you have filled all the tripe.

Bring a medium saucepan of water to the boil, add a pinch of salt, then reduce the heat to medium and wait until the water is simmering. Add the filled tripe to the pan and cook for 2 minutes. Remove from the pan and hang them to dry.

To serve, heat a large frying pan or skillet over a medium heat, add a knob of butter and the filled tripe and cook for 10 minutes, or until golden brown all over. Serve either warm or cold.

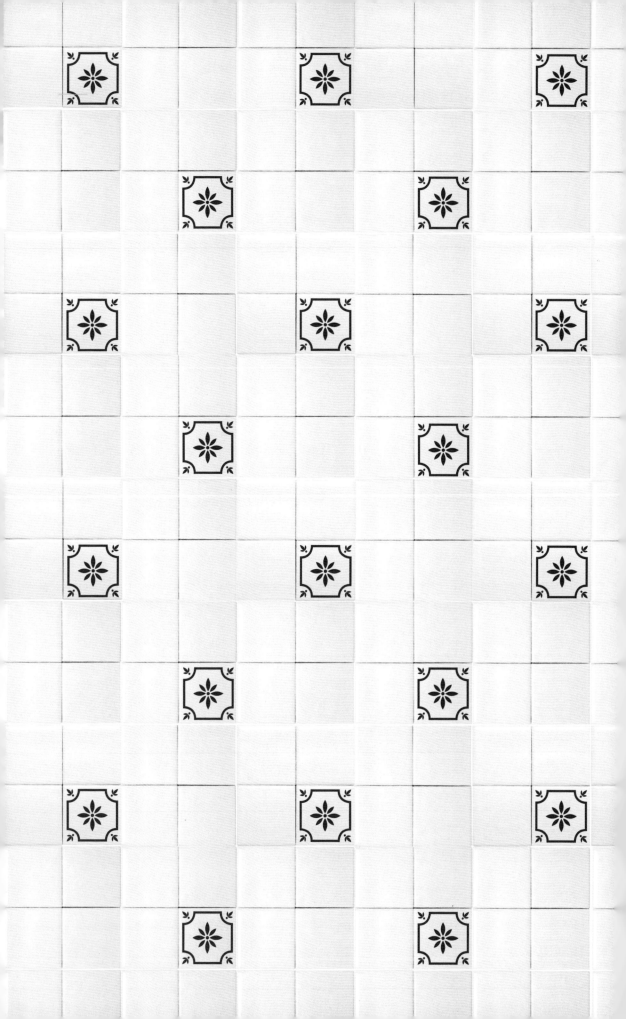

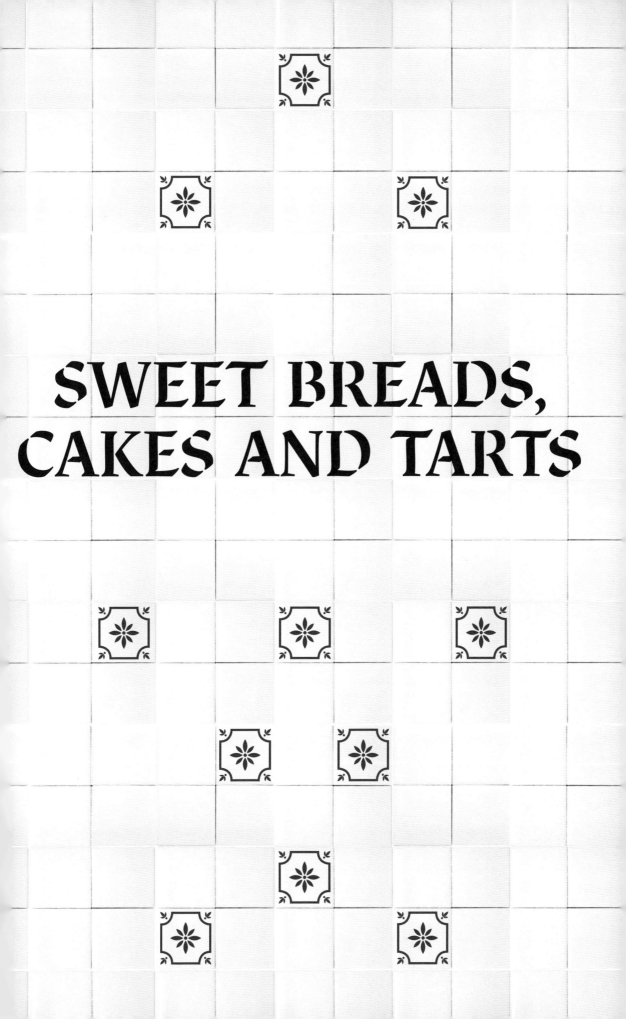

SWEET BREADS, CAKES AND TARTS

Sweet Bread Dough

••

Massa Sovada   ᴗ Açores

A light and airy bread with a subtle, sweet taste, eaten for breakfast or as a snack in the afternoon. In the Azores, it's also served alongside savoury dishes, especially with *Alcatra* (page 252). *Massa Sovada* is cooked across the archipelago throughout the year and is also a feature of the Festivals of the Holy Spirit — the parades that celebrate the first harvests, prosperity and abundance that are usually held between Easter and Whitsun (the seventh Sunday after Easter).

Preparation time: 1 hour 5 minutes, plus overnight standing and 7 hours 30 minutes rising
Cooking time: 1 hour 10 minutes
Makes: 2 loaves
⌀

For the starter:
180 g/6 oz sweet potatoes, unpeeled
20 g/¾ oz (1⅓ tablespoons) fresh yeast or
     5 g/¼ oz (1⅔ teaspoons) instant dried yeast
15 g/½ oz (4 teaspoons) caster (superfine) sugar
1 egg
90 g/3¼ oz (¾ cup) plain (all-purpose) flour

For the dough:
190 g/7 oz (1½ sticks plus 1 tablespoon) unsalted butter
700 g/1 lb 9 oz (5¾ cups) plain (all-purpose) flour, plus
     extra for dusting
2 teaspoons ground cinnamon
185 g/6½ oz (¾ cup plus 2 tablespoons) caster
     (superfine) sugar
5 eggs

The day before, make the starter. Preheat the oven to 180°C/350°F/Gas Mark 4.

Wrap the sweet potatoes in foil and bake in the oven for 45 minutes, or until soft. Remove the foil, peel off the skin and put the flesh into to a food processor and process to a purée. Set aside.

If using fresh yeast, mix it with a little warm water and leave at room temperature for 10 minutes.

Put the sweet potato purée, sugar, yeast, egg and flour into a large bowl and mix together until it is a smooth consistency. Cover the bowl with a tea (dish) towel and leave to stand overnight.

The next day, make the dough. Melt the butter in a small saucepan. Put the flour, cinnamon and sugar into a large bowl or a stand mixer fitted with a paddle attachment and mix together. Add the eggs, then pour in the melted butter, add the sweet potato starter and knead for 30 minutes, or until the dough is smooth and elastic and comes away easily from the sides of the bowl. Cover the bowl with a tea towel and leave to rise for 6 hours.

Divide the dough equally into two pieces and shape them into loaves. Sprinkle some flour over proving baskets or large bowls, add the bread and leave to prove for another 1 hour 30 minutes before baking.

Preheat the oven to 200°C/400°F/Gas Mark 6. Dust a large baking sheet with flour, tipping off any excess and place the dough onto the sheet. Bake for 25 minutes, or until golden brown and a toothpick inserted into the middle comes out clean. Leave to cool on a wire rack.

Brioche-style Buns

••

Bolos Lêvedos   🖾 p.353   ᴗ Açores

These rounded breads, shaped like small, flat cheeses, are similar to an English muffin. They are eaten at breakfast, as a snack, or as a side to savoury dishes. They can be enjoyed warm, spread with cold butter, fresh or soft cheese, and jam (jelly). In the past, *Bolos Lêvedos* were baked predominantly on the north coast of the island of São Miguel, stripped of sugar and eggs and linked to fasting during Lent, but these days the sweet version is commonplace.

Preparation time: 35 minutes, plus 2 hours rising
Cooking time: 15 minutes
Makes: 4
⌀

160 ml/5½ fl oz (⅔ cup) whole (full-fat) milk
550 g/1 lb 4 oz (4½ cups) plain (all-purpose) flour,
     plus extra for sprinkling
1¾ tablespoons instant dried yeast
115 g/4 oz (½ cup plus 1 tablespoon) caster (superfine)
     sugar
135 g/4¾ oz (1¼ sticks) butter, cut into small pieces
2 eggs
¼ teaspoon fine sea salt

To prepare the dough, heat the milk gently in a pan over a low heat, stirring frequently, for 5 minutes until warm. Remove from the heat.

Put the flour, yeast, sugar, butter, eggs, and the warmed milk into a large bowl and mix together until it forms a dough. Add the salt. Put the dough onto a lightly floured work counter and knead well for about 10 minutes.

Form the dough into a ball and sprinkle with flour, then put it back into the bowl and leave to rise for 2 hours, or until it has doubled in size.

Sprinkle a large baking sheet with flour. Divide the dough equally into 4 pieces and shape them into balls. Arrange them on the prepared baking sheet in a single layer, leaving space between.

Heat a sauté pan over a medium heat. Take one ball of dough and, using the palms of your hands, flatten it to about 1.5 cm/½ inch thick and put it into the dry pan. Cook for 8–10 minutes until golden on one side, then turn and cook for a further 5–6 minutes until golden on the other side and it feels light in your hand. Leave to cool on a wire rack. Repeat with the remaining dough.

Pointed Sweet Flatbreads

Bicas   ⛉ Beira Baixa

If any flour was left over from breadmaking, these light and crispy flatbread would often be made with the excess and then baked in a wood-fired oven. Occasionally, these sweet flatbreads were eaten instead of bread by the workers in the olive oil mills while they were processing the oil.

Preparation time: 20 minutes
Cooking time: 40 minutes
Makes: 14
⛛ ⌀

650 g/1 lb 7 oz Bread Dough (page 30)
80 ml/2¾ fl oz (⅓ cup) olive oil
1 large egg
60 g/2¼ oz (⅓ cup) caster (superfine) sugar,
    plus extra for sprinkling
plain (all-purpose) flour, for dusting

Preheat the oven to 180°C/350°F/Gas Mark 4. Sprinkle flour over one or two baking sheets.
    Combine all the ingredients, except the flour, in a bowl. Knead until a soft, smooth dough forms.
    Tip out the dough onto a floured work counter and shape into 14 oval balls, about 60 g/2¼ oz each. Flatten them until they are 5 mm/¼ inch thick, then dust with flour. Using a fork, prick holes all over the top. Arrange the flatbreads on the prepared baking sheets and bake in the oven for 40 minutes, or until golden. Leave to cool on a wire rack before serving.

Sweet Pumpkin Cornbread Rolls with Walnuts and Sultanas

**Pãezinhos de Milho
da Figueira da Foz**   ⛉ Leiria

Preparation time: 50 minutes, plus 4 hours rising
Cooking time: 45–50 minutes
Makes: 18
⌀

300 g/11 oz pumpkin, peeled, de-seeded and diced
270 g/9½ oz (2¼ cups) fine cornmeal
550 g/1 lb 4 oz (4½ cups) wholemeal flour, plus extra
    for dusting
10 g/¼ oz (2 teaspoons) fresh yeast or
    2.5 g (scant 1 teaspoon) instant dried yeast
60 g/2¼ oz (4 tablespoons) unsalted butter
170 g/6 oz (¾ cup plus 4 teaspoons) caster (superfine)
    sugar
60 g/2¼ oz (½ cup) walnut halves
75 g/2¾ oz (½ cup) sultanas (golden raisins)
sea salt

Put the pumpkin into a large saucepan and pour in enough water to cover, add a pinch of salt and cook over a medium heat for 15–20 minutes, or until soft. Using a slotted spoon, remove the pumpkin from the pan and put into a bowl. Set aside some of the pumpkin cooking water.
    Put both flours into a large bowl and mix together. Put the yeast into a small bowl, add a little of the pumpkin cooking water and stir until dissolved, then stir it into the flours.
    Put the butter into a small saucepan and heat over a low heat until melted.
    Mash the pumpkin, add the melted butter and the sugar and then combine with the flours. Knead for 5 minutes, adding a little of the pumpkin cooking water until a soft, smooth dough forms. Add the walnuts and sultanas (golden raisins) and knead into the dough until evenly distributed. Cover with food wrap and leave to rise for 4 hours.
    Preheat the oven to 160°C/325°F/Gas Mark 3. Lightly dust a large baking sheet with flour.
    Divide the dough equally into 18 small balls, about 65 g/2¼ oz each and arrange them on the prepared baking sheet. Bake in the oven for 30 minutes, or until golden. Leave to cool on a wire rack before serving.

Sweet Potato Buns

Broinhas de Batata Doce   ⛉ Leiria

Preparation time: 40 minutes, plus 2 hours rising
Cooking time: 1 hour 5 minutes
Makes: 26
⌀

600 g/1 lb 5 oz sweet potatoes, unpeeled
350 g/12 oz (1¾ cups) caster (superfine) sugar
6 g/¼ oz (1 teaspoon) ground cinnamon
1 teaspoon chopped wild fennel tops
zest of 1 lemon
¼ teaspoon fine sea salt
1 teaspoon instant dried yeast
500 g/1 lb 2 oz (4 cups plus 2 teaspoons) plain
    (all-purpose) flour, plus extra for dusting
unsalted butter, for greasing
2 eggs, for the egg wash
26 walnut halves, to decorate

Preheat the oven to 220°C/425°F/Gas Mark 7.
    Wrap the sweet potatoes in foil and bake in the oven for 45 minutes, or until soft. Remove the foil, peel off the skin and put the flesh into a food processor and process to a purée. Set aside.
    Put 120 ml/4 fl oz (½ cup) water and the sugar into a large saucepan and bring to the boil. Add the sweet potato purée, cinnamon, fennel tops, lemon zest and a pinch of salt and cook over a medium heat, stirring continuously, for 1 minute. Remove from the heat and leave to cool.
    Once cool, add the yeast and flour, and mix until a smooth, soft dough forms. Place the dough in a large bowl, cover with food wrap or a tea (dish) towel and leave to rise for 2 hours.

Preheat the oven to 200°C/400°F/Gas Mark 6. Grease a large baking sheet with butter and sprinkle with flour, tipping off the excess.

Put the eggs into a small bowl and lightly whisk with a fork. Divide the dough equally into small balls, about 40 g/1½ oz each. Brush the egg wash over them and top with a walnut half. Arrange the buns on the prepared baking sheet and bake in the oven for 20 minutes, or until golden. Leave to cool on a wire rack before serving.

Rolled Buns with Sugar and Cinnamon

••

Escarpiadas – Condeixa Ʊ **Beira Litoral**

Preparation time: 1 hour 30 minutes
Cooking time: 20 minutes
Makes: 22
Ø

1 kg/2 lb 4 oz (8⅓ cups) spelt flour, plus extra for
    dusting
75 g/2½ oz (5 tablespoons) fresh yeast or
    19 g/¾ oz (2 tablespoons) instant dried yeast
45 g/1½ oz (3 tablespoons) unsalted butter
425 g/15 oz (2 cups plus 2 tablespoons) caster
    (superfine) sugar, plus extra for sprinkling
4 teaspoons ground cinnamon
olive oil, for oiling
sea salt

Preheat the oven to 220°C/425°F/Gas Mark 7.

Put the flour, yeast, butter, 55 g/2 oz (¼ cup) of the sugar and a pinch of salt into a stand mixer fitted with a dough hook and mix together. Gradually incorporate 800 ml/27 fl oz (3¼ cups) water. Alternatively, mix in a large bowl with electric beaters. Mix at medium speed for 20 minutes or for 30 minutes by hand until a soft, smooth dough forms. Turn the dough out onto a floured work counter, dust with flour, then divide the dough into 22 equal portions, about 80 g/3 oz each.

Put 300 g/11 oz (1½ cups) of the sugar and the cinnamon into a bowl. Pour over a little olive oil and mix together.

Sprinkle a little extra sugar over a work counter then, using your hands, stretch one piece of dough into a square. Place the dough over the sugar and sprinkle more extra sugar over the top. Drizzle the olive oil over the sugar on the top of dough. Roll it up into a cylinder, then turn it by 90 degrees and roll the top of the cylinder to the bottom. Repeat with the remaining dough.

Put 400 ml/14 fl oz (1⅔ cups) water and the remaining sugar into a large bowl and stir well.

Arrange the *Escarpiadas* on a large rimmed baking sheet and pour the sugary liquid around them. Bake for 20 minutes, or until golden.

Remove from the oven, roll the *Escarpiadas* in the syrup that has formed on the sheet and serve.

Sweet Buns with Fennel Tops

••

Merendeiras dos Santos Ʊ **Leiria**

These are popular buns in my village during religious celebrations. The ladies who baked and then sold them would arrange them in large dried wooden baskets wrapped in plastic bags.

Preparation time: 1 hour, plus 6 hours rising and
20 minutes resting
Cooking time: 20 minutes
Makes: 12
Ø

80 ml/2¾ fl oz (⅓ cup) whole (full-fat) milk
30 g/1 oz (2 tablespoons) fresh yeast
500 g/1 lb 2 oz (4 cups plus 2 teaspoons) plain
    (all-purpose) flour, plus extra for dusting
3 eggs
180 g/6 oz (1 cup minus 4 teaspoons) caster (superfine)
    sugar
120 ml/4 fl oz (½ cup) olive oil, warmed
lemon zest
1 tablespoon ground cinnamon
2 tablespoons chopped wild fennel tops
unsalted butter, for greasing
2 egg yolks
150 g/5 oz (¾ cup) golden caster (superfine) sugar
sea salt

Heat the milk in a medium saucepan over a low heat for 5 minutes until warm. Remove from the heat, add the yeast and stir to dissolve. Mix in 150 g/5 oz (1¼ cups) of the flour. Cover with a clean tea (dish) towel and leave at room temperature for 2 hours.

Put the eggs, caster (superfine) sugar and a pinch of salt into a large bowl and whisk together, then add the warm olive oil together with the lemon zest. Add the milk and flour mixture and mix well until combined.

Put the remaining flour, the cinnamon and fennel tops into another large bowl and mix together. Add this mixture to the egg mixture and mix well until combined. Knead this dough for 20 minutes, then cover the bowl again and leave to rest at room temperature for 4 hours.

Preheat the oven to 200°C/400°F/Gas Mark 6. Grease one or two large baking sheets with butter and dust with flour, tipping off the excess.

Divide the dough equally into 12 small balls. Leave to rest on the work counter for 20 minutes.

Put the egg yolks into a small bowl and whisk lightly with a fork. Brush each bun with the egg and sprinkle some golden caster (superfine) sugar over the top. Arrange the buns on the prepared baking sheet and bake in the oven for 20 minutes, or until golden.

Leave to cool on a wire rack before serving.

Braided Sweet Bread

●●

Regueifa Doce ⏷ Beira Litoral

Preparation time: 1 hour, plus 5 hours rising
Cooking time: 30–40 minutes
Makes: 1
⌀

50 g/1¾ oz (3⅓ tablespoons) fresh yeast or
    12 g/½ oz (1⅓ tablespoons) instant dried yeast
1.5 kg/3 lb 5 oz (12½ cups) plain (all-purpose) flour,
    plus extra for dusting
330 g/11½ oz (1⅔ cups) caster (superfine) sugar
2 eggs
1 egg white
185 g/6½ oz (1⅔ sticks) unsalted butter,
    softened, plus extra for brushing
160 ml/5½ fl oz (⅔ cup) whole (full-fat) milk

Put the yeast into a large bowl, pour over 310 ml/
10 fl oz (1¼ cups plus 2 teaspoons) water and stir
until dissolved. Add 500 g/1 lb 2 oz (4 cups plus
2 teaspoons) of the flour and mix to a smooth
consistency. Cover with a clean tea (dish) towel
and leave to rest at room temperature for 1 hour.

Meanwhile, put the sugar, eggs and egg white
into a stand mixer fitted with a whisk attachment
and whisk for 10 minutes, or until doubled in
volume. Alternatively, whisk with electric beaters
in a large bowl. Add the softened butter and mix
until incorporated.

Add the remaining flour to the rested dough
and mix well, then add the milk and then the egg
mixture and mix to combine. Turn out onto a work
counter and knead for 15 minutes. Return to the
bowl, cover with a clean tea towel and leave to rise
at room temperature for 2 hours 30 minutes.

Line a large baking sheet with baking
(parchment) paper. Turn the dough out onto a
floured work counter and divide in half, then roll
each portion out into a thick rope. Twist together
both ropes to create a braid, then join the ends
to make a ring. Put onto the lined baking sheet
and leave to prove at room temperature for 1 hour
30 minutes.

Preheat the oven to 160°C/325°F/Gas Mark 3.

Put the butter for brushing into a small
saucepan and heat over a low heat until melted.

Brush the bread with the melted butter, then
bake for 30–40 minutes, or until golden and a
toothpick inserted into the middle comes out
clean. Leave to cool on a wire rack before serving.

Easter Bread

●●

Folar da Páscoa ⏷ Lisbon

**This light, sweet, brioche-style loaf, flavoured
with cinnamon and fennel, is always a part
of the Portuguese Catholic Easter celebrations
that bring a 40-day period of reflection and
fasting to a close. *Folar*, like other popular and
enriched breads, have long been made for these
special occasions, bread being the locals' staple
food. There are different recipes for this all over
Portugal, but all have the common cross, or criss-
cross, shape that represent the crucifixion. It
is also sometimes topped with hard-boiled eggs,
symbolising fertility and abundance.**

Preparation time: 45 minutes, plus 1 hour fermenting and
6 hours rising
Cooking time: 40 minutes
Serves: 10–12
⌀

120 ml/4 fl oz (½ cup) whole (full-fat) milk
30 g/1 oz (2 tablespoons) fresh yeast or
    7.5 g/¼ oz (2½ teaspoons) instant dried yeast
550 g/1 lb 4 oz (4½ cups) plain (all-purpose) flour T65,
    plus extra for dusting
100 g/3½ oz (½ cup) caster (superfine) sugar
85 g/3 oz (6 tablespoons) unsalted butter, plus extra
    for greasing
4 eggs
1 teaspoon chopped wild fennel tops
zest of ½ orange
zest of ½ lemon
1 teaspoon ground cinnamon
20 ml/¾ fl oz (4 teaspoons) firewater
2 egg yolks, for egg wash
3 hard-boiled eggs, shelled
sea salt

Heat the milk in a medium saucepan over a low
heat for 5 minutes until warm.

Put the yeast into a medium bowl and add
40 ml/1⅓ fl oz (2⅔ tablespoons) of the warm milk
and stir until dissolved. Add 120 g/4 oz (1 cup) of
the flour and 25 g/1 oz (2 tablespoons) of the sugar
and mix until smooth. Cover with a clean tea (dish)
towel and leave to ferment at room temperature
for 1 hour.

Heat the butter in a small saucepan over a low
heat for 5 minutes until melted.

Put the remaining flour, milk, sugar and the
eggs into a large bowl and mix together until
smooth. Add the melted butter, pinch of salt, the
fennel tops, citrus zest, cinnamon and firewater
and mix together until all the ingredients are
thoroughly incorporated. Add the yeast mixture
and mix well until it forms a smooth dough. Cover
the bowl with a clean tea (dish) towel and leave to
rise at room temperature for 6 hours.

Preheat the oven to 200°C/400°F/Gas Mark 6.
Grease a large baking sheet with butter, then dust
with flour, tipping off the excess.

Put the egg yolks into a small bowl and lightly whisk with a fork. Tip out the dough onto a floured work counter, then remove a little of the dough to make a long rope. Knead the remaining dough into a ball, then flatten it a little to make a round loaf. Press the hard-boiled eggs into the top of the dough, equally spaced apart. Cut the long rope of dough into 6 equal pieces. Arrange two pieces over each egg in a cross shape. Brush the dough all over with the egg wash, transfer to the prepared baking sheet and bake for 40 minutes, or until golden and a toothpick inserted into the middle comes out clean. Leave to cool on a wire rack before serving.

Easter Sweet Breads from Tramagal

Folares do Tramagal   ▽ Ribatejo

Preparation time: 30 minutes, plus 14 hours rising
Cooking time: 30 minutes
Makes: 2
Ø

400 ml/14 fl oz (1⅔ cups) whole (full-fat) milk
90 g/3¼ oz (6 tablespoons) unsalted butter
340 g/12 oz (1¾ cups) caster (superfine) sugar
4 eggs
460 g/1 lb Bread Dough (page 30)
850 g/1 lb 14 oz (7 cups) spelt flour, plus extra for dusting
1 egg, for egg wash
sea salt

Put the milk and a pinch of salt into a medium saucepan and heat over a low heat for 5 minutes, or until warm. Remove from the heat and set aside.
Put the butter into another medium saucepan and heat over a low heat until melted.
Put the sugar and eggs into a large bowl, add the melted butter and mix until well combined. Add the Bread Dough and stir until all the ingredients are well incorporated. Sift in the flour, then add the milk and mix well until it forms a smooth dough. Cover with a clean tea (dish) towel or food wrap and leave to rise for 12 hours.
The next day, dust one or two baking sheets with flour, tipping off the excess.
Divide the dough into two equal pieces and shape each piece into thick rings. Arrange them on the prepared baking sheets and leave to rest at room temperature for 2 hours.
Preheat the oven to 220°C/425°F/Gas Mark 7.
Put the egg for the egg wash into a small bowl and whisk lightly with a fork. Brush the bread cakes with the egg and bake in the oven for 30 minutes, or until a toothpick inserted into the middle comes out clean. Leave to cool on a wire rack before serving.

Easter Cake

Bolo da Páscoa   ▽ Beira Baixa

This cake is also called *Folar* and is indispensable during the Easter period all over the country.

Preparation time: 25 minutes, plus 3 hours rising
Cooking time: 35 minutes
Makes: 2
Ø Ø

zest and juice of 1 orange
60 ml/2 fl oz (4 tablespoons) olive oil
15 ml/½ fl oz (1 tablespoon) firewater
4 eggs, plus an extra 1 egg for egg wash
600 g/1 lb 5 oz (5 cups) self-raising (self-rising) flour
15 g/½ oz (1 tablespoon) fresh yeast or 4g/¼ oz (heaped 1 teaspoon) instant dried yeast
130 g/4½ oz (⅔ cup) caster (superfine) sugar, plus extra for sprinkling
1 teaspoon ground cinnamon

Put the orange juice, olive oil, firewater and 4 eggs into a medium bowl or jug (pitcher) and mix together.
Put the flour, yeast, sugar, orange zest and cinnamon into a large bowl and mix together until combined. Add the liquid ingredients and mix well to form a smooth, elastic dough. If the dough is too sticky, you may need to add a little more flour. Cover with a clean tea (dish) towel and leave to rise at room temperature for 3 hours, or until doubled in size.
Preheat the oven to 180°C/350°F/Gas Mark 4.
Put the egg for the egg wash into a small bowl and whisk lightly with a fork.
Divide the dough into two equal pieces and shape each piece into a loaf. Using a sharp knife, make a small cut along the tops, then brush all over with the egg wash. Bake in the oven for 35 minutes, or until golden all over. Halfway through the cooking time, sprinkle the cakes with sugar. Leave to cool on a wire rack before serving.

Easter Bread from Guarda

Bolo de Páscoa da Guarda ○ Beira Baixa

In the days leading up to Easter Sunday, local priests will bless the houses to offer the residents protection. In return, they will serve this Easter bread, which contains no sugar and so is like a cross between cake and bread. It is eaten in thick slices at any time of the day, spread with butter or olive oil.

Preparation time: 35–40 minutes, plus 3 hours 45 minutes rising
Cooking time: 45–50 minutes
Makes: 3

25 g/1 oz (2 tablespoons) fresh yeast or 7 g/¼ oz (2¼ teaspoons) instant dried yeast
800 g/1 lb 12 oz (6⅔ cups) plain (all-purpose) flour, plus extra for dusting
5 g/1/8 oz (1 teaspoon) sea salt
65 ml/2¼ fl oz (¼ cup) olive oil, plus extra for brushing
8 eggs
30 ml/1 fl oz (2 tablespoons) firewater or brandy

Put the yeast into a small bowl, add 3 tablespoons of warm water and stir until dissolved. Leave to stand at room temperature for 15 minutes.

Sift the flour into a large bowl and stir in the salt. Put the olive oil into a small saucepan and heat over a medium-low heat until it reaches 120°C/248°F on a thermometer. Pour the oil over the flour and stir with a wooden spoon. Add the yeast mixture and stir well to combine, then add the eggs and mix together. Pour over the firewater or brandy and knead for 5–10 minutes or until it forms a smooth, elastic dough. Cover the bowl with a clean tea (dish) towel and leave to rise at room temperature for 1 hour 30 minutes, or until doubled in size.

Oil two or three baking sheets. Turn the dough out onto a floured work counter and divide it into three equal pieces. Stretch each piece of dough into a flat rectangle, about 25 x 15 cm/10 x 6 inches. Brush each one with some olive oil, then fold one side over onto the other side and brush with oil over the top. Repeat with all the pieces. Transfer the pieces to the oiled baking sheets, cover with a clean tea (dish) towel and leave to prove at room temperature for 2 hours, or until doubled in size.

Preheat the oven to 200°C/400°F/Gas Mark 6.

Bake in the oven for 45–50 minutes or until golden brown all over. Insert a toothpick into the middle and if it comes out clean, they are ready. Leave to cool on a wire rack before serving.

Sweet Bread Buns

Arrufadas de Coimbra ○ Beira Litoral

Preparation time: 35 minutes, plus 7 hours rising
Cooking time: 18–20 minutes
Makes: 15

750 g/1 lb 10 oz (6¼ cups) strong bread flour, plus extra for dusting
160 ml/5½ fl oz (⅔ cup) warm whole (full-fat) milk
2 teaspoons instant dried yeast
90 g/3¼ oz (6 tablespoons) unsalted butter
180 g/6 oz (1 cup minus 4 teaspoons) caster (superfine) sugar
½ teaspoon ground cinnamon
5 large eggs

For the glaze:
1 egg yolk
1 tablespoon whole (full-fat) milk

Put the flour into a large bowl. Put the warm milk into a medium bowl, add the yeast and stir until dissolved, then add it to the flour and mix together.

Put the butter into a small saucepan and heat over a low heat until melted, then remove from the heat and set aside.

Put the sugar, cinnamon and eggs into another bowl and mix to combine, then add to the flour and mix until a ball-shaped dough has formed. Depending on the flour used, you may need to add a little more milk. Add the melted butter and knead it in for 10 minutes to form a smooth dough. Cover with food wrap and leave in a warm place for 4 hours, or until it has doubled in size.

Line a large baking sheet with baking (parchment) paper and dust with flour. Roll 60 g/2¼ oz of the dough into a long rope, then divide the remaining dough into 80 g/3 oz balls, shape them until they are round, then put them on the prepared baking sheet. Leave for 2 hours, or until doubled in size.

Cut small pieces from the long rope of dough and put them on top of each dough ball in a cross shape. Cover with a damp tea (dish) towel and leave to prove again for 1 hour, or until doubled in size.

Preheat the oven to 190°C/375°F/Gas Mark 5.

Combine the egg yolk and milk for the glaze in a small bowl, then brush over the top of the dough balls. Bake for 18–20 minutes, or until golden brown all over. Leave to cool on a wire rack before serving.

Sweet Bread Traybake

Boleimas   ◌ Alentejo

Boleimas is a golden brown rectangular cake made without eggs. It uses leftover bread dough, and in some villages of Alentejo, *Boleimas* have a cousin cake called *Bolo de Fundo de Alguidar* (bottom bowl cake) that is made from the leftover scraps of bread dough that stick to the sides and base of the bowl after the dough has fermented in it.

Preparation time: 15 minutes, plus 45 minutes resting
Cooking time: 45 minutes
Serves: 6–8
Ø

250 ml/8 fl oz (1 cup) olive oil, plus extra for oiling
265 g/9½ oz (1¼ cups) brown sugar
650 g/1 lb 7 oz (5¼ cups) self-raising (self-rising) flour
½ teaspoon salt
180 ml/6 fl oz (¾ cup) whole (full-fat) milk
zest of 1 lemon
⅕ teaspoon ground cinnamon
2 teaspoons instant dried yeast
4 eggs
caster (superfine) sugar, for dusting

Preheat the oven to 180°C/350°F/Gas Mark 4. Oil a 28 x 32-cm/11 x 12½-inch rimmed baking sheet.
   Put all the ingredients into a stand mixer fitted with a hook attachment and mix until a wet, sticky dough forms. Cover with food wrap and leave to rest at room temperature for 45 minutes.
   Using oiled hands, spread the dough over the prepared baking sheet, patting it out in a single layer to cover the sheet. Using a sharp knife, score the surface from top to bottom. Do the same horizontally, then sprinkle the top with caster (supefine) sugar. Bake for 45 minutes, or until golden. Leave to cool slightly before cutting into squares and serving while still warm. This cake can be stored in an airtight container for 3–4 days.

King's Cake

Bolo Rei   ◌ Lisbon

This cake is eaten at Christmas. Different versions are found all over Portugal. Some use crystallised fruits and nuts, while other versions mix them together. This traditional cake from Portugal is a take on the French Galette des Rois. A few years ago, this cake used to contain a hidden 'gift' of broad (fava) beans and whoever had the fava in their slice would have to buy the next cake. When I was growing up, my parents would cut the cake and give a slice to us children. It was amazing that we didn't break our teeth because the 'gift' in our cake was always made of cheap silver and the beans were very dry. For health and safety reasons, these 'gifts' have been removed from the cake.

Preparation time: 50 minutes, plus 4 hours soaking, 45 minutes fermenting and 6 hours 30 minutes resting
Cooking time: 30–40 minutes
Serves: 8
Ø

20 g/¾ oz (2 tablespoons) raisins, plus extra to decorate
120 g/4 oz (½ cup) crystallised fruits (shop-bought or home-made), plus extra to decorate
275 ml/9½ fl oz (1 cup plus 2 tablespoons) tawny port
45 g/1½ oz (3 tablespoons) fresh yeast or 11 g/½ oz (1¼ tablespoons) instant dried yeast
800 g/1 lb 12 oz (6⅔ cups) self-raising (self-rising) flour, plus extra for dusting
140 g/5 oz (1¼ sticks) unsalted butter
100 g/3½ oz (½ cup) caster (superfine) sugar
finely grated zest of ⅕ lemon
finely grated zest of ⅕ orange
5 eggs, 4 for the dough, 1 for the egg wash
30 g/1 oz (¼ cup) pine nuts
30 g/1 oz (¼ cup) walnut halves
20 g/¾ oz (2¼ tablespoons) blanched almonds
whole (full-fat) milk, warmed (optional)
sea salt
icing (confectioners') sugar, for dusting

Chop the raisins, then put them into a large bowl, add the crystallised fruit and mix together. Pour over the port, stir, then cover with food wrap and leave to soak for 4 hours. Drain the fruits, discarding any of the remaining port.
   Put the yeast, 200 g/7 oz (1⅔ cups) of the flour and 100 ml/3½ fl oz (⅓ cup plus 1 tablespoon) water into a medium bowl, mix together, then cover with a clean tea (dish) towel and leave to ferment at room temperature for 45 minutes.
   Put the butter, caster (superfine) sugar and the citrus rind into a stand mixer fitted with a paddle attachment and mix at medium speed for 5 minutes, or until pale and fluffy. Add the 4 eggs, one at a time, whisking after each addition. Once incorporated, add the yeast mixture and mix well. Sift in the remaining flour with a pinch of salt and mix at medium speed for 10 minutes. Add the chopped fruit and nuts and mix again for a further 5 minutes until incorporated. Depending on the kind of flour you are using the dough might be a bit dry. If so, you can add a small amount of warm milk to make the dough slightly sticky.
   On a floured work counter, shape the dough into a ball. Dust with flour and leave to rest for 6 hours.
   Line a baking sheet with baking (parchment) paper. Shape the dough into a round and put onto the lined baking sheet. Using your fingers, make a hole in the middle of the dough to shape it into a ring. To keep the hole open during baking, put an oiled 7.5-cm/3-inch cookie cutter in the centre of the ring. Leave to rest for a further 30 minutes.
   Preheat the oven to 190°C/375°F/Gas Mark 5.
   Put the egg into a small bowl and lightly whisk with a fork. Brush the dough with the egg wash, then decorate with more dried and crystallised fruits. Bake for 30–40 minutes, or until golden. Leave to cool on a wire rack. Once cool, dust icing (confectioners') sugar over the top before serving.

Dark Cake from Madeira

Bolo Preto da Madeira 📷 p.361　　🇺 **Madeira**

Preparation time: 20 minutes
Cooking time: 35–40 minutes
Makes: 1

∅

200 g/7 oz (1¾ sticks) unsalted butter, plus extra
　　for greasing
400 g/14 oz (3⅓ cups) plain (all-purpose) flour,
　　plus extra for dusting
150 g/5 oz lemon rind
200 g/7 oz (1⅓ cups) sultanas (golden raisins)
400 g/14 oz (2 cups) caster (superfine) sugar
8 eggs
1 teaspoon ground cinnamon
15 ml/½ fl oz (1 tablespoon) firewater
15 ml/½ fl oz (1 tablespoon) Madeira wine
1 teaspoon instant dried yeast
40 g/1½ oz (⅓ cup) blanched almonds
40 g/1½ oz (⅓ cup) walnut halves

Preheat the oven to 200°C/400°F/Gas Mark 6.
Grease a flat 32-cm/12½-inch cake pan with butter,
then sprinkle with flour, tipping out the excess.
　　Cut all the dried fruits into small pieces or pulse
them in a food processor. Set aside.
　　Beat the butter, a little at a time, in a stand mixer
fitted with a paddle attachment until it is creamy,
then gradually incorporate the sugar, keep the
machine on medium speed. While beating, add the
eggs, one at a time, whisking after each addition
　　Put the flour and dried fruit into a large bowl and
mix together, then add to the cake mixture with the
remaining ingredients and mix until well combined.
　　Pour the batter into the prepared pan and bake
for 35 minutes, or until until a toothpick is inserted
into the middle of the cake comes out clean. If
it doesn't, cook for a few more minutes and test
again. Leave to cool on a wire rack before serving.

Walnut Cake

Bolo de Nozes de Coruche　　🇺 **Ribatejo**

Preparation time: 20 minutes
Cooking time: 35 minutes
Makes: 1

∅

unsalted butter, for greasing
200 g/7 oz (2 cups) walnut halves
50 g/2 oz (½ cup minus 2 teaspoons) plain (all-purpose)
　　flour, plus extra for sprinkling
1 teaspoon instant dried yeast
5 eggs, separated
220 g/7½ oz (1 cup plus 4 teaspoons) caster (superfine)
　　sugar
¼ teaspoon salt

Preheat the oven to 180°C/350°F/Gas Mark 4.
Grease a 26-cm/10½-inch fluted cake pan with
butter, then dust with flour, tipping out the excess.
　　Put the walnuts into a food processor and blitz
into a 'flour', then tip them into a medium bowl,
add the plain (all-purpose) flour and yeast, then
mix together until combined. Add the walnut
mixture to the egg yolks and gently fold in well.
　　Put the egg yolks and sugar into a stand mixer
fitted with a whisk attachment and whisk at medium
speed until doubled in volume. Alternatively, whisk
with electric beaters in a large bowl.
　　Put the egg whites into a bowl with the salt
and, using electric beaters or a stand mixer fitted
with a whisk attachment, whisk until soft peaks
form, then gently fold them into the cake batter.
　　Pour the batter into the prepared pan. Bake
in the oven for 35 minutes, or until golden and a
toothpick inserted into the centre comes out clean.
Remove from the oven, leave to cool slightly, then
turn out of the pan and leave to cool on a wire rack.
The cake can be stored in a container for 5 days.

Family Cake from Madeira

Bolo de Familia da Madeira　　🇺 **Madeira**

Preparation time: 25 minutes
Cooking time: 45 minutes
Makes: 1

180 g/6 oz (⅔ stick) unsalted butter, plus extra for
　　greasing
350 g/12 oz (3 cups minus 2 teaspoons) self-raising
　　(self-rising) flour, plus extra for dusting
280 g/10 oz (1½ cups) caster (superfine) sugar
90 g/3¼ oz (½ cup minus 2 tablespoons) brown sugar
1 teaspoon bicarbonate of soda (baking soda)
1 teaspoon ground cinnamon
zest of 1 lemon
130 ml/4½ fl oz (½ cup) whole (full-fat) milk
2 eggs
40 g/1½ oz lard (pork fat)
150 g/5 oz (⅔ cup) honey
30 g/1 oz (¼ cup) sultanas (golden raisins), chopped
40 g/1½ oz (¼ cup) walnut halves, chopped

Preheat the oven to 200°C/400°F/Gas Mark 6.
Grease a 32-cm/12½-inch baking pan, 10 cm/4
inches deep, with butter, then sprinkle with flour,
tipping out the excess.
　　Put the flour, both sugars, bicarbonate of soda
(baking soda), cinnamon and lemon zest into a stand
mixer fitted with a paddle attachment and mix until
combined. Add the milk, eggs, butter, lard (pork fat)
and honey. Beat at maximum speed for 10 minutes,
then add the sultanas (golden raisins) and walnuts.
　　Pour the batter into the prepared pan and
bake in the oven for 30 minutes. Cover with foil,
reduce the oven temperature to 180°C/350°F/Gas
Mark 4 and bake for a further 15 minutes, or until
a toothpick inserted into the middle of the cake
comes out clean. Leave to cool before serving.

Dark Cake from Madeira

Honey Cake

Bolo de Mel ♡ Madeira

This dark, squidgy, richly spiced cake is made with sugarcane syrup rather than honey, as its name might suggest. It was created in the 15th century, during the expansion of sugar plantations in Madeira. Locals eat it as a snack or as a dessert with Madeira wine or liqueurs, tearing off pieces by hand. This cake was traditionally prepared for Christmas, but nowadays it can be found all year round in pastry shops and delicatessens (and some speciality shops in mainland Portugal).

Preparation time: 30 minutes, plus 5 days rising
Cooking time: 1 hour
Serves: 20–24

870 g/1 lb 15 oz (7 cups) self-raising (self-rising) flour, plus extra for dusting
15 g/½ oz (1 tablespoon) fresh yeast or 4 g/¼ oz (heaped 1 teaspoon) instant dried yeast
½ teaspoon white peppercorns
¼ teaspoon ground cloves
1 teaspoon ground cinnamon
½ teaspoon ground nutmeg
4 tablespoons chopped wild fennel tops
1½ teaspoons bicarbonate of soda (baking soda)
30 ml/1 fl oz (2 tablespoons) Madeira wine
170 g/6 oz lard (pork fat), at room temperature
130 g/4½ oz (1¼ sticks) unsalted butter, at room temperature, plus extra for greasing
450 g/1 lb (1½ cups) honey
280 g/10 oz (1½ cups minus 4 teaspoons) caster (superfine) sugar
350 g/12 oz (3½ cups) walnut halves, cut into pieces
80 g/3 oz (⅔ cup) blanched almonds, cut into pieces, plus extra to decorate
20 g/¾ oz cidrao, cut into small pieces, plus extra to decorate
zest and juice of 2 oranges

The day before, make the starter. Put 175 g/6 oz (1½ cups) of the flour into a large bowl. Dissolve the yeast in 250 ml/8 fl oz (1 cup) water, then add to the flour and mix well. Transfer the dough to a large floured bowl, cover with a clean tea (dish) towel and leave to rise for 12 hours.

Put the white peppercorns, cloves, cinnamon and nutmeg into a mortar and, using a pestle, mash together, then sieve into a small bowl, discarding the large bits remaining in the sieve (fine-mesh strainer). Stir in the fennerl tops. Set side.

Put the bicarbonate of soda (baking soda) into a small bowl, add the Madeira wine and stir together. Put the lard (pork fat) and butter into a medium heatproof bowl. Heat the honey in a saucepan over a low heat for 4–5 minutes, or until hot. Add the honey to the lard and butter and mix until they have melted.

Sift the remaining flour into a large bowl, then make a small hole in the middle and add the bread dough starter and knead for 2 minutes until

well incorporated. While mixing, add the honey mixture, until it is all incorporated, then add the sugar, chopped nuts and fruits, reserved spices, the Madeira wine mixture and the orange zest and juice. Knead the dough for 8–10 minutes, or until it comes away from the side of the bowl. Cover with a tea (dish) towel and 'blanket' and leave to rise in a cool place for 4 days.

On the fourth day, preheat the oven to 180°C/350°F/Gas Mark 4. Grease a 32-cm/12½-inch cake pan, which is 6 cm/2½ inches deep, with butter. Pour in the mixture. Decorate with some extra almonds and *cidrao* and bake for 50–60 minutes or until a toothpick inserted into the centre comes out clean.

Leave the cake in the pan to cool on a wire rack before serving. This cake lasts for at least a week when stored in an airtight container.

Honey Cake from Sagres

Bolo de Mel — Sagres 📷 p.363 ♡ Algarve

Preparation time: 20 minutes
Cooking time: 45–44 minutes
Serves: 12
⌀

unsalted butter, for greasing
220 ml/7½ fl oz (1 cup minus 2 tablespoons) olive oil
220 ml/7½ fl oz (1 cup minus 1 teaspoon) honey
300 g/11 oz (2½ cups) plain (all-purpose) flour, plus extra for dusting
260 g/9 oz (1⅓ cups) caster (superfine) sugar
1 tablespoon instant dried yeast
8 eggs, separated

Preheat the oven to 160°C/325°F/Gas Mark 3. Grease a 28 x 25-cm/10 x 8-inch baking pan with butter and dust with flour, tipping out the excess.

Bring the olive oil and honey to the boil in a medium saucepan, then reduce the heat to medium and simmer for 5 minutes. Remove from the heat and leave to cool.

Sift the flour and yeast into a bowl and set aside.

Put the egg yolks and sugar into a stand mixer fitted with a whisk attachment and whisk at medium speed for 2–3 minutes or until it has doubled in volume. Alternatively, whisk with electric beaters in a large bowl.

Add the cooled honey and oil mixture to the egg yolk mixture and stir until combined. Add the sifted flour and gently fold in until incorporated.

Put the egg whites into another bowl and, using either electric beaters or a stand mixer fitted with a whisk attachment, whisk until soft peaks form, then gently fold into the cake batter without losing any air. Pour the batter into the prepared pan and bake in the oven for 45–55 minutes, or until the top is dark. Remove from the oven, leave to stand for 5 minutes, then turn out of the pan and leave to cool on a wire rack.

Honey Cake from Sagres

Honey and Olive Oil Cake

Bolo de Mel – Castelo Branco   ⛉ Beira Baixa

Preparation time: 30 minutes
Cooking time: 1 hours 15 minutes
Makes: 1
Ø

280 ml/9¾ fl oz (1 cup plus 2 tablespoons) olive oil
290 g/10 oz (1¼ cups) honey
450 g/1 lb (3¾ cups) spelt flour, plus extra for dusting
1 teaspoon instant dried yeast
1 teaspoon ground cinnamon
9 eggs, separated
310 g/11 oz (1½ cups) caster (superfine) sugar
butter, for greasing

Put the olive oil and honey into a medium saucepan and bring to the boil. Remove from the heat and leave to cool. Combine the flour, yeast and cinnamon in a large bowl and set aside.

Put the egg yolks and sugar into a stand mixer fitted with a whisk attachment and whisk at medium speed until the mixture has doubled in volume. Alternatively, whisk with electric beaters in a large bowl. Add the cooled olive oil and honey mixture and mix until smooth. Gradually fold in the flour and yeast until it has all been fully incorporated.

Whisk the egg whites in another bowl to soft peaks, then gradually and gently fold them into the cake batter.

Preheat the oven to 180°C/350°F/Gas Mark 4. Grease a large rimmed baking sheet, about 35 x 38 cm/14 x 15 inches, with butter and dust with flour, tipping off the excess.

Pour the batter onto the prepared baking sheet and bake for 1 hour 15 minutes, or until the top is golden brown and a toothpick inserted into the cake comes out clean. Leave to cool on a wire rack before serving.

'Rotten' Cake

Bolo Podre   ⛉ Alentejo

This olive oil cake with a cross shape on top is brown on the outside and yellow inside, is not too sweet and has a soft and moist texture. Its name *podre* (meaning 'rotten') comes from one of its recipe steps, when the batter needs to be left to rise for about three to four hours (until it turns 'rotten'). Traditionally, *Bolo Podre* is eaten during family reunions throughout the year, or over the Easter period.

Preparation time: 35 minutes
Cooking time: 1 hour
Makes: 1
Ø

butter, for greasing
520 g/1 lb 2 oz (4⅓ cups) plain (all-purpose) flour,
     plus extra for dusting
7 eggs, separated
280 g/10 oz (1½ cups minus 4 teaspoons) caster
     (superfine) sugar
1 teaspoon instant dried yeast
400 g/14 oz (1¾ cups) honey
360 ml/12¾ fl oz (1½ cups plus 2 teaspoons) extra
     virgin olive oil
30 ml/1 fl oz (2 tablespoons) white brandy
zest of 1 lemon
1 teaspoon ground cinnamon
icing (confectioners') sugar, for dusting

Preheat the oven to 160°C/325°F/Gas Mark 3. Grease a fluted cake pan, 26 cm/11 inch in diameter and 8 cm/3¼ inches deep with butter, then dust it with flour, tipping out the excess.

Put 6 egg yolks, 1 egg white and the caster (superfine) sugar into a stand mixer fitted with a whisk attachment and whisk on medium speed for 15 minutes.

Meanwhile, combine the flour and yeast in another bowl.

With the mixer on medium speed, slowly add the honey and olive oil and keep mixing until both are fully incorporated. Add the brandy, lemon zest and cinnamon and mix until these are incorporated before slowly adding the flour.

Put the remaining egg whites into a clean bowl and whisk until soft peaks form, then gently fold them into the batter. Pour the cake batter into the prepared cake pan and bake for 1 hour, or until dark golden brown and a toothpick inserted into the cake comes out clean.

Remove the cake from the pan and leave to cool on a wire rack. Once cold, dust with icing (confectioners') sugar before serving.

'Rotten' Cake from Benavente

••

Bolo Podre de Benavente ◊ Ribatejo

Preparation time: 25 minutes
Cooking time: 1 hour 20 minutes
Makes: 1
◻ ⌀

50 ml/1⅔ fl oz (3½ tablespoons) olive oil, plus extra
  for oiling
250 g/9 oz (1¼ cups) caster (superfine) sugar, plus
  extra for dusting
6 eggs
50 g/2 oz (¼ cup minus 2 teaspoons) honey
250 g/9 oz (2 cups) self-raising (self-rising) flour
2 teaspoons ground cinnamon, plus extra for dusting
2 teaspoons ground cumin
3 teaspoons chopped wild fennel tops
1 teaspoon ground cloves
500 g/1 lb 2 oz (4 cups plus 4 teaspoons) coarse spelt
  flour

Preheat the oven to 190°C/375°F/Gas Mark 5. Oil
a 25 x 35-cm/10 x 14-inch square shallow cake pan
with olive oil.

Put the sugar and eggs into a stand mixer fitted
with a whisk attachment and whisk at medium
speed for 5 minutes, or until creamy. Alternatively,
whisk with electric beaters in a large bowl. Add all
the remaining ingredients, except the spelt flour,
and mix well until combined. Add the flour and
whisk at medium speed for 15 minutes.

Pour the cake batter into the prepared pan
and bake in the oven for 1 hour, or until golden
and a toothpick inserted into the middle of the
cake comes out clean.

Remove from the oven, then turn out of
the pan and leave to cool on a wire rack. Once
cool, sprinkle with caster (superfine) sugar and
cinnamon, then cut into slices before serving.

Horseshoe Cake

◆◆

Ferraduras – Bolo de Noivos   ◊ Lisbon
– Bombarral

**At the end of a wedding celebration, these
horseshoe-shaped cakes are offered to all guests
to take home.**

Preparation time: 30 minutes
Cooking time: 1 hour
Makes: 18
⌀

230 g/8 oz (2 sticks) unsalted butter, plus extra
  for greasing
500 g/1 lb 2 oz (4 cups plus 2 teaspoons) spelt flour,
  plus extra for dusting
220 g/7¾ oz (1 cup plus 4 teaspoons) caster
  (superfine) sugar
4 eggs
110 ml/3¾ fl oz (½ cup minus 4 teaspoons) olive oil
90 g/3¼ oz (½ cup minus 2 tablespoons) honey
1 teaspoon chopped wild fennel tops
2 egg yolks, for egg wash
sea salt

Preheat the oven to 200°C/400°F/Gas Mark 6.
Grease a large baking sheet with butter, then dust
with flour making sure it is uniformly covered,
tipping off the excess.

Put the sugar and eggs into a stand mixer fitted
with a whisk attachment and whisk at medium
speed for 5 minutes, or until creamy. Alternatively,
put them into a large bowl and whisk with electric
beaters. Add the flour, olive oil, honey, fennel
tops and a pinch of salt, then mix together until a
smooth dough forms.

Tip out the dough onto a lightly floured work
counter and divide it into 18 equal portions. Shape
each into a ball, then roll and shape them into
horseshoes. Put the egg yolks into a small bowl
and lightly whisk with a fork. Arrange them on the
prepared baking sheet and brush with egg yolk.
Bake for 1 hour, or until golden brown. Leave to
cool on a wire rack before serving.

Sponge Cake from Rio Maior

Pão de Ló de Rio Maior   ⛉ Ribatejo

Sponge cakes are a big thing in Portugal, from the slightly runny ones found along the west coast to the more cooked and fully dry ones found up in the north. They are all super delicious and are made with patience as they require time.

Preparation time: 15 minutes
Cooking time: 7 minutes
Makes: 1
∅ ✕ ⊠

unsalted butter, for greasing
14 egg yolks
30 g/1 oz (2 tablespoons) caster (superfine) sugar
4 egg whites
70 g/2½ oz (½ cup plus 2 teaspoons) plain
    (all-purpose) flour

Preheat the oven to 220°C/425°F/Gas Mark 7. Grease a 25-cm/10-inch cake pan with butter, then line the bottom and sides with baking (parchment) paper and grease the paper too.

Put the egg yolks, sugar and egg whites into a stand mixer fitted with a whisk attachment and whisk at medium speed for 8 minutes. Alternatively, whisk with electric beaters in a large bowl. Sift in the flour and whisk for a further 5 minutes.

Pour the batter into the prepared cake pan and bake in the oven for 7 minutes. Don't let it bake for any longer as it is meant to be runny in the middle and lightly baked on the outside.

Remove from the oven and leave to cool in the pan before serving.

Soft Sponge Cake from Alfeizerão

Pão de Ló de Alfeizerão   ⛉ Lisbon

This sponge cake is unusual as it is very runny in the middle. There is another sponge cake that's similar to this one from Ovar in the Beiria Litoral region called *Pão de Ló de Ovar* (Soft Sponge Cake from Ovar, see right).

Preparation time: 20 minutes, plus 10 minutes resting
Cooking time: 8–10 minutes
Makes: 1
⛉ ∅ ✕

7 egg yolks
2 whole eggs
90 g/3¼ oz (½ cup minus 2 teaspoons) caster
    (superfine) sugar
55 g/2 oz (½ cup) plain (all-purpose) flour, sifted

Preheat the oven to 200°C/400°F/Gas Mark 6. Grease a 25-cm/10-inch cake pan with butter, then line the bottom and sides with baking (parchment) paper and grease the paper too.

Put the egg yolks, whole eggs and sugar into a stand mixer fitted with a whisk attachment and whisk at medium speed for 8 minutes until light, fluffy and doubled in volume. Gradually add the sifted flour, gently folding it in with a silicone spatula in circular movements until incorporated into the batter.

Spoon the batter into the prepared cake pan and bake for 8 minutes, or until the outside is cooked but it is runny inside. However, if you prefer the inside to be more set, bake for 10 minutes.

Remove from the oven and leave to rest in the pan for 10 minutes. Remove the cake from the pan using the baking paper, otherwise it will fall apart.

Soft Sponge Cake from Ovar

Pão de Ló de Ovar 📷 p.367   ⛉ Beira Litoral

Preparation time: 30 minutes
Cooking time: 12 minutes, plus 3 hours standing
Makes: 1
∅

unsalted butter, for greasing
3 whole eggs
12 egg yolks
220 g/7½ oz (1 cup plus 4 teaspoons) caster
    (superfine) sugar
115 g/4 oz (1 cup minus 1 teaspoon) self-raising
    (self-rising) flour, sifted
pinch of salt

Preheat the oven to 180°C/350°F/Gas Mark 4. Grease a 35-cm/14-inch cake pan, which is 8 cm/3¼ inches deep, with butter, then line the bottom and sides with baking (parchment) paper and grease the paper with too.

Put the whole eggs, egg yolks and sugar into a stand mixer fitted with a whisk attachment and whisk at medium speed for 20 minutes, then increase the speed to full for a further 5 minutes, or until the mixture is light and fluffy. Gently fold in the flour until fully incorporated.

Pour the batter into the prepared cake pan and bake in the oven for 12 minutes, or until it has a soft, light caramel coloured layer on the top, is cooked round the edges and a skewer inserted into the middle of the cake comes out with bits of mixture still attached. The cake should be moist in the middle.

Remove from the oven and leave to cool in the pan for at least 3 hours or until completely cold before serving.

Soft Sponge Cake from Ovar

Rolled Sponge Cakes with Egg Cream from Azeitão

Tortas de Azeitão 📷 p.369 ⏷ Lisbon

These small sponge rolls with their shiny exterior and sweet egg-yolk filling are a delicacy usually associated with the village of Azeitão, south of Lisbon, although their origins lie in Alentejo. At the beginning of the 19th century the recipe was brought from the interior to Azeitão by a family who owned a pastry shop (which still exists; called O Cego). They were initially baked as one large cake in the shape of a roll, but soon they were changed to being shaped in the form of individual sweets. Locals make a point of visiting Azeitão in order to eat these *tortas*.

Preparation time: 35 minutes
Cooking time: 8–10 minutes
Serves: 4 / Makes: 1 large roll
🌱 🍃

For the sponge:
unsalted butter, for greasing (or use spray oil)
9 eggs, separated
150 g/5 oz (¾ cup) caster (superfine) sugar
60 g/2¼ oz (½ cup) cornflour (cornstarch)
1 teaspoon ground cinnamon, for dusting

For the filling:
150 g/5 oz (¾ cup) caster (superfine) sugar
8 egg yolks

Grease a 25 x 32-cm/10 x 12½-inch Swiss (jelly) roll pan or shallow rectangular baking pan with butter or spray with oil.

To make the filling, put the sugar and 230 ml/7¾ fl oz (1 cup minus 4 teaspoons) water into a large saucepan and heat over a medium heat for 10–12 minutes until it reaches 106°C/222°F on a sugar thermometer. Remove from the heat, add the egg yolks and mix well to combine, then put the pan over a medium heat and cook for a further 5 minutes, or until thick. Set aside.

To make the sponge, put the egg yolks and sugar into a stand mixer fitted with a whisk attachment and whisk at medium speed until it doubles in volume. Alternatively, whisk with electric beaters in a large bowl. Add the cornflour (cornstarch) and stir until the mixture is smooth.

Put the egg whites into another bowl and, using either electric beaters or a stand mixer fitted with a whisk attachment, whisk until soft peaks form, then add them to the egg yolk mixture and very gently fold them in until combined.

Pour the batter into the prepared cake pan, making sure it is no thicker than 1 cm/½ inch. Cover with a tea (dish) towel or food wrap and leave to rest for 10 minutes.

Preheat the oven to 200°C/400°F/Gas Mark 6.

Bake the sponge for 8 minutes, or until the top is firm to touch but the inside is still smooth and moist. Remove the cake from the oven.

Lay a clean tea (dish) towel on a work counter. Using a small sieve (fine-mesh strainer), sprinkle the cinnamon evenly over the towel, then flip the sponge onto the towel. Make sure the long side of the sponge is facing you. Spread the filling over the sponge in an even layer, then starting from the longest side nearest you and using the towel to help you, carefully roll up the sponge.

Put the rolled sponge cake onto a serving plate with the seam side downwards and set aside to come to room temperature. Cut into slices before serving.

Sponge Cake from Margaride

Pão de Ló de Margaride ⏷ Minho

Preparation time: 15 minutes
Cooking time: 45 minutes
Makes: 1
🍃

unsalted butter, for greasing
360 g/12¾ oz (1¾ cups plus 2 teaspoons) caster (superfine) sugar
15 egg yolks
4 whole eggs
190 g/6¾ oz (1½ cups) plain (all-purpose) flour
½ teaspoon baking powder

Preheat the oven to 190°C/375°F/Gas Mark 5. Line a 27-cm/10¾-inch fluted cake pan with baking (parchment) paper and grease the paper too.

Put the sugar, egg yolks and eggs into a stand mixer fitted with a whisk attachment and whisk at medium speed for 5 minutes. Alternatively, whisk with electric beaters in a large bowl. Remove the bowl from the machine and sift in the flour and baking powder, mixing it in well with a silicone spatula. It should have a light and creamy texture.

Pour the cake batter into the prepared cake pan and bake in the oven for 45 minutes, or until golden on the top and a toothpick when inserted into the middle comes out clean.

Remove from the oven, then carefully turn the cake out of the pan onto a wire rack and leave to cool before serving.

Rolled Sponge Cakes with Egg Cream from Azeitão

Rolled Orange Sponge Cake

••

Torta de Tondela　　　　　　　　ᴗ Beira Litoral

Preparation time: 20 minutes
Cooking time: 25 minutes
Makes: 1
⌀ ✕

unsalted butter, for greasing
200 g/7 oz (1⅔ cups) plain (all-purpose) flour, plus extra
　　for dusting
7 eggs, separated
240g/8½ oz (1¼ cups) caster (superfine) sugar, plus
　　extra for dusting
1 orange (or any other fruit depending on what is in
　　season), peeled, cut into wedges, then cut into
　　small pieces

Preheat the oven to 180°C/350°F/Gas Mark 4. Grease a large baking sheet with butter, then sprinkle with flour, tipping off the excess.

Put the egg yolks and sugar into a stand mixer fitted with a whisk attachment and whisk at medium speed for 5 minutes, or until doubled in volume. Alternatively, whisk with electric beaters in a large bowl.

Put the egg whites into another bowl and, using either electric beaters or a stand mixer fitted with a whisk attachment, whisk until soft peaks form.

Gently fold a little of the whites into the egg and sugar mixture, followed by a little of the flour and continue until everything is incorporated.

Pour the batter onto the prepared baking sheet and sprinkle with the fruit pieces, then sprinkle with extra sugar. Bake in the oven for 25 minutes. Leave to cool on a wire rack before serving.

Rolled Sponge Cake from Viana do Castelo

••

Torta de Viana　　　　　　　　　　ᴗ Minho

This sponge cake can be spread with any filling, really. Here, I give a recipe for the classic egg cream filling, but you can use any fruit coulis or jam (jelly) that you prefer.

Preparation time: 30 minutes
Cooking time: 10 minutes
Makes: 1
⌀

For the sponge:
unsalted butter, for greasing
8 eggs
150 g/5 oz (¾ cup) caster (superfine) sugar, plus extra
　　for sprinkling
1 teaspoon instant dried yeast
160 g/5¾ oz (1⅓ cups) plain (all-purpose) flour, sifted
ground cinnamon, for dusting

For the filling:
10 egg yolks
70 g/2½ oz (⅓ cup) caster (superfine) sugar
2 teaspoons cornflour (cornstarch)

Preheat the oven to 180°C/350°F/Gas Mark 4. Grease a shallow 35 x 38-cm/14 x 15-inch cake pan with butter, then line it with baking (parchment) paper and grease the paper too.

To make the filling, combine all the ingredients along with 150 ml/5 fl oz (⅔ cup) water in a medium saucepan and cook over a low heat, stirring continuously, for 10 minutes, or until thick. Transfer to a small container and leave to cool.

To make the sponge, put the eggs and sugar into a stand mixer fitted with a whisk attachment and whisk at medium speed for 4–5 minutes, or until pale and doubled in volume. Alternatively, whisk with electric beaters in a large bowl. Reduce the speed and add the yeast, then reduce the speed to the lowest speed possible and slowly add the flour until it is incorporated. You can fold the flour in with a silcone spatula, if you prefer.

Pour the batter into the prepared cake pan and and bake in the oven for 10 minutes. Remove the cake from the oven.

Lay a clean tea (dish) towel on a work counter. Sprinkle sugar evenly over the tea towel then flip the sponge onto the tea towel. Make sure the long side of the sponge is facing you. Spread the filling over the sponge in an even layer then, starting from the longest side nearest you and using the tea towel to help you, carefully roll up the sponge. Put the rolled sponge cake onto a serving plate with the seam side downwards. Sprinkle with more sugar and dust with cinnamon. Cut into slices before serving.

Almond Cake

•••

Bolo de Amêndoa   ☼ Alentejo

Preparation time: 40 minutes, plus 10 minutes resting
Cooking time: 15 minutes
Serves: 12–14
⌀

butter, for greasing
plain (all-purpose) flour, for dusting
12 egg yolks
420 g/14¾ oz (2 cups plus 4 teaspoons) caster
    (superfine) sugar
400 g/14 oz (3⅓ cups) almond flour
8 egg whites
100 g/3½ oz (¾ cup plus 2 teaspoons) spelt flour
crystallised sugar, for sprinkling

Grease a flat round 35-cm/14-inch baking pan with
butter, then dust it with plain (all-purpose) flour
and tip out the excess.
    Put the egg yolks and caster (superfine) sugar
into a stand mixer fitted with a whisk attachment
and whisk on medium speed for 4–5 minutes or until
pale and doubled in volume, then add the almond
flour. Alternatively, whisk with electric beaters in
a large bowl. Put the egg whites into a large clean
bowl and whisk until soft peaks form, then gently
fold them into the egg yolk mixture. Sift in the spelt
flour and mix gently until combined. Pour the cake
batter into the prepared pan and leave to rest for
10 minutes.
    Preheat the oven to 200°C/400°F/Gas Mark 6.
    Bake for 15 minutes, or until golden and a
toothpick inserted into the middle of the cake
comes out clean.
    Remove from the pan and leave to cool on a
wire rack, then sprinkle over the crystallised sugar
before serving.

Paradise Cake

•••

Bolo Paraíso   ☼ Alentejo

I'm always amused by the titles of some recipes,
such as this Paradise Cake. This name may be
related to the richness of this cake, which is
somehow light and very moreish.

Preparation time: 30 minutes
Cooking time: 40–45 minutes
Serves: 12–14
⌀

butter, for greasing
125 g/4¼ oz (1 cup) plain (all-purpose) flour, plus extra
    for dusting
10 eggs, separated
350 g/12 oz (1¾ cups) caster (superfine) sugar
1 teaspoon instant dried yeast
380 g/13½ oz (3¾ cups) almond flour

Preheat the oven to 190°C/375°F/Gas Mark 5.
Grease a 28-cm/11-inch springform baking pan, 3
cm/1¼ inches deep, with butter, then dust it with
plain (all-purpose) flour, tipping out the excess.
    Put the egg yolks and sugar into a stand
mixer fitted with a whisk attachment and whisk
on medium speed for 4–5 minutes or until pale and
doubled in volume. Alternatively, whisk with electric
beaters in a large bowl.
    Put the plain flour into another bowl, add the
yeast and mix together.
    Put the egg whites into a large clean bowl and
whisk until soft peaks form. Using a large metal
spoon, gently fold in a little of the egg whites
into the egg yolk mixture with a little of the flour,
then fold in some more egg whites and some of
the almond flour and repeat until you have used
up all the egg whites and flours.
    Pour the batter into the prepared baking pan
and bake for 40–45 minutes, or until risen, golden
brown and a toothpick inserted into the middle of
the cake comes out clean.
    Remove the cake from the pan and leave to
cool on a wire rack before serving. This cake can be
stored in an airtight container for up to 5 days.

Bacon from Heaven

▰▰▰▰▰▰▰▰▰▰▰▰▰▰▰▰▰▰▰▰▰▰▰▰▰▰▰▰▰▰▰▰▰▰▰▰

Toucinho do Céu   ⛉ Alentejo
– Portalegre 🖾 p.373

I particularly love this cake, as it is light and
crispy all over with a dense and rich texture.
It is very comforting. This was one of the first
desserts I baked as an apprentice in a local
restaurant in my home town.

Preparation time: 35 minutes
Cooking time: 55 minutes
Makes: 1
🌿

400 g/14 oz (2 cups) caster (superfine) sugar
7 egg yolks
2 egg whites
330 g/11½ oz (2¾ cups) almond flour
60 g/2¼ oz (½ cup) plain (all-purpose) flour,
     plus extra for dusting
40 g/1½ oz (3 tablespoons) unsalted butter,
     plus extra for greasing
icing (confectioners') sugar, for dusting (optional)

Put the caster (superfine) sugar and 200 ml/
7 fl oz (¾ cup plus 1 tablespoon) water into a
large saucepan and heat over a medium heat
for 10–12 minutes until it reaches 108°C/226°F
on a sugar thermometer. Remove the pan from the
heat and leave to cool.
  Put the egg yolks and whites into a large bowl
and mix together to combine.
  Add the almond flour to the cooled sugar syrup,
then add the eggs then the plain (all-purpose) flour.
Cook over a medium heat without letting it boil for
10 minutes, or until thick. Once you can see the
bottom of the pan while stirring, it is ready. Remove
the pan from the heat, add the butter and mix until
well incorporated. Cover and leave to cool.
  Preheat the oven to 180°C/350°F/Gas Mark 4.
Line a 28-cm/11-inch cake pan with baking
(parchment) paper, then grease with butter.
  Pour the cooled mixture into the prepared pan
and bake for 45 minutes, or until dark brown.
  Remove from the oven and turn out from
the pan, discarding the baking paper, and leave
to cool on a wire rack. Dust the top with icing
(confectioners') sugar, if liked, before serving.

Bacon from Heaven
with Figleaf Gourd Jam

▰▰▰▰▰▰▰▰▰▰▰▰▰▰▰▰▰▰▰▰▰▰▰▰▰▰▰▰▰▰▰▰▰▰▰▰

Toucinho do Céu de Guimarães   ⛉ Minho

Created by nuns in the 18th century, this cake is
a delight. It is rich, dense and moist with almond
paste and doce de chila (jam), which is then baked
in the oven to create a thin crust all round.

Preparation time: 35 minutes
Cooking time: 1 hour
Makes: 1
🌿

unsalted butter, for greasing
plain (all-purpose) flour, for sprinkling
450 g/1 lb (2¼ cups) caster (superfine) sugar
180 g/6 oz (1¾ cups plus 1 teaspoon) ground almonds
80 g/3 oz Figleaf Gourd Jam (Doce de Chila, page 414)
16 egg yolks
2 egg whites
icing (confectioners') sugar, for dusting

Preheat the oven to 160°C/325°F/Gas Mark 3.
Grease a 28-cm/11-inch cake pan, which is 3 cm/
1¼ inches deep, with butter, then sprinkle with
flour, making sure it is evenly covered. Tip out any
excess flour.
  Put the caster (superfine) sugar and 200 ml/
7 fl oz (¾ cup plus 1 tablespoon) water into a
large saucepan and heat over a medium heat for
10–12 minutes until it reaches 108°C/226°F on a
thermometer. Add the ground almonds and Doce
de Chila to the sugar syrup and stir. Reduce the
heat to low and cook for 10 minutes, or until
it boils. Remove from the heat and set aside.
  Put the egg yolks and whites into a medium
bowl and lightly whisk with a fork. Once the sugar
syrup mixture is cold, add the whisked eggs to
the syrup and mix until well combined. Cook over
a low heat, stirring continuously and not letting
it boil, for 5 minutes.
  Pour the mixture into the prepared pan. Bake
in the oven for 1 hour, or until a toothpick inserted
into the middle of the cake comes out clean. Turn
the cake out of the pan and leave to cool on a
wire rack. Brush off any flour, then dust with icing
(confectioners') sugar before serving.

'Sand' Cakes from Sines

Areias de Sines   ▯ Alentejo

Preparation time: 20 minutes
Cooking time: 20–25 minutes
Makes: 30
𝄃

20 g/¾ oz (1½ tablespoons) unsalted butter,
    plus extra for greasing
25 g/1 oz (3 tablespoons) plain (all-purpose) flour,
    plus extra for dusting
350 g/12 oz (1¾ cups) caster (superfine) sugar
110 g/3½ oz (1 cup minus 2 teaspoons) almond flour
1 whole egg
7 egg yolks
120 g/4 oz Figleaf Gourd Jam (*Doce de Chila*,
    page 414)

Preheat the oven to 230°C/450°F/Gas Mark 8.
Grease 30 8-cm/3¼-inch baking pans with butter,
then sprinkle with plain (all-purpose) flour, tipping
out any excess.

Put the sugar into a medium saucepan with
heat 140 ml/4¾ fl oz (½ cup) water and heat over
a medium heat for 10–12 minutes until it reaches
101°C/214°F on a thermometer. Remove the pan
from the heat, stir in the butter and then add the
almond flour and mix until combined. Set aside
to cool.

Put the whole egg into a medium bowl, add the
plain flour and whisk, then add it to the sugar and
almond mixture.

Put the egg yolks into another bowl and
whisk lightly. Add the *Doce de Chila* and mix to
combine, then stir into the almond mixture and
mix well. Divide the batter between the prepared
pans and bake for 10–12 minutes. Remove from the
oven and leave to cool on a wire rack.

'Prince' Cake from the Convent of Hope, Beja

Bolo Príncipe do Convento   ▯ Alentejo
da Esperança, Beja

Preparation time: 25 minutes, plus overnight standing
Cooking time: 40–45 minutes
Makes: 1
▯ 𝄃

550 g/1 lb 4 oz (2¾ cups) caster (superfine) sugar
550 g/1 lb 4 oz (4½ cups) almond flour
10 egg yolks
plain (all-purpose) flour, for dusting
250 g/9 oz Figleaf Gourd Jam (*Doce de Chila*,
    page 414)
300 g/11 oz Egg Yolk Noodles (*Encharcada do
    Convento de Santa Clara*, page 306) to cover the
    top or enough fondant
9 Egg Yolk Sheets (*Trouxas de Ovos*, page 306)

The day before, put the sugar into a large
saucepan with 280 ml/9½ fl oz (1 cup) water and
heat over a medium heat for 10–12 minutes until it
reaches 101°C/214°F on a thermometer. Remove
the pan from the heat, add the almond flour and
mix until combined. Set aside to cool.

Once the sugar and almond flour mixture is
cold, add the egg yolks. Put the pan over a low
heat and cook, stirring continuously, for 10 minutes,
or until thick. Once you can see the bottom of the
pan while stirring, it is ready. Remove the pan from
the heat, cover and leave to stand overnight.

The next day, preheat the oven to 140°C/
275°F/Gas Mark 1. Grease a 15-cm/6-inch cake pan
with butter and line the base with a circle of baking
(parchment) paper.

Dust a work counter with plain (all-purpose)
flour. Tip the dough onto the counter and divide
it equally into three pieces. Using floured hands,
shape each piece into a round, 15 cm/6 inches
in diameter. (This cake can have more than three
layers of sponge and two layers of filling, so if you
prefer more layers then stretch out the dough
thinly to make more rounds.)

Dust the cake pan very well with flour, then lay
one of the rounds of dough on the bottom. Cut a
large strip baking (parchment) paper into and use
it to line the sides of the pan. This is to prevent the
filling oozing out while baking.

Cover the dough in the cake pan with half
of the jam, and then add layers of the egg yolk
noodles and egg yolk sheets. Place another round
of dough circle on top, spread with the rest of
the jam and repeat the layers as before. Finish, by
placing the final round of dough on top. Place the
cake pan on a baking sheet and bake in the oven
for 40–45 minutes, or until a toothpick inserted into
the middle of the cake comes out clean.

Leave to cool on a wire rack before serving.

Almond Sponge with Figleaf Gourd Jam

Morgado   ○ Alentejo

Preparation time: 15 minutes
Cooking time: 40–45 minutes
Serves: 8–10

butter, for greasing
300 g/11 oz (3 cups) ground almonds
300 g/11 oz (1½ cups) caster (superfine) sugar
7 egg yolks
½ teaspoon salt
4 egg whites
130 g/4½ oz (½ cup) Figleaf Gourd Jam (*Doce de Chila*, page 414)
icing (confectioners') sugar, for sprinkling

Preheat the oven to 180°C/350°F/Gas Mark 4. Grease a 25-cm/10-inch springform baking pan with butter and line the base with a circle of baking (parchment) paper.

Put the almonds, sugar, egg yolks and salt into a stand mixer fitted with a whisk attachment and whisk on medium speed for 2 minutes or until combined. Alternatively, beat with a whisk in a large bowl.

Whisk the egg whites in another clean bowl to soft peaks. Gently fold the whisked egg white into the egg yolk mixture, making sure you do not lose any volume or air as the egg whites are incorporated.

Pour half of the batter into the prepared cake pan and then level evenly over the base. Spread the jam in a thin layer over the cake batter, then top with the remaining batter. Bake in the oven for 40–45 minutes, or until golden all over and a toothpick inserted into the middle of the cake comes out clean.

Remove the cake from the pan and leave to cool on a wire rack. Dust some icing (confectioners') sugar over the top of the cake before serving at room temperature.

Almond Sponge with Figleaf Gourd Jam and Egg Yolk Sheets

Pão de Rala   ○ Alentejo

Although this is called *pão* (bread), it is actually a round, whitish cake with the appearance of a loaf of bread. The outside is a paste made of almonds, sugar and egg yolks; inside is a yellow filling made of *Ovos Moles* (page 308) and *Doce de Chila* (page 414). It is served as a dessert during banquets and feasts, and so is usually adorned with strips of fringed tissue paper. *Pão de Rala* is another conventual sweet conceptualised and produced in Portuguese nunneries, and is mentioned in some 18th-century manuscripts of the Santa Clara de Évora Monastery, though these documents confirm that it was previously given by the nuns of the Santa Helena do Calvário convent.

Preparation time: 15 minutes, plus overnight standing
Cooking time: 30 minutes
Makes: 1

550 g/1 lb 4 oz (2¾ cups) caster (superfine) sugar
500 g/1 lb 2 oz (4½ cups) almond flour
5 eggs, whisked
plain (all-purpose) flour, for dusting
400 g/14 oz Figleaf Gourd Jam (*Doce de Chila*, page 414)
6 Egg Yolk Sheets (*Trouxas de Ovos*, page 306)

Put the sugar into a saucepan with 210 ml/7 fl oz (¾ cup plus 2 tablespoons) water and heat over a medium heat for 10–12 minutes, or until it reaches 108°C/226°F on a thermometer. Add the almond flour and stir well over the heat for 1 minute. Remove from the heat and set aside to cool.

Once the sugar and flour mixture is cold, add the whisked eggs, then put the pan over a low heat and cook, stirring continuously, for 10 minutes, or until thick. Once you can see the bottom of the pan while stirring, it is ready. Remove the pan from the heat, cover and leave to stand overnight.

The next day, preheat the oven to 200°C/400°F/Gas Mark 6. Dust a baking sheet with a good amount of plain (all-purpose) flour.

Tip out the dough onto a floured work counter and roll it out into a thin rectangle. Divide the dough equally into two pieces. Roll each half into a 22-cm/8½-inch round. Place one round onto the prepared baking sheet, lift the edges up a little so it can hold the filling, add a layer of the jam, then a layer of the egg yolk sheets. Repeat until both the jam and egg yolk sheets are used up. Place the remaining round of dough on top and carefully press the layers of dough together around the edges to seal in the filling. Bake in the oven for 8 minutes, or until golden brown. Transfer to a wire rack and leave to cool on before serving.

Almond Sponge Traybake with Figleaf Gourd Jam

••

Patudos de Alpiarça

⋃ Ribatejo

Preparation time: 15 minutes
Cooking time: 1 hour
Makes: 16

🌿 ⌀

unsalted butter, for greasing
260 g/9 oz (1⅓ cups) caster (superfine) sugar, plus
    extra for sprinkling
10 egg yolks
3 eggs
120 g/4 oz (1¼ cups) ground almonds
50 g/2 oz Figleaf Gourd Jam (*Doce de Chila*, page 414)
1 teaspoon pectin

Preheat the oven to 160°C/325°F/Gas Mark 3.
Grease a large rimmed baking sheet with butter.
    Put the sugar into a large saucepan with
80 ml/2¾ fl oz (⅓ cup) water and heat over a
medium heat for 10–12 minutes until it reaches
108°C/226°F on a thermometer.
    Put the egg yolks and eggs into a bowl and
whisk together.
    Add the almonds, jam and pectin to the pan
with the sugar syrup, and stir to combine. Remove
the pan from the heat, add the beaten eggs and
mix well until fully combined.
    Pour the cake batter onto the prepared baking
sheet, levelling it evenly across the sheet, and then
bake in the oven for 50 minutes, or until a toothpick
inserted into the middle of the cake comes out
clean. Leave to cool on a wire rack. Once cold,
sprinkle some extra sugar over the top and then
cut the cake into 16 squares before serving.

'Rancid Lard'

••

Toucinho Rançoso

⋃ Alentejo

When I attended culinary school, I also worked at
a local restaurant. It was a huge place that catered
for a lot of weddings and big parties. There I made
this cake several times a day for months. When I
made this cake again for the book, it brought back
so many memories.

Preparation time: 30 minutes
Cooking time: 1 hour 5 minutes
Makes: 1

⌀

200 g/7 oz (1 cup) caster (superfine) sugar
80 g/3 oz (⅔ cup) almond flour
9 egg yolks
100 g/3½ oz Figleaf Gourd Jam (*Doce de Chila*,
    page 414)
20 g/¾ oz (1½ tablespoons) unsalted butter, plus extra
    for greasing
1 egg white
30 g/1 oz (3⅔ tablespoons) plain (all-purpose) flour
icing (confectioners') sugar, for dusting
ground cinnamon, for dusting

Put the caster (superfine) sugar into a large
saucepan with 110 ml/3¾ fl oz (⅓ cup plus 2
tablespoons) water and heat over a medium heat
for 10–12 minutes until it reaches 101°C/214°F on
a thermometer. Add the almond flour and stir well
over the heat for 1 minute, or until the mixture is
smooth and dense. Remove from the heat and set
aside to cool.
    Add the egg yolks and jam to the pan with the
cooled almond mixture. Return the pan to over
a medium heat and cook, stirring continuously,
for 10 minutes, or until thick. Once you can see
the bottom of the pan while stirring, it is ready.
Remove the pan from the heat, cover with a tea
(dish) towel and set aside to cool.
    Preheat the oven to 140°C/275°F/Gas Mark 1.
Grease a 26-cm/10½-inch cake pan with butter.
    Whisk the egg white in a clean bowl to soft
peaks. Gently fold the whisked egg white into
the cooled almond mixture, making sure you do
not lose any volume or air as the egg white is
incorporated. Sift over the plain (all-purpose) flour
and fold in until fully incorporated.
    Pour the batter into the prepared cake pan
and bake in the oven for 45 minutes, or until
a toothpick inserted into the middle of the cake
comes out clean. Leave to cool on a wire rack.
Once cold, dust with icing (confectioners') sugar
and cinnamon before serving.

Baked Almond, Sweet Figleaf Gourd Jam and Egg Yolk Cream Cake

•••

Morgado de Amêndoas   ◡ Algarve

This cake, with its almond paste exterior and yellow egg yolk, sugar and a sweet squash jam (*Doce de Chila*) filling, resembles a large, round cheese — but the similarities end there. *Morgado* is usually cooked for festivities, especially weddings and baptisms, when it is decorated with sugar pearls and marzipan (sugared almond paste) figures, and/or different kinds of delicate decorative paper. There is also a smaller version of this cake, called *Morgadinho*, usually sold in pastry shops and restaurants in the Algarve, sometimes embellished with a sugar pearl top, other times with handmade, colourful marzipan flowers or fruits.

Preparation time: 30 minutes
Cooking time: 1 hour 10 miuntes
Makes: 1
🥜 ◻

380 g/13½ oz (3 cups plus 2 teaspoons) almond flour, plus extra for sprinkling
380 g/13½ oz (2 cups minus 4 teaspoons) caster (superfine) sugar
3 egg yolks
lard (pork fat), for greasing
royal icing (frosting), for decorating

For the filling:
250 g/9 oz Sweet Egg Yolk Strands (*Fios de Ovos*, page 312), plus extra for decorating
160 g/5¾ oz Soft Sweet Eggs (*Ovos Moles*, page 308)
250 g/9 oz Figleaf Gourd Jam (*Doce de Chila*, page 414)

Preheat the oven to 160°C/325°F/Gas Mark 3. Line the bottom of 28-cm/11-inch springform cake pan with baking (parchment) paper, then sprinkle with almond flour, tipping out the excess.

Put the sugar into a large saucepan with 190 ml/ 6¼ fl oz (¾ cup) water and heat over a medium heat for 10–12 minutes until it reaches 108°C/226°F on a thermometer. Reduce the heat to low, add the almond flour and cook for 5 minutes. Remove from the heat and set aside to cool.

Add the egg yolks, one at a time, to the pan with the cooled almond mixture, stirring well between each addition. Return the pan to over a low heat and cook, stirring continuously, for 10 minutes, or thick. Once you can see the bottom of the pan while stirring, it is ready. Remove the pan from the heat, cover with a tea (dish) towel and set aside to cool.

Divide the dough equally into two pieces. Shape one piece into a round large enough to cover the base of the cake pan and lay it in the pan, lifting the edges slightly. Add a layer of the sweet egg yolk strands, then a layer of the soft sweet eggs, then a layer of jam. Repeat until all the ingredients are used up. Roll out the remaining dough to a 28-cm/11-inch circle and lay it over the filling to cover. Grease the ring of the springform cake pan with the lard (pork fat) and tighten it around the cake. Sprinkle the top of the cake with flour and bake in the oven for 45 minutes, or until golden brown. Leave to cool on a wire rack, tip out the flour, then decorate with the royal icing (frosting) and the extra egg yolk strands.

Sweet Potato Cake

•••

Bolo de Batata Doce   ◡ Algarve

With its elongated shape, a purple or reddish-brown skin and yellow flesh, the Lira sweet potato variety from Aljezur in southwest Algarve is a delicacy in itself. It has a sweet taste and a slightly fibrous texture, with a raw flavour similar to that of chestnut. Sweet potato historically became the basis of the general populace of Aljezur's diet, earning it the nickname 'bread of the poor', with the stems and scraps used to feed cattle. Over the years it became the main ingredient of bread, sweets (candies), pastries, puddings and cakes, such as this one.

Preparation time: 30 minutes
Cooking time: 30 minutes
Makes: 1
⌀

unsalted butter, for greasing
530 g/1 lb 3 oz (4½ cups minus 2 teaspoons) self-raising (self-rising) flour, plus extra for dusting
500 g/1 lb 2 oz sweet potato, peeled
7 eggs
530 g/1 lb 3 oz (2⅔ cups) caster (superfine) sugar
1 teaspoon ground cinnamon
scant 1 teaspoon instant dried yeast

Preheat the oven to 180°C/350°F/Gas Mark 4. Grease a round 31-cm/12½-inch cake pan with butter and sprinkle with flour, tipping out the excess.

Grate (shred) the sweet potato on a box grater and set aside.

Put the eggs and sugar into a stand mixer fitted with a whisk attachment and whisk at medium speed until doubled in volume. Alternatively, whisk with electric beaters in a large bowl.

Put the flour, cinnamon and yeast into a large bowl and mix together. While whisking, gradually add the flour to the egg mixture, a little at a time, until it is all incorporated into the mixture. Add the grated sweet potato and fold it in gently until everything is combined.

Pour the cake batter into the prepared pan and bake in the oven for 30 minutes, or until a toothpick inserted into the middle of the cake comes out clean. Leave to cool on a wire rack before serving.

Sweet Potato Fudge Cake from Madeira

••

Fartes de Batata Doce da Madeira

ʊ Madeira

Preparation time: 25 minutes
Cooking time: 1 hour 15 minutes
Makes: 1

⌀

500 g/1 lb 2 oz sweet potatoes, unpeeled
80 g/3 oz (⅔ cup) blanched almonds
310 g/11 oz (1½ cups) caster (superfine) sugar,
    plus extra for dusting
2 eggs
35 g/1¼ oz (2 tablespoons) unsalted butter, plus extra
    for brushing
60 g/2¼ oz (½ cup) spelt flour
1 teaspoon bicarbonate of soda (baking soda)
40 ml/1⅓ fl oz (2⅔ tablespoons) orange juice
80 g/3 oz (⅔ cup) crystallised fruit, cut into small pieces

Preheat the oven to 190°C/375°F/Gas Mark 5.
Line a 21 x 28-cm/8¼ x 11-inch shallow baking pan
with baking (parchment) paper.
    Wrap the sweet potatoes in foil and bake in the
oven for 45 minutes, or until soft. Remove the foil,
peel off the skin and put the flesh into to a food
processor and process to a purée. Set aside. Keep
the oven on.
    Put the almonds into a food processor and blitz
until ground. Set aside.
    Put the sugar, eggs and butter into a stand
mixer fitted with a paddle attachment and mix well.
Alternatively, mix in a large bowl. Add the sweet
potato purée, flour, bicarbonate of soda (baking
soda), ground almonds, orange juice and the fruit
and mix for 2 minutes until all the ingredients are
well incorporated.
    Transfer the cake batter to a large saucepan
and cook over a low heat, stirring continuously, for
10 minutes, or until the moisture has evaporated
and the mixture is thick. Once you can see the
bottom of the pan while stirring, it is ready. Pour
the batter into the prepared cake pan and bake
for 18–20 minutes, or until golden on the top.
    Meanwhile, put the butter for brushing into
a small saucepan and heat over a low heat until
melted. Take off the heat. Remove the cake from
the oven, then brush with the butter and sprinkle
with sugar before serving.

Sweet Potato and Almond Cakes

••

Bolos de Batata Doce e Amêndoa de Benavente

ʊ Ribatejo

Preparation time: 20 minutes, plus 10 minutes standing
Cooking time: 35–45 minutes
Makes: 8

⌀

10 g/¼ oz (2 teaspoons) unsalted butter, plus extra
    for greasing
plain (all-purpose) flour, for sprinkling
90 g/3¼ oz sweet potatoes, peeled
210 g/7½ oz (1 cup plus 2 teaspoons) caster (superfine)
    sugar, plus extra for dusting
85 g/3 oz (¾ cup plus 1 tablespoon) ground almonds
3 egg yolks
15 g/½ oz (1 tablespoon) cornflour (cornstarch)
ground cinnamon, for dusting

Preheat the oven to 190°C/375°F/Gas Mark 5.
Grease 8 small cake pans, each measuring 10 cm/
4 inches in diameter, with butter, then sprinkle with
flour and tip out the excess.
    Put the sweet potatoes into a large saucepan,
pour in enough water to cover and cook over a
medium heat for 15–20 minutes, or until soft. Drain
and put into a food processor and process to a
purée. Set aside.
    Put the sugar and 100 ml/3½ fl oz (⅓ cup plus
1 tablespoon) water into a medium saucepan and
bring to the boil. Reduce the heat to medium and
simmer for 2 minutes, then remove from the heat
and add the puréed potatoes and ground almonds.
Cook over a medium heat for 5 minutes, stirring
continuously, until it is a light dry base. Remove
from the heat and leave to cool for 10 minutes.
    Once the sweet potato purée has cooled to
warm, add the egg yolks, stir well until combined,
then add the cornflour (cornstarch) and mix well
with a spatula.
    Pour the mixture into the prepared pans and
bake in the oven for 15–20 minutes, or until
golden. Remove from the oven, turn the cakes out
of the pans and leave to cool on a wire rack. Once
cold, combine the extra sugar and the cinnamon
on a large plate and roll the cakes in the cinnamon
sugar until coated before serving.

Dark Cake from Loriga

Bolo Negro de Loriga   ♡ Beira Baixa

This dark, rectangular cake comes from the village of Loriga in Serra da Estrela, the highest mountain range in continental Portugal. The recipe was inherited from an English colony that settled in the village in the 19th century, which accounts for the consistency, shape and colour being very similar to an English Christmas cake. And, indeed, it was first consumed in Loriga during religious festivals such as Christmas and Easter, but over time became a cake for every day. *Bolo Negro* can be found in bakeries and pastry shops in Serra da Estrela.

Preparation time: 15 minutes
Cooking time: 1 hour
Makes: 1
⌀

butter, for greasing
320 g/11¼ oz (2⅔ cups) self-raising (self-rising) flour, plus extra for dusting
1 teaspoon bicarbonate of soda (baking soda)
5 eggs
320 g/11¼ oz (1⅔ cups) caster (superfine) sugar
1 teaspoon ground cinnamon
140 ml/4¾ fl oz (½ cup) whole (full-fat) milk

Preheat the oven to 160°C/325°F/Gas Mark 3. Grease a 20 x 10-cm/8 x 4-inch loaf pan with butter, then dust with flour and tip out the excess.
    Put the flour and bicarbonate of soda (baking soda) into a bowl and mix together until combined.
    Put the eggs into a large bowl, add the sugar, cinnamon and milk and mix together gently without creating too many air bubbles. Do not whisk. Add the flour mixture and fold in gently until the batter is a smooth consistency.
    Pour the cake batter into the prepared pan, sprinkle some flour over the top and bake in the oven for 1 hour, or until it is a dark colour. Leave to cool on a wire rack before serving.

Cinnamon Layer Cake from Mirandela

Bola Doce Mirandesa   ♡ Trás-os-Montes e Alto Douro

This cake resembles the famous Goan recipe *Bebinca*, which is a layered cake made from ghee and coconut milk. The Portuguese version is a smooth, rich bread dough layered with lots of sugar and ground cinnamon.

Preparation time: 35 minutes, plus 1 hour 30 minutes– 2 hours rising
Cooking time: 50 minutes
Makes: 1
⌀

70 g/2¼ oz (4⅔ tablespoons) fresh yeast or 18 g/¾ oz (2 tablespoons) instant dried yeast
110 g/3¾ oz (1 stick) unsalted butter, plus extra for greasing
3 eggs
80 ml/2¾ fl oz (⅓ cup) olive oil, plus extra for oiling
1 kg/2 lb 4 oz (8⅓ cups) plain (all-purpose) flour
300 g/11 oz (1½ cups) caster (superfine) sugar
3⅓ tablespoons ground cinnamon

Put the yeast into a bowl and pour over 400 ml/ 14 fl oz (1⅔ cups) lukewarm water. (The water should be no more than 32°C/90°F, otherwise, the yeast won't activate.) Stir until dissolved. Set aside.
    Put the butter into a saucepan and heat over a low heat until melted. Put the eggs into a medium bowl and whisk lightly. Put the bowl in a warm place, then add the olive oil and melted butter.
    Put the flour into a large bowl, add the yeast mixture, stir, then add the olive oil mixture. Mix for 10 minutes until a dough forms. The dough is wet at first, but keep mixing. Cover with a clean tea (dish) towel and leave to rise at room temperature for 1 hour 30 minutes–2 hours or until doubled in size.
    Preheat the oven to 200°C/400°F/Gas Mark 6. Grease a 28 x 25-cm/11 x 10-inch baking sheet with butter.
    Combine the sugar and cinnamon in a medium bowl. Set aside.
    Using oiled hands, take a slab of the dough and spread it over the bottom of the baking sheet, making sure there are no holes. Stretch the edges of the dough up a little, then sprinkle with some of the cinnamon sugar. Repeat with the rest of the dough and cinnamon sugar, layering each dough on top of one another. Roll the edges of the last layer of dough with the edges of the bottom one to seal. Using a toothpick, poke holes into the cake without going through to the bottom layer.
    Bake in the oven for 50 minutes, or until dark brown on top and cooked through. Leave to cool on a wire rack before serving.

Sponge Cupcakes with Egg and Vanilla Cream

••

Fofos de Belas – Sintra   ⎁ Lisbon

Filled with cream and sprinkled with icing (confectioners') sugar, these small, cylindrical sponge cakes are an important sweet from the village of Sintra, just outside Lisbon, where they are almost exclusively sold at Casa dos Fofos de Belas, the pastry shop where they were created in 1850 with the original name of *Fartos de Creme* ('filled with cream'). The recipe remains unchanged.

Preparation time: 30 minutes
Cooking time: 30 minutes
Makes: 7
Ø

butter, for greasing
115 g/4 oz (1 cup minus 1 teaspoon) self-raising (self-rising) flour, plus extra for dusting
4 eggs, separated
160 g/5¾ oz (¾ cup plus 2 teaspoons) caster (superfine) sugar
zest of ½ lemon
pinch of instant dried yeast

For the filling:
45 g/1½ oz (⅓ cup) cornflour (cornstarch)
80 ml/2¾ fl oz (⅓ cup) cold whole (full-fat) milk
4 egg yolks
80 g/3 oz (½ cup minus 4 teaspoons) caster (superfine) sugar, plus extra for rolling

Preheat the oven to 190°C/375°F/Gas Mark 5. Grease 7 small round cake pans, each measuring 10 cm/4 inches in diameter, with butter then sprinkle with flour, shaking out the excess.

Put the egg yolks and sugar into a stand mixer fitted with a whisk attachment and whisk at medium speed until smooth and creamy. Alternatively, use electric beaters in a large bowl. Add the lemon zest.

Mix the flour and yeast together in a large bowl, then sift over the egg mixture and fold in until everything is well incorporated.

Put the egg whites into another bowl and, using either electric beaters or a stand mixer fitted with a whisk attachment, whisk until soft peaks form, then very gently fold into the egg yolk mixture.

Pour the batter into the prepared cake pans and bake in the oven for 12 minutes, or until golden on top and a toothpick inserted into the middle of the cake comes out clean. Carefully turn them out of the pans and leave to cool on a wire rack.

To make the filling, put the cornflour (cornstarch) and cold milk into a saucepan and whisk until the flour has dissolved. Put the pan over a low heat and cook for 5 minutes, or until it thickens, then remove from the heat, add the egg yolks and sugar, whisk, then put it back over a low heat and cook for 5 minutes, or until the egg yolks are cooked. The mixture should be thick at this point. Remove from the heat, transfer to a heatproof bowl, cover the surface with food wrap so it doesn't dry out and leave to cool.

When the sponges are cold, spread the extra sugar out over a large plate and roll the cakes in it. Cut the cakes in half and fill with the cold filling, then sandwich them back together before serving.

Honey and Cinnamon Cupcakes

••

Donas Amélias   ◎ p.381   ⎁ Açores

These cakes evolved from a recipe that used spices brought to the island from the Far East by travellers in early 1500. This version was made to celebrate a royal visit to the Azores in early 1900.

Preparation time: 30 minutes
Cooking time: 18–20 minutes
Makes: 24
Ø

90 g/3¼ oz (6 tablespoons) butter, plus extra for greasing
plain (all-purpose) flour, for sprinkling
250 g/9 oz (1¼ cups) caster (superfine) sugar
5 egg yolks
½ teaspoon ground cinnamon
zest of ½ small lemon
pinch of salt
80 g/3 oz (⅓ cup) honey
95 g/3½ oz (¾ cup) fine polenta (cornmeal)
3 egg whites
icing (confectioners') sugar, for dusting

Preheat the oven to 160°C/325°F/Gas Mark 3. Grease 24 small baking pans, each measuring 8 cm/3¼ inches in diameter and 2 cm/¾ inch deep, with butter and sprinkle with flour, tipping out any excess.

Melt 50 g/2 oz (3½ tablespoons) of the butter and keep warm. Cut the remaining butter into very small pieces and store in the fridge.

Put the caster (superfine) sugar and egg yolks into a stand mixer fitted with a whisk attachment and whisk until they have doubled their volume, then add the cinnamon, lemon zest and salt.

While whisking, gently pour the melted butter into the egg mixture, then add the cold butter and whisk again until it is all incorporated. Add the honey and polenta (cornmeal), then reduce the speed and keep whisking slowly until the honey and polenta are incorporated.

Whisk the egg whites into soft peaks, then gently fold the egg whites into the sugar base, making sure the mixture doesn't lose any volume.

Pour the batter into the prepared cake pans, then put them onto a baking sheet and bake in the oven for 18–20 minutes, or until golden brown on top. Remove from the pans and dust with icing (confectioners') sugar before serving.

Honey and Cinnamon Cupcakes

Fresh Cheese Tarts from Sintra

Queijadas de Sintra   ♡ Lisbon

Literally translated as 'cheesecakes', *queijadas* are small tarts prepared all over Portugal. However, these ones are a true speciality from the village of Sintra outside Lisbon, and are made of a thin, crispy dough filled with a paste of fresh cheese, eggs, sugar, flour and cinnamon. The snack-sized sweets started being mass produced in Sintra in 1756 by Maria Sapa, who produced 20 dozen per day. These days, they are usually packed and sold in paper rolls of six in many of the town's pastry shops.

Preparation time: 30 minutes, plus 12 hours resting
Cooking time: 20 minutes
Makes: 12
⌀

For the dough:
300 g/11 oz (2½ cups) plain (all-purpose) flour, plus
    extra for dusting
65 g/2¼ oz (4⅓ tablespoons) unsalted butter
    at room temperature
1 egg
sea salt

For the filling:
90 g/3¼ oz (6 tablespoons) cold unsalted butter
250 g/9 oz (1 cup plus 1 teaspoon) fresh cheese
7 egg yolks
200 g/7 oz (1 cup) caster (superfine) sugar
40 g/1½ oz (⅓ cup) plain (all-purpose) flour

To make the dough, put the flour and butter into a large bowl, and rub in until the mixture resembles breadcrumbs. Add the egg and 100 ml/3½ fl oz (7 tablespoons) water and mix well to form a smooth dough. Cover with food wrap or a damp tea (dish) towel and leave to rest in a cool place for 12 hours.

The next day, preheat the oven to 220°C/ 425°F/Gas Mark 7.

For the filling, put the butter into a saucepan and heat over a low heat for 2 minutes, or until melted. Remove from the heat and set aside. Put the cheese into a food processor and blend until smooth. Add all the remaining ingredients and whisk until creamy and smooth.

Roll out the dough on a floured work counter into a thin sheet, 2 mm/¹⁄₁₆ inch thick. Using a ring cutter, cut out 11-cm/3¼-inch circles of dough. Line the cake pans with the dough, stretching it to the sides but not going over the rim. Pour in the filling, leaving a 3-mm/¼-inch gap at the top, as the dough will puff up slightly during cooking. Put the pans onto 1 or 2 baking sheets and bake in the oven for 15 minutes, or until caramelised and golden. Leave to cool slightly, turn the tarts out of the pans and leave to cool on a wire rack before serving.

Fresh Cheese Tarts from Pereira

Queijadas de Pereira   ♡ Beira Litoral

Preparation time: 30 minutes, plus 1 hour 30 minutes resting
Cooking time: 20 minutes
Makes: 8
⌀

30 g/1 oz (2 tablespoons) unsalted butter
200 g/7 oz (1⅔ cups) plain (all-purpose) flour
sea salt

For the filling:
200 g/7 oz (¾ cup plus 1 tablespoon) fresh cheese
220 g/7½ oz (1 cup plus 4 teaspoons) caster
    (superfine) sugar
5 egg yolks
20 g/¾ oz (2⅓ tablespoons plain (all-purpose) flour

Put the butter into a saucepan and heat over a low heat for 2 minutes, or until melted.

Sift the flour into a large bowl, add the melted butter, 80 ml/¾ fl oz (⅓ cup) warm water and a pinch of salt and mix to a smooth dough. Cover with a tea (dish) towel or food wrap and leave to rest for 1 hour 30 minutes.

Preheat the oven to 200°C/400°F/Gas Mark 6.

For the filling, push the cheese through a sieve (fine-mesh strainer) into a bowl. Add the sugar, egg yolks and flour and mix well to combine.

Roll out the dough on a work counter into a long sheet. Cut out rounds from the dough large enough to line 8 small cake pans, 8 cm/3¼ inches in diameter and 2 cm/¾ inches deep.

Place the lined pans on a large baking sheet, pour in the filling and bake in the oven for 15 minutes, or until caramelised and golden. Leave to cool slightly, turn the tarts out of the pans and leave to cool on a wire rack before serving.

Fresh Cheese Tarts from Bárrio

Queijadas à Moda do Bárrio   ♡ Leiria

Preparation time: 30 minutes, plus 30 minutes resting
Cooking time: 45 minutes
Makes: 12
⌀

260 g/9 oz (2¼ cups minus 4 teaspoons) plain
    (all-purpose) flour, plus extra for dusting
unsalted butter, for greasing
250 g/9 oz (1 cup plus 2 tablespoons) cream cheese
220 g/7½ oz (1 cup plus 4 teaspoons) caster
    (superfine) sugar
3 egg yolks
1 teaspoon ground cinnamon

Put 200 g/7 oz (1⅔ cups) of the flour and 80 ml/2¾ fl oz (⅓ cup) water into a large bowl and mix well until a smooth dough has formed. Cover with food wrap and leave to rest in the fridge for 30 minutes.

Preheat the oven to 180°C/350°F/Gas Mark 4. Grease 12 small star-shaped or round pans, about 10 cm/4 inches in diameter and 1.5 cm/⅝ inch deep with butter.

Combine the cream cheese and sugar in a large bowl. Add the egg yolks and cinnamon and mix well. Sift in the remaining 60 g/2 oz (½ cup) flour and mix until smooth and there are no lumps.

Tip the dough out onto a floured work counter and roll out to a large thin rectangle. Cut out 12 rounds from the dough and use to line the prepared pans. Pour in the filling and bake for 15 minutes, or until caramelised and golden. Leave to cool slightly, turn the tarts out of the pans and leave to cool on a wire rack before serving.

Fresh Cream Cheese Tarts

Queijadas de Requeijão ♡ Alentejo

Preparation time: 30 minutes, plus 1 hour resting
Cooking time: 20 minutes
Makes: 12

For the pastry (pie dough):
75 g/7¾ oz lard (pork fat)
250 g/9 oz (2 cups) plain (all-purpose) flour

For the filling:
5 egg yolks
300 g/11 oz (1½ cups) caster (superfine) sugar
500 g/1 lb 2 oz (2¼ cups) requeijao cheese, or use a fresh cheese similar to ricotta
65 g/2¼ oz (4⅓ tablespoons) unsalted butter
2 tablespoons plain (all-purpose) flour
1 teaspoon ground cinnamon

To make the pastry (pie dough), put the lard (pork fat) into a small saucepan and heat over a low heat until melted. Put the flour into a large bowl, add the melted fat and mix together until a smooth dough is formed. Cover with food wrap and leave to rest for 1 hour.

For the filling, put the egg yolks and sugar into a stand mixer fitted with a whisk attachment and whisk until they are doubled in size and very fluffy. Push the cheese through a sieve (fine-mesh strainer) into a bowl, then add it to the eggs with the butter and mix until smooth and creamy. Sift the flour into the mixture and add the cinnamon.

Preheat the oven to 180°C/350°F/Gas Mark 4.

Tip the dough out onto a work counter and stretch it into a thin rectangle. Cut out 12 rounds of dough and use to line baking pans, each measuring 10 cm/4 inches in diameter.

Pour the filling into the pans and bake in the oven for 15 minutes, or until golden brown. Leave to cool slightly, turn the tarts out of the pans and leave to cool on a wire rack before serving.

Fresh Cream Cheese and Egg Tarts from Madeira

Queijadas de Requeijão da Madeira ♡ Madeira

Queijadas in Madeira are very different from the ones found on mainland Portugal. These are small, flattened round cakes with a very thin layer of dough for the base, folded to the centre to contain a cream cheese filling. *Queijadas* can be found in pastry shops all over the archipelago throughout the year, and in the 18th century were produced to celebrate religious ceremonies.

Preparation time: 20 minutes, plus 3 hours resting
Cooking time: 15 minutes
Makes: 15
∅

For the pastry (pie dough):
280 g/10 oz (2⅓ cups) self-raising (self-rising) flour
45 g/1½ oz (3 tablespoons) caster (superfine) sugar
260 g/9 oz (2¼ sticks) butter, at room temperature

For the filling:
400 g/1 lb requeijao cheese, or use a fresh cheese similar to ricotta
430 g/15 oz (2¼ cups minus 4 teaspoons) caster (superfine) sugar
10 egg yolks
50 g/2 oz (½ cup minus 2 teaspoons) plain (all-purpose) flour
unsalted butter, for brushing

Put the flour, sugar and butter into a large bowl and mix well to form a smooth dough, sprinkling with a little cold water, if necessary. Cover with a tea (dish) towel or food wrap and leave to rest for 3 hours.

Preheat the oven to 180°C/350°F/Gas Mark 4. Line a large baking sheet with baking (parchment) paper.

For the filling, mash the cheese with a fork then push it through a sieve (fine-mesh strainer) into a large bowl. Add the sugar, egg yolks and flour and mix together until well incorporated.

Stretch the pastry (pie dough) into a thin sheet, cut it into 15 squares, each measuring 10 cm/4 inches, and put a spoonful of the filling in the middle. Bring the four corners of the pastry up to each other and press together to seal. Put the pastries on the lined baking sheet and bake for 15 minutes, or until golden all over.

Meanwhile, put the butter for brushing into a small saucepan and heat over a low heat until melted. When the pastries come out of the oven brush them with the melted butter.

Fresh Cheese Tartlets from Évora

••

Queijadas de Évora 📷 p.385   🏷 Alentejo

Preparation time: 30 minutes, plus 1 hour resting
Cooking time: 30 minutes
Makes: 12
🌿

For the pastry (pie dough):
300 g/11 oz (2½ cups) plain (all-purpose) flour,
    plus extra for dusting
50 g/2 oz (3½ tablespoons) unsalted butter, plus extra
    for greasing
pinch of sea salt

For the filling:
11 egg yolks
400 g/14 oz (2 cups) caster (superfine) sugar,
    plus extra for dusting
200 g/7 oz (1⅔ cups) plain (all-purpose) flour
220 g/7¾ oz (1 cup minus 1 teaspoon) fresh ewe's
    cheese

To make the pastry (pie dough), put all the ingredients into a large bowl with 95 ml/3¼ fl oz (½ cup minus 4 teaspoons) warm water and mix together until smooth, adding a few more drops of water, if necessary. Knead the dough well for 10 minutes, then cover with food wrap and leave to rest for 1 hour.

Preheat the oven to 180°C/350°F/Gas Mark 4. Grease 12 baking pans, each measuring 9 x 2 cm/ 3½ x ¾ inches, with the butter then dust with flour, tipping out any excess. Set aside.

Tip the dough out onto a lightly floured work counter and stretch it into a rectangle, about 2 mm/¹⁄₁₆ inch thick or as thin as possible, then using a 10-cm/4-inch ring cutter, cut out 12 rounds and use to line the prepared baking pans. Place the pans on a large baking sheet.

To make the filling, put the egg yolks, sugar and flour into a stand mixer fitted with a whisk attachment and whisk on medium speed until smooth.

Put the cheese into another bowl and mash with a fork, then add the cheese to the egg yolk mixture and mix well until combined. Pour the filling into the lined pans and bake for 30 minutes, or until cooked. Leave to cool slightly, turn the tarts out of the pans and leave to cool on a wire rack. Sprinkle over some extra sugar before serving.

Egg Tartlets from Alpiarça

••

Queijadas de Alpiarça   🏷 Ribatejo

Preparation time: 10 minutes
Cooking time: 45 minutes
Makes: 12
🌿

unsalted butter, for greasing
plain (all-purpose) flour, for sprinkling
6 egg yolks
6 eggs
500 g/1 lb 2 oz (2½ cups) caster (superfine) sugar
120 ml/4 fl oz (½ cup) fresh orange juice

Preheat the oven to 160°C/325°F/Gas Mark 3. Grease 12 cake pans, each measuring 12 cm/4½ inches in diameter, with butter then sprinkle with flour, tipping out the excess.

Put the egg yolks, eggs, sugar and orange juice into a large bowl and whisk to combine. Pour the batter into the prepared pans. Put the pans into a large roasting pan and carefully pour hot water into the roasting pan so it reaches halfway up the sides of the cake pans. Bake in the oven for 45 minutes, or until golden brown.

Remove from the oven and leave the tarts to cool in the pans before serving.

Fresh Cheese Tartlets from Évora

Almond and Egg Yolk Tarts from Águeda

Pasteis de Águeda   ⏷ Beira Litoral

Preparation time: 20 minutes, plus 10 minutes resting
Cooking time: 30 minutes
Makes: 12

For the pastry (pie dough):
2 teaspoons unsalted butter, plus extra for greasing
16 g/½ oz lard (pork fat)
210 g/7½ oz (1¾ cups) plain (all-purpose) flour,
    plus extra for dusting
sea salt

For the filling:
250 g/9 oz (1¼ cups) caster (superfine) sugar
8 egg yolks
1 teaspoon unsalted butter
50 g/2 oz (½ cup minus 2 teaspoons) almond flour
1 egg white

Grease 12 cake pans, each measuring 10 cm/
4 inches in diameter and 2 cm/¾ inch high, with
butter.

Put all the ingredients for the pastry (pie
dough) into a large bowl, add 30 ml/1 fl oz (2
tablespoons) cold water and mix to a smooth
dough. Cover with food wrap and leave to rest
for 10 minutes. Turn the dough out onto a floured
work counter, then, using a rolling pin, roll out the
dough to a thin rectangle.

Press the dough down into the prepared pans,
then up the sides to the rim, making sure the pan is
evenly covered with the dough.

For the filling, put the sugar and 110 ml/4 fl oz
(½ cup) water into a medium saucepan and heat
over a medium heat for 10–12 minutes until it
reaches 110°C/230°F on a thermometer. Remove
from the heat and leave until nearly cold.

Put the egg yolks into a small bowl and whisk,
then add them to the cool sugar syrup and stir
in. Cook over a low heat for 5 minutes, or until
thick, add the butter and almond flour and stir to
combine. Transfer to a bowl, cover with food wrap
and leave to cool completely.

Preheat the oven to 200°C/400°F/Gas Mark 6.

Divide the cold filling evenly between the cake
pans and bake for 15 minutes.

Remove and leave to cool before serving.

Pastries from the Convent of Santa Clara

Pastéis de Santa Clara   ⏷ Beira Litoral

Pastéis de Santa Clara are easily recognisable in
the region of Coimbra from their different shapes:
half-moons, hearts or just rolls. Coimbra has some
of the oldest universities in the world, and it's said
that the nuns used to leave the convent and sell
the *pastéis* to the students in the city.

Preparation time: 30 minutes, plus 30 minutes resting
Cooking time: 15–20 minutes
Makes: 12
🌿

For the dough:
120 g/4 oz (1 stick) unsalted butter
250 g/9 oz (2 cups) plain (all-purpose) flour
2 eggs, for the egg wash
caster (superfine) sugar, for dusting

For the filling:
7 egg yolks
220 g/7½ oz (1 cup plus 4 teaspoons) caster
    (superfine) sugar
110 g/3¾ oz (1 cup minus 2 teaspoons) almond flour

Melt the butter in a small saucepan over a low heat.

Put the flour into a large bowl or into a stand
mixer fitted with a paddle attachment and mix,
slowly adding the melted butter until incorporated.
Add a few drops of cold water, a little at a time,
until a smooth dough forms. Cover with food wrap
and leave to rest for 30 minutes.

Turn the dough out onto a lightly floured work
counter and stretch it into a thin sheet, then cut a
long strip of dough, about 12 cm/4½ inches and
cover with a tea (dish) towel.

To make the filling, put the egg yolks into a
small bowl and whisk lightly with a fork.

Put the sugar and 100 ml/3½ fl oz (⅓ cup plus
1 tablespoon) water into a medium saucepan and
heat over a medium heat for 10–12 minutes until it
reaches 106°C/222°F on a thermometer. Remove
from the heat and add the almond flour. Stir, then
add the egg yolks. Cook, stirring frequently, over
a low heat for 10 minutes. It is ready when you can
see the bottom of the pan while stirring. Transfer
the filling to a large bowl and leave to cool.

Preheat the oven to 180°C/350°C/Gas Mark 4.

Roll the dough out on the work counter then
add a small amount of the filling down the length
of one-half of the dough. Flip the other half of the
dough over the filling and press down gently to
seal. Cut into 12 half-moon shapes and put onto a
large baking sheet.

Put the eggs for the egg wash into a small bowl
and lightly whisk, then brush over the pastries.
Sprinkle some sugar over the top and bake for
15–20 minutes, or until golden brown.

Egg and Almond Tarts

Brisas do Liz   ⋃ Leiria

Preparation time: 20 minutes
Cooking time: 20 minutes
Makes: 30
🌱 ⌀ ✕

40 g/1½ oz (3 tablespoons) unsalted butter, for
    greasing
255 g/9 oz (2 cups plus 1 tablespoon) icing
    (confectioners') sugar
115 g/4 oz (1 cup minus 1 teaspoon) almond flour
6 egg yolks
4 egg whites

Preheat the oven to 160°C/325°F/Gas Mark 3.
Grease 30 shallow tart pans, each measuring
7 cm/2¾ inches in diameter, with butter.
    Put 110 ml/3¾ fl oz (½ cup minus 2 teaspoons)
water and the icing (confectioners') sugar into
a large saucepan and bring to the boil. Cook for
2 minutes.
    Put the almond flour, egg yolks and whites into
a large heatproof bowl. Pour over the hot syrup
and stir well to combine.
    Pour the mixture into the prepared pans, don't
fill them up to the rim, leave some space, then
put the pans into several roasting pans and pour
in enough hot water to reach halfway up the sides
of the tart pans. Bake for 15–18 minutes, or until
they are firm. Once baked, the almonds sink to the
bottom of the tarts.
    Leave to cool slightly, turn the tarts out of the
pans, place them in paper cases and leave to cool
on a wire rack before serving.

Cinnamon Almond Tarts

Pasteis de Lorvão   ⋃ Beira Litoral

Preparation time: 25 minutes
Cooking time: 55 minutes
Makes: 14
⌀

unsalted butter, for greasing
plain (all-purpose) flour, for dusting
370 g/13 oz (1¾ cups plus 4 teaspoons) caster
    (superfine) sugar
9 egg yolks
1 whole egg
90 g/3¼ oz (1 cup minus 2 teaspoons) ground almonds
40 g/1½ oz (⅓ cup) self-raising (self-rising) flour
½ teaspoon ground cinnamon
zest of ½ lemon
15 g/½ oz (1 tablespoon) unsalted butter
icing (confectioners') sugar, for dusting

Preheat the oven to 180°C/350°F/Gas Mark 4.
Grease 14 cake pans, each measuring 8 cm/
3¼ inches in diameter and 2 cm/¾ inch deep,
with butter. Sprinkle with plain (all-purpose) flour,
tipping off the excess.
    Put the caster (superfine) sugar and 160 ml/
5½ fl oz (⅔ cup) water into a large saucepan and
heat over a medium heat for 10–12 minutes until it
reaches 108°C/226°F on a thermometer. Remove
from the heat.
    Put the egg yolks and whole egg into a stand
mixer fitted with a whisk attachment and whisk at
medium speed for 5 minutes, or until they have
doubled in size.
    Combine the ground almonds, self-raising
(self-rising) flour, cinnamon and lemon zest in a
large bowl. Add to the egg mixture and mix until
everything is well mixed with no lumps. Gradually
stir in the sugar syrup until it is incorporated.
    Pour the mixture into the prepared pans, then
put them into one or two large roasting pans and
carefully pour in enough water to reach halfway up
the sides of the pan. Bake for 40 minutes, or until
golden on the top. Remove from the oven and
sprinkle them with icing (confectioners') sugar.

Gooey Tartlets from Santarém

Queijadas de Santarém — ou de Espécie   ◡ Ribatejo

Preparation time: 10–20 minutes
Cooking time: 45 minutes
Makes: 10
⌀

unsalted butter, for greasing
plain (all-purpose) flour, for sprinkling
80 g/3 oz (⅔ cup) raw almonds or 75 g/3 oz (¾ cup)
    ground almonds (almond flour)
4 egg yolks
4 eggs
375 g/13 oz (2 cups minus 2 tablespoons) caster
    (superfine) sugar

Preheat the oven to 180°C/350°F/Gas Mark 4.
Grease 10 small cake pans, each measuring
10 cm/4 inches in diameter and 1.5 cm/⅝ inches
deep, with butter then sprinkle with flour, tipping
off the excess.

Have a large bowl of iced water ready nearby.
Bring a small saucepan of water to the boil. Once
the water is boiling, carefully add the almonds
and blanch for 1 minute, then transfer them with
a slotted spoon to the iced water and leave to
cool. Once they are cool, put them onto a clean
tea (dish) towel, gather up the corners and rub
the almonds together to remove the skins. Put the
almonds into a food processor and blitz until finely
ground. Set aside.

Put the egg yolks, eggs and sugar into a large
bowl and whisk until combined. Add the almonds
and gently fold in until they are incorporated.
Pour the batter into the prepared pans. Put the
cake pans into a large roasting pan and carefully
pour hot water into the roasting pan so it reaches
halfway up the sides of the cake pans. Bake in the
oven for 40 minutes, or until light golden brown.

Remove from the oven and leave the tarts to
cool in the pans on a wire rack before serving.

Lard Pastries

Pastéis de Toucinho   ◡ Alentejo

Preparation time: 30 minutes, plus 20 minutes standing
Cooking time: 1 hour 10 minutes
Serves: about 25 depending on your pans

For the dough:
unsalted butter, for greasing
95 g/3¼ oz lard (pork fat)
400 g/14 oz (3⅓ cups) plain (all-purpose) flour,
    plus extra for dusting
sea salt

For the filling:
200 g/7 oz (1⅔ cups) almond flour
180 g/6 oz (1 cup) lardo, cut into very small cubes
500 g/1 lb 2 oz (2½ cups) caster (superfine) sugar
7 egg yolks

To make the dough, grease 25 individual 8-cm/
3¼-inch cake pans with butter.

Put the lard (pork fat) into a small saucepan
and heat until melted. Put the plain (all-purpose)
flour into a large bowl and pour over the melted
pork fat. Sprinkle with a pinch of salt and mix
together, adding a little warm water, if necessary,
until a smooth dough forms. Cover with a clean tea
(dish) towel and leave to rest for 20 minutes.

Preheat the oven to 180°C/350°F/Gas Mark 4.

Dust a work counter with flour, tip the dough
onto it and stretch the dough into a thin rectangle.
Using a 10-cm/4-inch ring cutter, cut out circles of
the dough and use to line the prepared cake pans.

For the filling, put the almond flour into a bowl,
add the lardo and mix together. Set aside.

Put the sugar and 200 ml/7 fl oz (¾ cup plus
1 tablespoon) water into a large saucepan and
heat over a medium heat for 10–12 minutes until
it reaches 103°C/217°F on a thermometer. Add
the almond mixture and heat, stirring continuously
for 10 minutes, or until it reaches boiling point.
Remove from the heat and leave to cool.

Whisk the egg yolks in a bowl, then add to the
almond and sugar syrup mixture. Put the pan over
a medium heat and cook for 5 minutes, or until the
egg yolks are cooked.

Carefully pour the filling into the prepared
pans and bake for 15 minutes, or until golden
brown. Leave to cool slightly, turn the tarts out
of the pans and leave to cool on a wire rack
before serving.

Sweet Bean and Almond Tarts

Pastéis de Feijão   ⊽ Ribatejo

For this recipe, puff pastry can be used instead of the shortcrust pastry (pie dough). You can make the puff pastry according to the instructions on page 390 or use shop-bought.

Preparation time: 25 minutes, plus 30 minutes resting
Cooking time: 1 hour 20 minutes
Makes: 13

For the dough:
30 g/1 oz (2 tablespoons) butter
30 g/1 oz lard (pork fat)
250 g/9 oz (2 cups) plain (all-purpose) flour
sea salt

For the filling:
110 g/3¾ oz (¾ cup) cooked white beans
500 g/1 lb 2 oz (2½ cups) caster (superfine) sugar
120 g/4 oz (1 cup) almond flour
12 egg yolks

Put both fats into a small saucepan and heat over a low heat until melted. Remove from the heat.

Put the flour into a large bowl, add the melted fats and a pinch of salt and mix well with your hands, adding 30 ml/1 fl oz (2 tablespoons) cold water, if necessary, until a smooth dough forms. Cover with food wrap and leave to rest for 30 minutes.

For the filling, put the beans in a food processor and blitz until a smooth purée, then push the purée through a sieve (fine-mesh strainer) into a bowl.

Put the sugar and 250 ml/8 fl oz (1 cup) water into a large saucepan and heat over a medium heat for 10–12 minutes until it reaches 116°C/241°F on a sugar thermometer. Add the almond flour stir, then add the bean purée and mix until well combined. Reduce the heat to low and cook for 7 minutes. Remove from the heat and leave to cool.

Meanwhile, put the egg yolks into a medium bowl and whisk with a fork, then add them to the cooled filling mixture and cook over a medium heat, stirring continuously, for 10 minutes, or until thick. Remove from the heat.

Preheat the oven to 220°C/425°F/Gas Mark 7.

Roll the dough out on a lightly floured work counter into a thin sheet, then cut out 13 circles and use to line 13 small round cake pans, each measuring 8 cm/3¼ inches in diameter and 2 cm/¾ inch deep. Pour in the filling and bake in the oven for 25 minutes.

Remove from the oven, then turn the tarts out of the pans and leave to cool on a wire rack before serving.

Pastries from the Convent of Santa Clara

Pastéis de Santa Clara   ⊽ Alentejo
— Portalegre

Preparation time: 25 minutes
Cooking time: 55 minutes
Makes: 12
∅

For the dough:
100 g/3½ oz (7 tablespoons) unsalted butter, softened
400 g/14 oz (3⅓ cups) plain (all-purpose) flour
1 egg
sea salt

For the filling:
100 g/3½ oz sweet potato
8 egg yolks and 1 whole egg
300 g/11 oz (1½ cups) caster (superfine) sugar, plus
    extra 250 g/9 oz (1¼ cups) sugar for the syrup
320 g/11¼ oz (2⅔ cups) almond flour

Put the sweet potatoes into a small saucepan, cover with cold water and cook over a medium heat for 25 minutes, or until soft. Drain, remove the skin, then push the flesh through a sieve (fine-mesh strainer) into a bowl. You should have about 80 g/3 oz. Set aside.

Put the egg yolks and whole egg into a bowl and whisk with a fork.

Put the 300 g/11 oz (1½ cups) sugar and 90 ml/3 fl oz (6 tablespoons) water into a large saucepan and heat over a medium heat until it reaches 116°C/241°F on a thermometer. Remove from the heat and add the whisked eggs and sweet potato all at once. Mix well, then put the pan over a low heat and cook, stirring continuously, for 10 minutes, or until thick. Once you can see the bottom of the pan while stirring, it is ready. Remove the pan from the heat and set aside.

To make the dough, put all the ingredients into a bowl and mix together until a dough forms, adding a few drops of water, if necessary. Knead for 5 minutes until the dough is smooth, cover with a clean tea (dish) towel and leave to rest for 10 minutes.

Dust a work counter with flour, then stretch the dough into a rectangle, about 3 mm/⅛ inch thick. Put a spoonful of the filling into the middle of the dough as though making ravioli, repeat to all and close them.

Preheat the oven to 180°C/350°F/Gas Mark 4.

Place the tarts on a large baking sheet and bake in the oven for 18–20 minutes, or until golden. Leave to cool to room temperature in the pans.

To make the syrup, put the remaining sugar and 190 ml/6½ fl oz (¾ cup) water into a large saucepan and heat over a medium heat until it reaches 106°C/222°F on a sugar thermometer. Remove the pan from the heat and dip each tart into the sugar syrup to coat. Place them on a wire rack to drip and leave to cool before serving.

Custard Tarts

••

Pastéis de Nata 📷 p.391   ⋃ Lisbon

In 1982, Maria de Lourdes Modesto said the
following of the *pastel de nata* in her essential
cookbook *Traditional Portuguese Cooking*:
'These pastries are probably the most important
Portuguese speciality ever sold.' Almost four
decades later, they remain the ultimate national
symbol of Portugal. Today's *pastéis de nata*
recipes are adaptations of the original that dates
back to the 16th century, when they were made
in monasteries and convents all over the country.
These palm-sized tarts have a melt-in-the-mouth,
fragile, flaky crust and a not-too-sweet custard
that is caramelised and darkened in spots. Locals
visit their neighbourhood pastry shops in search
of the best-tasting *pastel de nata*. The cake pans
used to bake these tarts are not the same as
muffin pans – they are smaller and flatter. You can
find them online, or use a 10-cm/4-inch round
cake pan that is 2 cm/¾ inch high.

Preparation time: 3 hours 30 minutes, plus 2 hours
45 minutes resting and overnight chilling
Cooking time: 35 minutes
Makes: 35
Ø

For the filling:
320 g/11¼ oz (1⅔ cups) caster (superfine) sugar
50 g/2 oz (½ cup plus 2 teaspoons) cornflour
     (cornstarch)
4 egg yolks
600 ml/20 fl oz (2½ cups) whole (full-fat) milk
1 vanilla pod (bean), split lengthwise and seeds
     scraped out
pared rind of 2 lemons

For the puff pastry (or use ready-made puff pastry):
600 g/1 lb 5 oz (4¾ cups) plain (all-purpose) flour
480 g/1 lb 1 oz (4 sticks plus 1 tablespoon)
     unsalted butter
sea salt

To finish:
icing (confectioners') sugar, for dusting
ground cinnamon, for dusting

To make the puff pastry, put the flour into a mound
on a work counter. Put 320 ml/11 fl oz (1¼ cups plus
2 teaspoons) water into a jug (pitcher) or measuring
jug and season with a pinch of salt. Make a small
well in the middle of the flour and pour in the
water. Start mixing the flour into the water to form
a smooth dough, then cover with a tea (dish) towel
and leave to rest for 30 minutes.
    Divide the butter into three equal portions of
160 g/5¾ oz (1 stick plus 3 tablespoons). Lay a
large piece of food wrap on a work counter. Cut the
first portion of butter into thin slices and lay these
on the food wrap in a 20-cm/8-inch square. Put
a second piece of food wrap on top of the butter

and use a rolling pin to flatten the butter into a
thin 20-cm/8-inch square sheet. Repeat with the
remaining two portions of butter so that you have
three sheets of butter. The butter needs to be cool
but pliable when added to the dough, so chill the
sheets and remove each one from the fridge only
5 minutes before using it.
    Roll the dough out on a floured work counter
into a 21-cm/8½-inch square. Put a sheet of butter
in the centre of the dough, leaving a 5-mm/¼-inch
border. Fold the dough and butter in half by folding
the top half down, then fold in half again by folding
from left to right. Roll out into another 21-cm/8½-
inch square, then transfer to a baking sheet, cover
and rest in the fridge for 25 minutes. Repeat with
the remaining two sheets of butter. Rest the dough
each time you add the butter. When you have used
up all the butter, roll the dough into a rectangle
32 x 20cm/13 x 8 inches. Roll the dough tightly into
a cylinder, starting from the long edge. Cover the
dough in food wrap and leave to rest in the fridge
for at least 1 hour or overnight. If using ready-made
puff pastry pastry, roll the pastry out to a rectangle
32 x 20cm/13 x 8 inches. Roll the pastry tightly into
a cylinder, cover and rest in the fridge for 1 hour
    To make the filling, put the sugar into a sauce-
pan with 320 ml/11 fl oz (11/3 cups) water and heat
over a low heat until the sugar has dissolved. Turn
up the heat to medium and boil for 8–10 minutes
until it reaches 116°C/241°F on a thermometer.
    Meanwhile, put the cornflour (cornstarch), egg
yolks, milk, vanilla pod (bean) and seeds and lemon
rind into a large bowl and whisk until smooth. Once
the sugar has reached temperature, remove the
pan from the heat and whisk the syrup into the milk
mixture. Mix well, then pour the mixture back into
the pan and put over a low heat and cook for 4–5
minutes, or until it thickens. Remove and discard
the lemon rind and vanilla pod, then strain through
a chinois or sieve (fine-mesh strainer) into a clean
bowl and leave to cool. Cover and chill until needed.
    Using a sharp knife, cut slices from the dough
cylinder, about 5 mm/¼ inch thick, making a
downwards cut and not slicing. Each portion should
be about 25 g/1 oz, but this will depend on the size
of your pans or pan.
    Have a bowl of cold water nearby. Arrange all the
cake pans on several baking sheets and keep them
in the fridge. One at a time, place a circle of pastry
in the bottom of each pan, making sure the layers
of butter are seen when viewed from above. This
ensures the pastry will rise outwards and upwards
as it bakes. Wet your thumb in the cold water and
press the dough towards the outer edge of the pan,
filling up to the rim. Repeat with all the pans, then
put them back in the fridge to rest for 30 minutes.
    Preheat the oven to 240°C/475°F/Gas Mark 9.
    Fill the lined pans with the filling, almost to the
top. Bake in the oven for 13–15 minutes, or until the
filling is almost set with browned spots on the top
and the dough is crisp and golden. Remove from
the oven and dust with icing (confectioners') sugar
and ground cinnamon. Serve warm or cold. These
tarts are best eaten on the day they are made.

COOKIES, CANDIES AND JAMS

Flat Cookies

•••

Súplicas 📷 p.395   ▽ Trás-os-Montes
e Alto Douro

These cookies are lightly crispy on the outside but
have a soft texture on the inside.

Preparation time: 30 minutes
Cooking time: 25 minutes
Makes: 16
□ ∅ ✕

4 eggs
350 g/12 oz (1¾ cups) caster (superfine) sugar
370 g/13 oz (3 cups) plain (all-purpose) flour

Preheat the oven to 180°C/350°F/Gas Mark 4. Line
a large baking sheet with baking (parchment) paper.
    Put the eggs and sugar into a stand mixer
fitted with a whisk attachment and whisk at medium
speed for 25 minutes, then reduce the speed to
low and, while still whisking, slowly add the flour
until the mixture is fluffy.
    Working in batches, arrange tablespoonfuls
of the dough onto the prepared baking sheet,
spacing them well apart as they will spread.
Bake for 12 minutes, or until golden. Remove the
cookies from the baking sheet and repeat with
the remaining dough.

Cornmeal Cookies

•••

Bolachas de Milho   ▽ Açores

Preparation time: 15 minutes, plus 30 minutes resting
Cooking time: 20–25 minutes
Makes: about 30
🦋 ∅ ✕

330 g/11½ oz (2¾ sticks) butter, plus extra for greasing
330 g/11½ oz (2¾ cups) fine cornmeal, plus extra for
    dusting
310 g/11 oz (1½ cups) caster (superfine) sugar
3 eggs

Preheat the oven to 180°C/350°F/Gas Mark 4.
Grease a large baking sheet with butter, then dust
with fine cornmeal, shaking off any excess.
    Put all the ingredients into a stand mixer fitted
with a paddle attachment and mix on medium
speed for 10 minutes, or until a smooth dough
forms. Place in the fridge to rest for 30 minutes.
    Divide the dough into equal small balls, about
35 g/1¼ oz each. They can be slightly bigger if you
prefer, then place them on the prepared baking
sheet spaced apart and gently press them down
like a cookie, but not all the way, to flatten them.
    Bake in the oven for 20–25 minutes, or until
golden. Remove from the oven, leave for 5 minutes
then carefully transfer the cookies to a wire rack and
leave to cool before storing in an airtight container.

Polenta, Sweet Potato
and Cinnamon Cookies

•••

Broas Castelares   ▽ Lisbon

These small, elongated cookies have a golden
toasted egg yolk sheen. They are included on
every Portuguese Christmas table, especially in
the Lisbon region. Made using sweet potato and
polenta (cornmeal), they have a moist, dense
texture and are cooked in a very hot oven. They
are sometimes served on communion wafers or
orange leaves.

Preparation time: 50 minutes
Cooking time: 40 minutes
Makes: 30
□ ∅

225 g/ 8 oz sweet potatoes, unpeeled
60 g/2¼ oz (½ cup) plain (all-purpose) flour, plus extra
    for dusting
200 g/7 oz (1⅔ cups) fine cornmeal
300 g/11 oz (1½ cups) caster (superfine) sugar
1 egg and 2 egg yolks
zest of ⅓ orange
zest of ⅓ lemon
70 g/2½ oz (¾ cup) ground almonds
1 teaspoon ground cinnamon

Put the sweet potato into a saucepan, pour in
enough water to cover and cook over a low heat
for 15 minutes, or until soft. Drain, leave until
cool enough to handle, then peel off the skin
and discard. Put the flesh into a food processor
and blitz to a purée. Return to the saucepan.
    Put the plain (all-purpose) flour and fine
cornmeal into a large bowl and mix until combined.
    Using a silicone spatula, fold half of the sugar
into the sweet potato purée. Put the pan over
a medium heat and cook for 20 minutes, or until
the purée is coming away from the sides of the pan.
Remove from the heat and leave to cool a little.
    Add the remaining sugar to the pan, stir, then
add the whole egg and citrus zest and stir well
until everything is incorporated. Add the ground
almonds, and the cornmeal and flour mix. Put
the pan over a low heat and cook the mixture for
10 minutes, or until it is coming away from the sides.
Transfer the mixture to a large heatproof bowl and
leave to cool completely for a few hours.
    When ready to bake, preheat the oven to 220°C/
425°F/Gas Mark 7. Sprinkle flour over a large baking
sheet, tipping off the excess.
    Take small amounts of the mixture, about
35 g/1¼ oz each, and shape them into rugby balls.
Place on the prepared baking sheet.
    Put the egg yolks into a small bowl and beat
lightly with a fork. Brush the cookies with the
beaten egg and bake in the oven for 12 minutes, or
until golden. Remove from the oven, then carefully
transfer the cookies to a wire rack and leave to cool
before storing in an airtight container.

Olive Oil Cookies

•••

Biscoitos de Azeite   ⛉ **Beira Baixa**

Preparation time: 30 minutes, plus 10 minutes resting
Cooking time: 25 minutes
Makes: 30
⬚ ∅ ✕

550 g/1 lb 4 oz plain (all-purpose) flour
4 eggs, plus 1 egg for the egg wash
110 ml/3 ¾ fl oz (½ cup minus 2 teaspoons) olive oil
210 g/7½ oz (1 cup plus 2 teaspoons) caster (superfine)
    sugar, plus extra for dusting
35 ml/1¼ fl oz (2⅓ tablespoons) firewater or brandy

Sift the flour into a large bowl. Put the four eggs, the olive oil and sugar into a medium bowl and whisk until it is a creamy consistency.

Pour the egg and sugar mixture into the flour and mix with your hands to form a smooth dough. If the dough is sticky, add a little more flour and mix again. Cover with a tea (dish) towel and leave to rest at room temperature for 10 minutes.

Preheat the oven to 180°C/350°F/Gas Mark 4. Line 1 or 2 large baking sheets with baking (parchment) paper.

Divide the dough into 30 equal pieces, about 30 g/1 oz each and measuring 5 cm/2 inches in diameter. Arrange them on the prepared baking sheets, making sure there is space between each one as they spread during baking.

Put the egg for the egg wash into a bowl and beat lightly with a fork. Brush the cookies with the beaten egg and bake in the oven for 25 minutes, or until golden. Remove from the oven, then carefully transfer the cookies to a wire rack and leave to cool before storing in an airtight container.

'Drunken' Cookies

•••

Borrachões   📷 p.397   ⛉ **Beira Baixa**

The lack of food resources in the region of Beira Baixa made people creative when it came to food, and these cookies are an ingenious creation. Only a few ingredients are needed to create a delicious cookie and they can keep for a long time. *Borrachões* are made with alcohol, and their name translated as 'a little tipsy'. I usually make these cookies every month and they go well with a cup of tea.

Preparation time: 30 minutes, plus 20 minutes resting
Cooking time: 45 minutes
Serves: 4
⬚ ∅

220 g/7¾ oz (1 cup plus 4 teaspoons) caster (superfine)
    sugar, plus extra for sprinkling
220 ml/7½ fl oz (1 cup minus 2 tablespoons) olive oil
120 ml/4 fl oz (½ cup) white wine
120 ml/4 fl oz (½ cup) firewater or brandy
1 kg/2 lb 4 oz (8⅓ cups) self-raising (self-rising) flour
2 eggs, for the egg wash

Put the sugar, olive oil white wine and firewater into a large bowl and stir them together. While stirring, gradually add the flour, then mix with your hands to form a thick paste that doesn't stick to your fingers. Cover with a tea (dish) towel and leave to rest at room temperature for 20 minutes.

Preheat the oven to 200°C/400°F/Gas Mark 6.

Divide the dough in half and roll out each half on a work counter (the counter doesn't need to be floured) to a large square, about 3 mm/⅛ inch thick. Using a pasta cutter, cut out strips of the dough that are 4 cm/1½ inches wide and 10 cm/4 inches long. Arrange the strips on 1 or 2 large baking sheets.

Put the eggs for the egg wash into a small bowl and beat lightly with a fork. Brush the strips with the beaten egg, then prick holes all over them with a fork, sprinkle with sugar and bake in the oven for 45 minutes, or until golden. Remove from the oven, then carefully transfer the cookies to a wire rack and and leave to cool before storing in an airtight container.

Walnut and Wild Fennel Cookies

●●

Broas Secas dos ◊ Ribatejo
Santos de Abrantes

These cookies are usually made for the celebrations held on 1st November for *Dia dos Santos* (All Saints Day). They are typically found all over Portugal.

Preparation time: 20 minutes
Cooking time: 30 minutes
Makes: 30
◻ ∅

80 g/3 oz (⅔ cup) walnut halves
400 g/14 oz (3⅓ cups) plain (all-purpose) flour
120 g/4 oz (1 cup) fine corn flour
220 ml/7½ fl oz (1 cup minus 2 tablespoons) extra virgin olive oil
500 g/1 lb 2 oz (2¼ cups) honey
125 g/4¼ oz (½ cup plus 2 tablespoons) caster (superfine) sugar, plus extra for sprinkling
3 teaspoons ground cinnamon
10 g/¼ oz wild fennel tops, chopped
5 g/⅛ oz (1 teaspoon) sea salt
olive oil, for oiling

Preheat the oven to 200°C/400°F/Gas Mark 6.
Spread the walnuts out on a medium baking sheet and bake in the oven for 5 minutes, then remove and leave to cool. Chop into small pieces.
Put both flours into a large bowl, add the walnuts and mix together.
Bring the olive oil, 500 ml/17 fl oz (2 cups plus 1 tablespoon) water, the honey, sugar, cinnamon and wild fennel tops to the boil in a large saucepan. Once its starts to boil, reduce the heat to low and slowly add the flour mix, stirring continuously while cooking for 10 minutes. Add the salt, then transfer the mixture to a large heatproof bowl and leave to cool.
Once cold, divide the dough into 30 small balls and form them into small oval shapes.
Grease 1 or 2 large baking sheets with olive oil and arrange the cookies on the sheets, spacing them apart as they will spread during cooking. Bake in the oven for 10 minutes, or until golden. Remove from the oven, then carefully transfer the cookies to a wire rack and and leave to cool before sprinkling with sugar and serving.

Crispy Almond Cookies

●●

Palitos de Torres Novas ◊ Ribatejo

Preparation time: 20 minutes
Cooking time: 45 minutes
Makes: 26
∅

unsalted butter, for greasing
250 g/9 oz (2 cups) plain (all-purpose) flour, plus extra for dusting
3 eggs, separated
250 g/9 oz (1¼ cups) caster (superfine) sugar
zest of 1 lemon
40 g/1½ oz (⅓ cup) almond flour
1 teaspoon instant dried yeast

Preheat the oven to 180°C/350°F/Gas Mark 4. Grease a large rimmed baking sheet with butter, then sprinkle with flour, tipping out the excess.
Put the egg yolks and sugar into a stand mixer fitted with a whisk attachment and whisk at full speed for 5 minutes, or until doubled in volume. Alternatively, whisk with electric beaters in a large bowl. Add the lemon zest and almond flour, then sieve (sift) in the plain (all-purpose) flour and yeast and gently fold it in until it is all incorporated.
Put the egg whites into another bowl and, using either electric beaters or a stand mixer fitted with a whisk attachment, whisk until soft peaks form, then gently fold them into the flour mixture with a silicon spatula until they are incorporated. Pour the batter onto the prepared baking sheet and bake in the oven for 25 minutes, or until golden brown on top. Remove from the oven, then turn out of the baking sheet and cut into 26 pieces, each measuring 8 x 1 cm/3¼ x ½ inch.
Increase the oven temperature to 200°C/400°F/Gas Mark 6.
Arrange the cookie pieces on another large baking sheet and bake in the oven for 20 minutes, or until crispy. Remove from the oven, then carefully transfer the cookies to a wire rack and leave to cool before storing in an airtight container.

Almond Macaroons from the Convent of Almoster

Arrepiados do Convento de Almoster ⛨ Lisbon

Preparation time: 30 minutes
Cooking time: 1 hour
Makes: 20
⌀

280 g/10 oz (3½ cups) flaked (slivered) almonds
2 egg whites
260 g/9 oz (1⅓ cups) caster (superfine) sugar
1 teaspoon ground cinnamon
unsalted butter, for greasing
plain (all-purpose) flour, for dusting

Preheat the oven to 140°C/275°F/Gas Mark 1.
Spread the almonds out over a large baking sheet and toast in the oven for 8 minutes, or until golden. Remove from the oven and reduce the oven temperature to 130°C/250°F/Gas Mark ½.
Slice the almonds into flakes. Set aside.
Put the egg whites into a stand mixer fitted with a whisk attachment and whisk at medium speed until soft peaks form. Alternatively, whisk with electric beaters in a large bowl. While whisking, add the sugar, a tablespoon at a time, and whisk until it is a firm consistency. Add the almonds and fold in, then add the cinnamon and fold in until combined.
Line several large baking sheets with baking (parchment) paper and grease the paper with butter, then sprinkle with flour, tipping off any excess.
Using a tablespoon, make little heaps of the mixture onto the prepared baking sheet, leave space between them as they will spread during baking. Bake in the oven for 50 minutes. Remove from the oven and leave to cool before serving.

Almond Meringues

Tosquiados ⛨ Alentejo

These meringues are really easy to make and can be kept in an airtight container for a long while. They are perfect to enjoy with a cup of tea.

Preparation time: 5 minutes, plus overnight drying
Cooking time: 15 minutes
Makes: 30–40
🍮 ⬡ ⌀ V ✕

750 g/1 lb 11 oz (3¾ cups) caster (superfine) sugar
500 g/1 lb 2 oz (3¾ cups plus 2 teaspoons) blanched almonds, sliced

Put the sugar into a medium saucepan with 190 ml/6½ fl oz (¾ cup) water and heat over a medium-high heat for 10 minutes, or until it reaches 101°C/214°F on a thermometer. Add the almonds and stir well over the heat for 5 minutes.
Sprinkle a baking sheet or a marble stone with water. Using a tablespoon, make small piles of the mixture and place them on the prepared sheet or stone. Leave to dry out overnight. The next day, store in an airtight container.

Honey Cookies

Broas de Mel da Madeira ⛨ Madeira

Preparation time: 20 minutes, plus 45 minutes resting
Cooking time: 8–10 minutes
Makes: 26
⌀

1 egg
250 g/9 oz (1¼ cups) caster (superfine) sugar
70 g/2½ oz (5 tablespoons) unsalted butter, at room temperature
110 g/3¾ oz (½ cup minus 1 teaspoon) sugar cane honey or any other dark honey
250 g/9 oz (2 cups) self-raising (self-rising) flour
1 teaspoon ground cinnamon
1 teaspoon bicarbonate of soda (baking soda)

Put the egg, sugar and butter into a large bowl and, using your hands, mix together until they are well incorporated, then add the honey and mix again. Add the flour, cinnamon and bicarbonate of soda (baking soda) and knead the mixture until the flour is full incorporated. Cover with a clean tea (dish) towel and leave to rest for 45 minutes.
Preheat the oven to 220°C/425°F/Gas Mark 7. Line a baking sheet with baking (parchment) paper.
Divide the dough into 26 small balls, about 25 g/1 oz each, and place them, very well spaced out, on the prepared baking sheet. Bake for 8–10 minutes, or until deep brown and crispy around the edges. Remove from the oven, leave for 10 minutes, then transfer to a wire rack and leave to cool.

Honey Cookies
with Almonds

•••

Broas de Mel e Amêndoa   📷 p.401   🗒 **Leiria**

Preparation time: 15 minutes, plus 15 minutes resting
Cooking time: 35 minutes
Makes: 30
□ ⊘

200 ml/7 fl oz (¾ cup plus 1 tablespoon) olive oil
200 g/7 oz (¾ cup plus 2 tablespoons) honey
200 g/7 oz (1 cup) caster (superfine) sugar
320 g/11¼ oz (2⅔ cups) wholemeal flour, plus extra
    for dusting
320 g/11¼ oz (2⅔ cups) corn flour
75 g/2¾ oz (½ cup) blanched almonds, chopped
1 teaspoon ground cinnamon
2 cloves
30 whole blanched almonds, to decorate

Put the olive oil, honey, sugar and 600 ml/20 fl oz
(2½ cups) water into a large saucepan and bring
to the boil. Once it starts boiling, gradually add
both flours and cook for a further 10 minutes,
or until the flours are cooked out and a smooth
dough forms that comes away from the sides of
the bowl. Add the chopped almonds, cinnamon
and cloves and mix very well to combine. Remove
from the heat and leave to cool.

Divide the dough into 30 small balls, about 45 g/
1½ oz each, then top each one with a whole
almond. Put them onto a large chopping (cutting)
board, cover with a tea (dish) towel and leave to
rest for 15 minutes.

Preheat the oven to 160°C/325°F/Gas Mark 3.
Dust a large baking sheet with flour.

Put the cookies onto the prepared baking
sheet and bake for 15 minutes, or until golden.
Remove from the oven, then carefully transfer the
cookies to a wire rack and leave to cool before
storing in an airtight container.

Spiced Cookies
from São Jorge

•••

Espécies de São Jorge   🗒 **Açores**

**These round, white-and-brown cookies with
a hole in the middle are one of the best known
sweet treats of São Jorge. Made all over the
island, they are a guaranteed presence at popular
and family festivities. The recipe has a key
characteristic: it includes a filling made of sugar
and toasted breadcrumbs, as well as allspice and
fennel. The outside is a shortcrust, crispy dough,
with no added sugar, which contrasts with the
strong flavour and aroma of the spices, releasing
it from the weight of the sugar and breadcrumbs.**

Preparation time: 30 minutes, plus overnight chilling and
1 hour resting
Cooking time: 35–40 minutes
Makes: 30
⊘

For the *Massa Tenra* dough:
220 g/7¾ oz (1¾ cups plus 1 tablespoon) self-raising
    (self-rising) flour, plus extra for dusting
20 g/¾ oz (1½ tablespoons) unsalted butter, softened,
    plus extra for greasing
15 g/½ oz (4 teaspoons) caster (superfine) sugar
2 egg yolks

For the filling:
225 g/ 8 oz (1 cup plus 2 tablespoons) caster
    (superfine) sugar
3 teaspoons ground cinnamon
12 g/½ oz fennel tops, chopped
5 g/¼ oz Jamaican pepper
120 g/4 oz bread, toasted
15 g/½ oz (1 tablespoon) unsalted butter, softened
pared rind of 1 lemon

A day ahead, make the filling. Put the sugar and
120 ml/4 fl oz (½ cup) water into a small saucepan
and cook over a medium heat for 10–12 minutes
or until it reaches 106°C/223°F on a sugar
thermometer.

Put the spices, bread, butter and lemon rind
into a large bowl and mix together, then add this
to the sugar syrup. Stir and cook over a low heat
for 10 minutes, or until a smooth consistency is
achieved. Remove from the heat and leave to cool
in the fridge overnight.

The next day, make the dough. Sift the flour
onto a work counter, add the butter, sugar, egg
yolks and 35 ml/1¼ fl oz (2⅓ teaspoons) water
and mix everything together very well until a
dough forms. Using your hands, work this dough
for 10 minutes until the dough is smooth. Cover
with food wrap or a damp tea (dish) towel and
leave to rest for 1 hour.

Preheat the oven to 160°C/325°F/Gas Mark 3.
Grease a large baking sheet with butter and
sprinkle lightly with flour, tipping off the excess.

Stretch the dough out on a floured work
counter until it is about 3 mm/⅛ inch thick.
Remove the filling from the fridge, then take slabs
of this mixture and roll it between your hands like
a hotdog sausage, about 10 cm/4 inches long.
Set aside and repeat with the remaining filling.

Place the filling over the dough leaving a space
for the cut. Using a pasta cutter, cut rectangles
from the dough (4 cm/1½ inches wide) with the
filling in the middle. Take one of the ends and twist,
then fold the dough in a U shape and twist the
other end. Place on the prepared baking sheet and
repeat with the remaining dough and filling.

Bake for 15 minutes, or until golden. Remove
from the oven, then carefully transfer the cookies
to a wire rack and leave to cool before storing in
an airtight container.

Honey Cookies with Almonds

Christmas Cookies with Sweet Potato and Fennel

Broas de Natal ⌑ p.403   ♡ Lisbon

Preparation time: 30 minutes, plus 12 hours standing
Cooking time: 45 minutes
Makes: 22
◻ ∅

450 g/1 lb sweet potatoes, unpeeled
380 g/13½ oz (2 cups minus 4 teaspoons) caster
    (superfine) sugar
340 g/12 oz (2 cups minus 2 teaspoons) fine semolina
1 teaspoon chopped wild fennel tops
½ teaspoon ground cinnamon
zest of 1 lemon
olive oil, for oiling
plain (all-purpose) flour, for dusting
2 egg yolks
sea salt

Put the sweet potatoes into a large saucepan of cold water with a pinch of salt and cook over a low heat for 15 minutes, or until soft. Drain, setting 140 ml/4½ fl oz (⅔ cup) of the cooking water aside. Leave the sweet potatoes to cool for a few minutes, then peel off the skin and discard. Put the flesh into a food processor and process to a purée.

Put the sugar and reserved sweet potato cooking water into a large saucepan and heat over a medium heat for 10–12 minutes until it reaches 108°C/226°F on a sugar thermometer. Add the sweet potato purée, reduce the heat to low and cook, stirring continuously, for 10 minutes, or until all the water has evaporated and you can see the bottom of the pan. It is ready when the mixture is thick and pasty. Remove from the heat and set aside.

Put the semolina, chopped wild fennel tops, cinnamon, lemon zest and a pinch of salt into a large bowl and mix together. Add the hot sweet potato mixture and mix well to a smooth dough. Cover with food wrap or a tea (dish) towel and leave at room temperature for 12 hours.

The next day, preheat the oven to 220°C/425°F/Gas Mark 7. Oil a large baking sheet with olive oil and dust a chopping (cutting) board with plain (all-purpose) flour.

Put the egg yolks into a small bowl and beat lightly with a fork. Take pieces of the dough and shape them into round balls. Press them gently with the palm of your hand, they should have a pointed flat shape or you can just leave them round. Put them onto the prepared baking sheet and brush with the beaten egg. Bake in the oven for 10 minutes, or until golden brown. Remove from the oven, then carefully transfer the cookies to a wire rack and leave to cool before storing in an airtight container.

Spiced Butter Cookies from Madeira

Broas da Madeira   ♡ Madeira

Preparation time: 30 minutes
Cooking time: 20 minutes
Makes: 25
∅

350 g/12 oz (3 cups minus 2 teaspoons) self-raising
    (self-rising) flour, plus extra for dusting
300 g/11 oz (1½ cups) caster (superfine) sugar
½ teaspoon bicarbonate of soda (baking soda)
½ teaspoon ground cinnamon
½ teaspoon nutmeg
zest of ½ lemon
260 g/9 oz (2¼ sticks) unsalted butter
20 ml/¾ fl oz (4 teaspoons) Madeira wine
3 eggs

Preheat the oven to 200°C/400°F/Gas Mark 6. Dust a large baking sheet with flour.

Put the sugar, bicarbonate of soda (baking soda), cinnamon and lemon zest into a large bowl and mix together. Put the flour into another large bowl.

Put the butter into a small saucepan and heat over a low heat until melted. Remove from the heat, pour into the flour and mix together. Add the Madeira wine and mix together well. Alternatively, use a stand mixer fitted with a paddle attachment. Add the eggs and mix until a smooth dough forms.

Divide the dough into 25 medium-sized balls, about 40 g/1½ oz each, and place them on the prepared baking sheet. Press each one down gently to flatten them a little. Bake for 20 minutes, or until golden. Remove from the oven, then carefully transfer the cookies to a wire rack and leave to cool before storing in an airtight container.

Christmas Cookies with Sweet Potato and Fennel

Cinnamon Butter Cookies

Raivas de Lisboa   ⛂ Lisbon

Preparation time: 15 minutes, plus 1 hour resting
Cooking time: 10 minutes
Makes: 16
⊘ ✕

140 g/5 oz (¾ cup) caster (superfine) sugar
95 g/3¼ oz (6 tablespoons) unsalted butter,
    plus extra for greasing
4 eggs
330 g/11¾ oz (2¾ cups) plain (all-purpose) flour,
    plus extra for dusting
1 teaspoon ground cinnamon

Put the sugar and butter into a stand mixer fitted
with a whisk attachment and whisk at medium
speed until it is a smooth consistency. Alternatively,
whisk with electric beaters in a large bowl. Add
the eggs, one at a time, whisking until each one is
incorporated. Add the flour and cinnamon and fold
in until well mixed. Cover with food wrap and leave
the dough to rest in the fridge for 1 hour.
    Preheat the oven to 180°C/350°F/Gas Mark 4.
    Divide the dough equally into 16 small pieces,
then roll the pieces on a floured work counter
into thin strings. Grab the strings from one end
and roll them up into irregular snail shell shapes.
Put them on a large baking sheet and bake in the
oven for 10 minutes, or until golden. Remove from
the oven, then carefully transfer the cookies to
a wire rack and leave to cool before storing in an
airtight container.

Pork Lard Cookies

Broas Doces de Banha   ⛂ Alentejo

Preparation time: 30 minutes
Cooking time: 50 minutes
Makes: 30
⛂

olive oil, for oiling
300 g/11 oz (1½ cups) caster (superfine) sugar
350 g/12 oz lard (pork fat)
6 eggs, separated
zest of 1 lemon
1 teaspoon ground cinnamon
700 g/1 lb 9 oz (5¾ cups plus 2 teaspoons) plain
    (all-purpose) flour

Preheat the oven to 200°C/400°F/Gas Mark 6.
Oil a large baking sheet.
    Put the sugar and lard (pork fat) into a large
bowl and, using electric beaters, whisk very well.
Add the egg yolks, lemon zest and cinnamon and
whisk well until combined.
    Put the egg whites into another bowl and, using
either electric beaters or a stand mixer fitted with

a whisk attachment, whisk until soft peaks form,
then fold into the egg yolk mixture with the flour.
Divide the dough into 30 medium-sized round
balls, about 25 g/1 oz each, and place them on the
prepared baking sheet. Bake for 50 minutes, or
until golden. Remove from the oven, then carefully
transfer the cookies to a wire rack and leave to cool
before storing in an airtight container.

Pulled White
Sugarpaste Sweets

Alfenim — Ilha da Terceira   ⛂ Açores

**These medieval sweets (candies) have a long
history, brought to the islands of the Azores by
the Arabs who first settled there. Today they are
mainly made in the Ilha da Terceira. These sweets
required some technical skill and knowledge
of how to work and mould sugar into different
shapes including flowers and animals. They were
offered to noble people as a gift but also used as
an ornament in weddings. _Alfenims_ are rare these
days, but they can still be found in some religious
ceremonies, including in the _Festa do Espirito
Santo_ (The Holy Ghost festival).**

Preparation time: 20 minutes
Cooking time: 15 minutes
Makes: 30–40
🐝 ⊘ ✕

unsalted butter, for greasing
650 g/1 lb 7 oz (3¼ cups) caster (superfine) sugar
1 teaspoon white wine vinegar

Grease a stainless-steel bowl with the butter, then
prepare an inverted bain-marie (cold).
    Turn your oven on to 60°C/140°F/the lowest
possible Gas Mark to keep the sugarpaste warm
when ready, if necessary.
    Combine 280 ml/9½ fl oz (1 cup plus 2
tablespoons) water, the sugar and vinegar together
in a large saucepan and cook over a medium
heat for 10–12 minutes until the mixture reaches
108°C/226°F on a sugar thermometer.
    Once the sugarpaste reaches the temperature,
pour it over the inverted bain-marie and leave
to cool down gently. If the sugarpaste starts
to crystallise on the sides, pull it in. Once the
sugarpaste has reached a temperature that you
can handle, pull some of it out of the bowl and
work it, by pulling it and twisting it a few times
until it is opaque and white in colour.
    Using a pair of scissors, cut the sugarpaste
into small pieces and shape them into the form of
flowers or little birds. They can be also consumed
just like sweets (candies).

Wild Fennel Candies

Rebuçados de Funcho   ◡ Madeira

These small, cylindrical pale orange candies flavoured with fennel are a delicacy found all over the archipelago. Historically, yellow fennel flowers (*funcho*) covered the slopes of Madeira's capital Funchal, which is how settlers came to name the city. For locals today, *Rebuçados de Funcho* are eaten as a candy at any time of day, used to sweeten tea, or slowly melted in a glass of *aguardente*, or as a cough relief (due to the health properties of fennel).

Preparation time: 15 minutes
Cooking time: 30 minutes
Makes: 15
🥜 ⦸ ⬚ ✕

unsalted butter, for greasing
850 g/1 lb 14 oz (4¼ cups) caster (superfine) sugar
9 g/¼ oz fennel essence
sea salt

Grease a large baking sheet with butter and sprinkle with salt.

Put the sugar into a large saucepan with 400 ml/14 fl oz (1⅔ cups) water and heat over a medium heat for 10–12 minutes until it reaches 110°C/230°F on a thermometer. Add the fennel essence, then keep the pan over a medium heat and heat until the sugar reaches 125°C/257°F.

Once the sugar reaches the temperature, pour it onto the prepared baking sheet and leave to cool for a few minutes, then pull some off and stretch it out into long rolls 1 cm/½ inch in diameter. Cut the rolls into 2-cm/¾-inch pieces. Store in an airtight container.

Sugar-glazed Walnuts

Camafeus   ◡ Açores

The name of this small, delicate candy from Terceira island refers to *cameos*, objects made of chiselled stone with figures in relief. *Camafeus* are made of sugar syrup, grated (shredded) nuts and eggs, which form a paste that is thickened in a pan; the mixture is then moulded, covered with icing (frosting) and garnished with a half walnut. These nut-sized sweets (candies) are usually sold in small, crimped, paper boxes, they are eaten all year round but mostly at weddings and baptisms.

Preparation time: 20 minutes
Cooking time: 25 minutes
Makes: about 25 (depending on your chosen size)
🥜 ⬚ ⦸

420 g/14¾ oz (2 cups plus 4 teaspoons) caster (superfine) sugar
360 g/12¾ oz (2⅔ cups) walnut halves, grated (shredded)
7 egg yolks
3 egg whites
walnuts halves, to decorate

For the glaze:
500 g/1 lb 2 oz (2½ cups) caster (superfine) sugar
a few drops of lemon juice

Put the sugar into a large saucepan with 170 ml/5¾ fl oz (¾ cup minus 1 teaspoon) water and bring to the boil over a medium-high heat. Boil for 5 minutes, or until the mixture reaches 116°C/241°F on a sugar thermometer. Remove from the heat, add the walnuts and mix well. Leave to cool down a little.

Meanwhile, put the egg yolks into a bowl, add the egg whites and whisk with a fork until combined. Once the sugar mixture has cooled down slightly, add the eggs, then return the pan to the heat and cook gently over a low heat for 10 minutes, or until it thickens. Pour the mixture onto a baking sheet and leave to cool.

Meanwhile, to make the glaze, put the sugar in a medium saucepan with 300 ml/10 fl oz (1¼ cups) water and cook over a medium heat for 10 minutes, or until it reaches 112°C/234°F on a sugar thermometer. Remove the pan from the heat and whisk until the sugar is opaque. Add the lemon juice and keep the pan in a warm place, such as in a roasting pan half-filled with hot water.

Once the mixture is cool, using your hands, take small amounts of the mixture and shape into walnut-sized balls.

To finish, using two forks, dip each ball into the warm sugar syrup to coat and then place on a baking sheet. Put a walnut half on top of each ball to decorate.

Pine Nut Candies

Alcomonias   ▢ Alentejo

This diamond-shaped sweet (candy), made of toasted wheat flour, honey and pine nuts, can be found throughout the year in pastry shops in Alentejo, but is mostly sold in the town of Santiago do Cacém for traditional saints' days festivities such as *Feira do Monte* or *Feira de Santo André*. The origin of *alconomias* is not entirely clear, although their shape, the ingredients used and their Arabic prefixed name (that translates as 'cumin-coloured') all suggest that these date back to the period when the region was ruled by Arabic-speaking Muslims.

Preparation time: 15 minutes, plus 10 minutes drying
Cooking time: 40 minutes
Makes: 25–30
▢ ∅ ∨ ✕

850 g/1 lb 14 oz (7 cups) plain (all-purpose) flour, plus
    extra for dusting
800 g/1 lb 12 oz (4 cups) caster (superfine) sugar
120 g/4 oz (1 cup minus 2 teaspoons) pine nuts

Preheat the oven to 180°C/350°F/Gas Mark 4. Line several baking sheets with baking (parchment) paper.
Sprinkle the flour over the lined baking sheets, making sure it is in even thin layers, and toast in the oven for 8–10 minutes. Leave to cool.
Fill a saucepan with 420 ml/14¼ fl oz (1⅔ cups) water, add the sugar and bring to the boil. Once it starts boiling, add the pine nuts and simmer for 20 minutes.
Once the flour is cold, sift it into a large bowl, then stir it into the sugar water, a little at a time. Cook over a low heat, stirring continuously so the mixture doesn't catch on the bottom of the pan for 10 minutes, or until you stir and can see the bottom of the pan.
Dust a work counter with some flour and pour on the dough. Sprinkle more flour over the top and, using a rolling pin, roll it out until it is 5 mm/ ¼ inch thick. Cut the dough into small lozenges and leave them to air dry for 10 minutes on the work counter. Store in an airtight container.

Pine Nut Nougat

Pinhoadas   ▢ Alentejo

This sweet (candy) from Alcácer do Sal is made using one of the main ingredients produced in the region, harvested from the pine trees that developed in the long, sandy terrains of the Alentejo coastal area: pine nuts. *Pinhoadas* are caramelised, diamond-shaped candy bars in two lozenges, each covered in a thick white paper. They are usually served on top of pieces of communion wafer, or orange leaves, and are mostly eaten during popular festivals.

Preparation time: 15 minutes
Cooking time: 25 minutes
Makes: 40
▨ ▢ ∅ ✕

400 g/14 oz (3 cups) pine nuts
230 g/8¼ oz (1 cup) honey
almond oil, for oiling

Preheat the oven to 180°C/350°F/Gas Mark 4.
Spread the pine nuts out on a large baking sheet and roast for 10–12 minutes, or until golden. Remove from the oven and leave to cool until completely cold.
Bring the honey to the boil in a small saucepan over a low heat, stirring continuously to prevent the honey sticking to the pan. Once the pine nuts are cold, stir them into the honey until combined.
Oil a work counter with almond oil. Cut a large sheet of baking (parchment) paper and oil with almond oil. Pour the pine nut mix onto the oiled counter, then place the sheet of paper over the top to cover. Using a rolling pin, roll the pine nut mix out to a uniform thin sheet.
Peel the paper from the top of the nougat, then cut into strips using a warm knife.

Almond and Honey Nougat

Nogado Algarvio   ◻ Algarve

Similar to *Pinhoadas* from Alentejo (see left), *nogado* is a hard, golden-brown square of candy, prepared with equal parts almond and honey, usually served on top of green lemon or orange leaves, and produced in Baixo Alentejo and the Algarve interior. Almonds, widely used in desserts and pastries, have long played a key role in Portuguese cuisine, and in the Algarve in particular, with almond trees introduced to the region (and the Douro Valley) by the Arabs during their occupation of the Iberian Peninsula.

Preparation time: 10 minutes
Cooking time: 8–10 minutes
Makes: 80
🍯 ◻ ⬚ ◻ ✕

edible rice paper sheets
650 g/1 lb 7 oz (5 cups) blanched almonds
330 g/11½ oz (1 cups plus 1 tablespoon) honey
2 teaspoons ground cinnamon

Cut the rice paper into 3-cm/1¼-inch squares. Set aside.

Slice all the blanched almonds into very small pieces. (Do not use almond flour instead.)

Put the honey into a small saucepan and boil over a medium heat for 8–10 minutes, or until a paste starts to form. Add the almonds and stir until you can see the bottom of the pot as the mixture clumps together.

Pour the mixture onto a chopping (cutting) board then, using a wet rolling pin, roll out to a thin sheet. While still warm, cut into 3-cm/1¼-inch squares, then lay them on the rice paper squares. Dust with cinnamon before serving. Store in an airtight container (the nougat will soften over time).

Almond Nougat and Egg Yolk Noodles

Florados de Lagoa   ◻ Algarve

The recipe for these thin, crispy almond wafers topped with *Fios de Ovos* (Sweet Egg Yolk Strands, page 312) dates back to the 18th century and was a well-kept secret for many decades, known only to a handful of nuns in the convents of southern Portugal. In 2019, the Lago municipality took the decision to revive and preserve *florados* (named after flower ornaments), establishing them as the central pillar and symbol of the local gastronomy.

Preparation time: 15 minutes, plus 12 hours standing
Cooking time: 10–12 minutes
Makes: 28
🍯 ◻ ⬚ ◻ ✕

375 g/13 oz (3 cups minus 2 tablespoons) blanched almonds or 375 g/13 oz (3¾ cups) flaked (slivered) almonds
375 g/13 oz (1¾ cups plus 2 tablespoons) crystallised sugar
450 g/1 lb Sweet Egg Yolk Strands (*Fios de Ovos*, page 312)

If using blanched almonds, rinse them under cold running water, put them into a medium bowl and cover with water. Using a sharp knife, slice the almonds into flakes and keep them in a bowl of cold water so they don't go brown.

Put the sugar and 180 ml/6 fl oz (¾ cup) water into a large saucepan and heat over a medium heat for 10–12 minutes until it reaches 103°C/217°F on a thermometer. Drain the almonds and add them to the sugar syrup. Mix until the mixture is slightly dry. Remove from the heat.

Using a spoon, take a spoonful of the mixture and, with wet hands and over a wet surface, make a round 'cake', about 8 cm/3¼ inches in diameter. Put them onto the wet work counter and repeat until you have used up all the mixture. Leave them to stand for 12 hours.

The next day, remove them from the plate with a spatula and decorate them with a small amount of the *Fios de Ovos*.

Fig 'Cheese'

Queijos de Figo ⌂ p.409   � Algarve

Preparation time: 30 minutes
Cooking time: 35–40 minutes
Makes: 16
🍊 ▢ ⌀ V

220 g/7½ oz (1⅔ cups) almonds
220 g/7½ oz (1¾ cups) dried preserved figs
200 g/7 oz (1 cup) caster (superfine) sugar, plus extra
     for tossing
1 teaspoon ground cinnamon
1½ teaspoons very finely chopped wild fennel tops
25 g/1 oz (¼ cup) cocoa powder
zest of 1 lemon
icing (confectioners') sugar, for dusting

Preheat the oven to 180°C/350°F/Gas Mark 4.
  Spread the almonds out over a large baking
sheet and toast in the oven for 8 minutes, or until
golden. Keep checking them as they may burn.
Remove from the oven and leave to cool, then
transfer to a food processor and blitz until very
finely ground. Remove and set aside.
  Put the dried figs into the food processor and
blitz until it forms a fine paste. Set aside.
  Put the caster (superfine) sugar, cinnamon,
fennel tops, cocoa powder, lemon zest and 120 ml/
4 fl oz (½ cup) water into a large saucepan and
heat over a medium heat for 10–12 minutes until it
reaches 110°C/230°F on a sugar thermometer.
Add the ground almonds and cook for 8 minutes,
or until it boils. Reduce the heat to low, add the
fig paste and cook for a further 8 minutes.
  Dust a work counter with icing (confectioners')
sugar, then tip the fig dough out onto it and leave
to cool until completely cold.
  Once the dough is cold, divide it into small
'cakes', about 40 g/1½ oz each, and form them into
a round shape. Press them gently on the top so
they look like small cheeses.
  Put some caster sugar into a large shallow bowl
and toss the 'cheeses' in it until coated. Store in an
airtight container.

Almond Dough/Marzipan

Massa de Amêndoas / Maçapão   � Algarve

Marzipan (sugared almond paste) is used to
decorate lots of traditional desserts in the
Algarve. This part of Portugal is particularly well
known for the high-quality almonds that are
cultivated there. Most regional sweets (candies)
are made from marzipan and moulded into
incredible shapes resembling birds, fruit and
vegetables.

Preparation time: 15 minutes
Cooking time: 10 minutes
Makes: 800 g/1 lb 12 oz
🍊 ▢ ⌀ ▢ ✕

400 g/14 oz (3 cups) raw almonds
400 g/14 oz (2 cups) caster (superfine) sugar
1 egg white

Put the almonds onto a clean tea (dish) towel,
gather up the ends into a pouch and rub the
almonds together to remove the skins. Blitz in
a food processor.
  Put the sugar and 90 ml/3 fl oz (6 tablespoons)
water into a medium saucepan and bring to the boil
gently over a low heat for 10–12 minutes, or until
it is a thick paste. Remove from the heat, add the
almonds and mix in well, then add the egg white and
mix in.
  Tip out the mixture onto a work counter and
work the paste until it is a smooth 'dough'. Roll it
out, then cover with food wrap and leave it to rest
in the fridge.

Fig 'Cheese'

Marzipan and Sweet Egg Yolk Thread Cakes

••

Queijinhos de Amêndoas ⛩ Algarve

Queijinhos (or tiny cheeses), also known as 'fruits of the Algarve' or 'almond sweets', are small, very elaborate sweets (candies) made of marzipan (sugared almond paste), with a soft and sweet filling. It is common to see these in pastry shops and markets all over the Algarve, moulded and decorated to resemble every type of fruit and vegetable, sliced or whole cheeses, sausages, baskets and animals. Their preparation requires enormous expertise and perfectionism, involving many hours of specialised work.

Preparation time: 30 minutes, plus 4 hours resting
Cooking time: 5 minutes
Makes: 12
🫓 🗋 ⌀

1 egg white
280 g/10 oz (2 cups plus 2 teaspoons) blanched
    almonds
280 g/10 oz (1½ cups minus 4 teaspoons) caster
    (superfine) sugar
220 g/7½ oz Soft Sweet Eggs (*Ovos Moles*, page 308)
icing (confectioners') sugar, for dusting

Put the egg white into a small bowl and stir with a fork to break it down a little. Set aside.

Put the almonds into a food processor and blitz until finely ground. Transfer them to a large bowl and add the caster (superfine) sugar. Mix together until well combined then, while stirring, slowly add the egg white, a little at a time, until smooth. Pour the mixture into a large saucepan and cook over a low heat for 2 minutes. Remove from the heat and leave to rest for 4 hours.

Divide the dough into medium-sized balls, about 45 g/1½ oz each. Remove a bit of the dough from each ball and set aside. These will be the lids. Make a hole in the centre of the dough, without going all the way through and fill with the *Ovos Moles*. Use a knife to flatten the eggs. Roll the small pieces of dough out and use to cover the eggs. Repeat until all the balls are filled and covered with lids.

Put the icing (confectioners') sugar into a large shallow bowl, then roll the filled balls in it until coated. They should look like small round cheeses. Once they are all coated, gently press the top down on each one a little before serving.

Little Cheeses from Heaven with Almonds

••

Queijinhos do Céu de Constância 📷 p.411 ⛩ Ribatejo

Preparation time: 30 minutes, plus 12 hours chilling
Cooking time: 10–12 minutes
Makes: 14
🫓 🗋 ⌀

370 g/13 oz (3 cups) almond flour, finely ground
180 g/6 oz (1 cup minus 4 teaspoons) caster (superfine)
    sugar
2 egg whites
85 g/3 oz ft Sweet Eggs (*Ovos Moles*, page 308)

The day before, put the almond flour, sugar and egg whites into a bowl and mix well to combine.

Put a large heatproof bowl over a medium saucepan of gently simmering water, making sure the bottom of the bowl doesn't touch the water. Pour the almond mixture into the bowl and cook gently, stirring continuously, for 10–12 minutes, or until thick. Remove from the heat, pour into a container and leave in the fridge for 12 hours.

The next day, divide the chilled mixture into 14 small pieces, about 40 g/1½ oz each, then press each one in the middle with your thumb and fill it with a little of the *Ovos Moles*. Cover the filling with the dough from around the filling, then gently press it with your hand and roll it vertically so they look like little cheeses. Repeat with the rest of the chilled mixture and filling. Leave them to air-dry, then wrap them in baking (parchment) paper.

Little Cheeses from Heaven with Almonds

Little Cheeses from Heaven from the Convent of Donas

••

Queijinhos do Céu do Convento das Donas   ⏝ Ribatejo

Preparation time: 20 minutes
Cooking time: 20–25 minutes
Makes: 26
⌀ ◻ ⌀ ◻ ✕

330 g/11½ oz (1⅔ cups) caster (superfine) sugar
20 egg yolks
icing (confectioners') sugar, for sprinkling

Put the caster (superfine) sugar and 200 ml/
7 fl oz (¾ cup plus 1 tablespoon) water into a
large saucepan and heat over a medium heat for
10–12 minutes until it reaches 117°C/243°F on a
thermometer. Remove from the heat and carefully
add the egg yolks, stirring continuously. Bring to
the boil again, stirring continuously, until thick and
you can see the bottom of the pan while stirring.
Remove from the heat and leave the mixture to
cool completely.

   Once cold, sprinkle some icing (confectioners')
sugar over your hands and divide the mixture into
26 portions, then shape them into small round
balls. Put onto a large plate and sprinkle more
icing sugar over the top before serving.

Egg Yolk Sweets

••

Rebuçados de Ovos de Portalegre   ⏝ Alentejo

**These sweets (candies) from Alentejo are calorific
bombs. Whenever I'm in Lisbon, I love to visit the
shop that sells these but they can be easily made
at home.**

Preparation time: 20 minutes, plus overnight resting
Cooking time: 30–35 minutes
Makes: 30–40
◻ ⌀

14 egg yolks
350 g/12 oz (1¾ cups) caster (superfine) sugar
plain (all-purpose) flour, for dusting
almond oil, for oiling

For the syrup:
400 g/14 oz (2 cups) caster (superfine) sugar
20 ml/¾ fl oz (4 teaspoons) lemon juice

The day before, put the egg yolks into a bowl
and lightly beat with a fork. Put the sugar and
140 ml/4¾ fl oz (½ cup) water into a large saucepan
and heat over a medium heat for 10–12 minutes
until it reaches 108°C/226°F on a thermometer.
Remove the pan from the heat and leave to cool
before adding the whisked egg yolks. Return the
pan to a low heat and cook for 10 minutes, stirring
continuously, until the egg yolks are thick. Pour the
mixture onto a rimmed baking sheet and leave to
rest overnight.

   The next day, divide the egg yolk mixture equally
into 30 small balls, then dust flour over them,
shaking the balls to remove any excess. Set aside.

   Spread some almond oil over a marble stone.

   For the syrup, put the sugar, 140 ml/4¾ fl oz
(½ cup) water and lemon juice into a large saucepan
and heat over a medium heat for 10–12 minutes until
it reaches 102°C/216°F on a sugar thermometer.
Remove the pan from the heat then, using a fork
or a slotted spoon, dip the egg balls, one by one,
into the sugar syrup and leave to rest on the marble
stone until the sugar syrup hardens.

   Once dry, cut round pieces of baking
(parchment) paper and wrap them around the
sweets before serving.

Fake 'Chestnuts'

Castanhas de Viseu   ○ Beira Alta

Preparation time: 20 minutes, plus overnight cooling
Cooking time: 20 minutes
Makes: 15–20
◻ ⌀ ✕

220 g/7½ oz (1 cup plus 4 teaspoons) caster
    (superfine) sugar
22 egg yolks, plus 1 extra egg yolk for egg wash
plain (all-purpose) flour, for dusting

Put the sugar and 400 ml/14 fl oz (1⅔ cups) water
into a large saucepan and heat over a medium heat
for 10–12 minutes until it reaches 125°C/257°F on
a thermometer. Remove from the heat.

Add 19 of the egg yolks to the sugar syrup
and stir them in the same direction, then put
the pan over a low heat and cook, stirring
continuously, but avoid making circles so less air is
incorporated, for 10 minutes, or until thick and you
can see the bottom of the pan when stirring. Pour
the mixture into a large bowl, cover with food wrap
and leave to cool overnight.

The next day, put the extra egg yolk for the
egg wash into a small bowl and lightly beat with a
fork. Dust your hands with flour, then take a little of
the mixture and shape it into the size of chestnuts
or small round balls. Repeat until all the mixture is
used up. Brush them with the egg wash, then press
them down a little with a fork.

With a hot coal or flame, colour the top of
each 'chestnut', then wrap in baking (parchment)
paper pouches before serving.

Egg Sweets

Rebuçados de Ovos   ○ Beira Baixa

Preparation time: 20 minutes
Cooking time: 35–40 minutes
Makes: 17
◻ ⌀ ✕

260 g/9 oz (1⅓ cups) caster (superfine) sugar,
    plus an extra 200 g/7 oz (1 cup) for the syrup
30 g/1 oz (¼ cup) almond flour
4 egg yolks
sunflower oil, for oiling
plain (all-purpose) flour, for dusting

Put the sugar and 140 ml/4¾ fl oz (½ cup plus
4 teaspoons) water into a large saucepan and
heat over a medium heat for 10–12 minutes until
it reaches 108°C/226°F on a thermometer. Remove
from the heat, add the almond flour and stir, then
add the egg yolks and stir again. Put the pan over
a low heat and cook for 10 minutes, or until thick,
stirring continuously to prevent it sticking to the
bottom of the pan. Remove from the heat and pour
into a large heatproof bowl. Cover with a tea (dish)
towel or food wrap and leave to cool completely.

Grease a large baking sheet with oil. Dust your
hands with flour, then take a piece of the cold
paste, about 30 g/1 oz, and shape into a ball the
size of a walnut. Put it on the prepared baking
sheet and repeat with the remaining paste. You
should have 17 balls.

To make the syrup, put the extra sugar and
100 ml/3½ fl oz (⅓ cup plus 1 tablespoon) water
into a large saucepan and heat over a medium-high
heat for 10–12 minutes until it reaches 108°C/226°F
on a thermometer.

Using a fork, dip the balls into the syrup until
coated, then put them on another baking sheet
and leave to dry. Once cold and dry, cut out 17
small circles from a sheet of baking (parchment)
paper and place them on top.

Figleaf Gourd Jam

Doce de Chila/   ♡ Algarve
Doce de Gila   📷 p.415

This variety of squash, the figleaf gourd, is very sensitive to metallic objects, and reacts with it in a way that produces a very strange taste, so make sure you don't use anything metallic when making this recipe. The exact measurements for this recipe depend on the weight of the squash.

Preparation time: 45 minutes, plus 24 hours standing
Cooking time: 30 minutes
Makes: 1 x 500-ml/18 fl-oz jar
🔥 ▢ ⊘ ∨ ✕

1 figleaf gourd or any other squash
caster (superfine) sugar, the same weight of the peeled, cooked squash
rinds of 4 lemons
2 cinnamon sticks
sea salt

To prepare the gourd, throw it on the floor to break it open. Once broken, using either a wooden spoon or your hands, remove the seeds and the inside filaments, which taste bitter when cooked.

Fill a large bowl or plastic container with cold water, add a pinch of salt and wash the squash a few times. The gourd will produce foam and once it stops foaming it is ready to use. Put the squash into a large bowl, cover with cold water and leave to stand for 24 hours.

When you are ready to make the jam (jelly), drain the squash, then put it into a large saucepan, cover with cold water and add a pinch of salt. Cook over a medium heat for 15 minutes, or until soft. Drain and leave to drip on a perforated tray or in a colander, then dry it with a tea (dish) towel. Remove the skin, then weigh the squash. Pull it apart with your fingers or a wooden spoon.

Put the sugar, the same weight as the squash, into a large saucepan with half of the weight in water. Add the lemon rinds and cinnamon sticks and cook over a medium heat for 10–12 minutes, or until it reaches 112°C/234°F on a thermometer. Add the squash, reduce the heat to low and cook for 15 minutes, or until the texture is nice and compact.

Pour the jam into a large jug (pitcher) and leave to cool until it has a creamy, jam texture. Pour the jam into a sterilised 500 ml/18 fl oz glass jar, leaving a 1-cm/½-inch head space. Leave to cool, then cover the top of the jam with a disc of baking (parchment) paper and seal with the lid. Store in the fridge for up to 1 month.

Sweet Potato Jam

Doce de Batata Doce   ♡ Açores

Batata doce, or sweet potato, is also called *batata da ilha* (island potato) in the Azores, and is the main ingredient in this jam (jelly) made in Azorean homes. It is also often boiled, eaten in stews and soups, or roasted in the oven to be served as a snack or dessert. Sweet potatoes were brought to the Iberian Peninsula by the Spanish in the 15th century from the Yucatán region (Colombia, Ecuador and Peru today). As soon as the Portuguese King João III heard of these 'small, thin and withered potatoes', he ordered their cultivation in the Azores, especially on Terceira island. The Azorean population, surprised by the potential of this tuber which could act as a bread substitute, planted them in their backyards — a practice that expanded and flourished over the centuries.

Preparation time: 10 minutes
Cooking time: 1 hour 30 minutes
Makes: 3 x 300-ml/10 fl-oz (1¼-cups) jars
🔥 ▢ ⊘ ✕

450 g/1 lb sweet potatoes
1 cinnamon stick
400 g/14 oz (2 cups) caster (superfine) sugar
6 egg yolks, whisked

Put the sweet potatoes into a large saucepan, cover with cold water and cook over a medium heat for 35–45 minutes, or until soft. Drain, then leave to rest for 5 minutes before removing the skins. Discard the skins. Transfer the sweet potato flesh to a food processor and process until a purée forms. Set aside.

Put the sugar in a large saucepan with the cinnamon stick and 250 ml/8 fl oz (1 cup) water and put over a low heat until the sugar has dissolved, then increase the heat to medium and boil until it reaches 108°C/226°F on a thermometer. Remove and discard the cinnamon stick. Add the sweet potato purée, then warm everything through. Remove from the heat and add the whisked egg yolks. Put the pan back on the stove and cook over a low heat, stirring continuously, for 8–10 minutes, or until the mixture thickens.

Pour the jam (jelly) into a large jug (pitcher) and leave to cool until it has a creamy, jam texture. Pour the jam into three sterilised 300 ml/18 fl oz (1¼ cups) glass jars, leaving a 1-cm/½-inch head space. Leave to cool, then cover the top of the jam with a disc of baking (parchment) paper and seal with the lid. Store in the fridge for up to 1 week.

Figleaf Gourd Jam

Turnip Jam

••

Nabada de Semide   ⋂ Beira Litoral

Made of turnips, sugar and almonds, *nabade* is
a kind of jam (jelly) that can be eaten in a bowl
with a spoon, spread on slices of bread, paired
with fresh or cured cheese, and even used to fill
pies. It was created by the nuns of the Santa Maria
de Semide convent, near Coimbra, who used
to put turnips in a brine for eight days before
cooking them so that their intense flavour would
not prevail. Their oldest recipes included musk,
fennel, cinnamon, orange blossom and rose water.

Preparation time: 30 minutes, plus 4 days standing
Cooking time: 1 hour
Makes: 1 x 500-ml/18 fl-oz jar
🐟 🗋 🐟 ∨ ✕

1.3 kg/3 lb good-quality white turnips, peeled and sliced
    into medium-thick disks
550 g/1 lb 4 oz (2¾ cups) caster (superfine) sugar
110 g/3¾ oz (1 cup plus 2 teaspoons) ground almonds
1 teaspoon sea salt

Bring a medium saucepan of water to the boil, add
a pinch of salt, then add the turnips and cook for
30 minutes, or until soft. Remove them from the
pan and leave to cool in a bowl of cold water. Keep
the turnips in cold water for 4 days, changing the
water daily. (In Semide, the village where this jam
(jelly) was created, they call this process *corar*.
It removes the strong aromatic turnip flavour that
turnips usually have.)

When ready to cook, remove the turnips from
the water, put them into a clean tea (dish) towel
and squeeze to remove any excess water. Transfer
the turnips to a mortar and, using a pestle, mash
until a paste forms. Spread the paste over a
surface and remove any turnip strings or hard bits.

Put the sugar and 330 ml/11 fl oz (1⅓ cups)
water into a large saucepan and heat over a
medium heat for 10–12 minutes until it reaches
106°C/222°F on a sugar thermometer. Remove
from the heat, add the ground almonds and
turnip paste, then cook over a low heat, stirring
continuously to prevent burning, for 20 minutes,
or until it is a jam consistency.

Pour the jam into a large jug (pitcher) and leave
to cool until it has a creamy, jam texture. Pour
the jam into a sterilised 500 ml/18 fl oz glass
jar, leaving a 1-cm/½-inch head space. Leave to
cool, then cover the top of the jam with a circle of
baking (parchment) paper and seal with the lid.
Store in the fridge for up to 1 week.

Orange Rind Compote

••

Compota de Cascas de Laranja   ⋂ Alentejo

Preparation time: 25 minutes, plus overnight cooling
Cooking time: 45 minutes
Makes: 1 x 500-ml/18 fl-oz jar
🐟 🗋 🐟 ∨ ✕

10 whole oranges, washed and dried
280 g/10 oz (1½ cups minus 2 teaspoons) caster
    (superfine) sugar

Using a vegetable peeler, remove the rind from the
oranges. Remove only the rind and not the white
pith — if you take the pith too, the compote will be
bitter. (Set aside the orange flesh to use in another
recipe.) Slice the orange rind into long, thin strips.

Bring a saucepan of water to the boil. Add
the strips of orange rind and cook for 3 minutes,
then strain.

Put the strips of orange rind into another
saucepan, add the sugar and pour over 150 ml/
5 fl oz (⅔ cup) water. Cook over a low heat until
the temperature reaches 108°C/226°F on a sugar
thermometer. Remove from the heat and leave to
cool overnight before using.

Tangerine Liqueur

Licor de Tangerina   ▽ Açores

Preparation time: 15 minutes, plus 12 days infusing
Cooking time: 15 minutes
Makes: 3 or 4 x 500-ml/18 fl-oz jars
🐟 ▢ Ø ∨ ✕

15 tangerines
1.3 litres/44 fl oz (5¼ cups) plain alcohol
1.3 kg/3 lb (6½ cups) caster (superfine) sugar

Using a vegetable peeler, remove the rind from
the tangerines. (Set aside the flesh to use in
another recipe.)
    Put the alcohol and sugar into a large saucepan
with 1.3 litres/44 fl oz (5¼ cups) water and bring
to the boil. Once boiling, add the tangerine rind,
then remove the pan from the heat.
    Pour the liquid into a sterilised 500-ml/18 fl-oz
glass jars and seal with a lid. Leave to stand for
12 days, stirring the contents of the jar every day or
every other day. Once ready, strain the liqueur into
a sterilised bottle before serving.

Milk Liqueur

Licor de Leite   ▽ Açores

Made out of flavoured milk, this liquor is usually
consumed after meals or around Christmas
time. The recipe calls for alcohol, sugar, vanilla,
chocolate and lemon to be added to milk and
infused for 15 days. After that time, the mixture
is filtered and the solids retained so they can
be added to the Christmas pudding, which is
also traditionally prepared around this time. The
consumption of licor de leite is wrapped in a ritual:
during the Christmas season, groups of teenagers
from São Miguel go from door to door asking,
'o menino mija?' ('the little boy needs to pee?'),
offering a very small glass of liquor and a candy.

Preparation time: 15 minutes, plus 12 days infusing
Makes: 2 or 3 x 500-ml/18 fl-oz bottles
Ø 🐟

120 g/4 oz dark (semisweet) chocolate
1.3 kg/3 lb (6½ cups) caster (superfine) sugar
1 litre/34 fl oz (4¼ cups) ethanol alcohol
2 vanilla pods (beans)
pared rind of 2 lemons
1.3 litres/44 fl oz (5¼ cups) raw milk

Using a box grater, grate (shred) the chocolate
into a small bowl.
    Put the sugar, ethanol alcohol, vanilla pods
(beans), chocolate and lemon rind into a large
container. Add the milk, stirring with a wooden
spoon, then cover and leave to stand for 12 days
at room temperature, stirring every day.
    After 12 days, strain the liquid through a sieve
(fine-mesh strainer) lined with paper filters into a
jug (pitcher). Pour into a sterilised 500-ml/18 fl-oz
bottles, leaving a 1-cm/½-inch head space. Cover
and seal before storing.

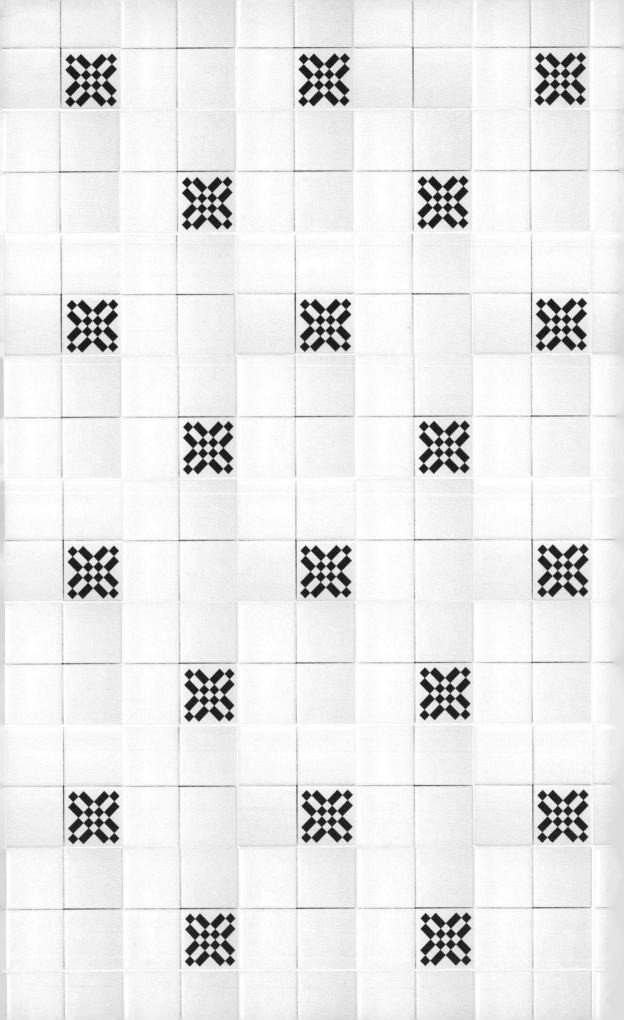

GUEST CHEFS
GLOSSARY
INDEX
RECIPE NOTES

José Avillez

Considered one of the greatest chefs in Portugal, José Avillez works to promote the cuisine of his native country and make it a top gastronomic destination. Currently Avillez has several restaurants in Portugal, in both Lisbon and Porto, and also in Dubai. With two Michelin stars, Belcanto has been named on the prestigious list of The World's 50 Best Restaurants. Located in Lisbon's historic centre, José Avillez offers contemporary Portuguese cuisine at Belcanto in a sophisticated and comfortable setting that takes us on a journey in time, from Chiado's old romatic feel to the future. Páteo is a popular fish and seafood bar and restaurant situated in the most spectacular courtyard in Lisbon, where dishes are designed to be shared and lingered over. Housed within Bairro do Avillez, this part-food hall and part-restaurant blurs the lines by also offering a gourmet deli, Taberna where you can share delicious small dishes, Pizzaria Lisboa that also serves amazing risotti and pastas, and a trendy restaurant, Mini Bar, where music plays a special role. Avillez has contributed to countless Portuguese and foreign language books, as well as hosting TV and radio shows.

Prawns with Garlic and Chillies

Preparation time: 15 minutes
Cooking time: 10 minutes
Serves: 4
🐟 ⬜ ⊠

extra virgin olive oil, for shallow-frying
1 garlic clove, peeled and germ removed
12 raw tiger prawns (shrimp), peeled but with the tail left on
flor de sal (fleur de sel), to taste

For the sauce:
1–2 red chillies, thinly sliced
80 ml/2¾ fl oz (⅓ cup) white wine
bunch of coriander, shredded
10 g/¼ oz unsalted butter

Heat the olive oil with the garlic clove in a sauté pan over a medium heat. Once the oil is shimmering, add the prawns and sauté for 4–5 minutes, or until they turn pink. Season with flor de sal (fleur de sel). Using a slotted spoon, transfer the prawns to a plate and set aside.

To make the sauce, add the chillies to the same pan and oil used to sauté the prawns and cook for a few seconds. Add the white wine to the pan with a splash of water, then add the butter and shredded coriander. Stir until the butter has melted and the sauce is well combined.

Divide the cooked prawns between four deep serving plates. Pour the sauce over the prawns and serve immediately.

Brás-Style Cod with Exploding Olives

Preparation time: 45 minutes, plus 12 hours soaking
Cooking time: 15 minutes
Serves: 4
🐟 ⬜

For the cod:
400 g/14 oz salt cod, desalted (see page 40)
500 g/1 lb 2 oz potatoes, peeled
3 onions, peeled and thinly sliced into rings
1 garlic clove, peeled and finely chopped
8 whole eggs plus 4 egg yolks, lightly beaten
3 teaspoons extra virgin olive oil, plus extra for deep-frying
bunch of parsley, shredded
sea salt and freshly-ground black pepper, to taste

For the exploding olives:
100 ml/3⅓ fl oz green olive juice (pitted green olives, mashed, strained and then squeezed through muslin/cheesecloth)
0.5 g/¹⁄₁₆ oz xanthan gum
0.2 g/¹⁄₃₂ oz calcium gluconolactate
500 ml/17 fl oz low-calcium water
½ teaspoon alginate
30 ml/1 fl oz olive oil macerated with orange, lemon, garlic, and thyme, filtered

The day before, prepare the exploding olives. Combine the green olive juice, xanthan gum and calcium gluconolactate in a bowl and then blend with a stick (immersion) blender. Store in the fridge for at least 12 hours.

The next day, combine 125 ml/4 fl oz of the low-calcium water with the alginate using the stick blender. Add the remaining water, blend thoroughly, pour into a deep, glass container and leave to rest in the fridge for at least 12 hours.

Take the olive juice mixture and the alginate mixture out of the fridge 30 minutes before continuing with the recipe.

Have a bowl of water nearby as well as the alginate mixture. Using a Parisian spoon or melon baller, scoop up a spoonful of the olive juice mixture, drawing it as near to the alginate mixture as possible (no more than 1 mm/¹⁄₁₆ inch away). Carefully lower the olive mixture into the alginate mixture and wait 30 seconds until a small sphere has formed. Using a slotted spoon, carefully lift the sphere and let it drip. Lower the sphere into a bowl of water, lift and let it drip again. Store in the filtered olive oil and set aside.

To prepare the cod, bring a large saucepan of water to the boil. Once boiling, add the cod and cook for 2 minutes. Remove the cod from the water, discard any skin or bones, then flake with a fork. Set aside.

Using a sharp knife, slice the potatoes into thin matchsticks. Rinse the potato matchsticks under cold running water to remove the starch and pat dry with paper towels.

When ready to cook, line a baking sheet with paper towels. Heat the olive oil for deep-frying in a large deep saucepan or fryer until it reaches 190°C/375°F on a thermometer. Working in batches, carefully lower the potato matchsticks into the hot oil and deep-fry for 2–3 minutes, or until golden. Remove with a slotted spoon and leave to drain on the lined baking sheet. Set aside.

Heat the olive oil in a heavy-based saucepan over a medium heat. Add the onions and garlic and cook for 5 minutes, or until the onion is translucent.

Add the flaked cod to the pan with the fried potato matchsticks, beaten eggs and egg yolks and stir to combine. Season with sea salt and black pepper. Fold half the shredded parsley through the mixture. Continue stirring until everything is creamy and well combined.

Scatter over the remaining parsley and add the exploding olives before serving immediately.

Olive Oil and Honey Pudding with Lemon Zest

•••

Preparation time: 10 minutes
Cooking time: 40 minutes
Serves: 4
🫒 ☐ ⌀

olive oil, for greasing
750 g/26½ oz caster (superfine) sugar
1 teaspoon ground cinnamon, plus extra for dusting
16 eggs
50 ml/1²⁄₃ fl oz extra virgin olive oil
280 ml/9½ fl oz rosemary honey
zest of 1 lemon

Preheat the oven to 180°C/350°F/Gas Mark 4 and grease a 27 x 13-cm/10½ x 5-inch cake pan with olive oil.

Combine the sugar and ground cinnamon in a bowl. Add the eggs, extra virgin olive oil and honey to the bowl. Using a stand (immersion) mixer, blend everything together until smooth.

Pour the batter into the prepared cake pan. Put the pan into a large roasting pan and carefully pour hot water into the roasting pan so it reaches halfway up the sides of the cake pan. Bake in the oven for 40 minutes, or until firm. Remove from the oven and leave to cool completely before releasing from the pan.

Dust the pudding with some extra cinnamon and decorate with the lemon zest before serving.

Vasco Coelho Santos

Euskalduna Studio, Porto

During the final year of his business management degree, Vasco Coelho Santos realised that his passion for cooking was stronger than his love for numbers, so he went to Lisbon to study at Atelier de Cozinha Michel and then did an internship at Restaurante Olivier and Tavares Rico. In 2010, Vasco left for Spain to work in some of the world's best restaurants: Mugaritz, Arzak and El Bulli. On his return to Porto, Vasco worked at Pedro Lemos and then travelled through Europe and Asia, working at Viajante and 2 am: Dessert Bar. Euskalduna Studio, the first space of his own, opened in Porto in 2016. Euskalduna – which means 'Basque' – is a tribute to Vasco's journey through the Basque country. At the restaurant, Vasco and his team invite everyone who visits to join their space of creation and share a gastronomic journey in the intimacy of the counter (a central space at the restaurant) and the two tables. Taking advantage of the intimate and welcoming environment, the team combines creativity and technique to break barriers, turning the fine dining concept into a fun experience that amazes all the senses.

John Dory Açorda

Preparation time: 1 hour 30 minutes
Cooking time: 45 minutes
Serves: 4
◻

For the bread porridge:
100 ml/3⅓ fl oz olive oil
400 g/14 oz onion, peeled and finely chopped
200 g/7 oz garlic cloves, peeled and finely chopped
500 g/17½ oz crusty bread, cut into small pieces

For the fish:
750 g/26½ oz John Dory
40 g/1½ oz fish roe
60 g/2 oz plain (all-purpose) flour
5 g/⅓ oz egg yolk
50 g/1⅔ oz cornflour (cornstarch)
20 g/¾ oz fine sea salt
10 g/⅓ oz freshly ground black pepper
1 litre/34 fl oz (4 cups) vegetable oil

For the coriander (cilantro) oil:
50 g/1⅔ oz coriander (cilantro) leaves
125 ml/4¼ fl oz rapeseed oil

To make the coriander (cilantro) oil, drop the coriander leaves into boiling water for a few seconds, then strain and place in a Thermomix or Bamix with the oil and grind for 10 minutes. Strain and set aside.

Clean and gut the fish and set aside the fish roe. Remove the head and set aside. Bone the fish and slice the flesh into tranches, each weighing 80 g/3 oz.

Make a brine with 2% salt, adding 20 g/¾ oz fine salt to every 1 litre/34 fl oz of water. Place the fish tranches and roe in the brine and leave for 35 minutes.

To make the fish broth, arrange the fish head and bones on a roasting tray and place in an oven at 190°C/375°F/Gas Mark 5 and roast them for 25 minutes. Transfer the roasted fish head and bones to a large saucepan and cover with water. Bring the water to the boil, then reduce the heat and cook for 30 minutes. Strain, discard the fish head and bones and set aside.

Heat the olive oil in a frying pan or skillet over a medium heat, add the onion and garlic and cook for 15 minutes or until well caramelised. Once caramelised, add the bread and mix to combine. Add the fish broth, little by little, crushing the bread until a porridge-like consistency forms.

Combine the flour, cornflour (cornstarch), egg yolk, salt and pepper with 115 ml/4 fl oz water in a bowl. Lightly whisk until the flour is fully incorporated to make a batter.

Heat 1 litre/34 fl oz (4 cups) vegetable oil in a heavy-based saucepan or fryer until it reaches 190°C/375°F on a thermometer. Coat each fish tranche in the batter and carefully lower into the hot oil and deep-fry for 4 minutes, or until golden.

To serve, ladle the bread porridge into four individual serving bowls. Place a piece of fried fish on top and spoon over the cured roe. Drizzle over the coriander (cilantro) oil before serving.

Rabbit Ravioli

Preparation time: 4 hours
Cooking time: 24 hours
Serves: 4

For the rabbit filling:
1 x 600-g/1 lb 5-oz rabbit
1 litre/34 fl oz (4 cups) red wine
500 ml/17 fl oz (2 cups) tawny port
2 onions
1 head of garlic, crushed
1 carrot
20 g/¾ oz rosemary
10 g/⅓ oz thyme
20 g/¾ oz salt

For the pasta dough:
1 egg
400 g/14 oz plain (all-purpose) flour
60 ml/2 fl oz oil
10 ml/⅓ fl oz milk
1 litre/34 fl oz (4 cups) vegetable oil, for deep-frying

For the parsley oil:
50 g/1¾ oz parsley leaves
125 ml/4¼ fl oz rapeseed oil

To make the parsley oil, drop the parsley leaves into boiling water for a few seconds, then strain and place in a Thermomix or Bamix with the oil and grind for 10 minutes. Strain and set aside.

The day before, place the rabbit in a bowl with the wine, port, onions, garlic, carrot, thyme, rosemary and salt. Leave to marinate for 24 hours.

The next day, strain the meat, vegetables and herbs, reserving the marinade. Place the onions, garlic, carrot, thyme and rosemary in the base of a large saucepan, then add the rabbit meat on top. Pour the reserved marinade into the pan and top up with some extra water to cover, if necessary. Place the pan over a low heat and leave to simmer gently for 3 hours or until the meat is tender.

Once cooked, shred the rabbit meat into small pieces, removing any bones, and set aside. Strain the rabbit cooking liquid into a freezer-proof container and place in a freezer until frozen.

Once frozen, thaw the cooking liquid over a fine muslin (cheesecloth) to obtain a consommé. Season with salt and pepper to taste.

Heat the olive oil in a frying pan or skillet over a medium heat, add the onion and garlic from the saucepan and cook for 15 minutes or until caramelised. Once caramelised, add the shredded meat to the pan.

To make the pasta dough, combine the flour, egg, oil and milk in a bowl. Add 115 ml/4 fl oz water and mix together until the flour is fully incorporated.

Divide the dough into two pieces. Roll out each piece into a thin sheet, about 40 x 20 cm/16 x 8 inches. Spoon the rabbit meat onto one sheet of pasta dough in 8 mounds, spacing each mound well apart. Lay the second sheet of pasta dough over the first and press down around the mounds

of rabbit meat to seal in the filling. Using a 6-cm/2-inch round pasta cutter, cut out 8 round ravioli.

Heat 1 litre/34 fl oz (4 cups) vegetable oil in a heavy-based saucepan or fryer to 190°C/375°F on a thermometer. Carefully lower the ravioli into the hot oil and deep-fry for 3–4 minutes or until golden.

Place two ravioli in the middle of four deep serving bowls and ladle over the consommé. Drizzle over the parsley oil before serving.

Egg Cream with Sweet Potato Strands

Preparation time: 24 hours
Cooking time: 1 hour
Serves: 4

350 g/12 oz almonds
350 g/12 oz sweet potato
1 litre/34 fl oz (4 cups) vegetable oil

For the egg cream:
10 eggs
250 g/8¾ oz caster (superfine) sugar
100 g/3½ oz whole almonds
20 g/¾ oz powdered sugar
10 g/⅓ oz ground cinnamon

Preheat the oven to 140°C/275°F/Gas Mark 1.

Spread the almonds out over a large baking sheet and toast in the oven for 12 minutes, or until golden. Place the toasted almonds in a bowl with 250 ml/8½ fl oz (1 cup) water. Crush the almonds as finely as possible. Strain the almond water into a freezer-proof container and place in the freezer until frozen.

To make the egg cream, separate the yolks and whites of 6 of the eggs into two bowls. Place the sugar in a saucepan with 250 ml/8½ fl oz water and bring to the boil until it reaches 108°C/226°F on a sugar thermometer. Pour the sugar syrup onto the egg yolks, stirring vigorously, and cook over a low heat until it reaches the desired thickness.

Cook the remaining 4 eggs sous-vide at 70°C/160°F for 2–4 minutes. Cool in iced water.

Using a mandolin, slice the sweet potatoes into matchsticks. Heat the oil in a heavy-based saucepan or fryer until it reaches 190°C/375°F on a thermometer. Carefully lower the sweet potato matchsticks into the hot oil and deep-fry for 5 minutes or until crispy. Leave to drain.

Divide the egg cream between four individual serving bowls, then add a sous-vide egg yolk to each bowl. Take the frozen almond mixture from the freezer and, using a fork, break it up to make a granita and add a spoonful to each bowl. Add a handful of sweet potato matchsticks and scatter over some almonds. Dust with icing (confectioners') sugar before serving.

George Mendes

Veranda, New York City

Acclaimed chef and cookbook author George Mendes is executive chef and partner at Veranda in downtown New York City. Mendes first introduced New York to elevated Portuguese cuisine in 2009 when he opened Aldea, a Michelin-starred fixture in the city's Flatiron District for over a decade. A first-generation American born to Portuguese immigrants, the Danbury, Connecticut native graduated from the Culinary Institute of America and worked for his mentor, David Bouley, at the chef's original namesake restaurant in Tribeca before honing his talent further at Alain Passard's Arpège in Paris. After more than three years running the kitchen at Toqueville near Union Square, Mendes left to chart his own course by opening Aldea to critical acclaim, which he followed with the opening of his popular Portuguese spot, Lupulo, in 2015. Mendes published his first cookbook, *My Portugal: Recipes and Stories* in 2014.

Salt Cod and Chickpea Salad

Salada de Bacalhau com Grão de Bico

Preparation time: 20 minutes
Cooking time: 5 minutes
Serves: 4

360 g/12¾ oz cooked salt cod, skin and bones removed
2 tablespoons extra virgin olive oil, plus extra to taste
660 g/23¼ oz (4 cups) cooked chickpeas (garbanzos)
2 tablespoons pickled shallots
2 teaspoons finely chopped flat-leaf parsley leaves
1 teaspoon grated orange zest
6 teaspoons sherry vinegar, plus extra to taste
85 g/3 oz (2 cups) baby watercress or rocket (arugula) leaves
parsley oil, to taste
flor de sal (fleur de sel), to taste
sea salt and freshly ground white pepper, to taste

Flake the salt cod into a bowl. Heat the olive oil in a medium saucepan over a medium-low heat. Add the flaked salt cod and cooked chickpeas (garbanzos) and cook, stirring gently, for 5 minutes to take the chill off both. Once warmed through, toss in the shallots, parsley, orange zest and 4 teaspoons of the vinegar. Season with salt and pepper.

Place the salad leaves in a bowl. Drizzle over more extra virgin olive oil and the remaining vinegar and then toss to dress the leaves. Season with salt and pepper. Taste and adjust the seasoning, if necessary, with more olive oil and vinegar.

Divide the salt cod and chickpea mixture between four deep serving plates, either piling the mixture into a mound or using a 15-cm/6-inch ring mould, if preferred. Drizzle over some parsley oil and sprinkle with a pinch of flor de sal (fleur de sel). Pile the dressed salad leaves on top of the salt cod and chickpeas before serving.

Green Peas Baked with Spicy Sausage and Poached Eggs

••

Ovos Escalfados com Linguiça e Ervilhas

Preparation time: 20 minutes
Cooking time: 20 minutes
Serves: 4
🖉 ◻

extra virgin olive oil, as needed
40 g/1½ oz smoked bacon, cut into 2.5-cm/1-inch
    pieces
1 small white onion, peeled and finely diced
3 garlic cloves, peeled and thinly sliced
1 bay leaf, torn
pinch of crushed red chilli flakes
3 tablespoons tomato purée (paste)
55 g/2 oz linguiça, sliced
20 g/¾ oz chouriço, sliced
240 g/8½ oz garden peas
4 eggs
7 g/¼ oz flat-leaf parsley leaves, chopped
sea salt, to taste

Preheat the oven to 180°C/350°F/Gas Mark 4.

Heat a large casserole dish (Dutch oven) or cast-iron cocotte over a medium heat. Drizzle in just enough oil to coat the base of the dish, then add the bacon. Cook, stirring occasionally, for 4 minutes or until the fat is rendered and the bacon is lightly browned. Transfer the bacon to a bowl.

Add the onion, garlic, bay leaf and chilli flakes to the casserole dish and cook, stirring, for 3 minutes or until the onion is soft but not coloured. Add the tomatoes and 1 teaspoon of oil and cook, stirring and scraping down the sides of the pan, for a further 4 minutes. The tomatoes should be steadily sizzling. Stir in the linguiça, chouriço, bacon and another 1 teaspoon of oil and cook, stirring occasionally, for 2 minutes, or until heated through. Stir in the peas and season with salt. Remove and discard the bay leaf.

Make four small wells for the eggs in the mixture, spacing them evenly apart. Carefully break an egg into each well, making sure each one is nestled in the stew and level with the surface. Bake in the hot oven for 8 minutes or until the egg whites are set but the yolks are still runny. Scatter over the parsley and season with lemon juice to taste before serving.

Beignets in Cinnamon Sugar

••

Sonhos

Preparation time: 20–25 minutes
Cooking time: 10 minutes
Serves: 4
𝒪

55 g/2 oz (¼ cup plus ¼ teaspoon) caster (superfine)
    sugar
½ teaspoon unsalted butter
150 g/5¼ oz (1 cup) plain (all-purpose) flour
4 large eggs
1 tablespoon ground cinnamon
canola oil, for deep-frying

Put ¼ teaspoon of the sugar and all the butter into a medium saucepan, pour in 240 ml/8 fl oz (1 cup) water and bring to the boil over a high heat. Add the flour and stir vigorously until the mixture forms a ball. Reduce the heat to medium and continue cooking, stirring vigorously, until the dough starts to puff up and a thin layer of dough sticks to the base of the pan. The dough will be very stiff, but keep working it.

Transfer the dough to the bowl of a stand mixer fitted with a paddle attachment and beat on medium-low speed to break up the ball of dough. Add the eggs, one at a time, beating until smooth after each addition. Increase the speed to high and beat for 1 minute, scraping down the sides of the bowl, until the eggs are fully incorporated and there are no lumps. Do not overwork the dough. Transfer the dough to a container, let it cool slightly and then chill in the fridge.

When you're ready to cook, combine the cinnamon and remaining 50 g/1¾ oz (¼ cup) sugar in a bowl and set aside. Fill a large saucepan with oil to the depth of 7.5 cm/3 inches and heat to 150°C/300°F on a thermometer. Working in batches and using a measuring teaspoon or small cookie scoop, carefully scoop and lower balls of dough into the hot oil. Do not overcrowd the pan. Cook for 8 minutes or until the beignets float on the surface of the oil, puff up and are golden. Remove the beignets from the oil using a slotted spoon and transfer immediately to the bowl of cinnamon sugar and gently turn to coat. Repeat until all the dough has been used up. Serve the beignets while still warm.

Ana Gonçalves and Zijun Meng

•••

TÃTÃ Eatery, London

Ana Gonçalves and Zijun Meng formed TÃTÃ Eatery in 2015 after years spent working with Nuno Mendes, first at The Loft Project, then at Viajante and Chiltern Firehouse. After a series of residencies and collaborations around London and Europe, the pair built a cult following thanks to their exciting blend of Asian and Mediterranean flavours and produce. With backgrounds in graphic design and fine art, the duo have a very particular approach to food. Project TÃTÃ Eatery has since progressed into a Nomadic brand travelling from place to place. The food is a fusion of the pair's heritage, where East meets West, and has always featured a menu focused on rice dishes, fresh (often raw) seafood, Iberian and British meat and fermented ingredients. TÃTÃ Eatery is about connecting people; connecting the guest to the chef and the supplier, and telling the story of where the produce comes from. In 2018, they introduced London to the Iberian Katsu Sando, which ultimately led to the launch of TÓU in 2019. A casual but refined brand in central London that specializes in katsu sandos and small dishes. In 2021, Ana and Meng redeveloped Mr Ji, an Asian eatery and bar in the heart of Soho, with a smart menu centred on small dishes, wines and cocktails.

Cuttlefish Chow Mei

••

Preparation time: 45 minutes
Cooking time: 10 minutes
Serves: 2
🖉 ▯

For the cuttlefish noodles:
1 x 300–400-g/10–14-oz cuttlefish, cleaned
sea salt
olive oil

For the dashi and egg yolk sauce:
50 g/1¾ oz egg yolk
large pinch of hon dashi powder

For the bean sprout salad:
200 g/7 oz bean sprouts
10 g/⅓ oz minced ginger
10 g/⅓ oz minced garlic
20 g/⅔ oz sake
40 g/1½ oz Japanese goma dressing
oil, for frying

For the caramelised onions:
2 heads of red onions, finely sliced
100 ml/3½ fl oz oil, for frying
sea salt

To serve:
heritage carrot, julienned
spring onion, sliced on the diagonal
marcona almonds, chopped
coriander stalks, chopped
aonori seaweed powder

To prepare the noodles, remove the skin and guts of the cuttlefish. (Reserve them along with the tentacles for another recipe – these trimmings will make a delicious stock with an amazing black colour.) Cut the cuttlefish body into 0.5-cm/¼-inch strips, season with a little sea salt and olive oil. Vacuum pack the cuttlefish strips and cook sous vide at 50°C/120°F for 20 minutes.

To make the sauce, whisk together the egg yolk and hon dashi powder until fully dissolved.

Have a bowl of iced water nearby. Bring a saucepan of water to the boil, drop in the bean sprouts and blanch for 20 seconds. Plunge the beans sprouts into the iced water, then drain.

Heat a frying pan or skillet over a high heat to smoking point, then add 2 tablespoons of oil. Once hot, add the minced ginger and sauté for 30 seconds, or until fragrant. Add the minced garlic and fry for a further 10 seconds. Add the sake and let everything simmer briefly before dropping in the bean sprouts. Stir for 30 seconds, remove from the heat and then stir through the goma dressing.

Heat a pan over a high heat, add the oil and bring it up until the oil just begins to smoke. Add the red onions and sauté, stirring continuously, for 2–3 minutes, or until softened. Reduce the heat to low and cook, stirring regularly, for a further 30 minutes, or until they slowly caramelise. Add a couple of pinches of salt, to taste.

Warm two deep serving plates. Mix the warm cuttlefish noodles, dashi and egg yolk sauce and caramelised onions together, then pile them into the middle of the plates. Add the bean sprout salad on top, then garnish with the julienned carrot, sliced spring onions and chopped almonds. Scatter over the chopped coriander stalks and sprinkle with the aonori powder. Serve immediately.

Iberico Pork Bone Broth

Preparation time: 26 hours
Cooking time: 20 minutes
Serves: 2
🌱 ⬜

For the pork neck:
600 g/1 lb 5 oz pork neck
oil, for grilling
sea salt

For the bone broth:
1 kg/2 lb 3 oz pork ribs
50 g/1¾ oz sliced ginger
100 g/3½ oz leeks
50 g/1¾ oz shiro dashi concentrate

For the sautéed greens:
500 g/17½ oz chopped Swiss chard
    (or any leafy green vegetable of your choice)
10 g/⅓ oz umeboshi paste
2 garlic cloves, peeled and finely sliced
oil, for frying
sea salt

To serve:
toasted sesame seeds
dried perilla powder (deulkkae-garu)

The day before, cold smoke the pork neck over apple wood chippings for 2 hours. Vacuum pack the smoked meat and cook sous vide at 65°C/150°F for 24 hours. Cool the meat in iced water and then remove any blood and gelatin with paper towels. Slice into 5-cm/2-inch steaks and set aside.

Bring a saucepan of water to boil, drop in the pork ribs and bring back to the boil, skimming the surface of any foam. Remove the pork from the pan and rinse under cold running water.

Pour 4 litres/135 fl oz (16 cups) water into a stock pot, add the boiled pork ribs and bring to a boil, frequently skimming the surface to keep the stock clean. Once boiling, reduce the heat, add the ginger and leek and simmer for 8 hours, or until thickened and reduced to about 500 ml/17 fl oz (2 cups). Strain and discard the pork rib bones and vegetables, then season the stock with the shiro dashi and set aside.

Have a bowl of iced water nearby. Bring a saucepan of water to the boil, drop in the greens and blanch for 30 seconds. Plunge the greens into the iced water, then drain.

In a frying pan or skillet, heat up some oil. Add the blanched greens and garlic at the same time, then stir in umeboshi paste and season with salt.

Prepare a grill (broiler). Once hot, brush the pork neck with oil and grill for 2 minutes on each side, turning frequently, or until golden all over but with a core temperature of 55°C/130°F.

Warm two deep plates. Slice the pork and arrange on one side of the plate. Pile the sautéed greens next to the pork. Pour the hot broth over and season with sesame seeds and perilla powder.

Brioche Pain Perdu

Preparation time: 24 hours
Cooking time: 10 minutes
Serves: 2
⬛

For the brioche pain perdu:
2 thick slices of brioche
50 g/1¾ oz caster (superfine) sugar
75 g/2⅔ oz egg yolk
150 ml/5 fl oz single (light) cream

For the milk ice cream:
180 g/6 fl oz whole (full-fat) milk
50 ml/1⅔ fl oz single cream
40 g/1½ oz trimoline inverted sugar
20 g/¾ oz caster (superfine) sugar
large pinch of cornflour (corn starch)
pinch of sea salt

For the sabayon:
40 g/1½ oz caster (superfine) sugar
40 ml/1⅓ fl oz water
1 whole egg plus 2 egg yolks

To serve:
extra virgin olive oil
black truffle
butter, for frying
caster (superfine) sugar, for dusting

The day before, remove and discard the crust from the brioche. Trim the slices to 5 cm/2 inches long by 3 cm/1 inch wide and 2 cm/¾ inch deep. Whisk together the sugar, egg yolk and cream until fully dissolved. Pour this mixture over the brioche and leave in the fridge overnight.

To make the ice cream, combine the sugar and cornflour (corn starch) and add to the milk and cream, along with trimoline inverted sugar. Bring the mixture to 85°C/185°F, whisking continuously until it thickens. Pass the mixture through a sieve (fine-mesh strainer), then pour into a Pacojet container and freeze.

To make the sabayon, whisk all ingredients in a bowl until smooth. Cook the mixture in a bain-marie until it reaches 55°C/130°F on a thermometer. Transfer to a stand mixer fitted with a balloon whisk attachment and whisk to stiff peaks.

Melt some butter in a non-stick frying pan or skillet. Once hot, add the soaked brioche and fry until coloured on all sides but without burning the butter. Transfer the brioche to a metal serving tray, dust over an even layer of caster (superfine) sugar and caramelise using a blowtorch.

Place a piece of brioche in the middle of four deep bowls and drizzle over a little extra virgin olive oil. Place a generous scoop of sabayon on top of the brioche. Place a scoop of milk ice cream in the middle of the sabayon, so it sits on top. Shave the fresh truffle over and serve immediately.

427

Nuno Mendes

•••

Bairro Alto Hotel, Lisbon and Lisboeta, London

Raised in Lisbon, Nuno Mendes combines his experience on the family farm in the Alentejo with innovative ingredients and techniques garnered during his travels to pioneer ideas as a chef. Nuno made his mark on the London food scene in 2006, when he opened Bacchus, receiving acclaim for this avant-garde offering. The Loft Project followed. It grew from an underground club, with Nuno hosting informal suppers in his own home, to a gallery for chefs with invited up-and-coming chefs using it as their own creative platform. In 2010, Nuno opened Viajante in the Town Hall Hotel. The restaurant received a Michelin star within nine months of opening, evolving from a local hotspot into an international destination. In 2011, Nuno launched an informal sister restaurant named the Corner Room. Nuno took up the position of executive chef at Chiltern Firehouse in 2014, and then in 2016, together with Andre Balazs, published *Chiltern Firehouse: The Cookbook*. Nuno returned to East London with the opening of Taberna do Mercado in 2015 at Old Spitalfields Market. A reinterpretation of food with wines from his native country, Taberna was the inspiration behind Nuno's first solo cookbook, *Lisboeta: City of Light*. Nowadays, Nuno splits his time between London and Lisbon. The Bairro Alto Hotel, located in the bohemian quarter of Lisbon, which Nuno joined as food and beverage creative director during a multimillion-euro expansion, was relaunched in 2019. Nuno continues to explore the rich diversity of Portuguese cuisine through his various projects, including his restaurant Lisboeta that will launch in central London in Spring 2022.

Pig Cheeks in Vinha d'Alhos

••

Preparation time: 40 minutes, plus 24–48 hours marinating
Cooking time: 2 hours 30 minutes
Serves: 4
🖉 ▢

For the pig's cheeks:
900 g/2 lb Iberico pig's cheeks with fat still attached
coarse sea salt, to taste
fine sea salt and finely ground white pepper
4 tablespoons rapeseed oil
100 g/3½ oz (1 stick) unsalted butter
3 garlic cloves, peeled and finely chopped
1 knob of ginger, peeled and finely chopped
1 large yellow onion, peeled and finely diced
1 head of fennel, finely diced
6 bay leaves, torn
2 sweet Valencia oranges, thinly sliced, to serve
1 bunch parsley, finely chopped, to serve
10 slices crusty bread, grilled, to serve
good-quality extra virgin olive oil, to serve

For the marinade:
200 ml/7 fl oz (¾ cup) red wine vinegar
200 ml/7 fl oz (¾ cup) dry white wine
100 ml/3½ fl oz (⅓ cup) orange juice
10 garlic cloves, smashed
10 bay leaves, torn
3 teaspoons chilli flakes
2 cinnamon sticks
2 tablespoons toasted ground cumin

For the paste:
3 garlic cloves
6 red chillies, finely chopped
1 teaspoon toasted ground cumin
1 teaspoon smoked paprika

To prepare the pig's cheeks, mix all the ingredients for the marinade together in a large bowl and add the meat. Leave to marinade in the fridge for 24–48 hours.

When ready to cook, remove the meat from the marinade. Strain the marinade and set aside.

Add 2 tablespoons of the rapeseed oil to a sauté pan over a high heat. Once hot, add half of the meat to the pan in a single layer and fry until all the meat is brown on both sides. Season the meat with salt and remove from the pan to a plate, saving the cooking oil. Wipe clean the pan and repeat with the rest of the oil and the remaining meat until all the meat is browned.

Add the reserved juices from the marinade and the reserved fat from cooking the meat to a food processor or blender. Add all the ingredients for the paste and process until smooth.

In a large saucepan melt the butter until brown and nutty. Add the garlic and ginger, fry gently until fragrant. Add the onion and fennel and cook down until very fragrant. Add the bay leaves and stir, then add the meat and sweat to incorporate. Raise the heat, add the paste so that it starts boiling and turn the heat down to a simmer. Cook for 2 hours 30 minutes or until the meat is very tender and fragrant.

Taste and adjust the seasoning, if necessary, and remove and discard the bay leaves. Garnish with the orange slices and scatter over the finely chopped parsley. Serve with the grilled crusty bread brushed with extra virgin olive oil.

This dish can also be eaten cold, and even served the next day.

Glossary

Açorda – A dish made with stale bread. Presented like a soup in Alentejo, in other parts *açorda* stands for bread porridge.

Alheira – A sausage made with pork, chicken, beef and bread from the north of Portugal, then smoked and air dried. Usually eaten grilled or pan fried.

Alimado/s – A term usually referring to horse mackerel (*Carapau Alimado*), *alimado* is the process of removing the skins and dorsal fin after the fish has been salted and poached in boiling water. An iconic dish from the Algarve and other coastal areas.

Azevias – Fried dough resembling a half moon, typically filled with chickpeas and almond or pumpkin compote, then tossed in sugar with cinnamon.

Bolo do Caco – A simple Madeiran bread recipe, shaped into a round disc and cooked over a hot brick.

Caldeirada – Known as fisherman's stew, this broth is made using a combination of different kinds of fish. Versions include both saltwater and freshwater fish, shellfish and vegetables.

Caldo Verde – Shredded kale green soup with potato and slices of chorizo, perhaps the most popular soup in the whole of Portugal.

Cataplana – A famous stewed dish that gains its name from the vessel in which it is cooked. A *cataplana* is a hermetic copper pot for stewing food. Recipes vary a lot, from shellfish to poultry.

Coentrada – A term for a dish cooked with lots of coriander and typically garlic. In Alentejo, the most famous version is pig trotters.

Cozido – The most popular dish in Portugal, this stew contains a soft-boiled vegetables, meats and charcuterie served with rice. The vegetables, meats and charcuterie vary depending on the region.

Escabeche – A marination method that can be applied to fish or meat, although fish is more popular. The *escabeche* consists mainly of a vinegar base, that can also take onion, garlic, olive oil and wine, it is a popular preserving method that is better served cold or at room temperature.

Estonado – A way of removing the hair from a kid goat without damaging the inner skin. When cooked, the skins become super crispy.

Estupeta – The name given to the less noble parts of tuna that have been cured in salt and airdried – the same process as Muxama.

Filhoses – Fried cakes usually made mainly with pumpkin, although there are versions with only flour and firewater. Typically fried and rolled in a sugar and cinnamon.

Mangusto – A combination of cabbage, bread and potatoes.

Míscaros – A wild mushroom called man on a horse back. It has a characteristic aroma and firm texture with a paled yellow colour. When in season, it is widely consumed across different parts of the country.

Pão de Ló – A light, moist sponge cake present throughout Portugal. The type varies from regionally.

Pastéis – Refers to something baked or fried, such as a casing, made to be filled as in *pastéis de massa tenra* or a mixture that is fried as in *pastéis de bacalhau*.

Papas – A dish that is made with fine cornflour, this creamy porridge can be made sweet or savoury.

Pica-pau – The name given to this snack dish made with cubes of meat, normally beef, garnished with mustard, pickles and parsley.

Queijada – A creamy cake, composed mostly of eggs and milk.

Sarapatel – A stew made with pig's offal and less premium cuts, it is usually thickened with pork blood that has been cooked previously and then crumbled.

Sarrabulho – A stew made with pig's or kid's blood in which offal cuts are used. There is a sweet variation, like a sweet pork blood porridge. Different versions are made with polenta and rice.

Sonhos – A light batter, almost like a doughnut or beignet, fried and rolled in sugar and cinnamon.

Trouxas – An egg yolk sheet cooked in syrup, which is then often filled with either creamy sweet eggs or broken *trouxas*.

Vinha d'Alhos – A marinade made with red wine and garlic. Different versions can contain paprika, vinegar, lemon and orange peel.

Index

Recipe Notes

Flour is plain (all-purpose) flour, unless specified otherwise.

Sugar is white granulated sugar, unless specified otherwise.

Butter is unsalted butter, unless specified otherwise.

Milk is whole (full-fat) milk, unless specified otherwise.

Cream is fresh double (heavy) cream, unless specified otherwise.

Eggs are assumed to be UK size medium (US size large) and preferably organic and/or free-range, unless specified otherwise.

Black pepper is freshly ground, unless specified otherwise.

Sea salt is unrefined, unless specified otherwise.

Breadcrumbs are fresh unless specified otherwise.

Chocolate is dark (bittersweet) chocolate and with a minimum of 70% cocoa solids, unless specified otherwise.

Individual fruits and vegetables are assumed to be of medium size, unless specified otherwise, and should be peeled and/or washed, unless specified otherwise.

When the zest of a citrus fruit is used, always use unwaxed organic fruit.

Herbs are fresh herbs, unless specified otherwise.

All herbs, shoots, flowers and leaves should be picked fresh from a clean source. Exercise caution when foraging for ingredients; any foraged ingredients should only be eaten if an expert has deemed them safe to eat. Mushrooms should be wiped clean.

Fish and shellfish are cleaned and gutted (and fish are filleted) before recipe preparation, unless specified otherwise.

When no quantity is specified for an ingredient – for example, oils for frying, herb for garnishing finished dishes – then quantities are discretionary and flexible.

Cooking and preparation times given are for guidance only, as individual ovens vary. If using a fan (convection) oven, follow the manufacturer's instructions concerning oven temperatures.

Exercise a high level of caution when following recipes involving any potentially hazardous activity. This includes the use of slaked lime, high temperatures and open flames, such as using a cook's blowtorch. In particular, when deep frying, slowly and carefully lower the food into the hot oil to avoid splashes, wear long sleeves to protect your arms and never leave the pan unattended.

When deep-frying, heat the oil to the temperature specified, or until a cube of bread browns in 15–30 seconds. After frying, drain the fried foods on paper towels.

Exercise caution when making fermented products, ensuring all equipment is spotlessly clean and seek expert advice if in any doubt.

When sterilising jars or bottles for preserves, wash them in clean, hot soapy water and rinse thoroughly. Heat the oven to 140°C/275°F/ Gas Mark 1. Place the jars or bottles on a baking sheet and place in the oven to dry. Fill the jars or bottles while they are still hot and seal immediately.

Imperial and metric measurements, as well as volumetric cup measurements, are given for each recipe. Follow only one set of measurements throughout a recipe, and not a mixture, as they are not interchangeable.

All volumetric cup measurements given are level. Flour cup measures are spooned and leveled. Brown sugar cup measures are packed, while other dry ingredient measures are loosely packed.

All tablespoon and teaspoon measurements given are level, not heaping, unless otherwise stated.
1 teaspoon = 5 ml
1 tablespoon = 15 ml

Australian standard tablespoons are 20 ml, so any Australian readers are advised to use 3 teaspoons in place of 1 tablespoon when measuring small quantities.

Some recipes include uncooked or very lightly cooked eggs, meat, or fish. These should be avoided by the elderly, infants, pregnant women, convalescents and anyone with an impaired immune system.

About the Author

•••

Leandro Carreira cut his culinary teeth at Andoni Luis Aduriz's restaurant, Mugaritz, in the Basque region of Spain, before arriving in London and working with Nuno Mendes at Viajante as Head Chef. His residency at Climpson's Arch in East London, an exploration of regional Portuguese cooking, received five-star reviews. Londrino, his first restaurant, opened in Bermondsey, London in 2017 and his current project, The Sea, The Sea, in Chelsea, London has been followed by The Sea, The Sea Chef's Table in late 2021.

•••

Phaidon Press Limited
2 Cooperage Yard
London E15 2QR

Phaidon Press Inc.
65 Bleecker Street
New York, NY 10012

phaidon.com

First published 2022
© 2022 Phaidon Press Limited

ISBN 978 1 83866 473 2

A CIP catalogue record for this book is available from the British Library and Library of Congress.

Publisher: Emilia Terragni
Commissioning Editors: Eve O'Sullivan and Emilia Terragni
Project Editor: Lisa Pendreigh
Production Controller: Sarah Kramer

Designed by João Mota
Layouts by Cantina, Ana Teodoro

All photography by Mário Ambrózio and Rafael Rodrigues at Raw Studio
All photography styling by Mariana Castello Branco and Barbara Freitas Ferreira at Raw Studio

Printed in China

The publisher would like to thank Miguel Andrade, Vanessa Bird, Julia Hastings, Sophie Hodgkin, Jo Ireson, Lucy Kingett, André Magalhães, Lesley Malkin, Ellie Smith, Tracey Smith, Sally Somers, Caroline Stearns, Kathy Steer and Albino Tavares for their contributions to this book.